ENCYCLOPEDIA OF MUHAMMAD'S (ﷺ) WOMEN COMPANIONS

AND THE
TRADITIONS THEY RELATED

SHAYKH MUHAMMAD HISHAM KABBANI

AND

LALEH BAKHTIAR

ABC INTERNATIONAL GROUP

© 1998, Laleh Bakhtiar

Book Designer
Liaquat Ali

Library of Congress Cataloging in Publication Data

Kabbani, Shaykh Muhammad Hisham and Bakhtiar, Laleh
    Encyclopedia of Muhammad's Women Companions and the
    Traditions They Related

    Includes bibliographical references.
    1. Women in the Hadith. 2. Hadith. 3. Biography. 3. Women in
    Islam.

    I. Title. BP134.W6576 1998
    297'.1228—dc30 94-3968

    ISBN: 1-871031-42-7

Published by

ABC International Group, Inc.

Distributed by

KAZI Publications
3023 W. Belmont Avenue
Chicago IL 60618
(T) 773-267-7001; (F) 773-267-7002
email: kazibooks@kazi.org

CONTENTS

PREFACE

The present work is divided into two books. Book I contains all of the Traditions related by the Prophet's women Companions (*sahabiyyat*). The Traditions (*ahadith*) are organized according to the Divine Law (*shariah*), but they begin with moral character development which is not traditionally included in books on the Law. A brief glance shows that women Companions related Traditions in many areas and not just in areas relating specifically to women. Where there is more than one Tradition on the same topic, one is presented and references to the the other versions are indicated below that specific Tradition.

The sources for these Traditions are the six canonical works, namely, *Sahih al-Bukhari, Sahih Muslim, Sunan Abu Dawud, Sunan Ibn Majah, Sunan al-Nisai,* and *Sunan al-Tirmidhi.* In order to help readers who are fluent only in English or only in English and Urdu, reference is also made to the *Mishkat al-masabih* (MM) translated into English by Robson and Urdu translations particularly of Tirmidhi (U).

Book II contains the biographies of over 600 women Companions of the Prophet including her name, her mother's name, name of her children, name of her husband (s) and where information is available from the earliest sources of Ibn Ishaq and Ibn Sad, a biography is included.

Ibn Sad's book, *Kitab al-tabiqat al-kubra* (Book of Classes), and in particular Book Eight on the female Companions of the Prophet is based on oral traditions as well as written works that preceded Ibn Sad. A major source used by Ibn Sad was that of his teacher, al-Waqadi (b. 130 AH/747 AD). Al-Waqadi's work compiled 150 years after the death of the Prophet was later lost but preserved to a large extent by his student, Ibn Sad. The genre of Books of Classes were originally written to identify transmitters of the Traditions of the Prophet. Ibn Ishaq (d. 767 AD/150 AH), the second main source for the biographies here, is author of the earliest biography of the Prophet.

The women whose Traditions and biographies appear here are women Companions who became models for later generations. The precedent they set of orally transmitting information, regardless of the fact that they were women, was extremely important to the process of recording the *sunnah*. It will become clear to the reader after reading Book I and Book II that women were given the same respect as men when commenting upon the Quran and relating the Traditions. It should also be noted that no traditional religion has ever held such a complete record of the women Companions of its prophet.

*****

My deepest gratitude goes to Shaykh Muhammad Hisham Kabbani for his inspiration and guidance throughout the preparation of this book. Without Shaykh Hisham's unswerving devotion to the Truth and the most Perfect Human Being, Prophet Muhammad (🕌), this work would never have been realized.

Laleh Bakhtiar
Chicago, 1998

FOREWORD

This work is devoted and dedicated to Muslim women. Without them, there would have been no Islam as women are honored to carry in themselves the greatest secret—that of human life.

Jalaluddin Rumi wrote:

> The Prophet said that women completely dominate men
> of intellect and possessors of hearts,
> But ignorant men dominate women, because [these men]
> are dominated by their animal nature.
> They have no kindness, gentleness, or love, because of the
> animality.
> Love and kindness are human attributes while anger and
> lust are animal qualities.
> Woman is the radiance of God. She is not your beloved.
> She is the Creator—you could say that she is not cre-
> ated.

What better example of a woman is there than the daughter of the Prophet (ﷺ), Fatima al-Zahra (ع)? When she saw that her father was constantly saying, "O my Community," she wanted to do something herself for the benefit of this Community. When God ordered the Prophet (ﷺ) to find a husband for his daughter, the Prophet (ﷺ) called all the Companions together and said to them, "God has ordered me to say that whoever recites the Quran from the beginning to end tonight may marry my daughter Fatima, if she consents."

That night, all the Companions tried to recite the Quran from beginning to end. All stayed at the mosque trying to finish except Ali ibn Abi Talib (ﷺ) who went home and slept.

Everyone, including the blessed Prophet (ﷺ) assembled at the mosque when Bilal (ؓ) recited the call for the dawn prayer. After performing the dawn prayer, Prophet Muhammad (ﷺ) asked, "Who finished the Quran last night so that I can marry him to my daughter Fatima?" No one was able to answer because it is difficult to finish the thirty parts of the Quran in only seven or eight hours. Ali ibn Abi Talib (ؑ) said, "O Messenger of God, I finished reciting the Quran last night."

The other Companions looked at him and said, "How is it that you finished the Quran? You slept all night."

He said, "No. I completed the Quran from beginning to end."

The Prophet (ﷺ) said to Ali, "Who is your witness?"

Ali (ؑ) said:

> God is my witness and you, O Prophet (ﷺ) are my witness that I completed it. O Messenger of God, I recited the following, "There is no god but God, Muhammad is the Messenger of God," three times, "I seek the forgiveness of God" seventy times, the Opening Chapter once, the Chapter of Sincerity three times, the Chapter of the Dawn one time, then the Chapter of Humanity one time, "there is no god but God" ten times and ten times "peace and the blessings of God be upon Muhammad and his family."

The Prophet (ﷺ) said, "As God bears witness, I also bear witness that Ali has completed the Quran. If you recite what he has recited, it is equivalent to having completed the Quran."

The Prophet (ﷺ) asked Fatima (ؑ), "O Fatima, do you accept Ali as your husband?" She said, "On one condition." All the Companions looked at Ali (ؑ), at Fatima (ؑ), at the Prophet (ﷺ). The Prophet's face changed as he wondered why Fatima said this? What could the condition be? The angel Gabriel came and told him, "O Prophet, do not make a quick decision concerning her. God tells you to ask her what her condition is." The Prophet (ﷺ) asked, "O Fatima, what is your condition?"

She said, "The condition does not concern Ali, but it is related to me. If that condition is fulfilled, I will accept. If not, I will never accept to marry Ali."

Again, the angel Gabriel went to the Prophet (ﷺ) saying, "God orders you to ask her what her condition is."

Now look at what God had put into her heart and consider the benefit and station of women in spirituality.

The Prophet (ﷺ) said, "O Fatima, what is your condition?" She said:

> I hear you continuously, day and night, praying for your Community. You say, "O my Lord! Give me permission to lead my Community to you! Forgive them! Purify them! Take away their sins and difficulties and burdens!" I hear you and know how much you suffer for your Community. I now from what you have said that when you pass away, you will still be saying, "My Community!" to your Lord, in your grave, and on Judgment Day. My father, I see you suffering so much for your Community. Since that love of your Community is also in my heart, I want your Community as my dowry. If you accept, I will marry Ali.

She asked for all of the Prophet's Community, everyone without discrimination. What could the Prophet (ﷺ) say? It was not in his hands to give such a dowry. He waited for Gabriel, but Gabriel did not come quickly. He kept him waiting for some time, then came and said, "God sends you His greetings and accepts Fatima's request. He gives her what she asked for as her dowry to marry Ali." The Prophet (ﷺ) immediately stood up and performed two cycles of prayer of thankfulness to his Lord.

Fatima (ع) was only concerned for the salvation of the Community of the Prophet (ﷺ). No one is going to be outside of her dowry because if God removes one person from the dowry, it will be as if her marriage to Ali (ﷺ) had been invalid. Therefore, she is going to take the entire Community under her wing and they shall enter with her into paradise. This is the power of one Muslim woman. She will take everyone with her into paradise.

The women whose biographies appear in this work are the female Companions of the Prophet. These women became models for later generations. They set the precedent for orally transmitted information through women as transmitters. This was crucial to the process of recording the hadith and would be a format used in later generations where women surrounded a spiritual person and then reported on his or her words and deeds. What will become obvious to the reader is the freedom of these first Muslim women and limits of their seclusion. While there were specific questions of the modest dress (*hijab*) which the women addressed based on the sayings and deeds of the Prophet (☆), it is clear that women were not prevented from engaging in the whole gamet of endeavors that men were engaged in. For instance, Umm Mani and Umm Umara (Nusayb bint Kab) were both at Aqaba, present where the Prophet (☆) was invited to Madina and Hawwa bint Zayd and Umm Sulaym, mother of Anas ibn Malik, converted before the migration to Madina.

Over 2000 Traditions have been related from more than 150 of these women. Traditions from nineteen of them relate directly to Quranic verses. The story of these women is amazing. It is a story far different from that of any other religious tradition. It is unique and yet often ignored in the contemporary feminist rush to condemn religion as something used to oppress women. In the case of the Islamic faith, believing women Companions of the Prophet (☆) who followed his *sunna* distinguished themselves in many ways. As a result, they became role models for future generations of women who were conscious of what it meant to submit to God's Will (*islam*).

These women realized the exceptional character of the Prophet of Islam (☆). They bore witness to the revelation as he received it. They memorized Quranic verses as soon as they were revealed and then tried to live their lives according to them. For the betterment of humanity, they subdued their egos, individual desires and personal wishes. While they occasionally failed the tests given to them, they would, at other times, reach towards their original pure nature (*fitra*) and once again be energized by the spirit. While close to the Prophet of Islam (☆)—some were in daily contact with him—they never lost their perspective on who he was. They never mistook him for anything other than a human being. They did, however, regard him as the most Perfect Human Being ever created by God and the very reason for creation. It was the Prophet's reminder to worship the One God that summarized, completed and fulfilled the previous monotheistic messages.

When the young wife of the Prophet, Ayisha, was exonerated by the revelation of a Quranic verse indicating her to be innocent of the slander cast against her, her parents told her to thank the Prophet. She replied that she would thank no one but Allah alone. This showed a tremendous sense of self-identity. At that moment of crisis, she knew who she was—a believing Muslim woman—and why she was created—to worship the One Allah alone.

While individual women are seldom mentioned in the Quran, the Traditions have shown how a number of verses relate directly to a particular woman.

Verses That Can Be Explained Through Women Biographies

* Verse 33:50 is commented upon by Maymuna bint al-Harith, Umm Hani Fakhida bint Abu Talib, and Umm Sharik Ghaziyya bint Jabir to the effect that the Prophet was permitted to marry his paternal and maternal cousins who emigrated with him "and a believing woman if she gives herself unto the Prophet." Maymuna bint al-Harith relates twenty-seven Traditions concerning the validity of the marriage of the Prophet and Zaynab bint Jahsh.

* Verses 66:1-4 relates to the Prophet's wives explaining the verse that tells of the Prophet's turning away from his wives and threatening to divorce them but that this threat was not considered as divorce.

*Verse 4:128 refers to how Sawda gives her day with the Prophet to Ayisha because she no longer had desire for sexual relations.

* Verses 24:2-20 tell of the slander against Ayisha and the harsh punishment against anyone who makes unsubstantiated allegations against a woman.

* The verses on seclusion of the Prophet's wives including 33:32, 53 and 59 are explained through the Traditions related from women.

* Verses 58:1-3 discuss a woman who complains to her husband that her husband had divorced her using the phrase, "be you to me as the back of my mother," a pre-Islamic phrase which the Prophet had prohibited.

* According to verse 60:10 it was Umm Kulthum bint Uqba, an early convert to Islam in Makka who remained in Makka after the migration, who is "she who is to be examined" refer-

ring to believing women who sought refuge among the Muslims.

* Verse 16:92 refers to Suayra where it says, "*she who unravels thread to thin filaments after she has made it strong.*"

Verses Linked to Specific Women

* Verse 33:37 relates to Zaynab bint Jahsh.

* Verse 60:7 refers to the Prophet's marriage to Umm Habiba bint Abu Sufyan where God said, "*God forbids you not those who warred not against you on account of religion and drove you not out from your homes.*"

* Verses 60:8-9 refer to Asma bint Abu Bakr who had received gifts from her disbelieving mother.

* Verse 3:27 refer to Khalida bint al-Aswad, the maternal aunt of the Prophet as related in the Traditions from women.

* Verse 4:43 relates to Ayisha, a verse that permits dry ablution when water is not available.

According to the six canonical works, over 150 Traditions gathered from the believing female Companions relate directly to the actual events of the revelation (*asbab al-nuzul*) and/or act as commentaries upon the verses themselves. These Traditions related by the women Companions are either from the Prophet's daughter Fatima or those whom were later called "the mothers of the believers"—that is, wives of the Prophet— or from other believing women.

The Traditions recorded from these female believers were recorded in exactly the same way that Traditions were recorded from male Companions: the exact words of one female Companion or one male Companion were preserved through a chain of transmission which, in the case of the six canonical works, was considered to be reliable.

*****

My special thanks goes to my wife, Nazihe Muhammad Nazim Adil, and to all mainstream Muslim women who have followed the Straight Path. I would especially like to thank Dr. Laleh Bakhtiar for helping me to jointly bring out this work. May Allah bless her and all women who are dedicated to His cause.

Shaykh Muhammad Hisham Kabbani
Fenton, Michigan 1998

BOOK 1:
TRADITIONS RELATED
FROM MUHAMMAD'S (ﷺ)
WOMEN COMPANIONS

PART I:
AN INTRODUCTION TO
MORAL-DEVELOPMENT

Chapter 1
Behavior: The Prophet as Model for All

Comprehensive Supplications
AYISHA RELATED:

God's Messenger liked comprehensive supplications and abandoned other kinds.

> AD v1 p388 n1477

Household Chores
AYISHA RELATED:

The Prophet used to mend his shoes, sew his clothes and work in his household just as one works in one's own house. She also reported that he was a man among men who used to patch his clothes, milk his goats and engage in work.

> T [H v4 p346]

Laughing
AYISHA RELATED:

When the Messenger of God arrived after the expedition to Tabuk or Khaybar [the narrator from Ayisha is doubtful as to which], the wind raised the end of a curtain which was placed before her storeroom revealing some dolls which belonged to her. He asked, 'What is this?' She said that they were her dolls. Among them he saw a horse with wings made of rags and asked, 'What is this I see among them?' She said that it was a horse. He asked, 'What does it have on it?' She said that it had two wings. He asked, 'A horse with two wings?' She asked if he had not heard that Solomon had horses with wings. The Messenger of God laughed so heartily that she could see his molar teeth.

> AD v3 p1373 n4914

5

Manner of Speech

AYISHA RELATED:

The Prophet used to speak so clearly that if somebody wanted to count the number of his words, he could do so.

SB v4 p494 n768

AYISHA RELATED:

The Messenger spoke in a distinct manner so that anyone who listened to him could understand.

AD v3 p1343 n4821

AYISHA RELATED:

The Prophet did not talk hastily as others do but used to pause at regular intervals. He who sat by him could remember what he had said.

T [H v4 p348]

AYISHA RELATED:

God's Messenger was not unseemly or lewd in his language, nor was he loud-voiced in the streets, nor did he return evil for evil, but he would forgive and pardon.

T [MMR v2 p1248]

Righteous Action

UMM SALAMA RELATED:

Towards the end of his life, the Messenger offered most of his prescribed prayers while he was sitting. The dearest of all deeds to him was the adherence by a servant to a righteous action, even if it were a small action.

IM v2 p225 n1225

Sitting

QAYLAH BINT MAKHRAMA RELATED:

The Prophet was sitting with his arms around his legs. When she saw the Prophet in such a humble position, she trembled with fear.

AD v3 p1353 n4829

Thankful Servant

AYISHA RELATED:

The Prophet used to offer prayer at night for such a long time that his feet would swell. She asked him why he did this since God had forgiven him all of his faults. He said, 'Should I not love to be a thankful servant of God?' When he grew old, he prayed while sitting, but when he wanted to bow forward, he would get up, recite [some other verses] and, then, perform the bow.

SB v6 p344 n361; SB v6 p34 n45; SM v4B p304 n2820

CHAPTER 2
COMPANIONS, COMPANIONS WHO WERE ALSO FAMILY OF THE PROPHET, COMPANIONS WHO WERE ALSO WIVES OF THE PROPHET: THEIR FINE QUALITIES

COMPANIONS

Abd Allah ibn Zubayr'

HAFSA RELATED:

The Messenger said, 'Abd Allah is a pious man.'

> SB v5 p61 n84

AYISHA RELATED:

The first child who was born in the Islamic land of Madinah among the Emigrants was Abd Allah ibn al-Zubayr. They brought him to the Prophet. The Prophet took a date and, after chewing it, put its juice in his mouth. So the first thing that went into this child's stomach was the saliva of the Prophet.

> SB v5 p169 n249; SB v5 p167 n248; SB v7 p272 n378; SM v3B p427 n2146 R2; SM v3B p428 n2148

AYISHA RELATED:

When the Prophet saw a lamp in Zubayr's house he said, 'Ayisha, I think that Asma must have given birth to a child. Do not give the child a name until I do so.' He named him Abd Allah and, with his own hand, rubbed his palate with moistened dates.

> T [MMR v2 p1373]
> SB v1 p276 n465

7

Abu Bakr Abu Qahafa

AYISHA RELATED:

Abu Bakr had married a woman, from the Kalb tribe, called Umm Bakr. When Abu Bakr migrated to Madinah, he divorced her, and she married her cousin, a poet, who recited a poem lamenting the disbelievers of the Quraysh.

SB v5 p177 n258

AYISHA RELATED:

During his last illness, God's Messenger asked her to call Abu Hurayra, her father [Abu Bakr], and her brother so that he might dictate a document, for God's Messenger feared that someone else might desire to succeed him and thus make a claim; therefore, God and the faithful do not accept the claim of anyone but that of Abu Bakr.

SM v4A p74 n2387

AYISHA RELATED:

The Messenger said, 'It is not suitable for a people among whom there is Abu Bakr to elect an Imam other than him.'

T [H v4 p515 rare]

AYISHA RELATED:

Abu Bakr went to the Prophet and told him that he [the Prophet] had been freed by God from the fire. On that day he [the Prophet] was named Atiq (freed man).

T [H v4 p516]

AYISHA RELATED:

Abu Bakr led the prayer, and the Messenger was not in the row.

N v1E p483 n789

AYISHA RELATED:

When God's Messenger went to Madinah, Abu Bakr and Bilal came down with a fever. She then went to them both and asked how they felt. Whenever Abu Bakr's fever worsened, he would say that every man would meet his death some morning while he was among his family, for death was really nearer to him than his leather shoe laces. Whenever Bilal's fever subsided, he would wish aloud to know whether he would spend a night in the valley [of Makkah] with *idhkhir* and *jalil* [kinds of grass] around him and whether he would drink one day the water of Mijannah and whether he would once again see the hills of Shamah and Tafil. Then she went to God's Messenger and told him what they had said. He said, 'O God, make us love Madinah as much or more than we used to love Makkah. O God, make it healthy and bless its measures and take away its fever to al-Juhfa.'

SB v5 p180 n263; SM v2B p326 n1376

Abu Salama ibn Abd al-Rahman

AYISHA RELATED:

The Messenger used to say to his wives, 'I am concerned about what will happen to you after I am gone, and only the self-sacrificing and truly generous will continue to care for you.' By this he meant those who give charity. Then she told Abu Salama ibn Abd al-Rahman that she hoped God would give his father drink from Salsabil in paradise! Ibn Auf [his son] had given as charity for the mothers of the faithful a garden which had been sold for forty thousand dinars.

T [MMR v2 p1347]

Ammar ibn Yasir

AYISHA RELATED:

God's Messenger said, 'Ammar [is a person] to whom if two things were offered, he would choose the best of the two.'

IM v1 p83] n148

Anas ibn Malek

UMM SULAYM RELATED:

She told the Messenger that since Anas was his servant, he should invoke God's blessing upon him. The Prophet said, 'O God! Increase his wealth and offspring and bless for him whatever You give him.'

SB v8 p258 n389; SM v4A p127 n2480

Asma bint Abu Bakr

ASMA BINT ABU BAKR RELATED:

When Zubayr married her, he had no real property or any slave or anything else except a camel, which drew water from the well, and his horse. She used to feed his horse with fodder, draw water, sew the bucket for drawing it and prepare the dough, but she did not know how to bake bread. Her neighbor Helpers used to bake the bread for her. They were honorable women. She used to carry the date stones on her head from Zubayr's land given to him by God's Messenger. This land was two miles from her home. One day while she was walking with the date stones on her head, she met God's Messenger who was traveling with some Companions. He called to her and then, directing his camel to kneel down, indicated that she should ride behind him on his camel. She felt embarrassed to travel with the men and remembered Zubayr and his jealousy, for he was one of those people who had the greatest sense of jealousy. God's Messenger noticed that she felt shy so he proceeded. She went to Zubayr and told him that she had met God's Messenger while she was carrying a load of date stones on her head and that he had some Companions with him. She told Zubayr that God's Messenger made his camel kneel so that she might ride, but that she felt embarrassed to do so since she remembered Zubayr's jealousy. Upon hearing this, Zubayr said that her carrying the date stones and being seen by the Prophet in such a state was more shameful to him than her riding with the Prophet [Zubayr meant he was more ashamed by the Prophet seeing his wife engaged in such hard work than he would have been had she ridden on the

Prophet's camel]. Finally, Abu Bakr sent her a servant to look after their horse; whereupon, she felt as if he had freed her.

SB v7 p111 n151; SM v3B p446 n2182; AD v2 p872 n3063

ASMA BINT ABU BAKR RELATED:

She prepared the food for Abu Bakr's house for the journey of God's Messenger when he intended to emigrate to Madinah. She could not find anything with which to tie the food container and the water skin. She told Abu Bakr that all she found was her waist belt. He told her to cut it into two pieces and tie the water skin with one and the food container with the other. She did this. [The sub-narrator states this is why she was called the Woman With the Two Waist Bands.]

SB v4 p141 n222; SB v5 p167 n246

Asma bint Umays

ASMA BINT UMAYS RELATED:

She had migrated to Abyssinia and had then migrated to Madinah (along with other emigrants to Abyssinia) and visited Hafsa. Umar had been sitting with Hafsa. When Umar saw Asma, he asked Hafsa who she was. Hafsa said that she was Asma, daughter of Umays. He mentioned to Asma that she was an Abyssinian and a sea-woman. Asma replied that it was so. Thereupon Umar said that they had preceded her in migration to Madinah and so had more right to God's Messenger than did her party [those who had migrated to Abyssinia and then to Madinah]. She felt annoyed at this and said that Umar was not stating the facts because he and the other Companions who had first migrated to Madinah had had the privilege of being in the company of the Messenger [in Makkah] who fed the hungry among them and instructed the ignorant; whereas, she and her fellow emigrants to Abyssinia had been far from [Makkah and Madinah] and among enemies, all for God and God's Messenger's sake. She said that she would mention to God's Messenger what Umar had said. She pointed out that her party remained in Abyssinia in constant trouble and dread. She said she would tell the Messenger, but she would not lie or add anything to what had taken place. When the Messenger came, she related that Umar had said so and so. Upon hearing this, God's Messenger said, 'His right is not more than yours. For he and his Companions there is one migration, but for you, the people of the boat, there are two migrations.' She said that she saw Abu Musa and the people of the boat coming to her in groups and asking her about this Tradition because there was nothing more pleasing and more significant to them than this. Abu Baurda reported that Asma had said that she saw Abu Musa asking her to repeat this Tradition to him again and again.

SM v4A p142 n2503

Hasan ibn Thabit

AYISHA RELATED:

God's Messenger said to Hasan, 'Satirize the Quraysh for it is more grievous to them than the hurt of an arrow.' The Messenger sent someone to Ibn Rawaha and asked him to satirize them. He composed a satire but it did not appeal to the Messenger. He then sent someone to Kab ibn Malik to do the same, but what he composed also did not appeal to the Prophet. He then sent another one to Hasan ibn Thabit. In the presence of the Messenger, Hasan said that the Messenger had called for a lion to strike the enemies with its tail. He lolled out his tongue and began to move it and swore that he would tear them with his tongue just as leather is torn. Thereupon God's Messenger said, 'Do not be hasty. Let Abu Bakr, who has the best knowledge of the lineage of the Quraysh, draw a distinction for you in regard to my lineage as my lineage is the same as theirs.' Hasan then went to Abu Bakr and, after making inquiry in regard to the lineage of the Messenger, returned to the Messenger and said that Abu Bakr had drawn a distinction in his lineage from that of the Quraysh. Hasan said that he would draw out from them the name of the Messenger as hair is drawn out from dough. The Messenger said to Hasan, 'Verily the spirit will continue to help you as long as you put up a defense on behalf of God and His Messenger.' The Messenger told her [Ayisha] that Hasan satirized the Quraysh and gave satisfaction to the Muslims and disquieted the non-Muslims.

SM v4A p134 n2490; SB v8 p111 n171; v4 p481 n731; SM v4A p133 n2489

AYISHA RELATED:

The Messenger of God used to set up a *minbar* in the mosque for Hasan [ibn Thabit] to stand on and satirize those who spoke against the Messenger of God. The Messenger of God would say, '[Gabriel] is with Hasan so long as he speaks in defense of the Messenger of God.'

AD v3 p1394 n4997

Helpers

AYISHA RELATED:

The day of fighting between the tribes of the Helpers, the Aws and the Khazraj [the battle of Buath] was brought to an end by God for the good of the Messenger. When the Messenger reached Madinah, the tribes had already separated, and their chiefs had been killed or wounded. God had brought about a battle for the good of His Messenger in order that they [the Helpers] would embrace Islam.

SB v5 p79 n121; SB v5 p111 n186; v5 p184 n267

Hudhayfa ibn Yaman

AYISHA RELATED:

On the day of the Battle of Uhud, the disbelievers were defeated. Then satan tempted them by shouting, 'O God's worshipers! Beware of what is behind you!' So the front lines attacked the back lines of the army. Hudhayfa looked and saw his father, al-Yaman, being attacked! He shouted to his fellow soldiers saying, 'My father! My father!', but by God they did not stop until they killed his father. Hudhayfa asked God to forgive the person who had killed his father. He continued to ask for forgiveness for that man until that man died.

SB v9 p18 n28; SB v9 p14 n22; SB v5 p102 n161; SB v5 p263 n391; SB v8 p430 n661

Sad ibn Abi Waqqas

AYISHA RELATED:

Sad prayed to God saying that God knew that there was none against whom he was more eager to fight for God's cause than those people who disbelieved His Messenger and drove him out [of his city]. He thanked God for ending the fight between them [the Aws and Khajraj tribes].

SB v5 p155 n241

AYISHA RELATED:

One night the Prophet was unable to sleep. He said, 'Would that a righteous person from my Companions guard me tonight.' Suddenly they heard the clatter of arms whereupon the Prophet asked, 'Who is there?' The reply came that it was Sad who had come to guard him. The Prophet then slept so soundly that they heard him snoring. Another time Ayisha said that Bilal prayed that the Prophet could spend the night in a valley with two kinds of good smelling grasses around him. She told this to the Prophet.

SB v9 p256 n337; SB v4 p88 n136; SM v4A p88 n2410 R1

Umar ibn Khattab

AYISHA RELATED:

God's Messenger said, 'There have been among the people before you inspired people, and if there were any such among my Community, Umar ibn Khattab would be one of them.'

SM v4A p79 n2398

Umm Hani bint Abu Talib

UMM HANI RELATED:

She went to God's Messenger in the year of the conquest of Makkah and found him bathing while his daughter, Fatima, was screening him with a garment. She greeted him, and he asked Fatima who it was. Fatima said that it was Umm Hani. He sent greetings of peace to Umm Hani. After he finished his bath, he got up, wrapped himself in a garment and offered eight cycles of prayer. When he was done, Umm Hani told him that she had given protection to two of her husband's male relatives. The Messenger replied, 'We have given security to those to whom you have given it.'

T [MMR v2 p846]; SB v4 p263 n396; SB v8 p116 n179; SB v8 p62 n98; SB v1 p216 n353; SM v1A p213 n336; SM v1B p406 n336R5; IM v1 p255 n465; IM v2 p284 n1323; N v1E p224 n228; T [H v2 p393]

Umm Khalid bint Khalid

UMM KHALID BINT KHALID RELATED:

When she came from Abyssinia to Madinah, she was a young girl. God's Messenger made her wear a sheet with designs on it. He rubbed those marks with his hands, saying, 'Good! Good!'

SB v5 p137 n214

Umm Sulaym

UMM SULAYM RELATED:

God's Messenger visited her house and took rest. She spread a piece of cloth for him, and he had a nap on it. He sweated profusely. She collected his sweat, and put it in perfume bottles. God's Messenger said, 'Umm Sulaym, what is this?' She said that it was his sweat which she had put in her perfume. God's Messenger sweated in cold weather when revelation came to him.

SM v4A p42 n2332

Usama ibn Zayd

AYISHA RELATED:

The people of the Quraysh tribe were concerned about a woman from the Makhzum clan [who had been found to have stolen something]. They said nobody but Usama ibn Zayd, who was the most beloved of God's Messenger, could intervene. Nobody dared speak to the Messenger but Usama ibn Zayd. The Prophet said, 'If a reputable person among the Children of Israel committed a theft, they used to forgive him, but if a poor person committed a theft, they would cut off his hand. But I would cut even the hand of Fatima if she committed a theft.'

SB v5 p58 n79

AYISHA RELATED:

Once when the Prophet wanted to wipe Usama's nose [when he was a small boy], she asked to be allowed to do it, and the Prophet said, 'Love him, Ayisha, for I love him.'

T [MMR v2 p1357]

Uthman ibn Affan

AYISHA RELATED:

Once Abu Bakr sought permission from God's Messenger to enter. The Messenger had been lying on his bed covered with his bed sheet. He gave permission to Abu Bakr and remained as he was. Abu Bakr, his need fulfilled, left. Umar sought permission, and it was given to him. The Messenger remained as he was. His need being fulfilled, Umar left. Uthman then sought permission to enter. The Messenger got up and said to me, 'Wrap me well with your cloth.' Uthman had his need fulfilled and left. I asked why the Messenger did not have any feeling of anxiety about not dressing properly in the presence of Abu Bakr and Umar but did with Uthman. The Messenger said,

'Verily Uthman is a man who is very modest, and I was afraid that if I permitted him to enter when I was in this state, he would not inform me of his need.'

SM v4A p81 n2402; SM v4A p80 n2401; AD v1 p65 n113

AYISHA RELATED:

God's Messenger one day said to Uthman, 'Uthman, if one day God entrusts you with this affair [of being caliph], the hypocrites will intend to strip off your shirt [of the caliphate] with which God dressed you. So do not take it off.' [Her nephew asked her what had prevented her from informing people of it at the time of the riots against Uthman. She said that she had forgotten it.]

IM v1 p64 n112; T [MMR v2 p1335]

Uthman ibn Mazun

UMM AL-ALAL-ANSARIYYAH RELATED:

When the Helpers drew lots as to which of the Emigrants should dwell with which of the Helpers, the name of Uthman ibn Mazun fell to Umm al-Alah's family. She said that Uthman stayed with her, and they nursed him when he got sick, but he died. They shrouded him in his clothes, and the Messenger came to their house. She said, addressing the dead Uthman, that she bore witness that he was blessed. The Messenger asked how she knew this. She said she did not know. The Messenger said, 'As regards Uthman, by God, he has died; and I really wish him every good, yet, by God, although I am God's Messenger, I do not know what will be done to him.' Umm al-Alal added that she never attested to someone's piety after that. Later she had a dream in which she saw a flowing stream for Uthman. She told the Messenger about her dream and he said, 'That is [the symbol] of his deeds.'

SB v3 p528 n852

Woman Slave

AYISHA RELATED:

A black woman slave embraced Islam. She had a hut in the mosque. She used to visit and talk to them. When she finished speaking, she would praise the day of the scarf as one of the Lord's wonders because it delivered her from the land of disbelief. Ayisha asked her what that day was. She said that once the daughter of one of her master went out. The girl was wearing a leather scarf [around her neck]. The leather scarf fell from her and a hawk descended and picked it up, mistaking it for a piece of meat. The master accused [the slave girl] of stealing it, and they tortured her to such an extent that they even looked for the scarf in her private parts. While they were gathered around her in her great distress, suddenly the hawk flew over their heads and dropped the scarf. They took it. She said to them that this was what they had accused her of stealing although she had been innocent.

SB v5 p111 n176

Zayd ibn Amr ibn Nufayl

ASMA BINT ABU BAKR RELATED:

She saw Zayd ibn Amr ibn Nufayl standing with his back against the Kabah and telling the people there that none among them was a follower of the religion of Abraham except him. He used to preserve the lives of female infants. If someone wanted to kill his daughter, Zayd would tell that person not to kill his [that person's] daughter. Zayd then promised that he would provide the daughter with food on that person's account. He would take her, and when she had grown up, he would say to her father that if her father wished, he would give his daughter back to him; but if he did not want her, he would continue to feed her on behalf of her father.

SB v5 p107 n169

Zayd ibn Haritha

AYISHA RELATED:

A person skilled in recognizing the lineage of a person through physiognomy and through examining the body parts of an infant came to her while the Prophet was present. Usama ibn Zayd and Zayd ibn Haritha were lying asleep. This expert said that the feet of Usama and his father were of persons belonging to the same lineage. The Prophet was pleased with that saying which won his admiration.

SB v5 p58 n78

AYISHA RELATED:

Abu Hudhayfa, one of those who fought the battle of Badr with God's Messenger, adopted Salim as his son. He married his niece, Hind bint al-Walid ibn Utba to him. Salim was a freed slave of a woman Helper. God's Messenger also adopted Zayd as his son. In the pre-Islamic period of ignorance, the custom was that if one adopted a son, the people would call him by the name of his adopted father from whom he would inherit until God revealed, 'Call them [adopted sons] by [the names of] their fathers' [33:5].

SB v5 p224 n335

Zubayr and Abu Bakr

AYISHA RELATED:

Zubayr and Abu Bakr were among those about whom it has been revealed, 'Those who responded to the call of God and His Messenger after misfortune had fallen upon them.'

SM v4A p92 n2418R2

COMPANIONS WHO WERE ALSO FAMILY OF THE PROPHET

Ali ibn Abi Talib

ASMA BINT AL-HAKAM RELATED:

She heard Ali say that he was a man when he heard a Tradition from the Messenger of God. God benefited him with it as much as He willed, but when one of the Companions narrated a Tradition to him, he adjured him. The Companion took an oath testifying that Abu Bakr narrated a Tradition to him, and Abu Bakr narrated truthfully. He said that he heard God's Messenger say, 'When a servant of God commits a sin and performs ablution well and stands and prays two cycles and asks pardon of God, God pardons him.' He then recited the verse, '*And those who, when they commit indecency or wrong their souls, remember God*' [3:134].

AD v1 p396 n1516

UMM ATIYA RELATED:

God's Messenger sent off an army of which Ali was a member, and she heard God's Messenger say with his arms upraised, 'O God, do not cause me to die before You let me see Ali [again].'

T [MMR v2 p1342]

UMM SALAMA RELATED:

God's Messenger said, 'A hypocrite does not love Ali and a believer does not hate him.' [Tirmidhi said this is a *hasan* Tradition whose line of transmission is *gharib*.]

T [MMR v2 p1342]

Fatima bint Muhammad

AYISHA RELATED:

She never saw anyone more like God's Messenger in respect to gravity, calm deportment, pleasant disposition, and speech than Fatima. When Fatima went to visit the Prophet, he stood up to welcome her, took her by the hand, kissed her, and made her sit where he was sitting. When he went in to visit her, she got up to welcome him, took him by the hand, kissed him, and made him sit where she was sitting.

AD v3 p1439 n5198

AYISHA RELATED:

She and the other wives of God's Messengers sent Fatima, his daughter, to him. Fatima sought permission to enter, as he had been lying with her [Ayisha] on her mantle. He gave Fatima permission and she said that his wives had sent her in order to ask him to observe equity in the case of the daughter of Abu Quhafa. She [Ayisha] remained silent. The Messenger said, 'O daughter, do you not love whom I love?' Fatima said that she did. He said, 'I love this one.' Fatima then stood up when she heard this and went to the wives of the Messenger and told them what she had said to her father and what he had said to her. The wives said that she had been of no avail to them. They asked Fatima to go again and say the same thing. She swore an oath that she would never speak to him about this matter again. The wives of God's Messenger then sent Zaynab bint Jahsh to the Messenger. She was one who was equal in rank with [Ayisha]. She [Ayisha] said she had never seen a woman more advanced in religious piety than Zaynab or more God-fearing or more truthful or more alive to the ties of blood or more generous or having more sense of self-sacrifice in practical life or having more charitable disposition or more closeness to God than Zaynab. Zaynab, however, lost her temper quickly but soon regained her composure. The Messenger permitted her to enter as she [Ayisha] was alone with him on her mantle in the same state as when Fatima had entered. Zaynab said that the Prophet's wives had sent her to seek equity in regard to the daughter of Abu Quhafa. Zaynab then came towards [Ayisha] and showed harshness. [Ayisha] looked at the Messenger to see if he would permit [Ayisha] to respond. Zaynab went on until [Ayisha] realized the Messenger would not disapprove if she [Ayisha] responded. [Ayisha] exchanged hot words with her until Zaynab became quiet. Thereupon the Messenger smiled and said, 'She is the daughter of Abu Bakr.'

> SM v4A p101 n 2442

AYISHA RELATED:

The Prophet in his fatal illness called his daughter Fatima and told her a secret because of which she started weeping. Then he called her and told her another secret. Fatima started laughing. When asked about that, Fatima replied that the Prophet told her that he would die in his fatal illness, and so she had wept. Then he secretly told her that from among his family, she would be the first to join him, and so she had laughed.

> SB v4 p527 n820; SB v4 p527 n899; SB v5 p16 n62; SB v8 p201 n301; SB v5 p513 n718; SB v8 p201 n301; SM v4A p109 n2450; IM v2 p463 n1621

AYISHA RELATED:

Fatima sent somebody to Abu Bakr asking him to give her her inheritance from the Prophet, an inheritance consisting of what God had given to His Messenger through booty gained without fighting. She asked for the wealth assigned for charitable purposes by the Prophet at Madinah and Fadak and for what remained of the one-fifth of the Khaybar booty. Abu Bakr said that God's Messenger had said, 'The property of we prophets is not inherited. Whatever we leave is for charity. Muhammad's family can eat from this property, but they have no right to take more than the food that they need." Abu Bakr added that he would continue to deal with the matter the way the Prophet had and dispose of it as the Messenger would have. Ali said that he bore witness to the oneness of God and to Muhammad, His Messenger. He added that the Companions acknowledged the superiority of Abu Bakr. He then described their relationship to the Prophet and their rights. Abu Bakr then said that he loved to do good to the relatives of God's Messenger even more than to his own relatives because if one was not good to the Messenger's family, then one was not good to him [the Messenger].

SB v5 p16 n60

AYISHA RELATED:

The Messenger said, 'Fatima is the chief mistress of the women in paradise.'

SB v5 p74 Title

Hasan and Husayn ibn Ali

AYISHA RELATED:

God's Messenger went out one morning wearing a striped cloak of black camel's hair. Hasan ibn Ali came along. He wrapped him under it. Then came Husayn and he wrapped him under it along with Hasan. Then came Fatima, and he took her under it. Then came Ali whom he also took under it. Then the Messenger said, "*God only desires to take away any impurity from you, O people of the household and purify you [through purifying].*" [33:33]

SM v4A p94 n2424

COMPANIONS WHO WERE ALSO WIVES OF THE PROPHET

Ayisha bint Abu Bakr

AYISHA RELATED:

When she was on a journey with the Messenger of God, she had a race with him. She outstripped him. When she became plump, she again had a race with the Prophet, and he outstripped her. He said, 'This is for that outstripping.'

AD v2 p709 n2572

AYISHA RELATED:

God's Messenger said to her, 'I can well discern when you are pleased with me and when you are annoyed with me.' She asked how. He said, 'When you are pleased with me you say, "No, by the Lord of Muhammad," but when you are annoyed with me, you say, "No by the Lord of Abraham."' She said that when she was annoyed with him, she left out his name altogether.

SM v4A p100 n2439; SB v8 p65 n101

AYISHA RELATED:

She went with the Messenger on one of the journeys. When they reached al-Baida or Dhat al-Jaysh, her necklace broke and was lost. The Messenger stopped to search for it, and the people also stopped with him. There was no water [for ablution] at that place, and they had no water with them. The people went to Abu Bakr and said that his daughter [Ayisha] had made the Messenger and the other people stop where there was no water. Abu Bakr went to the Messenger while the Messenger was sleeping with his head on [Ayisha's] thigh. Abu Bakr reprimanded her for delaying everyone in a place where there was no water. He then admonished her and said what God wished and pinched her on her flank with his hand, but she did not move because she did not wish to disturb the head of God's Messenger resting on her thigh.

SB v5 p16 n21

AYISHA RELATED:

She borrowed a necklace from Asma, and it was lost. The Messenger sent some of his Companions to look for it. During their journey, the time for prescribed prayer came. They offered the prescribed prayer without ablution. When they returned to the Messenger, they complained about it. The verse of dry ablution was revealed. Usayd ibn Hudayr blessed her [Ayisha] because it was through this incident that there came a blessing for Muslims.

SB v5 p75 n117

AYISHA RELATED:

Abu Bakr came to her while God's Messenger was sleeping with his head on her thigh. Abu Bakr reprimanded her saying that she had detained the people [who were searching for the necklace she had lost] in a place where there was no water. He admonished her and struck her flanks with his hand. She did not move because she did not wish to disturb the reclining of God's Messenger [on her thigh]. Then God revealed the divine verse of dry ablution [5:6].

SB v8 p552 n827

AYISHA RELATED:

Abu Bakr came towards her and struck her violently with his fist. He said that she had detained the people because of her lost necklance. She remained motionless as if she were dead lest she should wake God's Messenger although the blow was very painful.

SB v8 p553 n828

AYISHA RELATED:

God's Messenger said to her, 'O Ayisha! This is Gabriel sending his greetings to you.' She returned the greeting. Addressing the Prophet, she said that he [the Prophet] saw what they [others] did not see.

SB v8 p175 n266; SB v8 p141 n220; SB v8 p176 Title; SB v8 p178 n270; SB v5 p75 n112; SM v4A p104 n2447R3; AD v3 p1443 n5213

AYISHA RELATED:

God's Messenger said to her, 'You were shown to me twice [in my dream] before I married you. I saw an angel carrying you in a silken piece of cloth, and I said to him, 'Uncover her,' and behold it was you. I said to myself, 'If this is from God, then it must happen.'

SB v9 p115 n140; SB v9 p115 n139; SB v5 p152 n235; SM v4A p99 n2439; T MMR v2; SB v7 p42 n57; SB v7 p10 n15

AYISHA RELATED:

She told Abd Allah ibn Zubayr [her nephew] to bury her with the other wives of the Prophet in their house because she did not want to be sanctified. [It was also narrated that Umar asked Ayisha if he could be buried next to the Prophet and Abu Bakr and she agreed although it was not her habit to give permission to any of the Companions to be buried there].

SB v9 p319 n428

AYISHA RELATED:

She asked [her nephew Urwa] if he were not surprised at Abu Hurayrah. He came and sat down next to her apartment and began reciting the Traditions from the Messenger so that she could hear them. She was offering a superogatory prayer. He got up and left before she finished her prayer. Had she found him, she would have told him that the Messenger of God did not narrate Traditions quickly one after the other as he did.

AD v3 p1037 n3647; SM v4A p136 n2493

AYISHA RELATED:

She thought in her mind that she and the incident with the lost necklace were far too unimportant for God's words about her to be revealed in a command [for dry ablution] that would be [continuously] recited.

AD v3 p1320 n4717

AYISHA RELATED:

The Prophet said, 'Good tidings to you, Ayisha, for God Almighty has revealed your innocence.' He then recited to her the Quranic verses. Her parents told her to kiss the head of the Messenger of God. She praised God Almighty and not the Messenger [perhaps as he had taught her to praise God alone].

AD v3 p1440 n5200

Khadija bint Khuwalid

AYISHA RELATED:

God's Messenger gave glad tidings to Khadija bint Khuwalid of a palace in paradise.

SM v4A p98 n2434

AYISHA RELATED:

God's Messenger did not marry any other woman until Khadija died.

SM v4A p99 n2436

Zaynab

AYISHA RELATED:

Some of the wives of the Prophet asked him who among them would be the first to follow him. He said, "Whoever has the longest hand.' They started measuring their hands with a stick, and Sawda's hand turned out to be the longest. When Zaynab bint Jahsh died first during the caliphate of Umar, they came to understand that the 'long hand' was a symbol of practicing charity. Thus Zaynab was the first to follow the Prophet, as she used to love to practice charity.

SB v2 p286 n501; SM v4A p112

CHAPTER 3
COUNSELING AGAINST
WRONGDOING

ABUSING THE DEAD

Prohibition of Abusing the Dead

AYISHA RELATED:

The Prophet said, 'Do not abuse the dead for they have reached the result of what they have done.'

SB v8 p344 n523; SB v1 p270 n476

AYISHA RELATED:

God's Messenger said, 'When your companion dies, do not revile him.'

AD v3 p1365 n4881

Prohibition of Breaking the Bones of a Dead Body

AYISHA RELATED:

God's Messenger said, 'Breaking the bone of a dead body is just like breaking the bone of a living person.'

IM v2 p459 n1616; AD v2 p912 n1193

AVOID

Anger

AYISHA RELATED:

No one could cook food like Safiya. She cooked food for the Messenger of God and sent the food to him. She [Ayisha] became angry and broke the vessel. She asked the Messenger of God what atonement she must make. He replied, 'A vessel like this vessel and food like this food.'

AD v2 p1012 n3561

Backbiting

AYISHA RELATED:

The Messenger said, 'I do not like to speak of anyone's faults even if I should get such and such.'

T [MMR v2 p1011]

AYISHA RELATED:

Hasan ibn Thabit came and asked permission to visit her. She was asked how she could permit such a person to visit her. She replied that he had received a severe penalty [the loss of his sight]. Hasan then recited the following poem, 'A chaste pious woman who arouses no suspicion, she never talks about chaste heedless women behind their backs.' She then asked if he were not the same.

SB v6 p259 n279; SB v3 p501 n823A

Beating People

AYISHA RELATED:

God's Messenger never hit anyone with his hand—neither a woman nor a servant, but only when fighting in God's cause. He never took revenge for anything unless the things made inviolable by God were violated. He then took revenge for God, the Exalted and Glorious.

SM v4A p40 n2328; SB v8 p557 n836; AD v3 p1341 n4768; IM v2u p72 n136

AYISHA RELATED:

Whenever God's Messenger was given the choice of one of two matters, he would choose the easier of the two as long as it was not sinful to do so, but if it was sinful, he would not approach it. God's Messenger never took revenge against anybody for his own sake but did only when God's legal bounds were broken in which case he would take revenge for God's sake.

SB v8 p90 n147; SB v4 p491 n760; v8 p511 n777; SM v4A p40 n2327R3; AD v3 p1341 n4767

Boasting

ASMA RELATED:

A woman went to God's Messenger and said that she had a co-wife. She wanted to know if there was any harm in her giving the false impression of getting something from her husband which he had not in fact given her. God's Messenger said, 'The one who creates such a false impression of receiving what one has not been given is like one who wears a garment of falsehood.'

SM v3B p420 n2130; SB v7 p109 n146; SM v3B p420 n2129; AD v3 p1388 n4979

Cursing

AYISHA RELATED:

A man asked to enter the room where the Prophet was. The Prophet said, 'Admit him. What an evil brother of his tribe! What an evil son of his tribe!' When the man entered, the Prophet behaved in a nice, polite manner and was completely at ease with him. When the man left, she asked why the Prophet had showed the man such kind, polite behavior and had enjoyed his company when the Messenger had first said the other words. The Prophet said, 'O Ayisha! Have you ever seen me cursing. Remember that the worst people in God's sight on the day of resurrection will be those whom the people avoid in order to avoid the evil deeds they commit.'

SB v8 p36 n59A; SB v8 p95 n152; SB v8 p50 n80; SM v4A p184 n2591; AD v3 p1342 n4774; AD v3 p1342 n4775; AD v3 p1342 n4773

AYISHA RELATED:

When something of hers was stolen, she began to curse the thief. God's Messenger said to her, 'Do not lessen his sin.'

AD v3 p1368 n4891; AD v1 p390 n1492

UMM DARDA RELATED:

God's Messenger said, 'Those who curse will neither be witnesses nor intercessors on the day of resurrection.'

SM v4A p187 n2598R2

AYISHA RELATED:

Two men visited God's Messenger. They talked about a thing of which she was not aware, but it annoyed the Messenger. He cursed and reviled both of them. When they left, she asked if good would not reach everyone but these two. He asked why she said this. She replied because he had made it a condition with his Lord saying, 'O God, I am a human being. Make it a source of purity and reward for a Muslim whom I curse or revile.'

SM v4A p187 n2600

Disputing Over Allegorical Verses

AYISHA RELATED:

God's Messenger recited the verse, '*He it is Who has sent down upon you the Book wherein there are substantive verses—they are the essence of words and none takes heed, but the people endowed with understanding*' [3:7]. He said, 'Ayisha, you see those who dispute in these [allegorical verses]. It is they whom God alluded to [in the above verse]. Therefore guard yourselves against them.'

IM v1 p26 n47; SB v6 p53 n70; SM v4B p221 n2665; AD v3 p1290 n4581

Hypocrisy

AYISHA RELATED:

She said that the Prophet came to see her one day and said, 'O Ayisha! I do not think that so and so and so and so [the hypocrites] know anything about the religion which we follow.'

SB v8 p60 n94; SB v8 p59 n93

AYISHA RELATED:

The verse, '*And as for him among them who had the greater share. . .*' [24:11] refers to Abd Allah ibn Ubay ibn Salul.

SB v6 p247 n273

Imitating the Wrong Characteristics

AYISHA RELATED:

She asked God's Messenger if Safiya was enough for him [i.e. could satisfy him] because she was so short statured. He replied, 'You have said things which would pollute the sea if they were mixed with it.' She said that she had disgracefully imitated someone. He said, 'I would not imitate anyone even if I would get such and such.'

AD v3 p1359 n4857; T [MMR v2 p1011]

Innovation

AYISHA RELATED:

God's Messenger said, 'Whatever new is introduced to this affair of ours [the religion of submission to God's will], which does not form a part of it, is invalid.'

IM v1 p7 n14; SM v3A p154 n1718; AD v3 p1294 n4589; SB v3 p535 n861

Jealousy

AYISHA RELATED:

One night God's Messenger left her house, and she felt jealous. He came and saw her in this state of mind. He asked, 'Ayisha, what is wrong? Do you feel jealous?' She asked how a woman like she should not feel jealous with a husband like him. Thereupon God's Messenger said, 'It was your satan who came to you.' She asked if she had a devil, and he said that everyone did. She asked if he had one, and he said he did but that God helped him against satan and, therefore, he was absolutely safe from its mischief.

SM v4B p302 n2815

AYISHA RELATED:

She said that she never felt so jealous of any wife of God's Messenger as she did of Khadija because God's Messenger used to remember and praise her so often and because it was revealed to God's Messenger that he should give Khadija the glad tidings that she would have a palace made of pearls, gold, and precious stones in paradise.

SB v7 p115 n156; SB v9 p429 n576; SB v5 p104 n166; SB v5 p103 n164; SB v8 p22 n33; SM v4A p98 n2435; IM v2u p77 n150

Lying: "As you tell lies with your tongues. . ." 24:15

AYISHA RELATED:

She used to recite the verse, 'As you tell lies with your tongues' [24:15] and used to say al-walaq which means telling a lie. She knew this verse more than anybody else, as it was revealed about her.

SB v5 p331 n465

UMM KULTHUM BINT UQBA RELATED:

God's Messenger said, 'He who makes peace between people by inventing good information or saying good things is not a liar.'

SB v3 p533 n857

UMM KULTHUM BINT UQBA RELATED:

She did not hear God's Messenger give license for anything people say falsely, except in three matters. He said, 'I do not count as a liar a person who puts things right between people by saying a word intended only to put things right, nor a person who says something in war, nor a husband who says something to his wife or a wife who says something to her husband.' [The Tradition in Tirmidhi is by Asma bint Umays and does not include the part about wife to husband].

AD v3 p1371 n4903; T [MMR v2]

Minor Sins

AYISHA RELATED:

The Messenger of God said, 'O Ayisha! Take special care to guard yourself against sins that are regarded as minor, for even these will be brought to account by God.'

IM [MMT v1 p 216]

Miserliness

HIND BINT UTBA RELATED:

She went to God's Messenger and said that [before she embraced Islam] there was no family on the surface of the earth she wished to see degraded more than his family, but that today there was no family on the surface of the earth that she more honored than his family. The Prophet said, 'I thought so by Him in Whose Hand is my life.' She further said that Abu Sufyan was a miser. She wanted to know if it was sinful for her to feed her children from his property. The Messenger said, 'No as long as you take what is just and reasonable in terms of your needs.'

SB v5 p105 Title; SB v5 p105 title; SB v7 p216 n283; SB v7 p208 n277; SB v7 p208 n272; SB v3 p226 n413; SB v9 p203 n275; SB v8 p414 n636; SM v3A p150 n1714 R2-R3; IM v2u p188 n450; AD v2 p1003 n3525; SB v3 p382 n640; AD v1 p1003 n3526

Mistreatment of Animals

ASMA BINT ABU BAKR RELATED:

The Prophet prayed the eclipse prayer and then said, 'Hell was displayed so close that I said, "O my Lord! Am I going to be one of its inhabitants?"' Suddenly he saw a woman who was being scratched by a cat. He asked what wrong she had committed. He was told that she had imprisoned the cat until it died of hunger.'

SB v3 p323 n552

Prohibitions

AYISHA RELATED:

The Prophet said, 'A person who vowed to end a relationship or a bad habit should not be as concerned with keeping the vow as with refraining from doing something which is prohibited.'

IM v2u p127 n259

Pride

ASMA BINT UMAYS RELATED:

The Messenger of God said, 'Bad is the servant who is proud inwardly and outwardly and forgets God. Bad is the servant who boasts and forgets the most Powerful. The worst wrong-doer, however is the servant who is unmindful and forgets the grave. Bad is the servant who rebels, transgresses and forgets the beginning and the end. Bad is the servant who takes up this world in exchange for the next world. Bad is the servant who doubts the next world. Bad is the servant whom greed guides. Bad is the servant whom low desires misguide. Bad is the servant whom greed puts into disgrace.'

   T [H v1 p483 rare]

Quarreling

AYISHA RELATED:

The Prophet said, *'The most hated man in the sight of God is the one who is the most quarrelsome,'* and he said, *'Or do you think that you shall enter paradise without such [trials] as came to those who passed away before you?'* [2:214].

   SB v6 p37 n48; SB v9 p225 n298; SB v3 p381 n637; SM v4B p222 n2668

Slander

AYISHA RELATED:

When asked by her nephew about the meaning of the verse, *"[Respite will be granted] until when the messengers give up hope [of their people] and think that they are denied [by their people] . . ."* [12:110], she [Ayisha] replied that it meant that their communities did not believe them. Her nephew replied that the prophets had been sure that their communities treated them as liars, and it was not a matter of suspicion only. She agreed that no doubt they were sure about it. Her nephew asked if the verse could be interpreted to mean that the prophets thought that God did not help them [based on the word *kudhdhibu* or *kudhiku;* hence, the difference in interpretation]. She replied that that was impossible. She said that the prophets did not suspect their Lord of such a thing. This verse concerned the followers of the prophets who had faith in their Lord and who believed in their prophets and who suffered long periods of trial. She further added that God's Help was delayed until the prophets gave up hope for the conversion of the disbelievers among their community and suspected that even their followers were shaken in their belief. God's help then came to them.

   SB v4 p393 n603; SB v6 p38 n49

AYISHA RELATED:

Whenever God's Messenger wanted to go on a journey, he used to draw lots among his wives. He would take the one to whom the lot had fallen. Once he drew lots when he wanted to carry out an expedition, and the lot fell to her. She proceeded with God's Messenger after God's order of the modest dress had been revealed. She was carried in her *howdah* [on a camel] and dismounted. When the expedition was over and the Messenger had returned, they moved towards Madinah. The Messenger ordered the soldiers to move at night.

When the army was ordered to resume the homeward journey, she got up and walked on until she left the army camp behind. When she had answered the call of nature, she went towards her *howdah,* but she realized her necklace made of black beads had broken and fallen off. She began to look for it. This detained her. The group of peole who had been carrying her and her *howdah* came and put her *howdah* on the back of the camel on which she had been riding, thinking that she was inside. At that time women were light in weight as they ate little food; thus, no one noticed the lightness of the *howdah* while raising it up. They drove the camel forward.

She found her necklace after the army had gone. She found her way back to the camp, but there was nobody there. She went to the place where she used to stay thinking that they would at some point find her missing and return. While she was sitting at her place, she feel asleep. Safwan ibn al-Mutattil al-Sulami al-Dhakwani was behind the army. He had started in the last part of the night, reached her place in the morning, and saw the figure of a sleeping person. He came to her and recognized her, for he used to see her before the verses on the modest dress were revealed. She got up when he said, '*Truly to God we belong and truly to Him we shall return*' [2:156] [which he said upon recognizing her]. She covered her face with her garment, and by God he said nothing but repeated, "*Truly to God we belong and truly to Him we shall return*" [2:156]. He made his she-camel kneel down, and she mounted it. Then Safwan set out, leading the she-camel that was carrying her until they met the army resting during the hot midday. A false statement was made by Abd Allah ibn Ubayy ibn Salul.

After this she arrived in Madinah where she became ill for one month during which evil-doers spread the false statements of the people of the lie. She was not aware of any of this. Her suspicions were aroused when she no longer received the same kindness from God's Messenger that she did before she fell sick. God's Messenger would come to see her, greet her, and add, 'How is that lady?' and then depart. That worried her, but she did not become aware of the propogated evil until she recovered from her ailment.

She went out with Umm Mistah [to answer the call of nature] towards al-Manasi, the place where they relieved themselves at night before they had toilets in their homes. This habit was similar to that of the old Arabs who considered it troublesome and harmful to make toilets in their houses. She [Ayisha] went out with Umm Mistah who was the daughter of Abu Ruhm ibn Abd Manaf and whose mother was the daughter of Sakhr ibn Amir, the aunt of Abu Bakr as-Siddiq. Her son was Mistah ibn Uthatha. When they had finished, Umm Mistah and she went back towards the house. Umm Mistah stumbled over her robe; whereupon, she said, 'Let Mistah be ruined!' She [Ayisha] reproached her for using such language against a man who had taken part in the Battle of Badr. Umm Mistah then asked if she had not heard what he had said. She then asked what he had said. Umm Mistah told her the allegations of the people who lied about her. This added to her [Ayisha's] ailment.

When she returned home, God's Messenger came to her. After his greeting, she asked if he would allow her to return to her parents. [She wanted to see if they had heard the same lies]. God's Messenger showed her the way, and she went to her parents and asked her mother what the people were saying. Her mother told her not to worry because she was a wonderful lady loved by her husband, and none of her co-wives could find fault with her. She was surprised that people talked as they did. She cried the whole night. Her tears never stopped, nor did she sleep.

God's Messenger called Ali ibn Abu Talib and Usama ibn Zayd when revelation when no revelation come. Usama ibn Zayd told what he knew about her innocence and of the affection he had for her. He said that she was the Prophet's wife, and that they knew nothing of her but good. Ali ibn Abu Talib told the Messenger that God had imposed no restrictions upon the Messenger, and that there were many available women. He advised the Prophet to ask her slave girl who would tell him the truth.

God's Messsenger then asked Barira if she ever saw anything which might have aroused her suspicion in regard to Ayisha. Barira said that she had never seen anything blameworthy regarding her [Ayisha] except that, being a young girl, she sometimes slept leaving the family's dough unprotected so that the household goats ate it.

After this, God's Messenger addressed the people and asked who would take revenge on Abd Allah ibn Ubay ibn Salul. While on the *minbar*, he said, 'O Muslims! Who will help me against a man who has hurt me by slandering my family? By God, I know nothing except good about my family, and people have blamed a man [Safwan] of whom I know nothing but good. He never visited my family except when I was there.'

At this point, the tribe of the Aws and the tribe of the Khazraz began fighting with each other while God's Messenger was on the *minbar*. The Messenger quieted them until they became silent; whereupon, he also became silent. On that day she [Ayisha] continued weeping. Neither did her tears stop, nor could she sleep. After she had wept for two nights and a day without sleeping, her parents thought her liver would burst from weeping.

While they were together and she was crying, a woman Helper asked permission to see her. She gave her permission, and the woman Helper began crying along with her. At that point, God's Messenger entered, greeted them, and sat down. He had not sat with her since that day and had not received any revelation concerning the situation for one month. God's Messenger then recited, 'I bear witness that there is no god but God and that Muhammad is His Messenger,' and sat down. Then he said, 'O Ayisha, I have been told such and such a thing about you. If you are innocent, God will reveal your innocence, and if you have committed a sin, then ask for God's forgiveness and repent to Him, for when a slave confesses his sin and then repents to God, God accepts his repentance.'

When God's Messenger had finished, her tears ceased completely so that she no longer cried even a drop. Then she told her father to reply to God's Messenger on her behalf. Her father, Abu Bakr, said that he did not know what to say. She asked her mother to reply to God's Messenger, and her mother also said that she did not know what to say. She [Ayisha] continued saying that even though she was still a young girl with little knowledge of the Quran, she knew that they had heard the false statement and believed it; thus even if she insisted that she were innocent—and God knows she was innocent—they would not believe her, and if she were to admit to it—and God knows she was innocent—they would believe her. She said that the closest example she could think of was that of Prophet Joseph's father. She then prayed for patience and help from God. She said that she knew that she was innocent and that God would reveal her innocence. She had hoped that God's Messenger would have a vision which would prove her innocence.

God's Messenger had not left the house when the revelation came to him. He was overtaken by the same hard condition which overtook him when revelation came. Drops of his sweat ran down like pearls, although it was a cold winter day. That was due to the heaviness of the verse which was revealed to him. When that state ended and he smiled, the first word he said was, 'Ayisha, God has revealed your innocence.' Her mother told her to get up and go to the Messenger. She [Ayisha] said that she would not go to him and that she would thank no one but God who revealed, *'Verily, they who spread the slander are group among you. Think it not bad...'* [24:11-20].

When God revealed this to confirm her innocence, Abu Bakr, who used to give charity to Mistah ibn Uthatha because of the latter's kinship to him, vowed that he would never give Mistah anything after what he had said about her [Ayisha]. For this reason God revealed, *"Let not those among you who are good and are wealthy swear not to*

*give [help] to their kinsmen, those in need, and those who have left
their homes for God's cause. Let them pardon and forgive [not to punish them]. Do you not love that God should forgive you? And God is
Oft-forgiving, most Merciful'* [24:22]. Abu Bakr then asked God to forgive him and resumed giving charity to Mistah just as he had done
before. She further added that God's Messenger asked Zaynab bint
Jahsh about Ayisha's case. Zaynab replied that she [Zaynab]
refrained from telling lies, and that she [Zaynab] knew nothing but
good about Ayisha. Among the wives of God's Messenger, it was
Zaynab who had wanted to receive the same favor from him that she
once received. God saved Zaynab from telling lies becauase of her
piety, but her sister, Hamna, kept on fighting on her behalf; thus,
Hamna was destroyed as were those who invented and spread the
slander.

> SB v6 p247 n274; SB v4 p392 n602 (Umm Ruman); SB v9 p342 n462; SM v4B
> p280 n2770R2; SB v9 -342 n463; SB v6 p261 n281

Tricking the Prophet

AYISHA RELATED:

When God's Messenger went on a journey, he used to cast lots
among his wives. Once this lot came out in her favor and that of
Hafsa. They both went along with him. When it was night, God's
Messenger traveled along with her [Ayisha] and talked to her. Hafsa
proposed to her that they trade camels that night. That way each one
of them would see what she generally had not seen. She agreed. She
rode upon Hafsa's camel, and Hafsa rode upon her camel. The
Prophet greeted Hafsa and then rode with her until they dismounted. She [Ayisha] thus missed the company of the Prophet and felt
jealous. She put her foot in the grass and asked God to sting her with
a serpent or scorpion for what she had agreed to do.

> SM v4A p104 n2445; SB v7 p103; SB v4 p85 n130; SB v3 p529 n853; IM v2u
> p67 n123

CHAPTER 4
COUNSELING TO THE GOOD

ADOPTING A MIDDLE COURSE

Forgiveness

AYISHA RELATED:

Muslims were commanded to seek forgiveness for God's Companions, but they did not do so.

SM v4B p400 n3022

Good Deeds

ASMA BINT YAZID RELATED:

God's Messenger said, 'Shall I not tell you who are the best among you?' When they asked him to tell them, he said, 'The best of you are those who when seen are a means of God being brought to mind.'

IM [MMR v2 p1043]

AYISHA RELATED:

Once the Prophet came while a woman was sitting with her. He asked, 'Who is she?' She [Ayisha] replied that the woman was so and so and told him about the woman's [excessive] praying. He said disapprovingly, 'Do [good] deeds which are within your capacity [without being overtaxed], as God does not get tired [of giving rewards]. [Surely] you will get tired, and the best deed [act of worship] in the sight of God is that which is done rightly.'

SB v1 p36 n41; N v1E p471 n765; SB v1 p231 n378; SB v1 p391 n697; SM v1B p440 n782 R1; AD v1 p172 n656; IM v2 p105 n1028; AD v2 p74 n942; SB v2 p139 n251B

AYISHA RELATED:

Once Hawla bint Tuwait ibn Habib ibn Asad ibn Abd al-Uzza passed by when the Messenger was with her. She told him that people said that Hawla did not sleep at night. The Messenger said, 'She [Hawla] does not sleep at night! Choose an act which you are capable

31

of doing continuously. By God, God will not grow weary, but you will.'

SM v1B p441 n785, R1; AD v1 p358 n1365

AYISHA RELATED:

The Prophet was asked what deeds are most loved by God. He said, 'The most regular constant deeds even though they may be few.' He added, 'Only take deeds upon yourselves which are within your ability.'

SB v8 p314 n472; AD v1 p358 n1363

AYISHA RELATED:

She was asked if the Messenger chose a particular act for a particular day. She said that, no, his actions were continuous. Then she asked who among the people was capable of doing what the Messenger of God did.

SM v1B p441 n783, R1; AD v1 p358 n1365

AYISHA RELATED:

She never heard God's Messenger counseling anyone to anything except to religion.

AD v3 p1388 n4969

AYISHA RELATED:

She asked the Messenger concerning the verse, '*And those who bring what they have brought while their hearts are fearful*,' [23:60] were the people who drank wine and stole. He replied, 'No, daughter of the truthful one. They are those who perform the prescribed fast, pray and give charity while fearing that it may not be accepted from them. They are those who compete with one another in good deeds.'

IM [MMR v2 p1110]

AYISHA RELATED:

God's Messenger performed an act and held it to be valid. This news reached some of his Companions who did not approve of it and avoided it. Their reaction was conveyed to him. He stood to deliver an address and said, 'What has happened to people to whom there was conveyed on my behalf a matter for which I granted permission, and they disapproved it and avoided it. By God I have the best knowledge of God among them, and I fear Him most among them.'

SM v4A p51 n2356, R2; SB v9 p298 n404; SB v8 p79 n123

AYISHA RELATED:

The Prophet said, 'Perform good deeds properly, sincerely and moderately because good deeds [alone] will not make you enter paradise.' They asked if this also applied to him. He said, 'Even I, unless and until God bestows His pardon and mercy on me.'

SB v8 p315 n474; SB v8 p314 n471; SM v4B p304 n2818

AYISHA RELATED:

The Messenger of God said, 'Certainly the most perfect of the believers in faith is the one who is the best of them in conduct and the most affable of them to his family.'

T [H v1 p212]; T [Hv1 p200]

UMM DARDA RELATED:

Her husband reported that he heard God's Messenger say, 'When someone supplicates for his brother in his brother's absence, the angel commissioned for carrying the supplication to his Lord says, "Amen," and it is for the supplicater also.'

SM v4B p250 n2732R1

UMM HABIBA RELATED:

God's Messenger said, 'Everything a son of Adam says counts against him and not in his favor except recommending what is good, prohibiting what is objectionable or making mention of God.'

IM [MMR v1 p480]; T [MMR v1 p480]

Moderation

AYISHA RELATED:

The Prophet called Uthman ibn Mazun and said to him, 'Did you dislike my practice.' Uthman said that he did not but rather sought the practices of the Messenger. The Messenger said, 'I sleep. I pray. I keep the fast. I [sometimes] do not fast. I marry women. Fear God, Uthman, your wife has a right over you. Your guest has a right over you. Your "self" has a right over you. You should keep the fast and, sometimes, not fast. You should pray and sleep.'

AD v1 p358 n1364

AYISHA RELATED:

God's Messenger said, 'No one of you should say, "My soul has become evil," but he should say, "My soul has become insensitive."'

SM v4A p6 n2250; SB v8 p129 n198; AD v3 p1383 n4961

BLESSING A NEW BORN CHILD

Animal Sacrifice

UMM KURZ AL-KABIYYA RELATED:

The Messenger said, 'Two sheep are to be sacrificed for a boy and one for a girl, but it does you no harm whether they [the animal sacrifice] be male or female.' [Tirmidhi said this is a *sahih* Tradition.]

T [MMR v2 p884] N [MMR v2 p884]; AD v2 p797 n2829; AD v2 p797 n2828; AD v2 p797 n2830; T [MMT v4 p104]

Baby's First Food

AYISHA RELATED:

When new-born infants were brought to God's Messenger, he blessed them and rubbed their palates with dates.

SM v3B p428 n2147; AD v3 p1415 n5087; SB v7 p272 n377

AYISHA RELATED:

A woman went to God's Messenger and said she had given birth to a boy whom she called Muhammad and Abul-Qasim, but she had been told that the Messenger disapproved. He replied, 'What is it which has made my name lawful and my agnomen lawful or my

agnomen unlawful and my name unlawful?'
AD v3 p1382 n4950

GOD-WARINESS

UMM MUBASHSHIR RELATED:

She heard God's Messenger saying in the presence of Hafsa, 'God willing, the people who gave their allegiance under the Tree will never enter the fire of hell.' She asked why not and was scolded. Hafsa replied all among them would have to pass over the narrow bridge. Thereupon God's Messenger said, 'God, Exalted and Glorious, has said, "*We will rescue those persons who are God-wary and we will leave the tyrants to their fate there*"' [19:72].
SM v4A p138 n2496

Greetings and Salutations

AYISHA RELATED:

A group of Jews asked permission to visit the Prophet. When they were admitted, they said, 'Death be upon you' [*as-samu alayka*]. She said to them, 'Death and the curse of God be upon you!' The Prophet said, 'O Ayisha! God is kind and lenient and likes one to be kind and lenient in all matters.' She asked if he had not heard what they had said. He said that he had and that he responded, 'And upon you' [*wa alaykum*].
SB v9 p48 n61; SB v4 p114 n186; SB v8 p32 n53; SB v8 p269 n404; SB v8 p181 n273; SM v3B p438 n2165R2

ASMA BINT YAZID RELATED:

God's Messenger passed by her and a group of women and greeted them.
IM [MMR v2 p975]; AD v3 p1436 n5185

ASMA RELATED:

God's Messenger said, 'There is no one more jealous than God, the Exalted and Glorious.'
SM v4B p266 n2762R1

HEART-RENDERING TRADITIONS

Good Character

AYISHA RELATED:

She heard God's Messenger say, 'By his good character a believer will attain the degree of one who prays during the night and fasts during the day.'
AD v3 p1343 n4780

Kindness

AYISHA RELATED:

When the Prophet was informed about anything of a certain man, he would not say, 'What is the matter with so and so that he says such and such.' He would say, 'What is the matter with people that they say such and such.'

AD v3 p1341 n4770

AYISHA RELATED:

God's Messenger heard an altercation of two disputants at the door. Both of the voices were quite loud. One demanded some remission and desired that the other should show leniency to him; whereupon, the other said that he would not. The Messenger said to them, 'Where is he who swears by God that he will not do good?'" The men then agreed.

SM v3A p34 n1557

AYISHA RELATED:

Nomads went to God's Messenger and asked if he kissed his children. The Prophet said that he did. They replied that they did not. The Prophet said, 'He who does not show mercy [towards his children], no mercy will be shown to him.'

SM v4A p37 n2317; SB v8 p19 n27

AYISHA RELATED:

God's Messenger said, 'Ayisha, verily God is kind and He loves kindness. He confers kindness which he does not counter with severity and does not confer upon anything else besides it.'

SM v4A p185 n2593

AYISHA RELATED:

God's Messenger said, 'Kindness adds to the beauty of everything. Anything lacking kindness is defective.'

SM v4A p185 n2594
SB v8 p19 n27

AYISHA RELATED:

God's Messenger said, 'Among the believers who show most perfect faith are those who have the best disposition and who are most kind to their families.'

T [MMR v1 p692]

Hot Baths

AYISHA RELATED:

God's Messenger forbade men and women to enter hot baths. He then permitted men to enter them wearing their lower garments.

AD v3 p1122 n 3998; T [MMR v2 p936]

Living on Less

SAWDA RELATED:

The family of the Prophet [was so poor that they] never ate wheat bread with meat for three consecutive days to their fill until the Prophet died.

SB v8 p408 n678; SB v8 p307 n461; SM v4B p377 n2970, R1-R4

AYISHA RELATED:

The family of Muhammad used to spend months at a time without kindling a fire, as they had nothing to cook. They ate only dates and water [to fill their stomachs].

SM v4B p379 n2972, R1; SB v9 p310 n465

AYISHA RELATED:

God's Messenger died when the people could afford to eat only dates and water.

SM v4B p379 n2975

AYISHA RELATED:

When the Prophet died, no food was left on her shelf except some barley grain. She ate until it was gone.

SB v8 p306 n458; SM v4B p379 n2973, R2

AYISHA RELATED:

If the family of Muhammad ate two meals in one day, one of the two was of dates.

SB v8 p307 n461B

AYISHA RELATED:

The bed mattress of the Prophet was a leather case stuffed with palm fibers.

SB v8 p310 n463; SB v3 p313 n469

AYISHA RELATED:

They used to see three crescents in two months and still no fire was kindled in the house of God's Messenger [because they had nothing to cook].

SB v8 p310 n466

AYISHA RELATED:

The Messenger of God said, 'If you wish to reach me, you should then lead the life of the poor and be careful of the assemblies of the rich.'

T [H v1 p273 rare]

"Marriage is my way. . ."

AYISHA RELATED:

The Prophet said, 'Marriage is my way, and one who does not follow me is not among my followers. It is necessary for my followers to marry, so that I will be proud of my community. It is also necessary for followers who can afford to marry as well as for those who cannot afford to marry to fast, as fasting can suppress sexual desire.'

IM v2u p20 n2

Names: Good Meaning

ZAYNAB BINT UMM SALAMA

Her first name was Barra [goodness]. God's Messenger gave her the name of Zaynab. Then Zaynab, daughter of Jahsh, entered. Her name had also been Barra, and he had changed her name to Zaynab.

SM v3B p424 n2139

ASMA BINT YAZID RELATED:

The Messenger used to change a name that did not have a good meaning.

T [MMR v2 p998]

On Giving One's Agnomen to a Woman

AYISHA RELATED:

She told the Messenger of God that all of his wives had agnomens except her. He said, 'Give yourself the agnomen of Abd Allah, your [nephew].' She became known as Umm Abd Allah.

AD v3 p1383 n4952

Toothstick

AYISHA RELATED:

Abd al-Rahman ibn Abu Bakr was holding a toothstick with which he was cleaning his teeth. God's Messenger looked at him. She asked Abd al-Rahman to give the toothstick to her. After he gave it to her, she divided it, chewed it and gave it to God's Messenger. Then he cleaned his teeth with it while he was resting against her chest.

SB v2 p6 n15

AYISHA RELATED:

The Messenger of God was using a toothstick when two men, one older than the other, were with him. A revelation descended to him about the merits of using the toothstick. He was asked to show proper respect by giving it to the elder of the two.

AD v1 p12 n50

AYISHA RELATED:

The first thing God's Messenger did when he entered the house was to use his toothstick.

SM v1A p176 n253, R1

AYISHA RELATED:

Ablution water and a toothstick were placed by the side of the Prophet. When he got up during the night [for prescribed prayer], he relieved himself. Then he used the toothstick.

AD v1 p13 n55

AYISHA RELATED:

The Prophet did not get up after sleeping by night or day without using the toothstick before performing ablution.

AD v1 p14 n56

AYISHA RELATED:

The Messenger said, 'There are ten acts according to the nature originated by God (*fitrat*): clipping the moustache, letting the beard grow, using the toothstick, cutting the nails, washing the finger joints, plucking the hair under the arm pits, shaving the pubes, and cleansing one's private parts (after easing or urinating) with water.' [The narrator added that the tenth might be rinsing the mouth.]

AD v1 p12 n52; SM v1A p178 n261; IM v1 p169 n293

AYISHA RELATED:

The Messenger said, 'The toothstick is a means of purifying the mouth and is pleasing to the Lord.'

IM [MMR v1 p77]; N v1E p135 n5

AYISHA RELATED:

The Prophet used the toothstick and then gave it to her to wash. She would first use it herself and then wash it and hand it back to him.

AD v1 p12 n51

AYISHA RELATED:

God's Messenger asked [Khadija] about Waraqa. Khadija said to the Messenger that Waraqa had believed in the Messenger. The Messenger said, 'I was shown Waraqa in a dream wearing white clothes. If he had been one of the inhabitants of hell, he would have been wearing different clothing.'

T [MMR v2 p967]

CHAPTER 5
SUPPLICATION

REMEMBRANCE OF GOD

Middle of the Night of Shaban

AYISHA RELATED:

One night she found the Messenger missing. She found him in the Baqi cemetery. He said to her, 'Were you afraid that God and His Messenger would act wrongly towards you?' She replied that she thought he had gone to one of his other wives. He said, 'On the middle night of Shaban God most high descends to the lowest heaven and forgives more sins than the hairs of the goats of Kalb.'

IM [MMR v1 p271]; T [MMR v1 p271]; IM v2 p326; T [H v3 p426]

Purification by Snow and Hail

AYISHA RELATED:

The Messenger of God said, 'O God, wash away my sins with water of snow and hail. O God, purify me from sin as a white garment is purified from filth.'

N v1E p273 n336; N v1E p155 n62

Tone of Voice

AYISHA RELATED:

She said the verse, *'[O Muhammad!] Neither perform your prescribed prayer aloud nor say it in a low tone,'* [17:110] was revealed in connection with invocation.

SB v9 p464 n617; SM v1B p272 n447; SB v6 p180 n247; v8 p228 n339;

SPECIFIC TIMES

After Dawn Prescribed Prayer

UMM SALAMA RELATED:

The Prophet used to say after the dawn prescribed prayer, 'O God,

I ask You for beneficial knowledge, acceptable action and good provision.'

IM [MMR v1 p533]; T [MMR v1 p498]

Do Not Despair of God's Mercy

ASMA BINT YAZID RELATED:

The Messenger of God recited, 'O My servants, those that are reckless with their souls do not despair of the mercy of God. Verily God can forgive all sins, and He does not care.'

T [H v3 p761 [approved, rare]

God's Greatest Name

ASMA BINT ABU BAKR RELATED:

The Messenger said, 'God's greatest name is in these two verses, "And your God is one God; there is no god but He, the Compassionate, the Merciful," [2:163] and in the beginning of al-Imran, "A. L. M. God there is no god but He, the Living, the Eternal" [3:1].'

IM [MMR v1 p484]; AD v1 p390 n1491

Mentioning of God's Name

AYISHA RELATED:

God's Messenger used to mention Almighty God under all circumstances.

IM v1 p174 n302; SM v1A p228 n373; AD v1 p5 n18

Raising One's Eyes Towards the Sky When Supplicating

AYISHA RELATED:

In regard to the verses, 'Do they not look at the camels how they are created and at the heaven how it is raised,' [88:17-19], the Prophet raised his head towards the sky [when reciting them].

SB v8 p150

Reciting of "Glory Be to God" in the Morning and at the Time of Sleeping

JUWAYRIYA RELATED:

God's Messenger came out of her apartment in the morning as she was observing her dawn prescribed prayer in her place of worship. He came back in the forenoon, and she was still sitting there. He remarked that she was in the same position as when he had left her. She agreed. He said, 'I recited four words three times after I left you, and if these were to be weighed against what you have recited since morning, they would outweigh them. These words were, "Glory be to God because of the number of His creation; glory be to God because of the pleasure of His Self; glory be to God because of the weight of His Throne; glory be to God because of the ink used in recording His words"' [See 18:109].

SM v4B p248 n2726 R1

Remembering God and Taking His Name Before Eating

AYISHA RELATED:

The Messenger said, 'When anyone of you intends to eat, he

should recite, *"In the Name of God."* In case you forget to say it at the beginning, you should say, "In the Name of God, He is the First and the Last" at the end.'

N [MMT v4 p236]; T [H v2 p123]

Reward for Glorifying God

BUSAYRA RELATED:

One of the women Emigrants said God's Messenger told her, 'Apply yourselves to glorifying God, saying there is no god but He and declaring His holiness. Count them [these recitations] on your fingers for they [your fingers] will be questioned and asked to speak [on the day of judgment]. Do not be negligent and so be deprived of mercy.'

T [MMR v1 p490]

Seeking Reward and / or Forgiveness

AYISHA RELATED:

Ayisha related that the Prophet prayed, 'O God, make me one of those who, when they do good deeds, seeks reward, and who, when they commit evil, seeks forgiveness.'

IM [H v3 p764]

Supplication at Night

AYISHA RELATED:

God's Messenger prostrated himself at night when reciting the Quran. He said repeatedly, 'My face prostrates itself to Him Who created it and brought forth its hearing and seeing by His might and power.'

AD v1 p370 n1409; N [H v3 p332]; T [H v3 p332 n1098]

JASRA BINT DAJAJA RELATED:

She heard Abu Dharr say that the Prophet performed prayer [reciting] one single verse again and again until it was morning. The verse was, *'If You torment them, they are Your servants and if You forgive them, verily You are the Mighty, the Wise.'*

IM v2 p302 n1350

UMM HANI RELATED:

She listened to the recitation of the Quran by the Prophet during the night while she was on the roof [of her house].

IM v2 p301 n1349

Supplication for Pardon and Repentance

ASMA BINT UMAYS RELATED:

The Messenger of God liked to supplicate three times and to ask God's pardon three times.

AD v1 p396 n1520

AYISHA RELATED:

The Prophet said, 'O God, put me among those who when they do good are glad and when they do evil ask pardon.'

IM [MMR v1 p500]

Supplication in an Assembly

AYISHA RELATED:

Ayisha related that when God's Messenger sat in an assembly or offered prayer, he spoke some words. She asked him about them. He said they were, 'Glory be to You, O God, and I begin with praise of You. There is no god but You. I ask forgiveness of You and turn to You in repentance.' He told her that a good saying acts as a seal on one's words until the day of resurrection and atones for one's evil speech.

N [MMR v1 p522]; AD v3 p1404 n5043

Supplication Upon Leaving the Home

UMM SALAMA RELATED:

God's Messenger never left her house without raising his eyes to the sky and saying, 'O God, I seek refuge in You lest I stray or lead others astray [or be led astray] or cause injustice or suffer injustice or do wrong or have wrong done to me.'

IM [MMR v1 p520]; AD v3 p1413 n5075; IM [MMR v1]; N v1E p202 n178; T [MMR v1 p520]

Supplication Upon Sleeping

HAFSA RELATED:

When God's Messenger wanted to go to sleep, he put his right hand under his cheek and said three times, 'O God, guard me from Your punishment on the day when You raise up Your servants.'

AD v3 p1402 n5027

What a Person Should Say When Leaving the Toilet

AYISHA RELATED:

When the Prophet came out of the toilet, he used to say, 'Grant me Your forgiveness.'

AD v1 p7 n30

WHY ONE SEEKS REFUGE IN GOD

From Debt

KHAWLA BINT HAKIM SULAMIYYA RELATED:

God's Messenger said, 'When anyone stays in a place and says, "I seek refuge in the Perfect Words of God from the evil of what He has created," nothing will harm him until he leaves that place.'

SM v4B p241 n2708, R1

AYISHA RELATED:

One night she awoke to find God's Messenger not in the bed where he had been. When she began reaching out for him, her hand touched the lower part of his feet while he was in a state of prostration. His feet were raised and he was saying, 'O God, I seek refuge in Your pleasure from Your anger and in Your forgiveness from Your punishment. I seek refuge in You from Your anger. I cannot reckon Your praise. You are as You have lauded Yourself.'

SM v1B p289 n486; AD v1 p255 n878; N v1E p202 n171

AYISHA RELATED:

God's Messenger invoked God in prayer saying, 'O God, I seek refuge with You from all sins and from being in debt.' Someone asked why he so often sought refuge with God from being in debt. He said, 'If a person is in debt, he tells lies when he speaks and breaks his promises when he promises.'

SB v3 p323 n582

From Hellfire

AYISHA RELATED:

The Prophet used to supplicate with these words, 'O God! I seek refuge in You from the trial of hellfire, from the punishment of hellfire and from the evil of riches and poverty.'

AD v1 p400 n1538

From the Evils of the Moon

AYISHA RELATED:

The Messenger of God looked at the full moon and said, 'O Ayisha! I seek refuge in God from the evils of this moon. *It brings darkness when it overspreads [the moon being eclipsed]*" [113:3].

T [H v3 p806]; T MMR v1

From the Punishment of the Grave

UMM KHALID BINT KHALID RELATED:

She heard the Prophet seeking refuge in God from the punishment of the grave.

SB v8 p250 n375

From Winds and Storms

AYISHA RELATED:

She never saw God's Messenger laugh to such an extent that one could see his uvula. He only smiled. When he saw dark clouds or wind, the signs of fear could be seen on his face. She asked why it was that people were happy when they saw dark clouds hoping that they would bring rain, but when he saw clouds, there was anxiety on his face. He said, 'Ayisha, I am afraid that the wind may be bringing a calamity. People can be afflicted by the wind. When people saw his agony, they said, "It is a cloud which will give us rain." They saw it [only] as a cloud.'

SM v2A p31 n899R2; SB v8 p74 n114; SB v4 p286 n428; SB v6 p339 n269; AD v3 p1414 n5079

AYISHA RELATED:

When the Prophet saw something rising in the sky [i.e. clouds], he left what he was doing, faced them and said, 'O God, I seek refuge in You from the evil of what they contain.' If God cleared them away, he praised Him. If rain fell, he said, 'O God, give a beneficial fall.'

IM [MMR v1 p318]; AD v3 p1414

PART II
BELIEFS

CHAPTER 1
MONOTHEISM

CREATION

Angels

AYISHA RELATED:

She asked the Prophet if he had ever encountered a day more difficult than the day of the Battle of Uhud. The Prophet said, 'Your tribes have troubled me a lot. The worse trouble was the trouble on the day of Aqaba when I presented myself to Ibn Abd Yalail ibn Abd al-Kulal [in Taif], and he did not respond to my invitation. I departed, overwhelmed with great sorrow and proceeded on. When I found myself at Qarnath Thaalib, I lifted my head towards the sky to see a cloud unexpectedly shading me. I looked up and saw Gabriel in it. He called me saying, "God has heard your people's words and what you have replied to them. God has sent the Angel of the Mountains to you so that you may order him to do whatever you wish to these people." Then Angel of the Mountains called and greeted me and said, "O Muhammad! Order what you wish. If you like, I will cause two mountains to fall on them." The Prophet said, "No, but I hope that God will let them beget children who will worship God alone and will worship none besides Him."'

SB v4 p300 n454; SB v9 p360 n486

AYISHA RELATED:

Whoever claimed that the Prophet Muhammad saw his Lord was committing a great fault, for the Prophet only saw Gabriel in the genuine shape in which he was created, covering the whole horizon.

SB v4 p301 n457

AYISHA RELATED:

God's Messenger said, 'God and His angels bless those who are on

47

the right flanks of the rows.'
AD v1 p175 n676

AYISHA RELATED:

The Prophet said, 'Whoever recites the Quran and masters it by heart will be with the noble, upright recording angels. And whoever exerts himself to learn the Quran by heart and recites it with great difficulty will have a double reward.'
SB v6 p431 n459; SM v1B p447 n798, R1; AD v1 p381 n1449

AYISHA RELATED:

God's Messenger said, 'Angels are born out of light, and *jinn* are born out of the spark of fire. Adam was born as described in the Quran.'
SM v4B p385 n2996

AYISHA RELATED:

God's Messenger said, 'Verily God showers blessings on the right sides of the rows, and His angels [invoke favors on them].'
IM v2 p105 n1005

Jinn

AYISHA RELATED:

The Messenger of God asked her, 'Have the *mugharribun* been seen among you?' She asked what he meant. He replied, 'They are those in whom is a strain of the *jinn*.'
AD v3 p1415 n5088

INCLINATION OF SOULS

AYISHA RELATED:

The Prophet said, 'Souls are like recruited troops. Those who are of like qualities are inclined to each other, but those who have dissimilar qualities, differ from each other.'
SB v4 p348

JUDGMENT BY OTHERS OF THE PROPHET

AYISHA RELATED:

Whenever God's Messenger ordered the Muslims to do something, his orders were easy for them to carry out [according to their strength]. They said to the Messenger that they were not like him because God had forgiven him his past and future sins. God's Messenger became angry. It was apparent on his face. He said, 'I am the most God-war, and know God better than all of you do.'
SB v1 p22 n19

KNOWLEDGE

"AYISHA RELATED:

She was asked if the Prophet saw his Lord. She said the question made her hair stand on end. She said the questioner should know that whoever said the Messenger saw his Lord was a liar. Then she recited the verses, *"No vision can grasp Him but His grasp is over all vision. He is the most courteous, well-acquainted with all things"* [6:103] and *"It is not fitting for a human being that God should speak to him except by revelation or from behind a veil,"* [42:51]. She recited, *"No soul can know what it will earn tomorrow"* [31:34] and *"O Messenger! Proclaim [the message] which has been sent down to you from your Lord. . ."* [5:67]. She then said that the Prophet had seen Gabriel in his true form twice.

> SB v6 p359 n378; SB v9 p354 n477; SB v9 p467 n622; SB v6 p109 n136; SM v1A p125 n177

AYISHA RELATED:

God's Messenger said, 'He who loves meeting God, God loves meeting him. He who dislikes meeting God, God abhors meeting him.' He said, 'When a believer is given the glad tidings of the mercy of God and the pleasure of paradise, he longs to meet Him. When an unbeliever is given the news of his torment at the Hand of God and of the hardships to be imposed by Him, he does not want to meet God. God also abhors meeting him.'

> SM v4B p222 n2684, R2-R3

AYISHA RELATED:

Whenever she heard something she did not understand, she would ask again until she understood it completely. She said that once the Prophet said, *'Whoever will be called to account [about his deeds on the day of resurrection] will surely be punished.'* She responded with verse 84:8, *"He surely will receive an easy reckoning"* [84:8]. The Prophet replied, 'This means only the presentation of the accounts, but whoever will be called to argue about his account will certainly be ruined.'

> SB v1 p81 n103; SB v8 p356 n543; SB v8 p356 n544

CHAPTER 2
PROPHETHOOD

ABRAHAM

UMM SHARIK RELATED:

The Messenger ordered that the salamander should be killed. He said, 'It blew the fire on Abraham.'

SB v4 p370 n579

MIGRATION

AYISHA RELATED:

The Prophet and Abu Bakr employed a disbeliever from the the tribes of Dayl and the Abd ibn Adi as a guide. He was an expert guide. He broke his oath contract with the tribe of Asi ibn Dayl. He followed the religion of the disbelievers. The Prophet and Abu Bakr had confidence in him. Abu Bakr gave him their riding camels and told him after three days to take them to the cave of Thaur. Three days later, he brought them two riding camels, and both of them [the Prophet and Abu Bakr] set out accompanied by Amir ibn Fuhaiyra and the guide who guided them below Makkah along the road leading to the seashore.

SB v3 p253 n464; SB v3 p253 n465

AYISHA RELATED:

From the time she reached an age when she could remember things, she had seen her parents worshiping according to the right faith of Islam. Not a single day passed in which God's Messenger failed to visit them, both in the morning and in the evening. When the Muslims were being persecuted, Abu Bakr set out to migrate to Abyssinia. When he reached a place called Bark al-Ghimad, he met Ibn al-Daghna, the chief of the Qara tribe. He asked Abu Bakr where

51

he was going. Abu Bakr said that his people had turned him out of his country and that he would like to tour the world and worship the Lord. Al-Daghna replied that a man like Abu Bakr would not go out or be turned out, as he had helped the poor earn their living, kept good relations with his relatives, helped the disabled, provided guests with food and shelter, and helped people through their times of trouble. Al-Daghna said he would protect Abu Bakr. He told Abu Bakr to return to his home and worship his Lord in his own land. They went together to the Quraysh chiefs where al-Daghna said he would be the protector of Abu Bakr. Abu Bakr continued worshiping his Lord in his house and did not pray or recite the Quran outloud except in his house.

Later he had the idea to build a mosque in his courtyard. He did so and began reciting the Quran there. The disbelievers began to gather to watch him. He was soft hearted and could not help weeping while reciting the Quran. This horrified the Quraysh chiefs. They sent for ibn al-Daghna. They told him that Abu Bakr was not abiding by the conditions they had set out. They said that he either had to abide by them or Ibn al-Daghna had to revoke his protection of Abu Bakr. Ibn al-Daghna told Abu Bakr this, and Abu Bakr said that Ibn al-Daghna should revoke his protection because God's protection was sufficient for him. Ibn al-Daghna revoked his protection.

At that time, the Messenger was still in Makkah. He told his Companions, 'Your place of migration has been shown to me. I have seen salty land, planted with date-palms and situated between two mountains which are the two Harras.' When the Prophet told them, some of his Companions migrated to Madinah. Some of those who had migrated to Abyssinia went to Madinah. When Abu Bakr was preparing to migrate, the Messenger said to him, 'Wait. I expect to be permitted to migrate.' Abu Bakr asked if it were really true, and the Messenger said that it was. Abu Bakr postponed his departure in order to accompany God's Messenger and fed two camels [which he had] with the leaves of the samor trees for four months.

SB v3 p277 n494; SB v5 p158 n245; SB v7 p469 n698; AD v3 p1139 n4072; SB v1 p276 n465; SB v3 p1`96 n348; SB v5 p134 Title; SB v5 p114 Title; SB v8 p66 n102

AYISHA RELATED:

When the verse, 'And warn your nearest kin,' was revealed, the Messenger stood up on Safa and said, 'O Fatima, daughter of Muhammad, O Safiya, daughter of Abd al-Muttalib, O sons of Abd al-Muttalib, I have nothing which can avail you against God. You may ask me what you want of my worldly belongings.'

SM v1A p154 n205

REVELATION

"And invoke God for them. . ." [9:130]

AYISHA RELATED:

The Prophet heard a man reciting the Quran in the mosque. The Messenger said, 'May God bestow His mercy on him, for he made me remember such and such verse which I had missed in such and such a *surah*.'

> SB v8 p228 n347; SB v6 p507 n556; SB v6 p508 n562; SM v1B p442 n7881;
> AD v3 p1114 n3959; AD v1 p349 n1326

Beginning of Divine Revelation

AYISHA RELATED:

Revelation began for God's Messenger with true vision in sleep. The visions came like the bright gleam of dawn. Solitude became dear to him, and he used to seclude himself in the cave of Hira. There he would engage in worship, and as the monotheists before him had done (i.e. Prophet Abraham), the Messenger too worshiped for a number of nights before returning to his family to take provisions for his return to the cave. He returned to Khadija and took more provisions until revelation came to him while he was in the cave. Then the angel Gabriel came to him.

God's Messenger said, 'The angel said to me, "Recite," to which I replied, "I am unlettered." He took hold of me and pressed me until I was hard pressed. Thereafter he let me go and said, "Recite." Again I said I was unlettered. Three times he took hold of me and pressed me and said, "Recite." Then he let go and said, *"Recite in the Name of your Lord Who created, created the human being from a clot of blood. Recite and your most bountiful Lord is He Who taught the use of the pen, taught the human being what he did not know"* [96:1-4].

Then the Prophet returned immediately, his heart trembling. He went to Khadija and said, 'Wrap me up! Wrap me up!' She wrapped him until the fear had left him. He then said to Khadija, 'O Khadija! What has happened to me?' He told her about his experience saying, 'I feel awe over myself.'

She replied that he should be happy, for she knew God would never humiliate him, as he joined ties of relationship, spoke the truth, bore people's burdens, helped the destitute, entertained guests and aided people in their difficulties Khadija took him to Waraqa ibn Naufal ibn Asad, the son of her uncle [her paternal uncle]. He had embraced Christianity in the Age of Ignorance and wrote books in Arabic. He translated the New Testament into Arabic as God willed he should. He was very old and had grown blind. Khadija told God's Messenger that he should listen to the son of his brother.

Waraqa ibn Naufal asked Muhammad what he had seen. God's Messenger told Waraqa what he had seen. Waraqa said that it had been the same angel entrusted with the divine secrets which God revealed to Moses. He exclaimed that he wished he would be alive when his people would expel him. God's Messenger asked, 'Will my people drive me out?' Waraqa replied that they would because whenever had a man received revelation, he met with hostility. He said that if he lived long enough, he would help him.

SM v1A p108 n160, R1, R2; SB v1 p2 n3; SB v4 p395 n605; SB v6 p450 n478; SB v6 p454 n480; SB v6 p453 n479; SB v9 p91 n111; SB v6 p348 n?

AYISHA RELATED:

Al-Harith ibn Hisham had asked God's Messenger how divine revelation came to him. God's Messenger replied, 'Sometimes it is revealed like the ringing of a bell. This form of revelation is the hardest of all. This state passes away after I have grasped what has been revealed. Sometimes the angel comes in the form of a man and talks to me, and I grasp whatever he says.' She added that she saw the Prophet receiving revelation on a very cold day and noticed the sweat pouring down from his forehead [when the revelation ended].

SB v1 p2 n2; SB v4 p293 n438; SM v4A p42 n2333

Quranic Commentary

UMM SALAMA RELATED:

God's Messenger recited 1:1-4, 'In the Name of God, the Merciful and Compassionate, Merciful, Compassionate, Master of the Day of Judgment,' breaking its reading into verses one after another.

AD v3 p1120 n3990

UMM SALAMA RELATED:

She performed the circumambulation behind the people while the Prophet prayed and recited the Chapter of Tur (52).

SB v1 p48

AYISHA RELATED:

The Prophet sent an army unit under the command of a man who lead his companions in the prayers and finished his recitation with Chapter 112. When they returned from the battle and mentioned this to the Prophet, he asked the companions why the commander had done so. The companions said the commander did so because it mentions the qualities of the Merciful, and he loved to recite it in his prescribed prayer. The Prophet said to them, 'Tell him that God loves him.'

SB v9 p350 n472; SM v1B p453 n813

ASMA BINT YAZID RELATED:

She heard God's Messenger recite the verse, 'He acted unrighteously,' [11:46].

AD v3 p1116 n3971

UMM SALAMA RELATED:

The Prophet recited 39:59 in the following way, 'Nay, but there came to you [feminine pronoun referring to soul, nafs] My signs and you did reject them. You [feminine pronoun] were haughty and became

one of those who reject faith.'
AD v3 p1117 n3979

AYISHA RELATED:

God's Messenger recited 56:89, *'[There is for him] rest and satis-faction.'*
AD v3 p1118 n3980

AYISHA RELATED:

The revelation descended on God's Messenger, and he recited 24:1: *'A chapter which We have sent down and which We have ordained'* [instead of 'which we have described in detail.'
AD v3 p1121 n3997

AYISHA RELATED:

She was late one night after the night prescribed prayer. When she returned home, the Messenger asked where she had been. She said that she had been listening to the recitation of the Quran by one of the Companions. She said that she had not heard a recitation like his nor anyone with his sweet voice. He got up and she with him. The Prophet listened to the recitation and then turned to her and said, 'This is Salim, the freed slave of Abu Hudhayfa. Thanks be to God Who has created [people] like this in my *ummah.'*
IM v2 p294 n1338

AYISHA RELATED:

She did not recall the Prophet reciting the whole of the Quran until morning.
IM v2 p300 n1348

AYISHA RELATED:

The Prophet stayed for ten years in Makkah after the Quran was revealed to him, and he stayed in Madinah for ten years.
SB v5 p528 n741; SB v6 p473 n502

AYISHA RELATED:

Verses of the Quran referring to stoning to death and to breast feeding the adult were written on a paper and placed under her bed. When the Prophet died, they were busy with the funeral service, and their pet goat accidentally ate the paper.
IM v2u p57 n98

CHAPTER 3
RESURRECTION
AFFLICTION IN THE GRAVE

ASMA BINT ABU BAKR RELATED:

God's Messenger once stood up to deliver a sermon and mentioned the afflictions people will face in their grave. When he mentioned that, the Muslims started shouting loudly.

SB v2 p257 n455

ASMA BINT ABU BAKR RELATED:

God's Messenger arose to deliver an address in which he mentioned the trial a person endures in the grave. On hearintg this, the Muslims gave a shout of dismay which prevented her from grasping what God's Messenger had said. When the clamor died down, she asked the man next to her what the Messenger had said at the end of his address. The man replied that the Messenger had had a revelation that the trial they would endure in their graves would approximate that of the antichrist.'

N [MMR v1 p37]

AYISHA RELATED:

God's Messenger said, 'I saw hell wherein different portions were consuming each other. I saw Amr dragging his intestines [in it]. He was the first person to establish the policy of letting animals loose [for the idols].'

SB v6 p116 n148; SB v6 p177 n213

AYISHA RELATED:

A man asked God's Messenger who among the people were the best. He said, 'Of the generation to which I belong, then of the second generation, then of the third generation [until the time of the resurrection].'

SM v4A p157 n2503

AYISHA RELATED:

She asked God's Messenger what happened to the offspring of

57

believers. He said, 'They are joined with their parents.' She asked if this was so even though they may have done nothing. He replied, 'God knows best what they were doing.' She asked what happens to the offspring of polytheists. He replied, 'They are joined with their parents.' She asked if this were so even if they had done nothing. He replied, 'God knows best what they were doing.'

AD v3 p1320 n4695

AYISHA RELATED:

The Prophet was invited to the funeral of a boy who was among the Helpers. She asked if he was blessed, for he had done no evil, nor had he known it. The Messenger replied, 'It may be otherwise, for God created paradise and created those who will go to it. He created it for them when they were still in their father's loins. He created hell and created those who will go to it. He created it for them when they were still in their mother's womb.'

AD v3 p1320 n4696; SM v4B p218 n2662; IM v1 p48 n82

AYISHA RELATED:

God's Messenger used to invoke God in the prescribed prayer saying, 'O God, I seek refuge in You from the punishment of the grave and from the afflictions of the antichrist and from the afflictions of life and death. O God, I seek refuge in You from sins and from being in debt.' Somebody asked him why he so frequently sought refuge with God from being in debt. The Prophet said, 'A person in debt tells lies whenever he speaks and breaks promises whenever he makes them.' She also narrated that she heard God's Messenger in his prayer seeking refuge with God from the afflictions of the antichrist.

SB v1 p441 n795; SB v9 p184 n243; SM v1B p334 n587; v4B p240 n589R1;
v1B p335 n589; AD v1 p225 n879

AYISHA RELATED:

The Prophet said, 'They now realize that what I used to tell them was the truth. God said, "*Verily you cannot make the dead to hear nor can you make the deaf hear*" [27:80].'

SB v2 p256 n453

AYISHA RELATED:

The Prophet entered her house when a Jewess was with her. The Jewess asked if Ayisha felt she would be put on trial in the grave. The Messenger trembled on hearing this and said, "It is only the Jews who will be put on trial." Some nights passed, and the Messenger said, "Do you know that it has been revealed to me, 'You will be put on trial in the grave.'" She said she heard the Messenger of God seeking refuge from the torment of the grave after this.

SM v1B p333 n584; SB p251 n377; SM v1B p334 n58RR1

UMM MALIK AL-BAHJIYYAH RELATED:

She reported that the Messenger of God described a trial and brought it near. She asked the Messenger who would be the best of men therein. He replied, "A man who pays the dues of his beasts and

worships his Lord and a man who holds the head of his horse giving
threat to the enemy while they cause him fear.'

T [H v4 p15]

ANTICHRIST

FATIMA BINT QAYS RELATED:

She was asked to narrate a Tradition which she had heard directly from the Messenger in which there was no extra link between narrators. She said she would do that. She said that she married the son
of Mughira who was a chosen young man of the Quraysh at the time
but was martyred in the first struggle in the Way of God while fighting on the side of the Messenger. When she became a widow, Abd al-
Rahman ibn Auf, a Companion of the Messenger, proposed marriage
to her. God's Messenger also sent her such a message for his freed
slave, Usama ibn Zayd. It was conveyed to her that God's Messenger
had said about Usama, "He who loves me should also love Usama."
She told the Messenger that her affairs were in his hands and that he
could marry her to anyone he liked. He said to her, 'You had better
move now to the house of Umm Sharik' who was a wealthy woman
from among the Helpers. Then he said, "Do not do that for Umm
Sharik is a woman who is frequently visited by guests, and I do not
want your head to be uncovered or some stranger to see your legs
which you yourself abhor. You had better move to the house of your
cousin, Umm Maktum [who was blind]."

She moved there and when her waiting period ended, she heard
the call to prayer. She went to the mosque. She sat in the row of
women next to the row of men. When God's Messenger had finished
the prescribed prayer, he sat on the *minbar* smiling and said, 'Every
worshiper should remain sitting. Do you know why I have asked you
to assemble?' They said that they did not.

He said, 'By God, I have not assembled you for an exhortation or
to give a warning, but I have assembled you because Tamim Dari, a
Christian, who came and accepted Islam told me something which
agrees with what I was telling you about the antichrist. He told me
that he had sailed in a ship along with thirty men of the Lakhm and
Jutham clans. They had been tossed by waves in the ocean for a
month. Then the waves took them near an ocean island at the time of
sunset. They got into a small side boat and went to the island. There
was a beast with long thick hair and, because of this, they could not
distinguish his face from his back. They asked who it could be.

The beast said, "I am al-Jassasa [the beast who will spy for the
antichrist]." They asked what that meant. It said, "O people, go to this
person in the monastery as he is very eager to know about you." When
the beast told them to do this and gave them the name of the man

they should go to see, they were afraid because they thought the beast might be a devil. At any rate, they hurriedly went on until they came to that monastery and found a well built man there with his hands tied to his neck and his legs shackled up to his ankles. They asked who he was. He said that they would soon come to know about him and asked who they were. They said that they were sailors from Arabia, but the sea waves had driven them for a month and brought them near this island. They had gotten into the side boat and found this island where they met a beast with such thick hair that they could not see its face. It had told them to go to the monastery and said its name was al-Jassasa.

They had gone in haste to the monastery fearing that the beast might be the devil. The chained man asked them to tell him about the date palm tress of Baisan. They asked what he wanted to know. He asked whether or not these trees bore fruit. They said that they did. He said that he thought they would not bear fruit. He asked about the lake of Tabariyya [perhaps a spring in Balqa in Syria connected with the daughter of Lot]. They asked what he wanted to know. He asked if there was water in it, and they said that it had abundant water. He said that he thought that it would soon dry up. He asked about the spring of Zughar [a famous town near Syria].

They asked what he wanted to know about it. He said he wanted to know about the unlettered prophet and what he had done. They said that he had left Makkah and settled in Madinah. He asked if there was water there, sufficient to irrigate the land. They said there was. He asked if the Arabs fought him. They said that they did. He asked how they dealt with him. They said that he had overcome those in his neighborhood, and these had submitted themselves to him. He asked if it had actually happened, and they said that it had. He said it was better for them to show obedience to him.

Then he told them about himself. He said that he was the antichrist and would soon be permitted to leave there and travel in the land and not spare any town where he stayed for forty nights, except Makkah and Madinah, as these two areas were prohibited areas for him and so he would not make any attempt to enter either of these. An angel with a sword in his hand would confront him and would bar his way, and there would be angels to guard every passage leading to it.

Then the Messenger, striking the pulpit with the end of his staff said, 'This implies Taiba,' meaning Madinah. 'Have I not told you about the antichrist?' The people said that he had. He said, "I was happy to hear this account narrated by Tamim Dari, for it confirms the account which I gave you regarding the antichrist at Madinah and Makkah. Is the antichrist in the Syrian sea (Mediterranean) or the Yemen sea (Arabian sea)? No. On the contrary, he is in the East. He is in the East, and he pointed with his hand towards the East.' Fatima bint Qays said that she preserved this in her mind from the Messenger.

SM v4B p363 n2942, R1, R3; AD v3 p1203 n4311; AD v3 p1203 n4313; AD v3 p1203 n4312

UMM SHARIK RELATED:

She heard God's Messenger saying, 'The people will run away from the antichrist seeking shelter in the mountains.' She asked where the Arabs would be, and he said they would be insignificant in number.

SM v4B p366 n2945

DAY OF JUDGMENT

Divine Decree

AYISHA RELATED:

She heard the Messenger of God say, 'Whoso says anything about the divine decree shall be questioned about it on the day of resurrection, and whoso holds no talk about it will not be questioned.'

IM [H v3 p113]; IM [MMR v1]

Pertaining to the Day of Resurrection

AYISHA RELATED:

She asked God's Messenger about the words of God: *'The day when the earth will be changed for another earth and heaven will be changed for another heaven,'* [14:48]. She asked where the people would be that day, and he said they would be on the path.

SM v4B p290 n2770R2; SB v2 p256 n454 (Asma bint Abu Bakr)

Performing Prescribed Prayer in Jerusalem Mosque

MAYMUNA RELATED:

She asked the Messenger about the religious verdict on Jerusalem. He said, 'It is the land of the resurrection and gathering. Go to it and perform prescribed prayer there because a prescribed prayer performed there is equivalent [in reward] to one thousand prescribed prayers prayed in a mosque other than it.' She asked what to do if she was unable to make the journey. He said, 'Send oil [as a present] to it with which lamps are lit. He who does this is like he who visits it [and offers prescribed prayer].'

IM v2 p341 n1407

GOG AND MAGOG

ZAYNAB BINT JAHSH

The Prophet once came to her in a state of fear and said, 'None has the right to be worshipped but God. Woe upon the Arabs from a danger that has come near. An opening has been made in the wall of Gog and Magog like this,' making a circle with his thumb and index finger. Zaynab bint Jahsh asked if even believers and pious people would be destroyed. He said, 'Yes when evil persons will increase.'

SB v4 p361 n565; SB v9 p187 n249; SB v9 p148 n181; SM v4B p328 n2880R1

JUSTICE: SCALES OF

AYISHA RELATED:

Once a person went to the Messenger and sat in front of him. He then said that he had some slaves who sometimes told him a lie or stole his property or disobeyed him, and, that on such occasions, he scolded them and sometimes punished them. He asked how it would be for him on the final day of judgment [that is, how would God judge between him and the slaves]. The Prophet said, 'God will dispense justice correctly on the day of requital. If the punishment you gave to them was proportionate to their faults, you will neither get nor have to give anything. If the punishment was of a lesser degree than what they merited, you will be recompensed for it. If the punishment was excessive, you will have to recompense the slaves.' Upon hearing this, the man drew aside and began to cry. The Prophet then asked him if he had not heard the verse, '*We shall set up scales of justice for the day of judgment so that no soul will be dealt with unjustly in the least. And if there be [no more than] the weight of a mustard seed, We will bring it [to account] and enough are We to take account.*' The man then said to the Prophet that the best thing for him was to send the slaves away in the Name of God. He then declared that he has set them free with the Prophet as his witness, and that now his slaves were freed.

T [MMT v1 p159] n89; T [Hv4 p119]

UMM SALAMA RELATED:

She heard people mentioning the well, but she did not hear about it from God's Messenger. All she heard was him saying, 'O people!' A girl said that the Prophet had addressed the men only, and that he had not invited the attention of the woman. Umm Salama said that the Messenger had said, 'O people.' Therefore she had every right to listen to things pertaining to religion. God's Messenger had said, 'O people! I shall be your refuge at the well. Therefore, be cautious lest one of you should come to me and be driven away like a stray camel. I will ask the reasons, and it will be said to me, "You do not know what innovations they made after you." And I will then also say, 'Away with them.'"

SM v4A p28 n2295 R1; SB v9 p143 n172; SB v8 p385 n592

AYISHA RELATED:

She asked the Messenger of God if the fact that the son of Judan [Abdullah, a relative of hers] established ties of relationship and fed the poor would be of any avail to him. The Messenger said, 'It will be of no avail to him as he never said, "O my Lord, pardon my sins on the day of resurrection."'

SM v1A p157 n214

AYISHA RELATED:

She said to the Messenger of God that she knew the severest verse in the Quran. He asked, 'What verse is that?' She replied that it was God's words, *'If anyone does evil, he will be requited for it,'* [4:123].' The Messenger asked, 'Do you know Ayisha that when a believer is afflicted with a calamity or a thorn, it serves as an atonement for his evil deeds. He who is called to account will be punished.' She asked if God does not say, *'He truly will receive an easy reckoning'* [84:8]. He replied, 'This is what is presented. If anyone is questioned in reckoning, he will be punished.'

AD v2 p880 n3087; SB v6 p434 n461; SB v6 p434 n462; SB v6 p435 n463; SB v8 p357 n545; SM v4B p326 n2876

LAST HOUR

Approach of the Last Hour

AYISHA RELATED:

When the bedouins came to God's Messenger, they asked about their last hour. He looked towards the youngest among them and said, 'If he lives, he will not grow very old. He will find your last hour coming to you [he will see you dying].'

SM v4B p369 n2952; SB v8 p342 n518

Destruction of the Arabs

UMM AL-HARIR CLIENT OF TALHA IBN MALIK RELATED:

She heard that her patron said that God's Messenger said, 'One of the signs of the approach of the last hour will be the destruction of the Arabs.'

T [MMR v2 p1314]; T Hv4 p590

UMM SALAMA RELATED:

God's Messenger said, 'A band of rebels will kill Ammar.'

SM v4B p347 n2916R2

Demolishing the Kabah

AYISHA RELATED:

The Prophet said, 'At the last hour, an Ethiopian army will attack the Kabah and that army will sink down in the earth.'

SB v2 p390

AYISHA RELATED:

God's Messenger said, '[At the last hour] an army will invade the Kabah. When the invaders reach al-Baida, all the ground will sink and swallow the whole army.' Ayisha asked if the army would sink into the ground while among them would be people who worked in business [and their families] and who were not invaders. The Prophet replied, 'All of those people will sink, but they will be resurrected and judged according to their intentions.'

SB v3 p187 n329; AD v3 p1192 n4276

Imamate

SULAMA BINT AL-HURR
(SISTER OF KHARSHAH IBN AL-HURR AL-FAZARI) RELATED:

She heard God's Messenger say, 'One of the signs of the last hour will be that no person in a mosque will act as an Imam leader, and there will be no leader to lead the prescribed prayer.'

AD v1 p153 n581; IM v2 p93 n981; N [MMR v1 p231]

Returning of Idol Worship

AYISHA RELATED:

She heard God's Messenger say, 'The system of night and day will not end until the people begin to worship Lat and Uzza.' She recalled verse 9:33 in this regard, '*He Who has sent His Messenger with right guidance and true religion so that He may cause it to prevail upon all religions although the polytheists are averse to it.*' He said, 'It will happen as God likes. Then God will send a sweet fragrance and those only will survive who have no goodness in them. They will revert to the religion of their forefathers.'

SM v4B p343 n2907

Turmoil

AYISHA RELATED:

God's Messenger fiddled around while sleeping. She mentioned this to him when he woke up. He said, 'Strange it is that some people of my Community will attack the Kabah for killing one who would belong to the Quraysh tribe. He will try to seek protection in the Kabah. When they reach the desert, they will sink.' She asked if all sorts of people would take God's path. He said, 'Yes. There will be among them people who will come with definite designs and those who will come under duress and there will be travelers also, but they will all be destroyed through one stroke of destruction, although they will be raised in different states on the day of resurrection. God will, however, resurrect them according to their intention.'

SM v4B p330 n2884

PARADISE AND ITS INHABITANTS

Furtherest Lote Tree

ASMA BINT ABU BAKR

She heard the Messenger of God being reminded of the farthest lote tree. He said, 'A rider will travel in the shade of its branches for one hundred years, and one hundred riders will enjoy its shade [of which the narrator had doubt]. There are butterflies of gold therein, its fruits are as it were earth wares.'

T [Hv4p170]

Pertaining to the Destruction of the World

AYISHA RELATED:

She heard God's Messenger say, 'People will be assembled on the day of resurrection barefooted, naked, and uncircumcised.' She asked if male and female would be together on that day and looking at one another. He said, 'Ayisha the matter will be too serious for them to look at one another.'

SM v4B p319 n2859; SB v8 p350 n534

AYISHA RELATED:

She began to cry. God's Messenger asked her why she was crying. She said it was because she had begun to think of hell. She asked if he would remember his family on the day of resurrection. God's Messenger replied, 'There are three occasions when no one will remember anyone: at the scale, where his weight is either light or heavy; at the time of the examination of the book, when he is commanded, *"Take and read God's record,"* [21:47] and knows not whether his book will be put into his right hand or into his left hand or behind his back; and at the path, where it is placed over hell.'

AD v3 p1331 n4737

PROMISED SAVIOR

Descendant of Fatima

UMM SALAMA

God's Messenger said, 'The Guided One [savior, *mahdi*] will be of my family, among the descendants of Fatima.'

AD v3 p 1191 n4271

Islam Established on Earth

UMM SALAMA

God's Messenger said, 'Disagreement will occur at the death of a caliph, and a man of the people of Madinah will come forth flying to Makkah. Some of the people of Makkah will come to him, bring him out against his will, and swear allegiance to him between the corner of the Black Stone and the Station of Abraham. An expeditionary force will then be sent against him from Syria but will be swallowed up in the desert between Makkah and Madinah. When the people see that, the eminent saints of Syria and the best people of Iraq will come to him and swear allegiance to him between the Black Stone and the Station of Abraham. Then will arise a man of the Quraysh (whose maternal uncles belong to Kalb) who will send against them an expeditionary force which will be overcome. This is the expedition of the Kalb. Disappointed is the one who does not receive the booty of the Kalb. He will divide the property and will govern the people by the *sunna* of their Prophet and establish Islam on the earth. He will remain seven years, then die, and the Muslims will pray for him.'

AD v3 p1191 n4273

AYISHA RELATED:

The revelation, '*Nay, but the Hour of Judgment is theirs. . .*' 54:46 was revealed to Muhammad at Makkah while she was a playful little girl.

SB v6 p369 n399

RECORDING DEEDS

AYISHA RELATED:

The Prophet said, 'The pen has been stopped from [recording] the deeds and promises of three categories of people. The first is a sleeping person unless he is awake. The second is a minor until he reaches adulthood. The third is the insane until he becomes sane.' (According to Abu Bakr, until a person recovers from illness.)

IM v2u p98 n192

PART III:
PROGRAM OF ACTION:
ECONOMIC ISSUES

CHAPTER 1
CHARITY

Accepted by the Prophet
DUBAAH BINT AL-ZUBAYR IBN ABD AL-MUTTALIB RELATED:

Miqdad went to Baqi al-Khabkhabah for a certain need. He found a mouse taking out a dinar from a hole. It then continued to take out dinars one by one until it had taken out seventeen dinars. It then took out a red purse containing a dinar. There were then eighteen dinars. He took them to the Messenger and told him what had happened. He gave it to the Messenger as charity. The Prophet asked if he had extended his hand toward the hole. He said that he had not. God's Messenger then said, 'May God bless you.'

> AD v2 p878 n3081

JUWAYRIYA RELATED:

The Messenger went to her and asked, 'Is there anything to eat?' She said that the only food she had was a goat's bone which her freed maid-servant [Barira] was given as charity. Upon this, he said, 'Bring that to me for it (the charity) has reached its destination.'

> SM v2A p137 n1073; SM v2A p138 n1076; SM v2A p137 n1075 R1; T [Hv2]; T [Hv2 p16]; T [MMRv1]

UMM ATIYA RELATED:

A sheep was sent to her in charity. She sent some of it to Ayisha. The Prophet asked Ayisha for something to eat. Ayisha replied that there was nothing except what Nusayba al-Ansariya (Umm Atiya) had sent of that sheep. The Prophet said to her, 'Bring it as it has reached its place.'

> SB v2 p301 n525; SB v2 p332 n571; SB v7 p152 n202; SB v7 p154 n207; SB v3 p453 n753

And Heirs
UMM SALAMA RELATED:

She asked the Prophet if she would receive a spiritual reward if she spent for the sustenance of Abu Salama's offspring who were her sons. The Prophet replied, 'Spend on them and you will receive a spiritual reward for what you spent on them.'

SB v2 p317 n546; SB v7 p215 n282; SM v2A p93 n1001

As Atonement

AYISHA RELATED:

A man went to the Prophet in the mosque and said that he [the man] was ruined. The Prophet asked him what he had done. He said that he had had sexual relations with his wife during the month of Ramadan while fasting. The Prophet said, 'Give in charity.' The man said that he had nothing. The man sat down and, in the meantime, a man came driving a donkey carrying food to the Prophet. The Prophet asked, 'Where is the person who said he was ruined?' The man responded. The Prophet said, 'Take this food and give it in charity to someone.' The man asked if he should give the food to a family that was more poor than his own as his family had nothing to eat. The Prophet said, 'Then eat it yourselves.'

SB v8 p532 n811B

Begger's Rights

UMM BUJAYD RELATED:

She took the oath of allegiance to the Messenger of God and asked him what to do when a poor man stood at her door and she could find nothing to give him. The Messener of God said, 'If you do not find anything to give him, put something in his hand—even if it be a burnt hoof.'

AD v2 p437 n1663; T [H v2 p33]

Brings Blessings

ASMA BINT ABU BAKR RELATED:

The Prophet said, 'Do not shut your money bag otherwise God too will withhold His blessings from you. Spend in God's cause as much as you can afford.'

SB v2 p294 n513; SB v2 p294 n515

Given on Behalf of the Dead

AYISHA RELATED:

A person went to the Messenger of God and said that his mother died suddenly without leaving any will. He thought that she would have given charity if she could speak. He wanted to know if she would yet a reward if he gave charity on her behalf. The Prophet said, 'Yes.'

SM v2A p94 n1004, R4; SB v2 p266 n470; SM v3A p82 n1004 R1-2; AD v2 p812 n2875

Given Without Calculation

ASMA BINT ABU BAKR RELATED:

The Messenger said, 'Give in charity and do not give reluctantly otherwise God will give you in a limited amount. Do not withhold your money lest God should withhold it from you.'

SB v3 p461 n764; SM v2A p107 n1029, R1-R3

Includes All Types of Good Acts

AYISHA RELATED:

God's Messenger said, 'Every human being of Adam has been created with 364 joints. The one who declares the glory of God, praises God, declares God to be one, glorifies God, seeks forgiveness from God, removes stones or thorns or bones from people's path, enjoins what is good and forbids what is evil, to the number of those 364, will walk that day having removed himself from hell.'

> SM v2A p95 n1007, R2

"It is not righteousness..."

FATIMA BINT QAYS RELATED:

The Messenger of God said, 'Besides the poor-due, there is surely a duty upon property.' Then he recited, *'It is not righteousness that you turn your faces towards the East and the West, but righteousness is this that you believe in God and the day of judgment and the angels and the Book and the Prophets and give away wealth out of love for Him to the nearer of kin and the orphans and the needy and the wayfarer and the beggars and for emancipation of captives and keep up prayer and pay the poor-due'* (2:177).

> T [H v1 p275]; T [MMT v3]; t [MMR v1 p406]; IM [MMT v3 p24]

Protects From Hell-fire

AYISHA RELATED:

A woman and her two daughters went to her (Ayisha) asking for some charity. Ayisha found nothing except one date which she gave to the woman. The woman divided it between her two daughters and then got up and went away. When the Prophet came in and she had told him what had happened, he said, 'Whoever is responsible for these girls and treats them generously will be shielded by these girls from hell fire.

> SB v8 p17 n24; AD v4A p202 n2629

Rewards of

AYISHA RELATED:

When a woman gives in charity some of the foodstuff which she has in her house (without wasting her husband's property), she will receive the reward for what she has spent; and her husband will receive the reward because of his earning, and the storekeeper will also have a reward similar to it. The reward of one will not decrease the reward of others.

> SB v2 p290 n506; SB v3 p160 n279; SB v2 p297 n520; SB v2 p297 n521; SB v2 p297 n518; SM v2A p104 n1024 R2; SM v2A p104 n1024, R2; AD v2 p442 n1681

Spend in Charity from Her Husband's Earnings

ASMA BINT ABU BAKR RELATED:

She said to the Messenger of God that she had nothing of her own except what her husband, Zubayr, brought her. She asked if she could spend from it. The Messenger said, 'Give and do not hoard so your sustenance will not be withheld.'

AD v2 p445 n1695; SB v3 p461 n763

To Relatives Even If They Are Polytheists

ZAYNAB RELATED:

The Messenger of God said, 'O women, give charity even though it be some of your jewellery.' She returned to her husband, Abd Allah, [to whom she was giving charity] and said that he was a person with empty hands; whereas, the Messenger of God had commanded them to give charity. She said he should go to the Messenger and ask if this would suffice for her; otherwise, she would give it to someone else. Abd Allah told to her to go and ask. She went with another woman of the Helpers who had the same question that she had. Bilal came out, and they asked him to go to the Messenger and inform him that there were two women at the door asking whether it would serve them to give charity to their spouses and to orphans in their charge. They asked Bilal not to tell him who the women were. Bilal went to the Messenger of God and asked him what these women had instructed him to ask. The Messenger asked him who these women were. He said that they were women from the Helpers and Zaynab. Upon this the Messenger asked, 'Which Zaynab?' Bilal said the wife of Abd Allah. The Messenger said, 'There are two rewards for them, the reward of kinship and the reward of charity.'

SM v2A p93 n1000, R1; T [MMR v1]

What is Due

UMM SALAMA RELATED:

She wore gold ornaments. She asked if this was considered a treasure. The Messenger of God said, 'Whatever reaches a value on which the poor-due is payable is not a treasure when the poor-due is paid.'

AD v2 p406 n1559

CHAPTER 2
INHERITANCE

INHERITANCE OF PROPHETS

AYISHA RELATED:

Fatima, the daughter of the Messenger of God, sent a messenger to Abu Bakr asking from him the inheritance of the Messenger of God which God had bestowed on him at Madina and Fadak and what remained of the fifth of Khaybar. Abu Bakr said that the Messenger of God had said, 'We leave no inheritance. Whatever we leave is charity. The family of Muhammad will eat from this property.' Abu Bakr then said that he would not change this from what it had been at the time of the Messenger of God and that he would deal with it just as the Messenger of God dealt with it. Abu Bakr refused to give anything to Fatima from it.

AD v2 p833 n2962; AD v2 p833 n2963; AD v2 p833 n2964; SB v5 p381 n546

AYISHA RELATED:

When the Messenger of God died, the wives of the Prophet intended to send Uthman ibn Affan to Abu Bakr to ask him for their cost of living from the inheritance of the Prophet. Thereupon Ayisha repeated to them that the Messenger of God had said, 'We leave no inheritance. Whatever we leave is alms.'

AD v2 p841 n2970; SB v8 p472 n719

SHARES OF THE RELATIVES ON THE MATERNAL SIDE

AYISHA RELATED:

A client of the Prophet died and left some property but left no child or relative. The Messenger of God said, 'Give what he has left to a man belonging to his village.'

IM v2 p819 n2896; AD v2 p819 n2896; N v2u p357 n893; T [MMR v1 p652]; T [H v2 p333]

WILLS

JUWAYRIA BINT AL-HARITH RELATED:

When God's Messenger died, he did not leave a dirham or dinar [money], a slave or a slave women or anything else except his white mule, his arms and a piece of land which he had given in charity.

SB v4 p2 n2; SM v3A p84 n1635; AD v2 p805 n2857

CHAPTER 3
MISCELLANEOUS
ECONOMIC ISSUES

BOOTY

Acquiring Spoils Correctly

KHAWLA RELATED:

God's Messenger said, 'This property is fresh and sweet. One who attains it in a proper way will be blessed by it, but he who improperly acquires such property of God and His Messenger as his soul wishes will have nothing but hell on the day of resurrection.'

T [MMR v2 p855]

Best of Spoils

UMM AL-HAKAM OR DUBAAH (DAUGHTER OF HIS PATERNAL UNCLE), RELATED:

She and her sister, Fatima, daughter of the Messenger, went and complained to the Messenger about their living conditions. They asked for a captive of war. God's Messenger said, 'The orphans of the people who were killed in the Battle of Badr came before you, but I will tell you something better than that. You should say, "God is Greater," thirty-three times after each prescribed prayer. Also say, "Glory be to God" thirty-three times after each prescribed prayer and "Praise belongs to God" thirty-four times after each prescribed prayer. Then say once, "There is no god but God alone. He has no assocaite. The Kingdom belongs to Him. Praise belongs to Him. He has power over all things.'"

AD v2 p846 n2981

UMM SALAMA RELATED:

She sent a message to the teacher of the school saying, "Send me some boys to tease the wool, but do not send me a free boy."

SB v9 p34

Division of Spoils

AYISHA RELATED:

God's Messenger was brought a pouch containing beads and divided it among free woman and slave women. She said that her father used to divide things between free men and slaves.

AD v2 p833 n2946

Gained in Just Manner

KHAWLAH BINT QAYS RELATED:

The Messenger of God send, 'Verily this property (booty) is green, sweet. Whosoever gains it in a just manner, blessing is given to him; however, many extravagant men wish for it from the property of God and His Prophet. There will be nothing for them on the day of resurrection except hell.'

T [H v2 p420]

Not to Family

UMM AL-HAKAM [OR DUBAA BINT AL-ZUBAYR] RELATED:

The Messenger of God received some prisoners of war. She, her sister and Fatima, daughter of the Prophet, went to the Prophet. They complained to him about their condition and asked him to give them some prisoners [slaves]. The Messenger of God said, 'The orphans of Badr came before you [and took the prisoners of war].'

AD v3 p1406 n5048]

Special Portion of the Prophet From the Spoils

AYISHA RELATED:

Safiya was called after the word *safi* [a special portion of the Prophet].

AD v2 p848 n2988

BORROWING MONEY

MAYMUNA RELATED:

She borrowed money. Her family did not approve of her habit and asked her to stop doing it. She said the Prophet said, 'Any Muslim who borrows money with the intention of paying it back, God will help him repay it in this world.'

IM v2u p231 n568

PAWNING

AYISHA RELATED:

The Prophet purchased food grain from a Jew, placing his shield as collateral.

IM v2u p241 n597; SB v3 p414 n686; SB v3 416 n696; SB v3 p221 n404; SB v3 p161 n282; SB v5 p525 n743; SB v3 p174 n309; SB v4 p106 n165; SM v3A p61 n1603; IM v2u p242 n597

TRANSACTIONS

AYISHA RELATED:

God's blessings are in measurements [sa or three kgs and mudd or 2/3rd kg.].

SB v3 p192

WAGES

Children's Property

AYISHA RELATED:

The Messenger of God said, 'The children of a person are from what he earns. As a matter of fact, they are his most pleasant earning so he may take from their property.'

AD v2 p1002 n3522; IM v2 p1003 n3529; N v2u p187 n447; T {MMR v1

Income from a Slave

AYISHA RELATED:

A man bought a slave who remained with him as long as God wished him to remain. The man then found defects in the slave. He told his situation to the Prophet, and he returned the slave to his original owner. The original owner said that his slave had earned some wages. The Messenger said, 'He has the right to profit who is accountable for loss.'

AD v2 p997 n3501; IM v2u p171 n398; IM [MMT v4 p368]

PART IV:
PROGRAM OF ACTION:
INDIVIDUAL ISSUES

CHAPTER 1
PRESCRIBED FOR ATTAINING PURITY

ABLUTION

After Kissing One's Wife
AYISHA RELATED:

God's Messenger kissed some of his wives. He then went to perform the prescribed prayer without performing ablution. [It was said to her that it must have been none but her that he kissed]. Hearing this, she smiled.

IM v1 p272 n502; IM v1 p273 n503; AD v1 p54 n222

After Relieving Oneself
AYISHA RELATED:

God's Messenger directed women to tell their husbands to use water for the purpose of cleaning their private parts (because he hesitated to give such instructions to them) and to tell them that the Messenger of God used to clean his private parts with water.

N v1E p150 n46

After Touching the Male Organ
BUSRA BINT ABU SUFYAN

God's Messenger said, 'When anyone of you touches his sexual organ, he should perform ablution.'

IM v1 p262 n479; IM v1 p263 n481

Cleansing Oneself with Clods of Earth
AYISHA RELATED:

God's Messenger said, 'Whenever anyone of you goes to the desert to relieve himself, he should carry with him [at least] three clods of earth which he should use to clean himself. They are sufficient for him.'

N v1E p149 n44; AD v1 p10 n40

Clothes Stained With Semen

AYISHA RELATED:

She rubbed off the semen from the clothing of the Messenger of God and then offered the prescribed prayer wearing it.

AD v1 p96 n372; SBv1 p146 n230; SB v1 p146 n228; SB v1 p149 n229; SB v1 p147 n233; AD v1 p96 n373; IM v1 p293 n539; IM v1 p292 n537; IM v1 p292 n537; IM v1 p293 n539; N v1E n253 n299; N v1E p253 p300; N v1E p253 n301; N v1E p253 n302; N v1E p253 n303; N v1E p253 n304; N v1E p252 n298; N v1E p253 n299; N v1E p253 n300; N v1E p253 n302

Covering Utensils

AYISHA RELATED:

She used to cover three utensils for God's Messenger at night: a utensil for his ablution, a utensil for his tooth stick and a utensil for drinking water.

IM v1 p205 n361

Disapproval of Touching the Penis With the Right Hand

AYISHA RELATED:

The Prophet used his right hand to get water for ablution and take food and his left hand for purifying himself after urinating or defecating and for anything repugnant.

AD v1 p8 n33; SM v1A p180 n268R1; AD v1 p8 n34; AD v1 p8 n32

Eating That Which Fire Has Changed

UMM HABIBA RELATED:

God's Messenger said, 'Perform ablution to purify yourself after [eating] what fire has touched [i.e. cooked food].'

IM v1 p265 n486

How to Perform

AYISHA RELATED:

The Prophet liked beginning from the right in performing ablution, combing his hair, and putting on his shoes.

SB v7 p496 n745; SB v1 p250 n418; IM v1 p225 n401; SB v7 p530 n810; SB v1 p117 n169; SB v7 p223 n292; AD v3 p1153 n4128; N v1E p178 n113

AYISHA RELATED:

She never saw God's Messenger coming out of the toilet without having cleansed himself with water.

IM v1 p201 n354

AYISHA RELATED:

The Prophet used to wash his private parts three times. Ibn Umar said that they found that a remedy and means of purification.

IM v1 p203 n356

RUBAYYI BINT MUAWWIDH IBN AFRA RELATED:

The Messenger of God used to come to her. He once said, 'Pour ablution water on me.' She then described how the Prophet performed ablution by washing his hands up to his wrists three times and washing his face three times. He rinsed his mouth and snuffed up water once. Then he washed his forearms three times and wiped his head twice from the back to the front. He wiped his ears outside and inside. Then he washed his feet three times.

AD v1 p31 n126

Rubayyi bint Muawwidh ibn Afra related:

The Messenger of God performed the ablution in her presence. He wiped the whole of his head from its upper to its lower part, moving every side. He did not move his hair from its original position.

AD v1 p31 n128

Rubayyi bint Muawwidh ibn Afra related:

She saw the Messenger of God performing ablution. He wiped his head front and back, his temples, and his ears once.

AD v1 p31 n129

Rubayyi bint Muawwidh ibn Afra related:

The Prophet wiped his head with water left over in his hand.

AD v1 p31 n130

Rubayyi bint Muawwadh related:

God's Messenger performed ablution and then wiped the interior and the exterior of his ears.

IM v1 p244 n440; AD v1 p31 n131

Rubayyi bint Muawwadh related:

God's Messenger performed ablution and wiped his head twice.

IM v1 p243 n438

Rubayyi bint Muawwidh related:

She brought a basin to the Prophet for ablution. He said, 'Pour it for me.' She poured [water] for him. He washed his face and arms and then took some fresh water and wiped his head with it—front and back—and washed his feet. He washed every part three times.

IM v1 p220 n390

Not Essential When One Takes Something Cooked by Fire

Umm Salama

She said that the Messenger of God ate some meat of a goat's shoulder then went for the prescribed prayer and did not touch water.

N v1E p206 n184; SB v1 p138 n209; IM v1 p267 n491; N v1E p206 n184

On Inserting the Fingers Inside the Ears

Ayisha related:

God's Messenger would not go to sleep until he puffed out the wind from his mouth. He then would get up and offer his prescribed prayer without performing ablution. [That is, he would sleep while in prostration].

IM v1 p259 n474

Umm Ayyash related:

The slave girl of the daughter of the Messenger said that she used to help God's Messenger in performing ablution while she was standing and he was sitting.

IM v1 p221 n392

Performing Three Times

RUBAYYI BINT MUAWWADH RELATED:

God's Messenger performed ablution three times [washed the areas for ablution three times].

IM v1 p232 n418; AD v1 p29 n99; IM v1 p232 n418; v1 p231 n415

Person Sexually Defiled Can Eat and Drink

AYISHA RELATED:

When God's Messenger intended to take a meal while in a state of sexual defilement, he performed ablution.

IM v1 p319 n591; IM v1 p320 n594

Quantity of Water Desirable for Ablution

UMM UMARA RELATED:

A vessel containing 2/3rds *mudd* of water was brought to the Messenger. Suba told her that the Messenger rubbed and washed both his hands and wiped the inner side of his ears but he did not remember if the Prophet wiped the upper side of his ears.

N v1E p160 n75

Quantity of Water For Ablution and Bath Lustration

AYISHA RELATED:

She and God's Messenger used to performed ablution with a *mudd* of water. He performed the bath lustration with one *sa* of water.

N v1E p277 n349; IM v1 p155 n267; N v1E p277 n350

Remainders of a Cat

KABSHAH, WIFE OF IBN ABU QATADAH RELATED:

Abu Qatadah went to her. She poured water for him for ablution. Then a cat came to drink therefrom. He tipped the pot until it drank. She said that he saw her looking at him and asked if she was surprised. She said she was. He said that the Messenger of God had said, 'It is not impure. Verily it (the cat) is of those males or females who roam around you.'

T [H v1 p716]; AD v1 p19 n75; IM v1 p208 n367; N v1E p201 n168; N v1E p201 n169; N v1E p158 n69

Rinsing the Mouth After Drinking Milk

UMM SALAMA

God's Messenger said, 'When you drink milk, rinse out your mouths for it contains greasiness.'

IM v1 p271 n499

Sexually Impure Should Perform Before Sleeping

AYISHA RELATED:

She said that whenever the Messenger of God intended to sleep while he was sexually impure, he performed ablution as for the prescribed prayer before going to sleep.

N v1E p238 n261; IM v1 p316 n583; SB v1 p174 n286; N v1E p237 n258; AD v1 p55 n224; N v1E p238 n259

Sunnahs

AYISHA RELATED:

The Prophet had a piece of cloth with which he dried his limbs after performing ablution.

T [H v1 p699]; T [MMR v1 p86]

Washing the Feet

RUBAYYI BINT MUAWWADH RELATED:

Ibn Abbas went to her and asked her about the Tradition in which she mentioned that God's Messenger performed ablution and washed his feet.

IM v1 p251 n458

Washing the Heels

AYISHA RELATED:

God's Messenger said [in regard to ablution of washing the heels], 'Woe to the heels because of hellfire.'

IM v1 p247 n451

When to Perform After Relieving Oneself

AYISHA RELATED:

The Prophet urinated, and Umar was standing behind him with a jug of water. He asked, 'What is this Umar?' Umar replied that it was water for him to perform ablution. He said, 'I have not been commanded to perform ablution ever time I urinate. If I were to do so, it would become a part of the *sunna*.'

AD v1 p10 n42; IM v1 p187 n327

BATH LUSTRATION

Because of Sexual Defilement

UMM HABIBA RELATED:

The Messenger of God would offer the prescribed prayer in clothes in which he had had intercourse if he did not see any impurity on them.

AD v1 p95 n366

AYISHA RELATED:

When the Messenger of God used to perform the bath lustration because of sexual impurity, he called for a vessel like a vessel used for milking a camel. He then took a handful of water and began to pour it on the right side of his head and then on the left side. He took water in both his hands together and poured it on his head.

AD v1 p60 n240; SM v1A p205 n318

MAYMUNA RELATED:

She placed [the vessel of] water for the Prophet to purify himself because of sexual impurity. He lowered down the vessel and poured water on his right hand. He then washed it twice or three times. He then poured water over his private parts and washed them with his left hand. Then he put the vessel on the ground and wiped it. He then rinsed his mouth and snuffed up water and washed his face and hands. He then poured water over his head and body. Then he moved aside and washed his feet. She handed him a garment, but he began to shake off water from his body. She mentioned it to Ibrahim. He said that the Companions did not think there was any harm in using the garment [to wipe the water], but they disliked its use as a habit.

AD v1 p61 n245

Drying With a Towel

MAYMUNA RELATED:

She brought a cloth to God's Messenger when he performed a bath lustration after of sexual intercourse. He handed it back and began to shake off water [from his body].

IM v1 p256 n467

Experiencing Organism Without Moisture

AYISHA RELATED:

God's Messenger said, 'When anyone of you wakes up from his sleep and sees moistness but does not think that he has had a wet dream, he should perform the bath lustration. When he thinks that he has experienced [sexual discharge during sleep] but does not see the moistness, a bath lustration is not incumbent upon him.'

IM v1 p329 n612

Flow of the Fluid Between Man and Woman

AYISHA RELATED:

When asked about washing the fluid that flows between a husband and wife after sexual intercourse, she said that the Messenger of God used to take a handful of water and pour it on the fluid [that flows between a man and woman]. Again, he would take a handful of water and pour it over the fluid.

AD v1 p64 n257

Following Sexual Emission

AYISHA RELATED:

God's Messenger washed himself with water from a vessel [measuring seven to eight *sir*s] to purify herself after sexual intercourse.

SM v1A p205 n319, R1; SB v1 p162 n262

From a Brass Vessel

ZAYNAB BINT JAHSH RELATED:

She had a brass tub. She said that she used to wash the head of God's Messenger from water poured into it.

IM v1 p259 n472

From a Copper Vessel

AYISHA RELATED:

The big copper vessel used to be prepared for her and God's Messenger, and they would take water from it together [for bathing].

SB v9 p323 n439

How to Perform

AYISHA RELATED:

When God's Messenger bathed after of sexual intercourse, he first washed his hands. He then poured water with his right hand onto his left hand and washed his private parts. He then performed ablution as for prescribed prayer. He then took some water and wet his fingers and moved them through the roots of his hair. And when he found that these had been properly moistened, he poured three handfuls on his head. He then poured water over his body and subsequently washed his feet.

> SM v1A p203 n316, R2-R3; SB v1 p167 n273; SM v1A p204 n317R2; AD v1 p61 n242; AD v1 p61 n243; N v1E p231 n246

Husband and Wife Performing the Bath Lustration Together

AYISHA RELATED:

She pulled the water container placed between her and the Messenger of God. Their hands alternated taking water as she and the Messenger of God performed the bath lustration, following sexual impurity, from the same vessel.

> N v1E p227 n237; SB v1 p191 n319; SB v1 p162 n261; SB v1 p162 n263; SM v1A p206 n321; SM v1A p207 n322 by Maymuna; SM v1A p207 n324; AD v1 p59 n238; IM v1 p213 n376; N v1 p214 n380; N v1 p215 n383; N v1E p227 n235; N v1E p306 n415; N v1E p229 n242; N v1E p227 n236; N v1E p227 n238; N v1E p227 n238; N v1E p225 n231; N v1E p226 n234; N v1E p306 n413; N v1E p306 n414; N v1E p306 n415; AD v1 p21 n77; AD v1 p21 n78; N v1E p159 n73; N v1E p276 n347

UMM HANI RELATED:

The Prophet and Maymuna performed the bath lustration from one bowl [of water] having some trace of dough paste on it.

> IM v1 p213 n378; N v1E p229 n243; N [H v1 p718]

Male or Female

AYISHA RELATED:

When God's Messenger was asked about a man who noticed moisture but did not remember having had a wet dream, the Messenger said that he must wash. When asked about a man who thought he had had a dream but noticed no moisture, he said that the man did not need to wash. Umm Sulaym asked whether or not a woman must wash when she experienced [something similar] and the Messenger replied, 'Yes, women are of the same nature as men.'

> IM [MMR v1 p89]; SB v1 p171 n280 (Umm Salama); AD v1 p58 n236A; IM v1 p324 n602 (Khawala bint Hakim); N v1E p212 n200 (Khwala bint Hakim)

Modesty While Gaining Religious Knowledge

UMM SALAMA RELATED:

She said that verily God is not embarrased to [tell you] the truth and then asked if it were necessary for a woman to take a bath after she had had a wet dream [nocturnal sexual discharge]. The Prophet replied, 'Yes if she notices a discharge.' She then covered her face and asked if a woman has a discharge. He replied, 'Yes, of course; that is why a son may resemble his mother.'

SB v1 p96 n132

Obligatory for a Woman After Experiencing Orgasm in a Dream

UMM SULAYM (THE GRANDMOTHER OF IBN ISHAQ) RELATED:

She went to the Messenger in the presence of Ayisha and asked him if a woman experiences in a dream what a man experiences [orgasm]. Upon hearing this, Ayisha was appalled and told her that she had humiliated women. God's Messenger said, 'Ayisha, you are wrong to discourage her from seeking guidance.' He said to her [Umm Salaym], 'Umm Sulaym, she should take a bath lustration if she sees that [that is, experiences orgasm in a dream].'

SM v1A p199 n310; SB v8 p90 n; SB v8 p273 n113; SM v1A p200 n313R1; SM v1A p201 by Ayisha; AD v1 p59 n237; AD v1 p59 p236B; N v1 p323 n600; T v1E p211 n199

Obligatory When the Male and Female Have Sexual Contact

AYISHA RELATED:

A person asked the Messenger whether the bath lustration was obligatory for a husband who had sexual intercourse with his wife but without orgasm. She was sitting next to him. The Messenger said, 'She and I do it and then perform a bath lustration.'

SM v1A p219 n350

AYISHA RELATED:

When the sexual parts of a male and female have contact, performing the bath lustration becomes obligatory. She and God's Messenger did this, and both of them performed a bath lustration.

IM v1 p327 n608

Of a Woman After Sexual Defilement

KHUALA BINT HAKIM RELATED:

She said to the Messenger that she had closely plaited hair. Then she asked if she had to undo it for the bath lustration to purify herself after sexual intercourse? He said, 'It is enough for you to throw three handfuls of water on your head and then pour water over yourself. You will then be purified.'

IM v1 p325 n603; SM v1A p208 n330 by Umm Salama; AD v1 p63 n251; AD v1 p63 n252; N v1E p230 n244; N v1E p308 n418

Performing Ablution After Taking a Bath Is Not Necessary

AYISHA RELATED:

The Messenger performed a bath lustration and offered two

cycles of prescribed prayer and then offered the dawn prescribed prayer. She did not think that he performed ablution after performing the bath lustration.

AD v1 p62 n250; IM v1 p314 n579; N v1E p236; N v1E p315 n421; N v1E p 315 n432; N v1E p236 n255

Performing Ablution Before Taking a Bath Lustration

AYISHA RELATED:

Whenever the Prophet took a bath lustration after sexual intercourse, he began by washing his hands and then performed ablution as for the prescribed prayer. After that he would put his fingers in water and wet the roots of his hair and then pour three handfuls of water over his head and then pour water over his entire body.

SB v1 p156 n248; N v1E p233 n250

MAYMUNA RELATED:

God's Messenger performed ablution like that for the prescribed prayer but did not wash his feet. He washed off the discharge from his private parts and then poured water over his body. He withdrew his feet from that place [the place where he took the bath] and then washed them. And that was his way of taking the bath lustration following sexual intercourse.

SB v1 p157 n249

Person Defiled by Seminal Emission

AYISHA RELATED:

God's Messenger used to perform the bath lustration after sexual intercourse and then warm himself with her before she had taken a bath lustration.

IM v1 p315 n580

AYISHA RELATED:

God's Messenger used to have seminal emission and then sleep without touching water until he wore and performed the bath lustration.

IM v1 p315 n581

AYISHA RELATED:

If God's Messenger had any sexual desire for his wives, he would satisfy that. Then he would go to sleep in the same condition and would not touch water [for the purpose of the bath lustration] until waking.

IM v1 p315 n582

Person Who Is Sexually Impure May Postpone the Bath Lustration

AYISHA RELATED:

The Messenger would sleep while he was sexually defiled without touching water.

AD v1 p56 n228

Pouring Water with the Right Hand Over the Left Hand

MAYMUNA RELATED:

She placed water for the bath of God's Messenger and put up a screen. He poured water over his hands and washed them once or twice. [The sub-narrator added that he did not remember if she had said three or not]. Then he poured water with his right hand over his left one and washed his private parts. He rubbed his hands over the earth and washed them. He rinsed his mouth and washed his nose by putting water in it and blowing it out. He washed his face, forearms, and head. He poured water over his body and then withdrew from that place and washed his feet. She gave him a piece of cloth [towel]. He pointed with his hand [that he did not want it] and did not take it.

SB v1 p164 n266; SB v1 p162 n265; SB v1 p168 n275; SB v1 p160 n259; v1 p166 n272; IM v1 p311 n573; N v1E p313 n430; N p309 n420; N p307 n417; N p306 n412; p306 n422; N p233 n250; N p309 n421; N p312 n426; N p307 n417; N p309 n420; N p309 n421, 422, 423, 425, 426

AYISHA RELATED:

The Prophet would perform the bath lustration after sexual intercourse on Friday, after opening a vein, and after washing a dead body.

AD v1 p92 n348

Rubbing of Hands with the Earth to Thoroughly Purify

MAYMUNA RELATED:

The Prophet performed the bath lustration following sexual emission.

SB v1 p161 n260

Rubbing the Hair Thoroughly

AYISHA RELATED:

The Messenger of God first moistened his head and then poured three handfuls of water on his head.

N v1E p234 n252

Scenting With Perfume

AYISHA RELATED:

Whenever the Prophet performed a bath lustration following sexual discharge, he asked for *hilab* or some other scent. He took it in his hand, rubbed it first over the right side of his head, then over the left side and then rubbed the middle of his head with both hands.

SB v1 p160 n258

Sexual Impurity Before Fasting

UMM SALAMA RELATED:

The Messenger of God would be overtaken by the dawn when he was in a state of sexual impurity but would [still] perform the prescribed fast. [Ayisha also reports this Tradition.]

AD v2 p654 n2382

AYISHA RELATED:

A man said to the Messenger of God that he was overtaken by dawn while he was sexually defiled but had wanted to perform the prescribed fast. The Messenger of God said, 'I am also overtaken by dawn while I am in a state of sexual impurity. I also want to perform the prescribed fast. I take a bath and perform the fast.' The man replied that the Messenger was not like them. God had forgiven him his past and future sins. The Messenger became angry and said, 'I swear by God, I hope I shall be the most God-wary and most familiar of you with what I follow.'

AD v2 p655 n2383

Should a Woman Undo Her Plaited Hair

AYISHA RELATED:

When any of them were sexually impure, she took three handfuls of water with both hands together and poured water over her head. She took one handful of water and threw it on one side and the other on the other side.

AD v1 p63 n253; SB v1 p169 n276

AYISHA RELATED:

They took a bath lustration while having an adhesive substance over their head when preparing to dress for the sacred state of the prescribed pilgrimage and when wearing ordinary clothes.

AD v1 p63 n254

Sleeping After Sexual Intercourse

AYISHA RELATED:

Whenever the Messenger intended to sleep after having sexual intercourse, he performed ablution as for the prayer before going to sleep.

SM v1A p198 n305, R1

Taking a Bath By a Person Who Is Performing the Prescribed Fast

AYISHA RELATED:

At times in Ramadan the Prophet used to take a bath in the morning (not because of a wet dream) and continue his fast.

SB v3 p84 n152

Taking Because of Sexual Defilement

AYISHA RELATED:

She could show the marks of the hand of the Messenger of God on the wall where he took a bath lustration because of sexual impurity.

AD v1 p61 n244

AYISHA RELATED:

She was asked about the *witr* prayer of God's Messenger. A Tradition was mentioned, and she was asked what he did after having sexual intercourse: whether he took a bath lustration before going to sleep or slept before taking a bath lustration. She said that he did all these. Sometimes he took a bath and then slept. Sometimes he performed ablution only and went to sleep.

SM v1A p198 n307

When to Perform

AYISHA RELATED:

The Prophet used to wash his head with an adhesive substance while he was sexually impure. It was sufficient for him and he did not pour water on it.

AD v1 p63 n256

BATHING

Earth Can Purify

AYISHA RELATED:

People came to Madinah from their homes and from the outskirts of Madinah up to a distance of four miles or more. They passed through dust and were drenched with sweat which trickled from them. One of them went to God's Messenger who was in my house. The Prophet said to him, 'I want you to keep yourself clean on this day of yours [i.e. take a bath].'

SB v2 p12 n25; SM v2A p5 n847R1; AD v1 p272 n1050; AD v1 p287 n1109; AD v1 p92 n352

WOMAN FROM ABD AL-ASHHAL TRIBE RELATED:

She told the Messenger that between her home and the mosque there was a path full of filth. He asked, 'Is the path that follows it more clean than it?' She said that it was. He said, 'This serves as a substitute for that.'

IM v1 p290 n533; SB v3 p162 n285; AD v1 p99 n384; AD v1 p90 n342; AD v1 p92 n ; IM v1 p289 n531 by Umm Salama

One Should Draw a Curtain While Taking a Bath

MAYMUNA RELATED:

She placed water for the Messenger's bath, provided privacy for him, and he took a bath.

SM v1A p214 n337

Shoe Being Smeared With Impurity

AYISHA RELATED:

God's Messenger said, 'When any of you tread with his shoes upon something unclean, they will be purified with the earth.'

AD v1 p100 n387

CHILDBIRTH

AYISHA RELATED:

Asma bint Umays gave birth to Muhammad ibn Abu Bakr near Thul Hulayfa. God's Messenger commanded Abu Bakr to tell her that she should perform a bath lustration and then enter the sacred state.

SM v2B p224 n1209

DRY ABLUTION

AYISHA RELATED:

She borrowed a necklace from Asma and then lost it. God's Messenger sent some people from among his Companions to search for it. In the meantime the time for the prescribed prayer arrived, and they [the Companions] offered their prayer without ablution. When they went to the Prophet, they complained about it to him. Subsequently the verse regarding dry ablution was revealed. Usayd ibn Hudayr thanked her for the blessing saying that never did a difficulty happen in connection with her but that God made an escape from it for her and brought blessings for the Muslims.

SB 7 p69 n93; SM v1 p118 title; SM v6 p103 n131; SM v7 p510 n770; SM v6 p103 n132; SM v1 p200 n332; SM v1 p198 n330; SM v5 p75 n117; SM v5 p16 n21; SM v1 p118 title; SM v6 p88 n107; AD v1A p82 n317; N v1 p308 n568; T v1E p267 n326; T v1E p258 n313; T v1E p267 n326

FEMALE CIRCUMSCION

UMM ATIYYAT AL-ANSARIYA RELATED:

A woman used to perform circumcision in Madinah. The Prophet said to her, 'Do not cut severely, as that is better for a woman and more desirable for a husband.' [Abu Dawud remarks that this is not a strong Tradition because it had been transmitted in a form missing the link of the Companions].

AD v3 p1451 n5251; SB v7 p25 n36

MENSTRUATION

UMAYYAH BINT ABU AL-SALT RELATED:

She quoted a certain woman of the Ghifar tribe [whose name was Layla, the wife of Abu Dhar al-Ghifari according to Awn al-Mabud, I, 123] who said that the Messenger of God made her ride behind him on the rear of the camel saddle. The Messenger of God got down in the morning. He made his camel kneel down, and she got down from the back part of his saddle. There was blood on the saddle from her first menstruation. She stuck to the camel and felt ashamed. When the Messenger of God saw what had happened to her and saw the blood, he said, 'Perhaps you have begun menstruation.' She replied that she had. He then said, 'Set yourself right [that is, tie some cloth to prevent bleeding]. Then take a vessel of water and put some salt in it. Then wash the blood from the back part of the saddle and return to your mount.' When the Messenger of God conquered Khaybar, he gave her a portion of the booty. Therefore, whenever the woman wished to become purified from her menses, she would put salt in water. When she died, she left a will asking that her dead body be washed with salted water.

AD v1 p81 n313

Clothes

Cloth Touching a Menstruating Woman

MAYMUNA BINT AL-HARITH RELATED:

The Messenger of God offered the prescribed prayer while she was by his side in the state of menstruation. Sometimes his clothing would touch her when he prostrated. He would offer his prescribed prayer on a small mat.

AD v1 p172 n656; IM v2 p82 n956; SM v1B p298 n513

Coitus Above a Waist Wrapper

AYISHA RELATED:

When anyone among us (the wives of the Prophet) menstruated, the Messenger asked her to tie a waist-wrapper over her body, and then he lay with her.

SM v1A p193 n293, R1; N v1E p290 n373; N v1E p290 n375; N v1E p248 n288; N p248 n289; N v1E p248 n290; N v1E p248 n288

Everything But Sexual Intercourse Permissible

AYISHA RELATED:

When she menstruated, she left the bed and lay on the reed mat and did not approach the Messenger of God until she was purified. [Al-Tibi says that this Tradition was abrogated. A large number of Traditions permit a husband and wife to lie together and to embrace each other even when the wife is menstruating].

AD v1 p67 n271

Fondling a Menstruating Wife

AYISHA RELATED:

The Prophet and she used to perform the bath lustration from a single pot while they were in a state of impurity following sexual intercourse. When she was menstruating, he ordered her to put on a cloth worn below the waist and he fondled her. While in retreat in the mosque, he put his head near her, and she would wash it while she was menstruating.

SB v1 p180 n298; SM v1A p193 n293 R1; IM v1 p341 n635; SB v8 p115 n178

Impurity of Blood of Menses and How to Wash It

ASMA BINT ABU BAKR RELATED:

A woman came to the Messenger and asked what she should do if the blood of menses stained a garment of hers. The Prophet replied, 'You should scrape it, rub it with water, pour water over it, and then offer a prayer.'

SM v1A p191 n291; N v1E p299 n397 by Umm Qays bint Muhsin; N v1E p298 n396; N v1E p299 n397 by Qays bint Muhsin

Lying with One in Menstruation

AYISHA RELATED:

She and the Messenger of God passed the night together while she had one piece of cloth on her and was menstruating profusely. If any blood touched him, he would wash that spot and only that spot.

Then he would offer his prescribed prayer. If any blood touched his clothes, he would wash that place and only that place. Then he would offer his prescribed prayer.

N v1E p247 n287; SB v1 p179 n297; SM v1A p194 n296; N v1E p247 n286; N v1E p475 n776; N v1E p290 n374; N v1E p475 n776

Reciting the Prescribed Prayer in an Impure Garment

UMM JAHDAR AL-AMIRIYYA RELATED:

She asked Ayisha about the blood of menses which gets on clothes. Ayisha replied that she was lying with the Messenger of God. They had a garment over them, and they had put a blanket over the garment. When day broke, the Messenger of God took the blanket, wore it, and went out and offered the dawn prescribed prayer. He then sat [in the mosque among the people]. A man asked about the spot of blood. The Messenger of God caught hold of the blanket and sent it to me folded in the hand of a slave. The slave told her to wash it, dry it, and send it back to the Messenger. She sent for her vessel and washed the blanket. She then dried it and returned it to him. The Messenger of God came at noon with the blanket over him.

AD v1 p100 n388

Washing Clothes Worn During Menstruation

ASMA BINT ABU BAKR RELATED:

She heard a woman asking the Messenger of God what to do with her clothes after she became purified from menses. She wanted to know if she could pray in such clothes. He said, 'She should look for blood on them. She should rub them with some water and [in case of doubt] sprinkle them with more water and pray—so long as she did not find any blood.'

AD v1 p95 n360; SB v1 p144 n227; SB v1 p183 n304; AD p95 n361

UMM QAYS BINT MIHSAN RELATED:

She asked the Prophet about the blood of menstruation on clothes. He said, 'Remove it with a piece of wood and then wash it away with water and the leaves of the lote-tree.'

AD v1 p95 n363; IM v1 p338 n628; IM v1 p339 n629; IM v1 p340 n630

KHAWLAH BINT YASAR RELATED:

She went to the Messenger and said that she had only one dress, and that she had menstruated in it. She asked what she should do. He said, 'When you are purified, wash it and offer the prescribed prayer in it.' She asked what if the blood had not been removed. He said, 'It is enough for you to wash the blood. Its mark will not do any harm to you.'

AD v1 p95 n365; AD v1 p95 n360

AYISHA RELATED:

Each of the wives of the Prophet had only one cloth which she would wear during menstruation. Whenever it was stained with blood, she would moisten it with her saliva and rub the blood off.

AD v1 p94 n358; SB v1 p185 n309; AD v1 p95 n364

UMM QAYS RELATED:

A woman went to the Messenger and asked what she should do if the blood of menses stained her garment. He said she should scrape it with a flat stick [of wood] and wash it with water mixed with leaf of the jujube.

N v1E p251 n295

AYISHA RELATED:

She and the Messenger of God used to lie on the same cloth at night while she was menstruating. If anything from her stained him, he washed only the place that was stained. If anything stained his clothes, he washed the stained place only and prayed with the clothes.

AD v2 p581 n2161

AYISHA RELATED:

After they were purified from menses, they used to take hold of any blood spot on their clothes, rub the blood off their garment, pour water over it, wash that portion thoroughly and sprinkle water over the rest of the garment. After that they could pray wearing it.

SB v1 p184 n305

Eating

AYISHA RELATED:

She would drink when she was menstruating and would hand the vessel to the Messenger. He would put his mouth where hers had been and drink. She would eat meat from a bone when she was menstruating and then hand it to the Messenger of God, and he would put his mouth where hers had been.

N v1E p247 n285; SM v1A p195 n300; IM v1 p347 n643; N v1E p292 n380; N p293 n381; N v1E p293 n382; N v1E p293 n382; N v1E p245 n283; N v1E p158 n71; N v1E p275 n344

HENNA ON HANDS

AYISHA RELATED:

A woman asked her if a menstruating woman should dye her hands with henna. Ayisha said that they dyed their hands with henna in the presence of God's Messenger, and he did not forbid it.

IM v1 p354 n656

MODESTY

AYISHA RELATED:

The Messenger came to her whereupon her freed slave-girl concealed herself from the Prophet. The Prophet said, 'Is she menstruating?' She [Ayisha] replied that she was. Then he sliced off a piece from his turban for her and said, 'Cover your head with it.'

IM v1 p353 n654

MOSQUE

Getting Something From the Mosque

AYISHA RELATED:

The Messenger of God said, 'Get me the mat from the mosque.' She said that she was menstruating. He said, 'Your menstruation is not in your hand.'

> N v1E p243 n274; AD v1 p65 n261; IM v1 p340 n631; N v1E p295 n386; N v1E p295 n387; N v1E p295 n388

AYISHA RELATED:

She combed the Prophet's hair while she was menstruating, and he was in seclusion in the mosque. He would put his head near her in her room, and she would comb his hair while she was menstruating.

> SB v1 p178 n295; SB v1 p178 n294; IM v1 p340 n633

Laying a Mat in the Mosque

MAYMUNA RELATED:

She said that the Messenger of God used to recline in the lap of any of his wives and recite the Quran while she was in menses. Any one of them used to spread her mat in the mosque while she was menstruating.

> N v1E p244 n276; SB v1 p179 n296; SB v1 p244 n277; SB v1 p293 n383; SB v9 p477 n635; SM v1A p196 n301 by Ayisha; IM v1 p341 n634; N v1E p293 n383 by Ayisha

Seclusion

AYISHA RELATED:

One of the wives of God's Messenger joined him in the seclusion in the mosque during the last ten days of Ramadan. She noticed some blood and yellowish discharge [from her private parts]. She put a dish under her when she offered her prescribed prayer.

> SB v1 p185 n307; SB v1 p184 n306; SB p185 n308

Washing and Combing Her Husband's Hair

AYISHA RELATED:

When the Messenger was in seclusion in the mosque during the last ten days of Ramadan, he inclined his head towards her, and she combed his hair. He only entered the house to answer the call of nature.

> SM v1A p194 n297, R1-R4; SB v3 p147 n262; SB v7 p529 n808; SB v3 p136 n246; SB v7 p529 n809; SB v3 p136 n246; SB v3 p137 n245; N v1E p296 n390; N v1E n391; N v1E p295 n389; N v1E p244 n278; Nv1E p245 n280; N v1E p245 n281; N v1E p245 n279

NOT MENSES

UMM ATIYA RELATED:

They [the women] never considered yellowish discharge as a thing of importance [as menses].

SB v1 p194 n323; IM v1 p349 n647; N v1E p288 n370

AYISHA RELATED:

God's Messenger said regarding a woman who sees that which puts her in doubt after purification from menses: 'It is the blood of a vein or veins.'

IM v1 p349 n646

UMM ATIYYAH RELATED:

She took the oath of allegiance to the Prophet. She once said that they [the women] did not take into consideration brown and yellow [fluid] after purification.

AD v1 p79 n307; AD v1 p79 n308

PILGRIMAGE

"By the Mount and by a decree inscribed" [52].

UMM SALAMA

She complained to God's Messenger that she was sick. He said, 'Perform the circumambulation of the Kabah at Makkah while riding behind the people who are performing it on foot.' She performed the circumambulation while the Messenger offered a prayer by the side of the Kabah and recited, *'By the Mount and by a decree inscribed. . .'* [52].

SB v6 p357 n376; SB v2 p406 n698; SB v2 p400 n686; SB v2 p404 n692; SB v1 p269 n453; SM v2B p274 n1274; AD v2 p495 n1877

Getting Menses After the Final Circumambulation of the Kabah

AYISHA RELATED:

She told the Messenger that Safiya bint Huyai had gotten her menses. He said, "She will probably delay us. Did she perform the circumambulation with you?" We replied that she had. On hearing this, the Prophet told her to depart.

SB v1 p195 n325; SB v2 p470 n812; SM v2B p301 n1211 R32; AD v2 p531 n1998; N v1E p297 n393; SB v7 p1876 n246

Menstruating Woman Should Assume the Sacred State for the Prescribed Pilgrimage or Shorter Pilgrimage

AYISHA RELATED:

She and others set out with the Prophet on his farewell pilgrimage. Some of them intended to perform the shorter pilgrimage, while others intended the prescribed pilgrimage. When they reached Makkah, God's Messenger said, 'Whoever has assumed the sacred state for the shorter pilgrimage and has not brought the sacrifice with her should end her sacred state, and whoever has assumed the sacred state for the shorter pilgrimage and brought the sacrifice should not end the sacred state until she has slaughtered her sacrifice, and whoever has assumed the sacred state for the prescribed pilgrimage should complete her prescribed pilgrimage.' She said that she got her menses and kept on menstruating until the day of Arafat. She had assumed the sacred state only for the shorter pilgrimage. The Prophet ordered her to undo and comb her hair and assume the sacred state only for the prescribed pilgrimage and leave the shorter pilgrimage. Then the Prophet sent Abd al-Rahman ibn Abu Bakr with her and ordered her to perform the shorter pilgrimage from al-Tanim in place of the missed shorter pilgrimage.

SB v1 p189 n316; SB v7 p18 n26; SB v7 p324 n456; N v1E p250 n293; N v1E p230 n245

POSTPARTUM BLEEDING

UMM SALAMA RELATED:

A woman bleeding after delivery should refrain from prescribed prayer for forty days or forty nights. She should anoint her face with an aromatic herb called *wars* to remove dark spots.

AD v1 p80 n311; IM v1 p350 n648

UMM SALAMA RELATED:

Umm Bussah came to her [Umm Salama] and said that Samurah ibn Jundub commanded women to make-up the prescribed prayers missed during their menstrual period. She [Umm Salama] said they did not need to do so. The wives of the Prophet would refrain [from prescribed prayer] for the forty nights of bleeding after childbirth. The Prophet would not command them to make-up the prescribed prayers missed during the period of bleeding.

AD v1 p80 n312

PRAYERS MISSED

AYISHA RELATED:

A woman asked her if she [the woman] should offer the prescribed prayers which she did not offer because of menses. She [Ayisha] asked if she[the woman] was from the Huraura [a town in Iraq]. The woman said that they [the women of her group] were with the Prophet during their periods, but he never ordered them to offer the prescribed prayers during menses.

SB v1 p191 n318

AYISHA RELATED:

We women were commanded to make-up the days of the prescribed fast [missed due to menstruation] but were not commanded to make-up the prescribed prayers [missed] due to menstruation.

AD v1 p65 n263

AYISHA RELATED:

The Prophet said to her, 'Give up the prescribed prayer when your menses begins and when it has finished, wash the blood off your body [take a bath lustration] and perform the prescribed prayer.'

SB v1 p196 n327

PREDESTINED

UMM SALAMA RELATED:

She was lying with God's Messenger under his bed cover. She began to menstruate. She slipped out from under the bed cover. God's Messenger asked if she had begun to menstruate. She said yes. He said, 'This has been predestined for the daughters of Adam.' She said that was why she had slipped away. She put on the proper garment and came back. Hearing this, God's Messenger said to her, 'Come on and get under this cloak with me.' Then she got under it with him.

IM v1 p342 n637; SB v1 p192 n320; SB v3 p83 n151

PROLONGED FLOW OF BLOOD

FATIMA BINT QAYS RELATED:

She told the Messenger that she was suffering from intermittent bleeding. The Messenger of God said, 'The bleeding is from a blood vessel and not menses. Abandon the prescribed prayer when the real menses begins. When it ends, wash the blood from yourself and then offer your prescribed prayer.'

N v1E p213 n203; SB v1 p190 n317 by Ayisha regarding Fatima bint Abu Hubaysh; N v1E p182 n303 by Ayisha regarding Fatima bint Abu Hubaysh; N v1E p193 n322 by Ayisha; N v1E p280 n352; v1E p279 n351; p280 n353 by Ayisha; p280 n352; p281 n350 by Ayisha; p281 n355 by Ayisha; p282 n356 by Umm Salama; p282 n357 by Umm Salama; p283 n358 by Ayisha; p283 n359 by Ayisha; p283 n360 by Fatima bint Abu Hubaysh; p284 n361 by Ayisha; p284 n362 by Ayisha; p285 n363 by Zaynab bint Jahsh; p285 n364 by Ayisha; p286 n365 by Ayisha; p287 n366 by Ayisha; p287 n367 by Ayisha; p287 n368 by Ayisha; p287 n369 by Ayisha; p281 n354 by Ayisha regarding Umm Habiba bint Jahsh; p281 n355 by Ayisha regarding Umm Habiba bint Jahsh; p282 n356 by Umm Salama; p282 n357 by Umm Salama; SM v1A p211 n334, R1-R2, R5; SB v1 p195 n324; AD v1 p73 n288, AD v1 p73 n289, AD v1 p74 n290; AD v1 p79 n305; AD v1 p69 n279; AD v1 p75 n293; AD v1 p71 n285; IM v1 p337 n626; N v1E p283 n360 by Fatima bint Abu Hubaysh; N v1E p361 by Ayisha; 362 by Ayisha; N v1E p285 n363 by Zaynab bint Jahsh; N v1E p285 n364 by Fatima bint Abu Hubaysh; N v1E p286 n365 by Ayisha about Fatima bint Abu Hubaysh; N v1E p287 n366 by Ayisha about Fatima bint Abu Hubaysh; N v1E p287 n367 by Ayisha about Fatima bint Abu Hubaysh; N v1E p387 n368 by Ayisha re; N v1E p287 n369 by Ayisha re; N v1E p288 n370 by Ayisha re; N v1E p219 n216; N v1E v1E p218 n213; N v1E p217 n212; N v1E p218 n214; N v1E p214 n206; N v1E p215 n208; N v1E p214 n204; N v1E p215 n207; v1E p216 n209; N v1E p215 n208; N v1E p216 n209; N v1E p217 n212; v1E p214 n206; N v1E p215 n207; N v1E p213 n203; SM v1A p210 n333; N [H v1 p735]

Prescribed Prayer

AYISHA RELATED:

The Messenger of God said, 'Abandon the prescribed prayer when the menses begins, and when the period of menses ends, perform the bath lustration.'

N v1E p214 n204

Sexual Intercourse

UMM HABIBA RELATED:

She had a prolonged flow of blood during which her husband cohabited with her.

AD v1 p80 n309; AD v1 p80 n310

UMM SALAMA RELATED:

In the time of the Messenger of God, there was a woman who had a question about bleeding. She asked the Messenger to give a decision in this regard. He said, 'She should consider the number of nights and days during which she menstruated each month before she was afflicted with this trouble and abandon the prescribed prayer only during that period each month. When those days and nights were over, she should take a bath, tie a cloth over her private parts, and offer the prescribed prayer.

AD v1 p68 n274; AD v1 p75 n294; AD v1 p76 n300; IM v1 p335 n623; N v1E p216 n214; N v1E p216 n211; AD v1 p71 n284 (Bahiyyah)

AYISHA RELATED:

Sahla bint Shuayl had a prolonged flow of blood. She went to the Prophet. He commanded her to take a bath lustration before every prayer. When it became hard for her, he commanded her to combine the noon and afternoon prescribed prayers with one bath lustration and the sunset and night prescribed prayers with one bath lustration and to take one bath lustration separately for the dawn prescribed prayer.

AD v1 p75 n295

ASMA BINT UMAYS RELATED:

Women who have a prolonged flow of blood should take a bath lustration only once and then perform only ablution until their next menstrual period.

AD v1 p76 n299

FATIMA BINT ABU HUBAYSH RELATED:

She asked Asma bint Abu Bakr (or Asma narrated that Fatima bint Abu Hubaysh asked her) to question the Messenger of God. He advised her to refrain from prescribed prayer for a period of time equal to the length of her previous menses and then wash herself.

AD v1 p69 n281

FATIMA BINT ABU HUBAYSH RELATED:

Her blood kept flowing so the Messenger said to her, 'When the blood of menses comes, it is black blood which can be recognized. When that comes, refrain from prescribed prayer, but when a different type of blood comes, perform ablution and pray because this blood is from a blood vessel.

AD v1 p72 n286; AD v1 p75 n296; p76 n298; p78 n304; p70 n282; IM v1 p333 n621; p335 n624; N v1E p220 n219; p220 n218; p221 n220; p221 n221; p222 n222; p218 n214; p218 n215

HABIBA BINT JAHSH RELATED:

Her menstruation was great in quantity and severity. She went to the Messenger and told him. She found him in the house of her sister, Zaynab bint Jahsh. She asked what a woman who menstruates in great quantity and whose menstruation is very severe should do as it prevents her from offering the prescribed prayer and performing the prescribed fast. He said, 'I suggest that you use cotton for it absorbs the blood.' She said that it was too copious for that. He said, 'Then take a cloth.' She replied that it was too copious for that as well. The Messenger said, 'I shall give you two commands. It will be sufficient for you to follow one or the other, for you know best if you are strong enough to follow both of them. This is a trick of the devil so observe your menses for six or seven days. God alone knows which it should be. Then wash. When you see that you are purified, offer the prescribed prayer during the twenty-three or twenty-four days and nights [remaining in the month] and fast. That will be enough for you. Do this every month just as women who menstruate and are purified do. But if you are strong enough to delay the noon prescribed prayer and advance the afternoon prescribed prayer, then wash and combine the noon and the afternoon prayer. [Likewise] delay the sunset prescribed prayer and advance the night prescribed prayer and then wash and combine the two prayers. Then wash at dawn and fast if you are able to do so. Of the two commands, the second is more to my liking.'

AD v1 p72 n287; IM v1 p338 n627; T [MMR v1]

PURIFICATION

AYISHA RELATED:

The Prophet said, while she was in a state of menstruation, 'Untie your hair and perform the bath lustration.'

IM v1 p345 n641

AYISHA RELATED:

Asma asked the Messenger about the bath lustration necessitated by menstruation. He said, 'Let every one use water mixed with the leaves of the lotus tree to purify herself to attain a high degree [of purification]. Then [let her] pour water over her head and rub it intensely until it reaches the roots of her hair. Then let her pour water on her whole body. Then let her take a piece of musky cotton and purify herself with it.' Asma asked how she should do that. He said, 'Glory be to God! Purify yourself with it.' She [Ayisha] told her to rub the stains of menses blood with the cotton. Asma asked him about the bath lustration necessitated by seminal emission. He said, 'Let anyone of you take some water and purify yourself to attain the high degree of purification. Pour water on your head and then rub the water so it reaches the roots of your head. Then you should pour water on your entire body.' She [Ayisha] said that the best women are the women of the Helpers because their modesty did not prevent them from learning about their religion.

> IM v1 p346 n642; SB v9 p336 n456; SB v9 p335 n455; SM v1A p209 n332; AD v1 p81 n314; AD v1 p81 n315; N v1E p235 n254

QURANIC RECITATION

AYISHA RELATED:

The Prophet used to recite the Quran with his head in her lap while she was menstruating.

> SB v9 p477 n635; SM v9 p479 n639

WASHING

UMM QAYS BINT MIHSIN RELATED:

She took her young son who had not started eating [solid food] to God's Prophet who took him and sat him [the baby] on his lap. The child urinated on the garment of the Prophet. The Prophet asked for water and poured it over the soiled [area] and did not wash it.

> SB v1 p144 n223; SM v8 p244 n366; AD v3B p459 n287R1; AD v1A p189 n287R2; AD v1 p97 n374; IM v1 p283 n524; Nv1E p254 n305; SM v1A p180 n286, R1; SB v1 p144 n222; IM v1 p283 n523; N v1E p143 n29; SB v8 p19 n31; N v1E p254 n306

UMM KURZ RELATED:

God's Messenger said, 'Water should be sprayed [on the garment soilded by urine] of a baby boy, while that of a baby girl should be washed off.'

> IM v1 p286 n527

AYISHA RELATED:

It was mentioned to her that the Messenger had made a will in favor of Ali. She wondered when that could have happened, for as she recalled his last moments, the Messenger had asked for a vessel in which to urinate when he fell and breathed his last. So when could he have made a will?

> N v1E p145 n33

UMAYMAH BINT RUQAYQAH RELATED:

The Prophet kept a bed pan of wood beneath his bed in which he passed urine at night.

> N [H v1 p685]; AD v1 p6 n24; N v1E p145 n32; N v1E p145 n32

AYISHA RELATED:

Whoever informs you that the Prophet passed water standing, do not believe him. He passed water only while sitting.

> T [H v1 p685]; IM v1 p176 n307

CHAPTER 2
PRESCRIBED FAST

ATONEMENT FOR BREAKING

Breaking the Prescribed Fast Before Sunset

ASMA BINT ABU BAKR RELATED:

We broke the prescribed fast one day during Ramadan when it was cloudy. Then the sun rose. We were commanded to atone for that.

AD v2 p647 n2352

Broken Voluntary Fast

UMM UMARA BINT KAB RELATED:

She said that once when the Prophet visited her and she called for food for him, he told her that she should eat also, but she replied that she was fasting. He said, 'When people eat beside one who is fasting the angels invoke blessings on him until they finish eating.'

T [MMR v1 p440]; T [H v3 p550]

Making Up For Prescribed Fast During Ramadan

AYISHA RELATED:

Sometimes she missed some days of Ramadan but could not make them up except in the month of Shaban.

SB v3 p98 n171; AD v2 p658 n2393

Whoever Died and Ought To Have Performed the Prescribed Fast

AYISHA RELATED:

God's Messenger said, 'Whoever died and should have performed the prescribed fast but did not do so, his guardians must perform the prescribed fast on his behalf.'

SB v3 p99 n173; AD v2 p658 n2394; AD v2 p938 n3305

UMM HANI RELATED:

On one of the days of the conquest of Makkah, Fatima came and sat on the left side of the Messenger of God, and Umm Hani sat on the right side. A slave girl brought a vessel which contained something to drink. She gave it to him, and he drank it. He then gave it to Umm Hani who drank of it. She said to the Messenger that she had broken her fast. He asked her, 'Were you atoning for something?'

AD v2 p676 n2450; T [MMR v1 p439]

BEGIN FASTING

AYISHA RELATED:

The Messenger of God said, 'When Bilal calls the prescribed prayer [at the end of the night during the month of prescribed fast], keep on eating and drinking until Ibn Umm Maktum [who was blind] calls it out.' She said that the difference of time between their calls to prescribed prayer was not longer than it took one to climb down the minaret and the other to climb up.

N v1E p416 n642; SB v1 p342 n596; SB v3 p78 n142

IMPURITY AFTER DAWN

AYISHA RELATED:

A man went to the Messenger asking for a religious verdict. She [Ayisha] overheard it from behind the curtain. She added that he (the person) asked if the time of prescribed prayer overtook him while he was in a state of impurity, should he fast in that state? The Messenger said, 'At times the time of prayer overtakes me while I am in a state of impurity. I perform the prescribed fast in that very state.' The man said that the Messenger was not like other people for the Messenger had been pardoned for all of his sins— the previous ones and the later ones. Upon this he (the Prophet) said, 'By God I hope I am the most God-fearing of you and possess the best knowledge among you of those things against which I should guard.'

SM v2A p157 n1110; SB v3 p88 n156

UMM SALAMA RELATED:

God's Messenger at times got up in the morning in a state of ritual impurity from sexual intercourse (not from a wet dream) and then fasted on that day.

SB v3 p85 n153B; SB v3 p85 n153A; SM v2A p156n1109R1

INTENTION

HAFSA RELATED:

God's Messenger said, 'He who does not intend to perform the prescribed fast before dawn does not fast.'

AD v2 p675 n2448

NIGHT OF POWER

Looking for the Night of Power On Odd Nights

AYISHA RELATED:

God's Messenger practiced seclusion in the mosque during the last ten days of Ramadan [*itikaf*], and he said, 'Look for the Night of Power in the last ten nights of the month of Ramadan.'

SB v3 p132 n237; SB v3 p132 n236; SB v3 p131 n234

Supplication for the Night of Power

AYISHA RELATED:

She asked the Messenger of God if she came to know which night was the Night of Power, what prayer should she offer. He replied, 'Say: O God! You are, indeed, the most forgiving, the most merciful and to forgive is most pleasing to You so forgive me my sins.'

T [MMT v3 p57]; IM [MMR v1 p442]

SECLUSION

Dawn Prescribed Prayer

AYISHA RELATED:

When the Messenger of God intended to seclude himself, he offered the dawn prescribed prayer and then entered into his place of seclusion.

IM [H v3 p559]

Doing Good Deeds in the Last Ten Days of Ramadan

AYISHA RELATED:

When the last ten days of Ramadan came, the Prophet kept vigil and prayed during the whole night. He tied the wrapper tightly and awakened his family [to pray during the night].

AD v1 p360 n1371; SB v3 p134 n241; SB v3 p134 n241

It Is Excellent to Tell a Man When One is Accompanied by One's Wife

SAFIYA BINT HUYYAY RELATED:

One night while God's Messenger was in seclusion in the mosque, she went to visit him. She talked with him for some time. Then she stood up to go back, and he also stood up with her in order to bid her goodbye. She was at that time staying in the house of Usama ibn Zayd. Two people from among the Helpers happened to pass by him. When they saw the Messenger, they began to walk swiftly. The Messenger said to them, 'Walk calmly. She is Safiya, daughter of Huyyay.' Both of them apologized saying that they were not in doubt in regard to him. He said, 'Satan circulates in the body of people like the circulation of blood. I was afraid lest it should instill any evil in your heart.'

SM v3B p443 n2174; SB v8 p154n238: SB v4 p322 n501; SB v3 p139 n255; AD v3 p1388n4976

Last Ten Days of Ramadan in a Mosque

AYISHA RELATED:

The Prophet practiced seclusion in the mosque (*itikaf*) during the last ten days of Ramadan until he died, and then his wives practiced it after that.

SB v3 p135 n243

Man Who Observes Seclusion Is Allowed to Enter His House to Fulfil His Human Needs

AYISHA RELATED:

When the Messenger of God observed seclusion, he would put his head near her and she would comb his hair. He entered the house only to fulfil needs of nature.

AD v2 p680 n2461; AD v2 p681 n2462; AD v2 p681 n2463

On Visiting a Patient By a Person Who Is Observing Seclusion

AYISHA RELATED:

The *sunnah* for one who is observing seclusion [in a mosque] is not to visit a patient or to attend a funeral or touch or embrace one's wife or go out for anything but the call of nature. There is no seclusion without fasting, and there is no seclusion except in a congregational mosque.

AD v2 p682 n2467

SEEING THE NEW MOON

Fasting During Shaban and Ramadan

UMM SALAMA RELATED:

She did not see the Prophet fasting for two consecutive months except Shaban and Ramadan.

T [H v3 p520]

Laws About the Moon of Ramadan When the Weather is Cloudy

AYISHA RELATED:

God's Messenger counted the days in Shaban in a way he did not count in any other month. He fasted when he sighted the new moon of Ramadan, but if the weather was cloudy, he counted thirty days and then performed the prescribed fast.

AD v2 p636 n2318

TARAWIH PRAYER

During the Nights of Ramadan

AYISHA RELATED:

The people offered the *tarawih* prayer in the mosque during

Ramadan. The Messenger of God commanded her [to spread a mat]. She spread a mat for him and he prayed on it. He said, 'O people, praise be to God. I did not pass my night carelessly, nor did your position remain hidden from me.'

AD v1 p359 n1369

Superiority of Praying At Night in Ramadan

AYISHA RELATED:

God's Messenger prayed at night in the month of Ramadan.

SB v3 p127 n228

TIME OF PRESCRIBED FAST

AYISHA RELATED:

At times God's Messenger got up in the morning in a state of prescribed impurity after having sexual relations with his wives. He would then take a bath lustration and perform the prescribed fast.

SB v3 p81 n148A; SB v3 p81 n148B

TOUCHING ONE'S SPOUSE WHILE FASTING

HAFSA RELATED:

The Messenger of God kissed his wives while fasting.

SM v2A p156 n1107, R1; SM v2A p154 n1106; AD v2 p638 n2376; AD v2 p638 n2377; AD v2 p653 n2378; AD v2 p654 n2380

AYISHA RELATED:

A person performing the prescribed fast is forbidden to have sexual intercourse while fasting.

SB v3 p82

TRAVELER'S PRESCRIBED FAST

AYISHA RELATED:

Hamza ibn Amr al-Aslami asked the Prophet if he should perform the prescribed fast while traveling. The Prophet replied, 'You may perform the prescribed fast if you wish, and you may not fast if you wish.'

SB v3 p93 n163; SM v3 p93 n164

VOLUNTARY FAST

Ashura

AYISHA RELATED:

During the Age of Ignorance the Quraysh observed the prescribed fast on the day of Ashura [the 10th day of the month of Muharram]. The Prophet himself observed the prescribed fast on it as well. When he came to Madinah, he fasted on that day and ordered the Muslims to fast on it. When the order for the prescribed fast in Ramadan was revealed, prescribed fasting in Ramadan became an obligation and fasting on Ashura was given up. Whoever wished to fast did so, and whoever did not wish to fast, did not fast.

> SB v6 p24 n31; SB v6 p24n29; SB v3 p65 n117; SB v2 p388 n662; SB v5 p109 n172; SB v3 p103 n181; SB v3 p123 n219; SB v3 p123 n220; AD v2 p672 n2436

UMM FADL RELATED:

The people were in doubt whether or not the Prophet was fasting on the Day of Arafa. A wooden drinking vessel full of milk was sent to him, and he drank it.

> SB v7 p367 n540; SB v7 p359 n522; SB v7 p352 n509; SB v2 p421 n720; SB v3 p119 n210

Fasting Continuously is Prohibited

AYISHA RELATED:

God's Messenger prohibited the practice of performing the prescribed fast continuously—that is, without eating or drinking anything by day or night for a day or two. [He did this] out of mercy for people. They said to him that he practiced *al-wisal*. He said, 'I am not similar to you for my Lord gives me food and drink.'

> SB v3 p105 n185; SM v2A p154 n1105

Fasting in the Month of Shaban

AYISHA RELATED:

God's Messenger performed the prescribed fast until one might say that he would never stop fasting, and he would abandon fasting until one might say that he would never fast. She never saw God's Messenger fasting for a whole month except the month of Ramadan and did not see him fasting in any month more than in the month of Shaban.

> SB v3 p108 n190; SB v3 p108 n191; SM v2 p640 n2329; SM v2 p669 n2428

Particular Days

AYISHA RELATED:

She was asked if God's Messenger chose some special day for performing the prescribed fast. She answered that he did not, but that he used to be regular and constant in his worship. She then asked who among them could endure what God's Messenger endured.

> SB v3 p118 n208

AYISHA RELATED:

No one was allowed to fast on the 11th, 12th and 13th of Dhi Hajjah (days of *tashriq*) except those who could not afford to sacrifice an animal.

> SB v3 p122 n216

AYISHA RELATED:

She never saw the Messenger of God fast during the first ten days of Dhi Hajjah.

AD v2 p671 n2433; AD v2 p676 n2449

AYISHA RELATED:

God's Messenger used to fast on Saturday, Sunday and Monday of one month and on Tuesday, Wednesday and Thursday of the next.

T [MMR v1 p436]

AYISHA RELATED:

Some food was presented to her and Hafsa. They were fasting, but they broke their fast. Then the Messenger of God entered. They told him that a gift was presented to them, that they desired it, and broke their fast. The Messenger of God said, 'There is no harm to you. Fast another day in place of it.'

AD v2 p676 n2451

HAFSA RELATED:

She said that there were four things which the Messenger of God never omitted: 1) the fast of Ashura; 2) the fast of the 10th of Dhi Hajjah; 3) the three fasts of every month; and 4) the two cycles before the dawn prescribed prayer.

N [MMT v3 p85]

UMM SALAMA RELATED:

God's Messenger commanded her to fast three days every month beginning with Monday or Thursday.

N [MMR v1 p436]

CHAPTER 3
PRESCRIBED PRAYER

CALL TO PRESCRIBED PRAYER

Before Dawn

AYISHA RELATED:

When the caller to prescribed prayer pronounced the call for the dawn prescribed prayer and the dawn became evident, the Prophet ordered a two cycle light [quick?] prayer *[sunnah]* before the declaration of the prescribed prayer.

SB v1 p340 n592; SB v1 p343 n599; SB v2 p145 n262; SB v2 p153 n275B; SM v1B p408 n724 R2-6; IM v2 p209 n1198; IM v2 p180 n1145; N v1E p387 n586

Blind Person Calling the People to Prescribed Prayer

AYISHA RELATED:

Ibn Umm Maktum, who was blind, used to recite the call to prescribed payer at the request of God's Messenger.

SM v1B p233 n381; AD v1 p141 n535

What to Say

AYISHA RELATED:

When God's Messenger heard the caller to prayer uttering the testimony, he would say, 'And me too. And me too.'

AD v1 p138 n526

UMM SALAMA RELATED:

The Messenger of God taught her to say when the call to prayer for the sunset prayer was called, 'O God, this is the time when Your night comes, Your day retires, and the voices of Your summoners are heard, so forgive me.'

AD v1 p139 n530

UMM HABIBA RELATED:

When the Messenger spent a day and night with her and heard the call to prescribed prayer, she heard God's Messenger say what the caller said.

IM v1 p380 n719

CONGREGATION AND ITS EXCELLENCE

AYISHA RELATED:

The Messenger said, 'Prayer in a congregation is twenty-five times more excellent than prayer offered by a single person.'

N v1E p509 n842

In the Front Row

AYISHA RELATED:

God's Messenger said, 'The people will continue to keep themselves away from the front row until God will put them in hellfire.'

AD v1 p175 n679

Night and Dawn Prescribed Prayers in Congregation

AYISHA RELATED:

God's Messenger said, 'If people knew [the reward earned by attending] the night and dawn prescribed prayers in congregation, they would come [to the mosque to observe them]—even if it meant crawling to the mosque.'

IM v1 p437 n796

On the Returning of Women From Prescribed Prayer

UMM SALAMA RELATED:

When God's Messenger gave the salutations, he stayed for awhile. People thought that this meant that the women should leave sooner than the men.

AD v1 p267 n1035; SB v1 p458 n892

DECLARATION TO PERFORM THE PRESCRIBED PRAYER

AYISHA RELATED:

The Prophet said, 'If dinner is served and the declaration to perform the prescribed prayer is called, one should start with dinner.'

SB v1 p362 n640; SM v7 p269 n374; IM v2 p71 n933

ECLIPSE PRESCRIBED PRAYER

First Cycle of the Eclipse Prayer is Longer Than Second

AYISHA RELATED:

The Prophet led them and performed four bows forward in two cycles during the solar eclipse. The first cycle was longer.

SB v2 p98 n171

Freeing of Slaves at the Time of an Eclipse

ASMA BINT ABU BAKR RELATED:

The Prophet commanded them to free slaves on the occasion of an eclipse.

AD v1 p308 n1188; SB v2 p93 n163; SB v3 p420 n695; SB v3 p420 n696

Looking at the Leader During the Prescribed Prayer

AYISHA RELATED:

The Prophet, speaking about the prayer of the eclipse, said, 'I saw hell, and one of its sides was destroying the other. [And that was] when you saw me retreating during the prescribed prayer].'

SB v1 p399 Title

Paradise and Hell

ASMA BINT ABU BAKR RELATED:

She went to Ayisha while she was praying and asked her what had happened to the people. Ayisha pointed out towards the sky. [Asma looked towards the mosque] and saw the people offering the prayer. Ayisha said, 'Glory be to God.' Asma asked Ayisha if this was a sign. Ayisha nodded her head, meaning yes. Asma then stood [for the prayer of eclipse] until she nearly lost consciousness and had to pour water on her head. After the prayer, the Prophet praised and glorified God and then said, 'Just now at this place I have seen what I have never seen before, including paradise and hell. No doubt it has been given to me to know that you will be put to trials in your graves, and these trials will be like the trials of the antichrist—or nearly like it,' [the subnarrator is not sure which expression Asma used]. He continued, 'You will be asked, "What do you know about this man [Prophet Muhammad]?" Then the faithful believer will reply, "He is Muhammad, God's Messenger, who came to us with clear evidence and guidance, and so we accepted his teachings and followed him. He is Muhammad." And he will repeat it three times. Then the angels will say to him, "Sleep in peace as we have come to know that you were a faithful believer." On the other hand, a hypocrite or a doubtful person will reply, "I do not know, but I heard the people saying something and so I said it [the same]."'

SB v1 p70 n86; SB v1 p70 n86; SB v2 p92 n162; SB v2 p84 n154; SB v2 p170 n303; SB v4 p284 n428; SB v1 p70 n86; SB v2 p92 n162; SB v9 p288 n390; SM v2A p32 n901; SM v2A p37 n905 R1; SM v2 p185 n327; AD 1 p304 n1173; IM v2 p253 n1263; IM v2 p255 n1265

Recitation of the Quran in the Prayer at an Eclipse

AYISHA RELATED:

There was an eclipse of the sun during the lifetime of the Messenger of God. The Messenger of God came out and led the people in prayer. He stood up, and she guessed he recited Surah al-Baqarah. He prostrated himself twice and then stood up and prolonged the recitation. She guessed his recitation and knew that he recited Surah Ale-Imran.

AD v1 p307 n1183

Recite the Quran Aloud in the Eclipse Prayer

AYISHA RELATED:

The Prophet used to recite the Quran aloud during the eclipse prayer. When he had finished the eclipse prayer, he recited, 'God is Greater,' and bowed. When he stood straight from bowing, he said, 'Sami allahu liman hamidah rabbani wa laka-l-hamd.' He would again start reciting. In the eclipse prayer there were four bows forward and four prostrations in two cycles.

SB v2 p98 n172; AD v1 p307 n1184

Remember God During an Eclipse

AYISHA RELATED:

She narrated (concerning) the invocation during an eclipse.

SB v2 p96

ASMA BINT ABU BAKR RELATED:

The Messenger one day (they say because the sun was eclipsed) was so perturbed that he (in haste) took thw outer garment (of a female member of his family). It was later that his own cloak was sent back to him. He stood in prayer with people for such a long time that if a man came, he would not realize that the Messenger had already observed prostration.

SM v2A p38 n906, R2

Saying by the Imam of 'then after'

ASMA BINT ABU BAKR RELATED:

God's Messenger finished the eclipse prayer, and by then the sun had re-appeared. Then he delivered a sermon, praised God as He deserves, and said, "Then after [amma badu]."]

SB v2 p97

To Call the People for the Eclipse Prayer

AYISHA RELATED:

There was an eclipse of the sun. The Messenger of God commanded a man to summon people that the prescribed prayer could be held in congregation.

AD v1 p307 n1186

To Give Alms at an Eclipse

AYISHA RELATED:

The Prophet said, 'The sun and the moon are not eclipsed on account of anyone's death or on account of anyone's birth. When you see an eclipse, supplicate God. Declare His greatness. Give alms.'

AD v1 p308 n1187

FESTIVAL PRESCRIBED PRAYER

On the Number of 'God is Greater'

AYISHA RELATED:

God's Messenger would recite, 'God is Greater' seven times in the first cycle and five times in the second cyle on the day of the ending of the fast and on the day of sacrifice.

AD v1 p296 n1145; IM v2 p264 n1280

Women Offering the Festival Prescribed Prayer

UMM ATIYYA RELATED:

The Messenger of God commanded her to bring out the secluded women on the day of the festival. He was asked about the women who were menstruating. He said, 'They should be present at the place of virtue and the supplication of the Muslims.' A woman asked what they should do if one of them did not possess an outer garment. He said, 'Let her friend lend her a part of her garment.'

> AD v1 p293 n1132; SB v1 p214 n347; SB v2 p52 n97; SB v2 p47 n88; SM v2A p23 n890, R-R2; AD v1 p294 n1135; N v1E p297 n392

HAFSA RELATED:

They used to forbid their young women from going out for the two prescribed festival prayers. A woman came and stayed at the palace of the Khalaf tribe. She told them about her sister whose husband took part in twelve battles along side the Messenger. Her sister was with her husband in six [out of these twelve]. The woman's sister said that they used to treat the wounded and look after the patients. Once she asked the Messenger if there was any harm for any of them to stay at home if she did not have a veil. He said, 'She should cover herself with the veil of her companion and should participate in the good deeds and in the religious gatherings of Muslims.' When Umm Atiya came she asked her whether she had heard it from the Prophet. She said that she had. She said that she heard the Prophet say, 'The young unmaried virgins and the mature girls who practice modesty or the young unmarried virgins who often practice modesty and the menstruating women should come out and participate in the good deeds as well as the religious gatherings of the faithful believers, but the menstruating women should keep away from the place of prescribed prayer." Hafsa asked Umm Atiya if she had said menstruating women. She replied that she asked whether or not a menstruating woman could attend the ceremony at Arafat on the prescribed pilgrimage and such and such other deeds.

> SB v1 p192 n321

FRIDAY CONGREGATIONAL NOON PRAYER

New Clothes

AYISHA RELATED:

One Friday the Prophet delivered a sermon to the people. He had seen them putting on woolen garments. He said, 'There is no harm for any one of you who can afford it to have two garments for Friday in addition to having two garments worn out through use.'

> IM v2 p156 n1096

Shortness of Prayer and Sermon

UMM HISHAM BINT HARITHA IBN NUMAN RELATED:

The Messenger and her family shared an oven for some time. She learned the Chapter of Qaf from the tongue of the Messenger who used to recite it every Friday from the *minbar* when he delivered the sermon to the people.

SM v2A p15 n873R1; SM v2A p15 n873

PLACE OF PRESCRIBED PRAYER

On Offering the Prescribed Prayer Upon the Sheets of Cloth of Women

AYISHA RELATED:

The Messenger of God would not pray on their sheets of cloth or on their quilts.

AD v1 p169 n645

One Who Pronounces Salutation Only Once

AYISHA RELATED:

God's Messenger pronounced salutation only once facing forward [directing his face to the *qibla*].

IM v2 p63 n919

Passing in Front of a Person

AYISHA RELATED:

The things which annul the prescribed prayers were mentioned in her presence. People said that prescribed prayer was annulled by a dog, a donkey and a woman [if any of these passed in front of the people offering the prescribed prayer]. She said that they had made women into dogs. She had seen the Prophet praying while she lay in her bed between him and the *qibla*. Whenever she was in need of something, she would slip away, for she disliked to face him.

SB v1 p291 n490; SB v1 p289 n486; SB v1 p293 n493; SB v1 p294 n497

AYISHA RELATED:

The Prophet used to pray while she was sleeping across his bed in front of him. Whenever he wanted to pray *witr*, he would wake her up and she would pray *witr* with him.

SB v1 p292 n491; SB v2 p60 n111

MAYMUNA RELATED:

Her bed was beside the praying place [*musalla*] of the Prophet. Sometimes his garment fell on her while she lay on her bed.

SB v1 p294 n496

AYISHA RELATED:

God's Messenger was asked what constitutes an obstacle or screen for worshippers [that is, an item placed in front of the people performing the prescribed prayer so that someone might walk in front of them without interfering with their prayers]. He said, 'Equal to the height of the back of a saddle.'

SM v1B p293 n500, R1; N v1E p465 n749; N v1E p465 n749

Performing the Prescribed Prayer On a Mat

AYISHA RELATED:

She used to sleep in front of God's Messenger. Her legs were opposite the *qibla*. In his prostration, he pushed her legs, and she withdrew them. When he stood up, she stretched them out. In those days the houses were without lamps.

> SB v1 p232 n380; SB v1 p232 n381; SB v1 p292 n492; SB v2 p168 n300; SM v1B p373 n513 R1 (Maymuna); N v1E p468 n758; N v1E p202 n170

AYISHA RELATED:

God's Messenger offered his prayer while standing on the bed mat on the floor. She lay in front of him (between him and the *qibla*). If she had to get up (since she disliked facing him while he was in prescribed prayer), she would gradually slip away from the bed.

> SB v8 p195 n293; SB v1 p293 n494; SM v1B p298 n512; AD v1 p183 n712; AD v1 p183 n710; AD v1 p183 n713; IM v1 p82 n957; IM v2 p82 n958; N v1E p468 n758; N v1E p470 n762; N v1E p461 n741

AYISHA RELATED:

Had God's Messenger known what the women were doing, he would have forbidden them from going to the mosque as the Jewish women had been forbidden in Judaism.

> SB v1 p458 n828

Raising the Head After Prostration

ASMA BINT ABU BAKR

God's Messenger said, 'Whoever of you believes in God and the last day should not raise her head until the men raise their heads [after prostration] lest they should see the private parts of men.'

> AD v1 p217 n850

What Distracts Attention From the Prescribed Prayer

UMM SALAMA

The Prophet observed the prescribed prayer in the apartment of Umm Salama. Abd Allah or Umar ibn Abu Salama passed in front of him; whereupon, he made the [gesture] with his hand. Then he turned back. When Zaynab, the daughter of Umm Salama, passed [in front of him], he did the same with his hand, but she passed [in front of him]. When God's Messenger concluded the prescribed prayer, he observed, 'These [women] are dominant.'

> IM v2 p78 n948

PRESCRIBED PRAYER LEADER

Authorized to Appoint a Deputy

AYISHA RELATED:

God's Messenger was seriously ill. He asked whether the people had offered their prescribed prayer. They said that they had not because they were waiting for him. He said, 'Put some water in the tub for me.' His family did this, and he took a bath. When he was about to move, he fainted. When he came around, he asked again. This happened three times. The people waited in the mosque for God's Messenger to lead the night prescribed prayer. The Messenger sent instructions to Abu Bakr to lead the people in prescribed prayer. When the Messenger regained consciousness, he told Abu Bakr to lead the people in the prescribed prayer. Abu Bakr, who was a man of very tender feelings, asked Umar to lead the prescribed prayer. Umar said that Abu Bakr was more entitled. Abu Bakr led the prescribed prayers during those days. Afterwards the Messenger felt some relief. He left supported by two men. One of them was al-Abbas. He went to the noon prescribed prayer. Abu Bakr was leading the people in the prescribed prayer. When Abu Bakr saw him, he began to withdraw, but the Prophet told him not to withdraw. He told his two Companions to sit him down beside him. They seated him by the side of Abu Bakr. Abu Bakr offered the prescribed prayer while standing, following the prescribed prayer of the Prophet. The people offered the prescribed prayer standing while following the prescribed prayer of Abu Bakr. The Prophet was seated. [This was told to Abd Allah ibn Abbas for corroboration. The only addition was that the second person was Ali ibn Abi Talib.]

SM v1B p256 n418, R1-R5, R7

Imamate of Women

UMM WARAQAH BINT ABD ALLAH IBN AL-HARITH RELATED:

When the Prophet proceeded to the Battle of Badr, she asked him if she could accompany him in the battle. She said that she would act as a nurse for his patients, and perhaps she would attain martyrdom. He said, 'Stay at your home. God Almighty will bestow martyrdom upon you.' [The sub-narrator reported that because of this, she was called a martyr.] She read the Quran. She sought permission from the Prophet to have a caller to prayer in her house. He, therefore, permitted her to do so. She announced that her slave and slave girl would be freed after her death. One night they went to her and strangled her with a sheet of cloth until she died and then ran away. Umar told the people to find them, and they were crucified. This was the first crucifixion at Madinah. In this second Tradition, it is said that the Messenger used to visit her at her house. He appointed a caller to prayer for her, and he commanded her to lead the inmates of her house in prayer. Abd al-Rahman said that he saw her caller to prayer, and he was an old man.

AD v1 p156 n592; AD v1 p156 n591

Leader Is Appointed To Be Followed

AYISHA RELATED:

God's Messenger fell ill. Some of his Companions visited him to ask about his health. The Prophet performed the prescribed prayer sitting, and the people performed the prescribed prayer standing behind him. The Messenger indicated to them to sit down. When he finished the prescribed prayer, he said, 'Verily the leader is appointed only that he should be followed. As he performs the bending forward, you should perform the bending forward. As he raises himself erect, you should raise yourselves, and as he performs the prescribed prayer sitting, you too should perform the prescribed prayer sitting.

IM v2 p236 n1237; SB v1 p372 n656; SB v2 p185 n328; SM v1A p254 n412; SB v2 p18 n328; SB n657; SB n328; SB v7 p381 n562; SB v1 p656 n214; AD v1 p160 n605

Leading the Prescribed Prayer When the First Leader Comes

AYISHA RELATED:

If somebody was leading the prayer and (in the meantime), the first leader came, the prescribed prayer was valid whether the former leader retreated or not.

SB v1 p368

Waiting for the Imam to Stand Up

UMM SALAMA RELATED:

In the lifetime of the Prophet, the women would get up when they finished their prescribed prayers. The Messenger and the men would stay in their places as long as God willed. When the Messenger got up, the men would then get up.

SB v1 p457 n825; SB v1 p448 n809; SB v1 p457 n826; SB v1 p444 n799; IM v1 p70 n932

RAIN PRESCRIBED PRAYER

On Raising the Hands While Supplicating for Rain

AYISHA RELATED:

The people complained to the Messenger of the lack of rain. He gave orders for a *minbar*. It was then set up for him in the place of prayer. He fixed a day for the people to come out. When the rim of the sun appeared, the Messenger sat down on the *minbar*. Having pronounced the greatness of God, he expressed his praise. He said, 'You have complained of drought in your abodes and of delay in receiving rain at the beginning of its season. God has ordered you to supplicate Him and promised that He will answer your prayers. Praise be to God, the Lord of the Universe, the Compassionate, the Merciful, the Master of the Day of Judgment. There is no god but God Who does what He wishes. O God, You are God. There is no deity but You, the Rich, while we are the poor. Send down the rain upon us and make what You send down a strength and satisfaction for a time.' He then raised his hands and kept raising them until the whiteness under his armpits was visible. He then turned his back to the people and inverted or turned around his cloak while keeping his hands raised up. He then faced the people, descended and prayed two cycles of prayer. God then produced a cloud, and the storm of thunder and lightning came. Then the rain fell by God's permission, and before he reached his mosque, streams were flowing. When he saw the speed with which the people sought shelter, he laughed until his back teeth were visible. Then he said, 'I bear witness that God is Omnipotent, and that I am God's servant and His messenger.'

AD v1 p302 n1169

Raising of Both Hands While Asking God for Rain

AYISHA RELATED:

Whenever God's Messenger saw the rain, he used to say, 'O God! Let it be a strong, fruitful rain.'

SB v2 p78 n142

STRUCTURE OF THE PRESCRIBED PRAYER

UMM HANI RELATED:

The Messenger of God went to her home where he had a bath on the day of the victory of Makkah. He then offered eight cycles of prescribed prayer, and he carried out fully the bending forward and the prostration.

T [MMT v2 p215]

Moderation In What Is

AYISHA RELATED:

God's Messenger began by saying, 'God is Greater,' and the recitation, 'Praise be to God, the Lord of the Universe.' When he bowed, he neither kept his head up nor bent it down but kept it between these extremes. When he raised his head after bowing, he did not prostrate himself until he had stood erect. When he raised his head after prostration, he did not prostrate himself again until he sat up. At the end of every two prostrations, he recited the *tahiyya*. He used to place his left foot flat [on the ground] and raise up his right foot. He prohibited the satanic way of sitting on the heels, and he forbade people to spread out their arms like wild beasts. He ended the prescribed prayer with the salutations.

SM v1B p293 n498

On Offering Prescribed Prayer in Sitting Position

AYISHA RELATED:

God's Messenger used to pray standing at night for a long time and used to pray sitting at night for a long time. When he prayed standing, he bowed standing. When he prayed sitting, he bowed sitting.

AD v1 p243 n955

Salutations: Incline Towards the Left

AYISHA RELATED:

The Messenger of God offered the salutations in prescribed prayer facing forward and then inclined a little towards his right side.

T [H v3 p305]

Satan and His Soldiers Beware

AYISHA RELATED:

She asked the Prophet about one's looking here and there during the performance of the prescribed prayer. He replied, 'It is what satan steals from the prescribed prayer of any one of you.'

SB v4 p326 n511; SB v1 p401 n718; AD v1 p232 n910

Straightening the Rows

AYISHA RELATED:

God's Messenger said, 'God and His angels invoke blessing on those who arrange the rows [in prescribed prayer] in a compact form. He who fills some space [in the rows], God elevates him a degree on that account.'

IM v2 p100 n995

Supplications After Reciting, 'Peace and the Mercy of God be Upon You.'

AYISHA RELATED:

After God's Messenger sent salutations [to conclude the prescribed prayer], he sat only long enough to say, 'O God, You are the peace, and peace [emanates] from You. You are blessed, O the Lord of Majesty and Honor.'

IM v2 p65 n924; SM v1B p336 n592; AD v1 p394 n1507

What Has Been Said About the Children of Israel

AYISHA RELATED:

She hated anyone who kept his hands on his flanks while praying. She said that the Jews did this.

SB v4 p440 n664

What Is Recited After Takbir: Reciting Amin Aloud

AYISHA RELATED:

God's Messenger said, 'The Jews are not as envious of you for anything as they are envious of you for offering salutations [in prescribed prayer] and reciting, "Amen."'

IM v2 p28 n856

SUITABLE DRESS

Disapproval of Wearing Silk and Other Types of Clothes

AYISHA RELATED:

The Messenger of God once offered his prescribed prayer wearing a garment having designs on it. He then looked at its designs. When he offered the salutations [at the end of the prescribed prayer], he said, 'Take this garment of mine to Abu Jahm, for it turned my attention just now in my prescribed prayer. Bring a simple garment without designs.'

AD v3 p1132 n4041; SB v7 p475 n708; SB v1 p226 n369; SB v1 p226 n370; SB v1 p401 n719; SM v1B p318 n556; AD v3 p1132 n4042; AD v1 p232 n915; AD v1 p232 n914; N v1E p475 n774; N v1E p475 n774

Clothes Worn by a Woman Offering the Prescribed Prayer

UMM SALAMA RELATED:

She asked the Prophet if a woman could pray in a shirt and head covering without wearing a lower garment. He said, 'If the shirt is ample and covers the front of her feet.'

AD v1 p168 n640

Night Prescribed Prayer

ZAYNAB THAQAFIYA RELATED:

God's Messenger said, 'When any one of you [women] participates in the night prayer [in congregation], she should not perfume herself that night.'

SM v1B p271 n443, R1

Offering Prescribed Prayers With a Single Garment

UMM HANI RELATED:

The Prophet wrapped his body with a single garment and crossed its ends over his shoulders.

SB v1 p216

AYISHA RELATED:

The Prophet offered the prescribd prayer in a single [piece of cloth] of which one part was on her.

AD v1 p166 n631

SUNAN PRAYERS

After the Afternoon Prescribed Prayer

AYISHA RELATED:

The Messenger never missed two cycles after the afternoon prescribed prayer until he returned to God. He did not return to God until it became so difficult for him to offer the prescribed prayer while standing, that he used to offer most of these while sitting [the two cycles after the afternoon prescribed prayer]. He offered them in his house and never offered the prescribed prayers in the mosque [during his last illness] lest it might be hard for his followers. He loved what was easy for them.

SB v1 p325 n564; N v1E p384 n577

UMM SALAMA RELATED:

The Prophet offered two cycles of prayer after the afternoon prescribed prayer, but some people of the tribe of Abd al-Qays made her busy and did not let her offer the prescribed two cycle prayer after the afternoon prescribed prayer.

SB v1 p325; SB v1 p326 n565; N v1E p384 n577

AYISHA RELATED:

Whenever the Prophet came to her after the afternoon prescribed prayer, he always prayed two cycles.

SB v1 p326 n567; SB v1 p326 n566

AYISHA RELATED:

Umar misconstrued the fact and dissuaded people from observing two cycles after the afternoon prescribed prayer despite the fact that the Messenger of God had said, 'Let not any one of you intend to observe the prescribed prayer at the time of the rising of the sun or at the time of its setting, for it rises between the horns of satan.'

N v1E p383 n573; SM v1B p46 n8331

After the Evening Prescribed Prayer

AYISHA RELATED:

The Messenger of God said, 'God will build a house in paradise for whoever offers twenty cycles of prayer after the evening prescribed prayer.'

T [H v3 p383]

AYISHA RELATED:

The Prophet performed the evening prescribed prayer. Then he came back to her apartment and performed two cycles.

IM v2 p192 n1164

After the Noon Prescribed Prayer

UMM SALAMA RELATED:

The Messenger of God observed two cycles of prescribed prayer after the afternoon prescribed prayer in her house. She mentioned it to the Messenger of God; whereupon, he said, 'These are the two cycles which come after the noon prayer. I could not observe them [due to business] after I had offered the afternoon prescribed prayer.'

N v1E p386 n582; N v1E p385 n580; N v1E p385 n578; v1E p385 n579; N v1E p385 n583

Afternoon Prescribed Prayer

AYISHA RELATED:

God's Messenger offered the afternoon prescribed prayer when the light of the sun entered in her aprartment up until it left.

SM v1B p345 n611, R1-R3; SB v1 p298 n519; v1 p298 n518; SB v1 p298 n520; SB v1 p298 n521; AD v1 p107 n407; IM v1 p369 n683; N v1E p355 n508; SB v1 p298 n520

Before and After the Noon Prescribed Prayer

UMM HABIBA

She heard the Messenger of God say, 'God will make the fire unlawful for whoever performs four cycles of prayer before the noon prescribed prayer and four after it.'

IM [H v3 p381]; AD v1 p333 n1264; IM [MMTv2]; IM v2 p189 n1160

Before the Dawn and Noon Prescribed Prayer

AYISHA RELATED:

The Prophet never missed four cycles before the noon prescribed prayer nor two cycles before the dawn prescribed prayer.

SB v2 p153 n276; AD v1 p329 n1248

Before the Dawn Prescribed Prayer

AYISHA RELATED:

God's Messenger said, 'One who prostrates before sunset or at the dawn prescribed prayer before the rising of the sun in fact receives the reward of the prescribed prayer. When there is a prostration, this implies a bending forward.'

SM v1B p344 n609

AYISHA RELATED:

God's Messenger said, 'The two cycles at dawn are better than this world and all that it contains.'

SM v1B p409 n725, R1; SB v2 p145 n260; AD v1 p329 n1249

Before the Noon Prescribed Prayer

AYISHA RELATED:

Whenever she saw the Messenger observing the supererogatory prayer of the forenoon, but she herself observed it. If the Messenger abandoned any act which he in fact loved to do, it was out of fear that if the people practiced it constantly, it might become obligatory for them.

SM v1B p405 n718; SB v2 p151 n273; AD v1 p339 n1288

AYISHA RELATED:

God's Messenger observed two prostrations [that is, cycles of prescribed prayer] after the afternoon prescribed prayer, but then he became preoccupied or forgot them and so observed them after the afternoon prescribed prayer. Then he affirmed them. It was his habit that when he observed prescribed prayer, he then affirmed it.

SM v1B p464 n835, R1-R3

AYISHA RELATED:

The practice of the Messenger was that if he had not offered the four cycles before the noon prescribed prayer, he did so after he had completed his noon prescribed prayer.

T [MMT v2 p196]

Dawn Prescribed Prayer: Offering Two Cycles Before It

AYISHA RELATED:

When the Messenger of God ended his prayer late in the night, he would see if she was awake. If she was, he would talk to her. If she was asleep, he would awaken her and pray two cycles. Then he would lie down until the caller to prescribed prayer came to him and called him for the dawn prescribed prayer. Then he would offer two cycles lightly [quickly?] and leave for the prescribed prayer.

AD v1 p331 n1257; SB v2 p144 n258; SB v2 p144 n259; SB v2 p143 n257; SB v2 p122 n220; SM v1B p417 n743, R1; AD v1 p331 n1258; SM v1B p416 n739

AYISHA RELATED:

The earlier part of the dawn always found the Messenger of God sleeping in her house or near her.

SM v1B p417 n742; SB v2 p130 n234; IM v2 p209 n1197

AYISHA RELATED:

After the Prophet performed the ablution, he performed two cycles [of *sunna* prayer] and then went to the prescribed prayer.

IM v2 p181 n1146

AYISHA RELATED:

The deed which was most loved by the Prophet was a deed done continuously. When asked when the Messenger got up for the dawn prescribed prayer, she said that he got up upon hearing the crowing of a cock.

SB v2 p129 n232

Eight Cycles

UMM HANI

On the day of the conquest of Makkah, the Messenger offered eight cycles giving the salutations after every two cycles.

AD v1 p339 n1285

AYISHA RELATED:

The Messenger of God offered the night prescribed prayer. He then prayed eight cycles standing and two cycles between the call to prescribed prayer and the declaration to perform the prescribed prayer.

AD v1 p356 n1355; AD v1 p356 n1356

Eleven Cycles

AYISHA RELATED:

The Prophet prayed the supererogatory prayer in congregation.

SB v2 p154

AYISHA RELATED:

A woman from the Asad tribe was sitting with her when God's Messenger came to her house and asked who she was. She (Ayisha) said that she was so and so. She said that this woman did not sleep at night because she was engaged in prayer. The Prophet said disapprovingly, 'Do good deeds which are within your capacity, as God never tires of giving rewards until you get tired of doing good deeds.'

SB v2 p139 n251B

AYISHA RELATED:

God's Messenger used to offer eleven cycles as his prayer. He used to prolong the prostration to such an extent that one could recite fifty verses of the Quran before he would lift up his head. He used to pray two cycles [*sunnah*] before the dawn prescribed prayer, and then he used to lie down on his right side until the caller to prayer came and informed him of the time for prescribed prayer.

SB v2 p125 n223

AYISHA RELATED:

The Prophet performed the *tahajjud* prayer in her house. Then he heard the voice of Abbad who was praying in the mosque. He said, 'O Ayisha! Is this Abbad's voice?' She said that it was. He said, 'O God! Be merciful to Abbad.'

SB v3 p501 n823B

AYISHA RELATED:

Between the time when God's Messenger finished the night [*tahajjud*] prayer until dawn broke, he prayed eleven cycles, uttering the salutations at the end of every two and observing *witr* with a single cycle, during which he would prostrate himself about as long as one would take to recite fifty verses before raising his head. When the caller to prayer finished making the call for the dawn prescribed prayer, he would stand up and pray two short cycles. Then he would lay down on his right side until the caller to prayer came to him.

AD v1 p350 n1331; SB v1 p340 n592; SB v1 p343 n599; SB v2 p58 n108; SM v1B p415 n736R1; AD v1 p350 n1330; AD v1 p351 n1334; AD v1 p350 n1329; N v1E p435 n688; SB v2 p125 n223; SB v8 p215 n322

AYISHA RELATED:

The Prophet performed prayer, consisting of eleven cycles, between the night and dawn prescribed prayers [during the month of Ramadan]. He greeted [at the end of] every two cycles and observed one single cycle at the end [to render the total number of cycles an odd number] and maintained the prostration for a time equal to that taken by the recitation of fifty verses before he raised his head [from prostration]. When the caller to prescribed prayer fell silent after the first call to prayer of the dawn prescribed prayer, the Prophet would get up and perform two light cycles of prayer.

IM v2 p307 n1358; SB v3 p128 n230

Good Deeds

AYISHA RELATED:

God's Messenger gave up a good deed even though he loved doing it for fear that people might feel these actions were prescribed for them. The Prophet never prayed a prayer, but she offered it too.

SB v2 p127 n228

Night Prayer

AYISHA RELATED:

Anyone who offered the prayer at night regularly but on a certain night was overcome by sleep would, nevertheless, be given the reward of prayer. His sleep would be almsgiving.

AD v1 p345 n1309

AYISHA RELATED:

When God's Messenger missed the night prayer due to pain or any other reason, he observed twelve cycles during the daytime.

SM v1B p421 n746R4, R5

AYISHA RELATED:

God's Messenger stood up at night to pray. He began his prayer with two short prostrations.

SM v1B p434 n767

AYISHA RELATED:

God's Messenger did not sleep before observing the night prescribed prayer and did not chat at night after it.

IM v1 p380 n702

AYISHA RELATED:

Once the Messenger of God delayed the night prescribed prayer until Umar reminded him of it. The women and children had gone to sleep. The Messenger of God came out and said, 'None among the dwellers of the earth has been waiting for the prescribed prayer but you.' In those days no where except in Madinah was the prescribed prayer offered [because Islam had not as yet spread beyond the confines of Madinah].

N v1E p344 n485; SB v1 p312 n541; SB v1 p455 n821; SB v1 p455 n823; SM v1B p358 n638R2; N v1E p371 n538; N v1E n538; N v1E p371 n539; N v1E p371 n538

Nine Cycles

AYISHA RELATED:

The Messenger of God observed the *witr* prayer with nine cycles. He prayed seven cycles [of *witr* prayer] and he prayed two cycles sitting after the *witr* during which he would recite the Quran [sitting]. When he wished to bow, he stood up and bowed and prostrated.

AD v1 p354 n1346; IM v2 p308 n1360

On Time

AYISHA RELATED:

God's Messenger said, 'He who observes a cycle of morning prescribed prayer before the sun rises indeed observes it, and he who observes a cycle of the afternoon prescribed prayer before the sun sets indeed observes it.'

IM v1 p378 n700

Performing Superogatory Prayer in a Sitting Position

AYISHA RELATED:

She saw God's Messenger performing some of the night prescribed prayer in a standing position until he reached old age. [Once he had grown older] he began to observe prescribed prayer sitting until forty verses or thirty verses of his recitation were left. Then he stood up, recited them and performed prostration.

IM v2 p226 n1227; SB v2 p137 n249

Saying "then after" in the Sermon

AYISHA RELATED:

Once God's Messenger went out and prayed in the mosque with some men in the middle of the night. The next morning the people spoke about it. On the second night more people gathered and prayed with him. They circulated the news in the morning. The number of people increased greatly. On the third night God's Messenger came out, and they prayed behind him. On the fourth night, the mosque was crowded with the people that it could not accommodate them. God's Messenger came out only for the dawn prescribed prayer. When he finished the prayer, he faced the people and recited, 'I bear witness that there is no god but God and that Muhammad is His Messenger.' Then he said, 'Verily I realized you were also in the mosques but I did not acknowledge it because I was afraid that this prayer might be made prescribed for you and it might prove to be too difficult.' ;

SB v2 p23 n46; SB v1 p390 n696; SB v2 p128 n229; SM v1B p428 n761, R1; SB v3 p127 n229; AD v1 p359 n1368

Seven, Nine, Eleven Cycles

AYISHA RELATED:

The Prophet offered seven, nine or eleven cycles beside the two cycles of the dawn prescribed prayer.

SB v2 p132 n240

Sleeping In the First Part of the Night

AYISHA RELATED:

In regard to night prayer, the Prophet slept early at night and got up in its last part to pray. Then he returned to his bed. When the caller to prayer called the prayer, he would get up. If he needed a bath, he would take one. Otherwise he would perform ablution and then go out for the prayer.

SB v2 p136 n247

Ten Cycles

AYISHA RELATED:

God's Messenger offered the night prescribed prayer and then got up for the *tahajjud* prayer in which he offered eight cycles and then offered two cyles more while sitting. He then offered two cycles in between the call to prayer. He never missed them.

SB v2 p143 n256

AYISHA RELATED:

God's Messenger said, 'He who performs prayer [consisting of] ten cycles between the evening and night prescribed prayer, God will build a house for him in paradise.'

IM v2 p316 n1373

Thirteen Cycles

AYISHA RELATED:

God's Messenger prayed thirteen cycles, observing six cycles in pairs, including the two cycles of the dawn prescribed prayer. He observed *witr* with five cycles. He sat only in the last of them.

AD v1 p356 n1354; SB v2 p132 n241; SM v1B p415 n737R2; AD v p350 n1333

AYISHA RELATED:

The Prophet of God prayed thirteen cycles during the night. He would offer eight cycles, observing the *witr* with one cycle. Then he prayed two cycles after *witr* prayer in sitting position. When he wished to bow, he stood up and bowed. He prayed two cycles between the call to the dawn prescribed prayer and the declaration to perform the prescribed prayer.

AD v1 p351 n1335; SB v2 p145 n261; AD v1 p354 n1345; IM v2 p308 n1359

Twelve Cycles During the Day and Night

UMM HABIBA RELATED:

The Messenger of God said, 'Whoever will offer twelve cycles [in addition to the regular seventeen cycles] during the day and night for him a house will be built in heaven. [The twelve consisted of] four before and two after the noon prescribed prayer; two after the evening prescribed prayer; two after the night prescribed prayer; and two before the dawn prescribed prayer.'

T [MMT v2 p195]; SM v1B p410 n728, R2-R3; AD v1 p328 n1245; IM v2 p178 n1140; v2 p178 n1141; T MMT v2

Waking for the Dawn Prescribed Prayer

UMM SALAMA RELATED:

One night the Prophet got up and said, 'Glory be to God! How many afflictions God has revealed tonight and how many treasures have been sent down. Go and wake the sleeping women occupants of these dwellings for prescribed prayer. A well-dressed person in this world may be naked in the hereafter.'

SB v2 p127 n226

AYISHA RELATED:

The Messenger slept at dawn when he was with her.

AD v1 p346 n1313

SUPPLICATION

After Reciting 'God is Greater'

AYISHA RELATED:

When the Prophet began the prescribed prayer he used to say, 'Glory to You, O God! All praise is for you. Blessed is Your name and exalted is Your Majesty, and there is none to be served besides You.'

IM [H v3 p263]; AD v1 p199 n775; T [MMR v1]

AYISHA RELATED:

God's Messenger began the recitation with the words, '*All praise is due to God, the Lord of the universe*,' [1:2].

IM v2 p6 n812

Evening Prescribed Prayer

UMM FADL BINT AL-HARITH RELATED:

She heard her son [Ibn Abbas] reciting Surah 77 and said to him that his recitation had made her remember that this was the last chapter she heard the Messenger recite. He recited it in the evening prescribed prayer.

SB v1 p406 n730; SM v1B p272 n462; AD v1 p207 n809; SB v5 p509 n712

Making Supplication While Bowing and Prostrating

AYISHA RELATED:

The Prophet said, when bowing and prostrating, 'Glory be to You, O God, our Lord,' and 'Praise be to You, O God, forgive me,' thus interpreting the command in the Quran [Chapter 110:3].

AD v1 p224 n876; SB v6 p464 n491; SB v6 p464 n492; SM v1B p288 nR1-R3; SB v1 p434 n781; SB v1 p421 n760; IM v2 p43 n887; SB v5 p409 Title

Numbers of Prostrations in Quranic Recitation

UMM DARDA RELATED:

Abu Darda told her that he performed twenty-one prostrations with the Prophet. Among these [prostrations] was one performed [during the recitation] of Surah an-Najm [the Chapter on the Star].

IM v2 p130 n1055

Superogatory Prayers

AYISHA RELATED:

When the Messenger got up at night, he commenced his prayer with the words, 'O God, Lord of Gabriel and Michael and Israfil, the Creator of the heavens and the earth, Who knows the unseen and the seen, You decide among Your servants concerning their differences. Guide me with Your permission through the divergent views held about Truth, for it is You Who guides whom You will to the Straight Path.'

SM v1B p435 n770

Supplicating During the Prescribed Prayer

AYISHA RELATED:

A man prayed on his rooftop. When he recited the verse, 'Is not He able to bring the dead to life?' [Chapter 75:40], he would say, 'Glory be to You, then, why not?' People asked him about this, and he said that he had heard the Messenger of God say this.

AD v1 p225 n883

Supplications After Reciting, 'Peace and the Mercy of God be Upon You."

UMM SALAMA RELATED:

When God's Messenger performed the dawn prescribed prayer, he supplicated as he greeted [at the end of the prescribed prayer] saying, 'O God, I beg of You the knowledge that is beneficial, the provision that is pure and the deed that is accepted [and rewarded].'

IM v2 p65 n925

Reciting in Bowing and Prostration

AYISHA RELATED:

The Prophet said when bowing and prostrating, 'All-Glorious, All-

Holy, Lord of the angels and the spirit.'

AD v1 p223 n871; SM v1B p289 n487R1

TIME OF PRESCRIBED PRAYER

Afternoon Prescribed Prayer

AYISHA RELATED:

She asked her servant to write a passage from the Quran for her. She told the servant to tell her when he reached the verse, '*Be guardians of your prescribed prayers and of the midmost prescribed prayer*' [2:238]. He informed her. She asked him to write, 'Be guardians of your prescribed prayers and of the midmost prescribed prayer and of the afternoon prescribed prayer, and stand up with devotion to God' [2:238]. She then said that she had heard this from the Messenger of God.

AD v1 p107 n410

AYISHA RELATED:

The Messenger offered the afternoon prescribed prayer while the sun was still shinning in her dwelling place.

SB v4 p217 n335

Before the Noon Prescribed Prayer

AYISHA RELATED:

When God's Messenger missed the four cycles before the noon prescribed prayer he would observe them as two cycles after the noon prescribed prayer.

IM v2 p187 n1158

Dawn Prescribed Prayer

UMM SALAMA RELATED:

One night the Prophet woke up saying, 'None has the right to be worshipped but God. How many afflictions have been sent down tonight and how many treasures have been disclosed! Who will go and wake up the women dwellers of these rooms for the prescribed prayers? Many well dressed people in this world will be naked on the day of resurrection.'

SB v7 p491 n735; SB v8 p150 n237; SB v1 p87 n115; SB v9 p153 n189

Night Prayer

AYISHA RELATED:

No one should give up prayer at night. God's Messenger never put it aside. Whenever he felt ill or lithargic, he would offer it sitting.

AD v1 p344 n1302

AYISHA RELATED:

God, the Exalted would awaken God's Messenger at night. When the dawn came, he would finish his daily round of recital.

AD v1 p346 n1311

Noon Prescribed Prayer

AYISHA RELATED:

The middle prayer is the noon prayer.

T [H v3 p168]

On Time

UMM FARWA RELATED:

The Messenger of God was asked which deed is the best. He replied, 'Observing the prescribed prayer early in the time period.'

AD v1 p111 n426; T [MMRv1]; [Hv3p182]

UMM SALAMA RELATED:

God's Messenger observed the noon prescribed prayer much earlier than you, but you observed the afternoon prescribed prayer much earlier than he.

T [MMR v1 p125]

TRAVELER'S PRESCRIBED PRAYER

AYISHA RELATED:

When the prescribed prayers were first enjoined, they were two cycles each. Later the prescribed prayer in a journey was kept as it was, but the prescribed prayers for non-travelers were completed [increased to four cycles].

SB v2 p111 n196; SB v1 p214 n346; N v1E p331 n456

AYISHA RELATED:

Originally two cycles were prescribed in every prayer. When the Prophet migrated to Madinah, four cycles were enjoined, but the prescribed prayer of traveling remained unchanged [that is, two cycles].

SB v5 p187 n272; AD v1 p310 n1194

WHAT IS PERMITTED AND WHAT IS NOT

Before Dawn

AYISHA RELATED:

God's Messenger performed two cycles before the dawn prescribed prayer and said, 'The most excellent two chapters recited in the dawn prescribed prayer are, "*Say: He is God, the One,*" [112] and "*O you non-believers*"' [109].

IM v2 p182 n1148

Blowing in Prostration

UMM SALAMA RELATED:

The Messenger of God saw a servant of ours called Aflah. When he prostrated, he blew. The Messenger said to him, 'O Aflah! Cover your face with dust.'

T [H v3 p321]

Concerning Dozing Off in Prescribed Prayer

AYISHA RELATED:

God's Messenger said, 'When anyone among you dozes in prescribed prayer, he should sleep until his sleep is gone for when one of you offers the prescribed prayer while dozing, he does not know whether he may be asking for forgiveness or vilifying himself.'

N v1E p199 n164; SB v1 p139 n211; AD v1 p344 n1305; IM v2 p314 n1370

AYISHA RELATED:

God's Messenger said, 'When any one of you gets up at night for prayer and his tongue falters in the recitation of the Quran and he does not know what he is reciting, he should go to sleep.'

SM v1B p442 n786

Evening Prescribed Prayer

AYISHA RELATED:

The Messenger of God recited the whole of Sura Araf in the evening prescribed prayer by dividing it between two cycles.

N [MMT v2 p160]; N [MMRv1]

Hand Beckoning While in Prescribed Prayer

UMM SALAMA RELATED:

She heard the Prophet forbidding it [two cycles after the afternoon prescribed prayer]. Later she saw him offering them immediately after he offered the afternoon prescribed prayer. He then entered her house at a time when some of the women Helpers from the Haram tribe were sitting with her. She sent her slave girl to him and told the slave girl to stand beside him and tell him that Umm Salama said to him that she had heard he had forbidden the offering of these two cycles after the prescribed afternoon prayer, yet she has seen him offering them. She told her slave girl to wait for him if he waved his hand. The slave girl did this. The Prophet beckoned her with his hand, and she waited for him. When he had finished the prescribed prayer, he said, 'O daughter of the Umaya tribe. You have asked me about the two cycles after the afternoon prescribed prayer. The people of the tribe of Abd al-Qays came to me and kept me busy, and I could not offer the two cycle after the noon prescribed prayer. These two cycles that I have just offered are for those missed ones.'

SB v2 p183 n325

How to Prostrate Oneself

MAYMUNA RELATED:

When the Prophet prostrated himself, he kept his arms so far away from his sides that if a lamb had wanted to pass under his arms, it could have done so.

AD v1 p229 n897; SM v1 B p292 n496; SM v1BNJ p292 n497R1; IM v2 p40 n880

Night Prayers

AYISHA RELATED:

God's Messenger slept during the first part of the night and spent its last part in prayer.

IM v2 p311 n1365

Observing Supererogatory Prayers Standing or Sitting

AYISHA RELATED:

God's Messenger would pray during the night for a long time. When he prayed standing, he bowed in a standing posture. When he prayed sitting, he bowed in a sitting posture.

SM v1B p412 n730R1; AD v1 p243 n955

AYISHA RELATED:

She did not see God's Messenger reciting the Quran during the night prescribed prayer in a sitting position until he grew old. Then he recited it in a sitting position, but when thirty or forty verses were left out of the Chapter, he would then stand up, recite them, and bow.

SM v1B p412 n731, R1-R2; SB v2 p119 n219; AD v1 p243 n954; AD v1 p243 n953

AYISHA RELATED:

God's Messenger died in the state in which he observed most of his prescribed prayers in a sitting position.

SM v1B p412 n732R2

Offering Prescribed Prayer in Wives' Waist Wrappers

AYISHA RELATED:

The Messenger of God would not pray in their [his wives'] wrappers or in their quilts.

AD v1 p96 n367; AD v1 p96 n368

Opening a Door

AYISHA RELATED:

God's Messenger was praying with his door bolted. She came and asked to have the door opened [which faced the *qibla*]. He walked over and opened the door for her. He then returned to his place for prayer.

AD v1 p234 n922; IM [MMRv1]

Performing Superogatory Prayer in a Sitting Position

UMM SALAMA RELATED:

The Messenger performed prescribed prayer while sitting. When he intended to perform the bending forward, he would get up and stand erect for as long as it takes to recite forty verses.'

IM v2 p226 n1226

Performing the Bending Forward in Prescribed Prayer

AYISHA RELATED:

When God's Messenger performed the bending forward, he neither raised his head nor lowered it, but it was in between these extremes.

IM v2 p34 n869

Placing Hands on the Knees

AYISHA RELATED:

When God's Messenger performed the bending forward in prescribed prayer, he placed his hands on his knees and kept his arms apart from the sides.

IM v2 p37 n874

Recitation Following the Imam

Ayisha related:

God's Messenger said, 'Every prescribed prayer in which the first chapter of the Quran is not recited is deficient.'

IM v2 p20 n840

Resting During the Prescribed Prayer

Ayisha related:

God's Messenger said, 'He who suffers from vomiting or nose bleed or *qals* or emission of prostatic fluid should end the prescribed prayer and perform ablution. He then should depend on his prescribed prayer being accepted. He should not indulge in any talk during this [time].

IM v2 p223 n1221

Ayisha related:

God's Messenger said, 'When anyone of you performs the prescribed prayer and becomes impure, he should hold his nose firmly and then move [to seek purification].

IM v2 p224 n1222

Silent Recitation of 'In the Name of God, the Compassionate, the Merciful'

Ayisha related:

The Messenger began his prescribed prayer with 'God is Greater,' and 'Praise belongs to God, the Lord of the universe.' When he bowed, he neither raised up nor lowered down his head but kept it between the two. When he raised his head after bowing, he did not prostrate until he stood up straight. When he raised his head after prostration, he did not prostrate [the second time] until he sat down properly. He recited *al-tahiyyat* after every two cycles. When he sat, he rested his left foot laterally on the ground and raised his right. He forbad sitting like the devil [sitting on hips and raising one's knees like a dog] and spreading out the hands [on the ground in prostration] like animals. He used to end the prescribed prayer by uttering the salutation.

AD v1 p 201 n782

Sitting Between Two Prostrations

Ayisha related:

As God's Messenger raised his head from bending forward he did not perform prostration until he first stood erect. Then when he prostrated and lifted his head [from prostration], he did not prostrate [for the second time] until he sat erect and rested his left foot laterally on the ground..'

IM v2 p46 n893

WITR

AYISHA RELATED:

God's Messenger offered *witr* prayer on different nights at various hours extending from the night prescribed prayer up to the last hour of the night.

SB v2 p59 n110

AYISHA RELATED:

God's Messenger prayed in the night. When he prayed *witr*, he told her to get up and pray *witr*.

SM v1B p417 n744, R1; SM v1B p417 n740

AYISHA RELATED:

God's Messenger observed the *witr* prayer every night and completed *witr* at the time of dawn.

SM v1B p417 n745, R1-R2

AYISHA RELATED:

The Messenger observed *witr* with one cycle after which he performed two cycles reciting the Quran in the course of which he remained seated. When he wished to bow, he stood up and bowed.

IM [MMR v1 p267]

UMM SALAMA RELATED:

The Prophet prayed two cycles after *witr*.

T [H v3 p417]; T [MMTv2]

AYISHA RELATED:

God's Messenger offered salutation after every two cycles and made the number [of cycles] odd by [performing] one single cycle of *witr*.

IM v2 p198 n1177

UMM SALAMA RELATED:

God's Messenger performed seven or five single cycles [*witr*] without interrupting them with salutations or any talk.

IM v2 p207 n1192

UMM SALAMA RELATED:

The Prophet performed two light cycles after the single cycle while he was sitting.

IM v2 p208 n1195

CHAPTER 4
PRESCRIBED VISIT FOR
PILGRIMAGE

ANIMAL SACRIFICE

AYISHA RELATED:

On the 10th of Dhi Hajjah, the day of the sacrifice, no act of a child of Adam was more pleasing to the Lord than the sacrifice of an animal. On the day of judgment, the sacrificed animal reaches the place of the good pleasure of God before it falls on the ground; thus, the bondsmen of God should perform the sacrifice with full willingness of heart.

T [MMT v2 p244]; T [MMR v1 p306]; IM [H v3 p490]; T [Hv3 p490]

Deputizing Someone to Sacrifice an Animal

AYISHA RELATED:

She twisted the garlands of the animals the Messenger intended to sacrifice with her own hands. Then God's Messenger put them around their necks with his own hands and sent them with her father to Makkah. Nothing legal was regarded illegal for God's Messenger until the animals were slaughtered.

SB v3 p293 n510; AD v2 p461 n1753

Garlanding Sheep

AYISHA RELATED:

Once the Prophet sent a sheep as the sacrifical animal.

SB v2 p442 n759

"If I had formerly known what I came to know lately...."

AYISHA RELATED:

God's Messenger said, 'If I had formerly known what I have come to know, I would not have driven the sacrifical animal with me and would have ended the sacred state along with the people when they ended it.'

SB v9 p254 n335

It Is Meritorious to Sacrifice the Animal With One's Own Hand

AYISHA RELATED:

God's Messenger commanded that a ram with black legs, black belly and circles around its eyes should be brought to him so that he could sacrifice it. He told her to give him the large knife and then said, 'Sharpen it on a stone.' She did that. He then took the knife and then the ram. He placed it on the ground and then sacrificed it saying, 'In the Name of God. O God, accept this sacrifice on behalf of Muhammad and the family of Muhammad and the Community of Muhammad.'

SM v3B p321 n1967

Permission to Sacrifice a Cow

AYISHA RELATED:

The Messenger of God sacrificed a cow for his wives at the farewell pilgrimage.

AD v2 p459 n1746

Sacrifice of the First Ten Days of Rajab From the Age of Ignorance

AYISHA RELATED:

God's Messenger sacrificed one sheep out of every fifty sheep.

AD v2 p796 n2827

Shaving the Head

UMM SALAMA RELATED:

God's Messenger said, 'If anyone has a sacrifical animal and intends to sacrifice it and he sights the new moon of Dhi Hajjah, he must not cut any of his hair or nails until he sacrifices.'

AD v2 p784 n2785

Storing Up of the Meat of Sacrifice

AYISHA RELATED:

Some people of the desert came at the time of sacrifice during the lifetime of the Messenger of God. He said, 'Store up enough for three days and give the rest as alms.' After that the people said to him that they benefited from their sacrifices by dissolving the fat and thus making water bags from their skins. They said that he had prohibited the preserving of the meat for more than three days. He said, 'I prohibited you due to a group of people who came to you. Now eat, give it as alms and store it up.'

AD v2 p789 n2806

To Make an Incision in the Body of Sacrificial Animals

AYISHA RELATED:

The Messenger of God once brought sheep [or goats] for sacrifice to the Kabah and garlanded them.

AD v2 p459 n1751

ARAFAT

Merit of the Prescribed Pilgrimage and Shorter Pilgrimage

AYISHA RELATED:

God's Messenger said, 'There is no other day God sets free more servants from hell than the day of Arafat. He draws near, then praises them to the angels, asking, "What do they want?"'

SM v2B p314 n1348

"Then depart from the place..." [2:199]

AYISHA RELATED:

The Quraysh and those who followed their religion used to station at Mudalifah. They were called the Hums. The rest of the Arabs used to station at Arafat. When Islam came, God Almighty commanded His Prophet to go to Arafat and station there and to then go quickly from theret. That is in accordance with the words of God, 'Then go quickly from where the people went quickly.'

AD v2 p507 n1905; SB v6 p34 n45

CIRCUMAMBULATION

Circumambulation of a Pilgrim Who Performs the Pilgrimage of qiran

AYISHA RELATED:

The Messenger said that her observance of circumambulation of the Kabah and running between Safa and Marwah [only once] were sufficient for her prescribed pilgrimage and shorter pilgrimage.

AD v2 p499 n1892

Circumambulation on the Back of a Camel

AYISHA RELATED:

God's Messenger circumambulated the Kabah on the back of his camel on the occasion of the farewell pilgrimage and touched the corner of the Black Stone. He did not want people pushed away from him.

SM v2B p274 n1274; AD v2 p494 n1873

Circumambulation With Ablution

AYISHA RELATED:

When the Prophet reached Makkah, the first thing he began with was ablution. Then he performed the circumambulation of the Kabah. His intention was for both.

SB v2 p411 n705

Walk Proudly While Going Around the Kabah

AYISHA RELATED:

God's Messenger said, 'Going around the House [the Kabah], running between Safa and Marwa and stoning the pillars are meant for the remembrance of God.'

AD v2 p497 n1883

What is Needed of Circumambulation Pursuing and Staying in the Sacred State and Leaving It

ASMA BINT ABU BAKR RELATED:

Whenever she passed by Hajun, she would pray for peace and blessings upon God's Messenger. She said they used to stay with him. Few were their rides and small their provisions. She performed the shorter pilgrimage, and so did her sister, Ayisha, and Zubayr. As they touched the Kabah [performed circumambulation running between Safa and Marwa], they ended the sacred state and then again assumed the sacred state in the afternoon of the prescribed pilgrimage.

SM v2B p259 n1237

CONGREGATION

AYISHA RELATED:

God's Messenger completed the prescribed pilgrimage and the shorter pilgrimage in the company of his people.

SM v2B p253 n1228

DEPUTY

WOMAN OF THE KATHAM CLAN RELATED:

She told God's Messenger that her father was very old and he had not performed the prescribed pilgrimage. She said that he was too old to even sit on the back of a camel. The Messenger said, 'Perform the prescribed pilgrimage on his behalf.'

SM v2B p307 n1335

ENTERING AND LEAVING MAKKAH

Dhat Irq for People From Iraq

AYISHA RELATED:

God's Messenger appointed Dhat Irq as the place where the people of Iraq should assume the sacred state.

N [MMR v1 p539]

Entering Makkah

AYISHA RELATED:

God's Messenger entered Makkah from the side of Kuda, the upper end of Makkah, in the year of the conquest of Makkah. He entered from the side of Kida when he performed the shorter pilgrimage. Urwah entered Makkah from both sides but often entered from the side of Kuda as it was closer to his home.

AD v2 p4 n1863, n1864; SB v2 p379 n649

FESTIVAL OF SACRIFICE

SARA BINT NABHAN RELATED:

The Prophet addressed them on the second day of sacrifice and asked, 'What day is today?' They all said that God and His Messenger were better aware. He asked, 'Is this not the middle of the days of *tashriq?*'

AD v2 p518 n1948

FINAL CIRCUMAMBULATION

Circumambulation at the Time of Departure

AYISHA RELATED:

She assumed the sacred state for the shorter pilgrimage at Tanim. She entered Makkah and performed her shorter pilgrimage as an atonement. The Messenger of God waited for her at Abtah until she finished. He commanded the people to depart. The Messenger of God went to the Kabah, went around it, and left for Madinah.

AD v2 p532 n2000

AYISHA RELATED:

She went along with the Prophet during his last pilgrimage. He dismounted at Muhassab. [In another version she said that she went to the Messenger in the morning. He announced their departure to his Companions. He himself departed. He passed the Kabah before the dawn prescribed prayer and went round it and then proceeded. He then went away facing Madinah.]

AD v2 p532 n2001

AYISHA RELATED:

On the day of sacrifice, God's Messenger postponed the circumambulation of the pilgrimage until night.

T [MMR v1 p574]

AYISHA RELATED:

The Companions of God's Messenger who accompanied him did not circumambulate the Kabah until they had thrown pebbles at the *jamrah* [pillar at Mina].

AD v2 p499 n1891

May Be Deferred

AYISHA RELATED:

The Messenger allowed the deferment of the circumambulation of the pilgrimage until the night of the 10th of Dhi Hajjah.

T [MMT v3 p151]; T [H v3 p634]

Obligatory Circumambulation

UMM SALAMA RELATED:

The night which the Messenger of God passed with her was the one that followed the day of sacrifice. He came to her and Wahb ibn Zamah also entered. A man belonging to the lineage of Abu Umayya accompanied him. Both of them were wearing shirts. The Messenger said to Wahb, 'Did you perform the obligatory circumambulation?' He said that he did not. The Prophet told him to take off his shirt, and he did. His Companion too took off his shirt. They asked why. The Messenger replied, 'On this day you have been allowed to leave the sacred state and become as you were before you threw stones at the pillars until you perform the circumambulation of the Kabah.'

AD v2 p530 n1994

AYISHA RELATED:

The Prophet postponed the circumambulation on the day of sacrifice until the night.

AD v2 p530 n1995

Performing the Circumambulation After the Dawn and Afternoon Prescribed Prayers

AYISHA RELATED:

Some people performed the circumambulation of the Kabah after the morning prescribed prayer and then sat to listen to a preacher until sunrise. Then they stood up for the prescribed prayer. She commented that those people kept on sitting until the time in which praying the prescribed prayer is disliked. After that they stood up for the prescribed prayer.

SB v2 p405 n694

KABAH

AYISHA RELATED:

The Prophet left her in a happy mood, but he returned in a sad mood. He said, 'I entered the Kabah. If I had known beforehand what I came to know later, I would not have entered it. I am afraid I have put my community in hardship.'

AD v2 p538 n2024; AD v2 p468 n1780

MINA

AYISHA RELATED:

They asked God's Messenger whether they should not put up a building to shade him in Mina. He replied, 'No. Mina is a resting place for the camels of those who get there first.'

IM [MMR v1 p563]; AD v2 p536 n2014; T [H v3 p618]

MUDALIFA

Camping in Mahassab or Abtah

AYISHA RELATED:

Al-Abtah (al-Mahassab situated between Makkah and Mina or Hasba or Khaif Bani Kinana) was a place where the Prophet camped so that it might be easier for him to depart.

SB v2 p473 n818; SM v2B p292 n1298; AD v2 p532 n2003

Early Return from al-Mudalifa

AYISHA RELATED:

The Prophet sent Umm Salama on the night before the day of sacrifice, and she threw pebbles at the stone pillars before dawn. She hastened [to Makkah] and performed the circumambulation. That day was the one the Messenger of God spent with her.

AD v2 p514 n1937

AYISHA RELATED:

Sawda, who was bulky, sought permission from God's Messenger on the night of Mudalifa to move from there ahead of him and before the multitude set forth. He gave her permission. She then set forth before God's Messenger, but she [Ayisha] and the others stayed there until dawn and then moved on when the Messenger departed. She remarked that it would have been better for her if she had done what Sawda had done.

SM v2B p282 n1290, R1-R2; SB v2 p433 n740; SM v2B p283 n1292, R1

PREPARATIONS FOR THE PRESCRIBED PILGRIMAGE

DUBAAH BINT AL-ZUBAYR IBN ABD AL-MUTTALIB RELATED:

She asked God's Messenger if she could make a proviso as part of her intention to perform the prescribed pilgrimage. He said that she could. She asked what she should say. He said, 'Say: I am here, O God, I am here. The place where I leave the sacred state will be where You restrained me.'

AD v2 p465 n1772

SACRED STATE

Ending After the Sacrifice

HAFSA RELATED:

The Prophet ordered all his wives to end their sacred state during the year of the farewell pilgrimage. Upon hearing that, she asked the Prophet why he did not end his sacred state. He said, 'I have matted my hair and garlanded my animal to be sacrificed so I will not end my sacred state until I have slaughtered my animal.'

SB v5 p481 n681; SB v2 p441 n754; SB v7 p524 n798; SB v2 p372 n637; SM v2B p253; AD v2 p468 n1802

Farewell Pilgrimage

AYISHA RELATED:

They set out with God's Messenger. Some of them assumed the sacred state for the shorter pilgrimage and some for the prescribed pilgrimage and some for both. The Messenger assumed the sacred state for the prescribed pilgrimage. Those who had assumed the sacred state for the prescribed pilgrimage or for both did not end their sacred state until the day of the sacrifice.

SB v5 p483 n690

From Masjid al-Aqsa to the Kabah

UMM SALAMA RELATED:

She heard God's Messenger say, 'If anyone puts on the sacred dress for the prescribed pilgrimage or the shorter pilgrimage from the Aqsa mosque to the sacred mosque, his former and latter sins will be forgiven or he will be guaranteed paradise.'

AD v2 p457 n1737; IM [MMR v1]; IM [Hv3p577]

Miscellaneous

AYISHA RELATED:

They set out with the Messenger of God for the prescribed pilgrimage, and when they reached Sarif, she began to menstruate. When the Messenger of God went to her, she was weeping. He asked, 'Why are you weeping? Perhaps you began to menstruate?' She said that she had. He then said, 'This is the thing which God has ordained for all the daughters of Adam. Do what all the pilgrims do, except do not perform the circumambulation around the Kabah until you are purified.' The Messenger of God sacrificed a cow on behalf of his wives.

N v1E p250 n293; SB v1 p187 n313; SB v1 p177 n293; SB v1 p182 n302; SB v1 p188 n314; SB v7 p330 n466; SB v2 p417 n712; N v1E p279 n351; N v1E p230 n245

ASMA BINT ABU BAKR RELATED:

They set out for Makkah in the sacred state. God's Messenger said, 'He who has a sacrificial animal with him should remain in the sacred state.' She did not have a sacrifical animal. She changed her clothes and went out and sat by Zubayr [her husband]. He told her to get away from him. She asked him if he was afraid she would jump on him.

SM v2B p257 n1236, R1

HAFSA RELATED:

God's Messenger said, 'It is not sinful for a pilgrim to kill five kinds of animals: the crow, the hawk, the mouse, the scorpion and the rabid dog.'

SB v3 p34 n54; SB v4 p335 n531; SM v2B p215 n1198, R1-R2, R4-R6; SM v2B p216 n1200

On a Man Who Beats His Slave While He Is In the Sacred State

ASMA BINT ABU BAKR RELATED:

They came to perform the prescribed pilgrimage along with God's Messenger. When they reached al-Araj, the Messenger alighted from his camel, and everyone else did the same. Ayisha sat beside the Messenger, and Asma sat beside her father, Abu Bakr. The equipment and personal effects of Abu Bakr and the Messenger were placed with Abu Bakr's slave on a camel. Abu Bakr sat and waited for the Messenger's arrival. When he arrived, Abu Bakr saw no camel with him. He asked him where the camel was, and the slave replied that he had lost it the night before. Abu Bakr said that it was the only camel they had and began to beat him, while the Messenger was smiling and saying, 'Look at that man who is in the sacred state and what he is doing.'

AD v2 p480 n1814; IM v2u p437 n1098

On a Pilgrim Who is Provided Shelter From the Heat

UMM HUSAYN RELATED:

They performed the farewell pilgrimage along with the Prophet. She saw Usama and Bilal, one of them holding the halter of the she-camel of the Prophet while the other raised his garment and sheltered the Prophet from the heat until he had thrown pebbles at the stone pillars at Aqaba.

AD v2 p484 n1830

Performing Both Types Depends Upon

UMM SALAMA RELATED:

They went out with the Messenger during the farewell pilgrimage and assumed the sacred state for the shorter pilgrimage. Then God's Messenger said to them, 'Whoever has brought his animal for sacrifice should assume the sacred state for both the prescribed pilgrimage and the shorter pilgrimage and should not end his sacred state until he has performed both.' She arrived at Makkah along with the Messenger while she was menstruating so she did not perform the circumambulation around the Kabah or run between Safa and Marwa. She informed the Messenger of this, and he said, 'Undo your briads and comb your hair. Then assume the sacred state for the prescribed pilgrimage and leave the shorter pilgrimage.' She did so, and when they performed and finished the prescribed pilgrimage, God's Messenger sent her to al-Tanin along with her brother, Abd al-Rahman ibn Abu Bakr al-Siddiq, to perform the shorter pilgrimage. The Prophet said, 'This shorter pilgrimage is in place of your missed one.' Those who had assumed the sacred state for the shorter pilgrimage performed the circumambulation around the Kabah and the run between Safa and Marwa and then ended their sacred state. On their return from Mina, they performed another circumambulation around the Kabah and ran between Safa and Marwa, but those who combined their prescribed pilgrimage and shorter pilgrimage ran only once betweeen Safa and Marwa for both.

> SB v5 p479 n678; SB v2 p364 n632; SB v2 p364 n627; SB v2 p409 n702; SB v4 p126 n201; SB v2 p471 n815; SB v3 p5 n4; SB v3 p9 n16; SM v2B p225; AD v2 p468 n1777; AD v2 p467 n1775; AD v2 p468 n1778; AD v2 p467 n1774; AD v2 p528 n1990; SB v2 p371 n633

Perfume

AYISHA RELATED:

She scented God's Messenger both when he assumed the sacred state and ended the sacred state before the circumambulation around the Kabah.

> SB v2 p356 n612

AYISHA RELATED:

They were proceeding to Makkah along with the Prophet. They pasted the perfume called *sakk* on their foreheads at the time of assuming the sacred state. When one of them perspired, the perfume dripped down on her face. The Prophet saw but did not forbid it.

> AD v2 p483 n1826

AYISHA RELATED:

She could still see the glistening of the perfume where the hair parted on God's Messenger's head when he was in the sacred state.

> SM v2B p210 n1190, R1-R7; SB v7 p525 n800; v1 p166 n271; AD v2 p458 n1742

AYISHA RELATED:

She perfumed God's Messenger with a perfume containing musk before he assumed the sacred state, both on the day of sacrifice and upon the conclusion of the sacred state before circumambulating the Kabah.

> SM v2B p211 n1191

AYISHA RELATED:

She applied perfume to the Prophet with her own hands when he wanted to assume the sacred state. She also perfumed him at Mina before he departed from there to perform the final circumambulation of the Kabah.

> SB v7 p528 n805; AD v2 p458 n1741

AYISHA RELATED:

She perfumed the Prophet before he assumed the sacred state with the best scent available.

> SB v7 p531 n812

AYISHA RELATED:

During the final prescribed pilgrimage, she perfumed God's Messenger with *dharira* with her own hands, both on his assuming the sacred state and on finishing it.

> SB v7 p531 n814

AYISHA RELATED:

She put perfume on God's Messenger, and he went round his wives. In the morning he assumed the sacred state, and the fragrance of scent was still coming from his body.

N v1E p315 n433

Permissibility of Assuming the Sacred State Provisionally Because of Possible Illness

AYISHA RELATED:

God's Messenger went into the house of Dubaa bint Zubayr and asked her if she intended to perform the prescribed pilgrimage. She said that she wanted to but always remained ill. The Prophet said to her, 'Perform the prescribed pilgrimage but with a condition. Say, "O God, I shall be free from the sacred state when you detain me."'

SM v2B p223 n1207, R7

Talbiya

AYISHA RELATED:

The Prophet used to say talbiya in the following way, "Labbaika allahumma labbaik, labbaika la sharika laka labbaik, innal hamda wan-nimata laka wal-mulk, la sharika laka."

SB v2 p361 n622

SAFA AND MARWA

"And Manat the third..." [53:20]

AYISHA RELATED:

She was asked about running between Safa and Marwa. She said that those who assume the sacred state in the name of the idol Manat placed in al-Mushallal—out of reverence for it— used not to perform the running between Safa and Marwa so God revealed, "Verily Safa and Marwa are among the Signs of God" [2:158]. Thereupon God's Messenger and the Muslims performed the search betwen them. Sufyan said that Manat was at al-Mushallal in Qudaid. She added that the verse was revealed in connection with the Helpers. They and the tribe of Ghassan used to assume the sacred state in the name of Manat before they embraced Islam. She said that there were men from the Helpers who used to assume the sacred state in the name of Manat which was an idol between Makkah and Madinah. They told the Messenger that they did not perform the running or search between Safa and Marwa because of reverence for Manat.

SB v6 p362 n384

Reward of the Shorter Pilgrimage

AYISHA RELATED:

She said to the Messenger that people ran between Safa and Marwa after performing the two pilgrimages, but she only ran once.

He said, 'Wait until you become purified from menses and then go to al-Tanim, assume the sacred state, and after performing the shorter pilgrimage, join us at such and such a place. But it is according to your expenses or the hardship which you will undergo while performing it.'

SB v3 p8 n15

Running Between Safa and Marwa

AYISHA RELATED:

She was asked by her nephew how she interpreted the verse of the Quran, *"Verily Safa and Marwa are among the signs of God and whoever performs the prescribed pilgrimage to the Kabah or performs the shorter pilgriamge, it is not harmful for him to perform the circumambulation between them [Safa and Marwa]"* [2:158]. Her nephew felt that based on this verse, there was no harm if one did not run between Safa and Marwa. Ayisha said that his interpretation was not true. She said that had his interpretation been correct, the statement of God should have been: It is not harmful for him if he does not perform the running between them. However, in fact, the revelation concerned the Helpers who used to assume the sacred state to worship an idol called Manat which they worshiped at a place called Mushallal before they embraced Islam. Whoever assumed the sacred state [for the idol] would consider it not right to run between Safa and Marwa. When they accepted Islam, they asked God's Messenger about this. He referred to the above verse. She added that no one is allowed to omit the running between them.

SB v2 p412 n706

SHORTER PILGRIMAGE

Performing the Shorter Pilgrimage

UMM MAQIL RELATED:

When God's Messenger performed the farewell pilgrimage, Abu Maqil dedicated our camel to the path of God. Then we suffered from a disease. Abu Maqil died. The Prophet went out for the prescribed pilgrimage. When he finished it, she went to him. He asked her, 'Umm Maqil, what prevented you from coming out for the prescribed pilgrimage along with us?' She told him that she and her husband had made the intention to do that, but then her husband had died. They had a camel on which they could perform the prescribed pilgrimage, but Abu Maqil had bequeathed it for the path of God. The Messenger asked, 'Why did you not go out for the prescribed pilgrimage upon it for the prescribed pilgrimage is the path of God? If you missed this prescribed pilgrimage with us, perform the shorter pilgrimage during Ramadan, for it is like the prescribed pilgrimage.'

She said that the prescribed pilgrimage was the prescribed pilgrimage, and that the shorter pilgrimage was the shorter pilgrimage. She said that the Messenger told her this, and that she did not know if it was peculiar to her or not.

AD v2 p527 n1984

AYISHA RELATED:

God's Messenger performed two shorter pilgrimages: one in Dhi Qadah and the other in Shawwal.

AD v2 p527 n1986

To Go on the Prescribed Pilgrimage On the Pack Saddle of a Camel

AYISHA RELATED:

She said to the Messenger that he had performed the shorter pilgrimage, but she did not. The Messenger said, "O Abd al-Rahman! Go with your sister and let her perform the shorter pilgrimage from Tanim.' Abd al-Rahman let her ride over the pack-saddle of a she-camel, and she performed the shorter pilgrimage.

SB v2 p346 n593

STONING THE IDOLS

AYISHA RELATED:

God's Messenger performed the obligatory circumambulation of the Kabah at the end of the day of sacrifice after he had offered the noon prescribed prayer. He then returned to Mina and stayed there during the *tashriq* days. He threw pebbles at the pillars when the sun set. He threw seven pebbles at each of the pillars, uttering 'God is Greater' as he threw each pebble. He stood at the first and the second pillar and prolonged his stay there, making supplications with humility. He threw pebbles at the third pillar but did not stand there.

AD v2 p522 n1968

AYISHA RELATED:

God's Messenger said, 'When one of you throws pebbles at the last pillar [*jamrat al-Aqabah*], everything becomes lawful for him except his wife [sexual intercourse].'

AD v2 p524 n1973; T [MMR v1]; T [Hv3 p618]

UMM AL-HUSAYN RELATED:

She performed the prescribed pilgrimage along with God's Messenger on the occasion of the farewell pilgrimage and saw him throw pebbles at the Jamrat al-Aqaba and saw him riding a camel. Bilal and Usama were with him. One of them was leading his camel while the other was raising his cloth over the head of God's Messenger to protect him from the sun. God's Messenger said so many things. She heard him say, 'Even if a slave, having a missing limb and having a dark complexion, is appointed to govern you according to the

Book of God, listen to him and obey him.'
SM v2B p286 n1298, R1

TIME OF THE PRESCRIBED PILGRIMAGE

AYISHA RELATED:

They set out with God's Messenger in the months of the prescribed pilgrimage and on the nights of the prescribed pilgrimage and at the time and places of the prescribed pilgrimage and in the ritual state of the prescribed pilgrimage. They dismounted at Sarif [a village six miles from Makkah]. The Prophet then addressed his Companions and said, 'Anyone who has not brought his sacrificial animal and wants to perform the shorter pilgrimage instead of the prescribed pilgrimage or anyone who has the sacrificial animal should not end the sacred state after performing the shorter pilgrimage.' She added that the Companions of the Prophet obeyed the above order, and some of them ended the sacred state after the shorter pilgrimage. God's Messenger and some of his Companions were resourceful and had the sacrificial animal with them. They could not perform the shorter pilgrimage alone but had to perform both of them with one sacred state.
SB v2 p364 n631; SB v2 p446 n767; SB v2 p452 n778; AD v2 p468 n1779

TYPES

AYISHA RELATED:

God's Messenger performed the prescribed pilgrimage exclusively without performing the shorter pilgrimage at the beginning.
AD v2 p466 n1773

WOMAN'S JIHAD

AYISHA RELATED:

She said to the Prophet that Muslims consider *jihad* as the best deed. The Prophet said, 'The best *jihad* for women is the prescribed pilgrimage.'
SB v2 p347 n595

PART V:
PROGRAM OF ACTION:
POLITICAL ISSUES

CHAPTER 1
GOVERNMENT

ADMINISTRATION OF LAW

BURAYDA RELATED:

The Messenger said, 'Judges [officers of the court] are of three kinds: one of them deserves heaven and two deserve hell. Deserving of heaven is the judge who grasps the truth and decides accordingly, while the judge who does not decide justly, even after grasping the truth, is deserving of hell. The same is the case with the judge who lacks knowledge and is ignorant and, yet, ventures to pass judgment."

IM [MMT v4 p411]

EMIGRATION

AYISHA RELATED:

When the Messenger was asked about migration, he said, 'There is no more migration after the conqust of Makkah but struggle and sincere intention. When you are asked to set out for the cause of Islam, you should set out.'

SM v3A p268 n1864

RULERSHIP

Appointment of Ministers

AYISHA RELATED:

God's Messenger said, 'When God has a good purpose for a ruler, He appoints for him a sincere minister who reminds him if he forgets and helps him if he remembers. When God has a different purpose from that for him, He appoints for him an evil minister who does not remind him if he forgets and does not help him if he remembers.'

AD v2 p828 n2926; N [H v2 p585]

155

Justification for Hating the Amirs for Violating the Laws of the Shariah

UMM SALAMA RELATED:

God's Messenger said, 'In the near future there will be Amirs, and you will like their good deeds and dislike their bad deeds. One who sees their bad deeds [and tries to prevent their repetition by his hand or through his speech] is absolved from blame, but one who hates their bad deeds [in the heart of his heart being unable to prevent their recurrence by his hand or his tongue] is also safe [as far as God's wrath is concerned]; however, one who approves their bad deeds and imitates them is spiritually ruined.' People asked if they should not fight against them and the Messenger said, 'No as long as they offer their prescribed prayers.'

SM v3A p261 n1854, R1-R3

Chapter 2
Judicial Decisions

Judge Cannot Make Halal into Haram

Umm Salama related:

God's Messenger heard some people quarrelling at the door of his dwelling. He went out to them and said, 'I am only a human being. Litigants with cases of dispute come to me. One of you may happen to be more eloquent in presenting his case than the other; therefore, I might consider him truthful and pass a judgment in his favor. If ever I passed a judgment in favor of somebody whereby he took a Muslims' right unjustly, then whatever he took was nothing but a piece of fire. It is up to him to take it or leave it.'

> SB v9 p221 n292; SB v9 p79 n97; SB v9 p223 n295; SB v9 p212 n281; SB v3A p381 n638; SB v3 p542 n868; SB v3 p523 n845; SM v3A p149 n1713R2; AD v3 p1016 n3576; IM v2u p197 n475

Umm Salama related:

When two men were disputing over inheritance, the Messenger said, 'I decide between you on the basis of my opinion in cases about which no revelation has been sent down to me.'

> AD v3 p1016 n3578

Judicial Office

Umm Salama related:

Two men came to the Messenger of God who were disputing over their inheritance. They had no evidence except their claims. The Prophet noticed this. Thereupon, both the men wept, and each of them was concerned that his right might go to the other one. The Prophet then said, 'Now you have done whatever you have done so divide it up, aiming at what is right. Then draw lots, and let each of you consider the other to have what is legitimately his.'

> AD v3 p1016 n3577

OFFICES OF COMMANDER AND JUDGE

AYISHA RELATED:

The Messenger said, 'The testimony of a deceitful man or woman or of one who has been flogged for transgressing the bounds set by God or of one who harbors rancour against his brother or of one suspected regarding the patrons he claims or of one who is dependent on a family is not allowable.'

T [MMR v1 p804]

Chapter 3
Oaths

Commanders

UMM SALAMA RELATED:

God's Messenger said, 'You will have commanders some of whom you will approve and some of whom you will disapprove. He who expresses disapproval with his tongue is guiltless. He who feels disapproval in his heart is safe, but he who is pleased, follows them.' When asked if they should kill them the Prophet said, 'No so long as they pray.'

AD v3 p1332 n4742

Conditions

Allegiance of Women

AYISHA RELATED:

God's Messenger questioned women according to the verse, '*O you who believe! When the believing women come to you as emigrants, test them. . . for God is Oft-forgiving, Most Merciful*' [60:10-12]. She [Ayisha] then added when any of them agreed to those conditions [that they will not worship other than God, will not steal, will not commit illegal sexual intercourse, will not kill their children, will not slander others, and will not disobey the Prophet in just matters], God's Messenger would say to her, 'I have accepted your pledge of allegiance.' He would only say that. By God he never touched the hand of any woman [that is, never shook hands with them] while taking the pledge of allegiance, and he never took their pledge of allegiance except by his words only.'

SB v3 p548 n874; SB v6 p385 n415; SM v3A p268 n1866 R1

HAFSA RELATED:

When the verse, '*When believing women came to you giving you a*

159

pledge that they will not associate anything with God and will not disobey you in good,' was revealed, Umm Atiyya said that this pledge also included wailing. She said to the Messenger that members of such a tribe helped her (in lamentation) during pre-Islamic days and that she must, therefore, return the favor.' There was no alternative left for her but to help them. Upon this the Messenger of God said, 'Yes but only the members of such a tribe.'

SM v2A p53 n937; AD v2 p828 n2935; SB v9 p244 n321; IM v2u p415 n1038

Commandment For Fulfilling the Vow

MAYMUNA BINT KARDAM RELATED:

She went with her father for the prescribed pilgrimage. She saw the Meesenger of God and heard the people say that it was him. She fixed her eyes on him. Her father went near him while he was riding his she-camel. He had a rod like the rod of scribes. She heard the bedouins and the people indicating the rod. Her father went near the Messenger and held his foot. She said he accepted Islam and stood and listened to him. He told the Messenger of God that he had made a vow that if he had a male child, he would slaughter a number of sheep at the end of Buwanah in the dale of a hill. The Messenger of God said, 'Does it contain any idol?' He said that it did not. The Messenger said, 'Fulfill your vow that you have taken for God.' Her father then gathered them [the sheep], and began to slaughter them. A sheep ran away. He searched for it, asking God to help him find it so he could fulfil his vow. He found it and slaughtered it.

AD v2 p939 n3308; AD v2 p939 n3309; AD v2 p979 n3406

AYISHA RELATED:

The Prophet said, 'O followers of Muhammad. By God if you knew what I know, you would weep much and laugh little.'

SB v8 p408 n618; SB v8 p408 n627

Oaths Not Permitted

AYISHA RELATED:

The Prophet said, 'Whoever vows that he will be obedient to God should remain obedient to Him. Whoever made a vow that he will disobey God, should not disobey Him.'

SB v8 p448 n687; SB v8 p452 n691

AYISHA RELATED:

The Messenger of God said, 'No vow must be taken to do an act of disobedience, and the atonement for it is the same as for an oath.'

AD v2 p934 n3283

Violation of Oaths

AYISHA RELATED:

The verse, 'God will not call you to account for that which is unintentional in your oaths...' [2:225], was revealed concerning such oath formulas as, 'No by God!' and 'Yes by God!'

SB v8 p427 n656; AD v2 p924 n3248; SB v6 p79 n138; SB v6 p109 n137

CHAPTER 4
PRESCRIBED PUNISHMENT

Capital Crimes
AYISHA RELATED:

Only one woman of the Qurayzah tribe was killed. She was with Ayisha talking and laughing on her back and belly while the Messenger of God was killing her people with swords. Suddenly a man called her by name and asked where she was. The woman said that she was there. She (Ayisha) asked why the woman she had done that, and the woman said that she had [abused the Prophet]. The man took her and beheaded her. She (Ayisha) said that she would not forget that the woman was laughing although she knew that she would be killed.

AD v2 p709 n2665

AYISHA RELATED:

The Messenger of God said, 'The blood of a Muslim man who testifies that there is no god but God and that Muhammad is God's Messenger should not lawfully be shed except in three instances: a man who commits fornication after marriage in which case he should be stoned; one who goes forth to fight against God and His Messenger in which case he should be killed or crucified or exiled from the land; and one who commits murder for which he is killed.'

AD v3 p1212 n4339

Eighty Lashes
AYISHA RELATED:

When the verse about her innocence was revealed the Prophet went on the *minbar* and informed the audience of this. He ordered that two men and a woman be given eighty lashes for falsely accusing her.

IM v2u p291 n732

161

False Accusation

AYISHA RELATED:

When her vindication was revealed, the Prophet went on the *minbar*, mentioned that, and recited the Quran. Then when he came down from the *minbar,* he ordered the prescribed punishment for the two men and the woman [who had spread the lie about her].

> AD v3 p1249 n4459

Forgiveness

AYISHA RELATED:

The Prophet said, 'Disputants should refrain from taking retaliation. The one who is nearer should forgive first, and then the one who is next to him, even if [the one who forgives] is a woman.'

> AD v3 p1273 n4523

AYISHA RELATED:

The Prophet sent Abu Jahm ibn Hudhayfa as a collector of the poor-due. A man quarrelled with him about his share. Abu Jahm struck him and wounded his head. The people asked for retaliation. The Prophet made three offers, and finally the last offer was accepted. The Prophet said he was going to address the people in the afternoon and tell them that the parties had consented. He then asked the Emigrants if they accepted. They did not at first but did so when he increased the amount [of compensation]. He then told the people.

> AD v3 p1273 n4519

AYISHA RELATED:

God's Messenger said, 'Forgive the people of good qualities their slips but not faults to which prescribed penalties apply.'

> AD v3 p1219 n4362

AYISHA RELATED:

The Quraysh became very worried about the Makhzumi woman who had commited theft. They said that the only person who could speak in her favor to the Messenger was Usama as she was a favorite of his. When Usama spoke to God's Messenger about this matter, the Messenger said, 'Do you intercede with me to violate one of the legal punishments of God?' Then he got up and addressed the people. He said, 'O people! The nations before you went astray because if a noble person committed theft, that person what unpunished; but if a weak person among them committed theft, they inflicted the legal punishment on him. By God if Fatima, the daughter of Muhammad, committed theft, Muhammd would cut off her hand!'

> SB v8 p512 n779; SB v8 p512 n778; SB v4 p453 n681; SM v3A p130 n1688;
> AD v3 p1218 n4360; AD v3 p1218 n4361; AD v3 p1226 n4382; AD v3 p1226
> n4383; IM v2u p283 n712; IM v2u p298 n751; N [H v2 p569]

Repentance

AYISHA RELATED:

The Prophet cut off the hand of a woman. That woman used to come to her, and she (Ayisha) conveyed her message to the Prophet. She repented, and her repentance was sincere.

SB v8 p517 n792

Theft

AYISHA RELATED:

The hand of a thief was not cut off during the lifetime of the Prophet, except for stealing something equal to a shield in value.

SB v8 p516 n783; SB v8 p516 n784; SB v8 p516 n785; SB v8 p516 n786

AYISHA RELATED:

The Prophet said, 'The hand should be cut off for stealing something that is worth a quarter of a dinar or more.'

SB v8 p515 n780; SB v8 p515 n781; SB v8 p515 n782; SB v8 p516 n783; SM v3A p127 n1684; AD v3 p1222 n4370; AD v3 1222 n4371

Who is Exempt?

AYISHA RELATED:

God's Messenger said, 'There are three persons whose actions are not recorded: a sleeper until he awakens, an idiot until he is restored to reason and a boy until he reaches puberty.'

AD v3 p1226 n4384

TRY TO AVOID

AYISHA RELATED:

The Messenger said, 'Avert the infliction of prescribed penalties on Muslims as much as you can. If there is any way out, let a man go for it is better for a leader to make a mistake in forgiving than to make a mistake in punishing.'

T [MMR v1 p762]; T [Hv2 p545]

CHAPTER 5
STRUGGLE IN GOD'S WAY

ARMY EXPEDITION

Battle of Khandaq

AYISHA RELATED:

Regarding the verse, *'When they came on you from above and from below you [from East and West of the valley] and when the eyes grew wild and the hearts reached up to the throats,'* [33:10], this happened on the day of Khandaq [Battle of the Trenches].

SB v5 p299 n429; SM v4B p400 n3020

Battle of Khaybar

AYISHA RELATED:

When Khaybar was conquered, they said, 'Now we will eat our fill of dates.'

SB v5 p384 n547

Bringing Back the Wounded

RUBAYYI BINT MUAUWIDH RELATED:

They took part in the struggle in God's Way with the Prophet by providing the people with water and serving them and bringing the martyred and wounded back to Madinah.

SB v4 p87 n134

Clemency

AYISHA RELATED:

She asked the Messenger if there had come upon him a day more terrible than the day of Uhud. He said, 'I experienced from your people the hardest treatment. This was what I received on the day of [Taif]. I took myself to Ibn Abd Yalil Abd Kulal with the purpose of inviting him to Islam, but he did not respond to me as I desired so I departed with signs of deep distress on my face. I did not recover until I reached Qarn al-Thaalib. When I raised my head, near me was a cloud which had cast its shadow on me. I looked, and there was in it the angel Gabriel who called out to me and said, 'God, the Exalted and Glorious, has heard what your people have said to you, how they have reacted to your call. He has sent to you the angel in charge of the mountains so that you may order him in regard to them.' The angel in charge of the mountain then called out to me, greeted me, and said, 'Muhammad, God has listened to what your people have said to you. I am the angel in charge of the mountains, and your Lord has sent me to you so that you may order me as wish. If you wish me to bring together the two mountains that stand opposite each other at the extremities of Makkah to crush them, I will do that.' The Messenger said to him, 'I rather hope that God will produce from their descendants such persons as will worship God, the One, and will not ascribe partners to Him.'

SM v3A p213 n1795

Entering Makkah From the Upper Part

AYISHA RELATED:

During the year of the conquest of Makkah, the Prophet entered Makkah through the upper part.

SB v5 p408 n585

fitna

UMM MALIK AL-BAHZIYA RELATED:

When God's Messenger mentioned civil strife and its nearness, she asked him who would be the best of people during it, and he replied, 'A man with his cattle who pays the poor-due on them and worships his Lord and a man who holds his horse's head and causes fear for the enemy while they are causing him fear.'

T [MMR v2 p1126]

Martyr's Reward

AYISHA RELATED:

When Negus died, they were told that a light would be seen perpetually at his grave.

AD v2 p699 n2517

On a Woman Granting Protection to a Non-Muslim

AYISHA RELATED:

A woman believer would give security to a non-Muslim, and it would be allowed.

AD v2 p772 n2758

Responding to the Call

AYISHA RELATED:

Regarding the verse, 'Those who responded [to the call] of God and the Messenger after being wounded, for those of them who did good deeds and refrained from wrong, there is a great reward,' [3:172], she said to her nephew that his father, Zubayr, and Abu Bakr were among those who responded to the call of God and the Messenger on the day of the Battle of Uhud. When God's Messenger suffered what he suffered on the day of Uhud and the pagans left, the Prophet was afraid that they might return. He asked them who would follow the tracks of the unbelievers. He then selected seventy men from among them for this purpose [Abu Bakr and al-Zubayr were among them].

SB v5 p279 n404

Should a Polytheist Be Given a Share From the Booty If He Accompanies Muslims in Battle

AYISHA RELATED:

A man from the polytheists accompanied the Prophet to fight with him. He said, 'Go back.' Both the narrators then agreed that the Prophet said, 'We do not want any help from a polytheist.'

AD v2 p761 n2726

Struggle in God's Way for Women

AYISHA RELATED:

She asked the Prophet to permit her to participate in the struggle in God's Way. He said, "Your struggle is to perform the prescribed pilgrimage."

SB v4 p83 n127; SB v4 p83 n128; SB v4 n43; IM [Hv3 p578]]

Taking a Bath After Fighting

AYISHA RELATED:

When God's Messenger returned on the day [of the battle] of Khandaq, he put down his arms and took a bath. Then Gabriel, whose head was covered with dust, came to him saying "You have put down your arms! By God, I have not put down my arms yet." God's Messenger said, "Where should I go now?" Gabriel said, "This way," pointing towards the Qurayza tribe. God's Messenger went out towards them.

SB v4 p52 n68; SB v5 p306 n443

The Sitting of a Woman Behind Her Brother as a Companion-Rider

AYISHA RELATED:

She said to the Messenger that his Companions were returning with the reward of both the shorter pilgrimage and the prescribed pilgrimage while she was returning with the reward of the prescribed pilgrimage only. He told her to go with her brother Abd al-Rahman. "You sit behind him on the animal." He ordered Abd al-Rahman to let her perform the shorter pilgrimage from al-Tanim. Then he waited for her at the ihgher region of Makkah until she returned.

SB v4 p143 n227

To Set a Prisoner of War Free by Taking Ransom

AYISHA RELATED:

When the people of Makkah ransomed their prisoners, Zaynab

sent some property to ransom Abu al-As. Among this property was a necklace of hers which her mother, Khadijah, had given her when she married Abu 'l-As. When God's Messenger saw it, he felt great tenderness about it, and said, 'If you consider that you should free her prisoner for her and return to her what belongs to her, it will be well.' They said that they agreed. God's Messenger made an agreement with Abu 'l-As that he should let Zaynab come to him. The Messenger sent Zayd ibn Haritha and a man from among the Helpers and said, 'Wait in the valley of Yajia until Zaynab passes you. Then accompany her and bring her back.'

AD v2 p747 n2686; AD v2 p764 n2686

What is Permitted

AYISHA RELATED:

The Prophet said, 'Cunning and cheating is permissible in war. In fact, war is the name of cunning.'

IM v2u p398 n995

Who Can Participate

AYISHA RELATED:

God's Messenger set out for Badr. When he reached Harrat ul-Wabara [a place four miles from Madinah], a man met him who was known for his valor and courage. The Companions were pleased to see him. He said that he had come to follow the Messenger and get a share of the booty. The Messenger of God asked him, 'Do you believe in God and His Messenger?' He said, 'No. The Messenger of God said, 'Go back. I will not seek help from a polytheist.' He went on until we reached Shajara where the man met him again. He asked him the same question again, and the man gave him the same answer. He said, 'Go back. I will not seek help from a polytheist.' The man returned and overtook him at Gaida. He asked him what he had asked previously, 'Do you believe in God and His Messenger?' The man said that he did. The Prophet then said to him, 'Then come along with us.'

SM v3A p234 n1817

Women Participants

RUBAYYI BINT MUAUWIDH RELATED:

They were in the company of the Prophet providing the wounded with water and treating them and taking the marytred to Madinah [from the battlefield].

SB v4 p87 n133

UMM ATIYA RELATED:

She took part with God's Messenger in seven battles. She would stay behind in the camp of the men, cook their food, treat the wounded and nurse the sick.

SM v3A p232 n1812R6

NAVAL EXPEDITION

UMM HARAM, DAUGHTER OF MILHAN, WIFE OF UBADA IBN SAMIT [SISTER OF HIS FOSTER-MOTHER OR HIS FATHER'S AUNT, RELATED:

One day God's Messenger paid her a visit. She entertained him with food and then sat down to delouse his head. He dozed off, and when he woke up, he was laughing. He was asked what made him laugh. He said, 'Some people from my nation were presented to me who were fighters in the way of God and were sailing in this sea (gliding smoothly on the water). They appeared to be kings or like kings sitting on thrones.' She asked if she would be considered among the warriors. He prayed for her. He than placed his head down and dozed off again. He woke up laughing as before. She asked him what made him laugh. He replied, 'People from my nation were presented to me. They were fighters in God's way. He described them with the same words as he had described the first warriors. She asked him to pray to God that God might include her among these warriors. He said, 'You are among the first ones.'

SM v3A p268 n1912, R1-R2; AD v2 p875 n3074; AD v2 p676 n2486; AD v2 p689 n2487

CHAPTER 6
WITNESSES

INADMISSIBLE EVIDENCE

AYISHA RELATED:

The Messenger of God said, 'The deposition of a treacherous man or a treacherous woman is not admissible nor is that of a man who has been whipped for an ordained crime nor is that of a man who has enmity with his brother nor is that of a slave who attributes his freedom to a stranger nor is that of a relative nor is that of a man who is pleased with the members of his family.'

T [H v2 p623 rare]

WOMEN BEARING WITNESS TO EACH OTHER'S HONORABLE RECORD

AYISHA RELATED:

Buraira said that she had never seen anything faulty [in Ayisha] except that as a girl of immature age, she sometimes sleeps and leaves the dough for the goats to eat. That day the Messenger of God ascended the *mimbar* and asked somebody to support him in punishing Abd Allah ibn Ubay ibn Salul.

SB v3 p503 n829

PART VI:
PROGRAM OF ACTION:
SOCIAL ISSUES

CHAPTER 1
BEVERAGES

ALCOHOL

Any Drink That Intoxicates Is Forbidden

AYISHA RELATED:

The Prophet said, 'All drinks that produce intoxication are forbidden.'

SB v1 p153 n243

It Is Forbidden to Prepare Wine in Varnished Jar, Gourd, Green Pitcher or Hollow Stumps

AYISHA RELATED:

God's Messenger had forbidden the preparation of wine in gourd and varnished jars.

SM v3B p340 n1995R1, R4

Prohibition of Intoxicants

AYISHA RELATED:

God's Messenger was asked about an intoxicating drink made from honey. He said, 'Every drink that causes intoxication is forbidden.'

SM v3B p346 n2001, R1; SB v7 p343 n491; SB v1 p153 n243; SB v7 p343 n492; SB v7 p343; SB v3 p236 n429; SB v3 p168 n297; SM v3A p45 n1580R1; AD v3 p1044 n3674; AD v3 p1045 n3679

"Then be aware of taking a notice of war from God and His Messenger..." [2:279]

AYISHA RELATED:

When the last verse of Surah al-Baqara was revealed, the Messenger went out and recited the verse in the mosque and prohibited the trade of alcoholic liquors. *"If the debtor is in difficulty, grant him time until it is easy for him to repay..."* [2:280].

175

SB v6 p50 n66; SB v3 p236 n429; SB v3 p168 n297; SB v6 p49 n65; SB v6 p49 p64; SM v3A p45 n1580, R1

DATES AND RAISENS

Mixing of Various Kinds of Dates or Dates and Raisens

AYISHA RELATED:

Dates were steeped for the Messenger in a skin which was tied up at the top and had a mouth. What was steeped in the morning, he would drink in the evening; and what was stepped in the evening, he would drink in the morning.

AD v3 p1050 n3702; AD v3 p1049 n3699

AYISHA RELATED:

Amra would steep dates for the Messenger of God in the morning. When the evening came, he took his dinner and drank the date-water after his dinner. If anything remained, she poured it out. She then would steep more for him at night. When the morning came, he took his morning meal and drank the date-water after his morning meal. She said that the skin vessel was washed in the morning and in the evening. Her father [Hayyan] asked her if she did this twice a day, and she replied that she did.

AD v3 p1050 n3703; AD v3 p1045 n3697; AD v3 p1049 n3698; SM v3B p350 n2005R1

Prohibition of Intoxicants

UMM SALAMA RELATED:

The Messenger forbade them to boil dates so much that the kernels were spoiled and [forbade them] to mix raisins and dried dates.

AD v3 p1045 n3678

SAWDA RELATED:

One of their sheep died. They tanned its skin and kept on infusing dates in it until it was a worn out waterskin.

SB v8 p442 n677

SILVER UTENSILS

UMM SALAMA

God's Messenger said, 'He who drinks with silver utensils is only filling his abdomen with hell fire.'

SB v7 p367 n538; SM v3B p383 n2065

VINEGAR

AYISHA RELATED:

God's Messenger said, 'The best of condiments is vinegar.'

SM v3B p373 n2051

UMM HANI

The Prophet went to visit her and asked whether she had anything to eat. When she replied that she had nothing but some dry bread and vinegar, he said, 'Produce it. A house in which there is vinegar is not devoid of condiments.'

T [MMR v2 p894]

WELL WATER

AYISHA RELATED:

The water from al-Suqya was considered the sweetest by the Prophet [a well two days journey from Madinah].

AD v3 p1055 n3726

CHAPTER 2
DECORATION

BEDDING

In Front of Place of Prescribed Prayer

UMM SALAMA RELATED:

Her bedding was in front of the place of prescribed prayer of the Prophet.

AD v3 p1154 n4136

Prophet's Pillow

AYISHA RELATED:

The pillow of God's Messenger on which he slept at night was of leather stuffed with palm fibre.

AD v3 p1154 n4134; SM v3B p394 n2082R1; AD v3 p1154 n4135

CUSHION

ASMA RELATED:

She bought a cushion having pictures on it. When God's Messenger saw it, he stopped at the gate and did not enter. She noticed the signs of hatred on his face. She asked what she had done. He said, 'What about this cushion?' She said that she had bought it for him to sit on. God's Messenger said, 'The makers of these pictures will be punished severely on the day of resurrection when it will be said to them, "Bring to life what you have created."' He added, 'Angels do not enter a house in which there are pictures.'

SB v7 p545 n844; SB v7 p544 n842; SB v7 p542 n838; SB v7 p839; SB v7 p543 n840; SB v3 p181 n318; SB v7 p542 n838; SB v3 p397 n659; SB v7 p78 n110; SB v7 p545 n844; SB v8 p83 n130; SB v4 p297 n447; N v1E p471 n764; N v1E p471 n764

DECORATIONS

SAFINA RELATED:

A man invited Ali ibn Abi Talib to a feast. He prepared the feast for him. Fatima said that had they invited the Messenger of God, he would have taken food with them so the man called the Messenger and he came. He placed his hands upon the sides of the door but seeing a colored screen hung up in a corner of the house, he left. Then Fatima asked why he had turned back? He said, 'It is not for me or for a prophet to enter a decorated house.'

IM [H v2 p666]

UMM HABIBA

God's Messenger said, 'Angels do not go with a traveling company in which there is a bell.'

AD v2 p709 n2548

AYISHA RELATED:

Gabriel promised God's Messenger to come at a definite hour. That hour came, but he did not visit him. The Messenger had a staff in his hand. He threw it down and said, 'Never has God or His angels ever broken their promise.' Then he looked and found a puppy under his cot. He said, 'Ayisha, when did this dog enter her?' She said that she did not know. He commanded it to be put outside. Then Gabriel came and God's Messenger said to him, 'You promised me and I waited for you, but you did not come.' Gabriel said that it was the dog in his house which prevented him from coming, for angels do not enter a house in which there is a dog or a picture.

SM v3B p406 n2104; SM v3B p40 n2105

AYISHA RELATED:

Angels do not enter a hosue in which there is a picture or a dog. She said that she did not hear the Messenger narrate it herself, but that she based it on what she saw him doing. Once he set out for an expedition. She took a carpet and screened the door with it. When he returned he saw the carpet, and she perceived signs of disapproval on his face. He pulled it until it was torn or cut into pieces and said, 'God has not commanded us to clothe stones and clay.' She cut the curtain, and he did not find fault with that.

SM v3B p408 n2107, R1, R3, R5, R8-R9, R11-R14

AYISHA RELATED:

The Prophet never left anything having images or crosses in the house. He would destroy them.

SB v7 p541 n836; AD v3 p1155 n4139

CHAPTER 3
DIVORCE

ALIMONY

FATIMA BINT QAYS RELATED:

Abu Amr ibn Hafs divorced her absolutely when he was away from home. He sent his agent to her with some barley. She was displeased with him. When he said that she had no claim on the family, she went to God's Messenger and asked him. He said, 'There is no maintenance due to you from him.' He told her to spend her waiting period in the home of Umm Sharik, but then said that because many of his Companions visited her, it was better for her to spend the time with Umm Maktum [her relative] because 'He is blind and you can take off your garments. When the waiting period is over, let me know.' She did this and then mentioned that Muawiay ibn Abu Sufyan and Jahm had both sent proposals to her. God's Mesesnger said, 'As for Abu Hahm, he does not lower his staff from his shoulder, and as for Muawiya, he is a poor man, having no property so marry Usama ibn Zayd.' She objected to Usama, but when the Messenger said it a second time, she accepted. She said that God blessed them, and she was envied by others.

SM v2B p415 n1480, 1R1-R4, R7-R8, R10-R12, R15-R16, R19 ; SB v7 p185 n243; SM v2B p420 n1482; AD v2 p620 n2280; SB v7 p185 n244; SB v7 p187 n245; AD v2 p620 n2285; AD v2 p620 n2286

DIVORCE AND WAITING PERIOD OF A SLAVE WOMAN

AYISHA RELATED:

God's Messenger said, 'The divorce of a slave-woman consists in

saying it twice, and her waiting period is two menstrual courses.'
AD v2 p589 n2184; IM v2u p114 n233

DIVORCE FOR A CONSIDERATION

AYISHA RELATED:

Habiba bint Sahl was the wife of Thabit ibn Qays ibn Shimmas. He beat her and broke some part of her body. She went to the Messenger of God one morning and complained to him about her husband. The Prophet called on Thabit ibn Qays and said to him, 'Take part of her property and separate yourself from her.' Thabit asked the Messenger if this was right. The Messenger said that it was. Thabit said that he had given Habiba two gardens of his as dower which were already in her possession. The Prophet said, 'Take them and separate yourself from her.'

AD v2 p600 n2220; AD v2 p600 n2219

DIVORCE THREE TIMES

AYISHA RELATED:

The Messenger of God was asked about a man who divorced his wife three times. She married another who divorced her before having intercourse with her. He was asked if her first husband was lawful to her. The Messenger said, 'She is not lawful to the first husband until she tastes the honey of another husband, and he tastes her honey.'

AD v2 p629 n2302; SB v7 p137 n187; SB v7 p137 n2302; SB v7 p136 n186; v7 p182 n238; SB v7 p137 n193; SB v7 p137 n190; IM v2u p51 n86

SLAVE'S DIVORCE AND WAITING PERIOD

AYISHA RELATED:

Barira had to pass three menstrual periods as her waiting period when she divorced her husband.

IM v2u p114 n230

No Divorce by Force

AYISHA RELATED:

She heard the Messenger of God say, 'There is no divorce and no emancipation by force.'

IM [H v2 p705]; IM v2u p99 n197; IM [MMT v4 p313]

SUSTENANCE FOR A DIVORCEE DURING THE WAITING PERIOD

FATIMA BINT QAYS RELATED:

When her husband pronounced divorce three times, the Prophet said that she would not be provided with food and lodging.

IM v2u p95 n187; IM v2u p95 n186

WAITING PERIOD

UMM SALAMA RELATED:

The Messenger said, 'One whose husband has died must not wear garments dyed with saffron or red clay or be-jeweled garments. She must not apply henna or collyrium.

N [MMR v1 p710]

'YOU ARE AS MY MOTHER'S BACK...'

KHUWAYLAH BINT MALIK IBN THALABAH RELATED:

Her husband, Aws ibn Samit, pronounced the words, 'You are like my mother's back.' She went to the Messenger of God and complained to him about her husband. The Messenger of God said, 'Maintain your duty to God. He is your cousin.' She continued to complain until the verse was revealed, *'God has heard the saying of she who disputes with you concerning her husband'* [58:1]. The Messenger then said, 'He should set free a slave.' She said that he could not afford that. The Messenger said, 'He should fast for two consecutive months.' She said that her husband was an old man who could not fast.' The Messenger said, 'He should feed sixty poor people.' She replied that he has nothing to give in charity. At that moment a date-basket arrived holding fifteen or sixteen *sa*s. She asked if she should help him with another sixty *sa*s of dates. The Messenger said, 'You have done well. Go and feed sixty poor people on his behalf and return to your cousin.'

AD v2 p597 n2208; IM v1 p105 n188

CHAPTER 4
DRESS AND HAIR

DRESS

Black Decorated Square Garment

AYISHA RELATED:

When God's Messenger died, he was covered with a garment decorated with green squares.

SB v7 p474 n705

UMM KHALID BINT KHALID RELATED:

The Prophet was given some clothes including a black *khamisa*. The Prophet said, 'To whom shall we give this to wear?' The people were silent; whereupon, the Prophet said, 'Fetch Umm Khalid for me.' Umm Khalid was carried, as she was a small girl at that time. The Prophet took the *khamisa* in his hands and made her wear it. He said, 'May you live so long that your dress will wear out, and you will mend it many times.' On the *khamisa* there were some [green or pale] designs. The Prophet saw the designs and said, 'Umm Khalid! This is beautiful!'

SB v7 p478 n713; SB v7 p491 n736; AD v3 p1126 n4013; SB v4 p194 n305; AD v3 p1126 n4013

Extent of a Rider's Provisions

AYISHA RELATED:

The Messenger said to her, 'If you wish to join me, be satisfied with worldly things only to the extent of a rider's provision, avoid sitting with the rich, and do not consider a garment worn out until you have patched it.'

T [MMR v2 p916]

On Wearing a Shirt

ASMA BINT YAZID RELATED:

The sleeve of the shirt of God's Messenger came to his wrist.

AD v3 p1126 n4016; AD v3 p1126 n4015

UMM SALAMA RELATED:

The clothing which God's Messenger liked best was the shirt.

AD v3 p1126 n4014

Red Color

WOMAN OF THE ASAD TRIBE RELATED:

One day she was with Zaynab, the wife of the Messenger of God, and they were dyeing Zaynab's clothes with red ochre. The Messenger of God saw them. When he saw the red ochre, he turned back. When Zaynab saw this, she realized that the Messenger of God had disapproved of what she was doing. She then washed her clothes and concealed all redness. The Messenger of God then returned and saw the two of them. When he did not see anything [of what he had seen before], he entered.

AD v3 p1132 n4060

Sitting on a Mat Made of Date Palm Leaves

AYISHA RELATED:

The Prophet constructed a room with a straw mat in which to pray at night. During the day he used to spread it out and sit on it. The people began coming to the Prophet at night to offer the prayer behind him. When their number increased, the Prophet faced them and said, 'O people! Do only those good deeds which you can do for God does not get tired of giving reward, but you may get tired of performing good deeds. The best deeds to God are the ones done continuously—even though they are few.'

SB v7 p499 n752

Skins of Dead Animals

AYISHA RELATED:

The Prophet ordered that the skins of animals which had died a natural death could be used when they were tanned.

AD v3 p1150 n4112

MAYMUNA RELATED:

Some people of the Quraysh tribe passed by God's Messenger dragging a sheep as big as an ass. God's Messenger said to them, 'Would that you took its skin.' They said that it died a natural death. God's Messenger said, 'Water and leaves of the mimosa flava purify it.'

AD v3 p1150 n4114

Taken on Trust

AYISHA RELATED:

The Prophet wore two coarse striped garments, which when he sweated, felt heavy. A certain Jew received a consignment of cloth from Syria. She suggested the Messenger should send to the Jew and buy two garments from him to be paid when circumstances were easier. He did so. The Jewish man replied that he knew that the Prophet would only go off with his property and not pay. The Messenger said,

'He has lied. He knows I am one of the most pious of them and the most accoustomed to pay what is given on trust.'

T [MMR v2 p919]

Wearing Black Clothes

AYISHA RELATED:

She made a black cloak for the Prophet and he put it on. When he sweated in it, he noticed the odor of the wool and threw it away.

AD v3 p1137 n4063

Wearing Wool Clothes

AYISHA RELATED:

God's Messenger went out one morning wearing a variegated garment of black goat hair.

AD v3 p1127 n4021; SM v3B p394 n2081

HAIR

Dye Used by Women

AYISHA RELATED:

God's Messenger did not like the odor of henna.

AD v3 p1159 n4152

Lengthening Hair Artificially

ASMA RELATED:

A woman told the Prophet that her daughter had gotten measles and her hair had fallen out. The daughter was to be married and her mother wanted to know if her daughter could use false hair. The Messenger said, 'God has cursed the woman who lengthens hair artifically and the one who gets her hair lengthened artificially.'

SB v7 p534 n824; SB v7 p533 n818; SB v7 p534 n819; SB v7 p534 n824; SB v7 p101; SM v3B p416 n2122R2; SM v3 p416 n2123, R1

Messenger's Hair

AYISHA RELATED:

God's Mesenger and she used to perform the bath lustration from one vessel. He had hair which did not reach the shoulder but which came lower than the ear.

T [MMR v2 p934]; AD v3 p1164 n4175; T [H v1 p610]

Parting of the Hair

AYISHA RELATED:

When she parted the hair of God's Messenger, she made a part from the crown of his head and let his forelock hang between his eyes.

AD v3 p1164 n4177

Plaiting the Hair by Men

UMM HANI RELATED:

The Prophet came to Makkah with four plaits of hair.

AD v3 p1165 n4179

Women Shaving Their Head

AYISHA RELATED:

Ayisha reported that the Messenger of God forbade a woman to shave her head.

T [H v3 p625]

JEWELRY

Wearing Little Bells on Legs

BUNANA, FEMALE CLIENT OF ABD AL-RAHMAN IBN HAYYAN AL-ANSARI, RELATED:

She was with Ayisha when a girl came in wearing little tinkling bells on her legs. Ayisha ordered that they were not to bring her in unelss they took off her little bells. She said that she heard the Messenger of God say, 'The angels do not enter a house in which there is a bell.'

AD v3 p1165 n4219

Women Wearing Gold

AYISHA RELATED:

Some ornaments were presented to the Prophet as gifts from Negus. They contained a gold ring with an Abyssinian stone. God's Messenger called Umama, daughter of his daughter Zaynab, and said, 'Wear it my dear daughter.'

AD v3 p1175 n4223

ASMA BINT YAZID RELATED:

God's Messenger said, 'Any woman who wears a gold necklace will have a similar one of fire put on her neck on the day of resurrection, and any woman who puts a gold earring in her ear will have a similar one of fire put in her ear on the day of resurrection.'

AD v3 p1176 n4226; AD v3 p1176 n4225

PERFUME

Applying Scent to the Head and Beard

AYISHA RELATED:

She used to perfume God's Messenger with the best scent available until he saw the shine of the scent on his head and beard.

SB v7 p528 n806

CHAPTER 5
EMANCIPATION OF SLAVES

AGREEMENT TO PURCHASE FREEDOM

AYISHA RELATED:

Barira came to her seeking her help to purchase her freedom. Barira herself had not paid anything for her freedom. She (Ayisha) told her to return to her people and tell them that she would purchase Barira and inherit from her. Barira mentioned this to her people, but they refused and said that if she wanted to buy Barira's freedom, she could do so and receive a reward from God, but that they were the inheritors. She mentioned this to the Messenger of God. He said, 'Purchase her and set her free for the right of inheritance belongs only to the one who sets a person free.' He then stood up and said, 'What is the matter with people who make conditions which are not in God's Book? If anyone makes a condition which is not in God's Book, he has no right to it even if he stipulates it hundreds of times. God's condition is more valid and binding.'

> AD v3 p1102 n3918; SB v3 p445 n738; SB v3 p444 n737; SB v3 n443 p735; SB v3 p426 n713; SB v3 p443 n736; SB v8 p491 n743; SB v3 p209 n377; SB v3 p558 n889; SB v8 p495 n749; SB v8 p496 n752; SB v8 p495 n750; SB v3 p204 n364; SB v3 p204 n365; SB v3 p558 n889; SB v8 p465 n708; SB v2 p332 n570; SM v2B p434 n1504RI; AD v3 p1103 n3919; AD v2 p822 n2909; SB v3 p446 n739

AYISHA RELATED:

Juwyriyya bint al-Harith ibn al-Mustaliq fell to the lot of Thabit ibn Qays ibn Shammas or to her cousin. She entered into an agreement to purchase her freedom. She was a very beautiful woman most attractive to the eye. She [Juwyriyya] then went to the Messenger of God asking him for the purchase of her freedom.When she was standing at the door, she [Ayisha] looked at her with disapproval. She [Ayisha] realized that the Messenger of God would see what she had seen. Juwayriyya introduced herself to the Messenger of God and asked him to buy her freedom. The Messanger of God asked, 'Are you inclined to what is better than that?' She asked what it was. He replied, 'I shall pay the price of your freedom on your behalf and I shall marry you.' She agreed. She [Ayisha] said that when the people heard that the Messenger of God had married Juwayriyya, they released the capitves in their possession and set them free. They said that these people now were relatives of the Messenger of God by marriage. They added that they never saw another woman who brought such blessings to her people. One hundred families of the Mustaliq tribe were set free on account of her.

> AD v3 p1103 n3920

CHOICES OF A FREED SLAVEWOMAN

AYISHA RELATED:

When she set Barira free, the Prophet told her [Barira] that she had the choice to remain with her husband or leave him. She left him. Her husband was not a slave.

> IM v2u p113 n227

CONDITIONAL FREEDOM

SAFINA RELATED:

She was a slave of Umm Salama. Umm Salama said that she would emancipate her but stipulated that Safina must serve God's Messenger as long as he lived. Safina said to Umm Salama that she would not leave the Messenger, even if Umm Salama had not stipulated this.

> AD v3 p1103 n3921

DIVORCE

AYISHA RELATED:

Barira was freed. She was the wife of Mughith, a slave of Ale Abu Ahmad. The Messenger of God gave her a choice and said to her, 'If he has intercourse with you, then there is no choice for you.'

> AD v2 p602 n2228; AD v2 p602 n2227

FREEDOM

A Free Woman the Wife of a Slave

AYISHA RELATED:

Three principles were established because of Barira. First, when Barira was freed, she was given the option [to remain with her slave husband or not]. Second, God's Messenger said, 'The inheritance [wala] of a slave belongs to the one who frees the slave.' Third, when

God's Messenger entered the house, he saw a cooking pot on the fire but was given bread and meat soup from the soup of the home. The Prophet said, 'Did I not see the cooking pot [on the fire]?' They told him that the meat was given in charity to Barira, and that they thought he did not eat things given in charity. The Prophet said, 'It is an object of charity for Barira and a gift for us.'

SB v7 p22 n34

Freedom of Slave Mothers

SULAMA BINT MAQIL RELATED:

Her uncle took her to Madinah in pre-Islamic times. He sold her to Hubab ibn Amr. She bore Abd al-Rahman ibn al-Hubab, and then al-Hubab died. She was then told that she would be sold as a slave in order to repay the loan of her husband to his brother. God's Messenger told al-Hubab's brother, the guardian of her child, to free Sulama and that he would replace her with another slave. They did this, and she was set free. Later when the Messenger received other capitves in war, he gave one of them in place of Sulama.

AD v3 p1107 n3942

LAWS GOVERNING SLAVEWOMEN

AYISHA RELATED:

If a slave commits adultry, she should be lashed once. For a second offence, she should be lashed once. For a subsequent offence, she should again be lashed once. After the fourth offense, she should be sold for the price of a rope.

IM v2u p291 n731

MALE BEFORE FEMALE

AYISHA RELATED:

She intended to set free two of her slaves. She asked the Prophet who directed her to begin with the male.

N [H v2 p469]; N [MMRv1]

CHAPTER 6
FOOD

AGRICULTURE

AYISHA RELATED:

The Prophet said, "Whoever cultivates land that does not belong to anybody has more right to own it."

SB v3 p306 n528

BREAD

UMM SULAYM RELATED:

When Abu Talha told Umm Sulaym that the Prophet was hungry and asked if she had anything to eat, Umm Sulaym got out some loaves of bread and gave them to him. He took them to the Messenger. The Messenger asked if Abu Talha had come with some food. He said he had. The Messenger then told those who were with him to get up. They did so and went with him to Abu Talha's house. There the Messenger said, 'Umm Sulaym, bring whatever you have.' She brought that very bread. The Prophet told her to crush the bread into small pieces. Umm Sulaym pressed a skein of butter on it. Then God's Messenger said whatever God wished him to say to bless the food and then added, 'Admit ten [men].' So ten were admitted, ate their fill and went out. The Prophet then said, 'Admit ten more.' Ten more were admitted, ate their fill, and went out. He then again said, 'Admit ten more!' This happened again and again until eighty men had been fed.

SB v7 p224 n295

CONTAMINATION

MAYMUNA

The Prophet was asked regarding ghee in which a mouse had fallen. He said, 'Take out the mouse and throw away the ghee around it and use the rest.'

SB v1 p149 n236; SB v1 p149 n237; SB v7 p317 n446; AD v3 p1079 n3832

DATES

ASMA BINT ABU BAKR RELATED:

She carried date stones on her head from the land of Al-Zubayr given to him by the Messenger. It was a distance of 2/3 of a farsakh from her house.

SB v4 p249 n379

AYISHA RELATED:

God's Messenger said, 'A family which has dates will not go hungry.'

SM v3B p370 n2046, R1; AD v3 p1077 n3822

GOD'S NAMES

AYISHA RELATED:

The people told the Prophet that some people who had recently embraced Islam had brought them some meat as charity. They did not know whether or not the people had mentioned the name of God before slaughtering the meat. The Messenger said, 'You mention God's Name and eat.'

SB v9 p366 n495; SM v3 p156 n273; v7 p302 n415

AYISHA RELATED:

God's Messenger said, 'When one of you eats, he should mention God's Name. If he forgets to mention God's Name at the beginning, he should say, "In the Name of God," at the end of it.'

AD v3 p1065 n3758

HOSPITALITY

ASMA BINT YAZID RELATED:

The Prophet was brought some food which he offered to them. When they said they did not want it, he replied, 'Do not combine falsehood with hunger.'

IM [MMR v2 p901]

MEAT

Cured Meat

AYISHA RELATED:

The Prophet did not forbid the storage of meat sacrifices for three days in order that the rich could feed the poor. Later they kept even trotters to cook fifteen days later. The family of Muhammad did not eat enough wheat bread with meat or soup to satisfy them for three successive days.

SB v7 p255 n349; SB v7 p336 n477

Eating Meat

AYISHA RELATED:

God's Messenger said, 'Do not eat meat with a knife for it is a foreign practice but bite it for it is more beneficial and wholesome.' [Abu Dawud says that this Tradition is not strong.]

AD v3 p1066 n3769

MELON

AYISHA RELATED:

God's Messenger used to eat melon with fresh dates. He used to say, 'The heat of the one is broken by the coolness of the other, and the coolness of the one by the heat of the other.'

AD v3 p1078 n3827

MOTHERS OF THE BELIEVERS

AYISHA RELATED:

God's Messenger died and there was nothing in her house that a living being could eat except some barley lying on a shelf. She ate it, measured it and after a short period, it was consumed.

SB v4 p214 n329; SB v7 p243 n327

PROVISIONS

Water, Salt, Fire

AYISHA RELATED:

She asked the Messenger of God what are the things the refusal of which is not lawful. He said, 'Water, salt and fire.' She asked the Messenger what we know about water and about salt and fire. He said, 'O darling with reddish cheeks! Whosoever gives fire, gives in charity all that the fire cooks, and whosoever gives salt in charity gives all that the salt flavors. Whosoever gives a sip of water to a Muslim where water is available acts as if he set a slave free. Whosoever gives a sip of water to a Muslim where water is not available acts as if he gave him his life. '

IM [H v2 p313]; IM v2u p253 n634

AYISHA RELATED:

She and Asma prepared provisions when the Prophet and their father Abu Bakr migrated to Madinah.

SB v7 p246

SWEETS

AYISHA RELATED:

God's Messenger loved to eat sweet things and honey.

SB v7 p251 n342; SB v7 p397 n586

WATER

KABSHA RELATED:

God's Messenger went to visit her and drank, standing, from the mouth of a water-skin which was hung up, whereupon, she went and cut off its mouth.

T [MMR v2 p906]

CHAPTER 7
FUNERAL

BATH LUSTRATION AND SHROUDING THE DEAD

Concerning the Shroud of the Dead Body

AYISHA RELATED:

The Messenger was shrouded in three Yemeni cotton garments of white from Sahul, among which was neither a shirt nor a turban. As far as *hullah* was concerned, there was some doubt about it in the minds of people. It was brought in order to shroud him but was abandoned, and he was shrouded in the three cotton garments from Sahul. Then Abd Allah ibn Abu Bakr got the cloth and said that he would keep it in order to shroud himself. Then Abd Allah said that if God, the Exalted and Majestic, desired it for His Messenger, he would have been shrouded with it. Abd Allah sold it and gave the money to charity.

> SM v2A p56 n941, R1; SB v2 p206 n363; SB v2 p199 n354; AD v2 p896 n3146; AD v2 p888 n3114

Giving a Bath Lustration for the Dead by a Man to His Wife and a Wife to Her Husband

AYISHA RELATED:

God's Messenger returned from the Baqi cemetary and found her with a headache. He said, 'No, me! O my head, O Ayisha.' Then he said, 'Nothing will harm you if you pass away before me. I shall take care of you. I shall give you a bath lustration, wrap you in a shroud, invoke blessings on you [in the funeral prescribed prayer] and bury you.'

> IM v2 p376 n1465

How to Wash the Dead

UMM ATIYA RELATED:

The Messenger of God said to them while washing her daughter's body, 'Begin with the right side and the parts on which the ablution is performed.'

AD v2 p895 n3139; AD v2 p895 n3140

Observing Prescribed Prayer Over the Dead Bodies in the Mosque

AYISHA RELATED:

God's Messenger performed the funeral prayer for Suhail ibn Bayda inside the mosque.

IM v2 p404 n1518; AD v2 p905 n3184

On Covering Private Parts of the Dead While Washing

AYISHA RELATED:

They did not know whether or not to take off the Messenger's clothes and wash him. When they differed among themselves, God cast slumber over them until everyone of them had put his chin on his chest. Then someone spoke from a side of the house. They did not know who he was. He said, 'Wash the Prophet while his clothes are on him.' They stood and washed him while he had his shirt on him. They poured water on his shirt and rubbed him with his shirt and not with their hands. She said that if she had known beforehand about what she later came to learn, his wives would have washed his body.

AD v2 p894 n3135; IM v2 p375 n1464

Shrouding Without Using a Shirt

UMM ATIYA RELATED:

We were forbidden to accompany the funeral processions but not strictly.

SB v2 p206 n362; SB v2 p206 n368; SB v2 p206 n368; SM v2A p53 n938; AD v2 p898 n; IM v2 p434 n1577

Taking a Bath Lustration by a Man Who Washes the Dead

AYISHA RELATED:

The Prophet used to take a bath lustration because of sexual defilement, on Friday, for cupping and washing the dead.

AD v2 p898 n3154

Washing the Dead

UMM ATIYYA RELATED:

God's Messenger visited them when they were washing the body of his daughter, Umm Kulthum. He said, 'Wash her three or five times or for more than this [number]. If you consider it appropriate, [wash her] with water and [leaves of] the lotus tree. In the last [bath lustration] mix some camphor or something of the camphor tree. When you finish the bath lustration, then inform me.' As they finished the bath lustration for the dead, they informed him. He threw his cloak towards them and said, 'Take it as a undercloth that sticks to the body.'

> IM v2 p372 n1458; SB v2 p195 n345a; AD v2 p897 n3151; IM v2 p373 n1459; SB v2 p194 n344; SB v2 p196 n348; SB v2 p197 n351; SB v2 p194 n345; SB v2 p198 n353; SB v2 p196 n349; SB v2 p197 n350; SB v1 p117 n168; SB v2 p198 n352; ; SB v1 p117 n168; SB v2 p198 n352; SM v2A p53 n939; AD v2 p894 n3136; AD v2 p894 n3137; AD v2 p894 n3138; AD v2 p895 n3139; AD v2 p895 n3139

HAFSA RELATED:

The Messenger said to perform the bath lustration for the dead by washing the body an odd number of times. Three, five or seven were mentioned. She added that he said to start with the right side.

> SB v2 p195 n345a; SB v2 p195 n346; SB v2 p195 n347

What To Recite Over the Funeral Bier

UMM SHARIK AL-ANSARIYA RELATED:

God's Messenger commanded them to recite the first chapter of the Quran.

> IM v2 p392 n1495

GRAVES

AYISHA RELATED:

When God's Messenger breathed his last, the people differed on whether to prepare the niche [in the grave] or to cleave the grave until their voices became loud. Upon this Umar told them not to shout in the presence of God's Messenger, whether he be alive or passed away. They sent for all those who prepared the niche and dig graves. He who used to prepare the niche approached [first of all]. He prepared the niche for God's Messenger, and then he was buried.

> IM v2 p423 n1557

INTERCESSION FOR THE DEAD

AYISHA RELATED:

God's Messenger said, 'If a company of Muslims numbering one hundred pray for a dead person, all of them interceding for him, their intercession will be accepted.'

> SM v2A p59 n947

KISSING THE DEAD

The Prophet

AYISHA RELATED:

Abu Bakr came riding his horse from his dwelling in al-Sunh. He got off his horse, entered the mosque and did not speak to anybody until he came to her. Then he went directly to the Prophet who was covered with a marked blanket. Abu Bakr uncovered his face. He knelt down and kissed him and then began weeping. He said that God would not give two deaths to him. He said that the Prophet had died the death which was written for him.

SB v2 p188 n333; IM v2 p371 n1437

Uthman ibn Mazun

AYISHA RELATED:

God's Messenger kissed Uthman ibn Mazun when Uthman had passed away. It was as if she were looking at [the Messenger's] and tears flowing down his cheeks.

IM v2 p371 n1456; AD v2 p898 n3157; IM [MMR v1]; T [Hv3p19]

LAST ILLNESS

A Group of People Injuring a Patient

AYISHA RELATED:

They poured medicine into the mouth of God's Messenger during his illness. He pointed to them intending to say, 'Don't pour medicine into my mouth.' They thought that his refusal resulted from the aversion a patient usually has for medicine. When he improved and felt a bit better, he said to them, 'Did I not forbid you to pour medicine into my mouth?' They said that they thought he had done so because of the aversion one usually has for medicine. God's Messenger said, 'There is none of you but will be forced to drink medicine, except al-Abbas, for he did not witness this act of yours.'

SB v9 p23 n35; SB v5 p525 n735; SM v3 p1084 n3853

Arguing

AYISHA RELATED:

During his fatal illness, the Messenger said, 'Order Abu Bakr to lead the people in prescribed prayer.' She said to the Messenger that if Abu Bakr stood at his place in prayer, the people would not be able to hear him because of his weeping. She, therefore, suggested that Umar lead the people in prescribed prayer. Again the Messenger said, 'Order Abu Bakr to lead the people in prescribed prayer.' Then she [Ayisha] told Hafsa to tell the Prophet that if Abu Bakr stood in his place, the people would not be able to hear because of his weeping; therefore, Umar should lead the people in prescribed prayer. Hafsa said this whereupon God's Messenger said, 'You are like the brothers of Joseph [see 12:30-32]. Order Abu Bakr to lead the people in prescribed prayer.' Hafsa then said to her [Ayisha] that she had never received any good from her!

SB v9 p299 n406; SB v1 p383 n680; SB v1 p365 n647; SB v1 p358 n633; SB v5 p517 n727; SB v1 p384 n681; SB v1 p386 n684; SB v1 p367 n651; SB v4 p391 n598; IM v2 p229 n1232; IM v2 p230; IM v2 p229 n1232; N v1E p504 n836

Breathing His Last

AYISHA RELATED:

She saw God's Messenger while he was breathing his last, and there was a drinking bowl containing water in it near him. He would dip his hand into the bowl and wipe his face with water and then pray, 'O God, help me against the agonies of death.'

IM v2 p464 n1623

Charismata

AYISHA RELATED:

She was told when God's Messenger died that the people disagreed about his burial, but Abu Bakr said he had heard something from God's Messenger. He had said, 'God takes a prophet only in the place where he wishes to be buried.' So he told them to bury him where his bedding lay.

T [MMR v2 p1305]

Direction of the Grave

RELATIVE OF UMM SALAMA RELATED:

The bed of the Prophet was set as a man is laid in his grave. The mosque was towards his head.

AD v3 p1395 n5026

Illness of the Prophet

AYISHA RELATED:

She heard from the Prophet that no prophet dies until he is given the option to select either the worldly life or the life of the hereafter. She heard the Prophet in his last illness, when his voice was becoming hoarse, saying, "*In the company of those upon whom is God's Grace...*" [4:69]; thereupon, she thought that the Prophet had been given the option.

SB v5 p513 n719; SB v5 p513 n720; SB v5 p511 n715; SB v5 p515 n724; SB v6 p90 n110; SB v8 p340 n516; SB v8 p240 n359; SB v8 p340 n516; SB v7 p411 n612; SM v4A p102 n2443; SB v7 p392 n578

AYISHA RELATED:

It was one of the blessings of God towards her that the Messenger died in her house on the day of her turn while he was leaning against her chest. God made her saliva mix with his saliva at this death. Abd al-Rahman entered with a toothstick in his hand. She was supporting the back of the Messenger against her chest. She saw the Prophet looking at the toothstick. She knew that he loved the toothstick so she asked him if she should take it from him. He nodded in the affirmative. She took it. It was stiff for him to use so she softened it for him, and he cleaned his teeth with it. In front of him there was a jug or a tin containing water. He started dipping his hand in the water and rubbing his face with it. He said, 'None has the right to be worshipped except God. Death has its agonies.' He lifted his hands towards the sky and began saying, 'With the highest companion,' until he died and his hand dropped down.

SB v5 p520 n730; SB v5 p515 n722; SB v5 p527 n740; SB v4 p216 n332; SB v5 p523 n732; IM v2 p462 n1620

AYISHA RELATED:

God's Messenger died when he was sixty-three years old.

SB v5 p528 n742; SB v4 p481 n736

Mention of the Demise and Burial of the Prophet

AYISHA RELATED:

When God's Messenger passed away, Abu Bakr was with his wife, the daughter of Kharija, in the villages surrounding Madinah. People began to say that the Prophet had not died and that it was something that overwhelmed him at the time of revelation. Abu Bakr removed the cloth from his face, caressed him between his eyes, and said that he [Abu Bakr] was the most glorious in God's sight because he was caused to die twice. He told the people that the Messenger had died. Umar was in a corner of the mosque saying that God's Messenger had not passed away and that he would not depart until he cut off the hands and feet of the hypocrites. Abu Bakr ascended the *minbar* and said that whoever worshipped God should know that God is Alive and has not died. Whoever used to follow Muhammad should listen carefully and know that Muhammad had passed away, and that Muhammad was only a Messenger of God. He said that many messengers had passed away before him. He asked them if this meant that they would turn their heels or backs because of this. [He told them] none of this would harm God, and God would certainly reward the grateful. Umar said that he felt as if the Messenger had recited this verse only today.

IM v 2 p469; IM v2 p467 n1627; SB v5 p523 n734; SB v5 p523 n733; SB v2 p188 n333; T [H v3 p19]

UMM SALAMA RELATED:

During the lifetime of the Messenger, when a worshipper stood observing prescribed prayer, no one's glance would fall on the place of his feet. Then when God Messenger departed from this world [and Abu Bakr became caliph], when anyone stood to perform the prescribed prayer, no one's glance would fall upon the place where one's forehead is placed in prostration. Then Abu Bakr also passed away, and Umar became the caliph. Then when anyone stood for prescribed prayer, no one's glance fell beyond the place of the *qibla*. When Uthman ibn Affan became the caliph and turmoil prevailed, then people looked towards their right and left.

IM v2 p473 n1633

AYISHA RELATED:

God's Messenger said during his final illness, '[Beware of] the prayer and [the slaves] which your right hand possesses.' He ceaselessly said these words until his tongue did not utter them.

IM v2 p465 n1625

Severity of Death
AYISHA RELATED:

She did not envy anyone an easy death after having seen the severity of the death of God's Messenger.

T [MMR v1 p326]; IM v2 p464 n1622

Stupors of Death
AYISHA RELATED:

There was a leather or wood container full of water in front of the Prophet [at the time of his death]. He would put his hand into the water and rub his face with it saying, 'None has the right to be worshipped but God! No doubt, death has its stupors.' Then he raised his hand and began saying, 'O God with the highest companions [see 4:69],' and he kept on saying it until he died and his hand dropped.

SB v8 p341 n517; t [MMR v1 p327]; IM [H v1 p315]

The Aksiya and the Khama is. . .
AYISHA RELATED:

When the illness of God's Messenger worsened, he covered his face with a *khamisa*. When he became short of breath, he would remove it from his face and say, 'It is like that! May God curse the Jews and Christians who took the graves of their prophets as places of worship.' By that he warned his followers not to imitate them by doing that which they did.

SB v7 p474 n706; SB v4 p439 n660; SB v5 p516 n725

To Take a Bath or Perform Ablution From a Utensil, Tumbler or Wooden or Stone Tub
AYISHA RELATED:

When the ailment of the Prophet became aggravated and his disease became severe, he asked his wives to permit him to be nursed [treated] in her house. They gave him permission. Then the Prophet went [to Ayisha's house] with the help of two men. His legs were dragging on the ground between Abbas and the other man. Ubayd Allah [the subnarrator] said that he informed Abd Allah ibn Abbas of what Ayisha had said. Ibn Abbas asked if he knew who the other man was. He replied in the negative. Ibn Abbas said that he was Ali ibn Abu Talib. She further added that when the Prophet came to her house and his illness became aggravated, he ordered them to pour seven skins full of water on him so that he might be able to give some advice to the people. He was seated in a brass tub belonging to Hafsa. Then all of them began pouring water on him from the water skins until he beckoned to them to stop, showing that they had done what he wanted them to do. After that he went out to the people.

SB v1 p132 n197; IM v2 p461 n1618; AD v2 p572 n2132; AD v2 p572 n2133; SB v5 p517 n727

PRAYING FOR THE DEAD

Funeral Prayer in the Mosque

AYISHA RELATED:

The Messenger of God prayed in the mosque over the two bodies of the sons of al-Baida, Suhayl and his brother.

AD v2 p905 n3184; AD v2 p905 n3183

Praying for a Child Who Has Died

AYISHA RELATED:

Ibrahim, son of the Prophet, died when he was eighteen months old. God's Messenger did not pray at his burial.

AD v2 p905 n3181

What Is To Be Said While Visiting the Graveyard

AYISHA RELATED:

Whenever it was her turn for God's Messenger to spend the night with her, he would go out, towards the end of the night, to the Baqi cemetery and say, 'Peace be upon you, abode of a people who are believers. What you were promised you would get tomorrow, you will receive after some delay, and, God willing, we shall join you. O God, grant forgiveness to the inhabitants of Baqi al-Gharqad.'

SM v2A p71 n974; IM v2 p18 n1546

PROVIDE FOOD

ASMA BINT UMAYS RELATED:

When her husband, Jafar [ibn Abu Talib], was martyred, God's Messenger returned to his family and said, 'The people of Jafar are occupied in [the disposal of] their deceased so prepare food for them.'

IM v2 p455 n1611

WALKING AT A FUNERAL AND PRAYER FOR THE DEAD

AYISHA RELATED:

A Jewish woman had died. The Prophet heard them [her relatives] weeping for her. He said, 'Verily her family members are weeping for her, and she is being tormented in her grave [because of their wailing].'

IM v2 p445 n1595; SB v2 p213 n376

WEEPING FOR THE DEAD

Prohibited from Wailing

UMM SALAMA RELATED:

When Abu Salama died she [Umm Salama] said that he had been a stranger in a strange land. She said that she would weep for him in a manner that would be talked of. She made preparation for weeping for him when a woman from the upper side of the city came intending to help her weep. She happened to come across the Messenger of God. He said, 'Do you intend to bring the devil into a house from which God has twice driven him out?' Umm Salama, therefore, refrained from weeping.

SM v2A p44 n922

UMM SALAMA RELATED:

The Messenger interpreted the verse, '*And they should not disobey you in good practices,*' by saying that good practice here stood for wailing [in chorus].'

IM v2 p435 n1579

HAMNA BINT JAHSH RELATED:

She was told that her brother had been martyred. Upon hearing this, she prayed for God to have mercy on him for verily they had been told that to Him we are to return. She was told that her spouse had been martyred. She cried out in grief! God's Messenger said, 'The woman has [a strong] love for her spouse which she does not have for anything else.'

IM v2 p442 n1590

AYISHA RELATED:

When the Prophet received the news of the death of ibn Haritha, Jafar and Ibn Rawaha, he sat down and looked sad. She was looking at him through the crack in the door. A man came and told him about the crying of the women of Jafar. The Prophet ordered him to forbid the mourning. The man went and came back saying that he had told them, but they had not listened to him. The Prophet said, 'Forbid them.' So again he went and came back a third time and said that they did not listen to him at all. God's Messenger ordered him to go and put dust in their mouths. She [Ayisha] prayed that God might stick the man's nose in the dust [humiliate him] because he could neither persuade the women to fulfill the order of God's Messenger nor could he relieve God's Messenger from fatigue.

SB v2 p216 n386; SB v2 p221 n392; SB v5 p392 n562; SM v2A p52 n935; AD v2 p888 n3116

ASMA BINT YAZID RELATED:

When the son of the Messenger died, God's Messenger wept. He who was consoling [him], either Abu Bakr or Umar, said to him that he was the fittest of all those who glorify the right of God. The Messenger said, 'The eye sheds tears. The heart is grieved. We do not utter anything that makes the Lord distraught. Is not His word true who has promised to muster [all people].' Had not the last person followed his predecessor, we would have been sad for you, O Ibrahim, more than we have ever been. Verily we are grieved because of you.'

IM v2 p442 n1589

UMM ATIYA RELATED:
The Messenger of God made them promise, along with the pledge of allegiance, that they would not lament. Only five of them fulfilled the promise: Umm Sulaym, Umm al-Ala, the daughter of Abu Sabra, the wife of Muath or daughter of Abu Sabra and the wife of Muath.
SM v2A p53 n936, R1; SB v2 p222 n393; AD v2 p888 n3121

The Mourning of a Woman for a Dead Person Other Than Her Husband

UMM ATIYA RELATED:
One of the sons of Umm Atiya died. When it was the third day, she asked for a yellow perfume and put it over her body. She said that they were forbidden to mourn for more than three days except for their husbands.'
SB v2 p206 n369

WHAT TO SAY AT THE TIME OF A CALAMITY

Closing the Eyes of the Dead

UMM SALAMA RELATED:
The Messenger of God went to see Abu Salama (when he died). His eyes were fixed open. The Messenger closed them and said, 'When the soul is taken away, the sight follows it.' Some of the people of his family wept and wailed. He said, 'Do not invoke for yourselves anything but good, for angels say, "Amen," to what you say. O God forgive Abu Salama. Raise his rank among those who are rightly guided. Grant him a successor in his descendants who remain. Forgive us and him, O Lord of the Unverse, and make his grave spacious and grant him light in it.'
SM v2A p44 n920; AD v2 p888 n3112; IM v2 p370 n1454

Quran

UMM SALAMA RELATED:
Abu Salama told her that he heard the Messenger say, 'When a Muslim is afflicted with a calamity, he should take refuge in the words God has commanded: 'We are from God and to Him we return.' O God, I beg reward for my calamity from You. Confer upon me a reward on that account and give me [that which is better] than that [which I have lost due to the calamity];' for God rewards one who suffers [a calamity] and gives him in exchange [that which is] better.'
IM v2 p447 n1598; SM v2A p42 n918; AD v2 p888 n3113

WHAT TO SAY TO ONE WHO IS DYING

AYISHA RELATED:
God's Messenger went to her with a close relative of his. When

the Prophet saw [the grief] that had afflicted her, he said to her, 'Don't feel grief about your lost relative. Verily this [agony] is [a source] of his virtues.'

IM v2 p368 n1451

WISHING FOR DEATH

ASMA BINT ABU BAKR RELATED:

She went to Abu Bakr during his fatal illness. He asked her in how many garments was the Prophet shrouded? She said that he was shrouded in three *sahuliya* pieces of white cotton cloth, among which there was neither a shirt nor a turban. Abu Bakr further asked on what day the Prophet died. She said it was on Monday. He asked what day it was now. She said that it was Monday. He added that he hoped he would die some time between that morning and evening. Then he looked at the garment he was wearing during his illness. It had some stains of saffron. Then he said to wash his garment and add two more garments and shroud him in them. He said that it was worn out. He added that a living person has more right to wear new clothes than a dead one. The shroud is only for the body's pus. He did not die until it was the night of Tuesday, and he was buried before the morning.

SB v2 p263 n469

Chapter 8
Gift

Acceptance of a Gift

It Is Permissible for a Wife To Give Gifts To Other Than Her Husband

AYISHA RELATED:

Whenever God's Messenger wanted to go on a journey, he would draw lots as to which of his wives would accompany him. He would take her whose name came out. He fixed for each of them a day and a night, but Sawda bint Zama gave up her day and night to Ayisha in order to seek the pleasure of God's Messenger.

SB v3 p462 n766

Sending Gifts to the Prophet

AYISHA RELATED:

The people looked forward to the days of her turn [as hostess to the Prophet] to send gifts to God's Messenger in order to please him.

SB v3 p453 n748; SM v4A p101 n2441

Superiority of Giving Gifts

AYISHA RELATED:

She said to her nephew three crescents in two months had passed without a fire [for cooking] started in the houses of God's Messenger. She said that only two things sustained them: dates and water. Their neighbors from the Helpers gave them gifts of a she-camel or a sheep, temporarily so that its milk might be used. Then it was returned to the owner [*manaih*]. They gave this milk to the Messenger, and he made them drink it.

SB v3 p447 n741

Who is to be given a gift first?

AYISHA RELATED:

She told the Messenger that she had two neighbors and wondered

209

to which one should she give charity? He said, 'Give to the one whose door is nearest to you.'

SB v3 p463 n767

Whoever Gave a Gift to His Friend

AYISHA RELATED:

The wives of God's Messenger had formed two groups. One group consisted of herself, Hafsa, Safiya and Sawda. The other group consisted of Umm Salama and the other wives of the Messenger. Muslims knew that God's Messenger loved Ayisha; if any of them had a gift and wished to give it to the Messenger, he would delay it until the Messenger had come to her [Ayisha's] home. The group of Umm Salama discused the matter together and decided that Umm Salama should mention this to the Messenger. She did so three times. The last time he said, 'Do not hurt me regarding Ayisha as the divine revelations do not come to me on any bed except that of Ayisha.' Umm Salama said that she repented to God for hurting him. Then the group of Umm Salama asked Fatima to speak to the Messenger. Fatima told him that his wives asked him to treat them and the daughter of Abu Bakr equally. The Messenger said, 'O my daughter! Don't you love whom I love?' She replied in the affirmative. When she told the group of Umm Salama, they asked her to ask again, but she refused. Then Zaynab bint Jahsh went to him and used harsh words saying that his wives requested him to treat them and the daughter of Ibn Abu Quhafa on equal terms. She raised her voice and abused her [Ayisha] to her face so much that the Messenger looked at her [Ayisha] to see if she would respond. She [Ayisha] began to respond, but Zaynab silenced her. Looking at her [Ayisha], the Prophet said, 'She is really the daughter of Abu Bakr!"

SB v3 p454 n755; SB v3 p454 n754

COMPENSATION FOR A GIFT

AYISHA RELATED:

God's Messenger accepted gifts and gave something in return.

SB v3 p458 n758

GIVE GIFTS

A Present Generates Love and Removes Malice from the Heart

AYISHA RELATED:

The Messenger said, 'Exchange presents with one another. Presents remove ill-will from hearts.'

T [MMT v4 p387]

MAYMUNA RELATED:

She fed a slave girl and the Messenger said, 'You would have gotten more spritual reward if you had given the slave girl to one of your maternal uncles.'

SB v3 p462 n765; SB v3 p463 nTitle

To Borrow Something for the Bride At the Time of Her Wedding

AYISHA RELATED:

She wore a coarse dress costing five dirhams. She told a visitor to look at her slave girl who refused to wear it [the dress] in the house, although during the lifetime of God's Messenger, she (Ayisha) had a similar dress which no woman wishing to appear elegant [for her husband] failed to borrow from her.

SB v3 p480 n796

Chapter 9
Hunting

ANIMALS

Eating Horse Meat

FATIMA RELATED:

They slaughtered a horse and ate it during the lifetime of God's Messenger.

> SM v3B p308 n1942; SB v7 p305 n428; SM v3B p308 n1942; SB v7 p305 n419; SB v7 p305 n418; SB v7 p305 n420

Killing of Lizards

UMM SHARIK RELATED:

God's Messenger commanded her to kill lizards.

> SM v3B p472 n2237, R1; SB v4 p334 n526

Killing the Scorpion During the Prescribed Prayer

AYISHA RELATED:

A scorpion stung the Prophet while he was in [the state of] prescribed prayer. Thereupon he said, 'God curse the scorpion. It does not distinguish between a person engaged in prescribed prayer and a person not performing the prescribed prayer. Kill it in areas other than the sacred area.'

> IM v2 p241 n1246

Noxious Creature

AYISHA RELATED:

God's Messenger said that lizards were noxious creatures, but she did not hear the command to kill them.

> SM v3B p472 n2239; SB v4 p334 n525; SM v3B p472 n2237R1

Purification of the Skins of Dead Animals by Tanning Them

MAYMUNA RELATED:

Her slave girl was given a goat as charity, but it died. The Messenger happened to pass by the carcass. He asked, 'Why did you

213

not remove its skin? You could have put it to use after tanning it.'
They said that it was dead. He said, 'Only the eating of an animal
which has died is prohibited.'

SM v1A p222 n363

HUNTING BY A PILGRIM

AYISHA RELATED:

God's Messenger called the salamander a bad animal, but I did
not hear him ordering it to be killed.

SB v3 p35 n57

KILLING OF SNAKES AND SCORPIONS

AYISHA RELATED:

God's Messenger commanded the killing of the snake having
stripes on it, for it affects eyesight and causes miscarriages.

SM v3B p472 n2232

CHAPTER 1
MARRIAGE

ADMONISHING ONE'S MARRIED DAUGHTER

AYISHA RELATED:

Abu Bakr admonished her and poked her flank with his hands. The only thing which stopped her from moving at that time was the position of God's Messenger whose head was on her thigh.

SB v7 p127 n177

ADULTERY

AYISHA RELATED:

God's Messenger said, 'O followers of Muhammad! There is none who has a greater sense of zeal than God. He has forbidden His male servant to commit illegal sexual intercourse and His female servant to commit illegal sexual intercourse. O followers of Muhammad! If you but knew what I know, you would laugh less and weep more.'

SB v7 p109 n148; SB v7 p109 n149

BANNING WHAT IS ALLOWED

UMM ATIYA

God's Messenger drank honey in the house of Zaynab ibn Jahsh and would stay there with her. Hafsa and Ayisha agreed secretly that if he came to either of them, she would say to him that he must have eaten some bad smelling resin because they smelled it [on him]. They did this, and he replied, 'No but I was drinking honey in the house of Zaynab bint Jahsh, and I shall never take it again. I have taken an oath as to that, and you should not tell anybody about it.'

SB v6 p385 n434; SB v8 p446 n682; SB v9 p82 n102; SM v2B p405 n147; AD v3 p1050 n3706

215

COERCION

KHANSA BINT KHYDAM ANSARIYA RELATED:

Her father gave her in marriage when she was a matron, and she disliked that marriage. She went to the Prophet and complained, and the Prophet declared the marriage invalid.

SB v9 p64 n78; SB v7 p52 n69; AD v2 p562 n2096; IM [MMRv1]

CONSUMATION

AYISHA RELATED:

When the Prophet married her, her mother came to her and made her enter the house of the Prophet. Nothing surprised her, but the coming of God's Messenger to her in the forenoon.

SB v7 p66 n90

DOWRY

Negus Gave Her Dowery

UMM HABIBA RELATED:

She was married to Abd Allah ibn Jahsh [and had migrated with him to Abyssina]. It was there that her husband, Ubayd Allah ibn Jahsh, died. Negus married her to the Messenger of God and settled upon her a dowry of 5000 dirhams on behalf of the Messenger. He paid it to her from his own pocket. Negus then sent her to the Prophet in the company of Shurahbil ibn Hasana.

N [MMT v4 p294]

On a Man Who Has Sexual Intercourse With His Wife Before Giving Her Her Dowry

AYISHA RELATED:

God's Messenger commanded her to send a woman to her husband before her husband gave her dowery to her.

AD v2 p570 n2123

Wife Will Enter Paradise

UMM SALAMA RELATED:

She heard the Prophet say that when a woman died and her husband was happy with her, she would enter paradise.

IM v2u p23 n9; T [Hv1 p211]

EARLY MARRIAGE

On Marrying a Child Before Its Birth

MAYMUNA BINT KHARDAM REKATED:

She accompanied her father during the prescribed pilgrimage performed by the Messenger of God. She saw him. Her father went near him. He was riding on his she-camel. Her father stopped there

and listened to him. He had a rod like a teacher's rod. She heard the
bedouins and the people saying, 'Stay away from the flog.' Her father
went near him and took hold of his foot and acknowledged his
prophethood. He stopped and listened to him. Her father then said
that he participated in the army of Athran [in pre-Islamic times].
[The narrator Ibn al-Muthanna said that it was the army of Gathran.]
Tariq ibn al-Muraqqa asked who would give him a lance and receive
a reward. Her father asked what the reward was. Tariq replied that
he would marry the man to his first born daughter. Her father gave
him his lance and then disappeared until he found that a daughter
was born to Tariq, and that she had come of age. Her father went to
Tariq and told him to give him his wife. Tariq swore to him that he
would not do that until a new dower was fixed. Her father said that
he would not give a dower other than the one that he had previously
agreed to. The Messenger asked what her age was. Her father said
that she had grown old. The Messenger said that he thought he
should forget about her. Her father said that this gave him a feeling
of awe and fear when he looked at the Messenger. When the
Messenger felt this from him, he said, 'You will not be sinful, nor will
your companion be sinful.' [The translator comments that the marriage of a child not yet born is invalid, and that the agreement
between Kardam and Tariq was void. The narrator who asked the
Prophet about the marriage was afraid of sinfulness because both
parties had sworn that they would not go against their original agreement. It would have been sinful if they violated thier oaths.]

    AD v2 p563 n2098

On Marrying a Young Girl

AYISHA RELATED:

She played with dolls, and the Prophet let her play with her girl
friends.

    IM v2u p71 n134

AYISHA RELATED:

The Prophet was engaged to her when she was a girl of six. She
went to Madinah and stayed at the home of the Harith ibn Khazraj
tribe. Then she became ill, and her hair fell out. Later on her hair
grew again and her mother, Umm Ruman, came to her while she was
playing in a swing with some of her girl friends. She called her and
she went to her not knowing what her mother wanted her to do. Her
mother caught her by the hand and made her stand at the door of the
house. She was breathless. When her breathing normalized, her
mother took some water and rubbed her face and head with it. Then
she took her into the house. There in the house she saw some women
Helpers who wished her God's blessings. Her mother entrusted her to
them, and they prepared her for the marriage. Unexpectedly God's
Messenger came to her in the forenoon, and her mother handed her

over to him. At that time she was a girl of nine years of age.

SB v5 p152 n234; SB v8 p95 n151; SM v4A p101 n2440; AD v3 p1371 n4913; AD v3 p1374 n4915

❧ GIVING ONE'S WIFE THE OPTION TO DIVORCE OR NOT TO DIVORCE

AYISHA RELATED:

When God's Messenger granted the option to his wives, he began by saying, 'I am going to mention to you a matter which you should not decide in haste—that is, until you have consulted your parents.' She said that he already knew that her parents would never allow her to seek separation from him. He said, 'God, the Exalted and Glorious, said, "Prophet, say to your wives: If you desire this world's life and its adornment then come, I will give you a provision and allow you a good departure. If you desire God and His Messenger and the abode of the hereafter, then God has prepared for the doers of good among you a great reward."' All the wives agreed to stay married as she had done.

SM v2B p407 n1475; SB v6 p292 n308; SB v6 p293 n309; IM v2u p102 n203

AYISHA RELATED:

God's Messenger gave his wives the option to [either accept the situation as it was or] be divorced, but they did not choose divorce.

SM v2B p407 n1477, R2-R4; SB v7 p137 n189; SB v7 p137 n188; ; AD v2 p594 n2197

GUARDIAN

It Is Permissible for a Father to Give His Daughter in Marriage Even When She is a Young Girl

AYISHA RELATED:

God's Messenger married her when she was six years old, and she went to his house at the age of nine. She further narrated that they went to Madinah, and she had a fever for a month and her hair became as short as her earlobes. Her mother, Umm Ruman, went with her. At that time she was on a swing with her playmates. Her mother called her loudly. She went. She did not know what she wanted from her. Her mother took her hand and took her to the door. She gasped until the agitation of her heart was over. Her mother took her to a house where women of the Helpers had gathered. They all blessed her and wished her luck. She said they washed her head and embellished her. Nothing frightened her. God's Messenger came there in the morning, and she was entrusted to him.

SM v2B p352 n1422 R1-R3; SB v7 p32 n65; SB v7 p50 n64; IM v2u p32 n31; AD v2 p569 n2116

Marriage Without a Guardian is Not Valid

AYISHA RELATED:

If a woman has no close relative who can act as guardian, then the ruler of the land is her guardian.

IM v2u p34 n36

Permission Needed

AYISHA RELATED:

The Prophet said, 'If a virgin agrees to marriage without the permission of her guardian, her marriage is void, her marriage is void, her marriage is void. If there is intercourse with her, there must be a dowry for her because her private parts have been made lawful. If they dispute, then the ruler is the guardian for those who have no guardian.'

T [H v2 p651]; AD v2 p557 n2078; AD v2 p557 n2079; AD v2 p557 n2078; IM v2u p33 n35

PRE-ISLAMIC TYPES

AYISHA RELATED:

There were four types of marriage during the Age of Ignorance before Islam. One type was similar to that of the present day [that is, a man asked somebody else for the hand of a girl under his guardianship or asked a man for his daughter and gave her dowry and then married her.]

The second type occurred when a man told his wife, after she had become free from her period, to send for some man to have sexual relations with her. Her husband would then stay away from her and would not have sexual intercourse with her until she became pregnant from the other man with whom she had slept. When her pregnancy became evident, her husband would have sexual intercourse with her if he wished. Her husband did so [let his wife sleep with some other man] so that he might have a child of noble breed. Such marriage was called al-istibda.

Another type of marriage occurred when a group of less than ten men assembled. All of them had sexual relations with her. If she became pregnant and delivered a child and some days had passed after her delivery, she would send for all of them, and none of them would refuse to come. When they gathered before her, she would say to them that they all knew what they had done. Now she had given birth to a child so it was the child of so and so, naming whomever she liked. Her child would follow the man she named, and he could not refuse to take him.

The fourth type of 'marriage' occurred when many men had intercourse with a woman who never refused anyone who came to her. Such women were prostitutes who fixed flags at their doors as a sign, and anyone who wished could have sexual intercourse with them. If any prostitute became pregnant and delivered a child, then all the men would gather to call the persons skilled in recognizing the likeness of a child to his father (physiogonmists). The prostitute would let her child follow the man whom they recognized as his father. She would let him adhere to him and be called his son. The man could not refuse. When Muhammad was sent with the Truth, he abolished all the types of 'marriage' observed in the pre-Islamic Age of Ignorance, except the type of marriage people recognize today.

SB v7 p44 n37 Title; AD v2 p614 n2265

POLYGAMY

Abandoning One's Wife For a Time

AYISHA RELATED:

The camel of Safiya bint Huyayy was fatigued and Zaynab had a surplus mount. The Messenger of God said to Zaynab, 'Give her the camel.' She asked why she should give it to a Jewess. Thereupon, the Messenger of God became angry and stayed away from Zaynab during the months of Dhu al-Hijjah, Muharram and a part of Safar.

AD v3 p1293 n4585

Behavior of the Prophet Towards His Wives

AYISHA RELATED:

The Messenger said, 'Good among you are those who are good to their wives and I, for my part, am very good to my wives.'

T [MMT v4 p135]

Best Days for Marriage

AYISHA RELATED:

The Prophet married her in the month of Shawwal, and she was his favorite wife. She advised women to go to their husbands in the month of Shawwal.

IM v2u p74 n143

Division of Time Among One's Wives

AYISHA RELATED:

God's Messenger used to divide his time equally [among his wives]. He said, 'O God, this is my division concerning what I possess. Do not blame me concerning what You possess and I do not.'

AD v2 p572 n2129; IM v2u p67 n124; T [H v1 p204]

Gift to Co-Wife

AYISHA RELATED:

Sawda became old, and the Prophet wished to divorce her. She asked the Prophet not to divorce her because of her advanced age, as she wanted to be honored and respected as one of his wives on the day of judgment. She knew the Prophet was more inclined towards her (Ayisha) and voluntarily gave her marital rights to her. She was aware of the fact that the Prophet loved her (Ayisha), and this gift made it possible for the Prophet to stay with Ayisha one more night.

IM v2u p67 n125; SB v7 p104 n139; SM v2B p391 n1463

AYISHA RELATED:

One day the Prophet became angry with Safiya bint Huyayy. Safiya solicited her help to get her husband to forgive her. She [Ayisha] offered Safiya her turn with the Prophet. After the Prophet and Safiya made up, she [Ayisha] went to talk to him. The Prophet said that that day was not her day to be with him. She then told the Prophet the whole story, and he forgave her [Ayisha].

IM v2u p68 n126

Happy Life With Wives

AYISHA RELATED:

Once she and the Prophet ran a race together, and she won the race.

IM v2u p70 n131

AYISHA RELATED:

One day the Prophet returned to Madinah from Khaybar. Some woman from among the Helpers came from the marriage of Safyia bint Huyayy and described the occasion. She was not amused and covered her face. The Prophet looked at her and realized her anger. When she turned away from him, he caught her and placed her on his lap. He asked, 'What did you see?' She told him to leave her alone because Safiya was a Jewish woman.'

IM v2u p70 n132; IM v2u p75 n145

UMM SALAMA RELATED:

God's Messenger married her. He mentioned so many things in this connection that he said, 'If you desire that I spend a week with you, I shall have to spend a week with my other wives.'

SM v2B p390 n1460, R4

Husband's Delegation to His Wife

AYISHA RELATED:

The Prophet delegated to his wives the rights which they returned to him. Then he did not care much about it.

IM v2u p102 n202

Husband's Rights Over His Wife

AYISHA RELATED:

The Prophet said, 'If ever I ordered a woman to prostrate, it would have been to her husband.'

IM v2u p22 n7

If a Man Goes to All His Wives on the Same Day

AYISHA RELATED:

Whenever the Messenger finished his afternoon prescribed prayer, he visited his wives and stayed with one of them. One day he went to Hafsa and stayed with her longer than usual.

SB v7 p106 n143

Jealousy of Women and Their Anger

AYISHA RELATED:

God's Messenger said to her, 'I know when you are pleased with me and angry with me.' She asked him how he knew. He said, 'When you are pleased with me, you say, "No, by the Lord of Muhammad," and when you are angry with me you say, "No, by the Lord of Abraham."'

SB v7 p114 n155

Marrying a Virgin

AYISHA RELATED:

The Prophet did not marry any virgin except herself.

SB v7 p8 n2

Permissibility of Bestowing the Turn on One's Fellow Wife

AYISHA RELATED:

She felt jealous of the women who offered themselves to God's Messenger. Verse 33:51 was revealed, *'You may defer any one of them you wish and take to yourself any one you wish and if you desire any one you have set aside [no sin is chargeable to you].'* She said to God's Messenger that it seemed to her that his Lord hastened to satisfy his desire.

SM v2B p392 n1464, R1; SB v7 p35 n48; SB v6 p295 n311; SB v6 p295 n312; SM v2B p407 n1476; AD v2 p572 n2131; IM v2u p79 n153

REFUSED

AYISHA RELATED:

Once Umra bint Jaun was brought to the Prophet. Some of the wives of the Prophet told her to say that she sought God's protection from the Prophet because the Prophet would be happy to hear those words. Hearing this the Prophet said she should seek protection from one who was higher.

IM v2u p96 n188

REMARRIAGE OF A DIVORCEE

AYISHA RELATED:

The wife of Rifaa al-Qurazi went to God's Messenger while she [Ayisha] was sitting there. Abu Bakr was also there. Rifaa's wife said that after Rifaa had divorced her irrevocably [and the waiting period had passed], she married Abd al-Rahman ibn al-Zubayr who, by God had only something like a fringe of a garment [that is, a small penis], showing the fringe of her veil. Khalid ibn Said, who was standing at the door, because he had not as yet been admitted [to see the Messenger], heard her statement. He [Khalid ibn Said] asked why Abu Bakr did not stop this woman from saying such things openly before God's Messenger. He [Khalid ibn Said] said that the Messenger did nothing but smiled. Then the Messenger said to the woman, 'Perhaps you want to return to Rifaa. That is possible only if Abd al-Rahman consumates his marriage to you.'

SB v7 p459 n684; SB v3 p489 n807; SM v2B p369 n1433

REMARRIAGE OF A PREGNANT WIDOW

UMM SALAMA RELATED:

A women from the Aslam tribe called Subaia became a widow while she was pregnant. Abu al-Sanabil ibn Bakak demanded her hand in marriage, but she refused to marry him. She said that she could not marry him unless she has completed one of the two prescribed periods. About ten days later [after having delivered her child] she went to the Prophet, and he said that she could then marry.

SB v7 p182 n239; SB v7 p181 n237

UMM SALAMA RELATED:

God's Messenger went to visit her when Abu Salama died. She had put the juice of aloes on herself. He asked her what it was, and she told him it was only the juice of aloes and contained no perfume. He said, 'It gives the face a glow so apply it only at night and remove it in the daytime. Do not comb your hair with scent or henna for it is a dye.' She asked God's Messenger what she should use when combing her hair, and he told her to use lote-tree leaves and smear her head copiously with them.

N [MMR v1 p710]; N [H v3 p70]

RESTRAINT FROM WIVES 🦌

UMM SALAMA RELATED:

The Prophet vowed to keep aloof from his wives for a period of one month, and after the completion of twenty-nine days, he went either in the morning or in the afternoon to his wives. Someone said to him that he had vowed not to go to his wives for one month. He replied, 'This month was of twenty-nine days.'

SB v3 p73 n134; IM v2u p105 n209; SB v7 p99 n130

AYISHA RELATED:

Once the Prophet vowed not to have intercourse with his wife Zaynab because she had refused to accept a present from him.

IM v2u p106 n210

AYISHA RELATED:

Once the Prophet vowed to abstain from sex with his wife and to abstain from eating honey and paid expiation for it.

IM v2u p113 n226

TRADITION OF UMM ZARA

AYISHA RELATED:

Eleven women sat together promising each other that they would conceal nothing about their spouses. The first one said that her husband was like the meat of a lean camel placed at the top of a hill which was difficult to climb. The meat was not good enough that one had the urge to take it from the top of the mountain.

The second one said that her husband was so bad that she was afraid she could not describe his faults—visible and invisible—completely.

The third one said that her husband was a tall man but lacked intelligence. If she gave vent to her feelings about him, he would divorce her, but if she kept quiet, she would be made to live in a state of suspense [neither completely abandoned by him nor entertained as a wife].

The fourth said that her husband was like the night of Tihama [the night of the Hijaz and Makkah]—neither too cold nor too hot. She felt neither fear of him nor grief.

The fifth said that her husband was like a leopard as he entered the house and behaved like a lion when he left. He did not ask about that which he left in his house.

The sixth said that as far as her husband was concerned, he ate so much that nothing was left over, and when he drank, no drop was left behind. When he lay down, he wraped his body and did not touch her so that he might know his grief.

The seventh said that her husband was heavy in spirit, having no brightness in him, impotent, suffering from every conceivable disease, having such rough manners that he might break her head or wound her body or both.

The eighth said that her husband was as sweet as the sweet-smelling plant and as soft as the softness of the hare.

The ninth said that her husband was the master of a lofty building, tall, with heaps of ashes at his door; and his house was near the meeting place and the inn.

The tenth said that her husbad was Malik. How fine was Malik, much above appreciation and praise. He had many folds of camels, more in number than the pastures for them. When they heard the sound of music, they became sure that they were going to be slaughtered.

The eleventh said that her husband was Abu Zara. a fine man. He had suspended in her ears heavy ornaments and fed her liberally so that her sinews and bones were covered with fat. He made her happy. He had found her among the shepherds living by the side of the mountain and made her the owner of horses, camels, lands and heaps of grain. He found no fault with her. She further said that she slept and got up in the morning at her own sweet will and drank to her heart's content, that the mother of Abu Zara had heavily packed receptacles in her house, that the son of Abu Zara's bed was as soft as a green palmstick drawn forth from its bark or a sword drawn forth from its scabbard, and that Abu Zara's son was satiated with just the foreleg of a lamb. As far as the daughter of Abu Zara was concerned, how fine she was, obedient to her father, obedient to her mother, fleshy and a source of jealousy to her co-wife. The fine slave girl of Abu Zara did not disclose their affaris to other, did not remove the wheat or provision or take it forth or squander it but preserved it faithfully as a sacred trust. She did not let the house fill with rubbish.

She further recounted that once Abu Zara left the house when the milk had been churned in the vessels. He met a woman having two children like leopards playing with her pomegranates under her vest. He divorced her and married that woman whom he had met on the way. She later married another man, a chief, who was an expert rider and a fine archer. He bestowed upon her many gifts and gave her one pair of every kind of animal. He told her to make use of everything she needed and to send for her parents. Even if she combined all the gifts that the chief had bestowed on her, they would stand no comparision with the least gift of Abu Zara. She [Ayisha] then said to the Messenger that she was for him as Abu Zara was for Umm Zara.

SM v4A p105 n2448; SB v7 p82 n117

VIRGIN'S CONSENT

AYISHA RELATED:

God's Messenger said, 'It is essential to have the consent of a virgin [for marriage].' She said that a virgin feels shy. The Prophet said, 'Her silence means her consent.' Some people said that if a man fell in love with an orphan slave girl or a virgin and she refused him, then he would trick her by bringing two false witness to testify that he had married her. Then after she attained the age of puberty and a judge accepted the false witness, the husband (knowing that the witnesses were false) might consummate his marriage.

SB v9 p82 n101; SB v7 p52 n68; SB v9 p69 n79; SM v2B p352 n1420; IM v2u p309 n777

VIRGINS

AYISHA RELATED:

She asked the Prophet if he had landed in a valley where there was a tree from which something had been eaten and then found a tree of which nothing had been eaten, which tree would he let his camel grace? He said, 'I would let my camel graze the one of which nothing has been eaten before.'

SB v7 p10 n14

WAITING PERIOD OF A WIDOW

ZAYNAB BINT KAB RELATED:

The husband of her sister, Furaya bint Malik ibn Sinan, went in search of his slaves. The slaves killed him at Qadim village about six miles from the city of Madinah. When the news of her husband's death reached Madinah, she was visiting the family of the Helpers a little distance from her family's house. She went to the Prophet with the news of the death of her husband and informed him that he had left nothing for her to live on or any subsistence and, further, her family and near kin lived far from her. She asked if she could move back to her family. The Prophet said she could do as she wished. She was overjoyed to hear this. She had hardly left the mosque when the Prophet called her back and told her to stay in the house where she heard the news of the death of her husband to observe the waiting period. She stayed there for four months and ten days to complete the waiting period.

IM v2u p93 n182; AD v2 p625 n2293; T [MMR v1 p710]; IM [MMR v1]; N [MMR v1]

WEDDING FEAST

Fatima bint Muhammad

AYISHA RELATED:

The Prophet asked her and Umm Salama to prepare the dowry of Fatima. They escorted her to the house of Ali ibn Abu Talib. They took some soil from the Batha plain and plastered one room of Ali's house. They made two large pillows with date palm fibers and served the guests with dates, grapes and sweet water. They made a corner in the room where they placed a wooden stand for hanging clothes and a water bag. They had never seen such a wonderful occasion as Fatima's marriage feast.

IM v2u p44 n66

Giving a Banquet with Less Than One Sheep

SAFIYA BINT SHAYBA RELATED:

The Prophet gave a banquet with two mudds [one mudd = 3/4 kilo] of barley when marrying one of his wives.

SB v7 p52 n101

WIDOW'S MOURNING PERIOD

A Widow Should Mourn for Four Months and Ten Days

ZAYNAB BINT ABU SALAMA RELATED:

She went to Umm Habiba, the wife of the Prophet, when her father, Abu Sufyan ibn Harb had died. Umm Habiba asked for a perfume which contained yellow scent or some other scent and first perfumed one of the girls with it and then rubbed her own cheeks with it. She said that she was not in need of perfume but had heard God's Messenger say, 'It is not lawful for a lady who believes in God and the last day to mourn for a dead person for more than three days unless he was her husband for whom she should mourn for four months and ten days.' She [Zaynab] further said that she went to Zaynab bint Jahsh when her brother died. She asked for perfume, used some of it, and said that she was not in need of perfume but had heard God's Messenger saying from the *minbar* that it was not lawful for a lady who believed in God and the last day to mourn for more than three days—except for her husband for whom she should mourn for four months and ten days. She [Zaynab] further said that she heard her mother, Umm Salama, say that a woman went to God's Messenger and said that the husband of her daughter had died, and that [her daughter] was suffering from an eye disease. She wanted to know if she could apply collriyum to her eye. The Messenger replied, 'No,' two or three times. Then he added, 'It is just a matter of four months and ten days. In the pre-Islamic period of ignorance a widow among them had to throw a globe of dung when one year was elapsed.' The narrator asked what that meant and was told that when a woman was bereaved of her husband, she used to live in a wretched small room, put on the worst clothes she had, and not touch any scent for one year. Then she would bring an animal [donkey, sheep or bird] and rub her body against it. The animal against which she rubbed her body would scarcely survive. Only then could she come out of her room; whereupon, she would be given a globe of dung to throw away and would use the scent she liked.'

SB v7 p190 n251: SB v7 p192 n252A; SM v2B p423 n1488 R2; SM v2B p423 n489; AD v2 p626 n2298; IM v2u p116 n235A; SB v7 p194 n255; SM v2B p425 n938R2; SM v2B p425 n1491; SM v2B p424 n1490 R4-R5 ; AD v2 p626 n2295; AD v2 p626 n2296; IM v2u p117 n240; IM v2u p117 n241; IM v2u p117 n242; SB v7 p193 n254; SB v7 p194 n255; SM v2B p424 n1490R4-5

Can A Widow Leave Her Home During the Waiting Period

AYISHA RELATED:

Once Fatima bint Qays informed the Prophet that she was afraid of staying by herself while she observed the waiting period. He permitted her to change her residence.

IM v2u p95 n184

It Is Obligatory to Abstain from Adornment

ZAYNAB BINT ABU SALAMA RELATED:

She went to Umm Habiba when her father died. Umm Habiba sent for a yellowish perfume or something like it. She applied it to a girl and then rubbed it on her own cheeks saying she had no need of perfume, but had heard God's Messenger saying on the *minbar*, 'It is not permissible for a woman believing in God and the hereafter to mourn for the dead beyond three days. But in the case of the death of her husband, it is permissible for four months and ten days.'

SM v2B p423 n1486, R1, R3; SB v7 p194 n257; SB v7 p193 n252B; SB v7 p193 n253; SM v2B p423 n1487; AD v2 p624 n2292; SB v2 p207 n370; SB v1 p185 n310

ZAYNAB BINT ABU SALAMA RELATED:

When the husband of a woman died, she went into a hut and put on her worst clothes and did not apply perfume or something like it until a year was over. Then an animal like a donkey or a goat or a bird was brought to her, and she rubbed her hand over it. It once happened that the animal on which she rubbed her hand died. She then came out of her house and was given dung. She threw it and then made use of anything like perfume or something else as she liked.

SM v2B p423 n1489

Treating Diseases of the Eye

UMM SALAMA RELATED:

The husband of a woman died, and her eyes became sore. The people mentioned her story to the Prophet. They asked him whether it was permissible for her to use collyrium, as her eyes were exposed to danger. He said, 'Previously when one of you was bereaved by a husband, she would stay in her dirty clothes in a bad, unhealthy house for one year. When a dog passed by she would throw a clump of dung. No. She should observe the prescribed waiting period of four months and ten days.

SB v7 p408 n607

Things From Which a Widow Should Abstain

UMM SALAMA RELATED:

The Messenger of God said, 'A woman whose husband has died must not wear clothes dyed with safflower or with red ochre and ornaments. She must not apply henna and collyrium.

AD v2 p626 n2297; N [H v3 p71]

WIFE'S FEAR OF HUSBAND

AYISHA RELATED:

Regarding the verse, *'If a wife fears cruelty or desertion on her husband's part...'* [4:128], it concerns the woman whose husband does not want to keep her with him any longer but wants to divorce her and marry some other woman. She may tell him to keep her and not to divorce her but to marry another woman. She may say that he does not need to spend on her, nor does he need to sleep with her. This is indicated in the verse, *'There is no blame on them if they arrange an amicable settlement between them both and such settlement is better'* [4:128].

SB v7 p101 n134; SB v6 p99 n125; SB v3 p378 n630; SB v3 p378 n630; SB v3 p533 n859; SM v4B p400 n3021 R1; IM 2u p68 n127; SB v9 p360

CHAPTER 11
MEDICINE AND SPELLS

DISEASE AND TREATMENT

Blowing With a Slight Shower of Saliva While Treating with a Recitation of Quranic Verse

AYISHA RELATED:

Whenever God's Messenger went to bed, he recited the Chapters of Sincere Religion [al-Ikhlas], the Chapter of Dawn [al-Fajr] and the Chapter of Humanity [al-Nas] and then blew on his palms and passed them over his face and those parts of his body that his hands could reach. When he fell ill, he ordered her to do this for him.

SB v7 p430 n644; SB v7 p433 n647; SB v6 p495 n535; SB v6 p495 n536; SB v7 p433 n647; SB v7 p423 n631; SM v3B p451 n2192; AD v3 p1094 n3893; AD v3 p1402 n5038; SB v8 p223 n331

AYISHA RELATED:

Whenever the Messenger became ill, he recited the last two chapters of the Quran, and blew his breath over himself and rubbed his hands over his body. When he was afflicted with his fatal illness, she began reciting the last two chapters, blowing her breath over him [as he used to blow], and moving the hand of the Prophet over his body.

SB v5 p515 n723; SB v5 p510 n714

Cupping

SALAMA, THE PROPHET'S WOMAN SERVANT, RELATED:

Whoever complained to the Messenger about a headache was told to be cupped. If anyone complained of a pain in his legs, the Messenger told him to dye them with henna.

AD v3 p1084 n3849; T [MMR v2 p948]

KABSHA BINT ABU BAKR RELATED:

Abu Bakr forbade his family to be cupped on a Tuesday because the Prophet had told him, 'Tuesday is the day of blood in which there is an hour when it does not stop.' [Tuesday is ruled by the planet Mars].

AD v3 p1084 n3853

UMM SALAMA RELATED:

She asked for permission to be cupped, and God's Messenger asked Abu Tayba [her foster brother or a young boy before puberty] to cup her.

SM v3B p457 n2206

Excellence of Curing the Influence of the Evil Eye

AYISHA RELATED:

God's Messenger granted permission to the members of a family of the Helpers to make an incantation to remove the effects of the poison of the scorpion.

SM v3B p452 n2193R1

Fever is From the Heat of Hell

FATIMA BINT AL-MUNDHIR RELATED:

Whenever a women suffering from fever was brought to Asma bint Abu Bakr, she invoked God's name and sprinkled some water on the patient's chest. She said that God's Messenger ordered them to reduce fever with water.

SB v7 p415 n620

Hanging Amulets

ZAYNAB, THE WIFE OF ABD ALLAH IBN MASUD, RELATED:

Her husband, Abd Allah ibn Masud had heard the Messenger of God say, 'Spells, charms and love-spells are polytheism.' She asked her husband why the Prophet said this. Her eye had been discharging, and she had gone to the Jewish doctor who applied a spell to her. When he applied the spell, the inflammation in her eye had subsided. Abd Allah said that this was the work of the devil. He told her all she needed to do was to say what the Messenger of God said, 'Remove the harm, O Lord of people, and heal. You are the Healer. There is no remedy but Yours which leaves all diseases behind.'

AD v3 p1089 n3874

Incantations Against the Evil Eye

ASMA BINT UMAYS RELATED:

She asked the Messenger of God about the children of Jafar as they were easily susceptible to the evil eye. She asked if they could seek charms for them. He replied, 'Yes, because if there is anything which precedes pre-determination, it is surely the evil eye.'

IM [H v2 p81]

AYISHA RELATED:

When any person was ill with a disease or had an ailment or had an injury, God's Messenger placed his forefinger upon the ground and then lifted it reciting the Name of God and said, 'The dust of our ground with the saliva of any one of us serves as a means whereby our illness can be cured with the sanction of God.'

SM v3B p452 n2194; SB v7 p429 n641; SB v7 p428 n642; AD v3 p1092 n3886

AYISHA RELATED:

God's Messenger commanded the use of incantation for removing the influence of an evil eye.

SM v3B p452 n2195, R2

UMM SALAMA RELATED:

God's Messenger said to a small girl in the house of Umm Salama that the black stains on her face were due to the influence of an evil eye. He asked that she be cured with the help of incantation , made in the hope that her face should become spotless.

SM v3B p453 n2197; SB v7 p426 n635

Inserting Medicine in the Side of One's Mouth

UMM QAYS BINT MIHSAN RELATED:

She went to God's Messenger with her son whose palate and tonsils she had pressed with her finger as a treatment for a [throat and tonsil] disease. The Prophet asked, 'Why do you pain your children by pressing his throats? Use al-Hindi [a certain Indian incense], for it cures seven diseases, one of which is pleurisy. It is used as a snuff for treating throat and tonsil disease and is inserted into one side of the mouth of one suffering from pleurisy.'

SB v7 p411 n611; SB v7 p414 n616; SB v7 p412 n613; SM v3B p459 n2214R1; AD v3 p1088 n3868; SB v7 p402 n596

Invocation of the Visitor for the Patient

AYISHA RELATED:

Whenever God's Messenger paid a visit to a patient or a patient was brought to him, he invoked God saying, 'Take away the disease, O the Lord of the people! Cure him as You are the One Who cures. There is no cure but Yours, a cure that allows no disease.'

SB v7 p392 n579

Invocations to Take Away Epidemics and Disease

AYISHA RELATED:

The Prophet said, 'O God! Make us love Madinah as You made us love Makkah or more. Transfer the fever that is in it to al-Juhfa. O God! Bless our weights and measures.'

SB v8 p254 n383

Laxative

ASMA BINT UMAYS RELATED:

The Messenger asked her what laxative she used. She said whatt she used to purge; whereupon, he said that it [the laxative] was very hot. She then used senna as a purgative; and the Prophet said, 'If anything contained a remedy for death, it would be senna.'

IM [MMR v2 p948]; IM [Hv2]; T [Hv2 p77]

Magic

AYISHA RELATED:

Magic was worked on God's Messenger [by a Jewish man of the

Zurayq tribe called Labib ibn al-Asam] so that he thought that he had had sexual relations with his wives but actually had not. Then one day he said, 'O Ayisha! Do you know that God has instructed me concerning things I asked Him about? Two men came to me. One of them sat near my head, and the other sat near my feet. The one near my head asked the other what was wrong with me. The latter replied that I was under the effect of magic. The first one asked who has worked magic on him. The other replied that Labid ibn al-Asam from the Zurayq tribe (who was an ally of the Jews and was a hypocrite) had done this. The first one asked what he had used to do this. The other replied that he had used a comb and the hair stuck to it. The first one asked where it was. The other replied that it was wrapped in a skin of pollen of a male date palm tree kept under a stone in the well of Dharwan.' The Prophet then went to that well and took out those things and said, "This was the well which was shown to me in a dream. Its water looked like the infusion of henna leaves and its dates like the heads of devils." The Prophet added, 'Then that thing was taken out." He was asked why he did not treat himself with *nashra* [a special kind of treatment]. The Messenger replied, "God has cured me. I don't like to let evil spread among my people.'

> SB v7 p442 n658; SB v7 p443 n660; SB v7 p444 n661; SB v8 p56 n89; SB v8 p266 n400; SB v4 p267 n400; SB v4 p317 n490

Medicine for Making Women Fat

AYISHA RELATED:

Her mother intended to help her gain weight in order to send her to the Messenger of God, but nothing worked until her mother gave her cucumber with fresh dates to eat. Then she gained weight [as her mother had desired].

> AD v3 p1094 n3894

Men Treating Women / Women Treating Men

RUBAYYI BINT MUADH IBN AFRA RELATED:

They went with the Messenger on military expeditions, provided the people with water, served them, and took the dead and wounded back to Madinah.

> SB v7 p395 n583

There is a Remedy for Every Malady

AYISHA RELATED:

When any one among them was ill, God's Messenger rubbed him with his right hand and said, 'O Lord of the people, grant him health. Heal him for You are a great Healer. With Your healing power one is healed and illness is removed.' When God's Messenger was ill and his illness took a serious turn, she took his hand so that she could do what he used to do with it; but he withdrew his hand from her hand and said, 'O God, pardon me and make me join the companionship on high.' She said that she gazed at him constantly after he had passed away.

SM v3B p450 n2191, R2-R3, R5; SB v7 p432 n646; SB v7 p428 n639; SB v7 p428 n640; IM v2 p462 n1619

DIVINATION

SAFIYA RELATED:

God's Messenger said, 'When anyone visits a diviner and asks him about anything, for forty nights his prescribed prayers will not be accepted.'

SM v3B p472 n2230

FEVER

AYISHA RELATED:

The Prophet said, 'Fever is from the heat of hell fire so cool it with water.'

SB v4 p314 n485

GOOD AND EVIL OMENS

AYISHA RELATED:

A man casting an evil eye was commanded to peform ablution. Then the man affected by that evil eye was washed with the ablution water.

AD v3 p1088 n3871

HASA SOUP

For Sickness

AYISHA RELATED:

When the Messenger's family was exhausted from fever, God's Messenger ordered some soup made of flour, water and either oil or clarified butter [*hasa*] to be prepared. He then ordered them to sip some of it. He used to say, 'It heartens the sad and clears the heart of the invalid, as one of you clears dirt away from her face with water.'

T [MMR v2 p896]

ASMA RELATED:

A woman running a high fever was brought to her. She asked water to be brought and then sprinkled it on the uppermost part of the woman's chest. She (Ayisha) said that God's Messenger had said, 'Cool fever with water, for it comes from the vehemence of the heat of hell.'

SM v3B p458 n2211; SB v7 p416 n621; SB v4 p314 n485; SM v3B p458

Treating Snakebite or a Scorpion Sting With a Recitation of a Quranic Verse

AYISHA RELATED:

The Prophet allowed the treatment of poisonous sting with recitation of a Quranic verse.

SB v7 p427 n637

Visiting a Patient Who is Near Death

UMM SALAMA RELATED:

God's Messenger said, 'When you visit a patient or a dying person you should say good [words] because the angels say, "Amin" to whatever you say.' When Abu Salama passed away, she [Ayisha] went to the Messenger and told him. He said, 'Say: O God, forgive me and him. Grant me a better substitute.' She did and God granted [a substitute] who was better: he was Muhammad, God's Messenger.

IM v2 p366 n1447; SM v2A p43 n919; AD v2 p887 n3109

AYISHA RELATED:

She did not see anyone else being afflicted with more severe illness than God's Messenger.

SM v4A p176 n2570

MAGIC

UMM SALAMA RELATED:

She asked the Messenger if the pain of poisoned mutton which he had previously eaten had not ceased to afflict him. He said, 'Nothing affected me therefrom, but it [my illness] had already been decreed for me—even before Adam was created.'

IM [H v3 p115] ; MMR v1

PATIENTS

Severity of Disease

AYISHA RELATED:

She never saw anybody suffering as much from sickness as God's Messenger.

SB v7 p373 n549

Sick Men Visited by Women

AYISHA RELATED:

When God's Messenger migrated to Madinah, Abu Bakr and Bilal came down with a fever. She visited them and asked how they were. Whenever fever attacked Abu Bakr, he would recite the following poetic verses: everybody stays alive among his people, yet death is nearer to him than his shoe laces. Whenever the fever deserted Bilal, he would recite these lines of poetry: would that I could stay overnight in a valley wherein I might be surrounded by two kinds of good smelling grass and would that one day I might drink of the water of *majinna* and would that two mountains in Makkah might appear to me. When she [Ayisha] informed God's Messenger about this, he said, 'O God! Make us love Madinah as much or more than we love Makkah. O God! Make it healthy and bless its weights and measures for us and take away its fever and put it in al-Juhfa.'

SB v7 p378 n558; SB v7 p394 n581; SB v3 p62 n113

Sickness Is Expiation for Sins

AYISHA RELATED:

God's Messenger said, 'No calamity befalls a Muslim but that God removes some of his sins because of it—even though it were only the prick he receives from a thorn.'

SB v7 p371 n544; SM v4A p177 n2572R1, R2, R5-R6

PHYSIOGAMY

AYISHA RELATED:

God's Messenger came to her in a happy mood with his features gilttering with joy. He asked, 'Have you not heard what the expert in recognizing the son of another (by comparing some of the physical features of the purported father and son) has said about Zayd and Usama? He saw their feet and remarked that they belong to each other [that is, they are father and son].'

SB v4 p488 n755; SB v8 p502 n761; SB v8 p502 n762; SM v2B p388 n1459R1;
AD v2 p612 n2260; IM v2u p228 n508

PROPHETS

Children of Israel

AYISHA RELATED:

She asked the Prophet about the plague. He told her that it was a punishment sent by God on whom He wished. He told her that God made it a source of mercy for the believers because, if one during the time of plague stayed in his country patiently hoping for God's reward and believing that nothing would befall him except what God had written for him, he would receive the reward of a martyr.

SB v4 p452 n680

"Nothing will befall us except what God..."

AYISHA RELATED:

She asked the Messenger about the plague. He said, 'That was a means of torture which God sent upon whomsoever He wished, but He made it a source of mercy for the believers. He said that anyone who resided in a town in which this disease was present and remained there and did not leave that town but was patient and hoped for God's reward and knew that nothing would befall him except what God had written for him, would receive the reward of a martyr.'

SB v8 p402 n616; SB v7 p422 n630; SM v3A p292 n1916

Prevention

UMM AL-MUNDHAR BINT QAYS AL-ANSARIYAH RELATED:

God's Messenger came to visit her accompanied by Ali who was convalescing. They had some ripe dates hung from the ceiling. God's Messenger got up and began to eat from them. Ali also got up to eat, but God's Messenger kept on saying, 'Stop, Ali, for you are convalescing.' Ali stopped. She then prepared some barley and beet-root and brought it in. The Messenger said to Ali, 'Take some of that because it will be more beneficial for you.'

AD v3 p1083 n3847; IM [MMR v2 p893]

Quran

AYISHA RELATED:

When God's Messenger fell ill, Gabriel used to recite these verses, 'In the Name of God, may He cure you from all kinds of illness and safeguard you from the evil of a jealous person when he feels jealous and from the evil influence of the eye.'

SM v3B p448 n2185

Recitation of Quranic Verses Against the Evil Eye

AYISHA RELATED:

The Prophet ordered her or somebody else to recite the first Chapter of the Quran [ruqya means to recite verses from the Quran as a treatment for disease or to avert the evil eye].

SB v7 p426 n634

Spells

SHIFA BINT ABD ALLAH RELATED:

God's Messenger entered the room when she was with Hafsa. He said to Ayisha. 'Why don't you teach Hafsa the spell for skin eruptions as you have taught her how to write?'

AD v3 p1090 n3878

Talbina Gives Comfort to the Patient

AYISHA RELATED:

When there was any bereavement in her family, the women would gather there for condolence. She prepared a light food out of flour and water sweetened with honey and milk [talbina] in a small cauldron. It was cooked and then bread soaked in soup was prepared and poured over the talbina. She told the people to eat it because she had heard God's Messenger say, 'Talbina gives comfort to the aggrieved heart, and it lessens grief.'

SM v3B p461 n2216; SB v7 p401 n593; SB v7 p2434 n328

VISITING THE SICK AND REWARD FOR SICKNESS

On Praying for Recovery of the Sick When One Visits a Sick Person

AYISHA RELATED:

Her father had a complaint at Makkah, and the Messenger of God went to pay a sick visit to him. He put his hand on his forehead, wiped his chest and belly and then said, 'O God! heal Sad and complete his migration.'

AD v2 p883 n3098

On Visiting Sick Women

UMM AL-ALA RELATED:

God's Messenger visited her when she was sick. He said, 'Be glad Umm al-Ala, for God removes the sins of a Muslim by his illness as fire removes the dross from gold and silver.'

AD v2 p880 n3086

QURAN

AYISHA RELATED:

Some people asked the Prophet regarding the soothsayers. He said, 'They are nothing.' They said that some of the things soothsayers said came true. The Prophet said, 'That word which happens to be true is what a *jinn* snatches away [from angels] by stealth and pours into the ears of his friend [the fortune teller] with a sound like the cackling of a hen. The soothsayers then mix one hundred lies with that word.'

SB v9 p488 n650; SB v4 p325 n510; SB p291 n432; SB v4 p325 n; SB v7 p439 n657; SB v8 p150 n232; SM v3B p470 n2228R1

CHAPTER 12
MODESTY

DRESS

SAFIYYA RELATED:

Ayisha said that when the verse, *'They should cover their necks and bosoms not to reveal their beauty,'* was revealed, the women cut their waist sheets at the edges and covered their heads with the cut pieces.

SB v6 p267 n282

UMM SALAMA RELATED:

She was with God's Messenger when Maymuna was with him. Ibn Umm Maktum [who was blind] happened to come by after women had been ordered to observe the veil. The Prophet told them to cover around him. They said he was blind and could neither see nor recognize them. The Prophet said, 'Are both of you blind? Do you not see him?'

AD v3 p1147 n4100; T [Hv2 p694];T [MMR v1]

SAFIYA BINT SHAYBAH RELATED:

She said that Ayisha mentioned the women Helpers, praised them and said good words about them. She then said that when the verse of the Chapter of Light [surah al-nur] was revealed [24:31], they took their curtains, tore them, and made head covers of them.'

AD v3 p1144 n4089; AD v3 p1144 n4090; AD v3 p1144 n4091

Dawn Prescribed Prayer

AYISHA RELATED:

The believing women, modestly dressed, used to attend the dawn prescribed prayer in the Prophet's mosque. After finishing the prescribed prayer, they would return to their homes [in their sheets]. Nobody recognized them because of the darkness.

SB v1 p320 n552; SB v1 p458 n831; SM v1B p361 n645; AD v1 p111 n423; IM v1 p357 n669; N v1E p375 n548; N v1E p375 n549; N v1W p375 n548; SB v1 p225 n368

239

Effeminate Men

UMM SALAMA RELATED:

The Prophet came to her while there was an effeminate man sitting with her. She heard the effeminate man saying to Abd Allah ibn Abu Umaya that if he succeeded the next day in conquering Taif then he [the effeminate man] should take the daughter of Ghaylan in marriage because [she was so beautiful and fat that] she has four folds of flesh when facing front and eight when she turns her back. The Prophet then said, 'These [effeminate] men should never visit you [women].' That effeminate man was called Hit.

SB v5 p428 n613; SB v7 p118 n162; SM v3B p445 n2181; SM v3B p445 n2180; IM v2u p41 n57

Emancipated Slave

UMM SALAMA RELATED:

God's Messenger said, 'When a slave of one of you women has made an agreement to purchase his freedom and can pay the full price, you must wear the modest dress when with him.'

T [MMR v1 p725]; AD v3 p1101 n3917; IM [MMR v1]

Hanging Down of a Woman's Lower Garment

SAFIYA BINT ABU UBAYR RELATED:

When God's Messenger mentioned the lower garment, Umm Salama asked if it also referred to a woman. God's Messenger replied, 'She may hang it down a span.' She said that her foot would still show. He said, 'Then a forearm's length, not exceeding it.'

AD v3 p1148 n4105

AYISHA RELATED:

She prayed that God bestow His mercy on the early emigrant women who when God revealed, *'They should draw their veils over their necks and bosoms,'* tore their aprons and covered their heads with the pieces.

SB v6 p267

How much beauty can a woman display?

AYISHA RELATED:

Asma bint Abu Bakr, wearing think clothes, arrived where God's Messenger was. God's Messenger turned away from her and said, 'O Asma, when a woman reaches the age of menstruation, it does not suit her that she display parts of her body except this and this,' and he pointed to her face and hands.

AD v3 p1144 n4092

Offering the Prescribed Prayer Without Head Covering

AYISHA RELATED:

She visited to Safiya Umm Talhat al-Talhat and her daughers. Seeing her daughters she said that the Messenger of God entered her apartment and there was a girl there. He gave his lower garment to Ayisha, and said to tear it into two pieces and give one-half to this girl and give the other half to the daughter of Umm Salama. He said, 'I think they have reached puberty.'

AD v1 p168 n642

AYISHA RELATED:

God's Messenger said, 'God does not accept the prayer of a woman who has reached puberty unless she covers her head.'

AD v1 p168 n641; IM v1 p353 n655

Painting Nails With Henna

AYISHA RELATED:

A woman stood behind a screen with a letter (addressed) to the Messenger of God in her hand. The Prophet withdrew his hand and said, 'I know not whether it is the hand of a man or the hand of a woman.' She replied that it was the hand of a woman. He said, 'Had you been a woman, you would have painted your nails with henna.'

N [H v1 p610]; AD v3 p1159 n4154; AD v3 p1159 n4153

Permissibility of Women Going Out in the Fields to Answer the Call of Nature

AYISHA RELATED:

Sawda went out into the fields to answer the call of nature after the time that the partition had been prescribed for woman. She was a bulky woman and very tall. She could not easily conceal herself from anyone who knew her. Umar ibn Khattab saw her. He said that he recognized her, and she should be more careful. She turned back. God's Messenger was at that time in Ayisha's house, and there was a bone in his hand. Sawda came in and complained about Umar. Ayisha said that a revelation came to the Prophet. It ended, and the bone was still in his hand. He said, "Permission has been granted to you that you may go out for your needs."

SM v3B p441 n2170, R3; SB v8p170 n257; SB v6 p300 n318; SB v7 p119 n164

AYISHA RELATED:

The wives of the Messenger used to go to al-Manasi, a vast open place near Baqia at Madinah, to answer the call of nature at night. Umar used to say to the Prophet that his wives should be veiled, but the Messenger did not say to do so.

SB v1 p107 n148; SB v1 p108 n149

Veil of a Woman

UMM SALAMA RELATED:

The Prophet came to visit her when she was veiled and said, 'Use one fold, not two [so that it not resemble a turban].'

AD v3 p1147 n4103

Women Can Cover Face

ASMA RELATED:

Once they were with the Prophet and all of them were in the

sacred state. Whenever a stranger passed by, they used to cover their faces.

IM v2u p439 n1102

AYISHA RELATED:

Women can cover their face, but they should keep their veil away from their mouth when in the sacred state.

IM v2u p439 n1101

FOSTERAGE

Breast Feeding an Adult

AYISHA RELATED:

Once Sihla bint Suhayl went to the Prophet and reported that her husband, Abu Hudayfah, was annoyed seeing Salim in her home. The Prophet listened to her, and told her to breast feed Salim. She said that Salim was grown up, and it was not possible. The Prophet smiled, and said that he knew that. Then she breast fed him [expressing milk in a bowl from which he drank] and reported to the Prophet that her husband was now quite satisfied.

IM v2u p55 n97; SM v2B p384 n1453 R1-R4

AYISHA RELATED:

The Prophet said, 'Breast feeding turns a child into a blood relation.'

IM v2u p53 n90

Breast Feeding and Blood Relationship

UMM HABIBA RELATED:

She asked the Prophet to marry her sister. He asked if this would please her. She said that as she was not the Prophet's only wife, she would not mind having her sister in the family. The Prophet said, 'Two sisters as wives of a man are not permissible.' She said that she heard that he was going to marry Darrah bint Abu Salama. To this he said, 'She is the daughter of Abu Salama who is my blood relation because I shared the breast milk of his mother, Subia. The sister of one's wife and the daughter of one's wife from her previous husband are forbidden in marriage.'

IM v2u p54 n92; SB v7 p217 n285; SM v2B p381 n1449; AD v2 p547 n2051

Does Nursing Less Than Five Times Make Marriage Unlawful

AYISHA RELATED:

In what was sent down in the Quran, ten nursings made marriage unlawful, but they were abrogated by five known ones. When the Prophet died, these words were among what was recited in the Quran.

AD v2 p550 n2057; SM v2B p383 n1452

AYISHA RELATED:

God's Messenger said that one or two nursings of milk do not make marriage unlawful.

AD v2 p550 n2058

Female Unlawful for Marriage

UMM SALAMA RELATED:

The Messenger of God said, 'Nothing makes unlawful on account of fosterage but what unloosens the entrails of the breast. It occurs before weaning.'

T [H v2 p642]

Fosterage on the Part of a Father

UMM SALAMA RELATED:

She said that Aflah ibn Abu al-Quys went to see her. She hid herself from him. He asked why she was hiding herself since he was her paternal uncle. She asked how that was so. He said that the wife of his brother had nursed her. She said that the woman had nursed her and not the man. Thereafter the Messenger of God came, and she told him what had happened. He said, 'He is your paternal uncle. He may visit you.'

AD v2 p548 n2052; SB v3 p493 n812; SB v7 p120 n166; SB v8 p114 n177; SB v6 p301 n319; IM v2u p57 n103

Fosterage Through Hunger During Infancy

AYISHA RELATED:

God's Messenger visited her when a man was sitting near her. He seemed to disapprove of that. She saw signs of anger on his face. When she told him that he was her brother by fosterage, God's Messenger said, 'Consider who your brothers are because of fosterage since fosterage is through hunger [during infancy].'

SM v2B p385 n1455; SB v7 p27 n39; SB v3 p494 n815; SM v2B p378; AD v2 p548 n2053

Hafsa's Foster Uncle

AYISHA RELATED:

She told her uncle that once while the Prophet was in her house, she heard a man asking Hafsa's permission to enter Hafsa's house. She said to the Messenger that she thought that the man was Hafsa's foster uncle, and that he was asking permission to enter. The Messenger replied, 'I think the man is Hafsa's foster uncle.' She (Ayisha) asked if so and so were alive, would he be considered her foster uncle. The Messenger said, 'Yes he would [be treated] as foster relations are treated—that is, like blood relations [in marital affairs].'

SB v3 p495 n814; SB v4 p217 n337; SM v2B p378 n1444 R1

Nursing a Male Child

UMM SALAMA RELATED:

All of the wives of God's Messenger disliked the idea that one with this type of fosterage [having been nursed after the proper period] should come to them and told Ayisha that they only found that concession given to Salim. Umm Salama said that no one was going to be allowed to enter their houses with this type of fosterage, as they did not subscribe to this view.

SM v2B p385 n1454; IM v2u p58 n101

Nursing During Pregnancy or Intercourse With a Woman While She is Nursing a Child

ASMA BINT YAZID IBN AL-SAKAN RELATED:

She heard God's Messenger say, 'Do not inadvertly kill your children because the milk with which a child is nourished while his mother is pregnant overtakes the horseman and throws him from his horse.'

AD v3 p1089 n3872

Nursing From the Breast

UMM SALAMA RELATED:

The Messenger said, 'The only nursing which makes marriage unlawful is that which is taken from the breast and enters the bowels and is taken before the time of weaning.'

T [MMR v1 p674]

Nursing Once or Twice Does Not Prove Relationship

AYISHA RELATED:

Nursing once or twice does not prove relationship.

IM v2u p55 n95

One Gulp or Two of a Mother's Milk Does Not Make Marriage Unlawful

UMM AL-FADL RELATED:

A bedouin went to God's Messenger when he was in her house and said that he had one wife and had married another one besides. His first wife claimed that he had suckled once or twice with his newly married wife. God's Messenger said, 'One nursing or two do not make marriage unlawful.'

SM v2B p382 n1451, R1-R2, R4-R5; SM v2B p382 n1450; IM v2u p55 n96

Permissibility of Intercourse with a Nursing Mother

JUDAMA BINT WAHB AL-ASADIYYA RELATED:

She heard God's Messenger say, 'I intended to prohibit cohabitation with nursing women until I considered that the Romans and the Persians do it without any injury being caused to their children thereby.'

SM v2B p377 n1442, R1-R2; AD v3 p1089 n3873

Prohibition of the Daughter of the Brother by Fosterage

UMM SALAMA RELATED:

It was asked of the Messenger of God if he did not think that the daughter of Hamza was suitable for him. He said, 'Hamza is my brother by reason of fosterage [i.e. they were nursed by the same woman].'

SM v2B p380 n1448

Son of Slave Girl

AYISHA RELATED:

Utba ibn Abu Waqqas authorized his brother Sad to take the son of the slave girl of Zama into his custody. Utba said that he was his son. When God's Messenger arrived in Makkah during the conquest, Sad ibn Abu Waqqas took the son of the slave girl of Zama to the Prophet. Abd ibn Zama too came along with him. Sad said that he was the son of his brother, and the latter had informed him that he was his son. Abd ibn Zama said that he was his brother who was the son of the slave girl of Zama and who was born on his father's bed. God's Messenger looked at the son of the slave girl of Zama and noticed that he, of all the people, had the greatest resemblance to Utba ibn Abu Waqqas. God's Messenger then said to Abd, 'He is yours. He is your brother, O Abd ibn Zama, as he was born on the bed of your father.' At the same time, the Messenger said to his wife Sauda, 'Veil yourself before him [the son of the slave girl] O Sauda,' [because of the resemblance he noticed between him and Utba ibn Abi Waqqas]. God's Messenger added, 'The boy belongs to the bed where he was born, and stones are for the adulterer.'

SB v5 p414 n596; SB v3 p152 n269; SB v3 p232 n421; SB v4 p5 n8; SB v7 p17 n25; v8 p489 n741; SB v9 p221 n293; SB v8 p499 n757; SB v8 p356 n603; SB v8 p529 n807; SM v2B p387 n1457; AD v2 p614 n2266; SB v3 p426 n710

Unlawfulness of a Man of Age by Reason of Fosterage

AYISHA RELATED:

She and Umm Salama said that Abu Hudhayfa ibn Utbah ibn Rabia ibn Abd Shams adopted Salim as his son and married him to his niece Hind, daughter of Walid ibn Utba ibn Rabia. Salim was the freed slave of a woman from the Helpers. The Messenger of God adopted Zayd as his son. In pre-Islamic days when anyone adopted a man as his son, the people called him by his father's name, and he was given a share of his inheritance. God revealed the following: 'Call them by [the name of] their fathers, that is more just in the sight of God. And if you know not their fathers, then [they are] your brothers in the faith and your clients.' They were then called by the names of their fathers. A man whose father was not known remained under the protection of someone and was considered a brother in faith. Sahla, daughter of Suhayl ibn Amr al-Qurayshi, then said to the Messenger that they used to consider Salim their son, as he had dwelt with them and with Abu Hudhayfa in the same house and had seen her in her short clothes. She asked him what his opinion about this was. The Prophet said, 'Breast feed him.' She expressed her milk into a bowl five times from which he drank. He became like her foster-son. Thus she [Ayisha] asked the daughters of her sisters and the daughters of her brothers to nurse five times whatever male she wanted to see and who wanted to visit her—even though he might be of age. He then visited her. But Umm Salama and all other wives of the Propeht refused to allow anyone to visit them on the basis of such nursing, unless one was nursed during infancy. They told her that they did not know whether or not this arrangement was a special concession granted by the Prophet to Salim exclusively.

AD v2 p549 n596

What Is Unlawful by Reason of Consanguinity Is Unlawful by Reason of Fosterage

AYISHA RELATED:

God's Messenger said, 'What is unlawful by reason of consanguinity is unlawful by reason of fosterage.'

AD v2 p547 n2050

IN THE SACRED STATE

AYISHA RELATED:

Riders would pass them when they accompanied the Messenger of God while they were in the sacred state. When the riders came by them, one of them would pull her outer garment from her head over her face. When they had passed, she would uncover her face.

AD v2 p484 n1829; IM v2u p439 n1101

UMM HARITHA RELATED:

She went to God's Messenger after Haritha had been martyred on the day of the Battle of Badr by an arrow shot by an unknown person. She said that the Messenger knew the position of Haritha in her heart [how dear he was to her] so if he [Haritha] were in paradise, she would not weep for him, as he might see what she was doing. The Prophet said, 'Are you mad? Is there only one paradise? There are many paradises, and he is in the highest paradise.' The Prophet added, 'A forenoon journey or an afternoon journey in God's cause is better than the whole world and whatever is in it. A place equal to the size of an arrow's bow or a place equal to a foot in paradise is better than the whole world and whatever is in it. If one of the women of paradise looked at the earth, she would fill the whole space between earth and heaven with light and would fill whatever is in between them with perfume. The veil of her head is better than the whole world and whatever is in it.'

SB v8 p371 n572

NON-MAHRAM

Do Not Look Twice

BURAYDA RELATED:

Once the Prophet said to Ali, 'O Ali [if you see a non-mahram woman by chance] do not look at her twice. Your first glance [which is unintentional] is lawful [and will not be called to account], but the second is not.

T [MMT v4 p280]

The Looking of Women At Other People

AYISHA RELATED:

The Prophet screened her with his garment covering the upper part of his body while she looked at the Ethiopians who were playing in the courtyard of the mosque. She continued watching until she was satisfied. She added that one may deduce from this event how a young girl, [she was fifteen at the time according to some reports], who is eager to enjoy amusement should be treated in this respect.

SB v7 p119 n163

PRIVATE PARTS

AYISHA RELATED:

She never saw the Prophet's private parts.

IM v2u p48 n76; SB v1 p357 n662

CHAPTER 13
MOSQUES AND PLACES OF PRAYER

BUILDING MOSQUES IN DIFFERENT LOCALITIES

Keeping Them Clean and Perfumed
AYISHA RELATED:

God's Messenger commanded them to build mosques in different localities [that is, in the separate locality of each tribe] and commanded that they be kept clean and perfumed.

AD v1 p118 n455; IM v1 p418 n759

Scraping Off Sputum From the Mosque
AYISHA RELATED:

God's Messenger saw some nasal secretion, expectoration or sputum on the *qiblah* wall of the mosque, He scraped it off.

SB v1 p242 n401; SM v1B p316 n549; IM v1 p420 n764

ENTERING THE MOSQUE

FATIMA BINT MUHAMMAD RELATED:

When the Prophet entered the mosque, he would pray for blessings and safety and say, 'My Lord, forgive me my sins and open to me the gates of Your mercy.' And when he went out, he would pray for blessings and safety for himself and say, 'My Lord, forgive me my sins and open to me the gates of Your abundance.'

T [MMR v1 p147]

KABAH

Foundations Built by Abraham
AYISHA RELATED:

God's Messenger said to her, 'Do you not see that when your folk

249

built the Kabah, they did not build it on all the foundations built by Abraham?' She asked why he did not rebuild it on the foundations of Abraham. He said, 'But for the fact that your folk have recently given up infidelity, I would have done so.'

SB v4 p383 n587; SB v6 p12 n11; SB v9 p263 n349; SM v2B p307 n1333 R9; SM v2B p303 n1333

To Offer Prayer at the Hijr al-Hatim

AYISHA RELATED:

She wanted to enter the Kabah and pray there. God's Messenger caught her by the hand and admitted her to the *hijr*. He then said, 'Pray at the *hijr* when you intend to enter the Kabah for it is part of the Kabah. Your people shortened it when they built the Kabah, and they took it out of the House.'

AD v2 p538

MINBAR

WOMAN FROM AMONG THE HELPERS RELATED:

She asked the Messenger if she should make him something to sit on because she had a slave who was a carpenter. He said, 'If you wish.' She had a *minbar* made for him. When it was Friday, he sat on the *minbar*. The date-palm stem near which the Prophet used to deliver his sermons cried so much so that it was about to burst. The Prophet came down from the *minbar* to the stem and embraced it. It started groaning like a child being persuaded to stop crying, and then it stopped. The Prophet said, 'It has cried because of missing what it used to hear of religious knowledge.'

SB v3 p174 n308; SB v1 p262 n440

ON LIGHTING A LAMP IN THE MOSQUE

MAYMUNA, FREED SLAVE GIRL OF THE PROPHET, RELATED:

She asked God's Messenger to tell them the legal injunction about [visiting] Jerusalem. The Messenger of God said, 'Go and pray there. All the cities at this time are effected by war. If you cannot visit it and pray there, then send some oil to be used in the lamps [in the shrine].'

AD v1 p118 n457

PITCHING A TENT IN THE MOSQUE

AYISHA RELATED:

When the Messenger of God intended to observe seclusion, he prayed the dawn prescribed prayer and then entered his place of seclusion. Once when he intended to observe seclusion during the last ten days of Ramadan, he ordered a tent to be pitched for him, and it was done. When Hafsa saw it, she also ordered a tent pitched for her, and it was done. When Zaynab saw it, she ordered a tent to be pitched for her and it was done. When the Messenger of God saw the tents, he asked, 'What is this? Do you intend to do an act of virtue.' He then ordered his tent to be pulled down, and it was. Then his wives took their tents, and they were pulled down. He postponed the seclusion until the first ten days of Shawwal.

N v1E p448 n712; N v1E p448 n712

Seclusion of a Woman Who Is Bleeding Between Her Periods

AYISHA RELATED:

One of the wives of God's Messenger practiced seclusion in the mosque with him while she had bleeding in between her periods. She would see red blood or yellowish traces. Sometimes we put a tray underneath her when she offered the prescribed prayer.

SB v3 p141 n253; AD v1 p97 n375; IM v1 p283 n522; N MMR v1

"The earth has been made a place for prescribed prayer"

AYISHA RELATED:

There was a black slave girl belonging to an Arab tribe. They freed her, but she remained with them. The slave girl said that once one of the girls of that tribe came out wearing a red leather scarf set with precious stones. It fell from her head, or she misplaced it somewhere. A bird passed by that place, saw it lying there and, mistaking it for a piece of meat, flew away with it. The people searched for it, but they did not find it. They accused her of stealing it and started searching her and even searched her private parts. As she was standing there, the same bird passed by them and dropped the red scarf and it fell among them. She told them that this was what they had accused her of taking, and that she had been innocent. The slave girl went to the Messenger and embraced Islam. She had a tent or a small room with a low roof in the mosque. Whenever she called on her [Ayisha], she sat with her and would recite the following: The day of the scarf was one of the wonders of our Lord. Verily He rescued me from the disbelievers' town. She [Ayisha] added that she once asked her what was the matter with her because she always recited these poetic verses. It was then that she told her the whole story.

SB v1 p257 n430

SPEARMEN

AYISHA RELATED:

Once she saw the Messenger of God at the door of her home while some Ethiopians were playing in the mosque [displaying their skill with spears]. God's Messenger screened her with his cloak so as to enable her to see their display.

SB v1 p264 n445; SB v7 p86 n118

STRUGGLE IN GOD'S WAY

AYISHA RELATED:

Sad was wounded on the day of the Battle of the Ditch. A man from the Quraysh, called ibn al-Ariqah, shot him with an arrow which pierced the artery in the middle of his forearm. God's Mesenger pitched a tent for him in the mosque and would inquire after him as he was in close proximity. When the Messenger returned from the ditch and laid down his arms and took a bath, the angel Gabriel appeared to him as he was removing dust from his hair. Gabriel said to him, 'You have laid down your arms. By God, we have not yet laid them down so march against them.' The Messenger asked, 'Where?' He pointed to the Qurayza tribe. The Messenger fought against them. They surrendered at the command of the Messenger, but he referred the decision about them to Sad who decided that those of them who could fight should be killed, their women and children taken prisoners, and their properties distributed among the Muslims.

SM v3A p190 n1769, R2; SB v1 p269 n452; SB v5 p308 n448; AD v2 p883 n3095; N v1E p448 n713

VIRTUES OF THE PROPHET'S MOSQUE

Base of Minbar in Paradise

UMM SALAMA RELATED:

The Messenger of God said, 'The base of my pulpit [in the Madinah mosque] is in paradise.'

N v1E p441 n699

Prayer Said in Madinah Mosque

MAYMUNA RELATED:

She said that she heard the Messenger of God say, 'One prayer said in my mosque at Madinah is better than a thousand prayers said in other mosques—except for the Kabah in Makkah.'

N v1E p439 n694

WOMEN IN MOSQUES

On Strict Prevention of Women From Attending Prescribed Prayer in the Mosque

AYISHA RELATED:

If the Messenger of God had seen what the women had invented, he would have prevented them from visiting the mosque [for prescribed prayer], as the women of the Children of Israel were prevented. She was asked by her nephew if they were prevented, and she said that they were.

AD v1 p150 n569

Menstruating Woman Should Not Go to the Mosque

UMM SALAMA RELATED:

God's Messenger entered the courtyard of the mosque and exclaimed with a loud voice, 'The mosque is lawful neither for a sexually defiled male nor a menstruating woman.'

IM v1 p348 n645

WORSHIPPING AT GRAVES

AYISHA RELATED:

Umm Habiba and Umm Salama mentioned a church they had seen in Ethiopia in which there were pictures. They told the Prophet about it. He said, 'If any religious man dies among those people, they build a place of worship at his gravesite and draw these pictures on it. They will be the worst creatures in the sight of God on the day of resurrection.'

SB v1 p251 n419; SB v2 p233 n414; N v1E p445 n707

CHAPTER 14
MUSIC AND SINGING

Beating the Tambourine During the Marriage Ceremony

RUBAYYI BINT MUAWWIDH IBN AFRA RELATED:

After the consummation of her marriage, the Prophet came and sat on her bed as far from her as the transmitter was then sitting. Our little girls began beating the tambourines and reciting elegiac verses mourning her father who had been martyred in the Battle of Badr. One of them said that among us is a Prophet who knows what will happen tomorrow. On that the Prophet said, 'Leave this saying and keep on singing the verses you had been singing before.'

SB v7 p57 n77; SB v5 p225 n336; AD v3 p1371 n4904

Tambourines at Weddings

AYISHA RELATED:

The Prophet said, 'The event of marriage should be publically declared among the people, and tambourines should be played.'

IM v2u p39 n51

AYISHA RELATED:

She prepared a woman for a man from the Helpers as his bride. The Prophet said, 'O Ayisha! Have you prepared entertainment during the ceremony because the Helpers like entertainment?'

SB v7 p67 n92A

Tribal Music

AYISHA RELATED:

Her father, Abu Bakr, came to see her. She had two girls with her from among the girls of the Helpers. They were singing what the Helpers recited to one another at the Battle of Buath. They were not professional singers. Upon this Abu Bakr remarked that he was surprised to see the playing of a wind instrument of satan in the house of the Messenger on the day of a festival. Upon this the Messenger said, 'Abu Bakr, every people has a festival. This is our festival so let them play on.'

> SM v2A p25 n892, R1-R7; SB v2 p51 n96; SB v2 p37 n70; SB v2 p39 n72; SB v2 p56 n103; SB v5 p184 n268; SB v4 p480 n730; SB v4 p99 n155; IM v2u p40 n53

AYISHA RELATED:

When God's Messenger was seated, they heard confused sounds and boys' voices. He got up and saw an Abyssinian woman dancing with the boys around her. He said, 'Come and look, Ayisha.' She went and placed her chin on God's Messenger's shoulder and began to look over his shoulder, but Umar came along. When the people ran away from her, God's Messenger said, 'I am looking at the devils of *jinn* and men who have fled from Umar.' She then went back.

> T [MMR v2 p1327]

CHAPTER 15
ORPHANS

GUARDIAN

AYISHA RELATED:

The following verse, '*If a guardian is well-off, let him claim no renumeration [wages], but if he is poor, let him have for himself what is just and reasonable,*' [4:6], was revealed in connection with the guardian of an orphan. It means that if he [the guardian] is poor, he can take for himself [from the orphan's wealth] what is just and reasonable according to the orphan's share of the inheritance.

SB v4 p22 n27; SB v6 p79 n99

QURAN

AYISHA RELATED:

In regard to 4:6, God's Messenger said what it was revealed in connection with the custodian (of the property of an orphan) who is in charge of the orphan and looks after her. If he [the custodian] is poor, he is allowed to eat from [the orphan's property].

SM v4B p399 n3019, R1

AYISHA RELATED:

As regards the verse, '*And about what is recited unto you in the Book concerning orphan girls to whom you give not the prescribed portions and yet whom you desire to marry. . . .*' [4:127], the verse is about the female orphan who is under the guardianship of a man with whom she shares her property. He has more right [to marry] her [than anybody else]. But he may not want to marry her and so prevents her from marrying somebody else, lest he should share the property with him.

SB v7 p46 n59

AYISHA RELATED:

Regarding the verse, '*They ask your instruction concerning*

257

women. Say, 'God instructs you about them...,' it is about the female orphan who is under the guardianship of a man with whom she shares her property and who does not want to marry her and who does not want anyone else to marry her lest he [her husband] should share her property. He, therefore, prevents her from marrying. God forbade such a guardian to do so [to prevent her from marrying].

SB v7 p46 n62; SB v6 p98 n124

AYISHA RELATED:

She was asked about the meaning of the verse, 'If you fear that you shall not be able to deal justly with the orphan girls, then marry [other] women of your choice, two or three or four,' [4:3]. She said that it is about the orphan girl who lives with her guardian and shares his property. Her wealth and beauty may tempt him to marry her without giving her a dowry equal to what else might have been given by another suitor. Such guardians were forbidden to marry such orphan girls unless they treated them justly and gave them the most suitable dowry. Otherwise they were ordered to marry any other woman. After that verse, the people again asked the Prophet [about the marriage with orphan girls] so God revealed the following verse, 'They ask you instruction concerning the women. Say: God instructs you about them and about what is recited unto you in the Book concerning the orphan girls to whom you give not the prescribed protions and yet whom you desire to marry' [4:127]. About what is recited in the verse, 'If you fear that you shall not be able to deal justly with the orphan girls, then marry [other] women of your choice' [4:3], she said that Yet whom you desire to marry' [4:127] means the desire of the guardian to marry an orphan girl under his supervision who has little property or beauty in which case he should treat her justly. The guardians were forbidden to marry their orphan girls possessing property and beauty without being just to them, as they generally refrained from marrying them [when they were neither beautiful nor wealthy].

SB v3 p407 n674; SB v7 p19 n29; SB v9 p78 n95; SB v6 p79 n97; SB SB v6 p79 n98; SB v7 p53 n71; SB v4 p19 n25; SB v7 p23 n35; SM v4B p398 n301

WAGES

AYISHA RELATED:

She was asked by the aunt of Umara ibn Umayr about the orphan in his guardianship. He wanted to know if he could take from his property. She said that the Messenger of God said, 'The most pleasant things a person enjoys comes from what he earns, and his child comes from what he earns.'

AD v2 p997 n3521

CHAPTER 16
RELATIONSHIPS AND THEIR TIES

EVIL PROMPTINGS

AYISHA RELATED:

The Messenger of God said, 'It is not right for a Muslim to keep apart from another Muslim for more than three days. Then if he meets him and gives three salutations but receives no response, the other bears his sin.'

> AD v3 p1369 n4895

EXCELLENCE OF CHARITY

ASMA RELATED:

During the period of the peace treaty between the Quraysh and the Messenger, her mother visited her. Her mother was an idol worshipper. She consulted the Messenger and asked if her mother wished a gift from her, should she keep good relations with her mother or not. He said, 'Yes. Keep good relations with her.'

> SB v4 p272 n407; SB v3 p477 n789; SB v8 p8 n9; SM v2A p94 n1003R1; AD v2 p437 n1664

GOD'S KINDNESS TO THE ONE WHO IS KIND TO HIS RELATIVES

AYISHA RELATED:

The Prophet said, 'The word *al-rahm* [womb] derives its name from al-Rahman [one of God's Attributes meaning The Merciful]. So whoever keeps good relations with it [the womb, that is, relatives],

God will keep good relations with him and whoever severs [bonds of kinship], God will sever His relations with him.'
SB v8 p13 n18

JOINING THE TIES OF RELATIONSHIP AND PROHIBITION OF BREAKING THEM

AYISHA RELATED:

God's Messenger said, 'The tie of kinship is suspended to the Throne and says, 'He who unites with me, God unites with him. He who severs relations with me, God will sever relations with him.'
SM v4A p170 n2555

NEIGHBORS

Excellence of Spending and Giving Charity to Relatives
MAYMUNA BINT HARITH RELATED:

She set free a slave-girl during the lifetime of the Messenger of God. She mentioned this to the Messenger of God. He said, "Had you given her to your maternal uncles, you would have had a greater reward."
SM v2A p92 n999; AD v2 p444 n1686

One's Nearest Neighbor
AYISHA RELATED:

She said to the Messenger that she had two neighbors and would like to know to which one of them she should give presents. He said, 'To the one whose door is nearer to you.'
SB v3 p251 n460; SB v8 p30 n49; AD v3 p1424 n5136

RIGHTS OF NEIGHBORS

AYISHA RELATED:

The Messenger of God said, 'Gabriel kept on commending the neighbor to me so that I thought he would make him an heir.'
AD v3 p1424 n5132; SB v8 p27 n43; SM v4A p200 n2624

BOOK 2:
BIOGRAPHIES OF MUHAMMAD'S (ﷺ) WOMEN COMPANIONS

A

ABDA BINT AL-HARITH (SEE BUHAYNA)

ADAM BINT AL-JUMUH IBN ZAYD
Mother: Ruhm bint al-Qayn
Father: Jumuh ibn Zayd, al-
Sister of: Amr ibn al-Jamuh
Wife of: Haram ibn Muhayyisa
Tribe: Khazraj, Salama ibn Sad clan
Ibn Sad also relates the following:
She accepted Islam and gave her allegiance to the Messenger of God. Her brother was martyred at the Battle of Uhud.

ADAM BINT QURAT IBN KHANSA
Mother: Mawiya bint al-Qayn
Father: Qurat ibn Khansa
Children: Abd Allah, Numan, al-
Wife of: Tufayl ibn Malik, al-
Tribe: Khazraj, Salama ibn Sad clan
Ibn Sad also relates the following:
She accepted Islam and gave her allegiance to the Messenger of God.

AFRA BINT UBAYD IBN THALABA
Mother: Rua bint Adi, al-
Father: Ubayd ibn Thalaba
Children: Muadh, Muawwidh, Awf
Wife of: Harith ibn Rifaa, al-
Tribe: Khazraj, Malik ibn al-Najjar clan
Ibn Sad also relates the following:
She accepted Islam and gave her allegiance to the Messenger of God. Her sons were present at the Battle of Badr.

ALIYA BINT ZABYAN (SEE FATIMA BINT DAHHAK)

AMA BINT KHALID IBN SAID IBN AL-AS (SEE UMM KHALID BINT KHALID)

AMINA BINT QURAT IBN KHANSA
Mother: Mawiya bint al-Qayn
Father: Qurat ibn Khansa
Children: Abu Said
Wife of: Aws ibn al-Mualla
Tribe: Khazraj, Salama ibn Sad clan

Ibn Sad also relates the following:
She accepted Islam and gave her allegiance to the Messenger of God.

AMINA BINT RUQAYSH IBN RITHAB
Father: Ruqaysh ibn Rithab
Sister of: Yazid ibn Ruqaysh
Ibn Sad also relates the following:
She accepted Islam in Makkah, gave her allegiance to the Messenger of God and then migrated with her family to Madinah. Her brother was present at the Battle of Badr.

AMIRA BINT ABU HATHMA
Mother: Umm ar-Rabi bint Aslam
Father: Abu Hathma
Wife of: Yazid ibn Usayd; Yazid ibn Bardha
Tribe: Aws, Haritha ibn al-Khazraj clan
Ibn Sad also relates the following:
She accepted Islam and gave her allegiance to the Messenger of God.

AMIRA BINT AL-HARITH
Mother: Sawda bint Sawad
Father: Harith, al-
Sister of: Nasr ibn al-Harith
Wife of: Adi ibn Haram
Tribe: Aws, Zafar clan
Ibn Sad also relates the following:
She accepted Islam and gave her allegiance to the Messenger of God. Her brother was present at the Battle of Badr.

AMIRA BINT AL-RUBAYYA IBN AL-NUMAN
Mother: Her mother was a slave who gave birth to the child of her master
Father: Rubayya ibn al-Numan, al-
Tribe: Khazraj, Malik ibn al-Najjar clan
Ibn Sad also relates the following:
She accepted Islam and gave her allegiance to the Messenger of God.

AMIRA
Mother: Layla bint Sahba
Father: Hubbasha
Children: Bore children, names not mentioned

Wife of: Aws ibn Amr
Tribe: Aws, Khatma ibn Jusham clan
Alternative Name: Umm al-Quhayd bint Hubbasha
Ibn Sad also reports the following:
She accepted Islam and gave her allegiance to the Messenger of God.

AMIRA BINT KULTHUM
Wife of: Utba ibn Uwaym
Tribe: Aws, Amr ibn Awf clan
Ibn Sad also reports the following:
She accepted Islam and gave her allegiance to the Messenger of God.

AMIRA BINT MASUD IBN AWS
Mother: Layla bint al-Khutaym
Father: Masud ibn Aws
Children: Habiba, Umm Jundub
Wife of: Qays ibn Zayd
Ibn Sad also relates the following:
She accepted Islam along with her mother. They both gave their allegiance to the Messenger of God.

AMIRA BINT MASUD IBN ZURARA
Mother: Makhzum of Quraysh
Father: Masud ibn Zurara
Wife of: Alqama ibn Amr
Tribe: Khazraj, Malik ibn al-Najjar clan
Ibn Sad also relates the following:
She accepted Islam and gave her allegiance to the Messenger of God.

AMIRA BINT MUAWWIDH IBN AL-HARITH
Mother: Umm Yazid bint Qays
Father: Muawwidh ibn al-Harith
Children: Umara, Amr, Sariyya
Wife of: Abu Hasan ibn Abd Amr
Tribe: Khazraj, Malik ibn al-Najjar clan
Ibn Sad also relates the following:
She accepted Islam and gave her allegiance to the Messenger of God.

AMIRA BINT MUHAMMAD IBN UQBA
Mother: Family of Abu Farwa of Hudhayl
Father: Muhammad ibn Uqba

Children: Fadala
Sister of: Mundhir ibn Muhammad, al-
Wife of: Ubayd ibn Naqid
Tribe: Aws, Ubayd ibn Zayd clan
Ibn Sad also relates the following:
She accepted Islam and gave her allegiance to the Messenger of God. Her brother was martyred at the Battle of Badr.

AMIRA BINT MURSHIDA IBN JABR
Mother: Salama bint Masud
Father: Murshida ibn Jabr
Children: Thabit, Abu Jubayra, Abu Bakr, Umar Thubayta, Hammada, Safiyya
Wife of: Suwayd ibn al-Numan
Tribe: Aws, al-Haritha ibn al-Khazraj clan
Ibn Sad also relates the following:
She accepted Islam and gave her allegiance to the Messenger of God. Some of the Helpers said that Murshida ibn Jabr went on one of the Prophet's expeditions.

AMIRA BINT QAYS
Father: Qays
Tribe: Khazraj, Adi ibn al-Najjar clan
She is mentioned by Muhammad ibn Umar al-Waqadi as having accepted Islam.

AMIRA BINT SAD IBN AMIR
Mother: Umm Amir bint Sulaym
Father: Sad ibn Amir
Wife of: Kabbatha ibn Aws
Tribe: Aws, Haritha clan
Ibn Sad also relates the following:
She accepted Islam and gave her allegiance to the Messenger of God.

AMIRA BINT SAHL IBN THALABA
Mother: Umayma bint Amr
Father: Sahl ibn Thalaba
Children: Furaya, al-, Kabsha, Habiba
Wife of: Abu Umama Asad ibn Zurara
Tribe: Khazraj, Malik ibn al-Najjar clan
Ibn Sad also relates the following:
She accepted Islam and gave her allegiance to the Messenger of God.

AMIRA BINT THABIT IBN AL-NUMAN
Mother: Shumayla bint al-Harith
Father: Thabit ibn al-Numan
Tribe: Aws, Zafar clan
　　Ibn Sad also relates the following:
　　She accepted Islam and gave her allegiance to the Messenger of God.

AMIRA BINT YAZID IBN AL-SAKAN
Mother: Umm Sad bint Khuzaym
Father: Yazid ibn al-Sakan
Children: Harith, al-, Uthayra
Wife of: Manzur ibn Labid
Tribe: Aws, Abd al-Ashhal clan
　　Ibn Sad also relates the following:
　　She accepted Islam and gave her allegiance to the Messenger of God.

AMIRA BINT ZUHAYR
Mother: Fatima bint Bishr
Father: Zuhayr
Children: Zayd, Surara, Abd al- Rahman, Abd Allah
Wife of: Mirba ibn Qayzi of Aws
　　Ibn Sad also relates the following:
　　She accepted Islam and gave her allegiance to the Messenger of God. Two of her sons, Abd al-Rahman and Abd Allah, were killed on the Day of the Bridge without leaving children.

AMM SAIF ANSARIYYA
　　She is not mentioned by Ibn Sad. The wife of a blacksmith who lived a few miles from Madinah, she nursed the Prophet's son, Ibrahim, for a year and a half. The Prophet went occasionally to her home to see Ibrahim. He often found her house full of smoke but said nothing.

AMRA AL-KHAMISA BINT MASUD IBN QAYS
Mother: Amira bint Amr
Father: Masud ibn Qays
Children: Qays ibn Amr al-Najjari
Tribe: Khazraj, Malik ibn al-Najjar clan
　　Ibn Sad also relates the following:
　　She accepted Islam and gave her allegiance to the Messenger of God.

AMRA AL-THALITHA BINT MASUD IBN QAYS
Mother: Amira bint Amr

Father: Masud ibn Qays
Children: Abu Shaykh Ubayy
Wife of: Thabit ibn al-Mundhir
Tribe: Khazraj, Malik ibn al-Najjar clan
  Ibn Sad also relates the following:
  She accepted Islam and gave her allegiance to the Messenger of God. Her son is the half-brother of Hassan ibn Thabit by the same father. Abu Shaykh was present at Badr.

AMRA AL-THANIYYA BINT MASUD IBN QAYS
Mother: Amira bint Amr
Father: Masud ibn Qays
Children: Abu Muhammad (Masud); Amra, Rughayba
Wife of: Aws ibn Zayd; Sahl ibn Thalaba
Tribe: Khazraj, Malik ibn al-Najjar clan
  Ibn Sad also relates the following:
  She accepted Islam and gave her allegiance to the Messenger of God.

AMRA AL-ULA BINT MASUD IBN QAYS
Mother: Amira bint Amr
Father: Masud ibn Qays
Children: Sad, Thabit
Wife of: Zayd ibn Malik
Tribe: Khazraj, Malik ibn al-Najjar clan
  Ibn Sad also relates the following:
  She accepted Islam and gave her allegiance to the Messenger of God. Her son, Sad, was present at the Battle of Badr.

AMRA BINT ABU AYYUB IBN ZAYD
Mother: Umm Ayyub bint Qays
Father: Abu Ayyub ibn Zayd
Children: Khalid
Wife of: Safwan ibn Aws
Tribe: Khazraj, Malik ibn al-Najjar clan
  Ibn Sad also relates the following:
  She accepted Islam and gave her allegiance to the Messenger of God.

AMRA BINT HARITHA IBN AL-NUMAN
Mother: Umm Khalid bint Khalid
Father: Haritha ibn al-Numan
Wife of: Qays ibn Amr; Uthman ibn Sahl
Tribe: Khazraj, Malik ibn al-Najjar clan

Ibn Sad also relates the following:
She accepted Islam and gave her allegiance to the Messenger of God.

AMRA BINT HAZM IBN ZAYD
Mother: Khalida bint Anas
Father: Hazm ibn Zayd
Sister of: Umara, Amr, Mamar
Wife of: Sad ibn al-Rabi of Khazraj
Tribe: Khazraj, Malik ibn al-Najjar clan
Ibn Sad also relates the following:
She accepted Islam and gave her allegiance to the Messenger of God.

AMRA BINT HAZZAL IBN AMR
Father: Hazzal ibn Amr
Tribe: Khazraj, Qawaqila, Awf ibn al-Khazraj clan
Muhammad ibn Umar al-Waqadi mentions her as having accepted Islam.

AMRA BINT MASUD IBN AWS
Mother: Layla bint al-Khutaym
Father: Masud ibn Aws
Children: Abd Allah
Wife of: Muhammad ibn Maslama
Tribe: Aws, Zafar clan
Ibn Sad also relates the following:
She accepted Islam and gave her allegiance to the Messenger of God.

AMRA BINT QAYS
Mother: Naila bint Salama
Father: Qays
Wife of: Zayd ibn Thalaba
Tribe: Khazraj, Salama ibn Sad clan
Ibn Sad also relates the following:
She accepted Islam and gave her allegiance to the Messenger of God.

AMRA BINT RAWAHA IBN THALABA
Mother: Kabsha bint Waqid
Father: Rawaha ibn Thalaba
Children: Numan ibn Bashir, al-
Sister of: Abd Allah ibn Rawaha
Wife of: Bashir ibn Sad

Tribe: Khazraj
Ibn Sad also relates the following:
She accepted Islam and gave her allegiance to the Messenger of God. Her brother was present at the Battle of Badr.

AMRA BINT SAD IBN SAD
Mother: Hind bint Amr
Father: Sad ibn Sad
Children: Rifaa
Wife of: Mubashshir ibn al-Harith
Tribe: Khazraj, Saida ibn Kab clan
Ibn Sad also relates the following:
She accepted Islam and gave her allegiance to the Messenger of God.

AMRA BINT UBAYD (SEE UMAYRA)

AMRA BINT YAZID (SEE FATIMA BINT DAHHAK)

AMRA RABIA BINT MASUD IBN QAYS
Mother: Amira bint Amr
Father: Masud ibn Qays
Children: Sad ibn Ubada
Wife of: Ubada ibn Dulaym
Tribe: Khazraj, Malik ibn al-Najjar clan
Ibn Sad also relates the following:
She accepted Islam and gave her allegiance to the Messenger of God. She died while the Prophet was on the expedition of Dumat al-Jandal in Rabil Awwal, 5 AH/August, 626 CE. Sad ibn Ubada was with him. The Messenger arrived and went to her grave and prayed for her.

ANISA BINT ADI
Father: Adi
Children: Abd Allah ibn Salama
She is not mentioned by Ibn Sad. She accepted Islam most probably along with her son after the migration. Her son was martyred in the Battle of Uhud. When she heard of the martyrdom of her son, she went to the Messenger and asked if she could bury her son near her home so that she could pray at his gravesite. The Messenger accepted that she bury her son in Madinah.

ARBAB BINT KAB ANSARIYA
Father: Kab Ansariya

Children: Huzayifah
Wife of: Hasil al-Yaman ibn Jabir al-Asbi
She is not mentioned by Ibn Sad. Arbab accepted Islam before the migration as did her husband.

ARWA BINT ABD AL-MUTTALIB IBN HISHAM
Mother: Fatima bint Amr ibn Aidh of Makhzum, aunt of the Prophet
Father: Abd al-Muttalib ibn Hisham
Children: Tulayb; Fatima
Wife of: Umayr ibn Wahb ibn Abd al-Manaf; Arta ibn Sharahbil ibn Hashim
Tribe: Quraysh
Ibn Sad also relates the following:
She accepted Islam and gave her allegiance to the Messenger of God.

Muhammad ibn Ibrahim ibn al-Harith al-Taymi relates that Tulayb ibn Umayr accepted Islam in the home of Arqam ibn Abil Arqam al-Makhzumi. He then left and went to visit his mother, Arwa bint Abd al-Muttalib. He told his mother that he had given his allegiance to Muhammad and submitted to God.

His mother responded with support for his endeavors to help his uncle and added that if women were able to do what men do, they would also follow him and defend him as well. Her son asked what prevented her from accepting Islam and following the Prophet as her brother, Hamza had accepted. She responded saying that she would do whatever her sisters were doing. Her son began to insist that she should submit to the Prophet, believe in him and bear witness that there is no god but God and that Muhammad is the Messenger of God. She expressed her support of the Prophet and encouraged her son to help him and support him.

Barra bint Abu Tajra relates that Abu Jahl and a number of unbelievers of the Quraysh attacked the Prophet and injured him. Tulayb ibn Umayr went to Abu Jahl and hit him so hard that his head began bleeding. The Quraysh seized Tulayb and put him in chains. Abu Lahab had him released. Arwa was asked if she had seen that her son had made himself a target in place Muhammad? She said that the best of the days of her son were the days when he defended the son of his uncle. Muhammad had brought the truth from God. They asked her if she followed Muhammad. She replied that she did. Some of them went to Abu Lahab and told him what had happened. He went to visit her and said that he was surprised that she followed Muhammad and abandoned the religion of Abd al-Muttalib. She said that is was true and that he should take the side of his cousin, support and defend him. If the Prophet failed then Abu Lahab would have the choice of either staying with the Prophet or returning to his previous religion. She said that he would be able to use the excuse that he had supported him because he had been his cousin. Abu Lahab asked if she thought that they had power over all Arab tribes. [She said] Muhammad had brought a new religion. Then Abu Lahab left.

Muhammad ibn Umar al-Waqadi and others mentioned that Arwa said on that day that Tulayb helped his cousin and that she encouraged him to be steadfast in life and property.'

ARWA BINT AL-HARITH IBN ABD AL-MUTTALIB
Mother: Ghaziyya bint Qays
Father: Harith ibn Abd al-Muttalib, al-, uncle of the Prophet
Children: Muttalib, al-, Abu Sufyan, Umm Hakim, Rabi, al-
Wife of: Abu Widaa ibn Sabara
Tribe: Quraysh
    Ibn Sad also relates the following:
    She accepted Islam and gave her allegiance to the Messenger of God.

ARWA BINT AL-MUQAWWIM IBN ABD AL-MUTTALIB
Mother: Qilaba bint Amr
Father: Muqawwim ibn Abd al-Muttalib, uncle of the Prophet
Children: Abd Allah ibn Abu Masruh
Wife of: Abu Masruh (Harith ibn Yamar of Hawazin, al-)
Tribe: Quraysh
    Ibn Sad also relates the following:
    She accepted Islam and gave her allegiance to the Messenger of God.

ARWA BINT KURAYZ IBN RABIA
Mother: Umm Hakim al-Bayda bint Abd al-Muttalib
Father: Kurayz ibn Rabia
Children: Uthman, Aminah; Walid, al-, Ammara, Khalid, Umm Kulthum, Umm Hakim, Hind
Wife of: Uthman ibn Abil-Asi; Uqba ibn Abu Muayt
Tribe: Quraysh
    Ibn Sad also relates the following:
    She accepted Islam and gave her allegiance to the Messenger of God.

    Abd Allah ibn Kab, the freedman of the family of Uthman, relates that Abd Allah ibn Hanzala had said that they were present when the mother of Uthman ibn Affan died. She was buried at the Baqi cemetery. He returned and led the people in prayer at the mosque. Uthman prayed alone, and he prayed beside him. He heard him pray that God, have mercy on his mother or that God forgive his mother. This was during his caliphate.

Isa ibn Talha relates that he saw Uthman ibn Affan carrying the bier of his mother between the two pillars from the house of Ghutaysh until he put her down at the place of the prayer for the dead. After she was buried, he saw Uthman ibn Affan standing by her grave and praying for her.

ARWA BINT MALIK IBN KHANSA
Mother: Asma bint al-Qayn
Father: Malik ibn Khansa
Children: Khalid, Umm Mani
Sister of: Tufayl ibn Malik, al-
Wife of: Amr ibn Adi
Tribe: Khazraj, Salama ibn Sad clan
Ibn Sad also reports the following:
She accepted Islam and gave her allegiance to the Messenger of God. Her brother was present at the Battle of Badr.

ASMA BINT ABU BAKR AL-SIDDIQ
Mother: Qutayla bint Abd al-Uzza
Father: Abu Bakr al-Siddiq
Children: Abd Allah ibn Zubayr, Urwa, Mundhir, al-, Asim, Muhajir, al-, Khadija, Umm al-Hasan, Ayisha
Sister of: Abd Allah ibn Abi Bakr
Wife of: Zubayr ibn al-Awwam
Tribe: Quraysh, Amir ibn Luayy clan
Ibn Sad also reports the following:
She accepted Islam and gave her allegiance to the Messenger of God. Asma bint Abu Bakr al-Siddiq was known as 'the woman with the two waistbands'. She received this name when she was preparing provisions for the Messenger and her father, Abu Bakr, who had fled from the Quraysh and were hiding in a cave near Makkah, ready to begin the migration to Madina. She tore her cloth waistband into two, using one part to tie the Messenger's waterskin and the other to tie her father's.

Once people from Syria were fighting against her son, Urwa. They shouted at him that he was the son of 'the woman of the two waistbands'. He replied asking him what this had to do with them. When he told his mother, Asma, what had happened, she was surprised that they reproached him with this. He said that they did. She responded that it was true.

Abd Allah ibn al-Zubayr relates that Asma's mother, Qutayla bint Abd al-Uzza, whom Abu Bakr had divorced in the Age of Ignorance, remained an idolater. Once she came to visit her daughter,

Asma, bringing some gifts. Asma was not sure if she should accept these gifts or even allow her mother to enter her home. Asma sent a message to her half-sister, Ayisha, to ask the Messenger what to do. The Messenger sent the message, 'She should let her [mother] enter and accept her gifts.' Verse 60:89 was revealed in this regard, *"God does not forbid you in respect of those who have not fought you in religion's cause, nor expelled you from your habitations, that you should be kindly to them, and act justly towards them; surely God loves the just. God only forbids you as to those who have fought you in religions' cause and expelled you from your habitations and have supported in your expulsion, that you should take them for friends. And whosoever takes them for friends, those—they are the evildoers"* (60:8-9).

Asma married al-Zubayr after the migration. She relates that when she married al-Zubayr, he had nothing but a horse and a camel—neither property nor slaves nor any other possessions. She used to provide fodder for the horse and grind date-stones. She also grazed the camel, gave it water, patched the family's leather bucket and kneaded bread. She was not good at baking bread so her neighbors would help her. They were said to be sincere women. She used to carry date-stones on her head from the farm land the Messenger had given to al-Zubayr. It was about two miles from Madinah.

She related that one day she was walking back to Madinah carrying the date-stones on her head when she met the Messenger of God who was riding his camel. There was a group of Companions with him. He called her and said, 'Come on! Come on!' as he lowered his camel so that she could ride behind him. She was too embarrassed to travel with the men. She remembered al-Zubayr and his jealousy. He was one of the most jealous of people. The Messenger of God saw that she was embarrassed. He moved on.

When she saw her husband, al-Zubayr, she told him that she had met the Messenger of God while carrying date-stones on her head and that there was a group of Companions with him. The Messenger had made his camel kneel so that she could ride with him, but she was too embarrassed and remembered al-Zubayr's jealousy. Al-Zubayr told her that the thought of her carrying the date-stones was harder for him to accept than her riding with the Messenger.

Asma related that later her father, Abu Bakr, sent a slave who looked after the horse for her. She said it was as if she had been freed.

Abbas ibn Abd Allah ibn al-Zubayr related from Asma bint Abu Bakr that once she went to the Prophet and said that there was nothing in her house to eat except what al-Zubayr brought her. She wanted to know if she could give away some of what he brought her because there was nothing other than this to give. The Messenger said, 'Spend what you can. Do not hoard or God will withhold from you.'

Ubayd ibn Umayr related that Asma had a swelling on her neck. The Prophet began to stroke it, saying, 'O God, preserve her from his excess and harm.'

Ikrima relates that Asma bint Abu Bakr was married to al-Zubayr ibn al-Awwam. He was hard on her. She went to her father [Abu Bakr] and complained. He said that she should be patient because when a woman has a righteous husband who dies and she does not remarry, they will be re-united in the garden.

He also related that Asma ibn Abu Bakr was asked whether or not any of the *Salaf* fainted from fear. She replied that they did not faint from fear, but they used to weep.'

Ibn Abu Mulayka related that Asma bint Abu Bakr used to get headaches. She would put her hand on her head and ask God for forgiveness.

Muhammad ibn al-Munkadir related that the Messenger of God said to Asma bint Abu Bakr, 'Do not hoard or God will withhold from you.' She was a woman with a generous heart.

Abd Allah ibn al-Zubayr related that he never met anyone more generous than his mother.

Fatima bint Mundhir related that Asma bint Abu Bakr fell ill and that she set free every slave that she had. She used to say to her daughters and family that they should spend, give to charity and not wait for a surplus. If they waited for a surplus, she told them, they would not have any. However, if they gave to charity, they would not have less.

Al-Rukayn ibn al-Rubayyi related that he visited Asma bint Abu Bakr when she was a very old, blind woman. He found her praying. There was someone with her whom she was instructing to stand, to do that and to do this.

Abu Waqid al-Laythi, a Companion of the Prophet who was at the Battle of Yarmuk, related that Asma bint Abu Bakr was with al-Zubayr. He heard her say to al-Zubayr that a man of the enemy had passed by her tent running. Then his foot had hit the loop of her tent rope. He had fallen down dead, flat on his face without being hit by a weapon!

During the time of Said ibn al-As, Asma bint Abu Bakr took a dagger to use against thieves who were all over Madinah. She put it under her head when she slept.

Musab ibn Sad related that during the caliphate of Umar ibn al-Khattab, he alloted Asma bint Abu Bakr a thousand dirhams.

Hisham ibn Urwa related that al-Zubayr divorced Asma and took Urwa who was quite young at that time.

Mundhir ibn al-Zubayr arrived from Iraq and sent his mother,

Asma bint Abu Bakr, who by then was blind, a dress made of thin, fine, soft cloth. She touched it with her hand and asked the person who had brought it to return it to her son.

Her son went to see her. He told her that the dress had not been transparent. She said that it may not have been transparent, but it was translucent and that so did not want to wear it. He then bought her some soft, comfortable clothes which she wore.

Hisham ibn Urwa related that Asma wore clothes dyed with safflower when she was in the sacred state of the prescribed pilgrimage. The dye did not contain any saffron.

Fatima bint al-Mundhir related that she saw Asma only wearing garments dyed with safflower until she died. She wore outer garments that had been dyed with safflower.

Qasim ibn Muhammad al-Thaqafi related that Asma went to al-Hajjaj with her girls after she had gone blind. She asked where al-Hajjaj was. She was told that he was not there. She told them to tell her that she had heard the Messenger of God say that there would be two men in Thaqif after his death: a liar and an oppressor.

Abu Siddiq al-Naji related that al-Hajjaj went to Asma bint Abu Bakr and told her that her son had deviated in this House by opposing al-Hujjaj. He said that God had made her son, Abd Allah, taste a painful punishment from which he would die.

She responded by telling him that he lied. Abd Allah had always been dutiful to his parents. He performed the prescribed fasts and prayers. She said that the Messenger of God had informed her that two liars would emerge from Thaqif. One of them was worse than the first, who was an oppressor.

It is related that Asma bint Abu Bakr requested that when she died, she should be washed, shrouded and perfumed. She asked that no perfume be put on her shroud and that no one follow her with fire.

Fatima bint al-Mundhir related that Asma bint Abu Bakr said to fumigate her clothes over the clothes stand and to use *hanut* perfume on her body but not to leave any of it on her clothes.

It is said that Asma bint Abu Bakr died some nights after her son, Abd Allah ibn al-Zubayr, had been martyred. He was martyred on October 4, 692/the 17th of Jumada al-Ula in AH 73 AH.

Other Sources

Asma bint Abu Bakr was the eighteenth to embrace Islam according to Ibn Ishaq. Her son, Abd Allah ibn Zubayr, was the first Muslim born in Madinah. Later when Ibn Zubayr divorced her, she lived with her son. Her son was later to revolt against the corruption of the Umayyid leader al-Hujjaj and the caliphs Yazid and Abdul Malik ibn Marwan. Asma supported him in his endeavor.

She related fifty-six Traditions. Her transmitters include:
Abada ibn Hamza ibn Abd Allah ibn Zubayr
Abd Allah (son)
Abd Allah ibn Kaisar (freedman)
Abd Allah ibn Urwa (grandson)
Abu Bakr (son)
Abu Naufal
Amir (son)
Asad ibn Abd Allah (grandson)
Fatima bint Mundhir
Ibn Abbas
Ibn Abu Aqrab
Ibn Abu Malayka
Ibn Zubayr
Muhammad ibn Munkadir
Muslim
Muttalib ibn Hartib
Safiyya bint Shayba
Urwa (son)
Wahb ibn Kaysar

ASMA BINT AL-HARITH IBN HAZM (SEE LUBABA THE YOUNGER)

ASMA BINT AL-NUMAN IBN ABIL-JAWN
Father: Numan ibn Abil-Jawn, al-
Wife of: Her cousin; the Messenger of God
Tribe: Kindah, Jawn

Ibn Sad also related the following:
She accepted Islam and gave her allegiance to the Messenger of God. The Prophet married her, but never consummated the marriage.

Abu Awn al-Dawsi related that al-Numan ibn Abil-Jawn al-Kindi used to come and camp. His father's relatives were from the Najd near al-Sharba. He came to the Messenger of God as a Muslim and asked if he could marry the Messenger to the most beautiful widow among the Arabs. This woman had been married to her cousin who had died. She was a widow who he said desired to marry the Messenger. The Messenger of God married her for 400 dirhams.

Numan asked the Messenger not to give her such a small dowry. The Messenger said, 'I have not given any of my wives more than this, nor have any of my daughters had a higher dowry than this.'

Numan said that the Messenger was the best model and that he would send word to her family who would bring her to the Messenger. Numan said that he himself would go with the courier to ensure that the Messenger's wife was sent to him.

The Messenger of God sent Abu Usayd al-Saidi. When they reached her, she was sitting in her house. She told him to enter. Abu Usayd told her that, after the revelation of the verse about the wives of the Prophet speaking from behind a partition, none of the men would see the wives of the Messenger of God.

She asked him to please explain further. He told her that there should be a partition between herself and the men to whom she spoke, except for her close relatives. She accepted.

Abu Usayd al-Saidi related that he stayed three days. He then brought her with him in a camel-sedan. When they arrived in Madinah, he lodged her with the Saida clan. The women of the quarter visited and welcomed her. They then left her, talking about her beauty. The news of her arrival spread in Madinah.

He also related that he went to the Messenger who was with the Amr ibn Awf clan. He informed the Messenger of her arrival. Then Abu Usayd said that one of the Messenger's wives visited Asma bint al-Harith ibn Hazn and tricked her because of what they had heard about her beauty. She was an extremely beautiful woman. She was told by one of the other wives that as she, Asma, was descended from kings, if she wanted to succeed with the Messenger of God when he came to her, she should seek refuge with God from him. This way, she was told, she would have luck with him and he would desire her.

And he related that the Messenger of God sent him to the woman of Jawn. He brought her. They were in part of the Najd. He lodged her in the fortresses of the Saida clan. Then he went to the Messenger and informed him about her. The Messenger of God went out to her on foot. He squatted on his knees and then bent over to kiss her. That was what he did when he first married his wives. She said that she sought refuge with God from him. The Messenger of God pulled back from her and said to her, 'You have sought refuge with the Refuge.' He left her and ordered that she be returned to her family.

Said ibn Abd al-Rahman ibn Abza related that the Jawniyya woman sought refuge from the Messenger of God as she had been told that this would give her more luck with him. No woman except she had sought refuge from him. She was tricked because of her beauty. The Messenger was told about what had caused her to say what she had said. He said, 'They [my wives] are like the brothers of Joseph. Their deviousness is immense.'

Abd Allah ibn Jafar related that she was Umayya bint al-Numan ibn Abi 'l-Jawn.

Ibn Abi Awn related that the Messenger of God married the Kindite woman in the month of Rabi 'l Awwal in 9 AH/June, 630 CE.

Urwa related that Walid ibn Abd al-Malik wrote to him to ask him whether the Messenger of God married Qutayla, the sister of al-Ashath ibn Qays. He replied that the Messenger did not marry her at all. He did not marry any Kindite woman, except the woman of the

Awn tribe. He married her and then, when she was brought and reached Madinah, he looked at her and divorced her without consummating the marriage.

Zului related that the Messenger of God did not marry any Kindite woman except the woman of the Awn tribe. He did not consummate the marriage before he divorced her.

Ibn Abbas related that the Messenger of God married Asma bint al-Numan who was the most beautiful and youthful of the people of her time. When the Messenger of God began to marry foreign Arab women, Ayisha said that he had taken foreign women as his wives and that they would divert his attention from them [his non-foreign wives].

He asked Asma bint al-Numan's father for her hand when the Kinda came to him. When the wives of the Prophet saw her, they envied her. They told her that if she wanted to have luck with the Messenger, that she should seek refuge with God from him when he came to her. When he entered, drew back the partition, and stretched out his hand to her, she said that she sought refuge with God from him. He said, 'Who seeks refuge with God! Join your family!'

Abu Usyad al-Saidi, who had been at the Battle of Badr, related that the Messenger of God married Asma bint al-Numan al-Jawniyya. The Messenger asked Abu Usyad to bring her to him. Hafsa said to Ayisha or Ayisha to Hafsa that one should henna her while the other combed her hair. They did this. One of them said to the new bride that the Messenger liked it when a woman came to him and said that she sought refuge with God from him. When the new bride went to him and he closed the door, lowered the partition, and stretched his hand to her, she said that she sought refuge with God from him.

He brought his sleeve over his face and shielded himself from her. He said, 'You have sought refuge with the Refuge,' three times. Then he went out to Abu Usayd and told him to take her back to her family and provide her with two white dresses.

She used to say that people should call her "the wretch" because of what had happened.

Abu Usayd al-Saidi related that the Messenger of God married a woman from Jawn. The Messenger told Abu Usayd to bring her to Madinah. He brought her and lodged her in a fortress at the garden of al-Shawt beyond Dhubab. Then he went to the Messenger and told the Messenger that he had brought his wife.

The Messenger left on foot. Abu Usayd went with him. When the Messenger came to her, he bent down to kiss her. When the Messenger first married his wives, he used to kiss them. She said that she sought refuge with God from him. The Messenger said, 'You have sought refuge with the Refuge.' He commanded Abu Usayd to take her back to her family which he did.

When they reached her family, they shouted at her that she was not blessed! They asked what had come over her. She told them that she had been tricked. She had been told to say such and such the meaning of which she did not know. Her family told her that she had made them a laughing stock among the Arab tribes. She asked Abu Usayd what she should do. He told her to stay in her house and partition herself from any male relative because she was one of the Mothers of Believers.

So no one sought to marry her. She lived with her family at Najd and was not seen by anyone except a relative until her death during the caliphate of Uthman ibn Affan.

Zuhayr related that she died dispondent.

Ibn Abbas related that Asma bint al-Numan married al-Muhajir ibn Abi Umayya during the caliphate of Umar. Umar wanted to punish them. She claimed that the partition had not been set up for her and that she was not called Mother of the Believers so Umar left them alone.

Muhammad ibn Umar al-Waqadi related that Ikrima ibn Abi Jahl married her at the time of the apostasy during the caliphate of Abu Bakr. The partition of the Messenger of God had not been set up for her. This is not confirmed.

ASMA BINT MIHRAZ IBN AMIR

Mother: Umm Sahl bint Abu Kharija
Father: Mihraz ibn Amir
Children: Bashir, al-Jad
Wife of: Abu Bashir Qays ibn Ubayd
Tribe: Khazraj, Adi ibn al-Najjar clan

Ibn Sad also related the following:

She accepted Islam and gave her allegiance to the Messenger of God.

ASMA BINT MUKHARRABA IBN JANDAL OF TAMIM

Mother: Inaq bint al-Jabbar, al-
Father: Mukharraba ibn Jandal
Children: Abu Jahl, Harith, al-; Ayyash, Abd Allah, Umm Hujayr
Wife of: Hisham ibn al-Mughira; Abu Rabia ibn al-Mughira (brother of Hisham)
Tribe: Non-Qurayshi Emigrant

Ibn Sad also related the following:

She accepted Islam and gave her allegiance to the Messenger of God.

Rubayyi bint Muawwidh related that she went with some women Helpers to visit Asma bint Mukharraba, Umm Abi Jahl, during the time of Umar ibn al-Khattab. Her son, Abd Allah ibn Rabia, used to send her perfume from Yemen. She would then sell the perfume. She put some in Rubayyi's bottle and weighed it for her just as she weighed for her friends. As she did so, she asked Rubayyi to write down how much she owed.

Rubayyi wrote down how much she, Rubayyi bint Muawwidh, owed. Suddenly Asma told her to leave because she was the daughter of someone who had killed his master. Rubayyi said that in fact she was the daughter of someone who had killed his slave. Asma said that she would not sell anything to her. Rubayyi then told her that she would not ever buy anything from her, either, and that the perfume she was selling was neither good nor fragrant. Rubayyi then added that it was the best perfume she had ever smelled, but she was angry so she said that to Asma.

ASMA BINT MURSHIDA IBN JABR
Mother: Salama bint Masud
Father: Murshida ibn Jabr
Children: Thabit, Abu Jubayra, Abu Bakr, Umar, Thubayta, Bakra, Hammada, Safiyya
Wife of: Dahhak ibn Khalifa, ad-
Ibn Sad also related the following:
She accepted Islam and gave her allegiance to the Messenger of God. Her daughter, Thubayta, married Muhammad ibn Maslama.

ASMA BINT QURAT IBN KHANSA
Mother: Mawiya bint al-Qayn
Father: Qurat ibn Khansa
Children: Rubayya, al-
Wife of: Tufayl ibn al-Numan, al-
Tribe: Khazraj, Salama ibn Sad clan
Ibn Sad also related the following:
She accepted Islam and gave her allegiance to the Messenger of God.

ASMA BINT SALAMA OF TAMIM
Mother: Salma bint Zuhayr
Father: Salama
Children: Abd Allah ibn Ayyash
Wife of: Ayyash ibn Abu Rabia
Tribe: Non-Qurayshi Emigrant
Ibn Sad also related the following:
She accepted Islam early on in Makkah, gave her allegiance to the Messenger of God and migrated with her husband to Abyssinia.

ASMA BINT SHAQR

Father: Shaqr

She is not mentioned by Ibn Sad. Ibn Ishaq has her as a transmitter of a Tradition from the Prophet.

ASMA BINT UMAYS KHATHAMIYYA

Mother: Hind, Khawla bint Awf
Father: Umays Khathamiyya
Children: Abd Allah, Muhammad, Awm; Muhammad Abu Bakr; Yahya, Awn
Wife of: Jafar ibn Abi Talib; Abu Bakr al-Siddiqui; Ali ibn Abu Talib
Tribe: Non-Qurayshi Emigrant

Ibn Sad also related the following:

She accepted Islam after the Messenger had entered the house of Arqam in Makkah and gave her allegiance to the Messenger of God. She migrated to Abyssinia with her husband, Jafar ibn Abi Talib. There she gave birth to Abd Allah, Muhammad and Awn. Jafar was martyred at the Battle of Muta in September AD 629/Jumada al-Ula, AH 8.

When Asma bint Umays arrived in Madinah with her family from Abyssinia, Umar had said to her that he and the other Emigrants had migrated before her. She did not accept this as the truth. She said to Umar that the Messenger was feeding their hungry ones and teaching the ignorant ones in Makkah when she was far away in Abyssinia. She told Umar that she would go to the Messenger and ask him. The Messenger said to her, 'Some people migrated once, but you migrated twice.'

Asma bint Umays told the Messenger that some of the men were boasting to her, claiming that she was not among the first emigrants. The Messenger of God told her, 'Rather you have migrated twice. You migrated to Abyssinia when we were in Makkah, and then you migrated to Madinah after that.' She left Abyssinia with her husband and family and went to Madinah during the Battle of Khaybar.

Amir related that the first to suggest the bier for women was Asma bint Umays when she came back from Abyssinia. She had seen the Christians doing that there.

Asma bint Umays herself related that on the morning in which Jafar and the other Companions were martyred, the Messenger of God came to her. She had just tanned forty skins and was kneading bread. She took her sons, washed their faces and oiled them.

The Messenger of God came to her and asked, 'Asma, where are the sons of Jafar?'

She brought them to him. He embraced them and smelt them. Then his eyes overflowed with tears and he wept. Asma asked if perhaps the Messenger had some news of Jafar. The Messenger replied, 'Yes, he was martyred today.'

Asma began to shriek. The women gathered round her. The Messenger said, 'Asma, do not say rash words nor strike your chest.' He left and went toward his daughter, Fatima, who was crying for Jafar. The Messenger of God told her, 'For one like Jafar, let the weeper weep.' Then the Messenger of God said, 'Prepare some food for the family of Jafar. They are distracted today.'

Muhammad ibn Umar al-Waqadi related that Abu Bakr al-Siddiq married Asma bint Umays after Jafar ibn Abu Talib was martryed. She gave birth to Muhammad ibn Abu Bakr. Abu Bakr then died soon after.

Said ibn al-Musayyab related that Asma bint Umays was bleeding after the birth of Muhammad ibn Abu Bakr at Dhul Hulayfa when they were intending to make the farewell pilgrimage. Abu Bakr told her to take a bath lustration and then begin the pilgrimage.

Asma bint Umays gave birth to Muhammad ibn Abu Bakr at al-Bayda. Abu Bakr mentioned this to the Messenger of God who said, 'Let her perform the bath lustration and then assume the sacred state.'

Jabir related that when they were at Dhul-Hulayfa, Asma bint Umays gave birth to Muhammad ibn Abu Bakr. She asked the Messenger of God who commanded her to protect her private parts with a cloth, perform the bath lustration and then begin the prescribed pilgrimage.

Qays ibn Abu Hazim related that he visited Abu Bakr with his father. He was a thin white man. He saw the hand of Asma was tattooed.

Abu Bakr ibn Hafs related that Abu Bakr left instructions that his wife, Asma bint Umays, should wash him when he died. He asked that she not do it when she was fasting because she would not then be able to cope. She remembered his oath at the end of the day. She called for water and drank it. She was then ready to keep her promise to Abu Bakr.

Qasim related that Abu Bakr al-Siddiq left a will that his wife Asma should wash him. If she was unable to accomplish it, their son Muhammad should help her. This is a weak Tradition.

Ata related that Abu Bakr left a will saying his wife, Asma bint Umays, should wash him, and that if she were unable to do so, then Abd al-Rahman ibn Abu Bakr should do it.

Muhammad ibn Umar al-Waqadi asked how her son Muhammad could help her as he was bom at Dhul Hulayfa in the farewell pilgrimage, 10 AH/632 CE and so was only around three years old on the day that Abu Bakr died.

Ayisha related that Asma washed Abu Bakr.

Abd Allah ibn Abu Bakr related that Asma bint Umays, the wife of Abu Bakr al-Siddiq, washed Abu Bakr when he died. She went out and asked the Emigrants who were present if she had to perform the bath lustration. She was fasting and it was a very cold day. They told her it was not necessary.

Ata related that Asma washed him on a cold morning. She asked Uthman whether or not she had to perform a bath lustration. He said no. Umar heard that and did not object.

Umar allotted Asma bint Umays a stipend of 1000 dirhams.

Muhammad ibn Umar al-Waqadi said that after Abu Bakr died, Asma bint Umays married Ali ibn Abi Talib and gave birth to Yahya and Awn.

Notes

Asma related sixty Traditions: Her transmitters include:
Abd Allah ibn Shaddad ibn al-Had
Abu Musa Ashari
Abu Yazid Medri
Fatima bint Ali
Qasim ibn Muhammad
Umar ibn al-Khattab
Umm Aun bint Muhammad ibn Jafar
Urwa ibn Musayyib

ASMA BINT YAZID ANSARIYA

Father: Yazid Ansariya

Ibn Sad also related the following:

Asma related that she went to the Messenger of God with a group of women to offer him their allegiance. The Messenger stated the preconditions to them. A niece of hers stretched out her hand to take that of the Messenger of God. She was wearing a gold bracelet and gold rings. The Messenger of God withdrew his hand saying, 'I do not shake hands with women.'

She related that they gave their allegiance to the Messenger. He enjoined on them the verse, '*O Prophet, when believing women come to you swearing fealty to you upon the terms that they will not associate with God anything, and will not steal, neither commit adultery, nor slay their children, nor bring a calumny they forge between their hands and their feet, nor disobey you in aught honorable, ask God's forgiveness for them...*' (60:12). The Messenger said, 'I will not shake your hands, but I enjoin on you what God enjoins on you.'

Asma was among the women who went to the house of Umm Ruman to take Ayisha to the house of the Prophet as his bride. Asma related that after Ayisha's departure as a bride, she was present when the Messenger came. The Messenger drank some milk from a cup and then offered it to Ayisha. Ayisha was too embarrassed to take it. Asma said to her that she should take whatever God's Messenger gave her. She shyly took the cup of milk, drank one sip and put it down. The Messenger said, 'Give it to your friends.' (*Musnad* ibn Hanbal)

Once Asma was holding the rope of the Prophet's she-camel when revelation came to him. Asma related that the she-camel was crushed under the pressure of the revelation and that she was afraid that the camel's legs might break.

Asma fought in the Battle of Yarmuk during the caliphate of Umar al-Khattab. At one point the enemy pursued the Muslim forces right up to the tents of the women. Asma and the other women took the poles of the tents, fell upon the enemy and pushed them back. It is narrated that Asma alone killed seven enemy soldiers in this battle.

Asma narrated a few Traditions. Her transmitters are:

Mahmud ibn Umar Ansari

Muhajir ibn Abu Muslim

Shahr ibn Hushab Mujahid

Ishaq ibn Rashid

ASMA BINT YAZID (SEE UMM AMIR AL-ASHHALIYYA)

ATIKA BINT ABD AL-MUTTALIB IBN HASHIM
Mother: Fatima bint Amr ibn Aidh of Makhzum
Father: Abd al-Muttalib ibn Hashim
Children: Abd Allah, Zuhayr, Qurayba
Sister of: Abbas ibn Abd al-Muttalib
Wife of: Abu Umayya ibn al-Mughira of the Makhzum clan

Ibn Sad also related the following:

Atika had had a dream which alarmed and distressed her. She told her brother, Abbas ibn Abd al-Muttalib, about her dream asking him to keep it a secret as she feared that it might bring some evil and hardship to them. She said that she dreamt that before the Quraysh went out to Badr, a rider came on a camel and stopped at al-Abtah. He shouted as loudly as he could, 'O people! Go to your slain.' He shouted that three times.

She said she saw people gather around him. He entered the mosque. People followed him. His camel appeared on top of the Kabah. He shouted the same thing three times. His camel appeared on top of Abu Qubays. He shouted the same thing three times. He took a stone from Abu Qubays and dropped it. It came crashing down and stopped at the bottom of the mountain. There was not a house in Makkah in which a piece of it had not fallen yet none of that stone entered a house of the Hashim tribe nor the houses of the Zuhra.

Her brother al-Abbas said to her that she had had a vision. Worried, he left her. He met Walid ibn Utba ibn Rabia who was his friend. He mentioned his sister's dream to him and asked him to keep it secret.

The story of the dream spread among the people. They all talked about Atika's dream. Abu Jahl said to the Abd al-Muttalib tribe that they were not content with making their men prophets. Now they made their women prophets as well! He told them that Atika claimed that she saw such and such in a dream. He and the others agreed to wait three days to see if what she had said was true. If not, they would record the Muslims as the worst lying people of any tribe among the Arabs. Al-Abbas said that he, Abu Jahl, was yellow bellied and that he was more likely to lie and be censured than they.

The third day after Atika's dream, Damdam ibn Amr arrived in Makkah from Badr. Abu Sufyan ibn Harb had sent him to alert the Quraysh about the danger to their caravan. He had told him to slit the ears of his camel, slit open his shirt, front and back, and turn his saddle around in order to scare the people of Makkah into sending help to the Quraysh caravan.

Damdam ibn Amr shouted to the Quraysh that Muhammad and his Companions had attacked the Quraysh caravan. He called for help and said that he did not think that they would reach it in time.

They prepared to go to the rescue of their caravan. They went to Abu Lahab and asked him to go with them. Abu Lahab swore an oath to the two main idols, al-Lat and al-Uzza, that he would not go to Badr nor would he send anyone out either. He was only stopped by the fear of the dream of Atika. He said that Atika's dream had been fulfilled.

ATIKA BINT AWF

Mother: Shifa bint Awf, al-
Children: Miswar, al-, Safwan the elder, Umm Safwan
Sister of: Abd al-Rahman ibn Awf
Wife of: Makhrama ibn Nawfal
Tribe: Quraysh

Ibn Sad also related the following:

She accepted Islam along with her mother. They gave their allegiance to the Messenger of God.

ATIKA BINT KHALID OF KHUZAA (SEE UMM MABAD)

ATIKA BINT ZAYD IBN AMR

Mother: Umm Kurz bint al-Hadrami
Father: Zayd ibn Amr
Wife of: Abd Allah ibn Abu Bakr al-Siddiq; Umar ibn Khattab
Tribe: Quraysh

Ibn Sad also related the following:

She accepted Islam and gave her allegiance to the Messenger of

God. Atika bint Zayd ibn Amr was married to Abd Allah ibn Abu Bakr. He gave her part of his property provided that she would not re-marry after he died. He died. Umar told Atika that she had made unlawful for herself what God had made lawful for her. Therefore, she should return the property which she had taken not to remarry and re-marry. She did that. Umar proposed to her and she married him.

Ali ibn Zayd related that Atika bint Zayd ibn Amr was married to Abd Allah ibn Abu Bakr. Before he died, he asked that she should not re-marry after he died. She remained a widow. Men began to propose to her, but she rejected them. Umar asked her guardian to tell her about him.

The guardian did this, but she also rejected Umar. Umar then told the guardian to marry her to him. Her guardian married him to her. Umar went to her. He argued with her until he overcame her reservations, and she carried out the marriage with him. When he finished, he said, 'Bother! Bother! Bother! I say 'Bother!' to her!' Then he left her. He left her alone and did not go to her. She sent a freedman of hers to tell him to come back. She said that she would prepare herself for him.

Khalid ibn Salama related that Atika bint Zayd was married to Abd Allah ibn Abu Bakr. He loved her and assigned her part of his land, provided that she would not re-marry after he died.

Umar ibn al-Khattab married her. Ayisha told her to return the land to them. When Abd Allah ibn Abu Bakr died, Atika vowed that she would remain in grief and mourning for him.

When Umar ibn al-Khattab married Atika, Ayisha said to her that she (Ayisha) vowed that her eye would remain fixed on Atika, that her skin would continue to yellow, and that Atika should return the land she received from Ayisha's nephew to his heirs.

Yahya ibn Abd al-Rahman ibn Hatib related that Rabia ibn Umayya went to Umar ibn al-Khattab and said that he had a dream that Abu Bakr died. After him he proposed to this widow and married her. He went in to her as a bridegroom and at his door was a basket of clover. The woman was Atika bint Zayd ibn Amr. She had been married to Abu Allah ibn Abu Bakr. He had been killed on the day of Taif. He had assigned her part of his property provided that she did not re-marry after him.

Umar said to Rabia that he would not succeed in marrying Atika. She was determined not to remarry. Then Abu Bakr died. Umar succeeded him. He told Atika that she had made unlawful for herself what God had made lawful. He said she should return the property to its people and marry.

She did that. Umar proposed to her. She married him. Rabia ibn Umayya came and asked permission to visit Umar while he was her bridegroom. Umar gave him permission. He entered and began to look at the basket of clover at his door.

Umar's grandson related that Atika bint Zayd was married to Umar ibn al-Khattab. She kissed him while he was fasting, and he did not forbid her doing so.

Yahya ibn Sad related that Atika bint Zayd was the wife of Umar ibn al-Khattab. She used to kiss Umar's head while he was fasting. He did not forbid her doing so.

Hamid ibn Abd al-Rahman ibn Awf related that Atika bint Zayd, the wife of Umar ibn al-Khattab, asked permission to go to the mosque. When she asked for permission, Umar told her that she knew that he wanted her to stay at home. She said to Umar that she would continue to ask his permission. Umar did not object when she asked his permission. Umar was stabbed while in the mosque.

ATIYYA AL-QURAYZI

She is not mentioned by Ibn Sad.

According to Ibn Ishaq, she related a Tradition from the Messenger.

AUNT OF AS IBN AMR AL-TAFAWI

Tribe: Non-Qurayshi Emigrant

Ibn Sad also related the following:

She accepted Islam and gave her allegiance to the Messenger of God. She related a Tradition regarding the ear from the Prophet.

AUNT OF HUSAYN IBN MIHSAN

Tribe: Khazraj, Malik ibn al-Najjar clan

Ibn Sad also related the following:

She accepted Islam and gave her allegiance to the Messenger of God. She related a Tradition from the Messenger.

AYISHA BINT ABU BAKR IBN ABU QUHAFA

Mother: Umm Ruman bint Umayr of Kinana
Father: Abu Bakr ibn Abu Quhafa
Children: No children.
Wife of: Messenger of God
Tribe: Quraysh, Taym

Ibn Sad also related the following:

She accepted Islam and gave her allegiance to the Messenger of God.

Ibn Abbas related that the Messenger of God asked Abu Bakr for Ayisha's hand. Abu Bakr told the Messenger that Ayisha had been promised to Jubayr, Mutim ibn Adi's son. He asked to get a release from them which he did. She then married the Messenger. She was a virgin.

Ayisha related that the Messenger married her in Shawwal in the tenth year of prophethood, three years before the migration. She was six years old. The Messenger migrated and reached Madinah on the 12th of the month of Rabil Awwal. They had their wedding in the month of Shawwal, the eighth month after the migration. She was nine at that time.

Ayisha related that the Messenger of God married her at a time when she was playing with girls. She did not know that the Messenger of God had married her until her mother took her and made her sit in a room rather than outside playing. Then it occurred to her that she was married. She did not ask. Her mother was the one who told her.'

Ayisha related that the Messenger of God married her when she was six. He consummated the marriage when she was nine. He came in while she was playing with dolls with her girl friends. When he came in, her friends would leave and slip out. The Messenger of God would go out and bring them back.

Atiyya related that the Messenger of God asked for the hand of Ayisha bint Abu Bakr when she was a child. Abu Bakr asked if he would marry his brother's daughter. The Messenger said, 'You are my brother in faith.'

Abu Bakr gave her in marriage to the Messesnger for some household goods which were worth about fifty dirhams. Her nurse came to her while she was playing with the girls. She took her hand, brought her to the house, cleaned her up, took a veil with her and then took her to the Messenger of God.

Ayisha related that the Messenger of God married her when she was six. He consummated the marriage when she was nine. She was playing on a see-saw and had become disheveled. She was taken, cleaned up and then brought to him. He was shown her picture in silk.

Abd Allah ibn Abd Allah ibn Ubayd ibn Umayr related that the Messenger of God was so grieved about Khadija that people feared for him until he married Ayisha.

Abu Ubayda related that the Prophet married Ayisha when she was seven years old. He consummated the marriage when she was nine and died when she was eighteen.

Ayisha related that the Messenger of God married her in Shawwal. He consummated the marriage with her in Shawwal. She was to ask which of the Messenger's wives were more fortunate than she to have been married and then to have the marriage consummated in the month of Shawwal. She used to like it for women to have their marriage consummated in Shawwal.

Abu Asim related that people disliked to consummate marriage with women in Shawwal. The plague occurred in Shawwal for the first time.

Ayisha related that the Prophet married her when she was seven. He consummated the marriage with her when she was nine. She used to play dolls with her friends. When he came and they were with her, the Prophet would tell them to go on playing.

Ayisha related that the Messenger of God came in to her one day while she was playing with dolls. He asked, 'What are these, Ayisha?' She responded that they were horses of Solomon. He laughed.

Ayisha was asked when the Messenger consummated the marriage with her. She said that she had stayed behind in Makkah along with the Messenger's daughters when the Messenger migrated to Madinah. When he reached Madinah, he sent Zayd ibn Haritha and Abu Rafi, his freedman, to get them. He gave them two camels and 500 dirhams which the Messenger of God had received from Abu Bakr with which to purchase whatever camels they needed. Abu Bakr sent Abd Allah ibn Urayqit al-Dili with them along with two or three camels. He wrote to Abd Allah ibn Abu Bakr to order him to take Ayisha's mother, Umm Ruman, and his daughters, Asma and Ayisha. When they reached Qudayd, Zayd ibn Haritha purchased three camels with that 500 dirhams. Then they left Makkah together. They met Talha ibn Ubayd Allah who wanted to migrate with the family of Abu Bakr. They all left together. Zayd ibn Haritha and Abu Rafi left with Fatima, Umm Kulthum, and Sawda bint Zama. Zayd took Umm Ayman and Usama ibn Zayd. Abd Allah ibn Abu Bakr took Umm Ruman and his two sisters. Talha ibn Ubayd Allah set out. They all traveled together until Ayisha's camel bolted at al-Bayd. She was in a sedan with her mother. Her mother cried out to get the bride when finally the camel was caught. God Almighty preserved them. They reached Madinah. She dismounted with her father's family and the family of the Messenger. The Messenger on that day was building the mosque. There were houses around the mosque. His family stayed in one of them.

They stayed for some days in the house of Abu Bakr. Abu Bakr asked what prevented the Messenger of God from consummating his marriage to Abu Bakr's daughter. The Messenger of God said, 'The dower.'

Abu Bakr gave him 400 dirhams. The Messenger sent them to Ayisha and consummated the marriage with her in this house in which she later lived. The Messenger died in it.

The Messenger made himself a doorway into the mosque opposite the door of Ayisha. She said that the Messenger of God consummated the marriage with Sawda in one of the houses beside hers. The Messenger of God was with her.'

Ayisha related that Sawda gave her day to Ayisha saying that her day was for Ayisha. The Messenger gave Ayisha her own day and Sawda's day.

Ayisha related that she said to the Messenger that many of the women have agnomens. She asked the Messenger to give her one.

He said, 'Use the agnomen of your nephew, Abd Allah.'

Ayisha related that she asked the Messenger for an agnomen. The Prophet said, 'Use the agnomen of your nephew Abd Allah.' She was given the agnomen of Umm Abd Allah.

Ayisha related that there were ten reasons why she was preferred over the other wives of the Prophet. She was asked what the reasons were and Ayisha gave the following ten reasons: None of the other women he married were virgins. She was the only woman he married whose mother and father were both Emigrants. God Almighty revealed her innocence from heaven. Gabriel brought her picture from heaven in silk and said, 'Marry her. She is your wife.' He and she used to do the bath lustration from the same vessel. He did not do that with any of his wives except her. He prayed while she was stretched out in front of him. He did not do that with any of his wives except her. Revelation would come to him while he was with her. It did not come when he was with any of his wives except her. God took his soul while he lay against her chest. He died on the night when it was her turn, and he was buried in her room.

Ammar related that he and others knew that Ayisha was the wife of the Messenger in this world and the next.

Urwa related that the Messenger of God said to Ayisha, 'I saw you twice in a dream. I saw a man carrying you on a piece of silk. He said, "This is your wife." Then the silk was removed and it was you.' Ayisha said to him that if this were from God, He would bring it about.

Shabi related that Masruq when he reported from Ayisha, Umm al-Muminin, would say, 'The daughter of the truthful speaks the truth. Her innocence was proclaimed. She told me such and such.'

Another said in this Tradition, '[Ayisha is] the beloved of the beloved of God.'

Masruq related that a woman said to Ayisha, 'O Mother!'

She said, 'I am not your mother. I am the mother of your men.'

Ayisha related that she had dolls, i.e. toys. When the Prophet entered, she concealed them from him with her garment. Abu Awana said that she did not stop playing with her dolls.

Ayisha related that she was given characteristics which no other woman was given. The Messenger of God married her when she was seven. The angel put her picture in his hand, and he looked at it. He consummated that marriage when she was nine. She saw Gabriel, and no wife except she ever saw him. She was the most beloved of his wives, and her father was the most beloved of his Companions. The Messenger of God became ill in her house. She nursed him, and he died seen by no one but her and the angels.

Humayd ibn Urayb related that a man attacked Ayisha in the

Battle of the Camel. The people gathered against him.

Ammar asked what was happening. He was told that a man was attacking Ayisha. He told the man to stop and that he was attacking the beloved of the Prophet who would be the wife of the Messenger in the garden. She had asked the Messenger who would be in the garden and he had said that she would be among them.

Ayisha related that she asked the Messenger of God who would be his wives in the garden? He said, 'You are among them.'

Musab ibn Ishaq ibn Talha related that he was informed that the Messenger had said, 'I saw her in the garden so that my death would be easy for me on this account.' He spoke as if he were seeing her [Ayisha's] hands.

Muslim al-Batin related that the Messenger of God said, 'Ayisha is my wife in the garden.'

Masruq related that he was asked if Ayisha's views were reliable concerning the shares of inheritance. He said that there were. He had seen the old, great Companions of Muhammad ask her about the shares of inheritance.

Urwa said that he saw Ayisha giving 70,000 dirhams away as charity.

Umm Dharra said that Ibn al-Zubayr sent Ayisha some money in two sacks. They contained 100,000 dirhams. She called for a bowl. She was fasting that day. She began to divide it among people. In the evening, she told Umm Dharra to bring her food to end the fast. Umm Dharra told her that she could use some dirhams out of the money she had been given to buy some meat to end her fast. Ayisha told Umm Dharra not to scold her; and said if Umm Dharra had reminded her of this fact before, she would have done so.

Musab ibn Sad related that Umar allotted the wives of the Prophet 10,000 dirhams. He added 2000 more to Ayisha's lot. He said that she was the beloved of the Messenger.

Amr ibn al-As asked the Messenger who was the most beloved of people to him. The Messenger said, 'Ayisha.' Amr ibn al-As said that he was asking about men. The Messenger said, 'Her father.'

Masruq related that Ayisha said to him that she saw Gabriel standing in their room on a horse while the Messenger of God was talking to him. When he came in, she asked him to whom he was speaking? The Messenger asked, 'Did you see him?' She said that she had. He said, 'In what form?' She said that he had been like Dihya al-Kalbi. The Messenger said, 'You have seen a great blessing. That was Gabriel.' A short time later he said, 'Ayisha, this was Gabriel who conveys the greeting to you.' She sent him greetings and prayed that God may repay him with good to his guest.'

Ayisha related that the Messenger of God said to her, 'Gabriel conveys greetings to you.' She sent greetings to him.

Qasim related that Ayisha used to fast all the time.

Ibn Jurayh related that Ata said that he used to go to Ayisha with Ubayd ibn Umayr. She was near the water-course of Thabir. He asked her what the color of her curtain was that day. At that time she was in a tent which had a covering over it which acted as a partition between her and men; nevertheless, he saw her wearing a red garment when he was a child.

Ayisha related that the Prophet of God came and said, 'I will present something to you. You should not be hasty until you have consulted your parents.' She asked what it was. He recited to her, '*O Prophet, say to your wives, "If it is the life of this world and its finery you desire, come now and I will make you provision and set you free with kindliness. But if you desire God and His Messenger and the Last Abode, surely God has prepared for those among you such as do good, a mighty wage*" (33:28-29).'

Ayisha asked him why he told her to consult her parents because she desired God and His Messenger and the next abode. The Prophet was delighted with her response

He said, 'I will present to your companions what I have presented to you.' She asked him not to tell them what she had chosen which he did not do. He recited the same verse to them. Then he said, 'Ayisha chose God and His Messenger and the next abode.' Ayisha related that God gave them a choice, and they did not see that as a divorce.

Urwa related that his aunt Ayisha said to him that the Messenger of God had said to her, 'It is not hidden from me when you are angry and when you are pleased.' She asked how he knew.

He said to her, 'When you are pleased and you swear an oath, you say, "No, by the Lord of Muhammad." When you are angry, you say, "No, by the Lord of Abraham."' She confirmed that what he had said was the truth.

Ishaq al-Ama [the blind] related that he visited Ayisha and she veiled herself from him. He asked why she veiled herself from him when he could not see. She said that even if he did not see her, she saw him.

Abd al-Rahman al-Araj said in his assembly in Madinah that the Messenger used to assign Ayisha eighty weights of dates from Khaybar and twenty weights of barley or wheat.

Urwa said that Ayisha had a dress of rough silk given to her by her nephew, Abd Allah ibn al-Zubayr. Shumaysa related that she visited Ayisha, who was wearing clothes from wolf skin, a chemise, a head covering and a skirt. They were colored with safflower red.

It is related that a woman said that Ayisha used to wear safflower red clothes.

Abd al-Rahman ibn al-Qasim related that Ayisha used to wear safflower clothes when she was in the sacred state of the pilgrimage.

Qasim ibn Muhammad related that Ayisha used to wear the two red ones—gold and safflower red when she was in the sacred state.

Qasim ibn Muhammad was asked if it were true as people claim that the Messenger of God forbade two red things—safflower and gold.

He answered that they lied. He had seen Ayisha wearing safflower dye and wearing gold rings.

Ibn Abi Mulayka related that he saw Ayisha wearing a red chemise. Umm Shayba related that she saw Ayisha wearing a safflower red garment.

Ayisha related that a woman must have three pieces of clothing in which to pray—a chemise, a dress, and a head covering. Ayisha used to undo her wrapper and put it round herself.

The mother of Alqama ibn Abu Alqama related that she brought Hafsa bint Abd al-Rahman to Ayisha, the Mother of the Believers. Hafsa was wearing a thin head covering. Ayisha tore it in half and put a thick head covering on her head. The mother of Alqama ibn Abu Alqama related that she saw Hafsa bint Abd al-Rahman ibn Abu Bakr visit Ayisha wearing a thin head covering which showed her breast. Ayisha tore it in half and asked if she did not know what God had sent down in the Chapter of Light. Then she called for a head covering and put it on her.

Muadha related that he saw Ayisha wearing a safflower red wrap.

Safiyya related that she saw Ayisha doing the circumambulation of the Kabah with loose trousers.

Abd Allah ibn Abi Mulayka related that he saw Ayisha wearing a *muddarij* garment. He asked what *muddarij* meant and was told that it meant red.

Habiba bint Abbad al-Bariqiyya related that her mother had said that she saw Ayisha wearing a red chemise and a black head covering.

Umm al-Mughira, the freedwoman of the Helpers, related that she asked Ayisha about this. Ayisha said that they wore a garment during the time of the Messenger which was called "*sayra*" which contained some silk.

Qasim ibn Muhammad related that on a cold day he wore a garment of rough silk which he gave to Ayisha to wear. She did not remove it.

Urwa related that Ayisha gave Abd Allah ibn al-Zubayr a shawl of rough silk which she used to wear.

Muhammad ibn al-Ashath related that he asked Ayisha if he should give her a skin because it was warmer. She said that she disliked the skins of carrion. He told her that he would make sure to give her only one from an animal that had been slaughtered according to the Law. He arranged it for her and sent it to her, and she wore it.

Nerima related that Ayisha and the wives of the Prophet used henna when they were in the sacred state of the prescribed pilgrimage. That was after the death of the Prophet. They continued wearing safflower red garments.

Ayisha related that they set out with the Prophet until they were at al-Qaha. Yellow ran down her face from the scent she had put on her head when setting out. The Prophet said, 'Your color now, O fair-skinned one, is better!'

Ayisha related that she asked the Prophet about struggle in the Way of God (*jihad*). He said, 'Your struggle in the Way of God is the prescribed pilgrimage.'

Urwa related that sometimes Ayisha would recite a *qasida* of sixty or 100 verses.

Ikrima related that Ayisha covered herself from Hasan and Husayn. He said that Ibn Abbas had said that it was lawful for them to visit her.

Abu Jafar related that Hasan and Husayn did not visit the wives of the Prophet. Ibn Abbas said that it was lawful for them to visit the wives of the Prophet.

Abu Hanifa and **Malik ibn Anas** relate that when a man marries a woman, it is not lawful for his son or his grandson to marry her, nor their sons nor the sons of their daughters. This is agreed upon.

Abu Said related that someone visited Ayisha while she was mending her trousers. She said to Ayisha that God had given her much of wealth [that is, why mend your trousers? Get a new pair instead]. Ayisha answered that she had had enough of her because someone who has nothing old and worn has nothing new.

Qasim related that when Ayisha got used to wearing something, she did not like to get rid of it.

The mother of Abd al-Rahman ibn al-Qasim related that she saw Ayisha wearing a red garment while she was in the sacred state.

Ayisha related that she wished that when she died, she could be 'something discarded and forgotten' (19:23).

Abd Allah ibn Ubayd ibn Umayr related that Ayisha ordered people not to follow her bier with fire and not to place a red blanket under her.

Ayisha related that when she was dying she wished she had never been born or had been created as a tree glorifying God and doing what was obligatory for her to do.

Ayisha related that she wished that she had been born a tree or a cold clod of earth, or that she had not been created at all.

Isa ibn Dinar related that he asked Abu Jafar about Ayisha. Abu Jafar said that he asked God's forgiveness for her. She used to say that she wished she had been a tree or a stone or a clod of earth.

Isa ibn Dinar asked Abu Jafar why she had said these things. He said in order to repent.

Qays related that when Ayisha was dying she said that she had caused mischief after the Messenger, and that she should be buried with the wives of the Prophet.

Ibn Abi Mulayka related that Ibn Abbas visited Ayisha before she died and praised her, re-stating the good news that the Messenger did not marry a virgin other than her and that her vindication was sent down from heaven.

Ibn al-Zubayr visited her after him, and she told ibn al-Zubayr that Allah ibn Abbas had praised her. She said that she did not want anyone else to praise her that day and wished that she had been something discarded and forgotten.

Ibrahim related that Ayisha said that she wished she had been a leaf on a tree.

Khaythama said that when Ayisha was asked how she was, she would say that she was sound, all praises to God.

Dhakwan, Ayisha's doorman, related that he went in the house. Ayisha's nephew, Abd Allah ibn Abd al-Rahman, was standing by her head. He told him that Abd Allah ibn Abbas asked permission to visit her. Her nephew leaned down to her and said that Abd Allah ibn Abbas asked permission to visit her. She was dying. She asked her nephew to spare her this visit because she neither needed him nor did she wish to listen to his commendation. Her nephew told her that Ibn Abbas was one of the virtuous men who would greet her and bid her farewell! She finally agreed for Ibn Abbas to visit because of her nephew's insistence.

Ibn Abbas entered the room. When he entered the room, he greeted her and sat down. He then told her that he had good news. She asked what the good news was. Ibn Abbas told her that in a short time she would meet the Messenger again. Nothing stood between this except that her spirit was still in her body. He also said that she had been the most beloved wife of the Messenger. He emphasized how the Messenger of God loved only the good. He referred to how she had dropped her necklace on the night of al-Abwa and how the Messenger of God began to look for it until morning found him still in the campsite. The people had no water, and so God revealed that they should do dry ablution with good soil. What God allowed this community of lenience was because of her. God sent down her innocence from above the seven heavens. The spirit brought it. Therefore, there was no mosque of God in which He was remembered that did not recite [her innocence] at the ends of the night and day.

She asked Ibn Abbas to leave her. She said that she wished she had been something discarded and forgotten.

Ibn Abbas went to Ayisha about something which had made her cross with him. He told her that she was called Mother of the Believers because she would be fortunate. He told her it was her name before she was born.

Ayisha related that the Messenger of God said to her, 'Ayisha, if you want to join me, then enough for you of the provision of this world is the provision of a rider. Beware of sitting with the wealthy. Do not replace a garment unless you have already mended it.'

Ayisha related that after she had been shrouded and scented, [her servant] Dhakwan should lower her into her grave and level the earth over her. She said that after that, he was to be set free.

Abu al-Zinad related that Ibn Abi Atiq visited Ayisha when she was gravely ill. He asked her how she felt. She said that it was death. She insisted that her condition would not remain unchanged.

Salim Sablan related that Ayisha died on the night of the 17th of Ramadan after the *witr*. She commanded that she be buried on the same night. The people gathered and attended. He said that he had not seen a night with more people present than that. Even the people of al-Awali came down. She was buried in the Baqi cemetery.

Abu Atiq related that on the night that Ayisha died, a palm branch had rags wrapped around it. Then it was drenched in oil and ignited. It was carried with her.

Abu Atiq related that on the night that Ayisha died, he saw a palm branch with burning rags carried with her at night. He saw women at the Baqi cemetery as if it were a festival.

Nafi related that he saw Abu Hurayra pray for Ayisha at the Baqi cemetery. Ibn Amr was among the people who did not object. When Marwan performed the visit that year, he appointed Abu Hurayra as his deputy.

Abd Allah ibn Abu Bakr related that Abu Hurayra prayed for Ayisha in Ramadan in 58 AH. She was buried after the *witr*.

Urwa related that he was one of five people who went down into the grave of Ayisha: they were Abd Allah ibn al-Zubayr, al-Qasim ibn Muhammad, Abd Allah ibn Muhammad ibn Abd al-Rahman ibn Abu Bakr, and Abd Allah ibn Abd al-Rahman. Abu Hurayra prayed for her after the *witr* in the month of Ramadan.

Muhammad ibn Umar al-Waqadi related that Ayisha was buried on the night of Tuesday, the 17th of Ramadan, 58 AH/July 13, 678 CE, after the *witr*. On that day she was sixty-six years old.

Habib, the freedman of Urwa related that when Khadija died, the Prophet was terribly grieved over her. God sent Gabriel who brought him the picture of Ayisha. He told the Messenger that the one in the picture would remove some of his sorrow and had some of the qualities of Khadija. Then he took it back.

The Messenger of God used to frequent the house of Abu Bakr. He told Ayisha's mother, Umm Ruman, to take good care of Ayisha and watch over her for him.

On that account Ayisha had a special position among her family, but they were not aware that God had commanded that. The Messenger went to visit them one day as was his custom. He did not pass a single day without going to the house of Abu Bakr from the time he received the revelation until he migrated.

He found Ayisha hiding behind the door of the house of Abu Bakr, weeping with great distress. He asked her what was wrong. She complained about her mother, and said that she was after her. The eyes of the Messenger of God overflowed with tears. He went in to Umm Ruman and said, 'Umm Ruman, did I not tell you to watch over Ayisha for me?'

Umm Ruman replied that Ayishe had spoken to Abu Bakr al-Siddiq about Umm Ruman and made him angry. The Prophet asked, 'What difference does that make?' Umm Ruman then said that she would never trouble her again.

Ayisha was born at the beginning of the fourth year of prophethood. She married the Messenger of God in the 10th year, in Shawwal, when she was six. He married her a month after he had married Sawda.

Ayisha related that the Messenger of God said, 'The excellence of Ayisha over women is like the excellence of *tharid* over other foods.'

Ayisha related that the Messenger of God said one day, 'O Ayisha, this is Gabriel who greets you.' She sent greetings to him and added that she did not see Gabriel. The Messenger used to see what she did not see.

Rabia ibn Uthman related that the Messenger of God traveled by night. He then said to Ayisha, 'You are dearer to me than butter with dates."

Fatima al-Khuzaiyya related that she heard Ayisha say one day say that the Messenger had visited her. She asked him where he had been. He said, 'Humayra! I was with Umm Salama.' She asked if he had had his fill of Umm Salama. He smiled. She then asked him if he were to land on two slopes, one of which had been grazed and the other not grazed, on which one would he graze. He said, 'The one which was not grazed.' Ayisha then said that she was not like any of his other wives. She pointed out that each of his wives had had another husband, except for herself. The Messenger smiled.

Ayisha related that she and Safiyya insulted each other. Ayisha insulted Safiyya's father and Safiyya insulted Ayisha's father. The Messenger of God heard them. He asked, 'Safiyya, do you insult Abu Bakr! Safiyya! Do you insult Abu Bakr!'

Ibn al-Musayyab related that the Messenger of God asked Abu

Bakr, 'Abu Bakr, will you obtain my right from Ayisha?'

Abu Bakr raised his hand and struck Ayisha hard on the chest. The Messenger of God said, 'May God forgive you, Abu Bakr, I did not mean this!'

It is related that Ayisha recited this verse, *'Remain in your houses,'* (3333). She was heard to weep until her head covering was wet.

AYISHA BINT ABU SUFYAN IBN AL-HARITH

Mother: Salma bint Amr
Father: Abu Sufyan ibn al-Harith
Wife of: Muadh ibn Amir
Tribe: Aws, Amr ibn Awf clan
Alternative Name: Maryam bint Abu Sufyan ibn al-Harith

Ibn Sad also related the following:

She accepted Islam and gave her allegiance to the Messenger of God.

AYISHA BINT JAZ IBN AMR

Father: Jaz ibn Amr
Children: Mundhir, al-, Abd al-Rahman
Wife of: Abul Mundhir Yazid ibn Amir
Tribe: Aws, Zafar clan

Ibn Sad also related the following:

She accepted Islam and gave her allegiance to the Messenger of God. Her husband was the brother of Qutba ibn Amr who was present at the Battle of Badr.

AYISHA BINT UMAYR IBN AL-HARITH

Father: Umayr ibn al-Harith
Tribe: Khazraj, Salama ibn Sad clan

She is mentioned by Muhamamd ibn Umar al-Waqadi as having accepted Islam.

AYSA BINT AL-HARITH

Mother: Qilaba bint Sayfi
Father: Harith, al-
Children: Muhammad ibn Anas who had twenty-two sons and five daughters
Wife of: Anas ibn Fadala
Tribe: Aws, Zafar clan

Ibn Sad also related the following:

She accepted Islam and gave her allegiance to the Messenger of God.

AZDA BINT HARITH IBN KALADAH THAQAFI
Father: Harith ibn Kaladah Thaqafi
Wife of: Utba ibn Ghazqan

She is not mentioned by Ibn Sad. Tabari mentions that Azda's father was a well-known doctor. Her husband was a well-known Companion. She took part in many battles. In the battle between the people of Maysan and the Muslims near the Tigris river, fighting had become intense. The women had been left far behind the battlefield. Azda told the women that they could help the Muslim forces if they used their head coverings to make banners and then went to the battlefield as if they were fresh troops. They did this. Seeing what they thought to be reinforcements, the enemy fled the battlefield.

B

BAGHUM BINT MUADHDHIL, AL-
Father: Muadhdhil
Children: Abd Allah the younger, Safwan ibn Safwan, Amr ibn Safwan
Wife of: Safwan
Tribe: Non-Qurayshi

Ibn Sad also related the following:

She accepted Islam and gave her allegiance to the Messenger of God. Baghum accepted Islam at the farewell pilgrimage although some say that she did so on the day of the conquest of Makkah. Abd Allah ibn al-Zubayr related that on the day of the conquest, Baghum bint al-Muadhdhil of Kinana accepted Islam.

BARAKA (SEE UMM AYMAN)

BARAKA BINT YASAR
Father: Yasar, agnomen Abu Fukayha
Sister of: Abu Tajra, freedman of the Abd Dar clan
Wife of: Qays ibn Abd Allah al-Asadi
Tribe: Quraysh

Ibn Sad also related the following:

She accepted Islam and gave her allegiance to the Messenger of God. She was from Yemen and the Azd tribe. She became Muslim early on in Makkah and gave her allegiance to the Messenger. She migrated to Abyssinia in the second migration with her husband.

BARIRA, FREEDWOMAN OF AYISHA
Wife of: Mughith
Tribe: Quraysh

Ibn Sad also related the following:

She accepted Islam and gave her allegiance to the Messenger of God.

Ayman related that she visited Ayisha. She said to her that she belonged to Utba ibn Abi Luhayb. His wife and sons were willing to sell her provided that they maintain guardianship. She asked Ayisha whose freedwoman she would be [the one who sold her or the one who bought her]. Ayisha told the Messenger that Barira has come to her with her freedom contract (*kıtaba*). Barira had asked Ayisha to buy her freedom, and Ayisha agreed. Then Barira told Ayisha that her owners would not sell her unless they kept her guardianship. Ayisha then said that she had no need of her.

The Messenger of God heard this and said, 'What is the matter with Barira?' Ayisha told him. He said, 'Buy her and set her free. Agree to any condition that they want.' Ayisha bought her and set her free. The Messenger of God said, 'The guardianship belongs to the one who sets free, even if a hundred preconditions are made.'

Ayisha related that the Prophet got up and made a speech when Ayisha set Barira free after her people had made the precondition of keeping the guardianship.

He said, 'Why is it that some men make conditions which are not in the Book of God? Any condition which is not in the Book of God is invalid, even if it is stipulated a hundred times. The decision of God is even more binding, and the condition of God is even more firm.'

Ibn Abbas related that the husband of Barira was a black slave named Mughith. The Prophet made four judgments regarding her. First of all, her owners stipulated that they should keep the right of inheritance. Second, he judged that the right of inheritance belonged to the one who sets free. Third, she was given a choice as to whether or not to stay married to her husband. She herself made the choice to divorce him. Fourth, the Prophet ordered her to observe the waiting period. Ibn Abbas used to see her husband following her in the streets of Madinah with his eyes fixed on her.

She was given charity some of which she gave to Ayisha. She mentioned this to the Messenger. He said, 'It is charity for her, and a gift for us.'

Ayisha related that Barira was set free. She had a husband. The Messenger of God gave her the choice of remaining with him or separating from him.

Barira was given some meat as charity. They cut it up but offered the Messenger of God condiments without meat. He said, 'Didn't I see you had some meat?' They replied that it was meat which was given as charity to Barira. The Messenger of God said, 'It is charity for Barira and a gift for us.'

Barira went to Ayisha to ask for her help in obtaining her freedom contract from her people. Ayisha said that if her people agreed, she would buy her and pay her price all at once.

Barira went to her people and told them this. They said they would agree as long as they kept the right of inheritance. Barira went to Ayisha and told her what they had said and how they wanted to retain the right of inheritance.

The Messenger of God said to Ayisha, 'Buy her. What they have asked for will not effect you. The right of inheritance belongs to the one who sets free.'

Ata related that the husband of Barira was a slave named Mughith. He was from the Mughira tribe. When she was freed, the Messenger of God gave her a choice as to whether to stay with her husband. Ibn Abu Layla had thought that there was a choice in the case of a slave but not in the case of a free man.

Muhammad related that the Messenger of God gave Barira the choice of staying with her husband. The Messenger of God spoke to her. She asked the Messenger if it was obligatory for her to remain married to someone who was still a slave? He said, 'No. However, I am interceding for him.' Barira replied that she had no need of her slave husband.

Ibn Abbas related that the husband of Barira was a black slave of the Mughira tribe. On the day that Barira was set free, he saw him on the roads of Madinah following her, weeping and trying to appease her. She refused to change her mind.

Ayyub related that he did not know of anyone of the people of Madinah and Makkah who disagreed that Barira's husband was a slave.

Ibn Abbas related that on the day, when Barira was given a choice of staying with her husband or not, he was a black slave of the Mughira tribe called Mughith. He saw him following her in the streets of Madinah with tears running down into his beard. She kept saying to him that she had no need of him.

Ayisha [and others] relate that Barira's husband was a free man on the day she was given a choice.

BARRA (SEE JUWAYRIYYA BINT AL-HADITH IBN DIRAR)

BARRA BINT ABD AL-MUTTALIB IBN HASHIM
Mother: Fatima bint Amr ibn Aidh of Makhzum
Father: Abd al-Muttalib ibn Hashim
Children: Abu Salama ibn Abd al-Asad; Abu Sabra
Wife of: Abd al-Asad ibn Hilal;
      Abu Ruhm ibn Abd al-Uzza
Ibn Sad also related the following:

She accepted Islam and gave her allegiance to the Messenger of God. Her sons, Abu Salama and Abu Sabra, were martyred at the Battle of Badr. She was an aunt of the Prophet. Her son, Abu Salama, was married to Umm Salama before his martyrdom.

BARRA BINT ABU TAJRA IBN ABU FUKAYHA
Father: Abu Tajra ibn Abu Fukayha
Tribe: Quraysh
Ibn Sad also related the following:
She accepted Islam and gave her allegiance to the Messenger of God. She related Traditions from the Messenger.

BARZA BINT MASUD IBN AMR AL-THAQAFIYYA
Mother: Ama bint Khalaf ibn Wahb
Father: Masud ibn Amr al-Thaqafiyya
Children: Abd Allah the elder, Safwan Hisham the elder, Umayya and Umm Habib
Wife of: Safwan ibn Umayya
Tribe: Non-Qurayshi
Ibn Sad also related the following:
She accepted Islam and gave her allegiance to the Messenger of God. Her son, Abd Allah the elder, known as al-Tawil, was killed with Abd Allah al-Zubayr. She became Muslim at the time of the farewell pilgrimage.

BASHIRA BINT AL-NUMAN IBN AL-HARITH
Mother: Umm Sakhr bint Sharik
Father: Numan ibn al-Harith
Children: Rabi, al-, Umm al-Harith
Wife of: Sahl ibn al-Harith
Ibn Sad also related the following:
She accepted Islam and gave her allegiance to the Messenger of God.

BASHIRA BINT THABIT IBN AL-NUMAN
Mother: Shumayla bint al-Harith
Father: Thabit ibn al-Numan
Wife of: Abu Namla ibn Muadh
Tribe: Aws, Zafar clan
Ibn Sad also related the following:
She accepted Islam and gave her allegiance to the Messenger of God.

BAYDA BINT ABDUL MUTTALIB IBN HASHIM (SEE UMM HAKIM)

BINT AMR IBN WAHB

Father: Amr ibn Wahb
Wife of: Sad al-Aswad Sehmi
    She is not mentioned by Ibn Sad.
    One of the Companions of the Messenger, Sad al-Aswad Sehmi, was extremely unattractive. No one was prepared to have his daughter marry him. He explained his problem to the Messenger who then told him to go to Amr ibn Wahb and tell him that the Messenger had married his daughter to Sad. When Sad informed Amr ibn Wahb of the message from the Prophet, Amr ibn Wahb refused to accept. When his daughter heard the conversation, she went to the door and told Sad that if he were really sent by God's Messenger, she would happily and willingly marry him. Sad returned to the Messenger and told him what had happened. The Messenger then prayed for the girl who, in the meantime, had warned her father of God's punishment. Her father went to the Messenger and asked forgiveness. Sad ibn al-Aswad and bint Amr al-Wahb were married, but Sad was martyred in a battle before he could take his bride home.

BINT JUNDUB IBN SAMRA AL-JUNDI

Father: Jundub ibn Samra al-Jundi
Wife of: Prophet
Tribe: Kinana tribe
    Ibn Sad also related the following:
    She accepted Islam and gave her allegiance to the Messenger of God.
    Yazid ibn Bakr related that the Messenger married her, but the marriage was never consummated. Muhammad ibn Umar al-Waqadi said that the Companions denied that the Messenger married a woman from the Kinana tribe.

BINT KHABBAB IBN AL-ARATT

Father: Khabbab ibn al-Aratt
Tribe: Non-Qurayshi
    Ibn Sad also related the following:
    She accepted Islam and gave her allegiance to the Messenger of God. She related a Tradition regarding her sheep.

BUHAYNA

Mother: Umm Sayfi bint al-Aswad ibn al-Muttalib ibn Asad
Father: Harith, al-
Children: Abd Allah, Jubayr
Wife of: Malik of the Azd tribe
Tribe: Quraysh
Alternative Name: Abda bint al-Harith

Ibn Sad also related the following:
She accepted Islam and gave her allegiance to the Messenger of God. She accompanied the Messenger.

BUHAYSA BINT AMR IBN KHALIDA
Mother: Umm al-Hakam (Fukayha bint al-Muttalib)
Father: Amr ibn Khalida
Wife of: Numan ibn Ajlan, al-
Tribe: Khazraj, Zurayq ibn Amr clan
Ibn Sad also related the following:
She accepted Islam and gave her allegiance to the Messenger of God.

BURAYDA BINT BISHR IBN AL-HARITH
Mother: Umayma bint Amr
Father: Bishr ibn al-Harith
Children: Bore Muattab with third husband
Wife of: Abbad ibn Nahik;
　　　　　Maqil ibn Nahik (brother of Abbad);
　　　　　Abu Burda ibn Usayr
Ibn Sad also related the following:
She accepted Islam and gave her allegiance to the Messenger of God.

BUSAYRA, GRANDMOTHER OF HUMAYDA BINT YASIR
Tribe: Non-Qurayshi Emigrant
Ibn Sad also related the following:
She accepted Islam and gave her allegiance to the Messenger of God. She related a Tradition from the Messenger.

BUSHRA BINT MULAYL IBN WABRA
Mother: Umm Zayd bint Nadla
Father: Mulayl ibn Wabra
Children: Muhammad, Hamid, Khadija, Kulthum
Wife of: Hamza ibn al-Abbas
Tribe: Khazraj, Qawaqila, Awf ibn al-Khazraj clan
Ibn Sad also related the following:
She accepted Islam and gave her allegiance to the Messenger of God.

BUSRA BINT SAFWAN IBN NAWFAL
Mother: Salima bint Umayya ibn Haritha
Father: Safwan ibn Nawfal
Children: Muawiya ibn al-Mughira
Sister of: Half-sister of Uqba ibn Abi Muayt
Wife of: Mughira ibn Abil Asm al-

Tribe: Quraysh

Ibn Sad also related the following:

She accepted Islam and gave her allegiance to the Messenger of God. She related a Tradition from the Prophet.

BUTHAYNA BINT AL-NUMAN IBN AMR

Mother: Habiba ibn Qays
Father: Numan ibn Amr, al-
Wife of: Muhammad ibn Amr
Tribe: Khazraj, Zurayq ibn Amr clan

Ibn Sad also related the following:

She accepted Islam and gave her allegiance to the Messenger of God.

BUZAYA BINT ABU KHARIJA IBN AWS

Mother: Maryam bint Isma
Father: Abu Kharija ibn Aws
Wife of: Walid ibn Ubada, al-
Tribe: Khazraj, Qawaqila, Awf ibn al-Khazraj clan

Ibn Sad also related the following:

She accepted Islam and gave her allegiance to the Messenger of God.

D

DUBAA BINT AL-ZUBAYR IBN ABD AL-MUTTALIB

Mother: Atika bint Abu Wahb ibn Amr
Father: Zubayr ibn Abd al-Muttalib, al-
Children: Abd Allah, Karima
Wife of: Miqdad ibn Umar (Miqdad ibn al-Aswad)
Tribe: Makhzum

Ibn Sad also related the following:

She accepted Islam and gave her allegiance to the Messenger of God.

DUBAA BINT AMIR IBN QURAT

Children: From third husband: Salama ibn Hisham ibn al-Mughira
Wife of: Hawdha ibn Ali al-Hanafi; Abd Allah ibn Jidan al-Taymi;
Hisham ibn al-Mughira

Ibn Sad also related the following:

She accepted Islam and gave her allegiance to the Messenger of God. The Prophet proposed to her but never married her. Her first husband was very wealthy, and when he died, she remarried but later asked her second husband to divorce her. He did.

Ibn Abbas related that Dubaa bint Amir was married to Hawdha ibn Ali al-Hanafi. He died and she inherited a great deal of wealth. She married Abd Allahibn Jidan al-Taymi. They had no children. She asked him to divorce her, and he did so. She then married Hisham ibn al-Mughira. She gave birth to Salama. He was one of the best Muslims. Then Hisham died.

Dubaa was one of the most beautiful of Arab women and physically, very large. When she sat down, she took up a great deal of room. She used to cover her body with her hair. Her beauty was mentioned to the Messenger. He proposed to her through her son, Salama ibn Hisham ibn al-Mughira. Her son asked for permission to consult his mother. He went and told his mother that the Messenger had proposed to her. She asked him how he, her son, had responded. Her son said that he asked for permission to consult her. She told her son that there was no need to consult her in a situation like this and that he should go immediately and tell the Messenger that she accepted. He returned to the Prophet, but the Prophet was silent about it.

DUBAA BINT AMR IBN MIHSAN
Mother: Amra bint Hazzal
Father: Amr ibn Mihsan
Sister of: Thalaba ibn Amr; half of Abu Amr Bashir
Wife of: Ubayd ibn Umayr
Tribe: Khazraj, Malik ibn al-Najjar tribe

Ibn Sad also related the following:

She accepted Islam and gave her allegiance to the Messenger of God. Her brother was present at the Battle of Badr.

DUBAYYA BINT THABIT (SEE UMM SIMAK BINT THABIT)

DURRA BINT ABU LAHAB IBN ABD AL-MUTTALIB
Mother: Umm Jamil bint Harb ibn Umayya
Father: Abu Lahab ibn Abd al-Muttalib
Children: Walid, al-, Abul Hasan, Muslim
Wife of: Harith ibn Amr ibn Nawfal, al-; Dihya ibn Khalifa al-Kalbi

Ibn Sad also related the following:

She accepted Islam, gave her allegiance to the Messenger of God and migrated to Madinah. She related many Traditions.

Ibn Athir related that Durra, the daughter of Abu Lahab, uncle and staunch enemy of the Prophet, stayed with Rafi ibn Mualli Zuraiqi in Madinah. When the women of the Zuraiq tribe came to meet her, they said that, since she was the daughter of Abu Lahab about whom the chapter cursing Abu Lahab had been revealed, what blessings did she think she could possibly receive from the migration to Madinah.

Durra was deeply hurt by their comments and spoke to the Messenger of God about what had taken place. He comforted her and asked her to stay for awhile in the mosque. After the noon prescribed prayer, the Messenger addressed the people and said, 'O people, some of you have said hurtful things to members of my family. Know that, by God, they will surely have intercession through me and this includes the tribes like Sad, Hakam and Salhab with whom I have distant relations.'

Her husband was killed as an unbeliever at the Battle of Badr.

F

FARIA, AL-
Mother: Amira bint Sahl
Father: Asad ibn Zurara
Children: Abd al-Malik
Wife of: Nubayt ibn Jabir
Tribe: Khazraj, Malik ibn al-Najjar clan
Alternative Name: Furaya bint Asad ibn Zurara, al-
   Ibn Sad also related the following:
   She accepted Islam and gave her allegiance to the Messenger of God. The Prophet named her son.
   She was the oldest of the daughters of Asad ibn Zurara. When she came of age, Nubayt ibn Jabir proposed to her. The Messenger gave her in marriage to him. On the wedding night, the Messenger told them to say:
   We have come to you. We have come to you.
      Greet us. We greet you.
   If it were not for golden wheat,
      we would not have alighted in your valley.
   If it were not for red gold, we would not have come to you.
   She married Nubayt and became pregnant with Abd al-Malik. When she gave birth, his father took him to the Messenger of God and asked him to give him a name. The Messenger of God named him Abd al-Malik and blessed him.

FARIA BINT ISAM IBN AMIR, AL-
Father: Isam ibn Amir
Wife of: Amr ibn al-Numan
Tribe: Khazraj, Bayada ibn Amr clan
   Ibn Sad also related the following:

She accepted Islam and gave her allegiance to the Messenger of God.

FARIA BINT ZURARA, AL-
Mother: Suad bint Rafi
Father: Zurara, al-
Sister of: Abu Umama Asad ibn Zurara
Wife of: Qays ibn Qahd
Tribe: Khazraj, Malik ibn al-Najjar clan
Alternative Name: Furaya bint Zurara, al-
　　Ibn Sad also related the following:
　　She accepted Islam and gave her allegiance to the Messenger of God.

FATIMA
Mother: Atika bint Asad of Khuzaa
Children: Salit ibn Salit
Wife of: Salit ibn Umar
Tribe: Quraysh
Alternative Name: Umm Qihtam bint Alqama
　　Ibn Sad also related the following:
　　She accepted Islam and gave her allegiance to the Messenger of God. She migrated to Abyssina in the second migration with her husband.

FATIMA
Mother: Umm Habib bint al-As
Father: Mujallil, al-
Children: Muhammad and Harith, al-
Wife of: Hatib ibn al-Harith
Tribe: Quraysh
Alternative Name: Umm Jamil bint al-Mujallil
　　Ibn Sad also related the following:
　　She accepted Islam early on in Makkah, gave her allegiance to the Messenger of God and migrated to Abyssinia in the second migration with her husband and her two sons.

FATIMA BINT ABU HUBAYSH
Father: Abu Hubaysh
Children: Muhammad
Wife of: Abd Allah Jahsh
　　Ibn Sad also related the following:
　　She accepted Islam and gave her allegiance to the Messenger of God. She spoke to the Prophet about her constant bleeding. A Tradition was related by Ayisha regarding her.

FATIMA BINT AL-ASWAD IBN ABD AL-ASAD
Father: Aswad ibn Abd al-Asad
Tribe: Quraysh

Ibn Sad also related the following:

She accepted Islam and gave her allegiance to the Messenger of God. She stole something. The Messenger ordered the punishment for stealing which is to cut off the hand.

Habib ibe Abi Thabit related that Fatima bint al-Aswad ibn Abd al-Asad stole some jewelry in the time of the Messenger of God. More than one person interceded on her behalf with him. They asked Usama ibn Zayd to speak to the Messenger, as the Messenger of God used to accept his intercession. When Usama came and the Prophet saw him, the Messenger said, 'Usama, do not speak to me. When the laws are violated, there is no alternative. If the daughter of Muhammad had stolen, I would have cut off her hand.'

Muhammad ibn Sad related a transmission about Fatima bint al-Aswad. Included in the transmission of the people of Madinah and other people of Makkah was the story concerning the theft by Umm Amm bint Sufyan, whose hand was cut off by the Messenger of God. Her mother was the daughter of Abd al-Uzza ibn Qays, the sister of Huwaytib ibn Abd al-Uzza. Umm Amr went out at night during the farewell pilgrimage and came upon a camp of travelers. She took a bag of theirs. The people seized and bound her. In the morning, they took her to the Messenger. She sought refuge with Umm Salama, the wife of the Messenger. The Messenger orderedUmm Salama to let go of her. He said, 'By God, if Fatima, the daughter of Muhammad, had stolen, I would cut off her hand.'

Then he ordered that her hand be cut off. She left with her hand dripping blood. She went to the wife of Usayd ibn Hudayr, the brother of the Abd al-Ashhal tribe. Usayd ibn Hudayr's wife recognized her, took her in and made some hot food for her. Usayd ibn Hudayr came from the Messenger. Before he entered the house, he called to his wife and asked her if she had heard about what happened to Fatima bint al-Aswad. His wife answered that Fatima bint al-Aswad was with her.

Usayd ibn Hudayr went and told the Messenger who said, 'She has had mercy on her. May God have mercy on you.'

When Fatima bint al-Aswad went back to her father, he told his people to take her to the the Abd al-Uzza tribe because what she had done resembled what they did. They stated that her uncle, Huwaytib ibn Abd al-Uzza took her in.

FATIMA BINT AL-KHATTAB
Mother: Hantama bint Hashim
Father: Khattab, al-

Children: Abd al-Rahman
Sister of: Umar ibn al-Khattab
Wife of: Said ibn Zayd
Tribe: Quraysh
Alternative Name: Umm Jamil bint al-Khattab

Ibn Sad also related the following:

She accepted Islam and gave her allegiance to the Messenger of God. She became Muslim before her brother and before the Prophet went to the home of al-Arqam.

It was at the beginning of Islam before Fatima's brother, Umar al-Khattab, had converted to Islam. He told the story of his conversion which involved his sister who was a Muslim. He related that after the conversion of Hamza to Islam, he was going to find the Prophet in order to kill him. On the way he met one of the Messenger's Companion. Umar asked him if he had embraced Islam as a new religion thereby forsaking the ancient religion of his forefathers?

The Companion said that he had but added that Umar should be asking this question of his sister and brother-in-law because they had embraced Islam as well. Upon hearing this, Umar hastened to his sister's house. The door of the house was closed, but he could hear his sister reciting something. Hearing his footsteps, she became quiet.

When he entered her house, he asked her what she had been reciting. She did not want to tell him about the Quran. He began to beat her. She cried out that he could do what he wanted, but that she would not forsake Islam.

When he saw blood flowing from her head, he felt ashamed. His love overpowered his anger, and he asked her gently to recite for him what she had been reciting. She did so, and it had a deep impact on his heart. He had to delcare that there is no god but God.

FATIMA BINT ASAD IBN HASHIM

Mother: Fatima bint Haram ibn Rawaha
Father: Asad ibn Hashim
Children: Talib, Aqil, Jafar, Ali, Umm Hani, Jumana, Rayta
Wife of: Abu Talib ibn Abd al-Muttalib
Tribe: Quraysh, Asad

Ibn Sad also related the following:

She accepted Islam and gave her allegiance to the Messenger of God. The Prophet grew up in her home. He lived with her and her family from the age of eight until he married Khadija at the age of twenty-five. She was the daughter of the uncle of Zaida ibn al-Asamm, the grandfather of Khadija on her mother's side. The Prophet often spent midday resting in her house. He loved her very much, as she was the only mother he really knew. Fatima was very close to the Prophet both in worldly and spiritual relations.

FATIMA BINT DAHHAK
Tribe: Kilab tribe
Alternative Name: Amra bint Yazid; Aliya bint Zabyan; Saba ibn Sufyan; Nashah bint Rifaah
She is not mentioned by Ibn Sad.

Other sources say that she was married to the Messenger in 629 CE/ 8AH, but she sought refuge in God from him, and he divorced her. Others say that he divorced her because of the white marks of leprosy on her body.

FATIMA BINT MUHAMMAD IBN ABD ALLAH
Mother: Khadija
Father: Muhammad ibn Abd Allah
Children: Hasan, Husayn, Zaynab, Umm Kulthum
Sister of: Ruqiyya, Zaynab, Umm Kulthum
Wife of: Ali ibn Abi Talib
Tribe: Quraysh
Ibn Sad also related the following:

Her mother was Khadija bint Khuwaylid. She was born while the Quraysh were rebuilding the Kabah, five years before the mission was actualized.

It is related that Abu Bakr asked the Messenger for Fatima's hand in marriage. He said, 'Abu Bakr, wait for a decision about her.' Abu Bakr mentioned this to Umar. Umar told Abu Bakr that the Messenger had rejected him [Abu Bakr].

Then Abu Bakr told Umar that he, Umar, should ask the Messenger for Fatima's hand. So Umar asked to marry her. The Messenger said the same thing to him that he had said to Abu Bakr: 'Wait for a decision about her.'

Umar went to Abu Bakr and told him what had happened. Abu Bakr said to him that the Messenger had rejected him [Umar].

Then Ali's family told Ali to ask the Messenger of God for Fatima's hand in marriage. Ali proposed, and the Prophet gave her in marriage to him. Ali sold a camel he had and some of his goods. He then had 480 dirhams. The Messenger said to him, 'Invest two-thirds of it in scent and a third in goods.'

Musa ibn Qays al-Hadrami related that Hujr ibn Anbas said that Abu Bakr and Umar asked the Messenger of God for Fatima's hand. The Messenger said, 'She is yours, Ali. You are not a fraud' [meaning you are not a liar]. He did this because he had promised her to Ali before Abu Bakr and Umar had asked to marry her.'

Ata related that Ali asked to marry Fatima. The Messenger of God said to her, 'Ali is mentioning you.' She was silent, and so he gave his permission.

It is related that a man heard Ali say that he wanted to ask the

Messenger of God for his daughter, but that he had nothing to offer for her dowry. The man said that this was not true because their familes were connected in so many ways. Ali then asked to marry Fatima.

The Messenger asked, 'Do you have anything?' Ali said that he did not have anything. He asked, 'Where is your coat of chain mail which I gave you on such and such a day?' Ali said that he had that. The Messenger said, 'Give it to her.' He gave it to her.

Ikrima related that Ali proposed to Fatima. The Messenger said to him, 'What dowry will you give her?' Ali said that he did not have anything to give to her as dowry. The Messenger said, 'Where is your coat of chain mail which I gave you?' Ali responded that he did have that. The Messenger said, 'Give it to her.' He gave it to her and married her. It was worth four dirhams. Ikrima related that Fatima married Ali for an iron coat of chain mail.

Burayda related that a group of the Helpers said to Ali that he should marry Fatima. He went to the Messenger of God and greeted him. The Messenger asked him, 'What do you need, Ibn Abu Talib?'

Ali mentioned Fatima. The Messenger said, 'Welcome and greetings,' and did not say anything more.

Ali went back to that group of Helpers who were waiting for him. They asked what had happened. Ali replied that the Messenger had welcomed and greeted him. They said that one greeting from the Messenger was enough for him. They said that he had welcomed Ali and greeted him. Later Ali and Fatima were to be married. The Messenger said, 'Ali, there must be a wedding feast.'

One of the Companions said that he had a ram. A group of the Helpers collected some measures of millet for him. On the wedding night, the Messenger said, 'Do not begin anything until I join you.' The Messenger of God called for a vessel. He put his hands into it and then poured it over Ali. Then he said, 'O God, bless them and their offspring.'

It is related that Muhammad said that Ali gave Fatima a dowry of iron armor and a well-worn garmet.'

Muhammad ibn Ali related that Ali married Fatima for a sheepskin and a worn out garment.

Abu Jafar related something similar.

Ilya ibn Ahmar al-Yaskari related that Ali married Fatima. He sold a camel of his for 480 dirhams. The Prophet said, 'Invest two-thirds of it in scent and one third in clothes.'

Ali ibn Abi Talib related that he married Fatima when we had nothing to sleep on but a ramskin. They slept on it at night and fed the camel on it. She had no help.

Ibrahim related that the dower of the daughters of the Messenger of God and of his wives was 400 dirhams.

It is related that Ali ibn Abi Talib married Fatima, the daughter of the Messenger, in the month of Rajab five months after the Messenger arrived in Madinah. The marriage was consummated after Ali returned from the Battle of Badr. Fatima was eighteen on the day that the marriage with Ali was consummated.

Abu Jafar related that when the Messenger of God went to Madinah, he stayed with Abu Ayyub for a year or so. When Ali married Fatima, he told Ali to look for a house.'

Ali did so. He found something a little distant from the Messenger. He consummated the marriage there. The Messenger went to Fatima and said, 'I want to move you near me.'

She asked the Messenger to ask Haritha ibn al-Numan to move from his place for her. The Messenger of God said, 'Haritha has moved already for us. I am embarrassed to ask him again.'

Haritha heard about this. He moved. Then he went to the Messenger and said that he had heard that the Messenger wanted Fatima to move near himself. He told the Messenger that he was welcome to his house which was the nearest of the houses of the Najjar tribe. He said that both he and his wealth were for God and His Messenger and that he preferred the money which the Messenger took from him to that which remained.

The Messenger of God said, 'You have spoken true words. May God bless you.' The Messenger of God moved Fatima to Haritha's house.

It is related that Asma bint Umays said to Umm Jafar that she had prepared his grandmother, Fatima, for his grandfather, Ali. There was no stuffing in their bed and pillows except fibre. Ali prepared a wedding feast for Fatima. There was no better wedding feast in that time than his wedding feast. He left his armor in pawn with a Jew for half a measure of barley.

Muhammad ibn Umar related that when Ali married Fatima, their bed was a ramskin. When they wanted to sleep, they turned over its wool. Their pillows were made of leather stuffed with fibre.

Muhammad ibn Ali related that the dowry of Fatima was a worn out garment and a sheepskin.

Ikrima related that when the Messenger of God gave Fatima in marriage to Ali, part of the trousseau prepared for Fatima was a palm-leaf bed, a pillow of leather stuffed with fibre, a small leather vessel and a waterskin.

Umm Ayman related that the Messenger of God gave his daughter Fatima in marriage to Ali ibn Abi Talib. He told Ali not to co-habitate with Fatima until he had come to him. The Messenger of God went and stood at the door. He greeted the inhabitants. He asked for permission to enter. Permission was given. He asked, 'Is my brother here?'

Umm Ayman asked who was his brother. The Messenger replied,

'Ali ibn Abi Talib.' She asked how he could be his brother when he was married to the Messenger's daughter. The Messenger said to her, 'That is how it is, Umm Ayman.'

He called for water. It was brought in a vessel. He washed his hands in it. Then he called Ali who sat before him. He sprinkled some of that water on his chest and between his shoulders. Then he called Fatima. She came without a head covering, tripping on her garment. He sprinkled some of that water on her. Then he said, 'By God, I swear that I have married you to the best of my family.'

Umm Ayman said that she arranged Fatima's trousseau. Part of what was prepared for her was a cushion of leather stuffed with fibre. Soft sand was spread in her house.

Ikrima related something similar.

Darim ibn Abd al-Rahman ibn Thalaba al-Hanafi related that one of his uncles among the Helpers said that his grandmother had told him that she was one of the women who escorted Fatima to Ali. She said that Fatima was presented in two robes. The first had silver rings colored with saffron. They entered Ali's house. There was a sheepskin on a bench, a cushion stuffed with fibre, a waterskin, a sieve, a napkin and a cup.

Abd Allah ibn Amr ibn Hind related that on the night when Fatima was given to Ali, the Messenger of God said to Ali, 'Do not begin until I come to you.'

The Messenger of God soon followed them. He stood at the door and asked for permission to enter. He then entered. Ali stood apart from Fatima. The Messenger of God said, 'I know that you love God and His Messenger.' He called for water. He rinsed his mouth and then spit into the vessel. He then sprinkled it on Fatima's chest and Ali's chest.

Ali ibn Abu Talib related that when the Messenger of God married him to Fatima, he sent with her a woven cloth, a leather cushion stuffed with fibre, two mills, a water vessel, and two waterskins.

One day Ali said to Fatima that he had drawn water until his chest hurt. He asked Fatima to go and ask her father for a servant from the spoils. Fatima told Ali that her hands were blistered from grinding.

Fatima went to the Messenger of God. When he saw her, he asked her what she needed. She said she had come to greet him. Too embrarrassed to ask her father for anything, she returned home. Ali asked her what had happened. She told Ali that she was too embarrassed to ask her father for anything.

They went together. Ali told the Messenger that he had drawn water until his chest hurt. Fatima said that she had ground grain until her hands were blistered. Could he please give them a servant.

The Messenger said, 'By God, I will not give to you and leave the People of the Porch binding up their bellies from hunger. I have not found anything I can spend on them, but I will sell the booty and spend it on them.'

They returned to their home. The Messenger later went to them when they were under their blanket. When they covered their heads, their feet showed. When they covered their feet, their heads showed. They jumped up. The Messenger said, 'Stay where you are. Shall I tell you what is better than that for which you asked?' They asked him to please tell them.

The Messenger said, "Some words which Gabriel taught me: after every prayer say "Glory be to God," ten times; Praise be to God," ten times; and "God is greater," ten times. When you retire to your bed, then say "Glory be to God," thirty-three times; "Praise be to God," thirty-three times; and "God is greater," thirty-four times.'

Ali related that he did not forget these practices for even a day. Ibn al-Kiwa asked Ali if perhaps he might not have forgotten on the night of the Battle of Siffin. Ali said that he had not forgotten even on that night.

Amr ibn Said related that Ali had shown some harshness towards Fatima. Fatima complained to the Messenger of God. When the Messenger heard them talking, he stood up. She complained to the Messenger of God of Ali's roughness and harshness to her.

He said, 'Daughter, listen, give ear and understand. There is no cleverness in a woman who does not attend to her husband's affection when he is calm.' Ali said that he would refrain from his former behavior. He said he would never do anything which the Messenger disliked.

Habib ibn Abi Thabit related that some words passed between Ali and Fatima. The Messenger of God entered. Ali made him a bed. He lay down on it. Fatima came and lay down beside him. Ali came and lay down on the other side. The Messenger of God took Ali's hand and placed it on his navel. He took Fatima's hand and placed it on his navel and continued until he made peace between them. Then he left.

Someone asked the Messenger why he entered the house in a sad state and had joy on his face when he left.

The Messenger said, 'What would prevent me from being happy when I have made peace between the two I love the most?'

Abu Jafar related that al-Abbas came in to visit Ali ibn Abu Talib and Fatima. Fatima said to Ali that she was older. Al-Abbas told Fatima that she was born when the Quraysh were building the Kabah at the time the Prophet was thirty-five. He said that Ali was born a few years before that.'

Muhammad ibn Umar related that Fatima bore Ali, Hasan, Husayn, Umm Kulthum and Zaynab.

Ayisha related that she was sitting with the Messenger of God when Fatima came walking in with the same gait as the Messenger of God. He said, 'Welcome, my daughter.' He had her sit at his right or his left and whispered something to her. She wept. Then he whispered something to her and she laughed.

Ayisha asked Fatima why she laughed so soon after weeping? Ayisha said that the Messenger of God had singled out her [Fatima] for something, and then Fatima wept. Ayisha asked Fatima what the Messenger whispered to her. Fatima told Ayisha that she would not divulge the secret.

When the Messenger of God died, Ayisha again asked Fatima what had happened that day. Fatima told Ayisha that the Messenger had told her, 'Gabriel used to meet me every year and repeat the Quran to me once. This year he has come to me twice and repeated it to me. I think that my end is near. I am the best precursor for you.' He added, 'You will be the swiftest of my family to join me.' Fatima wept upon hearing this. Then he said, 'Are you not content to be the mistress of the women of this community or the women of the worlds?' She laughed upon hearing that.

Abd al-Rahman al-Araj related that he said in his gathering in Madinah that the Messenger of God assigned 300 weights of barley and dates to Fatima and Ali at Khaybar. Eighty-five weights were barley.

Amir related that Abu Bakr went to Fatima when she was ill. He asked permission to enter. Ali told Fatima that Abu Bakr was at the door. He asked if Fatima would give permission for him to enter. She asked Ali if he agreed. He said that he did. Abu Bakr went in to visit her. He comforted her and spoke to her. She was pleased with him.

Salma related that Fatima, the daughter of the Messenger of God, was ill while they were with her. On the day she died, Ali had gone out. She told Salma to prepare a bath for her. Salma poured a bath for her and she washed her in the best manner.

Then she told Salma to bring her new clothes. Salma brought them to her. She put them on. She told Salma to put her bed in the middle of the house. Salma did that. Fatima lay down on it and faced the *qiblah*. Then she said to Salma that she would soon die. Fatima said that she had been washed and asked that no one uncover her shoulder. She died. Ali came, and Salma told him. He said that no one would uncover Fatima's shoulder. He took her and buried her with that bath lustration.

Muhammad ibn Musa related that Ali ibn Abu Talib washed Fatima.

Ayisha related that after the death of the Messenger of God Fatima asked Abu Bakr for the inheritance due her from the booty left by the Messenger of God.

Abu Bakr said that the Messenger of God had said, 'We do not leave inheritance. What we leave is charity.' Fatima became angry. She lived only six months after the death of the Messenger of God.

Zuhri and **Abu Jafar** related that Fatima lived three months after the Prophet.

Abu Jafar and **Urwa** related it was six months.

Muhammad ibn Umar, whom I consider to be reliable, related that Fatima died on the 7th of Ramadan in the year 11/26th of November, 632 AH when she was about twenty-nine.

lbn Abbas related that Fatima was the first to be given a bier. Asma bint Umays made it for her. She had seen how it was constructed when she lived in Abyssinia.

Amra bint Abd al-Rahman related that Abbas ibn Abd al-Muttalib prayed for Fatima. Ali and Fadl ibn Abbas went down into her grave.

Urwa related that Ali prayed for Fatima.

Shabi related that Abu Bakr prayed for her.

lbrahim related that Abu Bakr al-Siddiq prayed for Fatima and said "God is greater," four times for her.

Zuhri related that Fatima was buried at night by Ali.

Ali ibn Husayn related that he asked Ibn Abbas at what time he buried Fatima. Ibn Abbas said that they buried her at night beyond Hada. Ali bin Husayn asked who prayed for her. He replied that Ali had prayed for her.

Muhammad ibn Umar al-Waqadi questioned Abd al-Rahman ibn Abi 'l-Mawali. He related that people said that the grave of Fatima was at the mosque in which funeral prayers were said at the Baqi cemetery. Abd al-Rahman said that was the mosque of Ruqayya, i.e. the woman who lived there. He said that Fatima was buried in the corner of the house of Aqil (which was next to the house of the Jahshi family) directly facing the exit of the Nabih tribe from the Abu 'l Dar tribe at the Baqi cemetery. There were seven cubits between her grave and the road.

Abd Allah ibn Hasan related that he found Mughira ibn Abd al-Rahman ibn al-Harith ibn Hisham waiting for him at the Baqi cemetery at midday in the intense heat. He asked Abu Hashim what made him stop there. Abu Hashim told Abd Allah ibn Hasan that he was waiting for him, and that he had heard Fatima was buried in this room in the house of Aqil next to the house of the Jahshi family. He wanted Abd Allah to buy it for himself, whatever the cost, so that he could be buried in it.

Abd Allah ibn Hasan agreed and made great efforts to purchase it from the Aqili family, but they refused to sell it. Abd Allah ibn Jafar said that he had not met anyone who had any doubts that her grave was located there.

FATIMA BINT MUNQIDH IBN AMR
Mother: A slave woman who bore her master a child
Children: Bore children, names not given
Wife of: Dawud ibn Abu Dawud
Tribe: Khazraj, Najjar clan
Ibn Sad also related the following:
She accepted Islam and gave her allegiance to the Messenger of God.

FATIMA BINT QAYS
Mother: Umayma bint Rabia of Kinana
Father: Qays
Sister of: Dahhak ibn Qays
Wife of: Abu Umar ibn Hafs; Usama ibn Zayd
Tribe: Quraysh
Ibn Sad also related the following:
She accepted Islam, gave her allegiance to the Messenger of God and migrated to Madinah. Fatima bint Qays related that in AD 631/AH 10, Abu Umar ibn Hafs divorced Fatima bint Qays irrevocably when he was away from her. His agent sent her some barley, but she exasperated him. He said, 'By God, you will have nothing from us!'

She went to the Messenger of God. The Messenger said, 'You have no right to maintenance from him.' He commanded that she observe her waiting period in the house of Umm Sharik. Then he said, 'Umm Sharik is a woman whom my Companions visit. Observe the waiting period in the house of your cousin Ibn Umm Maktum. He is blind. You can remove your garments. Let me know when you become lawful.'

She said that when her waiting period ended, she then told the Messenger that Muawiya ibn Abu Sufyan ibn Harb and Abu Jahm ibn Hudhayfa had both proposed to her.

The Messenger of God said, 'As for Muawiya, he is destitute with no property. Abu Jahm is always traveling. It is best to marry Usama.'

She disliked Usama, but the Messenger had said, 'Marry Usama,' so she married him. She said that God put good in Usama, and she was envied because of it.

Abu Salama related that Fatima bint Qays visited him. She said that she had gone to the Messenger of God desiring lodging and maintenance from her former husband. The Messenger said, 'Fatima, lodging and maintenance are owed by a husband who can take his wife back. Go to Umm Sharik and do not fail to let me know about yourself.' Then he said, 'Umm Sharik is visited by her brothers among the Emigrants. Go to Ibn Umm Maktum, He is blind.'

When her term came to an end, Muawiya, Abu Jahm ibn Hudhayfa, and Usama asked her to marry them. The Messenger of God said,

'Muawiya is destitute without property. Abu Jahm is always travel-ing. What is your position with Usama?'

It seemed that her family disliked him, but she said that she would marry the one whom the Messenger of God told her to marry.

Shabi related that he was informed by Fatima bint Qays that she was married to one of the members of the Makhzum tribe. He sent her word of her divorce when he was on the road from one of his expe-ditions in Yemen. She asked his family for maintenance and lodging and they refused. They said that he had not sent them anything for her.

She said she went to the Messenger of God and said that she was a daughter of the family of Khalid. Her husband has sent her word of her divorce. She asked his family for maintenance and lodging. They refused her. His family told the Messenger that her husband had sent three divorce pronouncements for her.

The Messenger of God said, 'Lodging and maintenance are owed by a husband who can take his wife back.'

It is related that Usama died in AD 673-74/AH 54 and that Fatima never married again but lived with her brother, Dahhak ibn Qays.

It is related that Fatima was a very capable, intelligent and schol-arly woman.

Muslim related that Fatima was generous and felt satisfaction in serving her guests. When Umar ibn al-Khattab died in AD 643/AH 23, the meeting of the consultative committee was held in her home because she was a woman of understanding, shrewd judgment and good opinions. The members of the committee thought that it would be appropriate to consult ther.

She narrated thirty-four Traditions. Among her narrators are:

Abd Allah al-Habi
Abd Allah ibn Abd Allah
Abd al-Rahman ibn Asim
Abu Bakr ibn Abu al-Jahm Said ibn Musayyib
Aswad
Muhammad ibn Abd al-Rahman ibn Thauban
Qasim ibn Muhammad
Shabi
Sulayman ibn Yasar
Tamim
Umm ibn Zubayr
Urwa

FATIMA BINT SAFWAN IBN MUHRITH

Wife of: Amr ibn Said ibn al-As
Tribe: Non-Qurayshi Emigrant

Ibn Sad also related the following:

She accepted Islam in Makkah, gave her allegiance to the Messenger of God and migrated to Abyssinia in the second migration with her husband.

FATIMA BINT UMARA

Father: Umara

Wife of: Abd Allah ibn Abu Bakr

She is not mentioned by Ibn Sad. Ibn Ishaq lists her as a transmitter of Traditions.

FATIMA BINT UQBA IBN RABIA

Mother: Safiyya bint Umayya

Father: Uqba ibn Rabia

Children: Walid, al-, Hisham, Ubayy, Utba, Muslim, Fatikha

Wife of: Quraza ibn Abd Amr ibn Nawfal; Abd Allah ibn Amir; Salim

Tribe: Quraysh

Ibn Sad also related the following:

She accepted Islam and gave her allegiance to the Messenger of God.

FATIMA BINT WALID IBN AL-MUGHIRA OF MAKHZUM

Mother: Hantama bint Shaytan

Children: Abd al-Rahman, Umm Hakim

Wife of: Harith ibn Hisham, al-

Tribe: Quraysh

Ibn Sad also related the following:

Abd Allah ibn al-Zubayr related that Fatima bint Walid ibn al-Mughira accepted Islam on the day of the conquest of Makkah and gave her allegiance to the Messenger of God.

FATIMA BINT YAMAN

Sister of: Hudhayfa ibn al-Yaman al-Abasi

Tribe: Aws, Abdul Ashhal clan

Ibn Sad also related the following:

She accepted Islam and gave her allegiance to the Messenger of God.

Fatima said that she visited the Messenger of God with some women. A waterskin hung above the Messenger which was dripping water on him to reduce the intensity of the heat of his fever. They said that if the Messenger of God were to ask God, He would remove the fever from him.

The Messenger said, 'The people with the most severe affliction are the Prophets and then those who follow them and then those who follow them.'

The sister of Hudhayfa, who had sisters who had met the

Prophet, related that the Messenger of God addressed them and said, 'Company of women, do you not have silver with which you can adorn yourselves? There is no woman among you who openly adorns herself with gold but that she will be punished by it.'

Mansur said that he mentioned that to Mujahid. He said that he met them. One of them would lengthen her sleeve in order to cover her ring.'

FATIMA BINT ZAIDA
She is not mentioned by Ibn Sad.

FUKAYHA
Mother: Hind bint al-Ajlan
Wife of: Rabi ibn Amir, Amr ibn Khalida, al-
Tribe: Khazraj, Bayada ibn Amr clan
Alternative Name: Umm al-Hakam bint al-Muttalib

FUKAYHA BINT AL-SAKAN IBN ZAYD
Mother: Zahra bint Aws, al-
Father: Sakan, al-
Wife of: Amr ibn Nabi
Tribe: Khazraj, Salama ibn Sad clan
Muhammad ibn Umar al-Waqadi mentions her.

FUKAYHA BINT UBAYD IBN DULAYM
Children: Qays, Umama
Wife of: Sad ibn Ubada
Tribe: Khazraj, Saida ibn Kab clan

FUKAYHA BINT YASAR
Sister of: Baraka
Wife of: Hattab ibn al-Harith
Tribe: Quraysh
Ibn Sad also related the following:
She accepted Islam early on in Makkah and migrated to Abyssinia in the second migration.

FUKAYHA (SEE UMM AMIR AL-ASHHALIYYA)
FURAYA, AL-
Mother: Kabsha bint Amr
Children: Abd Allah
Wife of: Abu Ahmad
Tribe: Aws, Ubayd ibn Zayd ibn Malik ibn Awf clan
Alternative Name: Qurayba bint Qays

FURAYA BINT AL-HUBAB IBN RAFI (SEE UMM AL-HUBAB)

FURAYA BINT KHALID IBN KHUNAYS, AL-
Mother: Hind bint al-Abarr
Father: Khalid ibn Khunays
Children: Hasan ibn Thabit al-Shayr
Wife of: Thabit ibn al-Mundhir
Tribe: Khazraj, Saida ibn Kab clan
Alternative Name: Umm Hasan ibn Thabit

FURAYA BINT MALIK IBN AL-DUKHSHAM, AL-
Mother: Jamila bint Abd Allah ibn Ubayy
Father: Malik ibn Dukhsham
Wife of: Hilal ibn Umayya of Aws
Tribe: Khazraj, Qawaqila, Awf ibn al-Khazraj clan

FURAYA BINT MALIK IBN SINAN, AL-
Mother: Unaysa bint Abi Kharija
Father: Malik ibn Sinan
Sister of: Abu Said al-Khudri; half-sister of Qatadaibn an-Numan
Wife of: Sahl ibn Rafi; Sahl ibn Bashir
Tribe: Khazraj
Ibn Sad also related the following:
She accepted Islam and gave her allegiance to the Messenger of God.
It is related that Furaya reported that her husband was killed at a place on the Madinah road called Tarf al-Qadum. Furaya mentioned this to the Messenger of God. She wanted to move from her husband's house to that of her family. She said that the Messenger of God had told her to do that. When she got up, he touched her with his cane and said, 'Stay in your house until the Book reaches its term.'
Zaynab bint Kab, who was married to Abu Said al-Khudri, said that Furaya ibn Malik, Abu Said's sister, informed her that she was married to a man of the Harith ibn al-Khazraj tribe. He had gone out to look for some runaway non-Arab slaves. He caught up with them at Tarf al-Qadum. They attacked and killed him.
She went to the Messenger of God. She told him that her husband had been killed and that he had not left her any maintenance nor lodging. She asked the Messenger of God for permission to join her brothers in their house. The Messenger of God gave her permission. Furaya said that when she had left the room or was still in it, the Messenger of God touched her with his cane. He told her to repeat her story to him. She did so. The Messenger then told her, 'Do not leave your dwelling in which the news of your husband's death had reached you until the Book reaches its term.'

She observed the waiting period there for four months and ten days. Uthman was asked about this. He sent for her. She went to him while he was with a group of people. He asked her about her situation and what the Messenger of God had commanded her. She told him what the Messenger had said. He sent word to a woman whose husband had died to tell her not to leave her house until the Book had reached its term [the waiting period had ended].

FURAYA BINT ZURARA, AL- (SEE FARIA BINT ZURARA, AL-)

FUSHUM BINT AWS IBN KHAWLI
Father: Aws ibn Khawli
Wife of: Itban ibn Murra
Tribe: Khazraj, Balhabla al-Habla is Salim ibn Ghanm ibn Awf
   Ibn Sad also related the following:
   She accepted Islam and gave her allegiance to the Messenger of God.

G

GHAZIYA BINT JABIR (SEE UMM SHARIK)

GHAZIYYA BINT SAD IBN KHALIFA
Mother: Salma bint Azib
Father: Sad ibn Khalifa
Children: Said
Wife of: Sad ibn Ubada
Tribe: Khazraj, Saida ibn Kab clan
   Ibn Sad also relates the following:
   She accepted Islam and gave her allegiance to the Messenger of God.

GHUMAYSA, AL- (SEE UMM SULAYM BINT MILHAN IBN KHALID)

H

HABBABA (SEE UMM AMIR BINT SULAYM)

HABIBA
Father: Muattab
Children: Abu Burda
Wife of: Usayr ibn Urwa
Tribe: Aws, Zafar clan

Alternative Name: Umm Habib bint Muattab
Ibn Sad also relates the following:
She accepted Islam and gave her allegiance to the Messenger of God.

HABIBA
Mother: Umayma bint Abd al-Muttalib
Father: Jahsh ibn Rithab
Children: No children
Wife of: Abd al-Rahman ibn Awf
Alternative Name: Umm Habib bint Jahsh ibn Rithab
Ibn Sad also relates the following:
She accepted Islam and gave her allegiance to the Messenger of God. She spoke to the Prophet about her constant bleeding and related Traditions.

HABIBA BINT ABU AMIR AL-RAHIB
Mother: Salma bint Amir
Children: Asma; Abd Allah
Wife of: Zayd ibn al-Khattab;
        Sad ibn Khaythama
Tribe: Aws, Amr ibn Awf ibn Malik ibn Aws clan
Ibn Sad also relates the following:
She accepted Islam and gave her allegiance to the Messenger of God.

HABIBA BINT ABU TAJRA
Father: Abu Tajra
Sister of: Barra
Tribe: Quraysh
Ibn Sad also relates the following:
She accepted Islam and gave her allegiance to the Messenger of God. She related Traditions from the Messenger.

HABIBA BINT ASAD IBN ZURARA
Mother: Amira bint Sahl
Father: Asad ibn Zurara
Children: Abu Umama
Wife of: Sahl ibn Hunayf
Ibn Sad also relates the following:
She accepted Islam and gave her allegiance to the Messenger of God. When she gave birth to her son, her husband took him to the Messenger of God. He said to the Messenger, 'Please name him.' The Messenger of God named him Sahl and gave him the agnomen of Abu Umama.

HABIBA BINT KHARIJA IBN ZAYD
Mother: Huzayla bint Utba
Children: Umm Kulthum
Sister of: Half-sister of Sad ibn al-Rabi
Wife of: Abu Bakr al-Siddiq; Khubayb ibn Asaf
Tribe: Khazraj
   Ibn Sad also relates the following:
   She accepted Islam and gave her allegiance to the Messenger of God.

HABIBA BINT MASUD IBN AWS
Mother: Shamus bint Amr, al-
Father: Masud ibn Aws
Children: Muqanna, al-, Umm al-Harith
Wife of: Sinan ibn Amr
Tribe: Aws, Zafar clan
   Ibn Sad also relates the following:
   She accepted Islam and gave her allegiance to the Messenger of God.

HABIBA BINT MASUD IBN KHALIDA
Mother: Faria bint al-Hubbab, al-
Father: Masud ibn Khalida
Wife of: Abd al-Rahman ibn Amr
Tribe: Khazraj, Zurayq ibn Amr clan
   Ibn Sad also relates the following:
   She accepted Islam and gave her allegiance to the Messenger of God.

HABIBA BINT MULAYL IBN WABRA
Mother: Umm Zayd bint Nadla
Father: Mulayl ibn Wabra
Children: Abd al-Rahman
Wife of: Farwa ibn Amr
Tribe: Khazraj, Qawaqila, Awf ibn al-Khazraj clan
   Ibn Sad also relates the following:
   She accepted Islam and gave her allegiance to the Messenger of God.

HABIBA BINT QAYS IBN ZAYD
Mother: Amira bint Masud ibn Aws
Father: Qays ibn Zayd
Children: Ubayd Allah; Kharija, Habiba bint Qays
Wife of: Muadh ibn al-Harith; Abu Fadala ibn Thabit

Tribe: Aws, Zafar clan

HABIBA BINT SAHL IBN THALABA
Father: Sahl ibn Thalaba
Wife of: Thabit ibn Qays; Ubayy ibn Kab
Tribe: Khazraj, Malik ibn al-Najjar clan

Ibn Sad also relates the following:

She accepted Islam and gave her allegiance to the Messenger of God. She requested and received a 'divorce for a consideration' and then lived with her family.

Yahya ibn Sad relates that the Prophet wanted to marry Habiba bint Sahl. He remembered the jealousy of the Helpers and decided against marrying her. She married Thabit ibn Qays.

Amra bint Abd al-Rahman relates that the Messenger had wanted to marry Habiba bint Sahl before she married Thabit ibn Qays. Thabit used to beat her. She went to the door of the Messenger of God in the early morning darkness to complain about her husband. She told the Messenger that she would not remain with Thalaba.

The Messenger of God said to Thalaba, 'Take back from her what you gave her and divorce her.' She received a divorce with consideration (*khul*) from him, giving him back whatever he had given her. She went and lived with her family.

It is related that Habiba bint Sahl was married to Thabit ibn Qays. Thabit had a violent temper. Habiba went to the Prophet in the darkness of the early morning to tell him about Thabit. When the Messenger went out of the mosque, he saw her. He asked, 'Who is it?' She said that she was Habiba.

He asked, 'What is wrong?' She said that she could no longer remain with her husband, Thabit. At that point Thabit arrived. The Messenger said, 'Take back from her whatever you have given her and give her a divorce.' She said that he had everything that he had given her. She remained with her family. Then she married Ubayy ibn Kab. The Messenger had wanted to marry her but thought better of it because of the jealousy of the Helpers.

It is related that Habiba was in the house of the Messenger of God. The Messenger entered and sat down. He said, 'There is no Muslim who dies with three of his children underage but that they will be brought on the day of resurrection to the gate of the garden and be told, 'Enter.' They will say. 'Not until our parents enter.' After the second or third time, it will be said, 'Enter, both you and your parents.' Ayisha asked her if she had heard, and she replied that she had.

Muhammad ibn Umar al-Waqadi reports that Muhammad ibn Sirin relates this from Habiba but does not give her lineage. Therefore it is not clear whether it was Habiba bint Sahl or someone else.

Ayisha relates that Thabit had beated Habiba so much that he had broken her bones. She complained to the Messenger and he ordered Thabit to take what he had given her and accept a divorce from her. His second wife, Jamila, made the same complaint and was also granted a divorce for a consideration.

Ibn Abbas relates that Habiba or Jamila complained of Thabit ibn Qays to the Messenger saying that nothing could bring them together. She put on her veil when she saw that he was coming toward her with some men. She saw that he was the darkest, the shortest and of the worst appearance of them all. She told the Messenger that she did not dislike him for any of his defects in morals or religion, but because he was so ugly. She wanted to spit in his face when he came to her.

Abd al-Razzaq in *Fath al-Bari* relates that she said to the Messenger that he could see how beautiful she was while Thabit was ugly.

Bukhari and Nasai report that she said she did not have anything against his religion and morals but she was afraid of breaking the limits of God regarding obedience to one's husband and protection of chastity and modesty while remaining his wife.

When the Messenger heard this complaint, he said to her, 'Will you return the garden he has given you?' She said to the Messenger that she would and that if Thabit desired even more, she would give him more.

The Messenger said, 'Not more but you must return the garden.' Then he ordered Thabit to accept the garden as consideration and agree to divorce her.

HABIBA (SEE JAMILA BINT KHUZAYMA IBN HAZMA)

HABTA BINT JUBAYR IBN AL-NUMAN
Mother: From Abd Allah ibn Ghatafan tribe
Sister of: Abd Allah, Khawwat Abu Jubayr
Tribe: Aws, Ubayd ibn Zayd ibn Malik ibn Awf clan
Ibn Sad also relates the following:
She accepted Islam and gave her allegiance to the Messenger of God. Her brothers were present at the Battle of Badr.

HAFSA BINT HATIB
Mother: Umama bint Samit
Father: Hatib
Sister of: Harith ibn Hatib, al-, Thalaba ibn Hatib
Tribe: Aws, Amr ibn Awf ibn Malik ibn Aws clan
Alternative Name: Umm Zurara

Ibn Sad also relates the following:

She accepted Islam and gave her allegiance to the Messenger of God.

HAFSA BINT UMAR IBN AL-KHATTAB
Mother: Zaynab bint Mazun
Father: Umar ibn al-Khattab
Sister of: Uthman ibn Mazun
Wife of: Khunays ibn Hudhayfa ibn Qays; Messenger of God
Tribe: Quraysh

Ibn Sad also relates the following:

She accepted Islam at the time that her father did.

Umar relates that Hafsa was born when the Quraysh were building the Kabah five years before the revelation.

Abul Huwayrith relates that Khunays ibn Hudhafa ibn Qays married Hafsa bint Umar ibn al-Khattab. She migrated with him to Madinah. He died childless as a result of wounds suffered at the Battle of Badr, leaving her a widow.

Ibn Umar relates that when Hafsa was widowed, Umar met Uthman and offered her to him. Uthman replied that he had no need of women. Umar met Abu Bakr and offered her to him. He was silent. He became angry with Abu Bakr. When the Messenger of God proposed to her, he gave her in marriage to him. Umar met Abu Bakr and said that he had offered his daughter to Uthman, and he had rejected the proposal. He had offered her to Abu Bakr, and Abu Bakr remained silent. Umar said that he was more angry when Abu Bakr had remained than when Uthman rejected the proposal. Abu Bakr said that the Prophet had mentioned something about her. It was a secret. He could not disclose the Messenger's secret.'

Abd Allah ibn Umar relates that when Hafsa bint Umar was widowed by the death of Khunays ibn Hudhafa as-Sahmi, one of the Companions of the Messenger of God who died in Madinah, Umar ibn al-Khattab said that he went to Uthman ibn Affan and offered Hafsa to him.

Uthman said that he would think about it. Umar met Uthman some days later. Uthman said that it seemed to him that he should not marry at this time.

Umar met Abu Bakr al-Siddiq. He said that if Abu Bakr agreed, he would marry him to Hafsa. Abu Bakr was silent. He did not reply at all. Umar was reportedly more hurt by the silence of Abu Bakr than he had been with Uthman's response. Some days later, the Messenger of God proposed to her. Umar gave her in marriage to him. Abu Bakr met him and said that perhaps he had become annoyed when he (Umar) had offered Hafsa to him (Abu Bakr), and he (Abu Bakr) had not replied but remained silent. Umar said that he had been hurt.

Abu Bakr replied that he had wanted to reply to the offer but had known that the Messenger had mentioned marrying her. He could not divulge the secret of the Messenger. If the Messenger had not married her, Abu Bakr would have done so.

Hasan relates that one of the Messenger's daughters was married to Uthman. She died. Umar met him and saw that he was desolate and grieved. He spoke to him and offered him Hafsa. Then he went to the Messenger and said that he met Uthman. He saw his grief so he offered him Hafsa.

The Messenger said to him, "Shall I show you a son-in-law better than Uthman? Shall I show Uthman a father-in-law better for him than you?' Umar replied that he would be most happy if the Messenger would do that. The Messenger of God married Hafsa and gave another of his daughter's in marriage to Uthman.

Umar relates that when Khunays ibn Hudhafa died, he offered Hafsa to Uthman. Uthman turned away from him. He mentioned this to the Messenger asking if the Messenger of God were not surprised by Uthman's response: that he offered him Hafsa, and that Uthman turned away from him!

The Messenger of God said, 'God will marry Uthman to better than your daughter. God will marry your daughter to better than Uthman.'

They say that Umar offered Hafsa to Uthman after the death of Ruqayya, daughter of the Messenger, but at that time Uthman wanted to marry Umm Kulthum, another daughter of the Messenger, and so Uthman turned away from Umar on that account. The Messenger of God married Hafsa and gave Umm Kulthum in marriage to Uthman ibn Affan.

Husayn ibn Abi Husayn relates that the Messenger of God married Hafsa in Shaban, thirty months before the Battle of Uhud.

Said ibn al-Musayyab relates that Hafsa was widowed by the death of her husband. Uthman was widowed by the death of Ruqayya. Umar saw that Uthman was depressed and sad. He asked if Uthman would marry Hafsa. She had finished her waiting period.'

Uthman did not reply. Umar went to the Messenger and mentioned what had happened to him. The Messenger said, 'There is something better than that. Marry Hafsa to me, and I will give my daughter, Umm Kulthum, in marriage to Uthman.' The Messenger of God married Hafsa, and Uthman married Umm Kulthum."

Said relates that God was good to both of them. The Messenger of God was better for Hafsa than Uthman, and the daughter of the Messenger of God was better for Uthman than Hafsa bint Umar.

Qays ibn Zayd relates that the Messenger of God divorced Hafsa bint Umar. Her uncles, Uthman and Quddama, sons of Mazun, went to her and found her weeping. She told them that the Messenger had not divorced her because he was fed up with her.

The Messenger of God went to visit her. She put on her outer garment. The Messenger said, 'Gabriel came to me and told me, "Take Hafsa back. She fasts and prays at night. She is your wife in the Garden."'

Qatada relates that the Messenger of God divorced Hafsa. Gabriel came and said, 'O Muhammad, take Hafsa back,' or he said, 'Do not divorce Hafsa. She fasts and prays at night, and she is one of your wives in the Garden.'

Ibn Abbas relates from Umar ibn al-Khattab that the Messenger divorced Hafsa and then took her back. This is also related from Anas ibn Malik.

Abu Bakr ibn Sulayman ibn Abu Hathma relates that the Messenger of God visited Hafsa where a woman called al-Shifa was with her making a charm against skin disease. The Messenger told al-Shifa to teach that art to Hafsa.

Bukayr relates that the Messenger of God intended to divorce Hafsa. He mentioned something of it. Gabriel appeared and said, 'Hafsa fasts and prays. She is a righteous woman.'

Ibn Sirin relates something similar.

Ayisha relates that the Messenger of God liked sweet things like honey. When he had prayed the afternoon prescribed prayer, he would go around to his wives and visit them. One day he visited Hafsa. He stayed with her longer than usual. She (Ayisha) asked what had happened. She was told that a relative of Hafsa had given her a jar of honey. Hafsa gave the Messenger of God a drink of it.

Ayisha told Sawda that she had a way to prevent this happening again. She said that when the Messenger visited Sawda and came near him, she should ask him if he has eaten manna gum [which has an unpleasant smell]. If he said no, Sawda should then ask him what the smell was. The Messenger of God would not like to have a smell issuing from him. He would say, "Hafsa gave me a drink of honey." Ayisha told Sawda to then say that its bees must have visited the mimosa (that the honey was bad). Ayisha said that she would do the same thing and so would Safiyya. Sawda said that she almost gave away their game. The Messenger was at her door. When the Messenger drew near, she asked him if he had been eating manna gum. The Messenger said, "No." She asked what the smell was. He said, "Hafsa gave me a drink of honey." She said that its bees must have visited the mimosa. When the Messenger visited Ayisha, she said something to the same effect. Then he visited Safiyya. She said something similar.

When he next visited Hafsa, she asked him if she should give him some of the honey to drink. He declined. Upon hearing this, Sawda was upset because their game had deprived him of the honey. Ayisha said that she told Sawda to be quiet.

Nafi relates that Hafsa died while she was fasting.

Muhammad ibn Umar al-Waqidi relates that the Messenger of God assigned Hafsa eighty weights of barley or wheat.

Salim relates from his father that Hafsa died and Marwan ibn al-Hakam prayed for her. He was the governor of Madinah at that time.

A freedwoman of the family of Umar relates that she saw a bier on the bed of Hafsa. Marwan prayed for her at the place of the funeral prayer. Marwan followed her to the Baqi cemetery and stayed until her burial was over.

The father of al-Maqburi relates that he saw Marvan between Abu Hurayra and Abu Said at the front of the funeral prayer for Hafsa. He saw Marwan carry the leg of her bed from the house of the Hazm tribe to the house of Mughira ibn Shuba. Abu Hurayra carried it from the house of Mughira to her grave.

Nafi relates that Abd Allah and Asim, the sons of Umar, went down into Hafsa's grave, as did Salim, Abd Allah and Hamza, the sons of Abd Allah ibn Umar.

Muhammad ibn Umar al-Waqadi relates that Hafsa died in Shaban, 45 AH during the caliphate of Muawiya ibn Abu Sufyan at the age of sixty.

She related sixty Traditions from the Messenger.

HALA BINT KHUWALID
Father: Khuwalid
Sister of: Khadija
Tribe: Khadija

She is not mentioned by Ibn Sad. She is the sister of Khadija. She went to Madinah and asked for permission to accept Islam. The Messenger was startled when he heard her voice because it sounded so much like that of her sister, Khadija. He was pleased to hear her voice. He said, 'This is Hala bint Khuwalid.'

Ayisha relates that upon hearing about this, she felt envy and asked if he meant one of the Quraysh women whose legs were lean and who died long ago because God has given him a better companion instead.

HALIMA
Mother: Rughayba bint Thalaba
Father: Urwa
Children: Rifaa
Wife of: Khadij ibn Rafi
Tribe: Khazraj, Bayada ibn Amr clan
Alternative Name: Jamila bint Urwa

Ibn Sad also relates the following:

She accepted Islam and gave her allegiance to the Messenger of God.

HALIMA BINT ABU DHUAYB

Father: Abu Dhuayb
Tribe: Sad clan

Ibn Sad does not mention her. Ibn Ishaq records the Tradition from her regarding the early life of the Messenger when he was in her care.

HAMNA BINT JAHSH IBN RITHAB

Mother: Umayma bint Abd al-Muttalib
Father: Jahsh ibn Rithab
Sister of: Abd Allah ibn Jahsh
Children: Muhammad ibn Talha al-Sajjad, Imran ibn Talha
Wife of: Musab ibn Umayr; Talha ibn Ubayd Allah

Ibn Sad also relates the following:

She accepted Islam and gave her allegiance to the Messenger of God.

Muhammad ibn Abd Allah ibn Jahsh relates that when the Messenger of God returned from Uhud, the women went to ask people about their relatives. They did not get any information until they went to the Messenger himself. When any woman asked him about her relatives, he informed her.

Hamna bint Jahsh went to him and asked about her brother, uncle and father. The Messenger said, 'Hamna know that your brother, Abd Allah ibn Jahsh, will be rewarded.' She recited,'We belong to God and to Him we return' [2:156]. She then asked God to have mercy on him and forgive him. The Messenger said, 'Hamna know that your uncle, Hamza ibn Abd al-Muttalib, will be rewarded.' She recited, 'We belong to God and to Him we return.' She then asked God to have mercy on him and forgive him. The Messenger then said, 'Hamna know that you husband, Musab ibn Umary, will be rewarded.' She replied that this was a great loss. The Messenger said, 'A husband has a place in a woman's heart which nothing else can replace.'

Muhammad ibn Umar al-Waqadi relates concerning this Tradition that the Messenger asked her, 'Why did you respond differently when you heard the news about Musab than when you heard about your brother and uncle?' She replied that she remembered that his children would be orphans.

She was present at the Battle of Uhud giving water to the thirsty and treating the wounded. The Messenger of God assigned her thirty weights from Khaybar. After that she married Talha ibn Ubayd Allah and gave birth to Muhammad ibn Talha al-Sajjad and Imran ibn Talha.

Harmala bint Abd of Khuzaa
Father: Abd of Khuzaa
Children: Hurmayla, Abd Allah, Amr
Wife of: Jahm ibn Qays
Tribe: Non-Qurayshi
Alternative Name: Umm Hurmayla

Her mother was a slave of Amr ibn Abd al-Shams. She migrated to Abyssinia in the second migration with her husband and died there.

Hasana
Children: Sharahbil ibn Hasana
Tribe: Non-Qurayshi Emigrant
Alternative Name: Umm Sharahbil

She accepted Islam early on in Makkah and migrated to Abyssinia with son on the second migration.

Hasana bint Thabit (see Raia)

Hawla bint Tuwayt ibn Habib, al-
Father: Tuwayt ibn Habib
Tribe: Quraysh

Ibn Sad also relates the following:

She accepted Islam after the migration and gave her allegiance to the Messenger of God.

Ibn Athir relates that Hawla was a very virtuous woman Companion who traded in perfumes. She once went to Ayisha and complained that her husband avoided her even though she used perfume every night. He turned away from her. When the Messenger came home and was told about this, he said, 'Go home and obey your husband.'

Ibn Hanbal in the *Musnad* relates that once Ayisha was with the Messenger when Hawla came in. Ayisha told the Messenger that people said that Hawla did not sleep at night but spent the night in prayer. He was surprised and said, 'One should work as much as one can without pain or hardship.'

Hawwa
Tribe: Khazraj, Malik ibn al-Najjar clan

She was the grandmother of Amr ibn Muadh al-Ansari and related a Tradition from the Messenger.

Hawwa bint Rafi ibn Imr al-Qays
Mother: Khuzayma bint Adi
Father: Rafi ibn Imr al-Qays
Sister of: Abul Haysar Anas ibn Rafi

Tribe: Aws, Abd al-Ashhal clan
Alternative Name: Saba, al
Ibn Sad also relates the following:
She accepted Islam and gave her allegiance to the Messenger of God.

HAWWA BINT ZAYD IBN SAKAN

Mother: Iqrab bint Muadh
Father: Zayd ibn Sakan
Children: Thabit
Sister of: Rafi ibn Yazid
Wife of: Qays ibn al-Khutaym
She became Muslim early on in Makkah between the first and second Aqabah and was a good Muslim. The Messenger of God heard about it. Qays ibn al-Khutaym went to Dhul Mijaz. The Messenger of God went to him and earnestly called him to Islam. Qays said to him that that to which he called was excellent and good, but war had distracted him from this news. The Messenger of God began to press him and said, 'Abu Yazid, I am calling you to God.'

Qays repeated what he had said the first time. The Messenger of God said, 'Abu Yazid, I have heard that you have treated your wife, Hawwa, badly since she left your religion. Fear God. Guard her for me. Do not oppose her.'

He said that he would do what the Messenger wanted. He would only treat her well.

Qays had behaved very badly towards her before that. Then Qays came to Madinah and told Hawwa that he had met Muhammad and that Muhammad had asked him to behave well towards her for him. He had promised the Messenger, and he would fulfil the promise. She must attend to herself because he would never harm her again.

Hawwa made public the fact she had been concealing her acceptance of Islam. Qays did not oppose her. People talked about this and said to him that his wife followed the religion of Muhammad! Qays would tell them that he has promised Muhammad that he would not harm her and would look after her for him.

HIND BINT ABU SUFYAN IBN HARB

Mother: Safiyya bint Abu Amr
Father: Abu Sufyan ibn Harb
Children: Abd Allah, Muhammad the elder, Rabia, Abd al- Rahman, Ramla, Umm al-Zubayr
Wife of: Harith ibn Nawfal, al-
Ibn Sad also relates the following:
She accepted Islam and gave her allegiance to the Messenger of God.

HIND BINT AL-HUSAYN IBN AL-HARITH
Father: Husayn ibn al-Harith
Sister of: Khadijah
Tribe: Quraysh
Ibn Sad also relates the following:
She accepted Islam and gave her allegiance to the Messenger of God.

HIND BINT AL-MUNDHIR IBN AL-JAMUH
Mother: Shamus bint Haqq, al-
Father: Mundhir ibn al-Jamuh
Children: Mundhir ibn Amr, al-
Sister of: Hubab ibn al-Mundhir, al-
Wife of: Amr ibn Khunays
Tribe: Khazraj, Salama ibn Sad clan
Ibn Sad also relates the following:
She accepted Islam and gave her allegiance to the Messenger of God. Her brother was martyred at the Battle of Badr, and her son was martyred at Bir Mauna.

HIND BINT AL-MUQAWWIM IBN ABD AL-MUTTALIB
Mother: Qilaba bint Amr
Father: Muqawwim ibn Abd al-Muttalib, al-
Children: Abd Allah, Abd al-Rahman
Wife of: Abu Amra (Bashir ibn Amr)
Ibn Sad also relates the following:
She accepted Islam and gave her allegiance to the Messenger of God.

HIND BINT AMR IBN AL-JAMUH
Mother: Hind bint Amr
Father: Amr ibn al-Jamuh
Wife of: Muhayyisa ibn Masud
Tribe: Khazraj, Salama ibn Sad clan
Ibn Sad also relates the following:
She accepted Islam and gave her allegiance to the Messenger of God.

HIND BINT AMR IBN HARAM
Mother: Hind bint Qays
Father: Amr ibn Haram
Children: Bore children names not given
Wife of: Amr ibn al-Jamuh
Tribe: Khazraj, Banu Salama ibn Sad

Ibn Sad also relates the following:
She accepted Islam and gave her allegiance to the Messenger of God.

HIND BINT AWS IBN ADI
Mother: Layla bint Ubayd
Father: Aws ibn Adi
Children: Abu Hanna; Sad
Wife of: Amr ibn Thabit of Aws; Khaythama ibn al-Harith
Tribe: Aws, Khatma ibn Jusham clan
Ibn Sad also relates the following:
She accepted Islam and gave her allegiance to the Messenger of God. Her son, Abu Hanna, was present at the Battle of Badr and her son, Sad, who became head of the Amr ibn Awf tribe, was martyred at this battle.

HIND BINT BARA IBN MARUR
Mother: Humayma bint Sayfi
Father: Bara ibn Marur
Wife of: Jabir ibn Atik
Tribe: Khazraj, Salama ibn Sad clan
Ibn Sad also relates the following:
She accepted Islam and gave her allegiance to the Messenger of God.

HIND BINT MAHMUD IBN MASLAMA
Mother: Shamus bint Amr, al-
Father: Mahmud ibn Maslama
Wife of: Amr ibn Said ibn Muadh
Tribe: Aws, Haritha ibn al-Khazraj clan
Ibn Sad also relates the following:
She accepted Islam and gave her allegiance to the Messenger of God.

HIND BINT SAD
Father: Sad
She is not mentioned by Ibn Sad. Ibn Ishaq relates a Tradition from her.

HIND BINT SAHL IBN ZAYD
Father: Sahl ibn Zayd
Tribe: Aws, Abdul Ashhal clan
She is mentioned by Muhammad ibn Umar al-Waqadi as having accepted Islam.

HIND BINT SIMAK

Mother: Umm Jundub bint Rifaa
Father: Simak
Children: Umar, Abd Allah; Harith, al-
Wife of: Sad ibn Muadh; Aws ibn Muadh (brother of her first husband)

Ibn Sad also relates the following:

She accepted Islam and gave her allegiance to the Messenger of God. Her son, al-Harith, was present at the Battle of Badr.

HIND BINT UQBA IBN RABIA

Mother: Safiyya bint Umayya
Father: Uqba ibn Rabia
Children: Aban; Muawiyya
Wife of: Hafs ibn al-Mughira of Makhzum; Abu Sufyan
Tribe: Quraysh

Ibn Sad also relates the following:

She accepted Islam and gave her allegiance to the Messenger of God.

Abd al-Malik ibn Nawfal, a shaykh of the people of Madinah from the Amir ibn Lutayy tribe, relates that Hind had said to her father that she was a woman who wanted to control her own affairs. She asked her father not to give her in marriage to a man until he had first let her consider the man. Her father agreed.

One day her father said to her that two men of their people have asked to marry her. He said that he would first describe them to her and then tell her their names. He then described the two men, saying that the first had nobility and noble lineage which would distract her from his foolish haste and heedlessness. His nobility atoned for his nature. He would be good company and was ready in response. If she followed him, he would follow her. If she made a decision, he would be with her. She could compel him as she liked in his property and not bother about his weakness.

He then described the second man as the paragon of his clan in his noble lineage and intelligence. He disciplined his family. They did not discipline him. If they followed him, it would be easier for them. If they opposed him, he was hard on them. He was very jealous. He was swift in regaining his composure and strong in defending his home. If he was hungry, he did not importune. If someone contended with him, he was not defeated.

She replied that as for the first, he was a master who wasted his noble woman, respecting her when she was unrepentant after her refusal. She wasted herself. If she gave him a child, she was foolish If she gave birth to noble sons, it would be from error. She asked her father not to mention this man and not to name him.

Hind said that the second one her father described was the proper husband of a noble free woman. She admired his character and she accepted him. She would accept the discipline of her husband. She would cling to her tent and care little. Their child would be worthy of defending the women of his clan and protecting its cohesion in adversity. She then asked who he was.

Her father replied that he was Abu Sufyan ibn Harb. She asked her father to marry her to him and to ask God for the best.

Muhammad ibn Sharahil al-Abdari relates that when Abu 'l-Sufyan ibn Harb consummated the marriage with Hind ibn Uqba ibn Rabia, Uqba ibn Rabia sent his son, al-Walid, to the Abu 'l-Huqayq tribe and borrowed their jewelery. Al-Walid gave himself as the pledge along with a group of the Abd al-Shams. He took the jewelery and was absent for a month. They returned it in full and the pledge was released.

Abd Allah ibn al-Zubayr relates that on the day of the conquest of Makkah, Hind bint Uqba accepted Islam as did other women. They went to the Messenger of God while he was at al-Abtah to give him their allegiance. Hind spoke and said to the Messenger that praise belongs to God who had given victory to the religion which He chosen for Himself so that she might benefit by the Messenger's mercy. She told the Messenger that she was a woman who believed in God and confirmed His Messenger. Then she removed her veil and said that she was Hind bint Uqba. The Messenger of God said, 'Welcome to you.'

She said to him that before there were no people of any land whom she had wanted to be abased more than his. Now there was no one on the earth who whom she wished be more exalted than his.

The Messenger of God said, 'And more.' He recited the Quran to them and took their allegiance. Hind spoke out among them and asked if they had taken his hand. He said, 'I do not take the hand of women. My word to a hundred woman is like my word to one woman.'

Muhammad ibn Umar relates that when Hind became Muslim, she struck down an idol in her house with an axe until she smashed it to pieces, saying that they had been deluded by the statues.

Ayisha relates that Hind went to the Messenger of God and said that Abu Sufyan was a stingy man who did not give what was adequate for her and her children unless she took it from his money without him knowing. The Messenger said, 'Take what is enough for you and your child in a correct manner.'

Maymun ibn Mahran relates that some women including Hind, the daughter of Utba ibn Rabia and the mother of Muawiya, came to the Prophet to give him their allegiance. When he said, 'Do not associate anything with God and do not steal,' Hind said that Abu Sufyan was a stingy man. She asked if anything would be held against her if she took some of his food without his permission. The Messenger sanctioned it in regard to fresh food but did not allow it in dry food.

He said, 'Do not fornicate.' She asked if a free woman fornicates.

He said, 'Do not kill your children.' She asked if he had left them a child that he did not kill at Badr.

He said, 'Do not disobey me in anything correct.'

Maymun relates that God did not counsel obedience to His Prophet except in what is correct, and what is correct is obedience to God Almighty.

al-Shabi relates that he mentioned that when the women gave allegiance, the Messenger of God said, 'Give allegiance on the basis that you do not associate anything with God.' Hind said that she agreed with that.

'Nor should you steal,' the Messenger said. Hind said that she took something from the property of Abu Sufyan. He said said that whatever she took of his property was lawful for her.

He said, 'You should not commit fornication.' Hind asked if a free woman fornicates.

He said, 'You should not kill your children.'

Hind said that the Messenger had killed them.

Ibn Ishaq related a poem that she recited upon hearing of the death of her father, an enemy of the Muslims, at the Battle of Badr.

> O eyes, be generous with your tears
> For the best of Khindif's sons
> Who never returned (home).
> His clan fell upon him one morning,
> The sons of Hashim and the sons of al-Muttalib,
> They made him taste the edge of their swords,
> They attacked him again when he was helpless,
> They dragged him stripped and spoiled
> With the dust upon his face;
> To us he was a strong mountain,
> Grass-clan, pleasing to the eye;
> As for al-Bara I do not mentioned him,
> May he get the good he counted on

> She also recited another poem:
> Fate is against us and has wronged us,
> But we can do nothingt to resist it.
> After the slain of Luayy bint Ghalib
> Can a man care about his death or the death of his friend?
> Many a day did he rob himself of wealth
> By lavishing gifts morning and evening.
> Give Abu Sufyan a message from me:
> If I meet him one day I will reprove him.

It was a war that will kindle another war
For every man has a friend to avenge.

Another poem she recited was:
What an eye which saw a death like the death of my men!
How many a man and woman tomorrow
Will join with the women;
How many did they leave behind on the day of the pit,
The morning of that tumultuous cry!
All generous men in years of drought
When the stars withheld their rain.
I was afraid of what I saw
And now my fear is realized.
I was afraid of what I saw
And today I am beside myself.
How many a woman will say tomorrow
Alas, Umm Muawiya!

And yet another poem:
O eye, weep for Utba, the strong-necked chief,
Who gave his food in famine,
Our defence on the day of victory.
I am grieved for him, broken-hearted, demented.
Let us fall on Yathrib with an overwhelming attack
With horses kept hard by,
Every long-bodied charger

Ibn Ishaq relates from Salih ibn Kaysan that Hind bint Utba and the women with her stopped after the Battle of Uhud to mutilate the bodies of the dead Companions of the Messenger of God. They cut off their ears and noses and Hind made them into anklets and collars and gave her anklets and collars and pendants to Wahshi, the slave of Jubayr ibn Mutim [who had martyred Hamza on orders from Hind to revenge the death of her father at the Battle of Badr]. Hind cut out Hamza's liver and chewed it, but she was not able to swallow it and threw it away. Then she mounted a high rock and shrieked at the top of her voice:

We have paid you back for Badr,
And a war that follows a war is always violent.
I could not bear the loss of Utba
Nor my brother and his uncle and my first-born.
I have slaked my vengeance and fulfilled my vow.
You, O Wahshi, have assuaged the burning in my breast.
I shall thank Wahshi as long as I live

Until my bones rot in the grave.

Ibn Ishaq also relates that she said:
    I slaked my vengeance on Hamza at Uhud.
    I split his belly to get at his liver.
    This took from me what I had felt
    Of burning sorrow and exceeding pain.
    War will hit you exceeding hard
    Coming upon you as lions advance.

HIND BINT UTHATHA IBN ABBAD
Mother: Umm Mistah bint Abi Ruhm ibn al-Muttalib
Father: Uthatha ibn Abbad
Children: Rayta
Sister of: Mistah ibn Uthatha
Wife of: Abu Jundub
Tribe: Quraysh

Ibn Sad also relates the following:

She accepted Islam and gave her allegiance to the Messenger of God.

Ibn Ishaq relates that lamenting the death of Ubayda ibn al-Harith ibn al-Muttalib, Hind bint Uthatha ibn Abbad ibn al-Muttalib recited the following poem.
    Al-Safra holds glory and authority
    Deep-rooted culture, ample intelligence.
    Weep for Ubayda, a mountain of strength to the strange guests,
    And the widow who suckles a dishevelled baby;
    To the people in every winter
    When the skies are red from famine;
    To the orphans when the wind was violent
    For whom he heated the pot which foamed with milk as it
        seethed;
    For whom when the fire burned low and its flame died
    He would revive it with thick brushwood.
    Mourn him for the night traveler or the one wanting food,
    The wanderer lost when he put at his ease.

In response to Hind bint Utba's poem after the Battle of Uhud where she had arranged for the martyrdom of the Messenger's uncle, Hamza ibn Abu Muttalib, Ibn Ishaq relates the poem that Hind bint Uthatha ibn Abbad ibn al-Muttalib composed [in response to Hind bint Utba] which follows:.

You were disgraced at Badr and after Badr,   .

O daughter of a despicable man, great only in disbelief.
God brought on you in the early dawn
Tall and white-skinned men from Hashim,
Everyone slashing with his sharp sword:
Hamza, my lion, and Ali, my falcon.
When Shayba and your father planned to attack me
They reddened their breast with blood.
Your evil vow was the worst of vows.

HUBBA BINT AMR

Mother: Habiba bint Qays
Father: Amr
Wife of: Sayfi ibn Aswad
Tribe: Khazraj, Bayada ibn Amr clan
Ibn Sad also relates the following:
She accepted Islam and gave her allegiance to the Messenger of
God.

HUMAYMA BINT AL-HUMAM IBN AL-JAMUH

Mother: Nuwwar bint Amir, al-
Father: Humam ibn al-Jamuh
Children: Masud
Sister of: Umayr ibn al-Humam
Wife of: Sinan ibn Qays
Ibn Sad also relates the following:
She accepted Islam and gave her allegiance to the Messenger of
God. Her brother was martyred at the Battle of Badr.

HUMAYMA BINT SAYFI IBN SAKHR

Mother: Naila bint Qays
Father: Sayfi ibn Sakhr
Wife of: Bara ibn Marur, al-; Zayd ibn Haritha al-Kalbi
Tribe: Khazraj, Salama ibn Sad clan
Ibn Sad also relates the following:
She accepted Islam and gave her allegiance to the Messenger of
God.

HUMAYNA BINT KHALAF IBN ASAD

Father: Khalaf ibn Asad
Wife of: Khalif ibn Said ibn al-As
Ibn Sad also relates the following:
She accepted Islam and gave her allegiance to the Messenger of
God. Her mother-in-law was Bint Khalid who married al-Zubayr ibn
al-Awwam and bore him Amr and Khalid.

HUNFA BINT ABU JAHL IBN HISHAM, AL-
Mother: Arwa bint Abil Is ibn Umayya
Father: Abu Jahl ibn Hisham
Children: Hind
Wife of: Suhayl ibn Amr of Banu Amir ibn Luayy; Usama ibn Zayd ibn Haritha
Tribe: Quraysh
Ibn Sad also relates the following:
She accepted Islam and gave her allegiance to the Messenger of God.

HUZAYLA BINT AL-HARITH IBN HAZM
Father: Harith ibn Hazm, al-
Tribe: Non-Qurayshi

HUZAYLA BINT MASUD IBN ZAYD
Mother: Mulayka bint Abd Allah
Father: Masud ibn Zayd
Wife of: Abd Allah ibn Unays
Tribe: Khazraj, Salama ibn Sad clan
Ibn Sad also relates the following:
She accepted Islam and gave her allegiance to the Messenger of God.

HUZAYLA BINT SAID IBN SUHAYL
Father: Said ibn Suhayl
Wife of: Shabbath ibn Khadij
Tribe: Khazraj, Dar ibn an-Najjar clan
Ibn Sad also relates the following:
She accepted Islam and gave her allegiance to the Messenger of God.

HUZAYLA BINT THABIT IBN THALABA
Father: Thabit ibn Thalaba
Wife of: Harith ibn Thabit, al-; Abu Masud Uqba ibn Amr; Abd al-Rahman ibn Saida
Tribe: Khazraj
Ibn Sad also relates the following:
She accepted Islam and gave her allegiance to the Messenger of God.

HUZAYLA BINT UTBA IBN AMR
Mother: Umayma bint Suhaym
Father: Utba ibn Amr

Children: Sad; Zayd ibn Kharija
Wife of: Rabi ibn Amr, al-; Kharija ibn Zayd
Ibn Sad also relates the following:
She accepted Islam and gave her allegiance to the Messenger of God.

I

IQRAB BINT AL-SAKAN IBN RAFI
Father: Sakan ibn Rafi, al-
Wife of: Thabit ibn Suhayb
Tribe: Khazraj
Ibn Sad also relates the following:
She accepted Islam and gave her allegiance to the Messenger of God.

IQRAB BINT MUADH IBN AL-NUMAN
Mother: Kabsha bint Rafi
Father: Muadh ibn al-Numan
Children: Rafi, Hawwa; Yazid, Thabit
Sister of: Sad ibn Muadh
Wife of: Yazid ibn Kurz; Qays ibn al-Khutaym
Tribe: Aws, Abd al-Ashhal clan
Ibn Sad also relates the following:
She accepted Islam and gave her allegiance to the Messenger of God. Her son, Yazid, was martyred on Day of the Bridge of Abu Ubayd.

IQRAB BINT SALAMA
Mother: Suhayma bint Abd Allah
Father: Salama
Children: Usayd
Sister of: Half-sister of Salama ibn Salama
Wife of: Rafi ibn Yazid
Tribe: Aws, Abd al-Ashhal
Ibn Sad also relates the following:
She accepted Islam and gave her allegiance to the Messenger of God.

IZZA BINT AL-HARITH IBN HAZM
Father: Harith ibn Hazm, al-
Children: Ziyad, Abd al-Rahman, Barza
Wife of: Abd Allah ibn Malik

J

JADA BINT UBAYD IBN THALABA
Mother: Rua bint Adi, al-
Father: Ubayd ibn Thalaba
Children: Haritha
Wife of: Numan ibn Nafi, al-; Hubab ibn al-Arqam, al-
Tribe: Khazraj, Malik ibn al-Najjar clan
Ibn Sad also relates the following:
She accepted Islam and gave her allegiance to the Messenger of God. Her son was present at the Battle of Badr.

JAMILA BINT ABD ALLAH IBN UBAYY
Mother: Khawla bint al-Mundhir
Father: Abd Allah ibn Ubayy
Children: Abd Allah ibn Hanzala after father's death; Muhammad
Sister of: Abd Allah ibn Ubayy
Wife of: Hanzala ibn Abi Amir al-Rahib; Thabit ibn Qays; Malik ibn al-Dukhshum; Khubayb ibn Yasaf
Tribe: Khazraj, Bal Hubla clan
Ibn Sad also relates the following:
She accepted Islam and gave her allegiance to the Messenger of God. Her first husband was martyred at the Battle of Uhud. Both of her sons were martyred at the Battle of al-Harra. Her son, Hanzala ibn Abu Amir, was reported to have been washed by angels.

JAMILA BINT ABU SASAA
Mother: Unaysa bint Asim
Father: Abu Sasaa
Children: Walid, al-; Abd Allah, Muhammad, Buthayna
Wife of: Ubada ibn al-Samit; Rabi ibn Suraqa, al-; Khalda ibn Abi Khalid
Tribe: Khazraj, Najjar clan
Ibn Sad also relates the following:
She accepted Islam and gave her allegiance to the Messenger of God.

JAMILA BINT KHUZAYMA IBN HAZMA
Mother: Amira bint Adi
Father: Khuzayma ibn Hazma
Wife of: Abd Allah ibn Sad
Tribe: Khazraj, Qawaqila, Awf ibn al-Khazraj clan
Alternative Name: Habiba
Ibn Sad also relates the following:

She accepted Islam and gave her allegiance to the Messenger of God.

JAMILA BINT SAD IBN AL-RABI

Mother: Amra bint Hazm
Father: Sad ibn al-Rabi
Children: Sad, Kharija, Yahya, Ismail, Sulayman, Umm Uthman, Umm Zayd
Wife of: Zayd ibn Thabit
Alternative Name: Umm Sad
Ibn Sad also relates the following:
She accepted Islam and gave her allegiance to the Messenger of God.

Umm Sad bint Sad relates that on the day of the Battle of the Trench, she was two years old. Her mother later told her about the battle. Her father, Sad ibn al-Rabi, was martyred at the Battle of Uhud when her mother was pregnant with her. Muhammad ibn Umar al-Waqadi includes her among those who gave their allegiance to the Messenger, in spite of her young age.

JAMILA BINT SAYFI IBN AMR

Mother: Nuwwar bint Qays, al-
Father: Sayfi ibn Amr
Sister of: Half-sister of Ghulba ibn Zayd
Wife of: Atik ibn Qays
Tribe: Aws, Haritha ibn al-Khazraj clan
Ibn Sad also relates the following:
She accepted Islam and gave her allegiance to the Messenger of God.

JAMILA BINT SINAN IBN THALABA

Father: Sinan ibn Thalaba
Children: Thabit
Wife of: Ubayd al-Sahham ibn Sulaym
Tribe: Aws, Banu Haritha ibn al-Khazraj
Ibn Sad also relates the following:
She accepted Islam and gave her allegiance to the Messenger of God.

JAMILA BINT THABIT IBN ABIL AFLAH

Father: Thabit ibn Abil Aflah
Children: Asim; Abd al-Rahman
Wife of: Umar ibn al-Khattab; Yazid ibn Jariyya
Tribe: Aws, Amr ibn Awf ibn Malik ibn Aws clan
Ibn Sad also relates the following:

She accepted Islam and gave her allegiance to the Messenger of God.

JAMILA BINT URWA (SEE HALIMA)

JARIYYA BINT AMR
Father: Amr
Tribe: Quraysh

She was tortured by Umar ibn al-Khattab before he accepted Islam. Ibn Sad also relates the following:

She accepted Islam early on in Makkah and gave her allegiance to the Messenger of God. She was one of those early Muslims tortured because of her religious belief. Umar ibn al-Khattab was the one who used to torture her to make her abandon Islam. [This was before he had accepted Islam.] He tortured her until he got tired. He said that he would stop simply because of boredom. She said to him that this was what the Lord would do with him.

JATHAMAH MASNIAH
Alternative Name: Hassanah

She is not mentioned by Ibn Sad.

Hakim reports in *Mustadrak* that Jathamah accepted Islam before the migration to Madinah. She was a friend of Khadija and used to often go and visit her. Many years after the death of Khadija, Jathamah went to Madinah to visit the Messenger. She had grown old and the Messenger did not at first recognize her. He asked her name. She said she was Jathamah. He said, 'No. Hassanah Masniah.' The Messenger then asked about her family and her general health. She answered that they were well and good.

When she left, Ayisha asked the Messenger about her because he had treated her with such honor and respect. He said, 'This old lady used to come to us during the time of Khadija. It is a sign of good faith to treat old acquaintances nicely.'

Ayisha relates that there was one old woman who used to come to the Messenger. He used to be very pleased when he saw her. One day she asked why he treated her with more respect and honor than anyone else.

He answered, 'This old lady used to come to see us during the lifetime of Khadija. Don't you know that to honor an old friend is also a sign of faith?'

JUDHAMA BINT JANDAL AL-ASADIYYA
Father: Jandal al-Asadiyya
Wife of: Unays bin Qatada

Tribe: Quraysh

Ibn Sad also relates the following:

She accepted Islam and gave her allegiance to the Messenger of God. She related a Tradition regarding having intercourse while being a nursing mother. Her husband was martyred at the Battle of Uhud.

Ibn Sad relates the following:

Uthman al-Jahshi relates that the Ghanim tribe were the allies of Harb ibn Uymayya who were Muslim. They accepted Islam at Makkah. Both the men and women migratedto Madinah. Among the women who left on the migration were Zaynab, Habiba and Hamna, the daughters of Jahsh and Judhama bint Jandal, Umm Qays bint Mihsan, Amina bint Ruqaysh and Umm Habib bint Nabbata.

Muhammad ibn Umar relates that Judhama bint Jandal was married to Unays ibn Qatada who was present at Badr and martyred at the Battle of Uhud. Judhama related Traditions from the Messenger of God.'

Ayisha relates that Judhama bint Jandal informed her that she had heard the Messenger of God say, 'I had wanted to forbid the practice of intercourse with one's wife while she breast-feeds her child (*ghila*). Then I remembered that the Greeks and Persians used to do it, and that it did not harm their children."

JUMANA BINT ABU TALIB

Mother: Fatima bint Asad ibn Hashim
Father: Abu Talib
Children: Jafar ibn Abu Sufyan
Wife of: Abu Sufyan ibn al-Harith ibn Abd al-Muttalib

Ibn Sad also relates the following:

She accepted Islam and gave her allegiance to the Messenger of God.

JUWAYRIYYA BINT ABU JAHL IBN HISHAM

Mother: Arwa bint Abil Is ibn Umayya
Father: Abu Jahl ibn Hisham
Wife of: Attab ibn Usayd ibn Abil Is; Aban ibn Said ibn al-As
Tribe: Quraysh

Ibn Sad also relates the following:

She accepted Islam and gave her allegiance to the Messenger of God. The tribe of Mughira tried to marry Juwayriyya to Ali while Fatima was alive and married to him. The Messenger did not allow it. saying, 'Fatima is part of me. What harms her, harms me.'

JUWAYRIYYA BINT ABU SUFYAN IBN HARB

Mother: Hind bint Utba

Father: Abu Sufyan ibn Harb
Wife of: Saib ibn Abu Hubaysh, al-; Abd al- Rahman ibn al-Harith
Tribe: Quraysh

Ibn Sad also relates the following:

She accepted Islam and gave her allegiance to the Messenger of God.

JUWAYRIYYA BINT AL-HARITH IBN DIRAR

Father: Harith ibn Dirar, al-
Wife of: Musafi ibn Safwan; Messenger of God
Tribe: Khuzaah, Mustalaq clan
Alternative name: Barra

Ibn Sad also relates the following:

She accepted Islam and gave her allegiance to the Messenger of God after the defeat of her tribe in 5 AH/627 CE, lead by her father, al-Harith ibn Abu Dirar. Her father escaped, but she was captured. The spoils of the expedition included 200 camels, 5000 goats and two hundred families.

Ayisha relates that the Messenger of God captured some of the women of the Mustalaq tribe. He took the one-fifth poor-due from them. This he divided them among the people. He gave a horseman two shares and a man on foot two shares. Juwayriyya bint al-Harith ibn Dirar fell to the share of Thabit ibn Qays al-Ansari. She had been married to her cousin, Safwan ibn Malik ibn Judhayma, who had been killed. Thabit ibn Qays gave her a deed for her redemption for nine *uqiyyas*. She was a beautiful woman. Whoever saw her was taken with her. While the Messenger was with Ayisha, Juwayriyya went to him to ask him for the money for her redemption. Ayisha said that as soon as she saw her, she [Ayisha] disliked the fact that she [Juwayriyya] had come in where the Prophet was. She [Ayisha] knew that the Messenger would see in her[Juwayriyya] what Ayisha had seen.

Juwayriyya introduced herself as Juwayriyya bint al-Harith. She said her father had been the master of his people. She pointed out that the Messenger could see what had befallen her. She fell into the share of Thabit ibn Qays. She said that Thabit ibn Qays has given her a certification for redemption for the sum of nine *uqiyyas*. She asked the Messenger to help her with her ransom.

The Messenger said, 'Or better than that?' She asked what that could be.

He said, 'I will pay your redemption for you and marry you.' She accepted.

The Messenger of God said, 'It is done.'

The people heard the news. It was announced to the in-laws of the

Messenger who were enslaved that they had been freed. They freed the prisoners from Mustaliq who were related to Juwayriyya. They set free a hundred people of a single house because the Messenger had married her. Ayisha relates that she knew of no other woman who had greater blessing for her people than she did. That took place when the Messenger finished the expedition of al-Mursayi.

Shabi relates that Juwayriyya was considered to be property as a prisoner of war. The Messenger of God set her free and married her.

Al-Hasan relates that the Messenger of God was gracious to Juwayriyya and married her.

Mujahid relates that Juwayriyya said to the Messenger that his wives will boast over her. They will say that he did not marry her.

The Messenger of God replied, 'Did I not make your dowry great? Did I not free forty of your people?'

Abu 'l-Abyad, the servant of Juwayriyya relates that the Messenger of God captured the Mustaliq tribe. Juwayriyya was among the captives. Her father came and ransomed her. Then the Messenger of God married her.

Abu Qilaba relates that the Prophet captured Juwayriyya bint al-Harith. Her father went to the Messenger and said that a person like his daughter should not be a slave. He was too noble for that. He asked for her release.

The Messenger said, 'Do you think that if we gave her a choice we would do well?' Her father agreed to pay what is due.

Her father went to her and told her that this man had given her a choice, so not to disgrace him. She said that she has chosen the Messenger of God. Her father told her that she had disgraced him.

Amir relates that the Messenger of God freed Juwayriyya bint al-Harith and married her. Her dowry consisted of the setting free of every captive of the Mustaliq tribe.

Al-Zuhri relates that Juwayriyya was one of the wives of the Messenger of God. He set up the partition for her and gave her what he gave his other wives.

Ibn Abbas relates that Juwayriyya bint al-Harith had been named Barra. The Messenger of God changed her name and called her Juwayriyya. He disliked the name Barra because he said, 'He has left *barra* (good).'

Zaynab bint Salama relates from Juwayriyya bint al-Harith that her name had been Barra. The Messenger of God changed it. He named her Juwayriyya. He disliked it to be said, 'He has left *barra* (good).

Ibn Abbas relates that Juwayriyya had been called Barra. The Messenger of God re-named her Juwayriyya. He prayed the dawn prescribed prayer and then left her. After he had prayed and stayed away until morning, he came back. She was still in her prayer place.

She told him that she had continued the superogatory prayer (*nawafil*) since he left.

The Messenger said, 'Let me teach you a prayer formula which, if you say it, will give you far more spiritual rewards than if you were to spend the entire day in the superogatory prayer: "Glory be to God as much as the number of His creations. Glory be to God according to His pleasure. Glory be to God according to the weight of His Throne. Glory be to God according to the ink of His words."

Abd Allah ibn Amr relates that the Messenger of God visited Juwayriyya bint al-Harith on a Friday. He found that she was fasting, He asked her, 'Did you fast yesterday?' She said that she had not.

He asked, 'Do you intend to fast tomorrow?' She said that she did not.

He said, 'Then break your fast.'

Abd al-Rahman al-Araj relates that in his assembly in Madinah, the Messenger of God assigned Juwayriyya bint al-Harith eighty weights of dates from Khaybar and twenty weights of barley or wheat.

Abu 'l-Abyad relates that Juwayriyya bint al-Harith, the wife of the Messenger, died in the month of Rabi al-Awwal in 56 AH/January-February 676 CE during the caliphate of Muawiya ibn Abu Sufyan. Marwan ibn al-Hakam, the governor of Madinah then, prayed for her.

Muhammad ibn Yazid's grandmother, who was the freed-woman of Juwayriyya bint al-Harith, relates that Juwayriyya said that the Messenger of God married her when she was twenty. Muhammad ibn Yazid's grandmother added that Juwayriyya died in 50/670 CE AH when she was sixty-five. Marwan ibn al-Hakam prayed for her.

Muslim reports that the Messenger loved her and often used to go to her house. One day he went to her and asked, 'Is there anything to eat?' She told him that her maid had given her some charity of meat and that this was all that she had.

The Messenger said, 'Bring it to me for charity has reached the one for whom it was given.'

Ibn Hisham reports that when the Messenger left the raid against Juwayriyya's tribe, he had married her. He entrusted her with one of the Helpers and went to Madinah. Her father came bringing the ransom for his daughter. While her father had been in al-Aqiq, on his way to Madinah to pay the ransom for his daughter, he looked at his camels and admired two of them so much that he decided to hide them and keep them for himself. When he saw the Messenger he said that he had brought his daughter's ransom. The Messenger asked him, 'What about the two camels which you have hidden in al-Aqia in such and such a pass?'

Al-Harith cried out that he bore witness that there is no god but God and that Muhammad is the Messenger of God. He added that no one could have known of this but God.'He and his two sons who were with him and some of his men accepted Islam. He sent for the two camels and gave them to the Messenger.

She related six Traditions from the Messenger.

KABSHA

Father: Abd al-Amr
Wife of: Abu Hamid Abd al-Rahman
Tribe: Khazraj, Saida ibn Kab clan
Alternative Name: Kubaysha bint Abd al-Amr

KABSHA

Mother: Her mother was a slave girl who gave birth to her master's child (*umm walad*)
Father: Farwa
Wife of: Abdur Rahman ibn Sad
Tribe: Khazraj, Banu Bayada ibn Amr
Alternative name: Kubaysha bint Farwa

Ibn Sad also relates the following:

She accepted Islam and gave her allegiance to the Messenger of God.

KABSHA BINT AL-FAKIH IBN QAYS

Mother: Salma bint Umayya
Father: Fakih ibn Qays, al-
Wife of: Masud ibn Sad; Ajlan ibn an-Numan, al-

Ibn Sad also relates the following:

She accepted Islam and gave her allegiance to the Messenger of God.

KABSHA BINT ASAD IBN ZURARA

Mother: Amira bint Sahl
Father: Asad ibn Zurara
Wife of: Abd Allah ibn Abi Habiba ibn al-Azar
Tribe: Khazraj, Malik ibn al-Najjar clan

Ibn Sad also relates the following:

She accepted Islam and gave her allegiance to the Messenger of God.

KABSHA BINT AWS IBN ADI

Mother: Layla bint Ubayd
Father: Aws ibn Adi

Children: Khuzayma and others not named; al-Waqsa
Wife of: Thabit ibn al-Fakih; Masud ibn Amir
Tribe: Aws, Khatma ibn Jusham clan

Ibn Sad also relates the following:
She accepted Islam and gave her allegiance to the Messenger of God.

KABSHA BINT HATIB IBN QAYS

Father: Hatib ibn Qays
Children: Bore children but names not given
Wife of: Abu Namla ibn Muadh; Bashir ibn Umayya
Tribe: Aws, Ubayd ibn Zayd ibn Malik ibn Awf clan

Ibn Sad also relates the following:
She accepted Islam and gave her allegiance to the Messenger of God.

KABSHA BINT MALIK IBN QAYS

Mother: Suhayma bint Umaymir
Father: Malik ibn Qays
Children: Zaynab
Wife of: Thalaba ibn Mihsan; Hubab ibn al-Harith, al-
Tribe: Khazraj, al-Najjar clan

Ibn Sad also relates the following:
She accepted Islam and gave her allegiance to the Messenger of God.

KABSHA BINT MAN ANSARIYA

Wife of: Abu Qays ibn Aslat Ansari

She is not mentioned by Ibn Sad.

When her husband died, her step-son claimed her in marriage as was the custom during the Age of Ignorance. Kabsha went to the Messenger and asked that he help her so that she would not have to marry her step-son but would be free to marry someone else. The following verse (4:19) was revealed, '*O you who believe! You are forbidden to inherit women against their will. Nor should you treat them with harshness that you may take away part of the dowry that has been given to them except where they have been guilty of open lewdness. On the contrary, live with them on a footing of kindness and equity.*'

Following the revelation of this verse, the Messenger gave a widow the full right to remarry anyone she wanted to marry after she completed the waiting period.

KABSHA BINT RAFI IBN MUAWIYYA

Mother: Umm al-Rabi bint Malik

Father: Rafi ibn Muawiyya
Children: Sad ibn Muadh, Amr ibn Muadh, Iyas, Aws, Iqrab, Umm Hizam
Wife of: Muadh ibn al-Numan
Tribe: Khazraj
Ibn Sad also relates the following:
She accepted Islam and gave her allegiance to the Messenger of God.

KABSHA BINT THABIT IBN ATIK (SEE UMM SAD BINT THABIT)

KABSHA BINT THABIT IBN HARITHA
Mother: Salama bint Hasan
Father: Thabit ibn Haritha
Tribe: Khazraj
Ibn Sad also relates the following:
She accepted Islam and gave her allegiance to the Messenger of God.

KABSHA BINT THABIT IBN AL-MUNDHIR
Mother: Sukhta bint Haritha
Father: Thabit ibn Mundhir
Children: Thalaba, Abu Amra, Abu Habiba; Ramla (Umm Thabit)
Sister of: Half-sister of Hassan ibn Thabit
Wife of: Amr ibn Mihsan; Harith ibn Thalaba, al-; Haritha ibn al-Numan
Tribe: Khazraj, Malik ibn al-Najjar clan
Ibn Sad also relates the following:
She accepted Islam and gave her allegiance to the Messenger of God.

KABSHA BINT WAQID IBN AMR
Mother: Hind bint Ruhm of Tayy
Father: Waqid ibn Amr
Children: Abd Allah ibn Rawaha, Amra (Umm al-Numan ibn Bashir); Thabit ibn Qays
Wife of: Rawaha ibn Thalaba; Qays ibn Shammas
Ibn Sad also relates the following:
She accepted Islam and gave her allegiance to the Messenger of God.

KHADIJA BINT HUSAYN IBN AL-HARITH
Father: Husayn ibn al-Harith
Sister of: Hind
Tribe: Quraysh

Ibn Sad also relates the following:

She accepted Islam and gave her allegiance to the Messenger of God.

KHADIJA BINT KHUWAYLID IBN ASAD

Mother: Fatima bint Zaida ibn al-Asamm
Father: Khuwaylid ibn Asad
Children: Hind (son), Hala (son); Hind (daughter); Qasim, Abd Allah
(Tahir), Tayyib, Zaynab, Ruqayya, Umm Kulthum and Fatima
Wife of: Abu Hala (Hind ibn al-Nabbash ibn Zurara); Atiq ibn Abid;
The Messenger
Tribe: Quraysh

Ibn Sad relates the following:

Ibn Abbas relates that the mother of Khadija bint Khuwaylid ibn Asad was Fatima bint Zaida ibn al-Asamm. Her mother was Hala bint Abd al-Manaf ibn al-Harith. Her mother was al-Araqa or Qilaba bint Suayd ibn Sahm. Her mother was Atika bint Abd al-Uzza ibn Qusayy. Her mother was al-Khutya or Rayta bint Kab. Her mother was Naila bint Hudhafa.

Before anyone married her, Khadija bint Khuwaylid was offered to Waraqa ibn Nawfal. No marriage took place between them. Then she married Abu Hala. His name was Hind ibn al-Nabbash ibn Zurara of Tamim. His father was a noble among his people. He settled in Makkah and formed an alliance there with the Abd al-Dar ibn Qusayy clan. The Quraysh used to marry their allies. Khadija bore Abu Hala a son called Hind and a son called Hala.

Then after the death of Abu Hala, she married Atiq ibn Abid of Makhzum. She bore him a girl called Hind who married her cousin, Sayfi ibn Umayya ibn Abid of Makhzum. She gave birth to Muhammad. This clan was called " Muhammad's tribe" because of the position of Khadija. It existed in Madinah but eventually died out. Khadija was called Umm Hind.

Mughira ibn Abd al-Rahman al-Asadi relates that his people said that they asked Hakim ibn Hizam which of them was older—the Messenger of God or Khadija? He said that Khadija was fifteen years older than him and that the prayer was unlawful for his aunt before the Messenger of God was bom [that is, that she had attained puberty].

Abu Abd Allah relates that Hakim's statement that the prayer was unlawful for her means she menstruated, but he was speaking as the people of Islam speak."

Ibn Abbas relates that the women of the people of Makkah met for a festival which they held in the month of Rajab. They did not think that anything was more important than attending that festival.

While they were in retreat with an idol, something in the shape of man appeared to them, came up to them, and then called out in his loudest voice to the women of Tayma that a Messenger would appear in their land who would be called Ahmad. He would be sent with the message of God. Any woman who was able to be his wife should do so.

The women threw stones at him. They denounced him and were harsh toward him. Khadija ignored what he said but did not treat him as the other women did.

Nafisa bint Umayya, the sister of Yala bint Umayya, relates that Khadija had nobility and great wealth. She used to send caravans of goods to Syria. Her caravan was equal to the general caravan of the Quraysh. She hired men and paid them on the basis of a partnership.

When Muhammad reached the age of twenty-five, he was known in Makkah as 'the Trustworthy' (*al-amin*). Khadija bint Khuwaylid sent for him. She asked him to take her caravan goods to Syria accompanied by her slave, Maysara. She said she would give him double what his people. had

Muhammad did this. He went to the market of Bosra in Syria and sold the goods which he had brought. He then bought other goods and took them back making double her normal profit. She gave the Prophet twice the amount she had said she would give.

Nafisa relates that she sent her to Muhammad secretly to ask him to marry her, and he agreed. Khadija sent for her uncle, Amr ibn Asad ibn Abd al-Uzza. He came. Muhammad came with his uncles. One of them performed the marriage. Amr ibn Asad said that this marriage should not be rejected.

Muhammad married her on his return from Syria when he was twenty-five. She bore Qasim, Abd Allah [who was Tahir], Tayyib[who was called that because he was born during the Islamic period], Zaynab, Ruqayya, Umm Kulthum and Fatima. Salma, Uqba's freed-woman, was her midwife. There were two years between each two children. She used to arrange for wet-nurses for them before they were born.

Ibn Abbas relates that the uncle of Khadija, Amr ibn Asad, gave her in marriage to the Messenger of God. Her father had died on the day of Fijar.

Muhammad ibn Umar al-Waqadi relates that our companions agree about this and there is no disagreement about it.

Muhammad ibn Umar al-Waqadi relates that Khadija was bom fifteen years before the Year of the Elephant. She was forty when she married the Messenger of God.

Hakim ibn Hizam relates that Muhammad married Khadija when she was forty. He was twenty-five. Khadija was two years older than Hakim ibn Hizam. She was bom fifteen years before the Year of the Elephant while Hakim was born thirteen years before the Elephant.

Ayisha and **Nafi ibn Jubayr** relate that Khadija was the first person to accept Islam from the Messenger of God.

Zuhri relates that the Messenger of God and Khadija prayed in secret for as long as God wished.

Afif al-Kindi relates that during the Age of Ignorance, he went to Makkah wishing to purchase clothes and perfume for his family. He stayed with Abbas ibn Abd al-Muttalib. While he was with him, looking at the Kabah when the sun was high, a young man came up to the Kabah. He raised his head towards the heavens and concentrated his attention. He faced the Kabah standing upright. A boy came and stood at his right. A woman soon came and stood behind them. The young man bowed. The boy and the woman bowed. The young man raised his head. The boy and the woman raised their heads. The young man went down in prostration. The boy and the woman went down in prostration. He told Abbas that he saw something amazing.

Abbas asked if he knew who the young boy was. He said that he did not know. Abbas said that he was his nephew, Ali ibn Abi Talib ibn Abd al-Muttalib.

He then asked if he knew who the woman was. When he replied that he did not know her. Abbas said that she was Khadija bint Khuwaylid, the wife of his nephew Muhammad. He said that his nephew, Muhammad, told them that his Lord was the Lord of the heavens and earth, who enjoined on him this religion which he followed. Abbas did not know if there was anyone on the face of the earth following his religion except these three.

Afif relates that he later wished that he had been their fourth.

Muhammad ibn Salih and **Abd al-Rahman ibn Abd al-Aziz** relate that Khadija died on the twentieth of Ramadan, three years before the migration. She was sixty-five.

Ayisha relates that Khadija died before the prescribed prayer was made obligatory. This was three years before the migration.

Hakim ibn Hizam relates that Khadija bint Khuwaylid died in the month of Ramadan in the tenth year of prophethood. She was sixty-five. He says that they took her out of her house and buried her at al-Hajun. The Messenger of God went down into her grave. At that time we did not have the *Sunnah* of the funeral prayer.

He was asked when this was. He told them that it was about three years before the migration. It was shordy after the Hashim clan left the ravine. She was the first woman the Messenger of God married. All his children were by her, except for Ibrahim, the child of Mariyah. Her agnomen was Umm Hind from her son by her first husband, Abu Hala al-Tamimi.

KHALIDA BINT ABU LAHAB IBN ABD AL-MUTTALIB
Mother: Umm Jamil bint Harb ibn Umayya

Father: Abu Lahab ibn Abd al-Muttalib
Children: Bore children, but names not given
Wife of: Uthman ibn Abil As ibn Bishr al-Thaqafi
Ibn Sad also relates the following:
She accepted Islam and gave her allegiance to the Messenger of God.

KHALIDA BINT AL-ASWAD IBN ABD AL-YAGHUTH
Mother: Amina bint Nawfal of Zuhra
Father: Aswad ibn Abd al-Yaghuth
Wife of: Abd Allah ibn al-Arqam
Tribe: Quraysh
Ibn Sad also relates the following:
She accepted Islam and gave her allegiance to the Messenger of God.
Zuhri relates that the Messenger of God visited one of his wives and there was a beautiful woman there when the verse 10:31, '*Who extracts the living from the dead and extracts the dead from the living?*' was revealed. The Messenger of God asked, 'Who is this?'
They said that she was one of his maternal aunts.
He said, 'My aunts in this land are foreigners. Which of my aunts is this?' They replied that it was Khalida bint al-Aswad ibn Abd al-Yaghuth.'
He said, 'Glory be to God who brings out the living from the dead!'
She was a righteous woman. Her father had died an unbeliever.
Muhammad ibn Umar al-Waqadi reports that the commentary of '*Who extracts the living from the dead*' means the believer from the unbeliever.

KHALIDA BINT AMR IBN WADHAFA
Mother: Hind bint Khalid
Father: Amr ibn Wadhafa
Sister of: Half-sister of Farwa ibn Amr
Wife of: Abu Ubada Sad ibn Uthman
Tribe: Khazraj, Bayada ibn Amr clan

KHALIDA BINT QAYS IBN THABIT
Father: Qays ibn Thabit
Children: Bishr
Wife of: Bara ibn Marur of Salama clan
Tribe: Non-Quraysh
Ibn Sad also relates the following:
She accepted Islam and gave her allegiance to the Messenger of God.
It is related that her son Bishr was present at the Battle of Badr.

He is the one who ate some of the poisoned sheep meat with the Messenger of God.

It is related that Khalida bint Qays was one of the Helpers who early on accepted Islam. It is reported that she visited the Messenger during his last illness. Placing her hand on his body, she said that she had never seen such a high fever.

The Messenger answered, 'Just as we [Prophets] receive more reward than others, so the severity of hardships is twice that of others.' Then he asked her what people thought of his illness. She replied that they thought that he was suffering from pleurisy.

The Messenger said, 'O God, protect me from that disease. My illness is the effect of that poison which your son and I ate at Khaybar. It continued working inside me.' The Messenger of God died a martyr.

It is related that once Khalida asked the Prophet if the dead also be recognized. He said, 'The soul of a pious person is like a green bird. If the bird is recognized among the leaves of the trees, the dead can also be recognized.'

She narrated a few Traditions from the Prophet.

KHANSA BINT AMR
Father: Amr
Sister of: Sakhr
She is not mentioned by Ibn Sad.

KHANSA BINT KHUDHAM AL-ANSARIYYA
Father: Khudham al-Ansariyya
Sister of: Unays ibn Qatada al-Ansari
Wife of: Abu Lubaba ibn Abu al-Mundhir
Tribe: Khazraj, Malik ibn al-Najjar clan
Ibn Sad also relates the following:

She accepted Islam and gave her allegiance to the Messenger of God. She related a Tradition. The Prophet said in regard to her that a father alone without his daughter's consent could not arrange marriage.

Nafi ibn Jubayr relates that Khansa bint Khudham was widowed. Her father gave her in marriage when she was unwilling. She went to the Prophet and said that her father has followed his own opinion and given her in marriage without consulting her.

He said, 'There is no marriage. Marry whom you wish.'

Her marriage was revoked. She married Abu Lubaba ibn Abul Mundhir.

Said ibn Abd al-Rahman al-Jahshi relates that there was a woman named Khansa bint Khudham who was married to Unays ibn

Qatada al-Ansari. He was killed at the Battle of Uhud. Her father gave her in marriage to a man. She went to the Prophet and said that her father had given her in marriage although she prefered her son's paternal uncle. The Prophet gave control of her life to her.

KHANSA BINT RABAB IBN AL-NUMAN
Mother: Adam bint Haram
Father: Rabab ibn al-Numan
Wife of: Amir ibn Adi;
      Numan ibn Khansa, al-
Tribe: Khazraj, Salama ibn Sad clan
Ibn Sad also relates the following:
She accepted Islam and gave her allegiance to the Messenger of God. She was the paternal aunt of Jabir ibn Abd Allah who was present at the Battle of Badr.

KHAWLA BINT HAKIM IBN UMAYYA
Mother: Duayfa bint al-As ibn Umayya
Father: Hakim ibn Umayya
Wife of: Uthman ibn Mazun Jamhi
Tribe: Banu Sulaym
Ibn Sad also relates the following:
She accepted Islam and gave her allegiance to the Messenger of God. The Prophet proposed to her but did not marry her.

Muhammad relates that Khawla bint Hakim was one of those who offered themselves to the Prophet. He put her off. She used to serve the Prophet. Uthman ibn Mazun married her and later left her a widow.

Said ibn al-Musayyab relates that it was Khawla bint Hakim who asked the Messenger of God about the woman who has the same sort of dream that a man has.

KHAWLA BINT HUDHAYL
Mother: Daughter of Khalifa ibn Farwa al-Kalbi**Father:** Hudhayl
Wife of: Prophet
Ibn Sad also relates the following:
She accepted Islam and gave her allegiance to the Messenger of God. The Prophet proposed but never married her. She died on the way to meet him.

al-Sharqi al-Qattami relates that the Messenger of God married Khawla bint al-Hudhayl, but she died before reaching him.

KHAWLA BINT KHAWLI IBN ABD ALLAH
Mother: Jamila bint Ubayy
Father: Khawli ibn Abd Allah

Sister of: Aws ibn Khawli
Tribe: Khazraj, Bal Hubla clan
Ibn Sad also relates the following:
She accepted Islam and gave her allegiance to the Messenger of God. Her brother was present at the Battle of Badr and at the washing of the body of the Prophet.

KHAWLA BINT MALIK IBN BISHR
Father: Malik ibn Bishr
Wife of: Ziyad ibn Zayd
Tribe: Khazraj, Zurayq ibn Amir clan
Ibn Sad also relates the following:
She accepted Islam and gave her allegiance to the Messenger of God.

KHAWLA BINT QAYS IBN QAHD
Mother: Furaya bint Zurara, al-
Father: Qays ibn Qahd
Children: Yala, Umara and two daughters who died as children; Muhammad
Wife of: Hamza ibn Abd al-Muttalib; Hanzala ibn al-Numan
Tribe: Khazraj, Malik ibn al-Najjar clan
Alternative Name: Khuwayla; Umm Muhammad
Ibn Sad also relates the following:
She accepted Islam and gave her allegiance to the Messenger of God.

KHAWLA BINT QAYS IBN AL-SAKAN
Mother: Umm Khawla bint Sufyan
Father: Qays ibn Sakan
Wife of: Hisham ibn Amir
Tribe: Khazraj, Adi ibn al-Najjar tribe
Ibn Sad also relates the following:
She accepted Islam and gave her allegiance to the Messenger of God.

KHAWLA BINT SAMIT IBN QAYS
Mother: Qurrat al-Ayn bint Ubada
Father: Samit ibn Qays
Children: Amir, Umm Uthman
Sister of: Ubada, Aws
Wife of: Abu Abd al-Rahman Yazid ibn Thalaba
Tribe: Khazraj, Qawaqila, Awf ibn al-Khazraj clan
Ibn Sad also relates the following:
She accepted Islam and gave her allegiance to the Messenger of God. Some have reported that she was the one who argued about her

husband before God revealed, *'God has heard the words of she who disputes with you about her husband'* (58:1). It has also been related that this is a mistake and that it is about Khawla bint Thalaba.

KHAWLA BINT THALABA
Father: Thalaba
Wife of: Aws ibn al-Samit
Tribe: Khazraj, Qawaqila, Awf ibn al-Khazraj clan

Ibn Sad also relates the following:

She accepted Islam and gave her allegiance to the Messenger of God.

Salih ibn Kaysan relates that the first Muslim that they heard about pronouncing the *zihar* divorce [that is, a husband saying to his wife that she is forbidden to him just as if she were the back of his mother] from his wife was Aws ibn Samit al-Waqifi. He was married to his cousin, Khawla bint Thalaba They said that he was a man who was somewhat crazy. He said to his cousin that she was to him like his mother's back.

She responded that he had said something terrible. She wanted to know what it meant so she went to the Messenger. She told him what had happened, what her husband had said. The Messenger of God sent for Aws ibn Samit. He came.

The Messenger of God asked, 'What do you have to say about what your cousin says?'

He said that she spoke the truth. He had pronounced *zihar* and made her like his mother's back. He then asked the Messenger what he should do.

The Messenger said, 'Do not go near her and do not have intercourse with her until I give you permission.'

Khawla said to the Messenger that her husband was penniless. She was the only one who spent on him.

There was some discussion between them about that for a time. Then God revealed this in the Quran, *'God has heard the words of she who disputes with you about her husband and lays her complaint before God. God hears the two of you talking together...'* (58:1) The Messenger commanded him to expiate the *zihar*. Aws said that if it had not been for Khawla, he would have been destroyed.

Imran ibn Abi Anas relates that in the Age of Ignorance there were those who made their wives unlawful to themselves for all time by *zihar*. The first to pronounce *zihar* in Islam was Aws ibn Samit. He was somewhat crazy. He had recovered and partially regained his senses when he courted his wife, Khawla bint Thalaba, the sister of Abu Abd al-Rahman Yazid ibn Thalaba, in one of his saner periods. He said to her that she was like his mother's back.' Then he regreted what he had said. He said to his wife that he thought that she was now unlawful for him.

She said to him that he had not mentioned divorce. He had said something that related to the time before God sent His Messenger. She told him to go to the Messenger and ask him about what he should do.

He told her that he was too ashamed to go and ask him about this. He asked if his wife could go to the Messenger. Perhaps in this way she would obtain some good for both of them.

She got dressed and went to him in Ayisha's house. She said to the Messenger that Aws was the father of her children, her cousin and the most beloved of people to her. She also mentioned the slight derangement which afflicted her husband, his lack of ability to express himself the way he wanted. God has said something about divorce, but her husband had not mentioned divorce. He had said that she was like his mother's back to him.

The Messenger of God said, 'I think that you are unlawful to him.'

She argued with the Messenger of God for a time. Then she prayed to God with intensity of feeling. She said it was very difficult for her to part from him. She prayed to God to send down something to the tongue of His Prophet which contained relief for them. Ayisha said she wept and those of the people of the house with her wept out of mercy and compassion for her.'

While she was talking to the Messenger of God, the revelation descended. His face trembled. He perspired until sweat fell from him like drops.

Ayisha told Khawla that what was being sent down to him can only be about her. She prayed to God saying that she only desired good from His Prophet. Ayisha said that when the revelation left the Messenger of God, she thought that Khawla's soul would depart out of fear of separation being revealed. It left the Messenger of God smiling.

He said, 'Khawla.' She replied. When the Messenger said, 'God has given revelation about you and him.' Then he recited to her '*God has heard the words of she who disputes with you about her husband ...*' (58:1) Then he said, '*Command him to free a slave.*' She leapt to her feet out of joy at the smile on the face of the Messenger of God. Then she said that he did not have a slave and had no servant except her.

Then he said, '*Command him to fast for two consecutive months.*'

She said that she knew that he would not be able to do that. He drank often in the day. His sight had gone. His body was weak.

He said, '*Then command him to feed sixty poor people.*'

She asked how it would be possible to do that since they only ate one meal a day.

He said, 'Tell him to go to Umm al-Mundhir bint Qays and take half a weight of dates from her and give it as charity to sixty poor people.'

She got up and went looking for her husband. She found him sitting at the door waiting for her. He asked her what had happened. She replied that good had been revealed. She told him that the Messenger told him to go to Umm al-Mundhir bint Qays and take from her half a weight of dates and give it as charity to sixty poor people.

Khawla said that he left her and brought the dates on his back. Her custom with him was that she would not let him carry five *sa's*. He began to feed two *mudds* of dates to every poor person.'

KHAWLA BINT UBAYD IBN THALABA
Mother: Rua bint Adi, al-
Father: Ubayd ibn Thalaba
Children: Muawiyya
Wife of: Samit ibn Zayd
Tribe: Khazraj, Malik ibn al-Najjar clan
Ibn Sad also relates the following:
She accepted Islam and gave her allegiance to the Messenger of God.

KHAWLA BINT UQBA IBN RAFI
Mother: Salma bint Amr
Father: Uqba ibn Rafi
Children: Sad; Amr
Wife of: Harith ibn al-Simma, al-; Abd Allah ibn Qatada
Tribe: Aws, Abd al-Ashhal clan
Ibn Sad also relates the following:
She accepted Islam and gave her allegiance to the Messenger of God.

KHAYRA BINT ABU UMAYYA IBN AL-HARITH
Father: Abu Umayya ibn al-Harith
Wife of: Miknaf ibn Muhayysa
Tribe: Aws, Salm ibn Imrul Qays clan
Ibn Sad also relates the following:
She accepted Islam and gave her allegiance to the Messenger of God.

KHIRNIQ BINT AL-HUSAYN OF KHUZAA
Father: Husayn of Khuzaa
Tribe: Non-Qurayshi
Ibn Sad also relates the following:
She accepted Islam and gave her allegiance to the Messenger of God.

KHULAYDA BINT ABI UBAYD (SEE UMM ABS BINT MASLAMA IBN SALAMA)

KHULAYDA BINT AL-HUBAB
Mother: Bint Mudlij
Father: Hubab, al-
Children: No children
Wife of: Abd Allah ibn Sad
Tribe: Aws, Zafar clan

Ibn Sad also relates the following:

She accepted Islam and gave her allegiance to the Messenger of God.

KHULAYDA BINT THABIT IBN SINAN
Father: Thabit ibn Sinan
Wife of: Kab ibn Amr; Abd Allah ibn Anas
Tribe: Khazraj

KHUWAYLA (SEE KHAWLA BINT QAYS IBN QAHD)

KILABI WOMAN
Wife of: Prophet
Alternative Name: Fatimah bint Dahhak; Amr bint Yazid; Aliyya bint Zabyan; Saba bint Sufyan

She is said by some to have married the Prophet, but that marriage was not consummated.

Ibn Sad relates the following:

There is disagreement about her name. Some say she is Fatima bint ad-Dahhak. Others say she is Amra bint Yazid. Yet others say she is Aliyya bint Zabyan and still others say that she is Saba bint Sufyan. Some say there was only one woman of Kilab. They disagree about her name. Others say that they are all involved and each of them has a different story from that of her companion. We will clarify that and record what we have heard.

Zuhri relates that she is Fatima bint al-Dahhak ibn Sufyan. She sought refuge from him and he divorced her. She used to collect the camels and said, 'I am a wretch.' The Messenger of God married her in Dhul Qida 8 AH and she died in 60 AH.

Ayisha relates that the Messenger of God married the Kilabiyya woman. When she came to him, he went up to her and she said, 'I seek refuge with God from you.'

The Messenger of God said, 'You have sought refuge with One Immense. Rejoin your family.'

Ibn Mannah relates that she sought refuge from the Messenger of God. She was out of her mind, and her wits had left her. She would say when she asked permission to visit the wives of the Prophet, 'I am the wretch.' She used to say, 'I was deceived.'

Amr relates that the Messenger of God went into her, but when he gave his wives a choice, she chose her people. He divorced her, and she used to collect the camels and say, 'I am the wretch.'

Musa ibn Said and **Ibn Abi Awn** relate that the Messenger of God divorced her because of some white leprosy she had.

Husayn ibn Ali relates that the Messenger of God married a woman of the Amir tribe. When he went out, she stared at the people in the mosque. His wives told the Messenger of God about this.

He said, 'You are against her.'

They said, 'We will show you her staring.'

The Messenger of God said, 'All right.'

So they showed her to him when she was staring at the people. So the Messenger of God divorced her.

Muhammad ibn Umar al-Waqadi reports that she sought refuge from him and he gave her refuge. The Messenger of God did not marry anyone from the Amir tribe except her. He did not marry other than the Jawniyya woman of Kinda.

Abu Wajza relates that the Messenger of God married her in Dhul Qida in 8 AH when he left al-Jifrana.

It is related from several people that she died in 60 AH.

Ibn Umar relates that one of the wives of the Messenger of God was Saba bint Sufyan. The Prophet sent Abu Usayd al-Saidi to propose on his behalf to a woman of the Amir tribe called Amra bint Yazid. He carried out the marriage to her and then the Prophet heard that she had some white leprosy and divorced her.

It is related from a man of the Banu Abi Bakr ibn Kilab that the Messenger married Aliyya bint Zabyan. She was with him for a time and then he divorced her.

KUAYBA BINT SAD ASLAMIYYA
Father: Sad Aslamiyya
Tribe: Non-Qurayshi Emigrant
Ibn Sad also relates the following:
She accepted Islam and gave her allegiance to the Messenger of God. She treated the wounded at the Battle of Khandaq. She set up a tent in the mosque to treat the sick and treated Sad ibn Muadh who had been wounded at the Battle of Khandaq.

KUBAYSHA BINT FARWA (SEE KABSHA)

KULTHUM BINT MIHRAZ IBN AMIR
Mother: Umm Sahl bint Abu Kharija
Father: Mihraz ibn Amir
Tribe: Khazraj, Adi ibn al-Najjar clan
Ibn Sad also relates the following:

She accepted Islam and gave her allegiance to the Messenger of God.

L

LAYLA BINT ABU SUFYAN IBN AL-HARITH
Mother: Salma bint Amr
Father: Abu Sufyan ibn al-Harith
Wife of: Hudhayl ibn Amir perhaps; Bukayr ibn Jariyya perhaps or perhaps both
Tribe: Aws, Amr ibn Awf ibn Malik ibn Aws clan
Ibn Sad also relates the following:
She accepted Islam and gave her allegiance to the Messenger of God.

LAYLA BINT AWS IBN ADI
Mother: Layla bint Ubayd
Father: Aws ibn Adi
Wife of: Harith ibn Ghiyath al-Khatmi, al-
Ibn Sad also relates the following:
She accepted Islam and gave her allegiance to the Messenger of God.

LAYLA BINT HATHMA IBN HUDHAYFA
Mother: A slave woman who gave birth to the child of her master
Father: Hathma ibn Hudhayfa
Children: Bore children, but no names given
Wife of: Amir ibn Rabia ally of Khattab ibn Nufayl
Tribe: Quraysh
Ibn Sad also relates the following:
She accepted Islam and gave her allegiance to the Messenger of God. She migrated to Abyssinia in both migrations.

LAYLA BINT KHUTAYM
Mother: Sharqat al-Dar bint Haysha
Father: Khutaym
Children: Amra, Amira
Sister of: Qays ibn al-Khutaym
Wife of: Masud ibn Aws
Tribe: Aws, Zafar clan
Ibn Sad also relates the following:
She accepted Islam and gave her allegiance to the Messenger of God. The Prophet married and divorced her because the Zafar clan of the Aws tribe asked for her release. She was an extremely jealous per-

son who was called "the one eaten by the lion." She was the first woman to give her allegiance to the Prophet along with her two daughters and two granddaughters.

Ibn Abbas relates that Layla bint al-Khutaym went up to the Messenger while he had his back facing the sun. She tapped his shoulder. He asked, 'Who is this whom the lion will eat?' He used to often say that.

She said that she was the daughter of the one who fed the birds and out stripped the wind. She was Layla bint al-Khutaym who had come to offer herself to him in marriage.

He said, 'Let it be done.'

So she went back to her people and said that the Messenger had married her.

They said to her that what she has done was evil because she was a jealous woman. They pointed out that the Messenger has several wives and that she would be very jealous. The other women would invoke God against her so she should asked to be released.

She went back and asked the Messenger to release her. He said, 'You are released.'

Masud ibn Aws married her. She gave birth to children. While she was washing in one of the gardens of Madinah, a wolf leapt at her, by the words of the Prophet, and ate part of her. She was found and then died.

Ibn Abi Awn relates that Layla bint al-Khutaym gave herself to the Messenger. Women had offered themselves to him before, but he had not paid any attention to them.

Asim ibn Umar ibn Qatada relates that it was Layla bint al-Khutaym who gave herself to the Messenger. He accepted her. She used to ride her mules in an objectionable way, and she had a bad character.

She said that she would make sure that Muhammad did not marry any other of the women Helpers in this area by offering herself to him in marriage. She went to the Prophet while he was standing with one of his Companions. He did not notice her until she put her hand on him.

He asked, 'Who is this whom the lion will eat?'

She said that she was Layla, the daughter of the master of his people and that she gave herself to him in marriage.

He said, 'I accept. Go back to your people, and my command will reach you.'

She went back to her people. They told her that she was a woman who would not be patient with co-wives. They pointed out that God had allowed His Messenger to marry whomever he wished.

She went back to the Messenger and said that she knew that God has allowed him to marry many women. Since she was a woman with a long tongue and no patience for co-wives, it would be better if he would release her. The Messenger of God said, 'I release you.'

LAYLA BINT NAHIK
Mother: Umm Abd Allah bint Aslam
Father: Nahik
Wife of: Sahl ibn al-Rabi
Tribe: Aws, Haritha ibn al-Khazraj clan
   Ibn Sad also relates the following:
   She accepted Islam and gave her allegiance to the Messenger of God.

LAYLA BINT RAFI
Mother: Umm al-Bara bint Salama
Father: Rafi
Children: Abu Abs
Wife of: Jabr ibn Amr
Tribe: Aws, Haritha ibn al-Khazraj, al- clan
   Ibn Sad also relates the following:
   She accepted Islam and gave her allegiance to the Messenger of God. Her son was present at the Battle of Badr.

LAYLA BINT RIBI IBN AMIR
Father: Ribi ibn Amir
Wife of: Tufayl ibn Malik, al-; Sayfi ibn Rafi ally of the Amr ibn Awf clan
Tribe: Khazraj, Zurayq ibn Amir clan
   Ibn Sad also relates the following:
   She accepted Islam and gave her allegiance to the Messenger of God.

LAYLA BINT RITHAB IBN HUNAYF
Mother: Amat Allah bint Ghanima
Father: Rithab ibn Hunayf
Children: Abd al-Rahman; Numan, al-, Umama, Umm Husayn; Sada
Wife of: Itban ibn Malik; Abd al-Rahman ibn Amir; Abd Allah ibn Amr
Tribe: Khazraj, Qawaqila, Awf ibn al-Khazraj clan
   Ibn Sad also relates the following:
   She accepted Islam and gave her allegiance to the Messenger of God.

LAYLA BINT SIMAK IBN THABIT
Father: Simak ibn Thabit
Tribe: Khazraj

Only Muhammad ibn Umar al-Waqidi mentions her as accepting Islam.

LAYLA BINT TIBA
Father: Tiba
Wife of: Wahb ibn Kalda
Tribe: Khazraj, Balhabla al-Habla is Salim ibn Ghanm ibn Awf
Ibn Sad also relates the following:
She accepted Islam and gave her allegiance to the Messenger of God.

LAYLA BINT UBADA IBN DULAYM
Mother: Amra al-Thalitha bint Masud
Father: Ubada ibn Dulaym
Children: Saib, al-
Sister of: Sad ibn Ubada
Wife of: Khallad ibn Suwayd
Tribe: Khazraj, Saida ibn Kab clan
Ibn Sad also relates the following:
She accepted Islam and gave her allegiance to the Messenger of God.

LUBABA BINT ABU LUBABA
Mother: Nusayba bint Faddala ibn al-Numan
Father: Abu Lubaba
Children: Bore both children but name not given
Wife of: Zayd ibn al-Khattab; Abu Said ibn Aws
Tribe: Aws, Amr ibn Awf ibn Malik ibn Aws clan
Ibn Sad also relates the following:
She accepted Islam and gave her allegiance to the Messenger of God. Her first husband was martyred at Yamama.

LUBABA BINT ASLAM IBN HARISH
Mother: Suad bint Rafi
Father: Aslam ibn Harith
Sister of: Salama ibn Aslan
Wife of: Zayd ibn Sad
Tribe: Aws, Haritha ibn al-Khazraj clan
Ibn Sad also relates the following:
She accepted Islam and gave her allegiance to the Messenger of God.

LUBABA THE YOUNGER
Mother: Fakhita bint Amr
Father: Harith ibn Hazm

Children: Khalid ibn al-Walid
Wife of: Walid ibn al-Mughira
Tribe: Non-Qurayshi Emigrant
Alternative Name: Asma bint al-Harith ibn Hazm
    Ibn Sad also relates the following:
    She accepted Islam after the migration and gave her allegiance to
the Messenger of God.

LUBNA BINT KHUTAYM

Mother: Qurayba bint Qays
Father: Khutaym
Children: Bore him children, but not named
Sister of: Qays ibn al-Khutaym
Wife of: Abd Allah ibn Nahik
Tribe: Aws, Zafar clan
    Ibn Sad also relates the following:
    She accepted Islam and gave her allegiance to the Messenger of
God.

LUBNA BINT QAYZI IBN QAYS

Mother: Umm Habib bint Qurad
Father: Qayzi ibn Qays
Wife of: Abu Thabit; Abu Ahmad ibn Qays
Tribe: Aws, Haritha ibn al-Khazraj, al-, clan
    Ibn Sad also relates the following:
    She accepted Islam and gave her allegiance to the Messenger of
God.

LUBNA BINT THABIT IBN AL-MUNDHIR

Mother: Sukhta bint Haritha
Father: Thabit ibn Mundhir
Tribe: Khazraj, Malik ibn al-Najjar clan
    Ibn Sad also relates the following:
    She accepted Islam and gave her allegiance to the Messenger of
God.

LUMAYS BINT AMR

Mother: Hind bint Qays
Father: Amr
Wife of: Zayd ibn Yazid
Tribe: Khazraj, Salama ibn Sad clan
    Ibn Sad also relates the following:
    She accepted Islam and gave her allegiance to the Messenger of
God.

M

MAHABBA BINT AL-RABI IBN AMR
Mother: Huzayla bint Utba
Father: Rabi ibn Amr
Children: Bilal
Sister of: Sad ibn al-Rabi
Wife of: Abu Darda
Tribe: Khazraj
Ibn Sad also relates the following:
She accepted Islam and gave her allegiance to the Messenger of God. Her brother was present at the Battle of Badr.

MANDWAS
Father: Khallad
Tribe: Khazraj
Alternative Name: Sadus bint Khallad
She is mentioned by Muhammad ibn Umar al-Waqidi as having accepted Islam.

MANDWAS BINT AMR
Mother: Hind bint al-Mundhir
Father: Amr
Children: Maslama
Sister of: Mundhir ibn Amr, al-
Wife of: Mukhallad ibn Samit
Tribe: Khazraj, Saida ibn Kab clan
Ibn Sad also relates the following:
She accepted Islam and gave her allegiance to the Messenger of God. Her brother, al-Mundhir, was present at Aqaba and Badr and martyred at Bir Mauna.

MANDWAS BINT QUBTA
Mother: Umayra bint Qurat
Father: Qubta
Children: Abu Amr; Utba, Umm Sad; Marwan
Wife of: Hubab ibn Sad, al-; Abd Allah ibn Kab; Abd Allah ibn Abi Salit
Tribe: Khazraj, Dar ibn al-Najjar clan
Ibn Sad also relates the following:
She accepted Islam and gave her allegiance to the Messenger of God.

MANDWAS BINT UBADA IBN DULAYM
Mother: Amra al-Thalitha bint Masud

Father: Ubada ibn Dulaym
Children: Thabit
Sister of: Sad ibn Ubada
Wife of: Simak ibn Thabit
Tribe: Khazraj, Saida ibn Kab clan

Ibn Sad also relates the following:

She accepted Islam and gave her allegiance to the Messenger of God.

MARIYAH THE COPT

Ibn Sad relates the following:

It is related that Abd Allah ibn Abd al-Rahman ibn Abi Sasaa said that in 7 AH, the governor of Alexandria, sent the Messenger of God, Mariyah and her sister, Serene, a thousand *mithqals* of gold and twenty soft garments, his mule, al-Duldul, and his donkey, Ufayr. A eunuch named Mabur (an old man who was the brother of Mariyah) accompanied them. He sent all of this with Hatib ibn Abi Baltaa.

Hatib ibn Abi Baltaa offered Islam to Mariyah and encouraged her to accept it. She and her sister became Muslim. The eunuch later accepted Islam in Madinah.

The Messenger of God liked Mariyah. She was fair and beautiful. He lodged her in al-Aliyya, the property which is now called Mashraba Umm Ibrahim. The Messenger of God used to visit her there. He set up the partition for her. He had intercourse with her on the basis that she was his slave. When she became pregnant, she gave birth there. Her midwife was Salma, the servant of the Messenger of God. Abu Rafi, the husband of Salma, came and gave the Messenger of God the good news of Ibrahim. He gave him a slave. That was in March-April AD 630/Dhul Hijja AH 8 AH.

Ayisha relates that she was not jealous of any woman except for Mariyah. 'This was because she was beautiful. The Messenger of God admired her. When she was first brought to him, he put her in the house of Haritha ibn al-Numan. She was our neighbor. The Messenger spent most of the day and night with her so that we became preoccupied with her. She became alarmed. He moved her to al-Aliyya. He used to visit there. It was hard on us. Then God gave him a son by her, and we were deprived of that.'

Anas ibn Malik relates that Umm Ibrahim was the favorite of the Messenger.

Qasim ibn Muhammad relates that the Messenger of God was alone with his slavegirl, Mariyah, in Hafsa's room. The Messenger came out, and Hafsa was sitting at the door. She was angry that the Messenger had been in her room with Mariyah on her day.

The Messenger said, 'She is unlawful for me. Get hold of yourself.'

Hafsa said that she would not accept this until the Messenger swore an oath to her.

So he said, 'By God, I will never touch her.'

Qasim considered that the words about her being unlawful were not binding.

Zuhri relates that Mariyah, the mother of Ibrahim, and her sister were given by the governor to the Messenger. The Messenger took the mother of Ibrahim and gave Serene to Hassan ibn Thabit."

Malik relates that the Messenger of God said, 'Protect the Copts. They are kinsmen. Their kinship is that Ismail ibn Ibrahim was from them and the mother of Ibrahim, the son of the Messenger, was from them.'

Anas ibn Malik relates that the mother of Ibrahim, the favorite of the Prophet, was in her upper room. A Copt used to go to her and takeher water and wood. The people talked about that, saying, 'A barbarian visiting a barbarian.'

The Messenger of God heard about this. He sent Ali ibn Abi Talib after him. Ali found him by a palm tree. When the Copt saw the sword, he was frightened. He took off the garment he was wearing and exposed himself. He was completely castrated. Ali went back to the Prophet and told him. He asked the Messenger if the Messenger commanded one of them to do something but that person thought something else would be better, should that person refer it back to the Messenger or not.

He said, 'Yes.'

Ali ibn Abi Talib told the Messenger about the Copt. Mariyah gave birth to Ibrahim. Gabriel came to the Prophet and said, 'Peace be upon you, Abu Ibrahim!' The Messenger was put at ease by that.'

It is related that Ali went out and met Mariyah's servant with a pot on his head bringing her some sweet water from a well. When Ali saw him, Ali unsheathed his sword and made for him. When the Copt saw Ali, he dropped the waterskin and climbed a palm tree exposing his private parts. He was completely castrated. Ali sheathed his sword and then went back to the Prophet and told him the news. The Messenger of God said, 'You were right. The witness sees what the one who is not present does not see.'

Ibn Abbas relates that when the mother of Ibrahim gave birth, the Messenger of God said, 'Her son has freed her.'

Ibn Abbas relates that the Messenger of God said, 'Any slavegirl who gives birth to her master's child is free when he dies unless he frees her before he dies.'

Abd al-Rahman ibn Hasan relates from his mother, Mariyah's sister whose name was Serene and who had been given by the Prophet to Hasan ibn Thabit and who bore him Abd al-Rahman. She said that she saw the Prophet when Ibrahim was dying. She and her sister were crying out. He did not forbid them doing so. When he died, he forbade them to cry out. Fadl ibn Abbas washed him while the Messenger of God was sitting down. Then she saw him at the side of the grave. Abbas was beside him. Fadl and Usama ibn Zayd went down into the grave. The sun was eclipsed on that day. The people said, 'It is because of the death of Ibrahim.'

The Messenger of God said, 'There has not been an eclipse because of the death or life of anyone.'

The Messenger of God saw a gap in between some bricks. He ordered that it be blocked up. He was asked the reason for this. He said, 'It neither harms nor benefits, but it satisfies the eye of the living. When the servant does something, God likes it to be done well.'

Ata relates that the mother of the child of the Messenger of God, Mariyah, was commanded to observe a waiting period of three menstrual periods.

It is related that Abu Bakr maintained Mariyah until his death. Umar then maintained her until she died during his caliphate. Muhammad ibn Umar relates that Mariyah, the mother of Ibrahim, son of the Prophet, died in the month of February-March AD 637/ Muharram AH 16. Umar ibn al-Khattab gathered the people to attend and prayed for her. Her grave is in the Baqi cemetery.

MARYAM BINT ABU SUFYAN IBN AL-HARITH (SEE AYISHA BINT ABU SUFYAN IBN AL-HARITH)

MAWIYYA, FREEDWOMAN OF HUJAYR IBN ABI IHAB
Tribe: Non-Qurayshi Emigrant

Ibn Sad also relates the following:

She accepted Islam and gave her allegiance to the Messenger of God. She is the woman in whose house Khubayb ibn Adi was imprisoned in Makkah until the end of the sacred months when they killed him. She used to recount his story and then she became a good Muslim.

Mawiyya relates that she never saw a better person than Khubayb. She looked at him through a crack in the door. He was in irons. It was a season when she did not know of any grapes in the land which could be eaten. In his hand was a bunch of grapes the size of a man's head. It had to be the provision of God.

Khubayb used to offer the special night prayers. The women would listen to him, weep and feel compassion for him. She asked Khubayb if he needed anything.

He answered that he did not need anything other than being given fresh water to drink, not being given what has been sacrificed to idols to eat and letting him know when they planed to kill him.

They decided to kill him at the end of the sacred months. She went to him and told him. He did not seem bothered. All he said to her was to send him something which he could use.

She sent him a razor with her son, Abu Husayn. [She used to care for him although he was not her natural son]. When the boy had left, she thought to herself that the man would have his revenge. She wondered what she had done. She realized she sent the boy with the weapon and he might kill him and say that he has taken a life for a life.

When her son took him the razor, he took it from him and then joked with him saying that the boy was very bold. He asked him if his mother was not afraid of his treachery that she sent him with a razor when they were planning to kill him.

Mawiya relates that she was listening to that. She said to Khubayb that she trusted him. She gave to him by his God and not so that he would kill her son.

Khubayb told her not to worry, that he would not kill her son or anyone because Muslims do not consider treachery lawful. Then she told him that they would take him out and kill him the following day. They took him out in irons to at-Tanim. The children, women and slaves and a group of the people of Makkah went with him. No one stayed behind. They were either someone seeking revenge and hoping to quench the desire for revenge by being present or someone who was not seeking revenge but was opposed to Islam and its people. They took him to al-Tanim along with Zayd ibn al-Dathima. They ordered that a tall piece of wood be set up. When they were about to put Khubayb on it, he asked if he could pray two cycles of prescribed prayer. They agreed. She says that he prayed two perfect cycles of prayer without extending them.

MAYMUNA BINT ABU SUFYAN IBN HARB
Mother: Lubaba bint Abil As
Father: Abu Sufyan ibn Harb
Children: Bore 1st husband children, but names not mentioned
Wife of: Urwa ibn Masud al-Thaqafi; Mughira ibn Shuba al-Thaqafi

MAYMUNA BINT AL-HARITH
Mother: Hind bint Awf ibn Zuhayr
Father: Harith, al-
Sister of: Umm al-Fadl bint al-Harith al-Hilaliyya
Wife of: Masud ibn Amr al-Thaqafi; Abu Ruhm ibn Abd al-Uzza;
Messenger of God
Ibn Sad also relates the following:
The Messenger of God married her at Sarif, ten miles from Makkah. She was the last wife the Messenger of God married. That was in 7 AH/April, 629 CE, during the shorter pilgrimage.

Muhammad ibn IbIahim relates that the Messenger of God married Maymuna bint al-Harith in Shawwal in 7 AH/February 629 CE.

Ikrama relates that Maymuna bint al-Harith was the woman who gave herself to the Messenger of God.

Amra relates that she was asked whether Maymuna was the one who gave herself to the Messenger of God. She said that the Messenger of God married her for 400 dirhams. The guardian for her marriage was al-Abbas ibn al-Muttalib.

Mujahid relates that Maymuna's name was Barra. The Messenger of God named her Maymuna.

Ibn Abbas relates that Maymuna and the Prophet used to perform bath lustration (*ghusl*) from the same vessel.

Umm Hani relates that the Messenger of God and Maymuna performed bath lustration from the same vessel, a bowl which had traces of dough in it.

It is related that Maymuna said that the Messenger of God used to pray in the mosque on a mat while she was sleeping beside him. His garment touched her when she was menstruating.'

Amr ibn Maymun ibn Mahran relates that the Messenger of God and she were both in a state of ritual impurity following sexual intercourse. She performed the bath lustration from a bowl. There was some water left over. The Messenger came and washed himself with it. She told him that she had washed from it.

He said, 'There is no ritual impurity in the water.'

Ibn Abbas relates that the Messenger of God said, 'These sisters are believers: Maymuna, Umm al-Fadl and Asma.'

Amr ibn Maymun ibn Mahran relates that the Messenger of God left Maymuna one night. She locked the door behind him. He came back and tried to open the door. She refused to open it for him. He said, 'I swear you will open it for me!' She insinuated that he had been visiting one of his other wives on her night.

He said, 'I did not. I left bursting from urine.'

Ubayd Allah al-Khawlani relates that he saw Maymuna, the wife of the Prophet, praying in a loose outer garment with no waist-wrapper.'

Muhammad relates that the Messenger of God asked Maymuna about a slavegirl of hers. She said she had freed her.

He said, 'You have short-changed yourself. If you had given her to your relatives, it would have been better.'

Yazid ibn al-Asamm relates that he and ibn Talha ibn Ubayd Allah met Ayisha once when she was coming from Makkah. He was her nephew. They stopped in one of the gardens of Madinah. They ate from the garden. Ayisha heard about it and came to her nephew to rebuke him. Then she turned to him and admonished him severely. She reminded them that God Almighty had brought them to the house of His Prophet. She insisted that Maymuna had given them free rein as a woman with great fear of God and someone who was constant in maintaining ties of kinship.

Yazid ibn al-Asamm relates that the toothstick of Maymuna bint al-Harith, the wife of the Prophet, was soaking in water while she was busy with work or prayer. Otherwise, she took it and cleaned her teeth with it.

Yazid ibn al-Asamm relates that a relative of Maymuna visited her. She sensed the smell of drink from him. She said that if her relative did not flog him, he could not enter her house ever again.

It is related from Maymuna that she saw a white snake in the earth. She took it, and said that God does not love corruption.

Kurayb, the freedman of Ibn Abbas, relates that Ibn Abbas sent him to lead Maymuna's camel. He could still hear her saying "There is no god but God," until she stoned the Jamra al-Aqaba.

Ubayd Allah al-Khawlani, who had been in the care of Maymuna, relates that he used to see Maymuna praying in an outer garment and head covering with no waist wrapper.

Yazid ibn al-Asamm relates that they buried Maymuna at Sarif in the tent in which the Messenger had consummated her marriage. The day she died she was shaven. She had shaved on the pilgrimage. He and Ibn Abbas went down into her grave. When they laid her down, her head was sloping down at an angle. She took her cloak and put it under her head. Ibn Abbas removed it and threw it aside. He put a stone under her head.

Ata relates that Maymuna died at Sarif. He went with Ibn Abbas to her. When they lifted her bier, they did not shake it nor rock it. The Prophet had nine wives. He allotted a share to eight and not to one.

Someone else relates that she died in Makkah, Abd Allah ibn Abbas carried her. He kept saying to those who were helping him carry her to be gentle with her because she was their mother. They buried her at Sarif.

Yazid ibn al-Asamm relates that he was present at the grave of Maymuna. Those who went down into it were Ibn Abbas, Abd al-Rahman ibn Khalid ibn al-Walid, Ubayd Allah al-Khawlani and myself. Ibn Abbas prayed for her.

Muhammad ibn Umar al-Waqadi relates that she died in 61 AH /680 or 681 CE during the caliphate of Yazid ibn Muawiya. She was the last of the wives of the Prophet to die. When she died, she was eighty or eighty-one. She died childless.

Abd al-Rahman al-Araj relates that in his assembly at Madinah, the Messenger of God assigned Maymuna bint al-Harith eighty weights of dates from Khaybar and twenty weights of barley.

It is related that when the Messenger of God wanted to leave for Makkh in the Year of the shorter pilgrimage, he sent Aws ibn Khawli and Abu Rafi to al-Abbas to marry him to Maymuna. Their camel got lost. They remained some days near Rabigh until the Messenger of God caught up with them at Qudayd. They went with him to Makkah. He sent to al-Abbas telling him what had happened. Maymuna entrusted her affairs to the Messenger of God. The Messenger of God came to the house of al-Abbas and asked al-Abbas for her hand in marriage. He married her to him.

Sulayman ibn Yasir relates that the Prophet sent Abu Rabi and a man of the Helpers. They married him to Maymuna before he left Madinah.

Muhammad ibn Ibrahim relates that the Messenger of God married her in Shawwal when he was out of the sacred state in the year of the shorter pilgrimage. He married her at Sarif. She also died at Sarif.

Amr ibn Maymun ibn Mahran relates that she visited Safiyya bint Shayba when she was a very old woman. He asked her if the Messenger of God married Maymuna when he was in the sacred state. She said that he had not but had married her when they were both out of the sacred state.

Amr ibn Maymun ibn Mahran relates that Umar ibn Abd al-Aziz wrote to his father to ask Yazid ibn al-Asamm about whether the Messenger of God was in the sacred state or out of it when he married Maymuna. His father summoned him. He wrote the letter for him. He said that the Messenger proposed to her when he was not in the sacred state and consummated the marriage when he was not in the sacred state. He had heard Yazid say that.

Amr ibn Maymun ibn Mahran relates that Umar ibn Abd al-Aziz wrote to him to ask Yazid ibn al-Asamm about the marriage of the Messenger to Maymuna. He wanted to know if he married her when he was in the sacred state or not. He asked him and Yazid ibn al-Asamm said that he married her when they were both out of the sacred state. He consummated the marriage with her when he was out of the sacred state.'

Amr ibn Maymun ibn Mahran relates that he was sitting with Ata when a man came and asked if someone in the sacred state can marry. Ata said that God has not made marriage unlawful since He made it lawful. Amr said that Umar ibn Abd al-Aziz wrote to him [Maymun was at that time in Mesopotamia] to ask Yazid ibn al-Asamm whether the Messenger of God married Maymuna when he was in the sacred state or out of it.

Yazid ibn al-Asamm responded that he married her when he was out of the sacred state.

Maymuna was the aunt of Yazid ibn al-Asamm. Ata said that he only takes this from Maymuna. He heard that the Messenger of God married her when he was in the sacred state.

Abu Rafi relates that the Messenger of God married Maymuna when he was out of the sacred state. He was the messenger between them.

Sulayman ibn Yasir relates that the Messenger sent Abu Rafi and a man of the Helpers to Maymuna. They married him to Maymuna while he was still in Madinah before he had set out.

Ata al-Khurasani relates that he said to Ibn al-Musayyab that Ikrima claims that the Messenger of God married Maymuna while he was in the sacred state.

He responded that he is a wicked liar. He said the man should go to him and curse him because the Messenger of God came in the sacred state. When he came out of the sacred state, he married her.

Ibn Abbas relates that the Messenger of God married Maymuna when he was in the sacred state. Also he was cupped at al-Qaha while he was in the sacred state.

Ibn Abbas that relates that the Messenger of God married Maymuna bint al-Harith at Sarif while he was in the sacred state. He then consummated it with her at Sarif on his return.

Yazid ibn Qarun relates that she died at Sarif and her grave is there.

Ibn Abbas relates that the Messenger of God married Maymuna, his aunt, at Sarif while he was in the sacred state. Ibn Abbas did not see anything wrong in this.

Ata al-Shabi and **Mujahid** relate that the Messenger of God married Maymuna while he was in the sacred state.

Fadl ibn Dukayn relates that the Messenger was cupped while he was in the sacred state.

Ibn Amir relates that the Messenger married Maymuna while he was in the sacred state. Also, he was cupped while he was in the sacred state.

Maymuna bint Kardam, slave of Yazid ibn Miqsam
Tribe: Non-Quraysh

Ibn Sad also relates the following:

She accepted Islam and gave her allegiance to the Messenger of God. She related a Tradition from the Prophet.

Maymuna bint Said, slave of the Prophet
Father: Said
Tribe: Non-Quraysh

Ibn Sad also relates the following:

She accepted Islam and gave her allegiance to the Messenger of God. She related a Tradition from the Prophet.

MUADHA BINT ABD ALLAH IBN AMR

Father: Abd Allah ibn Amr
Tribe: Khazraj
   Ibn Sad also relates the following:
   She accepted Islam and gave her allegiance to the Messenger of God.

MUHAYYA BINT SILKAN

Mother: Umm Sahl bint Rumi
Father: Silkan
Children: One daughter, name not given
Alternative Name: Ubada bint Abu Naila Silkan ibn Salama
   Ibn Sad also relates the following:
   She accepted Islam and gave her allegiance to the Messenger of God.

MULAYKA BINT ABD ALLAH IBN SAKHR

Mother: Busra bint Zayd
Father: Abd Allah ibn Sakhr
Children: Abu Jihad, Abd al-Rahman, Huzayla
Wife of: Masud ibn Zayd
Tribe: Khazraj, Salama ibn Sad clan
   Ibn Sad also relates the following:
   She accepted Islam and gave her allegiance to the Messenger of God.

MULAYKA BINT ABD ALLAH IBN UBAYY

Mother: Khalid ibn Sinan
Father: Abd Allah ibn Ubayy
Wife of: Hilal ibn Umayya of Aws
Tribe: Khazraj, Bal Hubla clan
   Ibn Sad also relates the following:
   She accepted Islam and gave her allegiance to the Messenger of God.

MULAYKA BINT KAB AL-LAYTHI

Father: Kab al-Laythi
   Ibn Sad also relates the following:
   She accepted Islam and gave her allegiance to the Messenger of God. The Prophet married her, but did not consumate the marriage.
   Abu Mashar relates that the Prophet married Mulayka bint Kab. She was known for her remarkable beauty. Ayisha visited her and asked if she was not ashamed to marry the person who killed her father.

She sought refuge from the Messenger of God, and he divorced her. Her people came to the Prophet and said that she was a young girl and had no judgment. She was deceived and so he should take her back.

The Messenger of God refused. They asked his permission to marry her to a relative of hers from the Udhra tribe. He gave permission and she married the man. Her father had been killed on the day that Makkah was conquered. Khalid ibn al-Walid killed him at al-Khandama.

Muhammad ibn Umar al-Waqadi relates that part of what is fabricated in this Tradition is the story that Ayisha asked her if she was not ashamed. Ayisha was not with the Messenger of God on that journey.

Yazid al-Jundi relates that the Messenger of God married Mulayka bint Kab al-Laythi in Ramadan, 8 AH/December 630-January 631 CE, and consummated it. She died with him.

Muhammad ibn Umar al-Waqadi relates that his companions deny this. They say that the Messenger did not marry a woman of Kinana at all.

MULAYKA BINT SAHL IBN ZAYD

Father: Sahl ibn Zayd
Children: Bore children, but names not given
Wife of: Abul Haytham ibn al-Tayhan
Tribe: Aws, Abd al-Ashhal clan
Ibn Sad also relates the following:
She accepted Islam and gave her allegiance to the Messenger of God.

MULAYKA BINT THABIT

Mother: Kabsha bint Aws
Father: Thabit
Wife of: Shutaym ibn Zayd
Tribe: Aws, Khatma ibn Jusham clan
Ibn Sad also relates the following:
She accepted Islam and gave her allegiance to the Messenger of God.

MULAYKAH BINT MALIK ANSARIYYA

Father: Malik Ansariyya
Children: Umm Sulaym, Umm Haram
She is not mentioned in Ibn Sad.
Bukhari reports that she once invited the Messenger to a meal at her home. She prepared the food herself. The Messenger accepted and after the meal, he told her that he would teach her the prescribed

prayer. There was only a worn-out mat in the house and it had faded. Anas first washed it with water and then spread it for the prayer. The Messenger led the prayer. Mulaykah, Anas and an orphan slave-boy stood behind in a row. The Messenger offered a two cycle prescribed prayer and then went home.

MUTIA BINT AL-NUMAN IBN MALIK
Father: Numan ibn Malik, al-
Wife of: Jaz ibn Malik, al-
Tribe: Aws, Ubayd ibn Zayd ibn Malik ibn Awf clan
  Ibn Sad also relates the following:
  She accepted Islam and gave her allegiance to the Messenger of God. The Prophet changed her name. She had been called Asiyya meaning rebel and the Prophet renamed her Mutia meaning obedient.

N

NAFISA BINT UMAYYA IBN UBAYY OF TAMIN
Mother: Munya bint Jabir
Father: Umayy ibn Ubayy of Tamin
Tribe: Quraysh
  Ibn Sad also relates the following:
  She accepted Islam and gave her allegiance to the Messenger of God. Her mother was the paternal aunt of Utba ibn Ghazwan, ally of al-Harith ibn Nawfal ibn Abd al-Manaf. She arranged for Khadija and the Prophet to marry.

NAILA BINT RABI IBN QAYS
Mother: Fatima bint Amr
Father: Rabi ibn Qays
Sister of: Abd Allah ibn al-Rabi
Wife of: Aws ibn Khalid
Tribe: Khazraj
  Ibn Sad also relates the following:
  She accepted Islam and gave her allegiance to the Messenger of God. Her brother was present at Aqaba and Badr.

NAILA BINT SAD IBN SAID
Father: Sad ibn Said
Sister of: Sahl ibn Sad al-Saidi
Tribe: Khazraj, Saida ibn Kab clan

She is mentioned by Muhammad ibn Umar al-Waqadi as having accepted Islam.

NAILA BINT SALAMA
Mother: Umm Amr bint Atik
Father: Salama
Children: Bore him children, names not mentioned; Sahl
Sister of: Half-sister of Salama ibn Salama
Wife of: Abd Allah ibn Simak of Ghassan; Kab ibn al-Qayn of Aws
Ibn Sad also relates the following:
She accepted Islam and gave her allegiance to the Messenger of God. Her son, Sahl, was martyred at the Battle of Uhud.

NAILA BINT UBAYD IBN AL-HURR
Mother: Rughayba bint Aws
Father: Ubayd ibn al-Hurr
Children: Abd al-Rahman
Wife of: Mamar ibn Hazm
Tribe: Khazraj, Najjar clan
Ibn Sad also relates the following:
She accepted Islam and gave her allegiance to the Messenger of God.

NASHAH BINT RIFAAH (SEE FATIMA BINT DAHHAK)

NUFAYSA BINT THALABA (SEE UNAYSA)

NUSAYBA BINT ABU TALHA
Mother: Umm Talha bint Mukhallad al-Khatmi
Father: Abu Talha
Children: Bore children, names not given
Wife of: Umayr al-Qari ibn Adi
Tribe: Aws, Khatma ibn Jusham clan
Ibn Sad also relates the following:
She accepted Islam and gave her allegiance to the Messenger of God.

NUSAYBA BINT KAB IBN AMR (SEE UMM UMARA)

NUSAYBA BINT NIYAR
Father: Niyar
Wife of: Uqba ibn Utuda
Tribe: Aws, Ubayd ibn Zayd ibn Malik ibn Awf clan

NUSAYBA BINT RAFI

Mother: From Abd Allah ibn Ghatafan tribe
Father: Rafi
Wife of: Abu Said ibn Aws
Tribe: Khazraj, Habib ibn Abd Haritha clan

NUSAYBA BINT SIMAK
Mother: Bassama bint Abd Allah
Father: Simak
Children: Bore children names not given
Wife of: Uthman ibn Talha; Bujad ibn Uthman
Tribe: Aws, Amr ibn Awf ibn Malik ibn Aws clan

NUWWAR BINT AL-HARITH IBN QAYS
Father: Harith ibn Qays
Children: Bore children names not given
Wife of: Qayzi ibn Amr
Tribe: Aws, Ubayd ibn Zayd ibn Malik ibn Awf clan

NUWWAR BINT MALIK IBN SIRMA
Mother: Salma bint Amir
Father: Malik ibn Sirma
Children: Zayd, Yazid; Malik
Wife of: Thabit ibn al-Dahhak; Umara ibn Hazm
Tribe: Khazraj, Adi ibn al-Najjar clan

Ibn Sad also relates the following:

She accepted Islam and gave her allegiance to the Messenger of God. She related Traditions from the Prophet.

Nuwwar bint Malik relates that when she was pregnant with Zayd ibn Thabit, she saw on the Kabah green and yellow silk shawls along with carpets and cloth woven by desert Arabs.

Umm Zayd ibn Thabit al-Nawwar relates that her house was the tallest house around the mosque. Bilal used to recite the call to prescribed prayer from the top of it. This lasted from the time when the first call to prayer was heard until the Messenger built his mosque. Then Bilal recited the call to prescribed prayer from the top of the mosque and something was raised up for him on top of it.

Thabit ibn Ubayd relates that Zayd ibn Thabit recited the funeral prayer for his mother when she died.

NUWWAR BINT QAYS IBN AL-HARITH, AL-
Father: Qays ibn al-Harith
Children: Azib
Wife of: Zayd ibn Nuwayra
Tribe: Aws, Haritha ibn al-Khazraj, al- clan

Ibn Sad also relates the following:
She accepted Islam and gave her allegiance to the Messenger of God.

Q

QAYLA
Tribe: Non-Quraysh
Alternative Name: Umm Bani Anmar
Ibn Sad also relates the following:
She accepted Islam and gave her allegiance to the Messenger of God. She related a Tradition about buying and selling.

QAYLA BINT MAKHRAMA AL-TAMIMIYYA
Father: Makhrama al-Tamimiyya
Children: Hizam
Wife of: Habib ibn Azhar
Tribe: Non-Qurayshi Emigrant
Ibn Sad also relates the following:
She accepted Islam and gave her allegiance to the Messenger of God. Her husband died at the beginning of Islam. Their paternal uncle took her children, all daughters, from her. She went to find Companions of the Messenger of God.

Abd Allah ibn Hassan relates that she went with Hurayth ibn Hassan al-Shaybani who headed a delegation of the Bakr ibn Wail clan to the Messenger of God. She questioned him, listened to him and prayed with him. She had a son named Hizam. He fought beside the Messenger in the expedition of al-Rabadha. He then went to collect grain in Khaybar, fell ill with a fever, and died, leaving daughters.

QUBAYSA BINT SAYFI IBN SAKHR
Mother: Naila bint Qays
Father: Sayfi ibn Sakhr
Children: Aisha; Aliyya, al-
Wife of: Jabir ibn Sakhr; Bishr ibn al-Bara
Tribe: Khazraj, Salama ibn Sad clan
Ibn Sad also relates the following:
She accepted Islam and gave her allegiance to the Messenger of God.

QURAYBA BINT ABU QUHAFA
Mother: Hind bint Nuqayd
Father: Abu Quhafa
Children: No children
Wife of: Qays ibn Sad ibn Ubada al-Saidi

Tribe: Quraysh

Ibn Sad also relates the following:

She accepted Islam and gave her allegiance to the Messenger of God.

QURAYBA BINT ABU UMAYYA IBN AL-MUGHIRA
Mother: Atika bint Utba ibn Rabia
Father: Abu Umayya ibn al-Mughira
Children: Abd Allah, Umm Hakim, Hafsa
Sister of: Half-sister of Umm Salama bint Abi Umayya (wife of the
   Messenger)
Wife of: Abd al-Rahman ibn Abi Bakr
Tribe: Quraysh

Ibn Sad also relates the following:

She accepted Islam and gave her allegiance to the Messenger of God. The harshness of her husband's character has been related.

Ibn Abi Mulayka relates that Abd al-Rahman ibn Abu Bakr married Qurayba bint Abi Umayya, the sister of Umm Salama. There was some harshness in his character. One day she said to him that she had been warned about him. He told her that her affairs were in her own hands. She responded that she did not prefer anyone over him, and they were not divorced.

QURAYBA BINT QAYS (FURAYA, AL-)

QURAYBA BINT ZAYD IBN ABD RABBIHI
Father: Zayd ibn Abd Rabbihi
Sister of: Abd Allah ibn Zayd
Tribe: Khazraj

Ibn Sad also relates the following:

She accepted Islam and gave her allegiance to the Messenger of God. Her brother saw the dream of the call to prescribed prayer.

QURRATUL AYN BINT UBADA IBN NADLA
Mother: Amira bint Thalaba
Father: Ubada ibn Nadla
Children: Ubada ibn al-Samit, Aws, Khawla
Wife of: Samit ibn Qays, al-
Tribe: Khazraj, Qawaqila, Awf ibn al-Khazraj clan

Ibn Sad also relates the following:

She accepted Islam and gave her allegiance to the Messenger of God. Her husband or son, Ubada, were present at Aqaba and the Battle of Badr.

QUTAYLA BINT AMR AL-KINANIYYA

Father: Amr al-Kinaniyya
Tribe: Non-Qurysh
  Ibn Sad also relates the following:
  She accepted Islam at the farewell pilgrimage and gave her allegiance to the Messenger of God.

QUTAYLA BINT QAYS
Father: Qays
Sister of: Ashath ibn Qays of Kinda
  Ibn Sad also relates the following:
  She accepted Islam and gave her allegiance to the Messenger of God.

  Ibn Abbas relates that when Asma bint an-Numan sought refuge from the Prophet, he left with anger showing on his face. Ashath ibn Qays told him not to be concerned. He asked if he could marry the Messenger to someone who was not less than her in beauty and lineage. The Messenger asked, 'Who?' He said that he was referring to his sister, Qutayla.

  The Messenger replied, 'I will marry her.'

  Ashath went to Hadramawt and then brought his sister. When they had traveled some distance from Yemen, he heard of the death of the Messenger. Ashath took his sister back to her country. They both apostasized. This is why she could re-marry. Her marriage was annulled due to apostasy. Qays ibn Makshuh al-Muradi married her.

  Dawud ibn Abi Hind relates that the Prophet died after marrying a woman of Kinda called Qutayla. She apostatised with her people. After that she married Ikrima ibn Abi Jahl. Abu Bakr was very upset. Umar said to him that she was not one of the Messenger's wives because the Messenger did not give her a choice nor did he veil her. God freed him from her by her apostasy with her people.

  It is related that Urwa used to deny this. He said that the Messenger did not marry Qutayla bint Qays. He did not marry any Kindite woman except for the sister of the Jawn tribe. He married her. She was brought to him. When he looked at her, he divorced her without consummating the marriage.

QUTAYLA BINT SAYFI AL-JUHANIYYA
Father: Sayfi al-Juhaniyya
Tribe: Non-Quraysh
  Ibn Sad also relates the following:
  She accepted Islam and gave her allegiance to the Messenger of God. She related a Tradition.

R

RABAB BINT AL-BARA IBN MARUR, AL-
Mother: Humayma bint Sayfi
Father: Bara ibn Marur, al-
Children: Sad
Wife of: Muadh ibn al-Harith
Tribe: Khazraj, Banu Salama ibn Sad
  Ibn Sad also relates the following:
  She accepted Islam and gave her allegiance to the Messenger of
God.

RABAB BINT AL-NUMAN IBN IMRUL QAYS, AL-
Mother: Muadha bint Anas ibn Qays
Father: Numan ibn Imrul Qays, al-
Children: Muadh (Abu Abi Namla); Bara, al-
Wife of: Zurara ibn Amr; Marur ibn Sakhr of Khazraj
Tribe: Aws, Abd al-Ashhal clan, B. Hudhayla
  Ibn Sad also relates the following:
  She accepted Islam and gave her allegiance to the Messenger of
God. She was the aunt of Sad ibn Muadh. Her son, al-Bara, was
one of the twelve chiefs but he died before the migration. The
Messenger went to his grave and prayed for him.

RABAB BINT HARITH IBN SINAN
Father: Harith ibn Sinan
Wife of: Kulayb ibn Yasaf
  Ibn Sad also relates the following:
  She accepted Islam and gave her allegiance to the Messenger of
God.

RABAB BINT KAB IBN ADI, AL-
Father: Kab ibn Adi
Children: Hudhayfa, Sad, Safwan, Mudlij, Layla
Wife of: Yaman ibn Jabir al-Abbasi, al-
Tribe: Aws, Abd al-Ashhal
  Ibn Sad also relates the following:
  She accepted Islam and gave her allegiance to the Messenger of
God.

RAIA
Mother: Kabsha bint Aws
Tribe: Aws, Khatma ibn Jusham clan
Alternative Name: Hasana bint Thabit (see Raia)
  Ibn Sad also relates the following:

She accepted Islam and gave her allegiance to the Messenger of God. Her name means "startling beauty."

RAMLA BINT ABD ALLAH IBN UBAYY
Mother: Lubna bint Ubada
Father: Abd Allah ibn Ubayy
Wife of: Isma ibn Zayd
Tribe: Khazraj, Bal Hubla clan
   Ibn Sad also relates the following:
   She accepted Islam and gave her allegiance to the Messenger of God.

RAMLA BINT ABU AWF IBN SUBAYRA
Mother: Umm Abd Allah (Surma bint al-Harith)
Father: Abu Awf ibn Subayra
Children: Abd Allah ibn Amr
Wife of: Muttalib ibn Azhar
Tribe: Quraysh
   Ibn Sad also relates the following:
   She accepted Islam in Makkah before the Messenger entered the house of al-Arqam. She gave her allegiance to the Messenger of God and migrated with her husband to Abyssinia in the second migration.

RAMLA BINT ABU SUFYAN IBN HARB IBN UMAYYA (SEE UMM HABIBA)

RAMLA BINT AL-HARITH IBN THALABA
Mother: Kabsha bint Thabit
Father: Harith ibn Thalaba
Wife of: Muadh ibn al-Harith
Tribe: Khazraj, Malik ibn al-Najjar clan
Alternative Name: Umm Thabit
   Ibn Sad also relates the following:
   She accepted Islam and gave her allegiance to the Messenger of God.

RAMLA BINT SHAYBA IBN RABIA
Mother: Umm Shirak bint Waqdan of Amir ibn Luayy clan
Father: Shayba ibn Rabia
Children: Aisha, Umm Aban, Umm Amr
Wife of: Uthman ibn Affan
Tribe: Quraysh, Amir ibn Luayy clan
   Ibn Sad also relates the following:
   She accepted Islam and gave her allegiance to the Messenger of God. Abul Zirah (Abd Allah ibn Dhakwan) was her freedman.

RAYHANA BINT ZAYD IBN AMR

Father: Zayd ibn Amr
Wife of: Hakam, al-; the Messenger of God

Ibn Sad also relates the following:

She accepted Islam and gave her allegiance to the Messenger of God.

She was married to a man of the Qurayza called al-Hakam. This is why some transmitters ascribe her lineage to the Qurayza tribe.

Thalaba ibn Abi Malik relates that Rayhana bint Zayd ibn Amr was from the Nadir tribe. She married al-Hakam. When the Qurayza tribe was captured, the Messenger of God took her as a captive. He freed her and married her. She died with him.

Umar ibn al-Hakam relates that the Messenger of God freed Rayhana bint Zayd ibn Amr. She had had a husband whom she loved and honored. She had said that no one would replace him. She was very beautiful.

Rayhana bint Zayd ibn Amr relates that when the Qurayza tribe was captured, the captives were presented to the Messenger of God. She said that she was among those who were presented to him. He commanded her and she drew back. He had the best of every booty. When she withdrew, God chose for her.

The Messenger sent me to the house of Umm al-Mundhir bint Qays for some days until the prisoners had been killed and the captives divided. He then came to me. I felt very shy. He called me and had me sit before him. He said, 'If you choose God and His Messenger, the Messenger of God will choose you for himself.'

I said that she chose God and His Messenger. When she became Muslim, the Messenger of God set her free. He married her and gave her a dower of 400 dirhams as he had given to his other wives. He married her in the house of Umm al-Mundhir. He allotted a share to her as he did to his wives. He put up a partition for her.

The Messenger of God liked her. She did not ask him for anything but that he gave it to her. She was told that if she had asked the Messenger of God for the Quryaza tribe, he would have freed them.

She said that he was not alone with her until after the captives had been divided. She remained with him until she died on his return from the farewell pilgrimage. He buried her at the Baqi cemetery. He married her in Muharram, 6 AH/May-June 627 CE.

Muhammad ibn Kab relates that Rayhana was part of the booty God gave him. She was a beautiful, graceful woman. When her husband was killed, she fell among the captives. The Messenger of God had the pick on the day of the Qurayza tribe. The Messenger of God gave her a choice between Islam and her religion. She chose Islam. The Messenger of God freed her and married her and set up the partition for her. She was very jealous, and so he divorced her with a single divorce. She remained in her place and did not go out. It was hard on her. She wept a lot. The Messenger of God visited her while she was in that state and took her back She remained with him. She died before he died.

Wahb relates that Rayhana was from the Nadir tribe. She was married to a man from the Qurayza tribe named al-Hakam. The Messenger of God freed her and married her. She was among his wives. He gave her a share as he did for his wives and set up a partition for her.

Zuhri relates that Rayhana bint Zayd bint Amr was from the Qurayza tribe. She was part of the spoils that went to the Messenger. He set her free, married her and then divorced her. She was part of his family. She said, 'No man ever saw me after the Messenger of God set up the partition for me.

Muhammad ibn Umar al-Waqadi relates that there is weakness in this Tradition on two points that she was from Nadir tribe and that she died during the lifetime of the Messenger of God. What is related about her being set free and her marriage is correct. It is the position of the people of knowledge that she was a captive and not set free before her death.

Ayyub ibn Bashir al-Maawi relates that when the Qurayza tribe was captured, the Messenger of God sent Rayhana to the house of Salma bint Qays, Umm al-Mundhir. She stayed with her until she had menstruated once and then become pure after her period. Umm al-Mundhir came and informed the Messenger of God. The Messenger of God went to her in the house of Umm al-Mundhir. He said to her, 'If you like, I will free you and marry you, or you can remain my property.' She said to the Messenger that it would be easier for her and him if she remained his property.' So she was the property of the Messenger. He had intercourse with her until her death.

Abu Bakr ibn Abd Allah ibn Abi Jahm relates that when the Messenger took Rayhana captive, he offered her Islam, but she refused. She said she would remain with the religion of her people.

The Messenger of God said, 'If you become Muslim, the Messenger of God will choose you for himself.' She refused. That was hard on the Messenger of God.

One day while the Messenger of God was sitting among his Companions, he heard the sound of sandals. He said, 'That is Ibn Saiyya coming to give me the good news of Rayhana's acceptance of Islam.' He came and informed him that she had become Muslim. The Messenger of God had intercourse with her by the right of ownership until she died.

RAYTA BINT ABD ALLAH
Father: Abd Allah

Wife of: Abd Allah ibn Masud
Tribe: Non-Qurayshi
   Ibn Sad also relates the following:
   She accepted Islam and gave her allegiance to the Messenger of God. A craftswoman, she shared her income with her husband.
   She told the Messenger that she was a craftswoman and that she sold her work. Neither her husband nor child nor she had anything. She asked him about maintenance for them. He said, 'You will be rewarded for what you spend on them.'

Rayta bint al-Harith ibn Hubayla of Taym
Mother: Zaynab bint Abd Allah ibn Saida
Father: Harith ibn Hubayla of Taym
Children: Musa, Ayisha, Zaynab
Sister of: Subayha ibn al-Harith
Wife of: Harith ibn Khalid
Tribe: Quraysh
   Ibn Sad also relates the following:
   She accepted Islam and gave her allegiance to the Messenger of God. Her son died in Abyssinia. She died on the way back to Madinah. She had migrated on the second migration with her husband.

Rayta bint Munabbih ibn al-Hajjaj
Mother: From Katham
Father: Munabbih ibn al-Hajjaj
Children: Abd Allah ibn Amr
Wife of: Amr ibn al-As al-Sahmi
Tribe: Quraysh
   Ibn Sad also relates the following:
   She accepted Islam on the day of the conquest of Makkah and gave her allegiance to the Messenger of God.

Rifaa
Mother: Kabsha bint Aws
Wife of: Mahmud ibn Wahwah
Tribe: Aws, Khatma ibn Jusham clan
Alternative Name: Umm al-Qasim bint Thabit

Ruayba bint Zurara
Mother: Suad bint Rafi
Father: Zurara
Wife of: Ghard (Khalid ibn al-Hashas), al-
Tribe: Khazraj, Malik ibn al-Najjar clan
   Ibn Sad also relates the following:

She accepted Islam and gave her allegiance to the Messenger of God.

RUBAYYI BINT AL-TUFAYL IBN AL-NUMAN, AL-
Mother: Asma bint Qurat
Father: Tufayl ibn al-Numan, al-
Wife of: Abu Yahya Abd Allah ibn Abd al-Manaf
Tribe: Khazraj, Salama ibn Sad clan
Ibn Sad also relates the following:
She accepted Islam and gave her allegiance to the Messenger of God.

RUBAYYI BINT NADR
Father: Nadr
Children: Haritha
She was the aunt of Anas ibn Malik. She is not mentioned by Ibn Sad. She accepted Islam either before or just after the migration. Her son was martyred in the Battle of Badr. Two Traditions are related about her.

RUBBAYI BINT HARITHA IBN SINAN, AL-
Father: Harith ibn Sinan
Wife of: Kulayb ibn Yasaf
Tribe: Khazraj
Alternative Name: Rabab bint Harith ibn Sinan (see Rubbayi bint Harith ibn Sinan)
She is mentioned by Muhammad ibn Umar al-Waqadi as having accepted Islam.

RUBBAYI BINT MUAWWIDH IBN AFRA
Mother: Umm Yazid bint Qays
Father: Muawwidh ibn Afra
Children: Muhammad
Wife of: Iyas ibn al-Bukayr
Tribe: Khazraj, Malik ibn al-Najjar clan
Ibn Sad also relates the following:
She became Muslim and gave allegiance to the Messenger of God. She related a reliable Tradition. She was divorced by a divorce for consideration (*khul*).
Abu Husayn Khalid ibn Dhakanan relates that he visited Rubayyi bint Muawwidh ibn Afra. She said that the Messenger visited her on the day of her wedding. He sat where her bed was. They had two slavegirls who were beating a drum and chanting about her people who were martyred at the Battle of Badr. Among the words they

were chanting was, 'Among us is a Messenger who knows what will happen tomorrow.'

The Messenger said, 'Stop that. Do not say that.'

Rubayyi bint Muawwidh ibn Afra al-Ansari relates that she asked her husband if he would give her a divorce of consideration in return for all she possessed. He agreed. She gave him everything except her wrap. He litigated with her before Uthman. Uthman said, 'It is his pre-condition.' So she gave it to him.

Rubayyi bint Muawwidh relates that some words or discussion passed between her cousin, who was her husband, and herself. She said to him that he could have all she owned if he divorced her. He agreed. He took everything of hers, even her bed. She went with him to Uthman ibn Affan. They explained what had transpired. Uthman was under siege and said that the condition stipulated was 'her property'. Her former husband should receive everything that was hers, even the locks of her hair if he liked.

RUFAYDAH ASLAMIYAH

She was an expert in traditional medicine and surgery. She looked after the sick and those wounded in the battles. She even took part in the battles. In the Battle of the Trench, her tent for medical assistance was placed in the Messenger's mosque. When Sad ibn Muadh was injured in the battle, she took care of him.

RUGHAYBA BINT SAHL IBN THALABA
Mother: Amra bint Masud
Father: Sahl ibn Thalaba
Wife of: Rafi ibn Abu Amr
Tribe: Khazraj, Malik ibn al-Najjar clan

RUMAYLA (SEE UMM SULAYM BINT MILHAN IBN KHALID)

RUMAYSA, AL- (SEE UMM SULAYM BINT MILHAN IBN KHALID)

RUMAYTHA (SEE UMM SULAYM BINT MILHAN IBN KHALID)

RUQAYQA BINT SAYFI IBN HASHIM
Mother: Hala or Tumadir bint Kalda ibn Abdu Manaf
Father: Sayfi ibn Hashim
Children: Makhrama, Safwan, Umayya
Wife of: Nawfal ibn Uhayb ibn Abd al-Manaf
Tribe: Quraysh

Ibn Sad also relates the following:

She accepted Islam and gave her allegiance to the Messenger of God.

Ruqayqa bint Sayfi ibn Hashim relates that she could recall her uncle Shayba [Abd al-Muttalib]. She was still a girl at that time. Muttalib ibn Abd Manaf visited her. She was the first to run to him. She clung to him and told her family that he was there. She became Muslim and joined the Messenger. She was the harshest of people towards her son, Makhrama, before he accepted Islam.

It is related that Ruqayqa bint Sayfi, the mother of Makhrama ibn Nawfal, warned the Messenger of God about the Quraysh's plot to kill the Messenger during the night. The Messenger of God left his bed and Ali ibn Abu Talib spent the night in it.

RUQAYYA BINT MUHAMMAD IBN ABD ALLAH

Mother: Khadija
Father: Prophet
Wife of: Uthman ibn Affan

Ibn Sad also relates the following:

She was promised to Utba ibn Abi Lahab ibn Abd al-Muttalib before the beginning of the mission. When God sent down the verses of Chapter 111, '*Perish the hands of Abu Lahab*,' his father, Abu Lahab, said to his son, 'My head is unlawful to your head if you do not divorce his daughter.'

They parted without the marriage ever being consummated. She became Muslim when her mother, Khadija bint Khuwaylid, became Muslim. She and her sisters gave allegiance to the Messenger of God when the women gave it.

She married Uthman ibn Affan. They made the migration to Abyssinia both times. The Messenger of God said, 'They are the first to migrate for God Almighty since the time of Prophet Lot.'

She suffered a miscarriage in the first migration and then bore Uthman a son after that whom they named Abd Allah. Uthman had that agnomen in Islam. The child lived to the age of two when a cock pecked his face. His face became swollen and he died. She did not bear any more children.

She migrated to Madinah after her husband, Uthman, when the Messenger had migrated. She fell ill when the Messenger was preparing for the Battle of Badr. The Messenger of God left Uthman ibn Affan behind to care for her. She died while the Messenger was at the Battle of Badr in the month of Ramadan, seventeen months after his migration. Zayd ibn Haritha brought the news of the Muslim victory at the Battle of Badr to the people of Madinah. When he entered the city with the news, the earth was being leveled over Ruqayya's grave.

Ibn Abbas relates that when Ruqayya, the daughter of the

Messenger of God, died, the Prophet said, 'Join our forerunner, Uthman ibn Mazun.'

The women wept over Ruqayya. Umar ibn al-Khattab came and began to hit them with his whip. The Prophet took hold of his hand and said, 'Let them weep, Umar.' Then he said, 'Weep, but beware of the braying of satan. Whatever comes from the heart and eye is from God and mercy. Whatever comes from the hand and tongue is from satan.'

Fatima sat on the edge of the grave beside the Prophet and began to weep. The Prophet wiped the tears from her eyes with the end of his garment.

Muhammad ibn Sad relates that he mentioned this Tradition to Muhammad ibn Umar al-Waqadi. Muhammad ibn Umar said that what he considered to be reliable from all transmissions was that Ruqayya died while the Messenger of God was at Badr and that he was not present at her burial. Perhaps this Tradition is about another of the daughters of the Prophet whose burial he attended. If it is about Ruqayya and it is confirmed, then perhaps he came to her grave after he arrived in Madinah, and the women wept for her after that.

RUQAYYA BINT THABIT IBN KHALID
Father: Thabit ibn Khalid
Tribe: Khazraj, Malik ibn al-Najjar clan
Muhammad ibn Umar al-Waqadi mentions her accepting Islam.

RUZAYNA, FREEDWOMAN OF THE PROPHET
Tribe: Non-Qurayshi Emigrant
Ibn Sad also relates the following:
She accepted Islam and gave her allegiance to the Messenger of God. She transmitted Traditions regarding fasting, Ashura, and the Dajjal.

S

SABA, AL (SEE HAWWA BINT RAFI IBN IMR AL-QAYS)

SABA BINT AL-SALT IBN HABIB
Father: Salt ibn Habib, al-
Wife of: Prophet
Alternative Name: Sana bint as-Salt ibn Habib
Ibn Sad also relates the following:
She accepted Islam and gave her allegiance to the Messenger of

God. She was proposed to the Prophet for marriage, but the marriage was never consummated.

It is related that a man from the group of Abd Allah ibn Khazim al-Sulami said that the Messenger of God married Sana bint al-Salt al-Sulamiyya, but she died before the marriage could be consummated.

Abd Allah ibn Ubayd ibn Umayr al-Laythi relates that a man from the Sulaym tribe went to the Prophet. He said to the Messenger that he has a daughter whose beauty and intelligence make him begrudge her to any but him. The Messenger wanted to marry her. Then he added that she has not been afflicted by any illness.

The Prophet said to him, 'We have no need of your daughter who comes to us bearing her errors. There is no good in property from which the poor-due is not taken and in a body which does not suffer harm.'

SABA BINT JABAL IBN AMR, AL-
Mother: Hind bint Sahl of Juhayna
Father: Jabal ibn Amr
Children: Ubayd
Sister of: Muadh ibn Jabal
Wife of: Thalaba ibn Ubayd
Tribe: Khazraj, Udi ibn Sad clan
    Ibn Sad also relates the following:
    She accepted Islam and gave her allegiance to the Messenger of God.

SABA BINT SAHL IBN ZAYD, AL-
Father: Sahl ibn Zayd
Tribe: Aws, Abd al-Ashhal clan
    Muhammad ibn Umar al-Waqadi mentions her accepting Islam.

SABA IBN SUFYAN (SEE FATIMA BINT DAHHAK)

SAFIYYA BINT ABD AL-MUTTALIB IBN HISHAM
Mother: Hala bint Wuhayb ibn Abd al-Manaf
Father: Abd al-Muttalib
Children: Safi; Zubayr
Sister of: Abd Allah, half-sister of Hamza
Wife of: Harith ibn Harb ibn Umayya; Awwam ibn Khuwaylid
Tribe: Quraysh
    Ibn Sad also relates the following:
    Safiyah, a paternal aunt of the Messenger, killed a Jew who was spying around their castle during the Battle of the Trenches. She was a very brave and fearless woman. The Prophet had great regard for

her. When Muslim forces lost at the Battle of Uhud, she left Madinah with a spear in her hand, arousing a sense of shame and dishonor among those who were returning from the battlefield. She said with anger to the soldiers that they had fled leaving the Messenger of God (on the battlefield).

When the Prophet saw her, he said to her brave son Zubayr, 'Do not let her see the dead body of her brother Hamzah.'

When she came to know of it, she said that she knew her brother's dead body had been mutilated. She said that she did not like that, but she would patiently bear it.

Hafiz Ibn Hajar relates that she recited funeral laments at his martyrdom. She and the Prophet grew up in same home. They were very close. At his death, she wrote,

O God's Messenger, you were our hope;

Today every mourner should weep for him;

Alas! Had God kept our master among us;

How fortuante we would have been

But the Command of God is not to be said again.

Historians have said she was a very intelligent, thoughtful, brave and patient woman. She held a distinctive position in respect of her genealogy, words and deeds.

Safiyya became Muslim and gave allegiance to the Messenger of God. She migrated to Madinah and the Messenger of God assigned her forty weights from Khaybar.

Urwa relates that when the Messenger of God went out from Madinah to fight his enemy, he left his wives and womenfolk in the fortress of Hasan ibn Thabit because it was the most secure fortress of Madinah. Hasan remained behind on the Day of Uhud. A Jew came up close to the fortress, listening and spying. Safiyya bint Abd al-Muttalib told Hasan to go down and kill him. Hasan seemed to dread doing that. She took a pole, went down and stealthily opened the door. She then attacked him, struck him with the pole and killed him.

Hisham ibn Urwa relates that Safiyya bint Abd al-Muttalib went out with a spear in her hand on the day of the Battle of Uhud when the Muslim troops were fleeing the battlefield. She shook the spear at the faces of the people, telling them not to flee from the Messenger of God.

When the Messenger saw her, he said to her son, 'Zubayr, the woman!' Hamza's belly had been slit open, and the Messenger of God did not want her to see him. She was his sister. Zubayr told his mother to go back. She refused to listen. She went and looked at Hamza.

Safiyya bint Abd al-Muttalib was buried in Baqi cemetery in the courtyard of the house of al-Mughira ibn Shuba at the place of ablution. Safiyya died during the caliphate of Umar ibn al-Khattab. She related Traditions from the Messenger of God.

SAFIYYA BINT AL-ZUBAYR
Mother: Atika bint Abu Wahb ibn Amr
Father: Zubayr, al-
Tribe: Makhzum
Ibn Sad also relates the following:
She accepted Islam and gave her allegiance to the Messenger of God.

SAFIYYA BINT BASHSHAMA IBN NADLA
Father: Bashshama ibn Nadla
Ibn Sad also relates the following:
She accepted Islam and gave her allegiance to the Messenger of God. The Prophet proposed to her, but never married her.

SAFIYYA BINT HUYAYY IBN AKHTAB
Mother: Barra bint Samwail
Father: Huyayy ibn Akhtab
Sister of: Rifaa ibn Samwail of Qurayza clan
Wife of: Sallam ibn Mishkam al-Qurazi; Kinana ibn ar-Rabi al-Nadiri;
 Messenger of God
Tribe: Jewish tribe of Harun ibn Imran
Ibn Sad relates the following:
When the Messenger of God attacked Khaybar and God gave him their property, Safiyya bint Huyayy and a cousin of hers were taken captive. He commanded Bilal to take them to his camel. The Messenger of God was given the best of all booty. Safiyya was part of what he chose on the day of Khaybar. The Prophet offered to free her if she chose God and His Messenger. She said that she chose God and His Messenger.

She became Muslim. He set her free. Her freedom was her dowry. He married her. He saw a greenish mark near her eye. He asked, 'What is this?'

She said that she had had a dream in which she saw the moon come from Yathrib and fall into her room. She mentioned it to her husband, Kinana. He said that it meant she wanted marry to the king from Madinah and struck her.

She observed a waiting period of one menstrual period. The Messenger of God did not leave Khaybar until she was free of menstruation. Then the Messenger of God left Khaybar without marrying her. When the camel was brought up to the Messenger so that he could leave, the Messenger placed his foot for Safiyya so that she could put her foot on his thigh. She refused and placed her knee on his thigh.

The Messenger shielded and carried her behind him. He put his cloak over her back and face. Then he tied it under his foot. He carried her and put her in the position of his wives. Then he went to a site called Tabbar six miles from Khaybar, meaning to marry her. She refused him. The Messenger of God felt annoyed on that account.

When he was at al-Sahba, which was about twelve miles from Khaybar, the Messenger of God said to Umm Sulaym, 'Attend to your companion and comb her hair.' The Messenger of God wanted to wed her there.

Umm Sulaym relates that they had no tent with them so she took two robes or cloaks and tied them to a tree to make a shelter. Then she combed her hair and perfumed her.

Umm Sulaym al-Aslamiyya also relates that she was among those who were present when the Messenger of God married Safiyya. She said that they combed her hair and perfumed her. A girl collected some jewelery from the women. There was no scent more fragrant than what was used that night. The Messenger of God came to her. She stood up for him. Umm Sulaym had told her to do that. They left her and the Messenger of God. They were married and he spent the night with her. In the morning she wanted to wash. They took her to the waters of the army. She took care of what she needed and washed. Umm Sulaym asked her about her night with the Messenger. She said that he was happy with her and did not sleep that night. He kept talking with her through the night. He said to her, 'What moved you to do what you did when I wanted to set up the first camp and consummate the marriage with you?'

She said that she was afraid for the Messenger because of the proximity of the Jews. That increased her position with the Messenger. The Messenger gave a wedding feast for her there. The feast consisted only of *hays*. Their bowls were only leather-mats. The people ate on that day and then the Messenger traveled to al-Qusabiyya which was a distance of sixteen miles.

Anas ibn Malik relates that Safiyya bint Huyayy had fallen to the share of Dihya al-Kalbi. The Messenger of God was told that a beautiful woman has fallen to the share of Dihya al-Kalbi. The Messenger bought her for seven camels. He gave her to Umm Sulaym to wait with her through her waiting period.

Abul-Walid relates in his Tradition that the wedding feast of the Messenger consisted of ghee, cheese and dates. Leather mats were placed on the earth and then the fat, cheese and dates were laid down on them.

Yazid ibn Harun relates in his Tradition, that the people said that they did not know whether the Messenger had married her, or whether she was his captive. When he carried her, he shielded her and put her behind him, so the people knew that he had married her. When they were near Madinah, the people hurried and the Messenger hurried. They used to do that. The camel stumbled. The Messenger fell, and she fell with him. The wives of the Messenger looked and prayed that God put this Jewess far away. The Messenger of God got up and shielded her and put her behind him.

Jafar relates that when Safiyya was brought to the Prophet, he said to her, 'Your father was one of the Jews with the strongest enmity towards me until God killed him.'

She said that God says in the Quran, *"No bearer shall bear another's burden"* (53:38).'

The Messenger said to her, 'Choose. If you choose Islam, I will keep you for myself. If you choose Judaism, then I will free you so that you can join your people.'

She said that she desired Islam and had believed in him before he called to sit on his mount. She said she had no desire for Judaism. She had neither father nor brother. She said to the Messenger that he had given her a choice between disbelief and Islam, and that she preferred God and His Messenger to freedom and returning to her people.

The Messenger kept her for himself. Her mother was one of the women of the Qaynuqa tribe of the Amr clan. The Prophet was never heard to mention her father with even a syllable which she might dislike. She had previously been married to Sallam ibn Mishkam who had divorced her. She had then married Kinana ibn Abil-Huqayq who died at the Battle of Khaybar.

Anas ibn Malik relates that Safiyya went to Dihya in his share of the spoils. He said that they began to praise her to the Messenger, saying that they had seen an unparalleled woman among the captives.

The Messenger of God sent for her. He paid Dihya a satisfactory amount and then handed her over to the mother of Anas ibn Malik. He told her to put Safiyya in order.

The Messenger of God left Khaybar and put her behind him. He stopped. Then he put a tent over her and said, 'Whoever has some extra provision should bring it.' They brought mash, dates and ghee until they had a pile of food. They made *hays* and began to eat and drink with him. That was the wedding feast of the Messenger for her.

When we saw the walls of Madinah, we were elated. We speeded up our mounts. We saw the walls and speeded up our mounts again. The Messenger speeded his mount with her riding behind him, but his mount stumbled. The Messenger of God fell and she fell.

He said, 'No one was looking at him or her. The Messenger shielded her. They went to him. He said, 'I'm not hurt' They entered

Madinah. The slavegirls of his wives came out looked at her, gloating at her fall.

Anas ibn Malik relates when he arrived with the Messenger of God, the Messenger had Safiyya behind him on his camel. Abu Talha and Anas ibn Malik were behind them. Suddenly the camel of the Messenger stumbled. Both he and the woman fell. Abu Talha rushed from his camel and went to the Prophet, asking if he was hurt.

He said, 'No. See to the woman.'

Abu Talha threw his garment over his face, went to Safiyya and threw his garment over her. She got up. He put her on his mount. They rode until they were at Madinah or looking down on Madinah.

The Messenger said, 'Coming, repenting, worshipping our Lord, praising.' This was recited until they reached Madinah.

Anas ibn Malik relates that the Messenger freed Safiyya and married her. Thabit al-Bannani asked him what her dowry was. Ansa ibn Malik said that her freedom was her dowry. The Messenger set her free and married her.'

Sahl ibn Sad relates that when the Messenger consummated his marriage with Safiyya bint Huyayy ibn Akhtab, he had a feast. He was asked of what the feast consisted. Sahl ibn Sad said of dates and mush. He said that on that day he saw Safiyya giving people *nabidh* to drink. Someone asked him what was this *nabidh* which she was giving them to drink.

They said that it was dates which were soaked overnight in a stone vessel or pot. In the morning Safiyya gave it to the people to drink.

Abd Allah ibn Umar relates that when the Prophet arrived with Safiyya, he saw Ayisha standing veiled in the middle of the people. He recognized her, joined her and took hold of her garment, saying, 'O fair one, what did you see?' Ayisha said that she had seen a Jewess.

Abu Hurayra relates that when the Messenger of God consummated the marriage with Safiyya, Abu Ayyub spent the night at the door of the Prophet. In the morning, the Messenger of God said the phrase 'God is Greater,' and Abu Ayyub appeared with his sword. He said that she was a girl new to Islam and marriage. The Messenger had killed her father, brother and husband so he did not trust her with him. The Messenger of God laughed and spoke kindly to him.

Ata ibn Yasir relates that when the Messenger of God came from Khaybar with Safiyya, he put her in one of the houses of Haritha ibn al-Numan. The women of the Helpers heard about her and her beauty. She began to stare at her. Ayisha came in a veil and went into the room where she was. The Prophet recognized her. When she left, the Messenger went after her. He asked, 'What did you think of her, Ayisha?' Ayisha responded by saying that she had seen a Jewess.

He said, 'Do not say this, Ayisha. She has become Muslim, and she is a good Muslim.'

Umm Sinan al-Aslamiyya relates that when they arrived in Madinah, they did not enter their houses until they had taken Safiyya to her house. The women Emigrants and Helpers had heard of her and went to her frequently. Umm Sinan says that she saw four of the wives of the Prophet in veils: Zaynab bint Jahsh, Hafsa, Ayisha and Juwayriyya. She heard Zaynab say to Juwayriyya that she could only think that this girl would consume all the time of the Messenger of God. Juwayriyya said that she was one of those who had little luck with husbands.

Ayisha relates that the Messenger of God was on a journey when Safiyya's camel got sick. Zaynab had some extra camels so the Messenger said, 'Safiyya's camel is sick. Could you give her one of your camels?' Zaynab refused to give a camel to a Jewess.

The Messenger did not go to Zaynab throughout the months of Dhul-Hijja and Muharram. Two or three months passed in which he did not go to her. She said that the Messenger did not come to her until she despaired of him and moved her bed. Then one day in the middle of the day she saw the shadow of the Messenger advancing.

Ibn Abi Awn relates that Ayisha and Safiyya insulted each other. The Messenger of God said to Safiyya, 'Why didn't you say, "My father is Aaron and my uncle is Moses?' Ayisha boasted about being better than her.

Said ibn al-Musayyab relates that Safiyya bint Huyayy came with some gold earrings and gave some of them to Fatima and the women with her.

Ata relates that the Messenger of God did not assign a share to Safiyya bint Huyayy.

Zuhri relates that Safiyya was one of his wives. He used to assign her a share as he did to his other wives.

Umar and **Abu Hurayra** relate that the Messenger of God set up a partition for her and used to allot her a share as he did for his other wives.

Muhammad ibn Umar al-Waqadi relates that the Messenger of God assigned her eighty weights of dates from Khaybar and twenty weights of *wasq* of barley or wheat.

Zayd ibn Aslam relates that when the Prophet of God was in his final illness, his wives gathered around him. Safiyya bint Huyayy said to the Messenger that she wished that she were suffering instead of him.

The other wives of the Prophet winced at that. The Messenger of God looked at them and said, 'Rinse out your mouths!' They asked why they should do that. He said, 'Whoever of you winked at her companion, by God, Safiyya spoke truthfully.'

Kinana relates that he was leading Safiyya to defend Uthman. Ashtar met her. He struck the face of her mule until it turned aside. She said to take her back because this one would not disgrace her.

Hasan relates that she then placed a plank between her house and that of Uthman to convey food and drink to him.'

Yahya ibn Said relates that Safiyya left a legacy to one of her Jewish relatives.

Husayn ibn Abd al-Rahman relates that he saw an old man who was an heir of Safiyya bint Huyayy. He became Muslim after her death, and thus he did not inherit directly from her.

Muhammad ibn Umar al-Waqadi relates that Safiyya bint Huyayy died in AD 670/AH 50 during the caliphate of Muawiya ibn Abu Sufyan.

Abu Salama ibn Abd al-Rahman relates that Safiyya bint Huyayy left 100,000 dirhams after the sale of her land and goods. She left a third of that as a legacy to her nephew who was Jewish. Abu Salama said that they refused to give it to him until Ayisha, the wife of the Prophet, spoke to them saying that they should fear God and give him his bequest. So he took a third of it, which amounted to thirty-three and a half thousand dirhams. She had a house which she gave as charity during her lifetime.'

Amina bint Abi Qays al-Ghifariyya relates that she was one of the women who conducted Safiyya to the Messenger of God. She heard Safiyya say that almost seventeen years had gone by since she was married to the Messenger.

Safiyya died in AD 672/AH 52 during the caliphate of Muawiya ibn Abu Sufyan and was buried at the Baqi cemetery.

SAFIYYA BINT THABIT

Mother: Kabsha bint Aws
Father: Thabit
Wife of: Abd al-Rahman ibn Aws al-Khatbi
Tribe: Aws, Khatma ibn Jusham clan
Ibn Sad also relates the following:
She accepted Islam and gave her allegiance to the Messenger of God.

SAFIYYAH BINT RABIA

Father: Rabia
Children: Shammas
Sister of: Utbah ibn Rabiah; Shaibah ibn Rabiah
Wife of: Uthman ibn al-Sharid Makhzumi
She is not mentioned by Ibn Sad. Her brothers were two of the

famous Quraysh leaders who were both killed in the Battle of Badr. She had been married to Uthman ibn al-Sharid Makhzumi who died before the beginning of the mission, leaving an infant son, Shammas. Shammas accepted Islam as did his mother in spite of the opposition of her brothers. She suffered a great deal at the hands of her brothers but remained steadfast. She migrated to Abyssinia with her son. They then migrated to Madinah and lived with Mubashir ibn Abd Muzar Ansari. Her son was wounded at the Battle of Uhud and later died.

SAHLA BINT SUHAYL IBN AMR
Mother: Fatima bint Abd al-Uzza
Father: Suhayl ibn Amr
Children: Muhammad; Salit; Amir; Salim
Wife of: Abu Hudhayfa ibn Utba; Abd Allah ibn al-Aswad; Shammakh
   ibn Said; Abd al-Rahman ibn Awf
Tribe: Quraysh
Ibn Sad also relates the following:
She accepted Islam early on in Makkah and gave her allegiance to the Messenger. She migrated to Abyssinia in both emigrations with her husband, Abu Hudhayfa ibn Utba. Sahla bint Suhayl had adopted Salim, the freedman of Abu Hudhayfa. He used to visit her. The Messenger allowed her to give him the amount of five nursings of her milk placed in a bowl from which he drank.

It is related that Sahla bint Suhayl, the wife of Abu Hudhayfa, told the Messenger that she used to consider Salim to be her son. He visited her when she was lightly dressed and he saw some of her.

The Messenger of God said, 'Give him five drinks of your milk and then he can visit you.'

Zuhri relates that Ayisha said that Salim informed her that he visited Umm Kulthum bint Abu Bakr so that she could give him five drinks of milk placed in a bowl so that he could visit Ayisha and record Traditions from her. He was given the equivalent of two or three drinks and then she became ill and he did not visit her.

Umm Salama relates that the wives of the Messenger refused to accept this. They said that this was a special allowance from the Messenger of God for Sahla bint Suhayl only.

Amra bint Abd al-Rahman relates that the wife of Abu Hudhayfa ibn Utba spoke about Salim, the freedman of Abu Hudhayfa, to the Messenger of God. She mentioned the fact that he came in where she was. The Messenger of God commanded her to give him some of her milk. She did so although he was old and had been present at the Battle of Badr.

Zuhri relates that she used to fill a vessel or a cup with her milk. Salim drank it for five consecutive days. Then he used to visit her when she was uncovered. It was an allowance which the Messenger of God made for Sahla bint Suhayl.

SAHLA (SEE UMM SULAYM BINT MILHAN IBN KHALID)

SAIDA BINT BASHIR IBN UBAYD
Father: Bashir ibn Ubayd
Tribe: Aws, Amr ibn Awf ibn Malik ibn Aws clan
Ibn Sad also relates the following:
She accepted Islam and gave her allegiance to the Messenger of God.

SAKHRA BINT ABU SUFYAN IBN HARB
Mother: Safiyya bint Abi Amr
Father: Abu Sufyan ibn Harb
Children: Children but no names mentioned
Wife of: Said ibn al-Akhnas
Ibn Sad also relates the following:
She accepted Islam and gave her allegiance to the Messenger of God.

SALMA
Wife of: Abu Rafi
Tribe: Quraysh
She accepted Islam and gave her allegiance to the Messenger of God. A freedwoman of the Prophet, she was the midwife for Khadija and Mariyah, the Copt. She is not mentioned by Ibn Sad.

SALAMA BINT AL-HURR
Father: Hurr, al-
Tribe: Non-Quraysh
Ibn Sad also relates the following:
She accepted Islam and gave her allegiance to the Messenger of God. She related a Tradition from the Prophet.

SALMA BINT AMR
Mother: Hind bint al-Mundhir
Father: Amr
Sister of: Mundhir ibn Amr, al-
Wife of: Uqba ibn Rafi
Tribe: Khazraj, Saida ibn Kab clan
Ibn Sad also relates the following:
She accepted Islam and gave her allegiance to the Messenger of God. Her brother at was present at Aqaba and the Battle of Badr.

SALMA BINT ASLAM (SEE UMM ABD ALLAH)

SALAMA BINT MASUD IBN KAB
Mother: Adam bint al-Jamuh
Father: Masud ibn Kab
Children: Bore children, names not given
Sister of: Huwaysa, Muhayyisa, Ahwas, al-
Wife of: Murshida ibn Jabr
Tribe: Aws, al-Haritha ibn al-Khazraj clan
Ibn Sad also relates the following:
She accepted Islam and gave her allegiance to the Messenger of God.

SALMA BINT UMAYS
Mother: Hind (Khawla bint Awf)
Father: Umays
Children: Umara; Abd Allah ibn Shaddad
Sister of: Asma
Wife of: Hamza ibn Abdul Muttalib;
　　　　　Shaddad ibn al-Had al-Laythi (half-brother of Hamza)
Tribe: Non-Qurayshi Emigrant
Ibn Sad also relates the following:
She accepted Islam and gave her allegiance to the Messenger of God. Shaddad was the son of the maternal aunt of Abbas by Umm Fadl and son of the aunt of Khalid ibn al-Walid.

It is related that Subaya al-Aslamiyya gave birth some days after the death of her husband. She went to the Messenger and asked for permission to marry. He gave her permission and she married.

Ubayd Allah ibn Abd Allah ibn Utba relates that Abu Sanabil ibn Bakak reproved Subaya bint al-Harith. She told him that she had gone to the Messenger of God and he had told her to marry.

Abu Salama ibn Abd al-Rahman relates that when he and Ibn Abbas argued about the Traditon of Subaya al-Aslamiyya. Ibn Abbas said to his slave, Kurayb, 'Go to Umm Salama and ask her.'

She said that Subaya bint al-Harith al-Aslamiyya gave birth twenty days after the death of her husband. The Messenger of God commanded her to marry. Abu Sanabil was one of those who proposed to her.

SALMA BINT YIAR
Father: Yiar
Sister of: Thubayta bint Yiar
Tribe: Aws, Ubayd ibn Zayd ibn Malik ibn Awf clan
Ibn Sad also relates the following:

She accepted Islam and gave her allegiance to the Messenger of God.

SALMA BINT ZAYD IBN TAYM
Mother: Rahhala bint al-Mundhir of Khazraj, al-
Father: Zayd ibn Taym
Wife of: Amr ibn Abbad
Tribe: Aws, Jaadira, Said ibn Murra clan
Ibn Sad also relates the following:
She accepted Islam and gave her allegiance to the Messenger of God.

SARRA BINT NABHAN AL-GHANAWIYYA
Father: Nabban al-Ghanawiyya
Tribe: Non-Quraysh
Ibn Sad also relates the following:
She accepted Islam and gave her allegiance to the Messenger of God. She related Traditions from the Prophet.

SAWDA BINT ABU DUBAYS AL-JAHMIYYA
Father: Abu Dubays al-Jahmiyya
Tribe: Non-Qurayshi Emigrant
Ibn Sad also relates the following:
She accepted Islam after the migration and gave her allegiance to the Messenger of God. Her father was also a Companion.

SAWDA BINT HARITHA IBN AL-NUMAN
Mother: Umm Khalid bint Khalid
Father: Haritha ibn al-Numan
Wife of: Abd Allah ibn Abi Haram
Tribe: Khazraj, Malik ibn al-Najjar clan

SAWDA BINT ZAMA IBN QAYS IBN ABD AL-SHAMS
Mother: Shamush bint Qays ibn Amr from al-Najjar, al-
Father: Zama ibn Qays ibn Abd al-Shams
Wife of: Sakran ibn Amr ibn Abd al-Shams, al-;
       Messenger of God
Ibn Sad also relates the following:
She accepted Islam and gave her allegiance to the Messenger of God. She migrated to Abyssinia in the second migration.
Bukayr relates that Sakran ibn Amr went to Makkah from Abyssinia with his wife, Sawda bint Zamia. He died in Makkah, leaving her a widow. When she became lawful [i.e. after the waiting peri-

od], the Messenger of God proposed to her. She said she would do whatever the Messenger wanted.

The Messenger of God said, 'Tell a man of your family to give you in marriage.' He told Hatib ibn Amr ibn Abd al-Shams to marry her to him. She was the first woman that the Messenger of God married after Khadija.

Abd Allah ibn Muslim relates that the Messenger of God married Sawda in Ramadan after the death of Khadija and before he married Ayisha. He consummated the marriage with her in Makkah. She migrated to Madinah.

Ayisha relates that Sawda bint Zama grew old. The Messenger of God did not have much to do with her. She knew her position with the Messenger. He spent a lot of time with Ayisha. Sawda was afraid that he would divorce her, and she would lose her place with him. She told the Messenger that she gave her day with her to Ayisha. The Prophet kissed her. The following verse was revealed: *"If a woman fears evil treatment or aversion, on the part of her husband..."* (4:128).

Ayisha relates that Sawda gave his day and night to Ayisha wanting to please the Messenger of God.

Numan ibn Thabit al-Taymi relates that the Messenger of God said to Sawda bint Zama, 'Begin a waiting period.'

She waited for him on his way in the night and said to him that she did not have any desire for men, but she wanted to be raised up among his wives, so for him to reconsider and take her back. The Messenger of God took her back.

Qasim ibn Bazza relates that the Prophet sent to Sawda about divorcing her. When he came to her, she waited on his way by Ayisha's room. When she saw him, she asked why he wanted to divorce her. She thought that perhaps he had ill feelings towards her. The Messenger said that this was not so. She then begged him not to divorce her. She said she knew she was old and had no need of men, but she wanted to be raised up among his wives on the Day of Judgment.

The Messenger took her back. She said to him that she had given her day and night to Ayisha.

Mamar relates that he heard that the Messenger wanted to divorce Sawda. She spoke to him about it, saying that she had no urge for a husband, but that she wanted God to raise her up as his wife on the Day of Judgment.

Ayisha relates that there is no woman whose skin she would more prefer to be in than that of Sawda bint Zema, except she was a woman with some envy.

Ibrahim relates that Sawda said to the Messenger of God that she prayed behind him the day before and bowed behind him until she held her nose fearing that blood would drip from it. The Messenger laughed. She sometimes used to make him laugh at things.

Ayisha relates that one day the wives of the Messenger of God gathered. They asked the Messenger which of them would be the quickest to join him. He said, 'The one with the longest hand.'

They took a cane to measure. Sawda bint Zama bint Qays had the longest hand. The Messenger of God died. Sawda was the swiftest of them to join him. Later they knew that the length of her hand meant charity. She was a woman who loved to give charity.

Muhammad ibn Umar al-Waqadi reports that this Tradition relating to Sawda is weak and concerns Zaynab bint Jahsh. She was the first of the wives of the Messenger of God to join him. She died during the caliphate of Umar ibn al-Khattab while Sawda bint Zama was still alive. Abd Allah ibn Muslim tells us that Sawda died in Shawwal, 54 AH/September-October 624 CE, in Madinah during the caliphate of Muawiya ibn Abi Sufyan. Muhammad ibn Umar al-Waqadi considered this Tradition to be reliable.

Abu Hurayra relates that the Messenger of God went on the pilgrimage with his wives in the year of farewell pilgrimage. He said, 'It is this pilgrimage, and then there is confinement'

Abu Hurayra relates that all the wives of the Messenger of God went on the pilgrimage again except for Sawda bint Zema and Zaynab bint Jahsh. They said that they would not ride an animal after the Messenger had died.

Sawda relates that she performed the prescribed pilgrimage and the visit and remained in her house as God Almighty has commanded her.

Ayisha relates that on the night of Muzdalifa, Sawda asked the Messenger for permission to go on before him and before the crush of people. She was a slow woman.

Qasim relates that this means she was heavy.

Ayisha relates that he gave her permission. She left before the surge of the people. They waited until morning, and then they set off with the Messenger. Ayisha says that she wanted to ask permission from the Messenger to do as Sawda had done. She waited to go ahead of the people with his blessings.

Ayisha relates that she wanted to ask permission of the Messenger as Sawda had asked permission so that he could pray the dawn prescribed prayer at Mina before the people came. They asked her if Sawda had asked his permission. She said that she had. She added that Sawda was a slow, heavy woman and so he gave her permission.

Abd Allah ibn Abi Farwa relates that he heard Abd al-Rahman al-Araj say in his assembly in Madinah that the Messenger used to assign Sawda bint Zama eighty weights of dates and twenty weights of barley or wheat from Khaybar.

Muhammad ibn Umar al-Waqadi reports that Umar ibn al-Khattab sent a sack of dirhams to Sawda bint Zama. She asked what it was and they said that it was dirhams. She said that a sack is a container for dates. She asked her maid to bring her a scarf. She divided them.

Ibn Abbas relates that Sawda bint Zama was married to al-Sakran ibn Amr, the brother of Suhayl ibn Amr. She dreamt that the Prophet came and walked on the back of her neck. She told her husband about it. He said to her that if her dream were true, he would die and she would marry the Messenger of God. She denied this to herself.

Then another night she dreamt that the moon swooped down on her from the sky while she was lying down. She told her husband, and he said that if her dream were true, then he would shortly die and she would remarry after him.

That very day al-Sakran fell ill and died. Shortly thereafter she married the Messenger.

Abu Salama ibn Abd al-Rahman and **Yahya ibn Abd al-Rahman** said, 'Khawla bint Hakim ibn al-Awqas as-Salamiyya, the wife of Uthman ibn Mazun, went to the Messenger of God and said, 'Messenger of God, 'I see you are experiencing a lack with the loss of Khadija.'

He said, 'Yes. She was the mother of the family and the lady of the house.'

She said, 'Shall I propose to someone on your behalf ?'

He said, 'Yes, women are better at that.'

She proposed on his behalf to Sawda bint Zama of the Amir ibn Luayy clan and to Ayisha bint Abi Bakr. He married them. He consummated the marriage with Sawda in Makkah. Ayisaha at that time was six years old. He consummated her marriage later when he was in Madinah.

Abd Allah ibn Muslim relates that Sawda bint Zama died in Madinah in Shawwal of 54 AH during the caliphate of Muawiya ibn Abi Sufyan.

SHAMUS BINT ABU AMIR AL-RAHIB, AL-
Mother: Amiq bint al-Harith
Father: Abu Amir al-Rahib
Children: Asim ibn Thabit, Jamila
Wife of: Thabit ibn Abil Aflah
Tribe: Aws, Amr ibn Awf ibn Malik ibn Aws clan
Ibn Sad also relates the following:
She accepted Islam and gave her allegiance to the Messenger of

God. Her son, Asim, was present at the Battle of Badr and martyred at al-Raji.

SHAMUS BINT AL-NUMAN IBN AMIR, AL-
Mother: Salima bint Mutarrif
Father: Numan ibn Amir
Children: Bore children, names not given
Wife of: Abu Sufyan ibn al-Harith
Tribe: Aws, Amr ibn Awf ibn Malik ibn Aws clan

SHAMUS BINT AMR IBN HARAM, AL-
Mother: Hind bint Qays
Father: Amr ibn Haram
Children: Bore children, names not given
Wife of: Mahmud ibn Maslama
Tribe: Khazraj, Salama ibn Sad clan

SHAMUS BINT MALIK IBN QAYS, AL-
Mother: Suhayma bint Umaymir
Father: Malik ibn Qays

SHANBA BINT AMR
Father: Amr
Tribe: Ghifar
She is not mentioned by Ibn Sad. According to Tabari, the Messenger divorced her because she made a sceptical remark on the death of the Messenger's son, Ibrahim.

SHAQIQA BINT MALIK IBN QAYS
Mother: Suhayma bint Umaymir
Father: Malik ibn Qays
Children: Abd Allah, Umm Ubayd
Wife of: Harith ibn Suraqa, al-
Tribe: Khazraj, Najjar clan
Ibn Sad also relates the following:
She accepted Islam and gave her allegiance to the Messenger of God.

SHARAF BINT KHALIFA
Father: Khalifa
Sister of: Dihya ibn Khalifa l-Kalbi
Ibn Sad also relates the following:
She accepted Islam and gave her allegiance to the Messenger of God. The Prophet proposed to her, but never married her.
Sharqi al-Qattami relates that when Khawla bint al-Hudhayl

died, the Messenger married Sharaf bint Khalifa, the sister of Dihya, but the marriage was not consurnmated.

Abd al-Rahman ibn Sabit relates that the Messenger of God proposed to a woman of Kalb. He sent Ayisha to look at her. She went and came back. The Messenger of God asked her, 'What did you see?'

She said, 'I did not see anything beneficial.'

The Messenger of God said to her, 'You saw something beneficial. You saw a mole on her cheek with every hair trembling on account of you.'

She said, 'Messenger of God, nothing is hidden from you.'

Mujahid relates that when the Messenger of God proposed and was rejected, he did not repeat the offer. When he proposed to a woman who first consulted her father, he would say to her, 'We have joined someone else.'

SHAYMA BINT HARITH

Father: Harith
Sister of: Foster-sister of Prophet

She is not mentioned by Ibn Sad. It is reported that Shayma was with the wet-nurse of the Messenger, Halima, at the same time that he was. She used to take care of Muhammad and sing lullabies to him.

When the Hawazin and Thaqif tribes were defeated in the Battle of Hunayn, Shayma was taken captive along with other members of these tribes. When she was brought before the Messenger, she told him that she was his foster-sister. She showed him a mark on her shoulder which the Messenger recognized. Recalling his childhood, tears filled his eyes. He spread his cloak on the ground for Shayma and treated her with great respect and honor. He said to her, 'Sister, if you want to stay with me, you are welcome. If you want to return to your tribe, you are free to do so.'

She chose to return to her tribe. He sent her along with some money, three slaves, one maid and a goat.

SHIFA BINT ABD ALLAH IBN ABD AL-SHAMS, AL-

Mother: Fatimah bint Wahb
Father: Abd Allah ibn Abd al-Shams
Children: Sulayman ibn Abi Hathma; Masruq ibn Hudhayfa
Wife of: Abu Hathma ibn Hudhayfa
Tribe: Quraysh

Ibn Sad also relates the following:

She accepted Islam and gave her allegiance to the Messenger of God. She is mentioned as having been very intelligent and learned. The Messenger used to visit her. Once she came to the Prophet and said she used to invoke spells against ant bites.

SHIFA BINT **A**WF, AL-
Mother: Salma bint Amir of Khuzaa
Father: Awf
Children: Abd al-Rahman, al-Aswad, Atika, Ama
Wife of: Awf ibn Abd al-Awf
Tribe: Quraysh
Ibn Sad also relates the following:
She accepted Islam and gave her allegiance to the Messenger of God. Her son freed a slave on behalf of his mother when she died. A Tradition is related regarding this.
Shifa was one of the women emigrants. The *Sunnah* about setting free on behalf of a dead person has come from her. She died during the lifetime of the Messenger.   •
Abd al-Rahman ibn Awf relates that he asked the Messenger if he could set a slave free on behalf of his mother. The Messenger of God said, "Yes," and he freed a slave on her behalf.

SHUMAYLA BINT AL-**H**ARITH
Mother: Uthayla bint Abd al-Mundhir
Father: Harith, al-
Children: Khalid, Bashira
Sister of: Abu Lubaba ibn Abd al-Mundhir
Wife of: Thabit ibn al-Numan
Tribe: Aws, Zafar clan
Ibn Sad also relates the following:
She accepted Islam and gave her allegiance to the Messenger of God.

SUAD BINT **R**AFI IBN **M**UAWIYYA
Mother: Umm al-Rabi bint Malik
Father: Rafi ibn Muawiyya
Children: Abu Umama Asad, chief of Najjar clan, Sad, Masud, Ruayba, Furaya
Wife of: Zurara ibn Adas
Tribe: Khazraj
Ibn Sad also relates the following:
She accepted Islam and gave her allegiance to the Messenger of God.

SUAD BINT **R**AFI (SEE **U**MM **S**ALAMA, WIFE OF **A**SLAM IBN **H**ARISH)

SUAD BINT **S**ALAMA IBN **Z**UHAYR
Mother: Umm Qays bint Haram
Father: Salama ibn Zuhayr
Wife of: Jubayr ibn Sakhr

Tribe: Khazraj, Salama ibn Sad clan

Ibn Sad also relates the following:

She accepted Islam and gave her allegiance to the Messenger of God. She asked the Prophet to receive the allegiance of what was in her womb. He said that she was the free of the free.

SUAYDA BINT ABD AL-AMR IBN MASUD

Mother: Sumayra bint Qays, al-
Father: Abd al-Amr ibn Masud
Children: Abd Allah, Jamila
Sister of: Numan, al-, Dahhak, al-
Wife of: Abul Yasar Kab ibn Amr of the Banu Salama of Khazraj; Kabibn Zayd
Tribe: Khazraj, Dar ibn al-Najjar, al-
Alternative Name: Umm Riya

Ibn Sad also relates the following:

She accepted Islam and gave her allegiance to the Messenger of God. Both of her brothers were present at the Battle of Badr.

SUBAYA BINT AL-HARITH AL-ASLAMIYYA

Father: Harith al-Aslamiyya
Wife of: Sad ibn Khawla
Tribe: Non-Qurayshi

Ibn Sad also relates the following:

She accepted Islam and gave her allegiance to the Messenger of God. She remarried twenty days after birth of a child when husband had died before the birth of child.

Subaya al-Aslamiyya relates that she gave birth some days after the death of her husband. She went to the Messenger and asked for permission to marry, and he gave her permission and she married.

Ubayd Allah ibn Abd Allah ibn Utba relates that Abu Sanabil ibn Bakak reproved Subaya bint al-Harith. She told him that she had gone to the Messenger, and that he had told her to marry.

Abu Salama ibn Abd al-Rahman relates that when he and Ibn Abbas argued about the Traditon of Subaya al-Aslamiyya. Ibn Abbas said to his slave, Kurayb to go to Umm Salama and ask her.

Umm Salama said that Subaya bint al-Harith al-Aslamiyya gave birth twenty days after the death of her husband. The Messenger commanded her to marry. Abu Sanabil was one of those who proposed to her.

SUDA BINT AWS IBN ADI

Mother: Layla bint Ubayd
Father: Aws ibn Adi
Children: Suwayd; Children, names not given

Wife of: Samit ibn Adi; Sahl ibn al-Harith
Ibn Sad also relates the following:
She accepted Islam and gave her allegiance to the Messenger of God.

SUHAILAH BINT MASUD ANSARIYAH (SEE SUHAYMA BINT MASUD IBN AWS)

SUHAYMA BINT ASLAM IBN HARISH
Mother: Suad bint Rafi
Father: Aslam ibn Harish
Sister of: Salama ibn Aslam
Wife of: Muhayyisa ibn Masud
Ibn Sad also relates the following:
She accepted Islam and gave her allegiance to the Messenger of God.

SUHAYMA BINT MASUD IBN AWS
Mother: Shamus bint Amr, al-
Father: Masud ibn Aws
Children: Abd al-Rahman, Umm Habib
Wife of: Jabir ibn Abd Allah, cousin
Tribe: Aws, Zafar clan
Alternative Name: Suhailah bint Masud Ansariyah
Ibn Sad also relates the following:
She accepted Islam and gave her allegiance to the Messenger of God.

SUKHTA BINT ASWAD IBN ABBAD
Mother: Humayma bint Ubayd
Father: Aswad ibn Abbad
Wife of: Mais ibn Qays; Ubayd ibn al-Mualla
Tribe: Khazraj, Salama ibn Sad clan
Ibn Sad also relates the following:
She accepted Islam and gave her allegiance to the Messenger of God.

SUKHTA BINT QAYS IBN ABU KAB
Mother: Naila bint Salama
Father: Qays ibn Abu Kab
Sister of: Sahl ibn Qays
Wife of: Harith ibn Suraqa, al-
Tribe: Khazraj, Salama ibn Sad clan
Ibn Sad also relates the following:
She accepted Islam and gave her allegiance to the Messenger of

God. Her brother was present at the Battle of Badr and martyred at the Battle of Uhud.

SULAFA BINT AL-BARA IBN MARUR

Mother: Humayma bint Sayfi
Father: Bara ibn Marur, al-
Children: Abd Allah, Abd al-Rahman
Wife of: Abu Qatada ibn Ribi
Tribe: Khazraj, Salama ibn Sad clan

Ibn Sad also relates the following:

She accepted Islam and gave her allegiance to the Messenger of God.

SUMAYKA BINT JABBAR IBN SAKHR

Mother: Umm al-Harith bint Malik
Father: Jabbar ibn Sakhr
Wife of: Numan ibn Jubayr
Tribe: Khazraj, Salama ibn Sad clan

Ibn Sad also relates the following:

She accepted Islam and gave her allegiance to the Messenger of God.

SUMAYRA BINT QAYS IBN MALIK, AL-

Mother: Salma bint al-Aswad
Father: Qays ibn Malik
Children: Numan, al-, Dahhak, al-, Qutba, Umm al-Riya; Salm, Umm al-Harith
Wife of: Abd Amr ibn Masud; Harith ibn Thalaba, al-

Ibn Sad also relates the following:

She accepted Islam and gave her allegiance to the Messenger of God. Her sons were present at the Battle of Badr and the Qutba expedition and killed at Bir Mauna. Her son, Salm, was present at the Battle of Badr and martyred at the Battle of Uhud.

SUMAYYA BINT KHUBBAT, CLIENT OF ABU HUDHAYFA

Children: Ammar ibn Yasar

Ibn Sad also relates the following:

She accepted Islam and gave her allegiance to the Messenger of God. She was one of those who was tortured for God to make her leave her faith. She did not do that but remained steadfast until Abu Jahl passed by her one day and stabbed her with a spear in her private parts causing her to die. She was the first to be martyred in Islam. She was a very old and frail woman. When Abu Jahl was killed in the

Battle of Badr, the Messenger of God said to Ammar ibn Yasar, 'God has killed your mother's murderer.'

Mujahid relates that the first person martyred in Islam was Sumayya, the mother of Ammar. Abu Jahl went to her and stabbed her with a spear in her private parts.

SUMAYYA BINT MABAD

Father: Mabad
Wife of: Abd Allah ibn Abi Ahmad
Tribe: Aws, Ubayd ibn Zayd ibn Malik ibn Awf clan

Ibn Sad also relates the following:

She accepted Islam and gave her allegiance to the Messenger of God.

SUNBULA BINT MAIS IBN QAYS

Mother: Sukhta bint Aws
Father: Mais ibn Qays
Sister of: Half-sister of Muadh and Aidh, sons of Mais
Wife of: Abu Ubada Sad ibn Uthman
Tribe: Khazraj, Zurayq ibn Amir clan

Ibn Sad also relates the following:

She accepted Islam and gave her allegiance to the Messenger of God. Her father, Mais, was present at the Battle of Badr.

T

TAMIMA BINT ABU SUFYAN IBN AL-HARITH

Mother: Shamus bint al-Numan, al-
Father: Abu Sufyan ibn al-Harith
Wife of: Abd Allah ibn Sahl
Tribe: Aws, Amr ibn Awf ibn Malik ibn Aws clan

Ibn Sad also relates the following:

She accepted Islam and gave her allegiance to the Messenger of God.

TAMIMA BINT WAHB

Father: Wahb
Wife of: Rifaa ibn Samwal; Abd al-Rahman ibn al-Zubayr
Tribe: Khazraj, Malik ibn al-Najjar clan

Ibn Sad also relates the following:

She accepted Islam and gave her allegiance to the Messenger of God. The Tradition regarding the necessity for a woman who has a final divorce from her husband to marry another husband before she is able to remarry the previous husband appeared in regard to her situation.

It is related that Rifaa ibn Samwal divorced his wife, Tamima bint Wahb, three times during the time of the Messenger of God. Then Abd al-Rahman ibn al-Zubayr married her and felt averse to her and could not consummate the marriage. He divorced her, and Rifaa, who had been her first husband, wanted to remarry her. This was mentioned to the Messenger of God, and he forbade him to marry her. He said, 'She is not lawful to you until she has tasted the sweetness [of intercourse].'

TAWAMA BINT UMAYYA IBN KHALAF, AL-
Mother: Layla bint Habib ibn Amr of Tamim clan
Father: Umayya ibn Khalaf
Children: Bore children, no names mentioned
Wife of: Asim ibn al-Jad al-Fizari
Tribe: Quraysh
Ibn Sad also relates the following:
She accepted Islam and gave her allegiance to the Messenger of God. Sulayman ibn Yasar relates that Tawama bint Umayya was divorced irrevocably and she asked Umar ibn al-Khattab about it and he made it a single divorce.

THUBAYTA BINT AL-RABI IBN AMR
Mother: Sahla bint Imrul Qays
Father: Rabi ibn Amr, al-
Children: Abd Allah, Kubbatha, Urraba
Wife of: Aws ibn Qayzi
Tribe: Aws, Haritha ibn al-Khazraj clan
Ibn Sad also relates the following:
She accepted Islam and gave her allegiance to the Messenger of God.

THUBAYTA BINT SALIT IBN QAYS
Mother: Sukhayla bint al-Simma
Father: Salit ibn Qays
Children: Abd al-Rahman, Salima, Maymuna
Wife of: Abd Allah ibn Sasaa
Tribe: Khazraj, Adi ibn al-Najjar clan
Ibn Sad also relates the following:
She accepted Islam and gave her allegiance to the Messenger of God.

THUBAYTA BINT YIAR
Father: Yiar

Wife of: Abu Hudhayfa ibn Utba
Tribe: Aws, Ubayd ibn Zayd ibn Malik ibn Awf clan
She freed Salim and then husband adopted him.
Ibn Sad also relates the following:
She accepted Islam and gave her allegiance to the Messenger of God. She is the one who freed Salim.

TUMADIR BINT AL-ASBAGH IBN AMR OF KALB

Mother: Juwayriyya bint Wabra of Kalb
Father: Asbagh ibn Amr of Kalb
Children: Abu Salama ibn Abd al-Rahman
Ibn Sad also relates the following:
She accepted Islam and gave her allegiance to the Messenger of God. She related Traditions from the Prophet.

Ibrahim ibn Abd al-Rahman relates that the Prophet sent Abd al-Rahman ibn Awf to Kalb. He said, 'If they respond to you, then marry the daughter of their king or the daughter of their chief.'

When Abd al-Rahman arrived, he called them to Islam. They responded. He established the *jiziya*. Then Abd al-Rahman ibn Awf married Tumadir bint al-Asbagh, the daughter of their king, and brought her to Madinah. She was the mother of Abu Salama ibn Abd al-Rahman.

Muhammad ibn Umar al-Waqadi reports that she was the first Kalbite woman to marry a Qurayshi. She only bore Abu Salama to Abd al-Rahman.

It is related that Tumadir had some bad qualities, and there were two divorce pronouncements against her. When Abd al-Rahman became ill, some words passed between him and her. He said to her that if she asked him for a divorce, he would divorce her. She asked for a divorce. He told her to tell him when she had menstruated.

When she had menstruated and become pure, she sent word to him. Her messenger passed by a member of his family. He called him and asked where he was going. He said that Tumadir had sent him to Abd al-Rahman to inform him that she had menstruated and become pure. He told him to go back and tell her not to do it because Abd al-Rahman would not take back his oath. He went and told her. She said that she would never take back her oath either and that he should go and tell this to her husband. He did so. Her husband divorced her as she had wanted.

Umm Kulthum relates that when Abd al-Rahman ibn Awf divorced his Kalbite wife, Tumadir, he gave her a black slave girl. He said that he gave her the use of her.

Talha ibn Abd Allah relates that Uthman ibn Affan let Tumadir bint al-Asbagh al-Kalbiyya inherit from Abd al-Rahman as he had divorced her in his final illness. It was a final divorce.

Sad ibn Ibrahim relates that Abd al-Rahman divorced Tumadir three times, and Uthman let her inherit from him after the end of the waiting period. Sad said that Abu Salama's mother was Tumadir bint al-Asbagh.

Muhammad ibn Umar al-Waqadi reports that when Zubayr ibn al-Awwam married Tumadir bint al-Asbagh al-Kalbiyya after Abd al-Rahman ibn Awf., she was only married to him a short time before he divorced her.

It is related that when Zubayr ibn al-Awwam divorced Tumadir bint al-Asbagh al-Kalbiyya, she had been with him for seven days. He did not delay divorcing her. She used to say that women should not be deceived by seven days considering what Zubayr has done to her.

U

UBADA BINT ABI NAILA SILKAN IBN SALAMA (SEE MUHAYYA BINT SILKAN)

UBAYYA BINT BASHIR (SEE UMAYYA)

UMAMA BINT ABIL AS IBN AL-RABI
Mother: Zaynab bint Muhammad
Father: Abil As ibn al-Rabi
Children: No children.
Sister of: Fatima, Umm Khulthum, Ruqiyya
Wife of: Ali ibn Abi Talib; Mughira ibn Nawfal, al-
Tribe: Quraysh
Ibn Sad also relates the following:

She accepted Islam and gave her allegiance to the Messenger of God. Abu Qatada was heard to say that while he was sitting at the door of the Messenger, he came out to them carrying Umama bint Abil As ibn al-Rabi. Her mother was Zaynab, daughter of the Messenger of God. She was a little girl.

He said that the Messenger of God prayed with her on his shoulder. He put her down when he bowed and picked her up when he stood up until he finished the prayer.

Abu Qatada ibn Ribi relates that he saw the Messenger of God pray while he was carrying Umama bint Abil As, his granddaughter, on his shoulder. He put her down when he bowed and picked her up when he stood up.

Abd Allah ibn al-Harith ibn Nawfal relates that the Messenger of God used to pray with Umama bint Abil As on his shoulder. He put her down when he bowed and picked her up when he stood up.

Ali ibn Zayd ibn Jidan relates that the Messenger of God went to his family with an onyx necklace. He said, 'I will give it to the one I love the most.'

The women thought that he would give it to Ayisha.

He called the daughter of Abul As by Zaynab and put it in her hand. There was a secretion from her eye, and he wiped it away with his hand.

Ayisha relates that the Negus gave the Messenger of God jewelery which included a gold ring. He accepted it but was about to turn away from it. He sent it to the daughter of his daughter Zaynab. He said, 'Adorn yourself with this, little daughter.'

It is related that Umama bint Abil As said to al-Mughira ibn Nawfal ibn al-Harith that Muawiya has proposed to her. He asked her if she would marry the son of the liver eater. She said she would. He said he would marry her and she agreed.

UMAMA BINT BISHR IBN WAQSH

Mother: Fatima bint Bishr of Khazraj
Father: Bishr ibn Waqsh
Children: Bore children. Ali ibn Asad al-Hadli
Sister of: Abbad ibn Bishr
Wife of: Mahmud ibn Maslama
Tribe: Aws, Abd al-Ashhal clan

Ibn Sad also relates the following:

She accepted Islam and gave her allegiance to the Messenger of God. Her brother was present at all the battles of the Prophet.

UMAMA BINT HAMZA IBN ABD AL-MUTTALIB

Mother: Salma bint Umays ibn Madd
Father: Hamza ibn Abd al-Muttalib
Sister of: Asma bint Umays
Alternative Name: Ammara bint Hamza

Ibn Sad also relates the following:

She accepted Islam and gave her allegiance to the Messenger of God. The Prophet proposed to her but never married her.

Ali relates that he asked the Messenger why he was choosy about the Quraysh women and did not want to marry one of them.

He said, 'Do you have someone then?' Ali said he did, the daughter of Hamza.'

He said, 'She is the daughter of my brother by nursing.'

Said ibn al-Musayyab relates that Ali asked the Messenger of

God why he did not marry the daughter of his uncle Hamza because she was the the most beautiful girl among the Quraysh.

He said, 'Ali, do you not know that Hamza is my foster-brother. God makes unlawful by suckling what lineage makes unlawful.'

Ibn Abbas relates that Ali spoke to the Prophet and asked why he left the daughter of his uncle an orphan among the idol-worshippers. The Prophet did not forbid him to bring her. He brought her out. Zayd ibn Haritha spoke up. He was the trustee of Hamza and the Prophet had formed brotherhood between them when he formed brotherhood between the Emigrants. He said that he was more entitled to look after his brother's daughter.

When Jafar ibn Abi Talib heard that, he said that the maternal aunt was like a mother. He was more entitled to look after her because her maternal aunt, Asma bint Umays, was his wife.

Ali said that he saw they were quarreling about a cousin. He was the one who brought her from among the idol-worshippers and had no tie of kinship with her closer than his. He felt he was more entitled to look after her.

The Messenger of God said, 'I will judge between you: You, Zayd, are the freedman of God and of His Messenger. You, Ali, are my brother and my Companion. You, Jafar, are the most like me in physique and character. You, Jafar, are more entitled to look after her since her aunt is married to you. A woman does not marry someone who is married to her aunt.' So he judged that Jafar was the one to care for her.

Muhammad ibn Umar al-Waqadi reports that Jafar hopped around the Messenger of God. The Prophet asked, 'What is this, Jafar?' He said that when the Negus wanted to please someone, they stood up and hopped around him.'

The Messenger of God gave her in marriage to Salama ibn Abi Salama. The Prophet used to ask, 'Have you repaid Salama?'

UMAMA BINT ISAM

Father: Isam
Wife of: Kabsha ibn Mabdhul
Tribe: Khazraj, Bayada ibn Amr clan

Ibn Sad also relates the following:

She accepted Islam and gave her allegiance to the Messenger of God.

UMAMA BINT KHADIJ IBN RAFI

Father: Khadij ibn Rafi
Sister of: Rafi ibn Khadij
Tribe: Aws, Haritha ibn al-Khazraj clan

Ibn Sad also relates the following:

She accepted Islam and gave her allegiance to the Messenger of God.

UMAMA BINT MUHARRITH IBN ZAYD

Mother: Salma bint Abi ad-Dahdaha
Father: Muharrith ibn Zayd
Wife of: Rabi ibn al-Tufayl, al-;Dahhak ibn Haritha, al-
Tribe: Khazraj, Salama ibn Sad clan
Ibn Sad also relates the following:
She accepted Islam and gave her allegiance to the Messenger of God. She is the grandaughter of the man who brought grapes to the Messenger in the garden in the outskirts of Taif.

UMAMA BINT QURAT IBN KHANSA

Mother: Mawiya bint al-Qayn
Father: Qurat ibn Khansa
Wife of: Yazid ibn Qayzi
Tribe: Khazraj, Salama ibn Sad clan
Ibn Sad also relates the following:
She accepted Islam and gave her allegiance to the Messenger of God.

UMAMA BINT RAFI

Mother: Halima bint Urwa of Khazraj
Father: Rafi
Children: Thabit, Muhammad, Umm Kulthum, Umm al-Hasan
Wife of: Usayd ibn Zhuhayr
Tribe: Aws, Haritha ibn al-Khazraj clan
Ibn Sad also relates the following:
She accepted Islam and gave her allegiance to the Messenger of God.

UMAMA BINT SAMIT IBN QAYS

Mother: Rabab bint Malik, al-
Father: Samit ibn Qays
Sister of: Half of Ubada ibn al-Samit
Wife of: Jumay ibn Masud
Tribe: Khazraj, Qawaqila, Awf ibn al-Khazraj clan
Ibn Sad also relates the following:
She accepted Islam and gave her allegiance to the Messenger of God.

UMAMA BINT SIMAK

Mother: Umm Jundub bint Rifaa
Father: Simak

Children: Abd Allah, Umm Sakhr, Umm Sulayman, Habiba
Wife of: Sharik ibn Anas
Tribe: Aws, Abd al-Ashhal clan
  Ibn Sad also relates the following:
  She accepted Islam and gave her allegiance to the Messenger of
God. She is the paternal aunt of Uzayd ibn Hudayr.

UMAMA BINT UTHMAN IBN KHALIDA
Mother: Umm Jamil bint Qutba
Father: Uthman ibn Khalida
Sister of: Abu Ubada ibn Sad
Wife of: Thabit ibn al-Jadha
Tribe: Khazraj, Zurayq ibn Amir clan
  Ibn Sad also relates the following:
  She accepted Islam and gave her allegiance to the Messenger of
God. Her brother were present at the Battle of Badr.

UMAMA (SEE UMAYMA BINT SUFYAN IBN WAHB)

UMARA BINT HUBBASHA IBN JUWAYBIR
Mother: Layla bint Sahba
Father: Hubbasha ibn Juwaybir
Tribe: Aws, Khatma ibn Jusham clan
  Ibn Sad also relates the following:
  She accepted Islam and gave her allegiance to the Messenger of
God.

UMAYMA
Mother: Umm Abd Allah
Wife of: Abu Sufyan ibn Harb
Tribe: Non-Quraysh of Kinana
Alternative Name: Umama (see Umayma bint Sufyan ibn Wahb)
  Ibn Sad also relates the following:
  She accepted Islam on the day of the conquest of Makkah or short-
ly after that and gave her allegiance to the Messenger of God.

UMAYMA BINT ABD AL-MUTTALIB IBN HASHIM
Mother: Fatima bint Amr ibn Aidh of Makhzum
Father: Abd al-Muttalib ibn Hashim
Children: Abd Allah, Ubayd Allah, Abd (Abu Ahmad), Zaynab bint
Jahsh (wife of the Prophet), Hamna bint Jahsh
Wife of: Jahsh ibn Riyab
  Ibn Sad also relates the following:
  She accepted Islam and gave her allegiance to the Messenger of

God. Her son, Abd Allah, was martyred at the Battle of Badr. She is an aunt of the Prophet.

UMAYMA BINT ABIL HAYTHAM
Mother: Mulayka bint Sahl ibn Zayd
Father: Abil Haytham
Tribe: Aws, Abd al-Ashhal clan
Muhammad ibn Umar al-Waqadi mentions her accepting Islam.

UMAYMA BINT ABU HATHMA
Mother: Hujja bint Umayr
Father: Abu Hathma
Wife of: Hilal ibn al-Harith; Abu Sindar ibn al-Husayn al-Aslami
Tribe: Aws, Haritha ibn al-Khazraj clan
Ibn Sad also relates the following:
She accepted Islam and gave her allegiance to the Messenger of God.

UMAYMA BINT AL-NUMAN IBN AL-HARITH
Mother: Umm Sakhr bint Sharik
Father: Numan ibn al-Harith, al-
Children: Numan, al-
Wife of: Ubayd ibn Aws
Tribe: Aws, Zafar clan

UMAYMA BINT AMR IBN SAHL
Father: Amr ibn Sahl
Tribe: Aws, Abd al-Ashhal tribe
Muhammad ibn Umar al-Waqadi mentions her accepting Islam.

UMAYMA BINT RUQAYQA BINT ABD ALLAH
Mother: Ruqayqa bint Khuwaylid sister of Khadija
Children: Nahdiyya, al-, Umm Umays, Zunnira
Sister of: Subayha ibn al-Harith
Wife of: Habib ibn Kuayb al-Thaqafi
Tribe: Quraysh
Ibn Sad also relates the following:
She accepted Islam and gave her allegiance to the Messenger of God. She related Traditions from the Prophet. She was among the slaves tortured in Makkah.
She is the one from whom Muhammad ibn al-Munkadir transmitted. She related from the Prophet the Tradition about him receiving the allegiance of the women. Abu Bakr bought her and her husband and children. His father, Abu Quhafa, asked his son why he devoted

himself to this man and left his people and purchased those weak-lings. Abu Bakr replied tha the knew best what he was doing.

When he purchased al-Nahdiyya, she had some flour she had ground for her mistress or some date-stones she had milled. Abu Bakr told her to return her flour or stones. She said she would not do so until she had milled it. That was after her mistress had sold her and Abu Bakr had set her free. Zunnira was afflicted in her sight and went blind. It was said to her that the gods, al-Lat and al-Uzza, had afflicted her. She said that they had not afflicted her and that this was from God. God restored her sight. The Quraysh said that this was some of the magic of Muhammad.

UMAYMA BINT UQBA IBN AMR
Mother: Umm Umayr bint Amr
Father: Uqba ibn Amr
Wife of: Sahl ibn Atik
Tribe: Aws, Haritha ibn al-Khazraj clan
Ibn Sad also relates the following:
She accepted Islam and gave her allegiance to the Messenger of God.

UMAYNA BINT ABU SUFYAN IBN HARB
Mother: Sufayya bint Abil As
Father: Abu Sufyan ibn Harb
Children: Abu Sufyan; Abd al-Rahman
Wife of: Huwaytib ibn Abd al-Uzza;
          Safwan ibn Umayya
Tribe: Quraysh
Ibn Sad also relates the following:
She accepted Islam and gave her allegiance to the Messenger of God.

UMAYRA
Children: Labid, Amra
Wife of: Thalaba ibn Sinan
Tribe: Aws, Banu Amr ibn Awf ibn Malik ibn Aws
Alternative Name: Amra bint Ubayd (see Umayra)
Ibn Sad also relates the following:
She accepted Islam and gave her allegiance to the Messenger of God.

UMAYRA BINT JUBAYR IBN SAKHR
Mother: Suad bint Salama
Father: Jubayr ibn Sakhr

Children: Abd Allah, Ubayd Allah, Faddala, Qahb, Mabad, Khawla, Suad

Wife of: Kab ibn Malik

Ibn Sad also relates the following:

She accepted Islam and gave her allegiance to the Messenger of God. She related the Tradition regarding raisens and dates.

UMAYRA BINT QURAT IBN KHANSA

Mother: Mawiya bint al-Qayn

Father: Qurat ibn Khansa

Children: Mandwas

Wife of: Qutba ibn Abd al-Amr

Tribe: Khazraj, Salama ibn Sad clan

Ibn Sad also relates the following:

She accepted Islam and gave her allegiance to the Messenger of God.

UMAYRA BINT UMAYR

Mother: Umama bint Bukayr

Father: Umayr

Wife of: Bujad ibn Uthman

Ibn Sad also relates the following:

She accepted Islam and gave her allegiance to the Messenger of God.

UMAYYA

Mother: Amra bint Rawaha

Sister of: Numan ibn Bashir, al-

Tribe: Khazraj

Alternative Name: Ubayya bint Bashir (see Umayya)

Ibn Sad also relates the following:

She accepted Islam and gave her allegiance to the Messenger of God.

UMAYYA BINT KHALIFA IBN ADI

Father: Khalifa ibn Adi

Children: Umm Sad

Wife of: Farwa ibn Amr

UMAYYA BINT QAYS IBN ABU AL-SALT AL-GHIFARIYYA

Father: Qays ibn Abu al-Salt al-Ghifariyya

Tribe: Non-Qurayshi Emigrant

Ibn Sad also relates the following:

She accepted Islam and gave her allegiance to the Messenger of God. She treated the wounded at Khaybar and related a Tradition.

Umayya bint Qays ibn Abi al-Salt al-Ghifariyya relates that

she went to the Messenger of God with some women of the Ghifar tribe. They told the Messenger that they wished to go out with him to Khaybar to treat the wounded and help the Muslims as much as they could. The Messenger of God said, 'With the blessing of God.'

They went with him. She was still a young girl. The Messenger put her behind the back of the saddle of his camel. He dismounted and made the camel kneel. She saw that the back of the saddle she had been on bore a trace of blood. It was the first time she had menstruated. She clung to the camel and was embarrassed. When the Messenger of God saw what she was doing and saw the blood, he said, 'Perhaps you have menstruated?' She said that she had.

He said, 'Attend to yourself. Then take a vessel of water and put some salt in it. Use it to wash off the blood which is on the saddle and come back.' She did that.

When God let us conquer Khaybar, the Messenger gave them some gifts from the booty but did not give them an actual share. He gave a necklace to her. He put it on her neck with his own hands. She said she would never take it off.

It remained on her neck until she died. She left instructions for it to be buried with her. Whenever she purified herself, she put salt in her water. She left instructions that salt be put in her water when she was ritually purified for burial.

UMM ABAN

Father: Utabh ibn Rabiyah
Wife of: Aban ibn Said ibn al-As

She is not mentioned by Ibn Sad. She took part in many battles after the death of the Messenger. Her husband was martyred in the Battle of Damascus. After that, she married Talha. When asked why she married him, she replied that she was acquainted with his good qualities, that he was someone who came home and smiled, went out and smiled. When you asked him something, he gave it happily and if you remained quiet, he did not wait for your request. If you did any work for him, he was grateful and if you made a mistake, he ignored and forgave it. [*Kanz al-Ummal*]

UMM ABD ALLAH

Mother: Umm Khalid bint Khalid
Sister of: Half-sister of Salama ibn Aslam
Wife of: Nahik ibn Adi
Tribe: Aws, Haritha ibn al-Khazraj clan
Alternative Name: Salma bint Aslam

Ibn Sad also relates the following:

She accepted Islam and gave her allegiance to the Messenger of God.

UMM ABD ALLAH BINT AZIB BINT AL-HARITH
Mother: Umm Habiba bint Abu Habiba or Umm Khalid bint Thabit
Sister of: Bara ibn Azib, al- ˙
Tribe: Aws, Haritha ibn al-Khazraj clan
Ibn Sad also relates the following:
She accepted Islam and gave her allegiance to the Messenger of God.

UMM ABD ALLAH BINT MILHAN
Tribe: Khazraj
Muhammad ibn Umar al-Waqadi mentions her accepting Islam.

UMM ABD ALLAH BINT MUADH IBN JABAL
Mother: Umm Amr ibn Khallad
Children: Amina
Wife of: Abd Allah ibn Amir
Ibn Sad also relates the following:
She accepted Islam and gave her allegiance to the Messenger of God.

UMM ABD ALLAH BINT SAWAD IBN RAZN
Mother: Umm al-Harith bint al-Numan
Wife of: Abu Muhammad ibn Muadh
Tribe: Khazraj, Salama ibn Sad clan
Ibn Sad also relates the following:
She accepted Islam and gave her allegiance to the Messenger of God.

UMM ABD ALLAH IBN MASUD
Mother: Hind bint Abd
Tribe: Non-Qurayshi
Alternative Name: Umm Abd bint Abd al-Wudd
Ibn Sad also relates the following:
She accepted Islam and gave her allegiance to the Messenger of God.

UMM ABD BINT ABD AL-WUDD (SEE UMM ABD ALLAH IBN MASUD)

UMM ABS BINT MASLAMA IBN SALAMA
Mother: Umm Sahm
Children: Bore children, names not given
Sister of: Muhammad and Mahmud ibn Salama

Wife of: Abu Abs ibn Jabr
Tribe: Aws, Haritha ibn al-Khazraj clan
Alternative Name: Khulayda bint Abu Ubayd
Ibn Sad also relates the following:
She accepted Islam and gave her allegiance to the Messenger of God.

UMM AL-ALA AL-ANSARIYYA
Tribe: Khazraj, Malik ibn al-Najjar clan
Ibn Sad also relates the following:
She accepted Islam and gave her allegiance to the Messenger of God. She related Traditions from the Prophet. She is the one who said that when the Helpers quarreled about the Emigrants, they drew lots for them. Uthman ibn Mazun was drawn. She was with the Messenger of God at Khaybar.

UMM AL-DAHHAK BIN MASUD AL-HARITHIYYA
Tribe: Aws, Haritha ibn al-Khazraj, al-, clan
Ibn Sad also relates the following:
She accepted Islam and gave her allegiance to the Messenger of God.

UMM AL-DARDA KHAIRA BINT ABU HADRAD ASLAMI
She is not mentioned by Ibn Sad.

UMM AL-HAKAM BINT AL-ZUBAYR
Mother: Atika bint Abi Wahb ibn Amr
Children: Muhammad, Abd Allah, Abbas, al-Harith, Abd al-Shams, Abd al-Muttalib, Umayya, a son and Arwa the elder
Wife of: Rabia ibn al-Harith ibn Abd al-Muttalib
Ibn Sad also relates the following:
She accepted Islam and gave her allegiance to the Messenger of God.

UMM AL-HAKAM BINT AL-MUTTALIB (SEE FUKAYHA)

UMM AL-HAKIM
Mother: Umm al-Banin bint Hudhayfa of Qudaa
Children: Bore children, names not given
Wife of: Qays ibn Makhrama
Tribe: Aws, Abd al-Ashhal clan
Alternative Name: Wadda bint Uqba ibn Rafi
Ibn Sad also relates the following:
She accepted Islam and gave her allegiance to the Messenger of God. Her mother was the paternal aunt of Mahmud ibn Labid.

UMM AL-HARITH
Mother: Umama bint Uthman
Wife of: Mirdas ibn Marwan
Tribe: Khazraj, Salama ibn Sad clan
Alternative Name: Umm Iyas bint Thabit
  Ibn Sad also relates the following:
  She accepted Islam and gave her allegiance to the Messenger of God.

UMM AL-HARITH BINT AL-HARITH
Mother: Sahla bint Imrul Qays
Tribe: Aws, Zafar clan
  Ibn Sad also relates the following:
  She accepted Islam and gave her allegiance to the Messenger of God.

UMM AL-HARITH BINT AL-HARITH IBN THALABA
Mother: Sumayra bint Qays, al-
Children: Harith, al-, Abd al-Rahman; Suhayma
Wife of: Amr ibn Ghaziya; Harith ibn Khazama, al-
Tribe: Khazraj, Dar ibn al-Najjar clan
  Ibn Sad also relates the following:
  She accepted Islam and gave her allegiance to the Messenger of God.

UMM AL-HARITH BINT MALIK IBN KHANSA
Mother: Asma bint al-Qayr
Sister of: Tufayl ibn Malik, al-
Wife of: Thabit ibn Sakhr
Tribe: Khazraj, Salama ibn Sad clan
  Ibn Sad also relates the following:
  She accepted Islam and gave her allegiance to the Messenger of God. Her brother was present at the Battle of Badr.

UMM AL-HARITH IBN AL-NUMAN IBN KHANSA
Mother: Khansa bint Rabab
Wife of: Sawad ibn Razn
Tribe: Khazraj, Salama ibn Sad clan

UMM AL-HUBAB
Children: Bore children, not named
Wife of: Masud ibn Khalda; Miri ibn Simak
Tribe: Khazraj
Alternative Name: Furaya bint al-Hubab ibn Rafi

UMM AL-HUSAYN AL-AHMASIYYA

Tribe: Non-Qurayshi Emigrant
Ibn Sad also relates the following:
She accepted Islam and gave her allegiance to the Messenger of God. She related a Tradition from the Prophet.

UMM AL-MUNDHIR BINT QAYS IBN AMR

Mother: Rughayba bint Zurara
Children: Mundhir, al-
Sister of: Salit ibn Qays
Wife of: Qays ibn Sasaa
Tribe: Khazraj, Adi ibn an-Najjar clan
Ibn Sad also relates the following:
She accepted Islam and gave her allegiance to the Messenger of God.

UMM AL-QASIM BINT THABIT (SEE RIFAA)

UMM AL-RABI BINT ABD IBN AL-NUMAN

Wife of: Kudaym ibn Adi
Tribe: Khazraj, Malik ibn al-Najjar clan
Ibn Sad also relates the following:
She accepted Islam and gave her allegiance to the Messenger of God.

UMM AL-RUBAYYI BINT ASLAM

Mother: Suad bint Rafi
Children: Sahl, Amira, Umm Damra
Sister of: Salama ibn Aslam
Wife of: Abu Hathma ibn Saida
Tribe: Aws, Haritha ibn al-Khazraj clan
Ibn Sad also relates the following:
She accepted Islam and gave her allegiance to the Messenger of God. Her brother was present at Badr.

UMM AL-SAIB

Ibn Sad also relates the following:
She accepted Islam and gave her allegiance to the Messenger of God. The Prophet visited her when she had a fever.

UMM AL-ZUBAYR BINT AL-ZUBAYR

Mother: Atika bint Abi Wahb ibn Amr
Tribe: Makhzum
Ibn Sad also relates the following:

She accepted Islam and gave her allegiance to the Messenger of God.

UMM AMIR AL-ASHHALIYYA
Mother: Umm Sad bint Khuzaym
Alternative Name: Fukayha; Asma bint Yazid
Ibn Sad also relates the following:
She accepted Islam and gave her allegiance to the Messenger of God. She related Traditions from the Prophet.

UMM AMIR BINT ABU QUHAFA
Mother: Hind bint Nuqayd
Children: Duayfa
Wife of: Amir ibn Abu Waqqas
Tribe: Quraysh
Ibn Sad also relates the following:
She accepted Islam and gave her allegiance to the Messenger of God.

UMM AMIR BINT SULAYM
Mother: Suad bint Amir
Children: Yazid, Umm Amir
Wife of: Usayd ibn Saida
Tribe: Aws, Haritha ibn al-Khazraj clan
Alternative Name: Habbaba
Ibn Sad also relates the following:
She accepted Islam and gave her allegiance to the Messenger of God.

UMM AMR BINT AL-MUQAWWIM
Mother: Qilaba bint Amr
Children: Abd Allah ibn Masud; Atika bint Abi Sufyan
Wife of: Masud ibn Muattib al-Thaqafi; Abu Sufyan ibn al-Harith ibn Abd al-Muttalib
Ibn Sad also relates the following:
She accepted Islam and gave her allegiance to the Messenger of God.

UMM AMR BINT AMR
Mother: Hind bint Qays
Wife of: Abul Yasr ibn Amr
Tribe: Khazraj, Salama ibn Sad clan
Ibn Sad also relates the following:

She accepted Islam and gave her allegiance to the Messenger of God.

UMM AMR BINT AMR IBN HADIDA
Mother: Umm Sulaym bint Amr
Sister of: Sulaym ibn Amr
Wife of: Qutba ibn Amir
Tribe: Khazraj, Salama ibn Sad clan
Ibn Sad also relates the following:
She accepted Islam and gave her allegiance to the Messenger of God. Her brother was present at Aqaba and the Battle of Badr.

UMM AMR BINT MAHMUD IBN MASLAMA
Mother: Umama bint Bishr
Children: Amr, Humayd
Wife of: Abd Allah ibn Muhammad ibn Maslama; Zayd ibn Sad
Tribe: Aws, Haritha ibn al-Khazraj clan
Ibn Sad also relates the following:
She accepted Islam and gave her allegiance to the Messenger of God.

UMM AMR BINT SALAMA
Mother: Salma bint Salama
Children: Bore children, names not given
Sister of: Salama ibn Salama
Wife of: Muhammad ibn Maslama
Tribe: Aws, Abd al-Ashhal clan
Ibn Sad also relates the following:
She accepted Islam and gave her allegiance to the Messenger of God. Her brother was present at Aqaba and the Battle of Badr.

UMM ANAS BINT WAQID IBN AMR
Wife of: Amr ibn Utba
Tribe: Khazraj, Qawaqila, Awf ibn al-Khazraj clan
Ibn Sad also relates the following:
She accepted Islam and gave her allegiance to the Messenger of God.

UMM ATIYYA AL-ANSARIYYA
Tribe: Khazraj, Malik ibn al-Najjar clan
Ibn Sad also relates the following:
She accepted Islam and gave her allegiance to the Messenger of God. She related Traditions from the Prophet.
Umm Sharahil, the servant of Umm Atiyya, relates that Ali ibn Abi Talib used to spend midday at Umm Atiyya's house.

Muhammad ibn Umar al-Waqadi relates that Umm Atiyya was present at Khaybar with the Messenger of God.

Umm Atiyya bint Harith
She is not mentioned by Ibn Sad.

Umm Aws Ansariya
She is not mentioned by Ibn Sad.

Umm Ayman
Children: Aiman
Wife of: Zayd ibn Haritha
Children: Ayman; Usama ibn Zayd
Wife of: Ubayd ibn Zayd; Zayd ibn Haritha al-Kalbi
Alternative Name: Umm Ayman
Ibn Sad also relates the following:
She accepted Islam and gave her allegiance to the Messenger of God. The Messenger of God inherited Baraka from his father along with five camels and some sheep. He freed her when he married Khadija bint Khuwaylid. Baraka then married Ubayd ibn Zayd of the al-Harith ibn al-Khazraj tribe and gave birth to Ayman. Ubayd ibn Zayd was a Companion of the Prophet who was martyred at Hunayn.

Zayd ibn Haritha al-Kalbi was the freedman of Khadija bint Khuwaylid. She gave him to the Messenger of God who freed him, and he married Umm Ayman after the mission. She gave birth to Usama ibn Zayd.

Uthman ibn al-Qasim relates that when Umm Ayman migrated, she was detained at al-Munsarif below al-Rawha. She became thirsty but did not have any water. She was fasting. Thirst was hard for her. A bucket of water descended from heaven with a white feather. She took it and drank from it until she had quenched her thirst. She used to say that no thirst afflicted her after that. She had been known among the Emigrants for being extremely thirsty when fasting, but after that drink, she was never overcome with thirst. She would not get very thirsty after that, even when she fasted on a hot day.

Sufyan ibn Uqba relates that Umm Ayman used to be kind to the Prophet and care for him. The Messenger of God said that whoever is happy to marry a woman of the Garden should marry Umm Ayman. Zayd ibn Haritha married her, and she bore him Usama ibn Zayd.

Mujahid relates that the Prophet said, 'Cover yourself with your head-covering, Umm Ayman.'

Muhammad ibn Qays relates that Umm Ayman went to the Prophet and asked for a mount.

He said, 'I will mount you on the off-spring of a she-camel.'

She said that it would not be able to support her. She did not want it. He said, 'I will only mount you on the off-spring of a she-camel.' He was joking with her. The Messenger of God used to joke, but he only spoke the truth. All camels are the offspring of she-camels.

It is related that when Umm Ayman visited the Prophet, she would say, 'Peace, not on you,' and so the Messenger of God allowed her to simply say, 'Peace.'

Abul Huwayrith relates that Umm Ayman prayed that God stop the feet of those who fled on the Day of Hunayn.

The Prophet said, 'Be quiet, Umm Ayman. You are harsh-tongued.'

Anas ibn Malik relates that a man had set aside some palm trees for him. When the Qurayza and al-Nadir tribes were defeated, he returned that property. Anas said that his family told him to go to the Prophet and ask him for that which he had to give or some of it.

The Prophet had given it to Umm Ayman. She said that she asked the Prophet and he gave those palm trees to her. Umm Ayman came and put a cloth on his neck and began to say that she would not give them to him because the Messenger had given them to her. The Prophet of God had said to her, 'You will have such and such.' She did not agree to give up the trees. He said, 'You will have the like of what he gave her.' She thought that he said ten times like it or about that.

Muhammad ibn Umar al-Waqadi reports that Umm Ayman was at the Battle of Uhud. She was carrying water and treating the wounded. She was also at Khaybar with the Messenger of God.

Zuhri relates that while Harmala, the freedman of Usama ibn Zayd, was sitting with Abd Allah ibn Umar, al-Hajjaj ibn Ayman entered and prayed the prescribed prayer in which he neither completed his bowing nor his prostration. Ibn Umar called him after he gave the greetings of peace and asked the man if he thought that he had offered the prescribed prayer. He said that he had not done so and was told he should repeat his prescribed prayer.

When Hajjaj turned away, Abd Allah ibn Umar asked who this was. Zuhri replied that he was Hajjaj ibn Ayman, the son of Umm Ayman.

Ibn Umar said that if the Messenger of God had seen this man, he would have loved him. Then he mentioned his love for the offspring of Umm Ayman. She was the nursemaid of the Prophet.

Tariq ibn Shihab relates that when the Prophet died, Umm Ayman wept. Someone asked her why she was weeping. She said she was weeping because there would be no more news from heaven.

Anas relates that Umm Ayman wept when the Prophet died. Someone asked why she was weeping. She said that she knew that the Messenger would die. She was crying for the revelation from heaven which would now be cut off.

Tariq ibn Shihab relates that when Umar was murdered, Umm Ayman wept and said that today Islam is dominant.

Qabisa relates in his version that Umm Ayman wept when the

Messenger died. She was asked about that and she said that she was weeping because of the end of news from heaven.

Muhammad ibn Umar al-Waqadi reports that Umm Ayman died at the beginning of the caliphate of Uthman."

Muhammad ibn Umar al-Waqadi reports that there was a dispute between Ibn Abil Furat, the freedman of Usama ibn Zayd and al-Hasan ibn Usama. In the course of the discussion, Ibn Abil Furat called him, saying, 'Son of Baraka!' referring to his mother, Umm Ayman. Al-Hasan told him to watch his words

The affair was taken to Abu Bakr ibn Muhammad ibn Amr ibn Hazm who was the judge of Madinah at that time or the governor of Umar ibn Abd al-Aziz. The story was recounted to him. Abu Bakr asked Ibn Abil Furat what he meant by the words, 'Son of Baraka?'

He said, 'I have called him by her name.'

Abu Bakr said that he had meant by this to belittle her. He asked if he did not realize her position in Islam and with the Messenger of God who had said to her, 'O mother,' and 'O Umm Ayman.' Abu Bakr said that God would not release him if he released Ibn Abil Furat. He, therefore, had him beaten with seventy lashes.

UMM AYYUB BINT QAYS IBN SAD
Tribe: Khazraj

Muhammad ibn Umar al-Waqadi mentions her accepting Islam.

UMM BANI ANMAR (SEE QAYLA)

UMM BISHR BINT AMR IBN ANMA
Mother: Umm Zayd bint Amir
Children: Bore children, names not given
Wife of: Abd al-Rahman ibn Khirash; Abd Allah ibn Bashir
Tribe: Khazraj, Salama ibn Sad clan

UMM BUJAYD
Tribe: Khazraj, Malik ibn al-Najjar clan

Ibn Sad also relates the following:

She accepted Islam and gave her allegiance to the Messenger of God. She was the grandmother of Abd al-Rahman ibn Bujayd. She related a Tradition.

UMM BURDA
Mother: Zaynab bint Sufyan
Wife of: Bara ibn Aws, al-
Alternative Name: Khawla bint al-Mudhir ibn Zayd

Ibn Sad also relates the following:

She accepted Islam and gave her allegiance to the Messenger of God. She was the nurse of Ibrahim.

UMM FADL
Mother: Hind (Khawla bint Awf) related to Hmyar.
Father: Harith ibn Hazm
Children: Fadl Lababat al-Kubra, Abd Allah, Ubayd Allah, Mabad, Qutham, Abdur Rahman , Umm Habib
Sister of: Maymuna bint al-Harith; Asma bint al-Harith, half-sis of Izza bint al-Harith etc.
Wife of: Abbas ibn Abdul Muttalib
Tribe: Non-Qurayshi Enigrant
Alternative Name: Lubaba the elder bint al-Harith ibn Hazm
Ibn Sad also relates the following:

She accepted Islam and gave her allegiance to the Messenger of God. She was the first woman after Khadijah to accept Islam. She was the wife of the Prophet's uncle Abbas. She was a woman of great status and station.

She was a brave and self-respecting woman. Once after the Battle of Badr, when Abu Lahab was beating Abu Rafi, a slave of Abbas, she struck him with a staff and wounded his head. She called Abu Lahab a shameless creature. She pointed out that his master was not there and yet Abu Lahab was beating him.

Abu Lahab dared not answer back and went away. The Prophet often went to her house. If it was noon, he rested there. She used to comb his hair to remove dust and blades of grass, etc.

Allama Ibn Abd al-Barr relates that Umm al-Fadl, Maymuna, Umm Salamah and Asma are four true believing women.

UMM FARWA, GRANDMOTHER OF AL-QASIM IBN GHANNAM
Tribe: Non-Quayshi Emigrant
Ibn Sad also relates the following:
She accepted Islam and gave her allegiance to the Messenger of God. She related a Tradition from the Messenger.

UMM FAWA BINT ABU QUHAFA
Mother: Hind bint Nuqayd
Father: Abu Quhafa or Uthman ibn Amir
Children: Muhammad, Ishaq, Ismail, Hubab, Qurayba
Wife of: Ashath ibn Qays al-Kindi
Tribe: Quraysh
Ibn Sad also relates the following:
She accepted Islam and gave her allegiance to the Messenger of God.

UMM HABIB BINT AL-ABBAS

Mother: Umm Fadl Lubana bint al-Harith al-Hilaliyya
Children: Zurqa and Lubana
Wife of: Aswad ibn Sufyan ibn Abd al-Asad
    Ibn Sad also relates the following:
    She accepted Islam and gave her allegiance to the Messenger of God.

UMM HABIB BINT JAHSH IBN RITHAB (SEE HABIBA)
    According to Ibn Sad, calling her Umm Habib is a mistake.

UMM HABIB BINT MUATTAB (SEE HABIBA)

UMM HABIBA

Mother: Safiyya bint Abil As
Children: Habiba
Wife of: Ubayd Allah ibn Jahsh of Khuzayma; Messenger of God
Alternative Name: Ramla bint Abu Sufyan ibn Harb ibn Umayya
    Ibn Sad also relates the following:
    She accepted Islam and gave her allegiance to the Messenger of God. Her mother was the aunt of Uthman ibn Affan.
    Ubayd Allah ibn Jahsh migrated with Umm Habiba to Abyssinia on the second migration. He apostatised from Islam and died there. Umm Habiba remained firm in her Islam and migration.
    Uthman ibn Muhammad al-Akhnasi relates that Umm Habiba bint Abu Sufyan bore her daughter Habiba by Ubayd Allah in Makkah before she migrated to Abyssinia. Muhammad ibn Sad said that she gave birth to her in Abyssinia.
    It is related that Sad said that she left Makkah when she was pregnant and gave birth to her daughter in Abyssinia.
    Ismail ibn Amr ibn Sad ibn al-As relates that Umm Habiba said that she saw her husband in a dream in the worst and ugliest form. She became alarmed. She said to him that he looked so different.
    In the morning he said to her that he had thought a lot about religion and found none better than Christianity yet accepted Islam. Now he had reverted to Christianity.
    She was upset and told him about the dream which she had had, but he paid no attention to it. He gave himself over to drinking wine until he died. Then she saw him in a dream as if he were calling her, saying, 'Mother of the Faithful!' She was alarmed and interpreted it as the Messenger of God marrying her.'
    She said that when her waiting period ended, she was aware of the messenger of the Negus at her door asking permission to enter. It was a slavegirl called Abraha who used to attend to his garments and oil him. Abraha told her that the Negus said that the Messenger of God

had written asking him to marry her to him. Umm Habiba was very happy with the news.

Abraha told Umm Habiba that the Negus asked her to appoint someone to give her away in marriage. Umm Habiba sent for Khalid ibn Said ibn al-As. He acted as her guardian. She gave Abraha two silver bracelets and two anklets she was wearing and the silver rings she was wearing out of joy at her good news. In the evening the Negus commanded Jafar ibn Abi Talib and the Muslims with him to attend.

The Negus spoke and said that he praises God, the King, the Most Pure, the Perfect Peace, the Trustworthy, the Safeguarder, the Almighty, the Compeller. He testified that there is no god but God and that Muhammad is His servant and Messenger. The Negus said that was the one about whom Jesus, the son of Mary, gave the good news.

He then told the group that the Messenger of God had written to instruct him to marry the Messenger to Umm Habiba bint Abi Sufyan. She had accepted the offer of the Messenger of God. The Negus said that he had assigned her a dower of 400 dinars. Then the dinars were poured before the people.

Khalid ibn Said spoke and said that all praise belonged to God. He bore witness that there was no God but God and that Muhammad was His servant and messenger. He said that he had replied to the messege of the Messenger of God and married him to Umm Habiba ibn Abi Sufyan. Then he called for God's blessings upon the Messenger of God.

He gave the dinars to Khalid ibn Said ibn al-As and he took them. Then the couple wanted to get up. The Negus told them to sit down. He said that the *Sunnah* of the Prophet is that when people marry, food should be provided for the marriage celebration. So he called for food, and they ate and then left.

Umm Habiba relates that when the money reached her, she sent for Abraha who had given her the good news. Umm Habiba said to Abraha that she, Umm Habiba, had given Abraha whatever money she had on the day when she gave her the good news. Now Umm Habiba wanted to give Abraha fifty mithqals.

Abraha refused. She brought out a box which contained what Umm Habiba had given her. She retumed it to her and said that the king has decided that Abraha should not take anything from Umm Habiba. Abraha said that she was the one who took care of the Negus' clothes and oiled him. She had followed the religion of Muhammad, the Messenger of God, and had surrendered to God. The king has commanded that his women send to Umm Salama all the scent they had.

Umm Habiba said that the following day Abraha brought her aloes, amber and much civet. Umm Habiba took all of them to the Prophet. He smelled it on her and did not object.

Umm Habiba said that Abraha had asked her to convey her greetings to the Messenger and inform him that she has been following his religion.

When Umm Habiba saw the Messenger, she told him how the proposal had taken place and what Abraha had done for her. She said that Abraha was kind to her and used to attend to her. Whenever she visited Umm Habiba, Abraha reminded her not to forget what she asked her to do.

The Messenger of God smiled. Umm Habiba gave him Abraha's greeting. He said, 'And peace upon her, and the mercy of God and His blessings.'

Muhammad relates that the Messenger sent Amr ibn Umayya al-Damri to the Negus to propose marriage to Umm Habiba bint Abi Sufyan who had been married to Ubayd Allah ibn Jahsh. She married the Messenger. The Negus gave her a dower of 400 dinars from him on behalf of the Messenger of God.

Abu Jafar relates that they thought that Abd al-Malik stipulated the dower of women at 400 dinars for that reason.

Abd Allah ibn Abi Bakr relates that the one who gave her in marriage and to whom the Negus presented the proposal was Khalid ibn Said ibn al-As. That was in 7 AH/628 CE. When she arrived in Madinah she was about thirty years old.

Zuhri relates that the Negus made the marriage arrangements for the Prophet and sent her with Sharahbil ibn Hasana.

Abd al-Wahid ibn Abi Awn relates that when Abu Sufyan heard about the marriage of the Prophet to his daughter, he said, 'That suitor is rejected!'

lbn Abbas relates about the verse, *"It may well be that God will place love between you and those of them who are your enemies,"* (60:7) in regard to the marriage of the Prophet to Umm Habiba bint Abi Sufyan.

Zuhri relates that when Abu Sufyan ibn Harb came to Madinah, he went to the Messenger when the Messenger was intending to retaliate against Makkah. He wanted to ask him to extend the truce of Hudaybiyya. The Messenger of God did not agree to that. So he got up and went to his daughter, Umm Habiba. When he went to sit on the bed of the Prophet, she rolled it up from under him. He asked his-daughter if he was too good for the bed or if the bed was too good for him. She told him that it was the bed of the Messenger while he, her father, was an unclean idol worshipper. He replied that his daughter had moved far from him.

Safiyya relates that when Abu Sufyan, the father of Umm Habiba, the wife of the Prophet, died, she called for scent. She put it on her arms and cheeks. Then she said that she had no need of this were it not that she heard the Messenger of God say, 'It is not lawful for a woman who believes in God and the Last Day to mourn for a dead person more than three days except for a husband. She mourns for him for four months and ten days.'

Ibn Shawwal relates that Umm Habiba bint Abi Sufyan informed him that the Messenger of God commanded her to avoid gatherings at night.

Muhammad ibn Umar al-Waqadi reports that the Messenger of God assigned Umm Habiba bint Abi Sufyan eighty weights of dates from Khaybar and twenty weights of barley.

Ayisha relates that Umm Habiba, the wife of the Messenger of God, called Ayisha when she was dying. She said that there was some bad feeling between the Messenger's wives. Umm Habiba asked God to forgive her and Ayisha for their part in this. Ayisha asked for God's forgiveness for all that. Umm Habiba thanked Ayisha and prayed that God might gladden her heart. Umm Habiba sent for Umm Salama and said the like of that to her.

Umm Habiba died in 46 AH/66 CE during the caliphate of Muawiya ibn Abu Sufyan.

Umm Habiba bint Nabbata al-Asadiyya
Tribe: Quraysh

Ibn Sad also relates the following:

She accepted Islam and gave her allegiance to the Messenger of God.

Umm Hakam
Father: Abd al-Rahman ibn Masud
Wife of: Abu Masud Uqba ibn Amr
Tribe: Khazraj
Alternative Name: Umm Hakim bint Abd al-Rahman ibn Masud

Ibn Sad also relates the following:

She accepted Islam and gave her allegiance to the Messenger of God.

Umm Hakam bint Abu Sufyan ibn Harb
Mother: Hind bint Utba
Father: Abi Sufyan ibn Harb
Children: Abd al-Rahman called Ibn Umm al-Hakam
Wife of: Abd Allah ibn Uthman of Thaqif

Ibn Sad also relates the following:

She accepted Islam and gave her allegiance to the Messenger of God.

Umm Hakim
Mother: Fatimah bint Amr of Makhzum
Father: Abd al-Muttalib ibn Hashim

Children: Amir, Arwa, Talha, Umm Talha
Wife of: Kurayz ibn Rabia
Alternative Name: Bayda bint Abd al-Muttalib ibn Hashim
Ibn Sad also relates the following:
She accepted Islam and gave her allegiance to the Messenger of God.

UMM HAKIM BINT ABD AL-RAHMAN IBN MASUD (SEE UMM HAKAM)

UMM HAKIM BINT AL-HARITH IBN HISHAM
Mother: Fatima bint al-Walid ibn al-Mughira
Wife of: Ikrima ibn Abu Jahl
Tribe: Quraysh
Ibn Sad also relates the following:
Abd Allah ibn al-Zubayr relates that on the day of the conquest of Makkah, Umm Hakim bint al-Harith, the wife of Ikrima ibn Abu Jahl, became Muslim and went to the Messenger of God and gave him her allegiance. She related a Tradition from the Messenger.

UMM HAKIM BINT AL-NADR
Mother: Hind bint Zayd
Children: Abu Hakim, Abd al-Rahman, Umm Hakim (Sahla)
Wife of: Amr ibn Thalaba
Tribe: Khazraj, Adi ibn al-Najjar clan
Ibn Sad also relates the following:
She accepted Islam and gave her allegiance to the Messenger of God.

UMM HAKIM BINT HARITH
Wife of: Ikrimah ibn Abu Jahl; Khalid ibn Said
She is not mentioned by Ibn Sad.

UMM HAKIM BINT TARIQ AL-KINANIYYA
Tribe: Non-Qurayshi Emigrant
Ibn Sad also relates the following:
She accepted Islam at the farewell pilgrimage and gave her allegiance to the Messenger of God.

UMM HAKIM BINT WIDA AL-KHUZAIYYA
Tribe: Non-Quraysh
Ibn Sad also relates the following:
She accepted Islam and gave her allegiance to the Messenger of God. She related a Tradition from the Prophet.

UMM HANI AL-ANSARIYYA
Tribe: Khazraj, Malik ibn al-Najjar clan
Ibn Sad also relates the following:
She accepted Islam and gave her allegiance to the Messenger of God. She related a Tradition from the Prophet.

UMM HANI BINT ABU TALIB IBN AL-MUTTALIB
Mother: Fatima bint Asad
Father: Abu Talib ibn al-Muttalib
Alternative Name: Fakhita
Ibn Sad also relates the following:
She accepted Islam and gave her allegiance to the Messenger of God. The Prophet proposed to her but never married her.

Her name was Fakhita. Hisham ibn al-Kalbi used to say that her name was Hind, but Fakhita is more common.

Ibn Abbas relates that the Prophet proposed marriage to Abu Talib for his daughter, Umm Hani, during the Age of Ignorance. Hubayra ibn Abu Wahb also proposed to her. He married her to Hubayra.

The Prophet said, 'Uncle, do you marry her to Hubayra and ignore me?' He replied that they had in-law-ship with them, and the noble is an equal for the noble.

She accepted Islam, and this split her from Hubayra. The Messenger of God proposed to her. She said that she used to love him during the Age of Ignorance and loved him much more in the age of Islam! She said she was an older woman and did not want to burden him.

The Messenger of God said, 'The best of women who ride camels are the women of the Quraysh. How kind they are to children in their youth and how careful of their husband's property!'

Abu Aqrab relates that the Messenger of God proposed to Umm Hani. She said that he was more beloved to her than her sight and hearing. She said that the right of the husband was immense and so she feared that if she devoted herself to her husband, she would fall short in her duty to her children. If she devoted herself to her children, she pointed out, she might fall short in her duty to her husband.

The Messenger of God said, 'The best of women who ride camels are the women of the Quraysh. How kind they are to children in their youth and how careful of their husband's property!'

Abu Aqrab relates that the Messenger of God visited Umm Hani and proposed to her. She asked how she could lie with this one and nurse that one referring to the two children in front of her.

He asked for something to drink. He was brought some milk. He drank some and then handed it to her. She drank the rest. She told him that she drank it even though she was fasting.

He said, 'What moved you to do that?'

She said that she did it for the sake of his left-overs. She said she would not leave them for anything. Since she was able, she drank it.

The Messenger of God said, 'The best of women who ride camels are the women of the Quraysh. How kind they are to children in their youth and how careful of their husband's property! If Mary, the daughter of Imran, had ridden the camel, no one would have been preferred to her.'

Umm Hani bint Abi Talib relates that the Messenger of God proposed to her. She made an excuse to him and he excused her. Then God sent down, 'O Prophet! We have made lawful for you your wives you have given dowries to...' to 'and the daughters of your maternal aunts, who have migrated along with you' (33:50). According to this, she was not not lawful to him. She had not migrated with him. She was one of those brought into Islam.

Abu Salih, the servant of Umm Hani, relates that the Messenger of God proposed to Umm Hani bint Abi Talib. She told the Messenger that she was older than him and that she had young children.

When her sons came of age, she offered herself to him and he said, 'Now, no,' because God had sent down to him, 'O Prophet! We have made lawful for you your wives you have given dowries to...' to 'and the daughters of your maternal aunts, who have migrated along with you' (33:50).' She was not one of the women who migrated.

Another said that her children by Hubayra were Jada, Umar, Yusuf and Hani.

UMM HANZALA BINT RUMI

Mother: Suhayma bint Abd Allah ibn Rifaa
Children: Bore c hildren, names not given
Wife of: Thalaba ibn Anas
Tribe: Aws, Abd al-Ashhal clan

Ibn Sad also relates the following:

She accepted Islam and gave her allegiance to the Messenger of God.

UMM HARAM BINT MILHAN

Mother: Mulayka bint Malik
Children: Haram (?), Muhammad; Qays, Abd Allah
Sister of: Umm Sulaym; Haram ibn Milhan (?)
Wife of: Ubada ibn as-Samit; Amr ibn Qays
Tribe: Khazraj, Adi ibn al-Najjar clan

Ibn Sad also relates the following:

She accepted Islam and gave her allegiance to the Messenger of God. She related a Tradition from the Prophet.

UMM HARITHA AL-RUBBAYI BINT AL-NADR
Mother: Hind bint Zayt
Children: Haritha; Umm Umayr
Wife of: Suraqa ibn al-Harith
Tribe: Khazraj, Adi ibn al-Najjar clan
Ibn Sad also relates the following:
She accepted Islam and gave her allegiance to the Messenger of God. Her son was martyred at the Battle of Badr.

UMM HASAN IBN THABIT (SEE FURAYA BINT KHALID IBN KHUNAYS, AL-)

UMM HIBBAN BINT AMIR
Mother: Fukayha bint Sakan
Sister of: Uqba ibn Amir
Wife of: Haram ibn Muhayyisa
Tribe: Khazraj, Salama ibn Sad clan
Ibn Sad also relates the following:
She accepted Islam and gave her allegiance to the Messenger of God.

UMM HISHAM BINT HARITHA IBN AL-NUMAN
Mother: Umm Khalid bint Khalid
Wife of: Umara ibn al-Jahhab
Tribe: Khazraj, Malik ibn al-Najjar clan
Ibn Sad also relates the following:
She accepted Islam and gave her allegiance to the Messenger of God. She related a Tradition from the Prophet.

Umm Hisham bint Hareitha ibn al-Numan relates that the Messenger of God stayed with them for a year or part of a year. He illuminated their dwelling for one year. She learned, 'Qaf' directly from the tongue of the Messenger of God who recited it to the people every Friday when he addressed them in the sermon.

UMM HUFAYD AL-HILALIYYA
Tribe: Non-Qurayshi Emigrant
Ibn Sad also relates the following:
She accepted Islam and gave her allegiance to the Messenger of God. She gave a lizard to the Prophet.

UMM IYAS BINT ANAS IBN RAFI
Mother: Umm Sharik bint Khalid of Khazraj
Wife of: Abu Sad ibn Talha
Tribe: Aws, Abd al-Ashhal clan
Ibn Sad also relates the following:

She accepted Islam and gave her allegiance to the Messenger of God.

UMM IYAS BINT THABIT (SEE UMM AL-HARITH)

UMM JAMIL BINT ABI AKHZAM IBN ATIK
Mother: Daughter of Khabbab ibn al-Aratt
Children: Abd Allah, Khalid, Jamil, Ubayda
Sister of: Umar Faruq
Wife of: Said ibn Ubayd
Tribe: Khazraj, Malik ibn al-Najjar clan
Ibn Sad also relates the following:
She accepted Islam and gave her allegiance to the Messenger of God. She was the cause of her brother's conversion to Islam. She was a woman of great determination and loved the Prophet more than her life. She was very intelligent and had attained a very high station in the sight of God's Messenger. The Prophet had also a close relation with her and put great trust in her.

UMM JAMIL BINT AL-HUBBAB IBN AL-MUNDHIR
Mother: Zaynab bint Sayfi
Wife of: al-Mundhir ibn Amr
Tribe: Khazraj, Salama ibn Sad clan
Ibn Sad also relates the following:
She accepted Islam and gave her allegiance to the Messenger of God.

UMM JAMIL BINT AL-JULLAS
Wife of: Salim ibn Utba
Tribe: Aws, Ubayd ibn Zayd ibn Malik ibn Awf clan
Ibn Sad also relates the following:
She accepted Islam and gave her allegiance to the Messenger of God.

UMM JAMIL BINT AL-KHATTAB (SEE FATIMA BINT AL-KHATTAB)

UMM JAMIL BINT QUTBA IBN AMIR
Mother: Umm Amr ibn Amr
Children: Umama
Wife of: Uthman ibn Khalda; Zayd ibn Thabit; Anas ibn Malik
Tribe: Khazraj, Salama ibn Sad clan
Ibn Sad also relates the following:
She accepted Islam and gave her allegiance to the Messenger of God.

UMM JAMIL BINT AL-MUJALLIL (SEE FATIMAH)

UMM JUNDUB AL-AZDIYYA
Tribe: Non-Quraysh
Alternative Name: Umm Sulaym ibn Amr ibn al-Ahwas
Ibn Sad also relates the following:
She accepted Islam and gave her allegiance to the Messenger of God. She related a Tradition from the Prophet regarding the prescribed pilgrimage.

UMM JUNDUB BINT MASUD IBN AWS
Mother: ash-Shamus bint Amr
Children: al-Harith
Wife of: Nasr ibn al-Harith; Adi ibn Haram
Tribe: Aws, Zafar clan
Ibn Sad also relates the following:
She accepted Islam and gave her allegiance to the Messenger of God.

UMM KABSHA
Tribe: Qudaa
Ibn Sad also relates the following:
She accepted Islam and gave her allegiance to the Messenger of God. She related a Tradition from the Prophet.

UMM KHALID BINT KHALID
Mother: Humayma bint Khalif Khuzaa
Father: Khalid ibn Said ibn al-As
Children: Umar, Khalid
Wife of: Zubayr ibn al-Awwam
Tribe: Quraysh, Khuzaa
Alternative Name: Ama bint Khalid ibn Said ibn al-As
Ibn Sad also relates the following:
She accepted Islam and gave her allegiance to the Messenger of God. She was born in Abyssinia. She related a Tradition from the Prophet.
Muhammad ibn Umar al-Waqadi reports that Zubayr ibn al-Awwam married Ama bint Khalid and she gave birth to Umar and Khalid. Ama was therefore called Umm Khalid.

UMM KHALID BINT KHALID AL-ANSARIYYA
Mother: Umm Thabit bint Thabit
Children: Abd Allah, Abd al-Rahman, Sawda, Amra, Umm Hisham
Wife of: Haritha ibn al-Numan
Tribe: Khazraj, Malik ibn an-Najjar clan

Ibn Sad also relates the following:

She accepted Islam and gave her allegiance to the Messenger of God.

UMM KULTHUM BINT MUHAMMAD IBN ABD ALLAH

Mother: Khadijah

Father: the Prophet

Ibn Sad also relates the following:

She was married to Utayba ibn Abi Lahab ibn Abd al-Muttalib before prophethood. When the Messenger of God was sent and God sent down, *'Perish the hands of Abu Lahab,'* (111) his father, Abu Lahab, said to him that he must not marry the .daughter of the Messenger. So he parted from her without having consummated the marriage. She remained with the Messenger in Makkah and became Muslim when her mother became Muslim. She and her sisters gave allegiance to the Messenger of God with the women. She migrated to Madinah when the Messenger of God emigrated. She left for Madinah with the family of the Messenger of God and remained there.

When Ruqayya, the daughter of the Messenger of God, died, Uthman ibn Affan then married Umm Kulthum, who was a virgin. That was in Rabi al-Awwal 3 AH/August-September, 624 CE. He consummated the marriage with her in this year in Jumada al-Akhira. She remained with him until she died without bearing any children. She died in Shaban, 9 AH/November-December, 630 CE. The Messenger said, 'If I had had ten [i.e. daughters], I would have married them to Uthman.'

Anas ibn Malik relates that he saw Umm Kulthum, daughter of the Messenger of God, wearing a striped silk cloth.

Asma ibn Umays relates that Safiyya bint Abd al-Muttalib and she washed the dead body of Umm Kulthum, daughter of the Messenger of God. She put her on a bier which she ordered be made from freshly cut palm boughs and buried her.

Amra bint Abd al-Rahman relates that the women of the Helpers washed her, including Umm Atiyya. Abu Talha went down into her grave.

Anas ibn Malik relates that he saw the Prophet sitting on her grave with his eyes flowing with tears. He said, "Who among you did not have intercourse last night?" Abu Talha said that he had not.

The Messenger said to him, "Go down into her grave.'

Muhammad ibn Abd al-Rahman ibn Sad ibn Zurara relates that the Messenger of God prayed for her and sat on her grave. Ali ibn Abi Talib, al-Fadl ibn Abbas and Usama ibn Zayd went down into her grave.

UMM KULTHUM BINT SUHAYL IBN AMR

Mother: Fakhita bint Amir ibn Nawfal
Children: Abu Sabra Muhammad, Abd Allah
Wife of: Abu Sabra ibn Abi Ruhm
Tribe: Quraysh

Ibn Sad also relates the following:

She accepted Islam and gave her allegiance to the Messenger of God.

UMM KULTHUM BINT UQBA IBN ABI MUAYT

Mother: Arwa ibn Kurayz
Father: Uqba ibn Abi Muayt
Children: Children (no names); Zaynab; Ibrahim, Hamid
Sister of: Uthman
Wife of: Zayd ibn Harith al-Kalbi; Zubayr ibn al-Awwam; Abd al-Rahman ibn Awf; Amr ibn al-As
Tribe: Quraysh

Ibn Sad also relates the following:

She accepted Islam and gave her allegiance to the Messenger of God. She was the first woman to migrate to Madinah alone after the Messenger migrated.

We do not know of any other Qurayshi woman who left her parents as a Muslim to migrate for God and His Messenger except for Umm Kulthum bint Uqba. She left Makkah alone. She accompanied a man of Khuzaa and arrived in Madinah after the truce of Hudaybiyya. Her brothers, Walid and Ammara, the sons of Uqba, set out after her. They arrived in Madinah the day after she arrived. They asked the Messenger to fulfill their precondition on which basis they concluded the treaty.

Umm Kulthum said to the Messenger that she was a woman, and the state of women is among those who are weak as he well knew. She said that if the Messenger returned her to the unbelievers, they would test her in her religion, and she might not be able to endure it.

So God broke the contract regarding women in the truce of Hudaybiyya, sent down the test about them and gave a judgment about that which pleased all of them. He sent down about Umm Kulthum, *"Submit them to a test. God has best knowledge of their belief"* (60:10). So the Messenger of God tested her and tested the women after her, saying, 'By God, is it only love of God and His Messenger and Islam which has brought you out, or have you left for a husband or for money?'

When they made a satisfactory reply, they were kept and not returned to their families. The Messenger of God said to al-Walid and

Ammara, 'God has broken the treaty regarding women by what you know, so leave.'

Umm Kulthum did not have a husband in Makkah. When she came to Madinah, she married Zayd ibn Haritha al-Kalbi and she bore him children. He was killed on the Day of Muta. Then she married Zubayr ibn al-Awwam and bore him Zaynab.

Maymun relates that Kulthum bint Uqba ibn Abi Muayt was married to Zubayr ibn al-Awwam. He had some harshness towards women, and she disliked him. So she asked him for a divorce. He refused her until he divorced her unwittingly. Once she pestered him while he was doing ablution for the prescribed prayer. He divorced her with a single divorce. She left and gave birth. One of his family met him and told him that she had given birth.

He said that she had tricked him. He went to the Prophet and mentioned that to him. The Messenger said, 'The Book of God has decided regarding her position, so propose to her again.' He said that he knew she would never come back to him.

Muhammad ibn Umar al-Waqadi reports that then she married Abd al-Rahman ibn Awf and bore him Ibrahim and Hamid. Abd al-Rahman then died while she was married to him. Then she married Amr ibn al-As, and she died while married to him.

UMM KURZ AL-KHUZAIYYA
Tribe: Non-Quraysi Emigrant
Ibn Sad also relates the following:
She accepted Islam and gave her allegiance to the Messenger of God. She related a Tradition from the Prophet.

UMM MABAD
Wife of: Tamim ibn Abdul Uzza (cousin)
Tribe: Non-Qurayshi Emigrant
Alternative Name: Atika bint Khalid of Khuzaa
Muhammad ibn Umar al-Waqadi and others report that she came later and became Muslim and gave her allegiance.

UMM MALIK BINT UBAYY IBN MALIK
Mother: Salma bint Matruf
Children: Rifaa, Khallad
Wife of: Rafi ibn Malik
Tribe: Khazraj, Bal Hubla clan
Ibn Sad also relates the following:
She accepted Islam and gave her allegiance to the Messenger of God. Her grandfather was Ubayd ibn Malik who was the poet al-Murammaq.

UMM MANI BINT AMRI IBN ADI
Mother: Arwa bint Malik
Children: Shibath
Wife of: Abu Shibath Khadij ibn Salama
Tribe: Khazraj, Salama ibn Sad clan
Alternative Name: Umm Shibath
Ibn Sad also relates the following:
She accepted Islam and gave her allegiance to the Messenger of God. She bore Shibath on the night of Aqaba, and she was also present at the Battle of Khaybar.

UMM MANZUR BINT MAHMUD IBN MASLAMA
Mother: ash-Shamus bint Amr
Children: Mahmud ibn Labid al-Faqih, Manzur, Maymuna
Wife of: Labid ibn Uqba
Tribe: Aws, Haritha ibn al-Khazraj clan
Ibn Sad also relates the following:
She accepted Islam and gave her allegiance to the Messenger of God.

UMM MAQIL AL-ASADIYYA
Tribe: Non-Quraysh
Ibn Sad also relates the following:
She accepted Islam and gave her allegiance to the Messenger of God. She related a Tradition from the Prophet.

UMM MIHJAN
She is not mentioned by Ibn Sad. Shibli Numani in *Sirat al-Nabi*, (vol. 1, p. 396) reports that Umm Mihjan cleaned and swept the Prophet's mosque in Madinah. The Messenger greatly respected her and honored her. She got sick and died. She was buried without infomring the Messenger. Afterwards when he came to know of her death, he asked his Companions why he had not been told of it. They said that as the Messenger was fasting and resting, they did not want to disturb him.
The Messenger asked where her grave was. He went there and offerent a funeral prayer for her.

UMM MISTAH BINT ABI RUHM IBN AL-MUTTALIB
Mother: Rayta bint Sakhr
Children: Mistah, Hind
Wife of: Uthatha ibn Abbad
Ibn Sad also relates the following:
She accepted Islam and gave her allegiance to the Messenger of

God. Her son spoke with the people of the lie about the wife of the Prophet, Ayisha, and she spoke against her son.

UMM MUADH BINT ABD ALLAH
Tribe: Khazraj, Salama ibn Sad clan
She is mentioned by **Muhammad ibn Umar al-Waqadi** as having accepted Islam.

UMM MUBASHSHIR AL-ANSARIYYA
Wife of: Zayd ibn Haritha
Tribe: Khazraj, Malik ibn al-Najjar clan
Alternative Name: Umm Bashir
Ibn Sad also relates the following:
She accepted Islam and gave her allegiance to the Messenger of God. She related a Tradition from the Prophet.

UMM MUHAMMAD (SEE KHAWLA BINT QAYS IBN QAHD)

UMM MUSLIM AL-ASHJAIYYA
Tribe: Non-Quraysh
Ibn Sad also relates the following:
She accepted Islam and gave her allegiance to the Messenger of God. She related a Tradition from the Prophet.

UMM MUTA AL-ASLAMIYYA
Tribe: Non-Qurayshi Emigrant
Ibn Sad also relates the following:
She accepted Islam after the migration and was present with the Messenger at the Battle of Khaybar. She gave her allegiance to the Messenger of God.

UMM NIYAR BINT ZAYD IBN MALI
Sister of: Sad ibn Zayd al-Ashhali
Tribe: Aws, Banu Abdul Ashhal
Muhammad ibn Umar al-Waqadi mentions her accepting Islam.

UMM QAYS BINT HISN IBN KHALIDA
Sister of: Qays ibn Hisn
Tribe: Khazraj, Banu Bayada ibn Amr
Ibn Sad also relates the following:
She accepted Islam and gave her allegiance to the Messenger of God. Her brother was present at the Battle of Badr.

UMM QAYS BINT MIHSAN
Sister of: Ukkasha ibn Mihsan of Badr

Ibn Sad also relates the following:

She accepted Islam and gave her allegiance to the Messenger of God. She related a Tradition from the Prophet.

UMM QAYS BINT UBAYD (SEE UMM SALIT AN-NAJJARIYYA)

UMM RAFI BINT UTHMAN IBN KHALIDA
Mother: Umm Jamil bint Qutba
Sister of: Abu Ubada Sad
Wife of: Khallad ibn Rafi
Tribe: Khazraj, Bayada ibn Amr clan

Ibn Sad also relates the following:

She accepted Islam and gave her allegiance to the Messenger of God.

UMM RAZN BINT SAWAD IBN RAZN
Mother: Umm al-Harith bint al-Numan
Wife of: Yazid ibn al-Dahhak
Tribe: Khazraj, Salama ibn Sad clan

Ibn Sad also relates the following:

She accepted Islam and gave her allegiance to the Messenger of God.

UMM RIMTHA
Father: Amr ibn Hashim
Children: Hakim, Abul Qaqa ibn Hakim
Tribe: Quraysh
Alternative Name: Umm Rumaytha bint Amr ibn Hashim

Ibn Sad also relates the following:

She accepted Islam and gave her allegiance to the Messenger of God.

UMM RUMAN BINT AMIR IBN UMAYMIR
Children: Tufayl; Abd al-Rahman, Aisha, Ruman
Wife of: Harith ibn Sakhbara; Abu Bakr
Tribe: Non-Qurayshi Emigrant

Ibn Sad also relates the following:

She accepted Islam and gave her allegiance to the Messenger of God. Umm Ruman was a righteous woman. She died in the time of the Prophet in Madinah in Dhul Hijjah, 6 AH/April-May 628 CE.

Muhammad ibn al-Qasim relates that when Umm Ruman was lowered into her grave, the Messenger of God said, 'Whoever is pleased to look at a woman of the *houris* should look at Umm Ruman.'

Affan relates that the Messenger of God went down into her grave.

UMM RUMAYTHA BINT AMR IBN HASHIM (SEE UMM RIMTHA)

UMM SABA
Tribe: Non-Qurayshi Emigrant
Ibn Sad also relates the following:
She accepted Islam and gave her allegiance to the Messenger of God. She related a Tradition from the Prophet.

UMM SAD
Mother: Lubna bint Ubada
Wife of: Jubayr ibn Thabit
Tribe: Khazraj, Bal Hubla clan
Alternative Name: Umm Said
Ibn Sad also relates the following:
She accepted Islam and gave her allegiance to the Messenger of God.

UMM SAD BINT MASUD
Mother: Kabsha bint al-Fakih
Tribe: Khazraj, Zurayq ibn Amir clan
Ibn Sad also relates the following:
She accepted Islam and gave her allegiance to the Messenger of God.

UMM SAD BINT QAYS IBN HISN
Mother: Khawla bint al-Fakih
Wife of: Qays ibn Amr; Masud ibn Ubada
Tribe: Khazraj, Bayada ibn Amr clan
Ibn Sad also relates the following:
She accepted Islam and gave her allegiance to the Messenger of God.

UMM SAD BINT SAD IBN AL-RABI
Mother: Khallada bint Anas
Father: Sad ibn al-Rabi
Children: Sad, Kharija, Sulayman, Yahya, Ismail, Uthman, Umm Zayd
Wife of: Zayd ibn Thabit
Alternative Name: Jamila
Ibn Sad also relates the following:
She accepted Islam and gave her allegiance to the Messenger of God. She was born after her father died at the Battle of Badr. She relates that she and Zayd used to perform the bath lustration from the same vessel.

Zayb ibn al-Said relates the he saw Umm Sad wearing an ivory bracelet on her wrist and an ivory ring.

UMM SAD BINT THABIT

Mother: Muadha bint Anas
Children: Said, Abd al-Rahman, Umar Kathir
Wife of: Yazid ibn Abi Yusr
Alternative Name: Kabsha bint Thabit ibn Atik

Ibn Sad also relates the following:

She accepted Islam and gave her allegiance to the Messenger of God.

UMM SAD BINT UQBA IBN RAFI

Mother: Salma bint Amr
Wife of: Qays ibn Makhrama after her sister, Wadda bint Uqba
Tribe: Aws, Abd al-Ashhal clan

Ibn Sad also relates the following:

She accepted Islam and gave her allegiance to the Messenger of God. Her mother was the paternal aunt of Mahmud ibn Labid.

UMM SAD JAMILAH BINT ASAD ANSARIYA

Father: Asad ibn Rabi Ansari

Ibn Sad also relates the following:

She accepted Islam and gave her allegiance to the Messenger of God. Her father was martyred at the Battle of Uhud. At the time of his death, she said to the Helpers that if the Messenger is martyred today and even one of them survives, they will not be able to show their faces to God. No excuse of theirs will be accepted by Him. She told them that they had all sworn to sacrifice themselves for God's Messenger.'

Umm Jamila reached a high station in knowledge and scholarship. Abu Bakr greatly respected her. Once she went to see him during his caliphate, and he spread his garment on the floor for her. Umar Faruq was there and asked Abu Bakr who she was. Abu Bakr replied that she was the daughter of the one who was better than both of them.

Umar was surprised and asked how this was so.

Abu Bakr said that because her father, Sad ibn Rabi, took the way of paradise during the time of the Messenger of God while they two were still sitting here in this world.'

Historians have greatly eulogized Umm Sad. They have written that she was not only a narrator of Traditions but was also well acquainted with commentary on the Quran. She taught the Companion, Dawud ibn Husayn, the Quran. It is also said that she had memorized some parts of the Quran and gave regular lessons on it (Ibn Athir).

UMM SAD (SEE JAMILA BINT SAD IBN AR-RABI)

UMM SAHL
Mother: Umayma bint Uqba
Children: Bore children, names not given
Wife of: Sinan ibn al-Harith; Abd Allah ibn Zayd
Alternative Name: Umm Thabit bint Sahl
    Ibn Sad also relates the following:
    She accepted Islam and gave her allegiance to the Messenger of God.

UMM SAHL BINT AL-NUMAN IBN ZAYD
Sister of: Qatada ibn an-Numan
Tribe: Aws, Zafar clan
    Ibn Sad also relates the following:
    She accepted Islam and gave her allegiance to the Messenger of God.

UMM SAHL BINT AMR
Mother: Amina bint Aws
Wife of: Mihraz ibn Amir
Tribe: Khazraj, Adi ibn an-Najjar clan
    Ibn Sad also relates the following:
    She accepted Islam and gave her allegiance to the Messenger of God. Her brother was present at the Battle of Badr.

UMM SAHL BINT MASUD
Mother: Kabsha bint al-Fakih
Tribe: Khazraj, Banu Zurayq ibn Amir
    Ibn Sad also relates the following:
    She accepted Islam and gave her allegiance to the Messenger of God.

UMM SAHL BINT RUMI
Mother: Suhayma bint Abd Allah
Children: Bore children, names not given
Wife of: Silkan bibn Salama
    Ibn Sad also relates the following:
    She accepted Islam and gave her allegiance to the Messenger of God.

UMM SAID (SEE UMM SAD BINT ABD ALLAH IBN UBAYY)

UMM SALAMA
Mother: Atika bint Amir ibn Rabia of Kinana

Father: Suhayl (Zad ar-Rakib)
Wife of: Abu Salama (Abd Allah ibn Abd al-Asad of Makhzum);
Messenger of God
Alternative Name: Hind bint Abi Umayya
Ibn Sad also relates the following:
She accepted Islam and gave her allegiance to the Messenger of God.

Umar ibn Abu Salama relates that his father went to Uhud. Abu Salama al-Jashami shot him in the arm with an arrow. His wound was treated for a month, and then the wound healed. The Messenger of God sent his father to Qatan in Muharram at the beginning of the thirty-fifth month [after the migration]. He was away for twenty-nine days. He then returned and entered Madina on the 8th of Safar 4 AH/July 20, 625 CE. His wound had become septic. He died from it on the 8th of Jumada al-Akhira in 4 AH/November 16, 625 CE. His mother observed her waiting period and became lawful on the 10 Shawwal in 4 AH/March 15, 626 CE. Then the Messenger of God married her at the end of the month of Shawwal 4 AH/ April, 626 CE. She died in Dhul Qida, 59AH/September-October 676 CE.

Umm Salama relates that the Messenger of God said to her, 'When you are afflicted by a calamity, you should say, "O God, reward me for my affliction and give me something better than it in return."' She said that he said this on the day that Abu Salama died. Then she asked who will she have to replace Abu Salama. God soon gave her someone better than Abu Salama in return.

Umm Salama, the wife of the Prophet, relates that Abu Salama said that he had heard the Messenger of God say, "'If anyone is afflicted by a calamity and he says what God has commanded him to say: '*Surely we come from God and surely to Him we return!*' (2:256) and then 'O Lord, reward me for my affliction and give me something better than it in return,' God will reward him for his affliction. He is then worthy of God giving him something better than it in return.'

She said that when Abu Salama died, she remembered what he had reported to her from the Messenger of God. She said the Messenger had said to Abu Salama, "*Surely we come from God and surely to Him we return!*, O Lord, reward her for her affliction something better than it in return.' Then she asked what replacement could be given to her who is better than Abu Salama? She was given someone better than Abu Salama in return, and she hoped that God will reward her for her affliction.

Ziyad ibn Abi Maryam relates that Salama said to Abu Salama that she has heard that there is no woman whose husband dies as one of the people of the garden while she is one of the people of the garden who does not marry anyone after his death, but that God reunites them in the garden. This is also the case when a woman dies and the man remains after her. She asked him to make a pact with him so that neither of them would remarry if one of them died. He asked if she would obey him. She said that she would. He then told her that when he dies, she is to remarry. He prayed, 'O God, provide Umm Salama after me with a man better than me who will not grieve her nor injure her!'

She said that when Abu Salama died, she asked what man would be better for her than Abu Salama? After some time the Messenger of God came and stopped at the door. He mentioned the proposal to her nephew or her son and to her guardian. Umm Salama said that she would have to either reject the Messenger of God or bring him her family.

The following day he repeated the proposal and she said the same thing. Then she said to her guardian that if the Messenger of God returned, then marry her to him. The Messenger of God returned and married her.

Umm Salama said that the Messenger of God said that when you are near death, speak well. The angels say "Amin" to what you say. When Abu Salama died she went to the Prophet and told him that Abu Salama had died. She asked what prayer she should recite.

He said, 'Say: O God, forgive me and him and give me better than him after him.'

She said this, and God gave her the Messenger.

Damra ibn Habib relates that the Messenger of God visited Umm Salama to console her for the loss of Abu Salama. He prayed that God comfort her for her loss and replace him with someone better. God did comfort her for her loss and replaced him with someone better. She married the Messenger of God.

Umm Salama relates that Abu Salama said that the Messenger of God had said, "Whenever any of you is afflicted by a calamity, he should say, 'Surely we come from God and surely to Him we return! O God, I expect the repayment for my calamity from You, so reward me for it.'

She had wanted to say this so he would give her someone better in exchange. Then she thought who could be better than Abu Salama? Nevertheless, she said it.

The narrator said that when her waiting period was over, Abu Bakr proposed to her, and she rejected him. Then Umar proposed to her and she rejected him. The Messenger of God sent to her, and she welcomed him and his messenger. She said to tell the Messenger of God that she was a jealous woman, had young children, and that none of her relatives who could act as guardian was present.

The Messenger of God sent to her, 'As for what you say about having young children, God will provide you with enough for your children. As for what you say about your being jealous, I will pray to God to remove your jealousy. As for relatives, none of them, present or absent, will not be pleased with me.'

The Messenger of God said, 'I will not give you less than what I gave your sister so and so: two mills, two jars, and a leather cushion stuffed with fibre.'

He said that the Messenger of God came to her. When he arrived, she had taken Zaynab to her room to nurse her. The Messenger of God was shy and noble and went back. He did that several times. Then Ammar ibn Yasir realized what she had done. She said that she would go that day. Ammar came. He was her brother by the same mother. He went in where she was and took her from her room. He told her to stop this ugly foul thing by which she injured the Messenger of God. He then entered and began to direct his gaze around the room, asking where little Zaynab was. She told him that Ammar had come and taken her.

The Messenger of God consummated the marriage with his wife and then said, 'If you like, I will give you the seven days which I give women."

Umm Salama said that when her waiting period for Abu Salama was over, the Messenger of God came to her and spoke to her with a partition between her and him. He proposed to her. She asked what the Messenger wanted with her? She said that she said this only to discourage him in regard to her because she was an older woman and the mother of orphans. She also mentioned her intense jealousy while the Messenger had several wives.

The Messenger of God said, 'That should not stop you. As for what you said about jealousy, God will remove it. As for what you said about your age, I am older than you. As for what you said about your orphans, they are the business of God and His Messenger.'

She agreed and he married her. On the night when they had arranged the consummation, she went in the day to her mill and took some extra barley for her family and ground it and some excellent fat and made a paste for the Messenger of God. When the Messenger of God, came to her, the food was offered to him and he took some of it. He spent that night and in the morning, he said, 'You are an honor to your family, and you have a position with them. If you would like for this to be your night and day, it will be that. If you wish, I will give you seven nights. If I give you seven, then I will give seven to your co-wives.' She said the Messenger should do as he liked.

Abu Bakr ibn Abd al-Rahman related that the Messenger of God proposed to Umm Salama and part of what he said to her was, 'What prevents you, Umm Salama?' She told him that she had three qualities which prevented her from giving a positive response: she was old; she had children; and she was jealous.

He said, 'As for what you say about jealousy, we will pray to God to remove it from you. As for what you say about age, I am older than you. Children are the business of God and His Messenger.'

So he married her and spent time with her without touching her because she was breast-feeding. He did this until Ammar ibn Yasir came one day and said to give him this child who distracted the wife of the Messenger of God. So he took the child and found her a nurse at Quba.

The Messenger of God entered and asked about the little girl. 'Where is little Zaynab?'

A woman was sitting with Umm Salama. She told him that Ammar had taken the child to be nursed. He said, 'We will allot you tomonow.'

So he came the following day and was with his wife. When he was about to leave, he said, 'Umm Salama, you have honor with your family. If you want me to allot you seven days, I have not allotted seven to any woman before you. If I allot you seven, 1 will allot them seven.'

Umm Salama relates that when the Messenger proposed to her, she said that she had some qualities which had made her not fit to marry the Messenger: She was an older woman. She was the mother of orphans. She was intensely jealous.

The Messenger of God sent for her and said, 'As for what you say about being an older woman, I am older than you, and it is no fault for a woman to marry someone older than her. As for what you say about being the mother of orphans, all of them are the business of God and His Messenger. As for what you say about intense jealousy, I win pray to God to remove it from you.'

She said the Messenger of God married her and moved her to the room of Zaynab bint Khuzayma, Mother of the Poor, after she had died. There was a jar. She looked in it and there was some barley. There was a mill, an earthenware pot and a cooking pot. She looked and it contained some knobs of melted fat. She took that barley and ground it and then mixed it in the earthenware pot. She took the knobs of melted fat and seasoned it with it. That was the food of the Messenger of God and the food of his wife on the night of his wedding.

Al-Muttalib ibn Hantab said that the widow of the Arabs (Umm Salama) visited the Master of the Muslims at the beginning of the evening as a bride, and she spent the end of the night grinding.

Muhammad ibn Umar ibn Abi Salama said that the Messenger of God proposed marriage with Umm Salama to her son, Umar ibn Abi Salama. He accepted the marriage on behalf of his mother when he was a young boy at that time.

Abu Bakr ibn Abd al-Rahman relates that when the Messenger of God consummated his marriage with Umm Salama, he said to her in the morning, "If you would like, I will spend seven days with you and seven days with them," meaning his other wives. "If you like, three with you, and then the turns will resume." She responded that she wanted three.

Salih ibn Ibrahim relates that when Umm Salama began her marriage to the Messenger of God, she was nursing the daughter of Abu Salama.

Ammar ibn Yasir relates that the little child was keeping the Messenger of God from his wife. He took her and found her a nurse-maid.

Abd al-Malik ibn Abi Bakr relates that Umm Salama, the wife of the Prophet, told him that when she went to Madinah, she told them that she was the daughter of Abu Umayya ibn al-Mughira. They called her a liar. This went on until some people went on the pilgrimage and asked her if she wanted to send a letter to her family. So she wrote and sent it with them. When they returned to Madinah, they said that she was telling the truth and she had more respect from them.

She said that when she gave birth to Zaynab, the Messenger of God came and proposed to her. She responded that a person like herself does not marry. She would have no more children, and she was a jealous woman with a family. The Messenger said, "I am older than you. As for the jealousy, God will remove it from you. As for the family, they are the business of God and His Messenger." So she married him, and he began to come to her, saying, "Where is little Zaynab?" until Ammar came and took the child. He said, 'This child is obstructing the Messenger of God!" She was nursing her. So the Prophet came and said, "Where is little Zaynab?" She replied, "She is with Qurayba bint Abi Umayya Ammar ibn Yasir took her." The Prophet said, "I will come to you tonight."

She said that she set out the skin and brought out some grains of barley which were in her jar and brought out some fat and mixed them together. Then he spent the night and said in the morning, "If you wish, I will spend seven nights with you, and if I spend seven, I will give seven to my wives." It is related that Ayisha said that when the Messenger of God married Umm Salama, she felt very unhappy when her beauty was mentioned to them. She was civil to her until she saw her. Ayisha said that Umm Salama was even more beautiful than the description of her. She mentioned this to Hafsa. Hafsa said that this was just jealousy, and that Umm Salama was not as she had been described. Hafsa was civil about her until she saw her, and then she said that Umm Salama was not as she had been described but much more beautiful than that. Ayisha saw her later and agreed that she was as Hafsa had said, and she was jealous."

Abu Bakr ibn al-Harith al-Makhzumi relates that the

Messenger of God married Umm Salama in Shawwal and consummated the marriage in Shawwal.

Umm Kulthum relates that when the Prophet married Umm Salama, he said to her, "I sent the Negus some *uqiyyas* of musk and jewelery, and I believe that he has died. I think that the gift I sent to him will be returned to me. If it is returned to me, it is yours," [meaning Umm Kulthum]. It was as the Prophet had said. The Negus had died and his gift was returned to him and he gave each of his wives an *uqiyya* of musk, and gave the rest to Umm Salama, and he gave her the jewelery.

Abd al-Rahman ibn al-Harith relates that the Messenger of God was on one of his journeys, and he was accompanied by both Safiyya bint Huyayy and Umm Salama on that journey. The Messenger of God went to the *howdah* of Safiyya, thinking that it was the *howdah* of Umm Salama. It was Umm Salama's day. The Messenger of God began to chat with Safiyya and Umm Salama became jealous. Then the Prophet realized that it was Safiyya and went to Umm Salama.

She said, 'You were chatting with the daughter of the Jew on my day when you are the Messenger of God!' She said, 'Then I regretted those words.' She used to ask forgiveness for them. She said, 'Messenger of God, ask forgiveness for me. Jealousy provoked me to it.'"

Muhammad ibn Umar relates that the Messenger of God assigned Umm Salama eighty *wasq*s of dates from Khaybar and twenty *wasq*s of barley, or wheat."

Nafi relates that Umm Salama, the wife of the Prophet, died in AH 59 and Abu Hurayra prayed for her at al-Baqi. It is related that she was 84 when she died.

Umm Salama
Mother: Rughayba bint Sahl
Children: Salama
Wife of: Aslam ibn Harish
Tribe: Khazraj, Malik ibn al-Najjar clan
Alternative Name: Suad bint Rafi

Ibn Sad also relates the following:

She accepted Islam and gave her allegiance to the Messenger of God. Her sons were present at the Battle of Badr.

Umm Salama bint al-Mukhtar ibn Abi Ubayd
Mother: Umm al-Walid bint Umayr
Wife of: Abd Allah ibn Abd Allah ibn Umar ibn al-Khattab
Related Traditions from Umar

UMM SALAMA BINT MASUD IBN AWS
Mother: Shamus bint Amr, al-
Children: Harith, al-
Wife of: Aws ibn Malik
Tribe: Aws, Zafar clan

UMM SALIT AL-NAJJARIYYA
Mother: Umm Abd Allah bint Shibl
Children: Salit, Fatima
Wife of: Abu Salit ibn Abi Haritha
Alternative Name: Umm Qays bint Ubayd

UMM SHARAHBIL BINT FARWA IBN AMR
Mother: Umm walad
Wife of: Yaqazan ibn Ubayd, al-
Tribe: Khazraj, Banu Bayada ibn Amr

UMM SHARIK
Alternative Name: Ghaziya bint Jabir

The Prophet proposed to her, but never married her.

Ibn Sad relates the following:

She was one of the famous and well-respected women Companions who were close to the Messenger and for whom the Messenger had great affection. It is reported that she was a very wealthy woman who generously fed people. She made her home into a guest house. People who came to see the Messenger often stayed in her home.

Muslim also reports that before the migration, Umm Sharik was responsible for looking after all the new converts. When Fatima bint Qays was divorced by her husband, she was first ordered by the Messenger to remain with Umm Sharik for her waiting period. However, since her home was often full of guests and her own relatives, the Messenger later said she should stay with her cousin.

It is related by various people that she was from the Daws.

Ibrahim al-Taymi relates that Umm Sharik was a woman of the Amir ibn Luayy tribe. She offered herself to the Messenger of God who did not accept her. She never married after that.

Amir relates about the verse, "*You may defer any of them you will,*" [33:51] that it relates to all of the women who offered themselves to the Prophet. He accepted some of them but did not accept others. They did not marry after him. One of them was Umm Sharik.

Shabi relates that the woman whom the Messenger of God did not accept was Umm Sharik al-Ansariyya.

Ali ibn Husayn relates that the woman who gave herself to the Prophet was Umm Sharik, a woman from al-Aws.

Mujahid relates that she did not give herself to the Prophet.

Ikrima relates regarding this verse, '*And any believing woman who* *gives herself to the Prophet if the Prophet desires to marry her exclusively for you, not the believers as a whole,'* [33:50] that he said, 'She was Umm Sharik al-Dawsiyya.'

Munir ibn Abd Allah al-Dawsi relates that the husband of Umm Sharik became Muslim. Her name was Ghaziya bint Jabir al-Dawsiyya. He was Abu 'l- Akar. He migrated to the Messenger of God with Abu Hurayra when the Daws migrated. Umm Sharik said that the family of Abu 'l- Akar came to her and asked if she had embraced Islam? She told them that she had. They then said to her that they would torture her severely because of this.

They took her from their house at Dhu Khalasa They set out for a place and put her on a slow camel with the worst of their saddles. They fed her bread with honey. They would not let her drink a drop of water until midday when the sun was burning overhead. It was midsummer. They set up their tents and left her in the sun until her mind, sight and hearing left her. They did that to her for three days. On the third day, they told her to renounce Islam. By then she did not know what they were saying so she pointed with her finger towards heaven to indicate the oneness of God. She was exhausted by then. Then she felt the coolness of a bucket on her chest. She took it and drank from it. Then it was snatched from her. She looked up, and it was hanging between heaven and earth. She was unable to reach it. Then it came down to her a second time. She drank from it another time. Then it went up. She looked at it between heaven and earth. Then it came down to her a third time. She drank from it until she quenched her thirst. She poured it on her head, face and clothes. Her husband's relatives came and looked at her calling her an enemy of God and asking where she had gotten the water. She told them that God's enemies were other than she and that it was they who opposed His religion. When asked where the water came from, she said that it came from God and that God had provided for her.

They rushed to their waterskins and containers and found them unopened. They said, "We bear witness that your Lord is our Lord and that the One who gave you water in this place after what we did to you is the One who prescribed Islam." So they became Muslim and all emigrated to the Messenger of God. They used to acknowledge her excellence over them and what God had done for her.'"

She is the one who offered herself to the Prophet. She was from the Aws. She was beautiful and advanced in years. She offered herself to the Prophet. The Prophet accepted her. Ayisha remarked that there was no good in a woman who gave herself to a man. Umm Sharik said that she was that. Then God called her a believer. He said, *'And any believing woman who gives herself to the Prophet.'* [33:50]. When this verse was revealed, Ayisha said that God was swift in what the Messenger desired.

Muhammad ibn Umar al-Waqadi relates that he saw those who said that 33:50 was revealed about Umm Sharik. It was established with them that it was a woman from Daws from Aws.

Musa ibn Muhammad ibn Ibrahim relates that Umm Sharik related Traditions from the Messenger of God.

Ibn al-Musayyab relates from Umm Sharik said that the Messenger of God commanded lizards to be killed.

It is related from Umm Sharik that she heard the Messenger of God say when he was mentioning the Dajjal, "People will flee from him into the mountains." She asked the Messenger where the Arabs will be on that day. He said, 'They will be few.'"

Yahya ibn Said relates that Umm Sharik al-Dawsiyya migrated and came across a Jew on the road. She was fasting. The Jew said to his wife, 'If you have something to drink, give it to her.'

She spent the entire night like that until the end of the night. Then a bucket was placed on her chest and a pouch [for drawing water]. She drank and later woke them up when setting out before dawn. The Jewish man said that he heard the voice of a woman saying, "I have to." His wife said that she did not give Umm Sharik anything to drink.

He also relates that once Umm Sharik had a butter container which someone had lent to her, and a man haggled with her over it. She said that there was not much in it. She blew in it and hung it in the sun and then it was full of ghee. It was said that the butter container of Umm Sharik was one of the Signs of God.

Jabir relates that Umm Sharik had a butter container in which she gave ghee to the Messenger of God. One day her children asked her for ghee, but there was none. She went to the butter container to look into it, and there it was flowing. She poured out some of it for them. They ate from it for a time. Then she looked at what remained and poured it out and it ended. Then she went to the Messenger of God and he said to her, "Did you pour it out? If you had not poured it out, it would have remained with you."

UMM SHARIK BINT KHALID

Mother: Hind bint al-Abarr
Wife of: Anas ibn Rafi
Tribe: Khazraj, Saida ibn Kab clan
  She is not mentioned by Ibn Sad.

UMM SIMAK BINT FADALA

Mother: Sawda bint Suwayd
Sister of: Anas and Munis

Tribe: Aws, Zafar clan
Ibn Sad also relates the following:
She accepted Islam and gave her allegiance to the Messenger of God.

UMM SIMAK BINT THABIT
Mother: Adam bint Amr
Children: Umara
Wife of: Yazid ibn Thabit
Tribe: Khazraj, Malik ibn al-Najjar clan
Alternative Name: Dubayya bint Thabit
Ibn Sad also relates the following:
She accepted Islam and gave her allegiance to the Messenger of God.

UMM SINAN AL-ASLAMIYYA
Tribe: Non-Qurayshi Emigrant
Ibn Sad also relates the following:
She accepted Islam and gave her allegiance to the Messenger of God.

Umm Sinan al-Aslamiyya relates that when the Messenger of God wanted to go to Khaybar, she went to him and said that she would go with him to sew the waterskins and treat the sick and wounded as well as see to the camels. The Messenger of God said, "Come with the blessings of God. Your companions are both from your people and I have given them permission. If you wish, go with your people or if you wish, go with us." She said that she wanted to go with the Messenger. He said, 'You can be with Umm Salama, my wife.' So she went with Umm Salama.

Umm Sinan al-Aslamiyya was present at the conquest of Khaybar with the Messenger of God. She said that they did not go out to the Friday prayer and Festival prayers until they despaired of finding husbands.

UMM SUBAYYA KHAWLA BINT QAYS AL-JAHMIYYA
Tribe: Non-Qurayshi Emigrant
Ibn Sad also relates the following:
She accepted Islam and gave her allegiance to the Messenger of God.

Umm Subayya Khawla bint Qays al-Jahmiyya relates that her hand and the hand of the Messenger of God alternated in the same vessel for ablution.

Umm Subayya Khawla bint Qays al-Jahmiyya relates that she used to listen to the sermons of the Messenger of God on Friday while she was in the back with the women. She would listen to him recite Surah Qaf from the *minbar*.

Sawda bint Abi Dubays al-Jahmiyya, who met the Prophet, relates that Umm Subayya Khawla bint Qays said that during the time of the Prophet and Abu Bakr and the beginning of the caliphate of Umar, the women used to socialize in the mosque. Sometimes they spun wool and sometimes some of them would work with palm leaves. Umar said that he would make them free women [i.e. make them stay at home]. They stayed at home although they used to attend the prescribed prayers at their time. Umar used to go out when he had prayed the final night prayer. He would go around and whip anyone who was in the mosque. He would look at them, note their faces, check on them and ask them whether they had prayed the night prayer, or he would take them out and give them supper.

UMM SUHAYL BINT ABU HATHMA
Mother: Hujja bint Umayr
Children: Mukhallid
Wife of: Yazid ibn al-Bara ibn Azib
Tribe: Aws, Haritha ibn al-Khazraj clan
Ibn Sad also relates the following:
She accepted Islam and gave her allegiance to the Messenger of God.

UMM SULAYM BINT AMR IBN UBBAD
Sister of: Abul Yasar Kab ibn Amr
Wife of: Nabi ibn Zayd
Tribe: Khazraj, Salama ibn Sad clan
Ibn Sad also relates the following:
She accepted Islam and gave her allegiance to the Messenger of God. Her brother was present at Aqaba and the Battle of Badr.

UMM SULAYM BINT KHALID
Children: Sulaym
Wife of: Qays bin Qahd
Tribe: Khazraj, Malik ibn al-Najjar clan
Ibn Sad also relates the following:
She accepted Islam and gave her allegiance to the Messenger of God.

UMM SULAYM BINT MILHAN IBN KHALID
Mother: Mulayka bint Malik
Children: Anas ibn Malik; Abd Allah, Abu Umayr
Wife of: Malik ibn al-Nadr; Abu Talha
Tribe: Khazraj, Adi ibn al-Najjar clan

Alternative Name: Ghumaysa, al-; Rumaysa, al-; Sahla; Rumayla; Unayfa; Rumaytha

Ibn Sad also relates the following:

She accepted Islam and gave her allegiance to the Messenger of God. She was present at the Battle of Hunayn while she was pregnant with Abd Allah ibn Abi Talha. Before that she had been present at the Battle of Uhud giving water to the thirsty and treating the wounded.

Umm Sulaym relates that she was with the Prophet on the day of Uhud carrying a dagger.

Umara ibn Ghaziya relates that Umm Sulaym was present with the Messenger of God while she was pregnant with Abd Allah. She had a dagger which she had strapped to her waist.

Anas relates that Umm Sulaym took a dagger on the day of Hunayn. Abu Talha told the Messenger of God that Umm Sulaym was there with a dagger.

She said to the Messenger of God that she had a dagger in case one of the idol-worshippers came near her. She said she would slit open his stomach. She told him to kill those brought into Islam by power and strike off their heads if they retreated from him. The Messenger of God smiled and said, "Umm Sulaym, God is enough and better."

It is related that Umm Sulaym believed in the Messenger of God. Abu Anas came. He asked if she had become a heretic. She said that she had not become a heretic but believed in Muhammad. She said that she had begun to teach Anas and taught him to say: "There is no god but God," and to say: "I bear witness that Muhammad is the Messenger of God." He did that. She was told not to corrupt his son. She responded that she was not corrupting him. Then her husband left and was killed by an enemy of his. When she heard that he had been killed, she decided that she must wean Anas. She said that she would not marry until Anas told her to and said that she had done her duty.

Once Anas was weaned, Abu Talha, who was an idol-worshipper, proposed to her. She refused. One day she asked him if he thought that a stone should be worshipped when it can neither harm nor benefit him. She also asked about a piece of wood which he took to a carpenter who carves it for her. She wanted to know if it helped or harmed him. What she said had a profound effect on him. He went to her and told her that what he had said had had a profound effect on him and he became a believer. She told him that she would marry him and would not take any dower from him except his belief in God.

Anas ibn Malik relates that Abu Talha proposed to Umm Sulaym. She said to Abu Talha that she believes in the Oneness of God and in the Messenger of God. She said if he followed the Prophet, she would marry Abu Talha. He said that he believed as she did so Umm Sulaym married him. Her dowry was his Islam.

Abd Allah ibn Abd Allah ibn Abi Talha relates that Abu Talha proposed to Umm Sulaym bint Milhan. Umm Sulaym had said that she would not marry until Anas came of age and could ask for God's blessings upon her.

Abu Talha relates that Anas had sat and had spoken in the assemblies. Umm Sulaym asked what he would give her to marry him. She said that either he followed her in what she believed or withdrew his marriage proposal because she believed in the Messenger of God. Abu Talha told her that he also believed what she believed. So the dower between them was his Islam.

Anas ibn Malik relates that the Messenger of God visited Umm Sulaym and prayed a *sunnah* prayer in her house. He said, "Umm Sulaym, when you pray the prescribed prayer, say, 'Glory be to God,' ten times, 'praise be to God' ten times, and 'God is greater' ten times, and then ask whatever you wish of God. He will say to you, 'Yes, yes, yes.'"

Anas relates that Talha went to propose to Umm Sulaym. She said that she would not marry an idol-worshipper. She asked him if the god whom he worships was carved by the carpenter slave of such and such a family? She said that if he were to kindle a fire under it, it would burn up. He went away, but it had a profound effect on his heart She said the same thing to him every day he went to see her. One day he went and said he had accepted what she had offered him. Her dowry was the Islam of Abu Talha.

Thabit relates that Umm Sulaym asked Abu Talha if he not know that the god which he worshiped was only a tree which grew from the earth which was carved by an Abyssinian of a certain tribe. He said that he did. She asked if he was not ashamed to prostrate himself to a piece of wood which grew from the earth which was carved by an Abyssinian of a certain tribe. She said that if he bore witness that there was no god but God and that Muhammad was the Messenger of God, she would marry him without desiring any other dower from him. He asked her to let him think about it. He left, thought about it and then returned and said that he bore witness that there was no god but God and that Muhammad was the Messenger of God. She called out to her son to get up and marry her to Abu Talha.

Anas ibn Malik relates that the Prophet sometimes used to visit Umm Sulaym. When the time for the precribed prayer came, he would pray on a carpet of theirs. It was a mat moistened with water.

Anas ibn Malik relates that the Prophet used to visit Anas' mother, Umm Sulaym, and give her something to prepare for him. Anas said that he had a younger brother named Abu Umayr. One day the Prophet visited them and asked Umm Sulaym why her son, Abu

Umayr, was depressed. She told the Prophet of God that a bird he used to play with had died. The Prophet began to stroke his head, saying, "Abu Umayr, what did the little songbird do?'"

Anas ibn Malik relates that the Prophet did not enter a house without the husband being present except for that of Umm Sulaym. He was asked about that. He said, "'I have compassion for her. Her brother was killed when he was with me."

Umm Sulayrn relates that the Messenger of God used to spend midday in her house. She would spread out a leather mat and he would spend midday on it and perspire. She used to mix some perfume with his sweat.

Anas ibn Malik relates that the Prophet visited Umm Sulaym in her house. There was a waterskin hanging in the house which contained water. He took it and drank from it while standing. Umm Sulaym took it and cut off its mouth and kept it.

Anas ibn Malik relates that the Prophet visited Umm Sulaym. She brought him some dates and ghee. He said, "Put your ghee back in your skin and your dates back in your vessel. I am fasting." Then he stood in a corner of the house and prayed a *sunan* prayer. He supplicated for Umm Sulaym and the people of her house. Umm Sulaym told him that she had a private request to ask of him. He asked, "What is it?" She asked him to pray for his servant Anas. The Messenger did not omit any of the good of either of the next world or of this world without praying for it for Anas. He said, "O God, provide him with wealth and children and bless him."

Anas relates that he was the Helper with the greatest wealth. His daughter, Umayna, told her that some one hundred and twenty of his offspring had been buried before al-Hajjaj came to Basra.

Anas relates that Umm Sulaym sent him to the Messenger of God with a basket of dates, but he was not home. There was a tailor who was doing something for him. He had made some stew for him of meat and squash. He invited him. When he saw that he liked pumpkin, he began to put it near him. When he returned to his house, he placed the basket before him. He began to eat from it and divide it up until he finished it.

Anas relates that the Prophet said, "I entered the Garden and heard a rustling sound, and there was al-Ghumaysa bint Milhan." The Prophet said to Umm Sulaym, "Why don't you go on the pilgrimage with us this year?" She said to the Prophet that her husband had only two camels. He would make pilgrimage on one of them, and the other was left to irrigate his palm trees. He said, "Go on the shorter pilgrimage in Ramadan. Make the visit. It is like the prescribed pilgrimage or takes the place of the prescribed pilgrimage."

Ibn Abbas relates that Umm Sulaym told the Messenger of God that Abu Talha and his son were going on the pilgrimage on their camel leaving her behind. The Messenger of God said, "'The shorter pilgrimage in Ramadan will compensate for the pilgrimage with me."

Anas relates that Umm Sulaym was with the wives of the Prophet. They were being driven on by a camel-driver. The Prophet came to them and said, "Anjasha! Take it easy when driving the glass vessels!"

Anas relates that Abu Talha had a son called Abu Umayr. The Prophet used to meet him and say, "Abu Umayr, what did the bird do?" Anas said that Abu Umayr became ill while Abu Talha was away in one of his gardens, and the child died. Umm Sulaym washed him, shrouded him, perfumed him and covered him with a cloth. She said that no one should tell Abu Talha before she told him. Abu Talha came home. She had perfumed herself for him and prepared herself for him. She brought supper. He asked how Abu Umayr was. She said that he had had his supper and finished.

Abu Talha had supper and had relations with her as a man does with his wife. Then Umm Sulaym asked Abu Talha what he thought about the people of a house who make a loan to the people of another house. When its owner asks for it back, should the debtor return it or keep it. He said that the debtor should return it. She then said to him that he should expect a reward for the loss of Abu Umayr. He went straightaway to the Prophet and told him what Umm Sulaym had said.

The Prophet said, 'May God bless you in the result of your night!' She became pregnant and gave birth to Abd Allah ibn Abi Talha. On the seventh day, Umm Sulaym told him to take the child and a basket which contained some dates to the Messenger of God so that he could be the one to put the dates in the child's mouth and name him. Abu Talha took him to the Prophet. He stretched out his feet and laid him down. He took a date and chewed it and then put it in the child's mouth. The child began to suck it. The Prophet said, "The Helpers have a deep love for dates."

Anas relates that Abu Talha's son died and Umm Sulaym told him not to tell Abu Talha until she had told him. She wrapped the child a cloth. When Abu Talha came, she put food before him and he ate. Then she perfumed herself for him. He had sex with her and she became pregnant with a boy. She asked him what if a family borrows something from another family; and when the family who has loaned, asks for the return of their loan, and the indebted family refuses to retum it, what should they do? Abu Talha said that the loan must be returned to its people. She then told him that his son was a loan from God, and God had taken him back. He said that we belong to God and to Him we return!

The Prophet was informed and he said, "May God bless them in their night!" Anas said that Umm Sulaym had a boy and sent him with him to the Prophet. The Prophet was wearing a cloak and was tending to some camels of his. The Messenger of God asked, "Do you have some dates with you?"

He said that he did. He took the dates and put them in his mouth, chewed them and then gathered it from his mouth and put it in the child's mouth. The child began to suck. The Messenger of God said, "The Helpers love dates." He put the date in his mouth and named him Abd Allah. None grew up among the Helpers better than he.

UMM SULAYM BINT QAYS IBN AMR
Tribe: Khazraj, Adi ibn al-Najjar clan

Muhammad ibn Umar al-Waqadi mentions her accepting Islam.

UMM SULAYM IBN AMR IBN AL-AHWAS (SEE UMM JUNDUB AL-AZDIYYA)

UMM SUNBULA AL-MALIKIYYA
Tribe: Non-Qurayshi Emigrant

Ibn Sad also relates the following:

She accepted Islam and gave her allegiance to the Messenger of God. She related a Tradition from the Prophet.

Ayisha relates that when they went to Madinah, the Messenger of God forbade them to taket gifts from the Bedouins. Umm Sunbula al-Aslamiyya came with some milk but they refused it. The Messenger of God and Abu Bakr reached Madinah after migrating from Makkah. He asked, 'What is this?' She told him that Umm Sunbula had broughtthem some milk and because he had forbidden them from accepting anything from the Bedouins, they did not touch it.'

The Mesenger of God said, "Take it. When they become Muslim, they are not Bedouins. They are the people of our desert and we are the people of their towns. When we call them, they answer. When we ask for their help, they give it. Pour it, Umm Sunbula!"

She poured it, and he told her to give it to Abu Bakr. He drank and told her to pour it. She poured it and the Messenger of God drank. Then he said, "Pour it." She poured, and he gave it to Ayisha who drank it. Ayisha remarked that it was cool on the liver.

UMM TALIB BINT ABU TALIB ABD AL-MUTTALIB
Mother: Fatima bint Asad
Father: Abi Talib

Ibn Sad also relates the following:

She accepted Islam and gave her allegiance to the Messenger of God. Hisham ibn al-Kalbi does not mention her in his *Book of Lineages* as being among the daughters of Abu Talib. He mentions Umm Hani, Jumana and Rayta. It may be that Rayta is Umm Talib as Muhammad ibn Umar al-Waqadi states In the *Book of the Feeding of the Prophets.* He says that the Messenger assigned Umm Talib bint Abu Talib forty *wasqs* at Khaybar.

UMM TARIQ, FREEDWOMAN OF SAD
Tribe: Non-Qurayshi Emigrant
Ibn Sad also relates the following:
She accepted Islam and gave her allegiance to the Messenger of God. She related a Tradition from the Prophet.

UMM THABIT BINT HARITHA IBN ZAYD
Mother: Hind ibn Malik
Wife of: Abd Allah ibn al-Himyar
Tribe: Khazraj, Salama ibn Sad clan
Ibn Sad also relates the following:
She accepted Islam and gave her allegiance to the Messenger of God.

UMM THABIT BINT JABR IBN ATIK
Mother: Hadba bint Amr
Wife of: Atik ibn al-Harith
Tribe: Aws, Ubayd ibn Zayd ibn Malik ibn Awf clan
Ibn Sad also relates the following:
She accepted Islam and gave her allegiance to the Messenger of God.

UMM THABIT BINT MASUD
Mother: Kabsha bint al-Fakih
Tribe: Khazraj, Zurayq ibn Amir clan
Ibn Sad also relates the following:
She accepted Islam and gave her allegiance to the Messenger of God.

UMM THABIT BINT QAYS IBN SHAMMAS
Mother: Khawla bint Amr ibn Qays
Children: Simak
Sister of: Half-sister of Thabit ibn Qays
Wife of: Thabit ibn Sufyan
Tribe: Khazraj
Ibn Sad also relates the following:
She accepted Islam and gave her allegiance to the Messenger of God.

UMM THABIT BINT SAHL (SEE UMM SAHL)

UMM THABIT BINT THABIT IBN SINAN
Tribe: Khazraj
  Muhammad ibn Umar al-Waqadi mentions her accepting Islam.

UMM THABIT BINT THALABA IBN AMR
Mother: Kabsha bint Malik
Wife of: al-Ala ibn Amr
Tribe: Khazraj, Malik ibn al-Najjar clan
  Ibn Sad also relates the following:
  She accepted Islam and gave her allegiance to the Messenger of God.

UMM THABIT (SEE RAMLA BINT HARITH IBN THALABA)

UMM THALABA BINT ZAYD IBN AL-HARITH
Mother: Umama bint Khalid
Sister of: Thalaba ibn Zayd
Wife of: Amr ibn Aws
Tribe: Khazraj, Banu Salama ibn Sad
  Ibn Sad also relates the following:
  She accepted Islam and gave her allegiance to the Messenger of God.

UMM UBAYD BINT SURAQA IBN AL-HARITH
Mother: Umm Harith al-Rubayyi
Sister of: Haritha ibn Suraqa
Wife of: Rafi ibn Zayd; Tamim ibn Ghaziya
Tribe: Khazraj, Adi ibn al-Najjar clan
  Ibn Sad also relates the following:
  She accepted Islam and gave her allegiance to the Messenger of God. Her brother was martyred at the Battle of Badr.

UMM UMARA
Mother: Rabab bint Abd Allah ibn Habib, al-
Children: Abd Allah, Habib; Tamim, Khawla
Sister of: Abd Allah ibn Kab, Abu Layla Abd al-Rahman ibn Kab
Wife of: Zayd ibn Asim; Ghaziya ibn Amr
Tribe: Khazraj, Banu Najjar
Alternative Name: Nusayba bint Kab ibn Amr
  Ibn Sad also relates the following:
  She accepted Islam at the time of the pledge of Aqaba and gave her allegiance to the Messenger of God. She was present at the pledge of Aqaba. She was present at Uhud, Hudaybiyya, Khaybar, the shorter

pilgrimage to the Kabah, Hunayn and the Battle of Yamama in which her hand was cut off. She heard Traditions from the Prophet.

It is related that Nusayba bint Kab said that she was present at the pledge with the Prophet when allegiance was given to him on the night of Aqaba. At that time,she gave allegiance with the people.

Muhammad ibn Umar al-Waqadi reports that Umm Umara bint Kab was present at Uhud with her husband, Ghaziya ibn Amr, and her two sons. She set out with them at the beginning of the day with a waterskin with the intention of giving water to the wounded. On that day she fought and proved herself courageous. She received twelve wounds, either from a spear or a sword. Umm Sad bint Sad ibn Rabi said that she went to visit her and asked her to tell him about the Battle of Uhud.

She said that she went out at the beginning of the day to Uhud to see what the people were doing. She took a skin with some water in it. She went to the Messenger of God who was with his Companions when things were going in favor of the Muslims. When the Muslims were dispersed, she joined the Messenger of God and began to take part in the fighting. She defended the Messenger of God with a sword, and shot with the bow until she was wounded. He saw the scar of a deep wound on her neck. He asked Umm Umara who gave them this.

She said that Ibn Qumaya advanced when the people left the Messenger of God. He was shouting to be shown the Prophet. Musab ibn Umayr and some people confronted him. She was among them. He dealt her this blow, and she dealt him several blows in exchange, but the enemy of God was wearing double armour.

Damra ibn Said al-Mazini relates that his grandmother, who was present at Uhud giving water, said that she heard the Messenger of God say, "The stand of Nusayba bint Kab today was better than the stand of so and so." On that day, he saw her fighting fiercely. She kept at it until she had received thirteen wounds. She saw Ibn Qumaya strike her neck and that was the worst of her wounds. She was treated for a year. Then the caller of the Messenger of God called out, "To Hamra al-Asad," and she tried to go but was unable to move because of loss of blood. They put compresses on the wound through the night until morning. When the Messenger of God returned from Hamra, he did not go to his house before sending Abd Allah ibn Kab al-Mazini to ask about her. He returned with the news that she was safe. The Prophet was happy about that.

Umm Umara relates that when the people left the Messenger of God exposed, only a group of not more than ten remained. She, her two sons and her husband were in front of him, defending him. The people were passing by him in their flight. He saw that she did not have a shield, and he saw a man retreating with a shield. He said to the man with the shield, "Give your shield to the one who is fighting."

So he handed over his shield to her. She took it and used it to shield the Messenger of God. The horsemen attacked them. She commented that if they had been on foot as the Muslims were, they would have trounced them, God wiling. A man would come on his horse and strike her and she would use the shield against him and his sword. Then she would strike the hocks of his horse. The Messenger of God began to shout, "Umm Umara! Your mother! Your mother!" She said that he helped her against the enemy until she finished him off.

Abd Allah ibn Zayd relates that she was wounded in her left arm that day. A man like a great tree struck her but did not stay and went on. The blood would not stop. The Messenger of God said, "Bind your wound." My mother came with some bandages in her bag which she had prepared for wounds. The Prophet was standing looking at me. Then she told me to go and fight the people. The Prophet said, "Who can endure what you can endure, Umm Umara!"

She said that the man who had struck her son advanced. The Messenger of God said, "That is the one who struck your son." She confronted him and struck his leg. He went down on his knees. She saw the Messenger of God smiling broadly so that she could see his teeth. He said, "You have retaliated, Umm Umara!" Then they advanced on the enemy with weapons until they finished him off. The Prophet said, "Praise be to God who has given you victory and delighted you over your enemy and let you enjoy your revenge directly."

Abd Allah ibn Zayd relates that she was present at Uhud with the Messenger of God. When the people dispersed from around him, he and his mother went close to him to defend him. He said, "Is it the son of Umm Umara?" She said that he was. He said, "Throw!" So, standing in front of him, she threw a stone at one of the idol-worshippers who was on horseback. She hit his horse's eye, and the horse bolted so that both it and its rider fell. She began to overwhelm him with stones until she had made a pile. The Prophet was looking and smiling. He saw that she was wounded on her neck and said, "Your mother! Your mother! Bind her wound! May God bless you, the people of a house! The stand of your mother is better than the stand of so and so. May God have mercy on you, the people of a house! The stand of your foster father (meaning his mother's husband) is better than the stand of so and so. May God have mercy on you, the people of a house!" She asked him to pray to God to make them his companions in the Garden. He prayed, "O God, make them my companions in the Garden!" She said that she no longer cared about what might afflict her in this world.

It is related that Damra ibn Said said that Umar ibn al-Khattab was given some silk garments among which was an excellent a garment One of them said that the garment was worth such and such and that he should send it to the wife of Abd Allah ibn Umar, Safiyya bint Abi Ubayd. He said that it was something whichhe would not give to Ibn Umar, adding that he will send it to someone who is more entitled to it than her—Umm Umara Nusaba bint Kab. On the day of Uhud, he heard the Messenger of God say, "Whenever I looked to the right or the left I saw her fighting in front of me."

Nusayba bint Kab relates that the Messenger of God came to visit her, and she offered him a vegetable dish and barley bread. He took some of it. He said, "Come and eat." She told him that she was fasting. He said, "When someone eats in the presence of someone who is fasting, the angels continue to bless him until he finishes his food."

Umm Umara relates that the Messenger of God went to visit them. They brought him some food. Some of those present were fasting. The Prophet said, "When food is eaten in the presence of the faster, the angels bless him."

Muhammad ibn Yahya ibn Hibban relates that Umm Umara received twelve wounds at Uhud, and her hand was cut off at Yamama. In addition to the loss of her hand, in the Battle of Yamama, she received eleven wounds. She went to Madinah where they were treated. Abu Bakr thought he should go to her to ask about her. He was the caliph at that time. He said that she married three men and had children from all of them. From Ghaziya ibn Amr al-Mazini she had Tamim. She married Zayd ibn Asim and from him had Habib who was cut up by Musaylima, and Abd Allah who was killed at al-Hana The child of the third man died without issue.

UMM WALAD SHAYBA
Tribe: Non-Qurayshi Emigrant

Ibn Sad also relates the following:
She accepted Islam and gave her allegiance to the Messenger of God. She related a Tradition from the Prophet,

UMM WARAQA BINT ABD ALLAH IBN AL-HARITH
Tribe: Khazraj, Banu Malik ibn an-Najjar

Ibn Sad also relates the following:
She accepted Islam and gave her allegiance to the Messenger of God. She related a Tradition from the Prophet.

UMM WARAQA BINT NAWFAL (ABD ALLAH)

She is not mentioned in Ibn Sad. Ibn Athir indicate that she accepted Islam after the migration and learned to recite the Quran. She memorized the entire Quran. She asked permission of the Messenger to go to the Battle of Badr to care for the sick and wounded with the hope that she might attain martyrdom. The Messenger told her, "You should remain in your home; perhaps God will give you the blessing of martyrdom there."

She is said to have been a devote. As she knew the Quran by heart, the Messenger made her the *imam* of women. He also made her a caller to prayer as she had requested. Upon hearing the call, women used to gather in her home for prescribed prayer.

The Messenger was very kind to her. He used to sometimes visit her home with his Companions, saying, "'Let us go to the house of the martyr."

She had one slave and one maid to whom she promised freedom upon her death. One night they murdered her and ran away. In the morning, Umar Faruq mentioned to the people that he had not heard the voice of Umm Waraqa reciting the Quran. She was found murdered. Her murderers were caught and beheaded. This was the first instance of *qisas* in Madinah.

UMM ZAYD BINT AL-SAKAN IBN UTBA
Children: Zayd
Wife of: Suraqa bint Kab
Tribe: Khazraj
Ibn Sad also relates the following:
She accepted Islam and gave her allegiance to the Messenger of God.

UMM ZAYD BINT AMR
Tribe: Khazraj, Malik ibn al-Najjar clan
Muhammad ibn Umar al-Waqidi mentions her accepting Islam.

UMM ZAYD BINT QAYS IBN AL-NUMAN
Mother: Adam bint Haram
Wife of: Khalid ibn Adi
Tribe: Khazraj, Salama ibn Sad clan
Ibn Sad also relates the following:
She accepted Islam and gave her allegiance to the Messenger of God.

UMM ZURARA (SEE HAFSA BINT HATIB)

UMRA BINT RAWAHA
Children: Numan
Wife of: Bashir ibn Sad Ansari
She is not mentioned in Ibn Sad.

UNAYFA (SEE UMM SULAYM BINT MILHAN IBN KHALID)

UNAYSA
Mother: Unaysa bint Wafid
Wife of: Saib ibn Khallad, al-
Tribe: Khazraj
Alternative Name: Nufaysa bint Thalaba (see Unaysa)
Ibn Sad also relates the following:
She accepted Islam and gave her allegiance to the Messenger of God.

UNAYSA BINT ABD ALLAH IBN AMR
Wife of: Abbas ibn Ubada; Amr ibn Aws
Tribe: Khazraj, Bayada ibn Amr clan
Ibn Sad also relates the following:
She accepted Islam and gave her allegiance to the Messenger of God.

UNAYSA BINT AMR IBN QAYS
Mother: Amina bint Aws
Children: Qatada, Umm Sahl; Abu Said al-Khudri, al-Furaya
Sister of: Abu Salit, Usayra ibn Amr
Wife of: Numan ibn Amir;
      Malik ibn Sinan
Tribe: Khazraj, Adi ibn al-Najjar clan
Ibn Sad also relates the following:
She accepted Islam and gave her allegiance to the Messenger of God. Her brother and son were present at the Battle of Badr.

UNAYSA BINT ANMA IBN ADI
Mother: Jahiza bint al-Qayn
Sister of: Thalaba ibn Anma
Wife of: Abd Allah ibn Amr
Tribe: Khazraj, Salama ibn Sad clan
Ibn Sad also relates the following:
She accepted Islam and gave her allegiance to the Messenger of God. Her brother was present at Aqaba and the Battle of Badr.

UNAYSA BINT HILAL
Mother: Salma bint Taliq
Wife of: Ajlan ibn al-Numan, al-
Tribe: Khazraj, Banu Habib ibn Abd Haritha
Ibn Sad also relates the following:
She accepted Islam and gave her allegiance to the Messenger of God.

UNAYSA BINT KHUBAYB IBN YASAF

Mother: Zaynab bint Qays
Children: Abd Allah, Muhammad, Umm Kulthum
Wife of: Zayd ibn Kharija
Ibn Sad also relates the following:
She accepted Islam and gave her allegiance to the Messenger of God. She related a Tradition from the Prophet.

Khubayb ibn Abd al-Rahman, Unaysa's uncle, that she went on the prescribed pilgrimage with the Messneger of God. She said that during Umar's caliphate, the men went seeking the shade of the gardens with their cloaks over their heads, and there they spent the midday after the Friday prescribed prayer."

Khubayb ibn Abd al-Rahman reports that she said, 'We girls of the quarter used to take our sheep to Abu Bakr al-Siddiq.'

UNAYSA BINT MUADH IBN MAIS

Mother: Umm Thabit bint Ubayd
Wife of: Amir ibn Amr
Tribe: Khazraj, Zurayq ibn Amir clan
Ibn Sad also relates the following:
She accepted Islam and gave her allegiance to the Messenger of God.

UNAYSA BINT RUQAYM IBN AL-HARITH

Mother: Salma bint Amr
Wife of: Wahwah ibn Thabit al-Khatmi
Tribe: Aws, Khatma ibn Jusham clan
Ibn Sad also relates the following:
She accepted Islam and gave her allegiance to the Messenger of God.

UNAYSA BINT SAIDA IBN AISH

Mother: Amira bint Salim
Sister of: Uwaym ibn Saida
Wife of: Amr ibn Suraqa
Tribe: Aws, Amr ibn Awf ibn Malik ibn Aws clan
Ibn Sad also relates the following:
She accepted Islam and gave her allegiance to the Messenger of God.

UNAYSA BINT URWA IBN MASUD

Mother: Rughayba bint Thalaba
Wife of: Hanzala ibn Malik
Tribe: Khazraj, Bayada ibn Amr clan
Ibn Sad also relates the following:

She accepted Islam and gave her allegiance to the Messenger of God.

USAYMA BINT ABIL AFLAH
Mother: Faria bint Sayfi, al-
Children: No children
Wife of: Amir ibn Abu Amir ar-Rahib
Tribe: Aws, Amr ibn Awf ibn Malik ibn Aws clan
Ibn Sad also relates the following:
She accepted Islam and gave her allegiance to the Messenger of God.

USAYMA BINT JABBAR IBN SAKHR
Tribe: Khazraj, Banu Salama ibn Sad
Muhammad ibn Umar al-Waqidi mentions her accepting Islam.

UTHAYLA BINT AL-HARITH IBN THALABA
Mother: Fatimah bint Zayd Manat
Tribe: Khazraj, Najjar clan
Ibn Sad also relates the following:
She accepted Islam and gave her allegiance to the Messenger of God.

UZZA BINT ABU LAHAB IBN ABD AL-MUTTALIB
Mother: Umm Jamil bint Harb ibn Umayya
Children: Ubayda, Said, Ibrahim
Wife of: Awfa ibn Hakim ibn Umayya
Ibn Sad also relates the following:
She accepted Islam and gave her allegiance to the Messenger of God.

W

WADDA BINT UQBA IBN RAFI (SEE UMM AL-HAKIM)

WAQSA BINT MASUD IBN AMIR, AL-
Mother: Kabsha bint Aws
Wife of: Numan ibn Malik
Tribe: Aws, Haritha ibn al-Khajraj clan
Ibn Sad also relates the following:
She accepted Islam and gave her allegiance to the Messenger of God.

WIFE OF SAFWAN IBN MUATTAL
She is not mentioned by Ibn Sad. Imam Malik mentions that she

accepted Islam before her husband did so after the Battle of Taif. However, the Messenger did not remarry them.

She is reported to have been a very sincere and devout worshipper who was often engaged in the remembrance of God. Once she went to the Messenger and told the Messenger that her husband, Safwan, treated her harshly because of her praying; and tht when she fastedt, he made her end the fast while he himself offered the prescribed dawn prayer after sunrise.' Safwan was with her. The Mesenger asked if this was so. Safwan told the Messenger that she recited two long surahs in prescribed prayer, and he forbade her doing this.

The Messenger said to her, "The recitation of one Surah is enough." Safwan then added that she said that he made her end her fast. The fact is that when she intended to perform the optional fast, she continued it on and on. It became a hardship for me [being a young man]. The Messenger said, "No wife should perform optional fasting without her husband's consent."

Then Safwan said that his offering prescribed dawn prayer after sunrise was true. He said it was because they were workers, and this has been the habit of his family for ages. The Messenger said, "Safwan, when you get up, you must offer the prescribed prayer." (Abu Dawud and Ibn Majah)

Z

ZAYNAB BINT ABU MUAWIYA AL-THAQAFIYYA
Wife of: Abd Allah ibn Masud
Tribe: Non-Qurayshi Emigrant

Ibn Sad also relates the following:

She accepted Islam and gave her allegiance to the Messenger of God. She related a Tradition from the Prophet.

It is related from Busr ibn Said that the Messenger of God said to Zaynab al-Thaqafiyya, the wife of Abd Allah ibn Masud, "When you go out for the night prescribed prayer, do not put on perfume."

ZAYNAB BINT ABU MUAWWIYAH
Wife of: Abd Allah bin Masud

She is not mentioned in Ibn Sad.

ZAYNAB BINT ABU SALAMA
Father: Abu Salama
Mother: Umm Salama

Ibn Sad also relates the following:

She accepted Islam and gave her allegiance to the Messenger of God.

Muhamnmad ibn Amr ibn Ata relates that he named his daughter Barra. Zaynab bint Abu Salama told him that the Messenger of God forbade this name. She had been named Barra, and the Messenger of God said, "Do not proclaim yourselves pure. God knows best who is pious (*barr*) among you." They asked what they should name her and he said, "Zaynab."

It is related that Zaynab bint Abu Salama died when Tariq was the *amir* of the people. Her bier was brought after the dawn prescribed prayer and placed in the Baqi cemetery. Tariq performed the dawn prescribed prayer in the dark.

Ibn Abi Harmala relates that he heard Abd Allah ibn Umar say to her family that either they pray for the dead now or wait until the sun has risen.

ZAYNAB BINT AL-HUBAB IBN AL-HARITH
Children: Said
Wife of: Qays ibn Amr
Tribe: Khazraj, Najjar clan

ZAYNAB BINT JAHSH AL-ASADIYYA
Mother: Umayma bint Abd al-Muttalib ibn Hashim
Wife of: Zayd ibn Haritha; Messenger of God

Ibn Sad also relates the following:

She accepted Islam and gave her allegiance to the Messenger of God. Her mother was Umayma bint Abd al-Muttalib ibn Hashim.

Uthman al-Jahshi relates that the Prophet left for Madinah. Zaynab bint Jahsh was one of those who migrated with the Messenger of God to Madinah. She was a beautiful woman. The Messenger of God proposed to her on behalf of Zayd ibn Haritha. She told theMessenger that she was not pleased with him for herself. She was a widow of the Quraysh. He said, "I am pleased with him for you," and so Zayd ibn Haritha married her.

Muhammad ibn Yahya ibn Hibban relates that the Messenger of God went to the house of Zayd ibn Haritha to look for him. Zayd had been called Zayd ibn Muhammad. The Messenger of God had missed him for a time and asked, "Where is Zayd?" He went to his house to look for him but did not find him. Zaynab bint Jahsh, his wife, came out to him wearing a single garment. The Messenger of God turned away from her. She told the Messenger that Zayd was not there and asked him to enter their home.

The Messenger refused to enter. Zaynab made haste to put on more clothes because of what the Messenger had said to her at the door. She leapt up quickly. The Messenger admired her. He turned away muttering something which could hardly be understood, although he said aloud, "Glory be to God the Immense! Glory be to the One who turns hearts."

Zayd went to his house and his wife told him that the Messenger had been there. Zayd asked if she had invited him to come in. She said that she had invited him, but that he refused. He asked if she had heard him say anything. She said that when he turned away she heard him say, "Glory be to God the Immense! Glory be to the One who turns the hearts."

Zayd went to the Messenger of God and asked the Messenger why he had not gone into Zayd's house when Zaynab had invited him. He then added that perhaps Zaynab pleased the Messenger and that he should divorce her.

The Messenger of God said, "Hold on to your wife." Zayd could not find any way to her after that day. So he went to the Messenger of God and informed him. The Messenger of God said, "Hold on to your wife."

Zayd told the Messenger that he would divorce Zaynab. The Messenger of God said, "Hold on to your wife."

Zayd separated from her and disassociated himself from her. She became lawful, meaning her waiting period came to an end. Some time later while the Messenger of God was sitting and talking with Ayisha, suddenly he was overcome by a swoon that left him smiling. He said, "Who will go to Zaynab to give her the good news that God has married her to me from the heaven?" and the Messenger of God recited, "When you said to the one God had blessed and you yourself had blessed, "Keep hold of your wife and fear God". . ." [33:37]

Ayisha relates that far and wide they had heard about Zaynab's beauty and another of the most noble of matters is what was done for her when God married the Messenger to her from heaven. She was asked if she would boast to them because of this.

Ibn Abbas relates that when Zaynab was informed of her marriage with the Messenger of God to her, she prostrated.

Muhammad ibn Abd Allah ibn Jahsh relates that Zaynab bint Jahsh said that when the servant brought her the message of her marriage to the Messenger of God, she vowed to fast for two months for God. When the Messenger of God visited her, she could not fast at home or on a journey for which lots were drawn. When she drew the lot to remain at home, she fasted the two months.

Ibn Abi Awn relates that Zaynab bint Jahsh said one day to the Messenger that she was not like any of his wives because all of his wives had her father or brother or family give her in marriage to the Messenger except for her. [She said] God had married her to the Messenger from heaven.'

Zaynab bint Umm Salama relates that she heard her mother, Umm Salama, say that Zaynab bint Jahsh was mentioned, and she asked for mercy on her. She mentioned some of what had gone on between her and Ayisha. Zaynab said that she was not like any of the wives of the Messenger of God because they were married with dowry and they were given in marriage by relatives, while God married her to His Messenger. There was revelation in the Book about her which the Muslims recite and which is not changed or altered, *"When you said to the one God had blessed.. ."* [33:37].

Umm Salama relates that the Messenger of God liked her. He also used to become vexed with her. She was a righteous woman who fasted, prayed, worked and gave all of that as charity to the poor.

Anas relates that Zayd ibn Haritha came to complain about Zaynab to the Prophet. The Messenger of God said, "Hold on to your wife," and it was revealed, *". . . while keeping hidden something in yourself that God wished to bring to light"* [33:37].'

Arim relates in his version of the Tradition that the Messenger of God married Zaynab. The Messenger of God did not have a wedding feast for any of his wives as he had for her. He sacrificed a sheep.

Anas relates that it was revealed about Zaynab bint Jahsh, *"When Zayd no longer had any need of her, We married her to you"* [33:37]. She used to boast to the wives of the Prophet, saying that their families gave them in marriage while God, from above the seven heavens, gave her in marriage.'

Asim al-Ahwal relates that a man of the Asad tribe was boasting. The Asadi asked if he had among them a woman for whom God from above the seven heavens ordered marriage. He was referring to Zaynab bint Jahsh.

Anas ibn Malik relates that when the waiting period of Zaynab bint Jahsh ended, the Messenger of God said to Zayd ibn Harithia, "I do not find anyone I consider more trustworthy and reliable than you. Go to Zaynab and propose to her for me." Zayd went to her while she was mixing her dough. Zayd said that when he saw her, his breast was constricted and he could not look at her since he knew that the Messenger of God had mentioned her. He turned his back on her and backed away. He told her that he had good news and that the Messenger of God was mentioning her.

She responded that she would not do anything until her Lord commanded her. She went to her place of prayer and the verse was revealed to the Messenger, *"When Zayd no longer had any need of her, We married her to you"* [33:37]. He said that the Messenger came and entered without permission.

Thabit al-Bannani relates that he asked Anas ibn Malik how long he served the Messenger of God. He replied ten years, and that the Messenger did not change his manner towards him because of anything he did bad or good. He was asked what the most extraordinary thing that he saw in these ten years was. Anas answered that it was when the Messenger marriaged Zaynab bint Jahsh who had been married to his servant, Zayd ibn Haritha.

Umm Sulaym relates that she told her son, Anas, that the Messenger of God had married that morning and that she did not think he had any food. She asked for the jar. He handed it to her and she made some *hays* paste from pressed dates in a clay vessel which would be enough for him and his wife. She then told her son to take it to the Messenger. He went to him. That was before the verse of the partition had been sent down.

The Messenger told him, "Put it down." So he put it down between him and the wall. He told me, "Invite Abu Bakr, Umar, Uthman and Ali." He went on to mention some of his Companions by name. He was astonished at the number of people he told him to invite, given the lack of the food. It was a very small amount of food. But he did not want to disobey him, went and invited them.

He said, "See who is in the mosque and invite them." So he went to every man, whether he was praying or asleep and said told him to respond to the invitation of the Messenger of God on his wedding morning, until the house was full. He asked him, "Is there anyone left in the mosque?" Anas said that there was not. He said, "Go see who is in the street and invite them." Anas invited people until the room was full. He asked, "Is there anyone left?" Anas told him that there was no one left. He said "Bring the vessel." Anas placed it before him and he put three of his fingers in it and squeezed it. He said to the people, "Eat in the Name of God." Anas began to see the dates growing, or the fat as if it were springs bubbling up, until all who were in the house and in the room had eaten and there still remained in the vessel the same amount he had brought. He placed it before his wife and then went to his mother to astonish her with what he had seen.

She told him not to be surprised because if God had wished all of the people of Madinah to eat from it, they could have eaten from it. Anas was asked how many people he thought were there. He said seventy-one men or possibly seventy-two.

Anas ibn Malik relates that he was the person who has the most knowledge of the verse of partition. When Zaynab was given to the Prophet, some food was prepared. He invited the people. They came. Zaynab was with the Messenger of God in the house. They began to chat and the Messenger went out and then came back. They were still sitting there.

He said that then it was sent down: "*So you who believe! Do not go into the Prophet's rooms except after being given permission to come and eat, not waiting for the food to be prepared. However, when you are called go in and, when you have eaten, then disperse and do not remain wanting to chat together. If you do that it causes injury to the Prophet though he is too reticent to tell you so. But God is not reticent*" *with the truth. When you ask his wives for something, ask them from behind a partition"* [33:53]. The people got up and the partition was set up."

Anas relates that the Messenger of God gave a feast when he consummated his marriage with Zaynab. He gave the Muslims their fill of bread and meat. Then he went to the rooms of the Mothers of the Believers to greet them and supplicate for them. They greeted him and made supplication for him. He used to do that on the morning he consummated a marriage. He returned. He was with him. When he reached Zaynab's room, there were two men in the corner of the room chatting. When the Messenger of God saw them, he left his room. When the two men saw the Prophet leave his room, they got up quickly.

Anas said that he does not know whether he told him that they had left or he was told. He went back and entered the room and dropped the curtain between him and the Messenger. God sent down the verse of the partition.

Anas ibn Malik relates that he was the person with the most knowledge of the partition. Ubayy ibn Kab used to ask me about it.

Anas relates that the Messenger of God became a bridegroom of Zaynab bint Jahsh. He said that he married her in Madinah. He invited the people to some food after midday. The Messenger of God saw that some men remained sitting with him after the people had left. The Messenger of God went out. He went with him as far as Ayisha's room. He thought that the men had gone out and come back, and he returned with him. The men were still sitting there so the Messenger went back, and Anas went with him a second time as far as Ayisha's room. Then the Messenger went back and the men were gone. The Messenger set up a partition between Anas and himself and the verse on partition was revealed.

Ubayd ibn Umayr relates that he heard Ayisha state that the Prophet used to linger with Zaynab bint Jahsh and drink honey with her. Ayisha said that she and Hafsa decided that the Prophet would not visit her because they would say that they detected the smell of manna gum from him. He went to one of them and she said that to him. He said, "But I have drunk honey with Zaynab bint Jahsh. I will not do it again." So it was sent down, *"So Prophet! Why do you make forbidden what God has made lawful for you?"* to *"If the two of you would turn to God"* [66:14]. The two were Ayisha and Hafsa. *"When We confided a certain matter to one of his wives"* [66:3] was his words, "I have drunk honey."

It is related that Abd al-Rahman al-Araj was heard to say in his assembly in Madinah that the Messenger of God assigned Zaynab bint Jahsh eighty *wasqs* of dates from Khaybar and twenty *wasqs* of barley or wheat."

Ayisha blesses Zaynab and said that she obtained unsurpassed honor in this world. God married her to His Prophet in this world and the Quran described it. The Messenger of God said to his wives, "The swiftest of you to join me will be the one with the longest armspan." So the Messenger of God gave her the good news of the swiftness of her joining him. She was his wife in the garden."

Ayisha relates that the Prophet said to his wives, "The one among you with the longest hand will follow me first." They used to meet in one of their rooms after the Prophet's death and stretch out their hands on the wall to measure their length. They continued to do that until Zaynab bint Jahsh died. She was a small woman, may God have mercy on her. She did not have the longest hand among us. So then we knew that by the length of the hand the Prophet had meant charity. Zaynab was a woman who did handiwork and tanned and pierced leather and gave charity in the way of God.'

Al-Qasim ibn Muhammad relates that when Zaynab bint Jahsh was dying, she said that she had prepared her shroud. She said perhaps that Umar would send a shroud for her. She said that if he did send a shroud, then give one of the shrouds away as charity. She added that if they could give away her waist wrapper as charity when they lowered herdown into the grave, they should do so.'

Muhammad ibn lbrahim al-Taymi relates that Zaynab bint Jahsh gave instructions that she be carried on the bed of the Messenger of God and the bier be carried on it. Before that, Abu Bakr had been carried on it. When a woman died, she was carried on it until Marwan ibn al-Hakam forbade that any but a noble man be carried on it. In Madinah they muttered in groups about the dead being carried on it.

Zaynab's grave was in Baqi cemetery at the house of Aqil between the house of Aqil and the house of Ibn al-Hanafiyya. Milk was brought from Sumayna and placed at the grave. It was a hot summer day.

Baraza bint Rafi relates that when the allowance was paid out, Umar sent Zaynab bint Jahsh her share. When it was brought to her, she said that others among her sisters were more entitled to a share of this than she was. They told her that it was hers. She shielded herself from it with a garment and told them to pile it up and put a cloth over it. Then she said to Baraza to put her hand in and take a handful of it and take it to the so and so tribe referring to her relatives and orphans, until only a little remained under the cloth. Baraza bint Rafi said to her that they had a right to it.

She told her to take what was under the cloth. They found eighty-five dirhams. Then Zaynab lifted her hands towards heaven and prayed that the allowance of Umar not reach her after that year. She died. Abd al-Wahhab said in his Tradition that she was the first of the wives of the Prophet to join him.

Muhammad ibn Kab relates that the allowance of Zaynab bint Jahsh was 12,000 dirhams. She only received it one year. When 12,000 dirhams were brought to her, she told them not to let the next lot of this money reach her because it was a temptation. Then she divided it between her relatives and people in need.

Umar heard about that and said that she was a woman who sought good. He stopped at her door and gave the greeting and said that he had heard that she had distributed the money. So he sent her 1000 dirhams to spend, and it went the same way as the other money.

Amra bint Abd al-Rahman relates that when Zaynab bint Jahsh was dying, Umar ibn al-Khattab sent her five garments from the treasury which she could choose from. She was shrouded in one of them and her sister Hamna gave away the shroud which she had prepared for her burial.

Amra bint Abd al-Rahman relates that she heard Ayisha say that Zaynab departed in a praiseworthy manner and was a great loss for the orphans and widows.'

Abd al-Rahman ibn Abza relates that Zaynab was the first of the wives of the Messenger of God to join him. She died in the time of Umar ibn al-Khattab. They asked Umar who would go down into her grave. He said whoever was able to visit her when she was alive. Umar prayed for her and did four *takbir*s."

Al-Qasim ibn Abd al-Rahman relates that they said that when Zaynab bint Jahsh died, she was the first of the wives of the Prophet to join him. When she was carried to her grave, Umar went to her grave and praised God. He then said that he sent for the women [meaning the wives of the Prophet], when this woman fell ill to ask who should nurse her and attend to her. They said that they would. When she died, Umar asked who would wash, perfume and shroud her. They said that they would. Then he asked who would enter the grave. They said that it should be whoever could visit her when she was alive. He agreed with them. He told the people to move back and two men from her household put her in her grave.

It is related from Nafi and others that people used to go out for both men and women. When Zaynab bint Jahsh died, Umar commanded that it be announced that none should go out for Zaynab except her relatives. Umays' daughter asked if she should show him something which she saw the Abyssinians do for their women. She made a bier and covered it with a cloth. When he saw it, he said that it was an excellent idea. He commanded that it be announced to be brought out for their mother.

Abd al-Rahman ibn Abza relates that he prayed with Umar for

Zaynab bint Jahsh. She was the first of the wives of the Messenger of God to die. He recited 'God is Greater' four times for her and then sent to the wives of the Messenger of God asking who should enter her grave. They said whoever could see her while she was alive should put her in her grave. Umar said that they spoke the truth.

Muhammad ibn al-Munkadir relates that Umar ibn al-Khattab passed by the grave diggers who were digging Zaynab's grave on a hot summer day. He said that he should pitch a tent over them. It was the first tent pitched over a grave.

Muhammad ibn al-Munkadir relates that Umar commanded that a tent be pitched at the Baqi cemetery over her grave due to the intensity of the heat on that day. It was the first tent pitched over a grave at Baqi.

Thalaba ibn Abi Malik relates that on the day that al-Hakam ibn al-As died during the caliphate of Uthman, he saw a tent pitched over his grave on a summer day. People started talking and criticising the tent. Uthman remarked how quicklt people move to evil and confuse one another. He asked if all who were present were aware that Umar ibn al-Khattab had set up a tent over the grave of Zaynab bint Jahsh? They said that they were. He asked if there had been any criticism. They said they had not heard any.

Abd Allah ibn Abi Salit relates that he saw Abu Ahmad ibn Jahsh carrying the bed of Zaynab bint Jahsh. He was blind and weeping. He heard Umar say to leave the bed and people would not fail to help him. They crowded to the bed. Abu Ahmad said to Umar that this woman was the one by whom they obtained every blessing. This cooled the heat of what he felt.

Amir ibn Rabia relates that he saw Umar ibn al-Khattab pray for Zaynab bint Jahsh in AH 20 on a summer day. He saw a cloth stretched over her grave. Umar was at the edge of the grave. Abu Ahmad, who had gone blind, was with him at the edge of the grave. Umar ibn al-Khattab and the great Companions of the Messenger of God were present. Umar ibn Muhammad ibn Abd Allah ibn Jahsh and Usama and Abd Allah the sons of Abi Ahmad ibn Jahsh, and Muhammad ibn Talha ibn Ubayd Allah, who was the son of her sister Hamna bint Jahsh, went down into the grave of Zaynab bint Jahsh

Uthman ibn Abd Allah al-Jahshi relates that the Messenger of God married Zaynab bint Jahsh at the beginning of the month of Dhul Qida in AH 5. She was thirty-five at the time.

Amra bint Abd al-Rahman relates that he asked Ayisha about the marriage of the Messenger of God to Zaynab bint Jahsh. She said that it took place on their return from the expedition of al-Muraysi or shortly after it.

Uthman ibn Abd Allah al-Jahshi relates that Zaynab bint Jahsh did not leave a dirham nor dinar. She gave away as charity all that she could. She was the refuge of the poor. She left her house, and they sold it to al-Walid ibn Abd al-Malik when the mosque was destroyed for 50,000 dirhams.

Urwa relates that when Zaynab bint Jahsh died, Ayisha, began to weep and mention Zaynab and ask for mercy on her. Ayisha was asked about that, and she said that Zaynab was a righteous woman.

Urwa relates that she asked which of the wives of the Messenger of God did he prefer? She said that he was with him a lot, and Zaynab bint Jahsh and Umm Salama had a position with him. I reckoned they were the dearest of his wives to him after her.

Abd Allah ibn Muhammad relates that Umm Ukkasha ibn Mihsan was asked how old Zaynab bint Jahsh was when she died. She said that they arrived in Madinah in the migration when she was about thirty and she died in AH 20.'

Uthman relates that Zaynab bint Jahsh died when she was 35.

ZAYNAB BINT KHUZAYMA

Wife of: Tufayl ibn al-Harith ibn al-Muttalib, al-; Ubayda ibn al-Harith; Messenger of God

Ibn Sad relates the following: She was the Mother of the Poor.

Zuhri relates that Zaynab bint Khuzayma al-Hilaliyya was called the Mother of the Poor. She had been married to Tufayl ibn al-Harith ibn al-Muttalib who divorced her.

Abd al-Gahid ibn Ali Awn relatese that Ubayda ibn al-Harith married her. He was martyred in the Battle of Badr.

Muttalib ibn Abd Allah ibn Hantab relates that Zaynab, Mother of the Poor, was married to Ubayda ibn al-Harith who was killed at Badr.

Quddama relates that the Messenger of God proposed to Zaynab bint Khuzayma al-Hilaliyya, the Mother of the Poor. She entrusted her business to him, and the Messenger of God married her. He called witnesses and gave her 500 dirhams as a dowry. He married her in Ramadan at the beginning of the thirty-first month of the migration. She remained with him for eight months. She died at the end of Rabi al-Akhir at the beginning of the thirty-ninth month. The Messenger of God prayed over her and buried her at Baqi cemetery.

Muhammad ibn Umar relates that he asked Abd Allah ibn Jafar who went down into her grave. He replied that it was three of her brothers. When asked how old she was when she died, he was told thirty or thereabouts.

It is related from Ata ibn Yasir that the Hilaliyya woman who was married to the Messenger of God had a black slavegirl. She said that she wanted to free this girl. The Messenger of God said to her, "Will you not offer her to your nephews to tend sheep?"

ZAYNAB BINT MUHAMMAD
Mother: Khadijah
Father: Messenger of God

Ibn Sad relates the following:

Her mother was Khadija bint Khuwaylid. She was the oldest of the daughters of the Messenger of God. He married her to his cousin, Abul-As ibn al-Rabi before prophethood. She was the first of the daughters of the Messenger of God to marry. Abul Aas' mother was Hala bint Khuwaylid, Zaynab's maternal aunt. Zaynab and Abul As had two children: Ali and Umama. Ali died when he was still a child and Umama grew up and later married Ali ibn Abi Talib after Fatima's death.

It is related from Amr al-Shabi that Zaynab, the daughter of the Messenger of God, was married to Abul As ibn al-Rabi. She became Muslim and emigrated with her father, while Abul As refused to become Muslim.

It is related from Ayisha that Abul As ibn al-Rabi was one of those who was with the idol-worshippers at Badr. He was captured by Abd Allah ibn Jubayr al-Ansari. When the people of Makkah ransomed their captives, his brother, Amr ibn al-Rabi, came to ransom his brother. Zaynab, the daughter of the Messenger of God, was still in Makkah at that time, and she sent her necklace made of Zafar onyx which had belonged to Khadija bint Khuwaylid. Zafar is a mountain in Yemen. Khadija bint Khuwaylid had given her the necklace when she consummated her marriage to Abul As ibn al-Rabi. She sent it as part of her husband's ransom. When the Messenger of God saw the necklace, he recognized it. It moved him and he remembered Khadija and felt sad. He said, "If you can see the way to releasing her captive to her and returning her goods to her, then do it."

They said they were. They released Abu 'l-Aas and returned Zaynab's necklace to her. The Prophet made Abu 'l-Aas promise that he would let Zaynab join him. He made that promise and he kept it.

Muhammad ibn Umar al-Waqadi, whom I consider reliable, reports that Zaynab made migration with her father.

Muhammad ibn Umar al-Waqadi reports that the Messenger of God used to say, 'We find no fault in Abul As as an in-law.'

Yazid ibn Ruman relates that the Messenger of God led the people in the dawn prescribed prayer. When he stood up for the prescribed prayer, Zaynab, daughter of the Messenger of God, said that she had given safe conduct to Abul As ibn al-Rabi. When the Messenger of God finished, he asked, "Did you hear what I heard?" They said that they did. He said that he did not know anything about what was going to happen until she heard what he heard. Safe conduct can be given by the least of people.

Ismail ibn Amir relates that Abul As ibn al-Rabi came from Syria His wife, Zaynab, had become Muslim with her father and migrated. Then he became Muslim later on, and the Prophet did not separate them.

Qatada that Zaynab relates that the daughter of the Messenger of God was married to Abul As ibn al-Rabi. She migrated with the Messenger of God. Then her husband became Muslim and migrated to the Messenger of God, and he returned her to him.

Qatada said that Surat Baraa was sent down after that. So when a woman became Muslim before her husband, he had no means to her except by proposing again. Her accepting Islam amounted to a definitive divorce.

Shuayb relates that the Prophet returned his daughter to Abul As ibn al-Rabi with a new marriage.

Ibn Abbas relates that the Messenger of God returned his daughter to Abul As after two years had passed, by virtue of the first marriage, without any new dowry.

Muhammad ibn Ibrahim al-Taymi relates that Abul As ibn al-Rabi went to Syria in the caravan of the Quraysh. The Messenger of God heard that that caravan was returning from Syria. He sent Zayd ibn Haritha with 170 horsemen. They intercepted and seized the caravan and its goods in the vicinity of al-Is in Jumada al-Ula, AH 6. They captured some of the people who were in the caravan, including Abul As ibn al-Rabi. He went to Madinah to his wife, Zaynab, daughter of the Messenger of God, before daybreak. He asked for her protection and she granted it to him. When the Messenger of God prayed the dawn prescribed prayer, she stood at the door and called out in her loudest voicethat she had given protection to Abu 'l-Aas ibn al-Rabi.'

The Messenger of God said, "O people, did you hear what I heard?" They said that they did. He said, 'By the One who has the soul of Muhammad in His hand, I did not know anything about what was going to happen until I heard what you heard. The believers are one hand against others. The least of them grants their protection. We protect the one she protects.

When the Prophet went to his house, Zaynab came to him and asked him to return to Abul As what had been taken from him. He did that. He also commanded her not to go near him for she was not lawful to him as long as he remained an idol-worshipper. Abul As returned to Makkah and settled all his obligations. Then he became Muslim and returned to the Prophet as a Muslim, migrating in the month of Muharram, AH 7. So the Messenger of God returned Zaynab to him by virtue of that first marriage.

Anas ibn Malik relates that he saw Zaynab, the daughter of the Messenger of God, wearing a striped silk cloak.

Abd Allah ibn Abi Bakr ibn Muhammad ibn Amr ibn Hazim relates that the daughter of the Messenger of God died at the beginning of AH 8.

Abu Rafi relates that those who washed Zaynab, the daughter of the Messenger of God, included Umm Ayman, Sawda bint Zama and Umm Salana, the wife of the Messenger of God.

Umm Atiyya relates that when one of the daughters of the Prophet died, the Messenger of God commanded us, "Wash her an odd number of times—three or five or more than that if you think it better. Wash her with water and lotus. Put some camphor in the last washing. When you finish, inform me." She said that they informed him and he gave them his wrapper and said, "Shroud her with it."

Umm Atiyya relates that when they washed the daughter of the Messenger of God, they braided her hair into three braids (on the sides and in front) and put them behind her.

Umm Atiyya relates that when they washed the daughter of the Prophet, the Messenger of God said to them when they were washing her, 'Begin with the right side and the places of ablution.'

ZAYNAB BINT QAYS IBN SHAMMAS
Mother: Khawla bint Amr ibn Qays
Children: Unaysa
Sister of: Half-sister of Thabit ibn Qays
Wife of: Khubayb ibn Asaf
Tribe: Khazraj
Ibn Sad also relates the following:
She accepted Islam and gave her allegiance to the Messenger of God.

ZAYNAB BINT SAHL IBN AL-SAB
Wife of: Wadia ibn Amr
Tribe: Khazraj, Bal Hubla
Ibn Sad also relates the following:
She accepted Islam and gave her allegiance to the Messenger of God.

ZAYNAB BINT SAYFI IBN SAKHR
Mother: Naila bint Qays
Children: Khishrim, al-Mundhir
Wife of: Hubab ibn al-Mundhir, al-
Ibn Sad also relates the following:

She accepted Islam and gave her allegiance to the Messenger of God.

ZAYNAB BINT UTHMAN IBN MAZUN
Wife of: Abd Allah ibn Umar; Mughira ibn Shuba, al-
Tribe: Quraysh

Ibn Sad also relates the following:

She accepted Islam and gave her allegiance to the Messenger of God.

Nafi relates that Abd Allah ibn Umar married Zaynab bint Uthman ibn Mazun after her father had died. Her uncle, Quddama ibn Mazun, gave her in marriage to him. The girl's mother said to the girl not to permit it. The girl disliked the marriage. She and her mother mentioned that to the Messenger of God. The Messenger of God ended her marriage and al-Mughira ibn Shuba married her.

ZUNNIRA BINT ABD ALLAH
Mother: Umayma bint Ruqayqa
Tribe: Quraysh slave

Ibn Sad also relates the following:

She accepted Islam and gave her allegiance to the Messenger of God.